African Americans on Television

African Americans on Television

Race-ing for Ratings

David J. Leonard and
Lisa A. Guerrero, Editors

 PRAEGER

AN IMPRINT OF ABC-CLIO, LLC
Santa Barbara, California • Denver, Colorado • Oxford, England

Library of Congress Cataloging-in-Publication Data

African Americans on television : race-ing for ratings / David J. Leonard and Lisa A. Guerrero, editors.
    p. cm.
  Includes index.
  Includes bibliographical references.
  ISBN 978-0-275-99514-0 (hardcopy : alk. paper) — ISBN 978-0-275-99515-7 (ebook)   1. African Americans on television.   2. Television broadcasting—Social aspects—United States.   3. Television broadcasting—Political aspects—United States.   I. Leonard, David J. editor of compilation.
II. Guerrero, Lisa editor of compilation.
  PN1992.8.A34A48   2013
  791.45'08996073—dc23   2012047895

ISBN: 978-0-275-99514-0
EISBN: 978-0-275-99515-7

17   16   15   14   13   1   2   3   4   5

This book is also available on the World Wide Web as an eBook.
Visit www.abc-clio.com for details.

Praeger
An Imprint of ABC-CLIO, LLC

ABC-CLIO, LLC
130 Cremona Drive, P.O. Box 1911
Santa Barbara, California 93116-1911

This book is printed on acid-free paper ∞

Manufactured in the United States of America

For our families
To the intellectual giants and mentors upon whose shoulders we
stand upon each and every day
and
To the future scholars whose work, commitment to the field, and
determination inspires us each and every day

Contents

Acknowledgments

Every cultural production, from a film to television show, represents a collective effort, a merging together of artistic and creative impulses from a spectrum of individuals. A book is no different, with a myriad of voices and individuals coming together in an effort. With this book, our reliance on our colleagues and the brilliant minds we are in community with has been tremendous. As a project that originally started as a coauthored text that evolved into a multivolume history of African American television, which then morphed into a single-volume collection, we have experienced more twists and turns than are typical—even for academia. We are thus appreciative of the support and patience of the many people at Praeger. We could not have completed this journey without their continued support and their willingness to wait and wait and wait for its completion. We also would like to acknowledge the financial support of the College of Liberal Arts and Washington State University, who allowed us to purchase many DVDs all of which provided us with hours of research material and entertainment.

Of course, we must acknowledge the brilliant scholars included in this collection. Every anthology represents an effort to bring together an array of voices, perspectives, and critical points of analysis. That is no different here. We salute these authors for their dedication to black cultural studies, to televisual examinations, and to the ongoing conversations about race and representation. We also wish to thank them for their contributions, many of which were done with short time lines and pressure to fill in gaps within the text. Their efforts are much appreciated.

While we have each been influenced by an array of cultural critics, scholars, cultural activists, and intellectuals inside and outside the world of popular culture and African American studies, we think it is important to acknowledge the specific influence of Herman Gray and Mark Anthony Neal. While Lisa had the opportunity to study under Herman Gray, his conceptualization of black cultural moves that pushes the conversation beyond the dyad of positive/negative representations has been immensely helpful to both of us. Mark Anthony Neal has been a mentor to both of us; his friendship, guidance, and mentorship are greatly appreciated. Likewise, his work on "post-soul aesthetics" and the discourses surrounding representations of blackness in a post–civil rights America have been influential. This work, in our estimation, works to advance these conversations paying tribute to these intellectual giants.

Over the last few years, we have each been influenced tremendously by our "virtual family." Although some of the people we have never met in person, these friends, allies, and support system have been instrumental in the completion of this book. Props and love to: James Peterson, Stephanie Troutman, Guthrie Ramsey, Scott Poulson-Bryant, Tanisha Ford, Theresa Runstedtler, Treva Lindsey, Regina Bradley, Marc Lamont Hill, Dream Hampton, Heidi Renee Lewis, Shantrelle Lewis, Darnell Moore, Tamura Lomax, Joan Morgan, Anita Manuur, Alicia D. Bonaparte, Tanya Golash-Boza, Danielle Dirks, Emery Petchauer, Simone Browne, Riche Richardson, Monica Miller, Yaba Blay, Nicole Fleetwood, Koritha Mitchell, LaCharles Ward, Kyra Gaut, Crystal Fleming, Sarah J. Jackson, Ebony Utley, Gaye Theresa Johnson, Lester Spence, Jaylah Burrell, Imani Perry, Sohail Daulatzai, John Jennings, Danielle Herd, Jay Smooth, Leigh Reiford, Byron Hurt, Adam Mansbach, Nitasha Sharma, Salamishah Tillet, Monica Casper, Jamilah King, Kaila Afrekete Story, Jamilah Lemiux, Rahiel Tesfamariam, Jeff Chang, Therí Alyce Pickens, Juliana Chang, Kiese Laymon, Andrea Plaid, Vera Cruz-Swinton, Stephany Spaulding, Chris LeBron, Andreana Clay, Darryl Dickson-Carr, Dawn-Elissa Fischer, Jelani Cobb, R L'Heureux Lewis-McCoy, Julius Dion Bailey, Mark Naison, Honorée Fanonne Jeffers, Jose Alamillo, H. Samy Alim, Britney Cooper, Joe Schloss, Anamaría Flores, Aishah Shahidah Simmons, and Alondra Nelson. You and so many others inspire, encourage, and sustain us each and every day.

In our daily lives, we are members of a very dynamic and forward-moving department. Love and respect to our colleagues, specifically Mary Bloodsworth-Lugo, Carmen Lugo-Lugo, and Richard King, whose support, friendship, and mentorship have been unbelievable in good times and in bad. We are a fierce team, and I am thankful for each and every opportunity to work with you, just as I am equally thankful for every lunch and conversation.

David would like to give a special shout-out to Jared Sexton, Oliver Wang, Alejandro Jose Gradilla, Dylan Rodriguez, Rani Neutill, David Hernandez, Nerissa Balce, Vernadette Gonzalez, Mimi Thi Nguyen, Minh-ha T.

Phan, Josh Kun, and his other Berkeley grads who are holding things down. Thanks also go out to Anna, Rea, and Sam, as well as every member of the Leonard and Chow families for constant and unrelenting support. And of course, thanks to Lisa Guerrero, who is truly a Pullman treasure. We could have not finished this project without you.

Lisa would like to give special thanks to Aureliano DeSoto for his intellectual magic touch and true friendship. Thanks also to Mariah Maki, Joanne Greene, and Kim Mueller for being constant cheerleaders and for providing much needed breaks from academia. Thanks and love to Emily Limbach, Michael Gibbons, Kate Biagini, Sonia Patel Dalton, and Gina Giammona for always being there. All love, appreciation, and respect to my colleague, coeditor, and dear friend, David J. Leonard, for his unwavering support and for doing ALL of the heavy lifting for this project. Without you, this book wouldn't exist. Finally, thanks to Nana for being my number one fan and for absolutely everything else.

Introduction

Our Regularly Scheduled Program . . .

David J. Leonard and Lisa A. Guerrero

Born amid the shifting landscapes of the 1960s and 1970s and raised in the cultural saturation of the 1980s, African Americans' place on television operated as an important pedagogical tool within our socialization. In particular, our relationship with the African Americans on our television screens during this coming-of-age period began to shape our understanding of complex sociocultural and sociopolitical systems based on race and class before we ever had the critical vocabulary to express an opinion about these systems. For Lisa, it began with the heartthrobs: Linc on *The Mod Squad*, Isaac on *The Love Boat*, and, of course, Tubbs on *Miami Vice*. "Cool pose" wasn't an idea that she had words for at the time, but she knew it when she saw it and wondered if everyone else was seeing it too. (As she would eventually discover as a scholar, not only did everyone else see it, but for many people, that *was all they saw*.) She remembers crying and wondering why Kunta Kinte would endure a beating rather than just call himself "Toby" and having her grandmother say simply, "because Toby isn't his name. No one has the right to tell you that you have to be someone else because it's easier for *them*," her very first lesson in the history of the racial politics of naming. She cried too when James Evans died because it didn't seem fair, only to learn much later in life just how unfair it really was and on how many levels it was unfair. She also laughed at Flip Wilson, George Jefferson, and Benson, all of whom appeared to be much smarter than the people who surrounded them. And while in her lifetime she has certainly

This chapter contains parts of a prior book written by David J. Leonard entitled *Screens Fade to Black: Contemporary African American Cinema*, 2006. Said prior material is included herein with the permission of Praeger Publishers, © 2004.

watched more programs that feature white characters due to the overall lack of diversity in television programming, she *remembers* more of the black characters that have populated her screen and their impact on her thinking about the world.

For David, television marks different moments in his life, clearly having an impact that results in this book. To this day, he still remembers the endless conversations that resulted from the release of *Roots;* he still recalls watching *What's Happening* and *Diff'rent Strokes,* both of which represented a sight of uncritical consumption and generational conflict. Whereas his parents shunned shows like these, David found himself uncritically watching shows like *What's Happening, The White Shadow,* and even *The Jeffersons* in part because these represented a break from his parents' sense of respectability and cultural appropriateness. Yet, the inability to understand the broader implications of these shows, or *The Cosby Show,* which was a family event, also encapsulates this project as we, along with the other authors, return to shows that largely define our shared cultural memory, that raised us, and our consciousness, in many ways, some of which we still work to understand and, finally, to speak back at them. We use this space to offer critical readings of those shows that warranted intervention, that necessitate the imposition of a critical gaze, and that were dreams deferred for us, as not yet emergent scholars and cultural critics. This book is a returning home to many of the shows, bringing with us the baggage of scholarly experiences, critical media literacy, and a broader understanding of the relationship between popular culture and society at large. Yet, it also represents a bridging together of these shows of yesteryear, shows defined by our nostalgia and memory, with more recent productions, ones that we have never consumed outside our scholarly gaze. Television matters, and it always has for us; its meaning, though, transcends the pleasurable and the entertainment; it extends beyond nostalgia and communal meaning to a place defined by the impact of representations, accepted narratives, and societal framing. This book works to highlight how the last 30 years of history for African Americans in television matters both inside and outside our homes, within and beyond the imagined spaces on television, and toward an understanding of the themes and shifts that continue to shape new developments in the modes of blackness within the cultural sphere of televisual media.

While ideologies of color blindness emanate from a spectrum of state institutions, ranging from the media to the academy, popular culture represents a crucial site in the deployment of frames of color blindness. Television, since its advent, given its reach and given its entrenched connection to both commercial advertisements and the hegemony of whiteness, has been a crucial site for teaching the ideologies, dominant understandings, and meanings surrounding race, class, gender, and sexuality. Historically, through the dual discursive practices of erasure and the perpetuation of racist stereotypes, evident in shows like *Amos 'n Andy* or *The Jack Benny Show,* television has been a space for the dissemination of some of the most racist caricatures of blackness. Normalizing race relations and inequalities, as well as the dominance of whiteness, the history of television has largely been one of disparagement, demonization, and ridicule. Beginning in the 1960s, activists and others within the community protested the ubiquity of stereotypes and the overall lack of diversity on television. Agitation and pressure did contribute to the golden age of black television, with the success of shows like *Good Times, Sanford and Son,* and *The Jeffersons,* all of which, in different ways, gave voice to the range of identities and experiences within the black community. Yet, this moment was short-lived, with the Reagan revolution, the growing acceptance of a "race doesn't matter narrative," and an overall environment hostile to discussions of race, turning television into a vessel through which to perpetuate color-blind ideologies and uncritical multiculturalism. In many senses, television has become a site of celebration, wherein traditional discourses pay tribute to America's progress and possibilities, using popular culture as an exemplar for what various individuals have described as the "browning of America," a "racing of American culture," or an "explicit darkening, blackening and coloring of American culture, at least in terms of operation of its dominant institutions of cultural production and legitimation."[1] In other words, popular culture isn't looked at as merely embodying a changed or color-blind moment for America; it is also, paradoxically, seen as facilitating a more equitable racial politics given the widely accepted notion that popular culture breaks down barriers, whether through the participation of artists from different social groups or through the shared adoration experienced by a diversity of fans.

As a source of the rhetoric of progress, the entertainment world exists as one of the most powerful disseminators of color blind ideology, employing and deploying "evidence" of both structural and individual transformation toward a color blind society.[2] Herman Gray, in *Cultural Moves: African Americans and the Politics of Representation,* laments the ways in which the visibility of blackness on America's screens, televisions, airwaves, and sports fields contributes to a discourse of progress, as part of maintaining hegemony.

> Indeed, these representations of black people can just as easily be used to support political project that deny any specific claim or warrant on the part of black folks to experiencing disproportionately the effects of social justice,

economic inequality, racism, and so on. As state and national campaigns for "color blindness" and against affirmative action indicate, black visibility is often the basis for claims to racial equality, the elimination of social and economic injustice, and the arrival of the time for racial invisibility. So, liberals use media representation of black achievement (rather than images of, say, criminality) to persuade constituents of the importance of diversity, while conservatives use the same representations to celebrate the virtues of color-blindness and individual achievement.[3]

In other words, where politicians, educators, and leaders have failed in selling Martin Luther King's dream, and even failed to foster integration, the world of popular culture has seemingly broken down the walls of racism, demonstrating the merits of people of color to whites, while facilitating an erosion of the social, cultural, and racial distance that has long helped to maintain racism. This understanding of popular culture as the great equalizer is convincing because of the impact that the visual image has on how people interpret social formations. "I am seeing it; therefore it must be real/true/accurate." The primacy granted to visibility in relation to our ways of knowing is the reason why underrepresented groups have historically fought the battle for inclusion, especially in pop culture on the basic, and largely uncritical plane of visibility. But as Gray argues, not only is this a short-sighted battle plane, but, in fact, generally works at counter purposes to achieving equality because it cultivates the powerful illusion that we already have it. We must already live inside equality because we can point to it . . . on our billboards, our movie screens, and our television sets. That is to say that despite others' failures, the rest of society has caught on, appropriating the message that popular culture has not only provided opportunity, but serves as a virtual space of integration, whereupon whiteness meets the other. Leon Wynter, in *American Skin,* encapsulates this discourse, arguing that the last 30 years have seen a major transformation in American identity. "We live in a country where the 'King of Pop' was born black and a leading rap M.C. is white, where salsa outsells ketchup and cosmetic firms advertise blond hair dye with black models. Whiteness is in a steep decline as the primary measure of Americanness. The new, true American identity rising in its place is transracial, defined by shared cultural and consumer habits, not skin color or ethnicity."[4] This shifting definition of American identity, as well as the manner in which race fits within American society, is heavily linked to popular culture and consumption. The increasing popularity of celebrities of color is thus both a sign and an instigator of racial discursive shifts. According to this view, something had to give, and that thing was the systematic naturalization of whiteness as the defining cultural element of American life. "It's taken a long time, but American identity has finally begun to reach the truth of its composition. The artificial walls between American and being like an African or Hispanic or Asian American are coming down faster than anyone imaged even ten years ago," writes Leon Wynter. "Today, we wouldn't think of trying to describe 'American' by first excluding what is 'nonwhite.'"[5] Ellis Cashmore concurs, arguing that through popular culture whites embrace difference, thereby limiting antipathy and hatred, whereas prior to the rise of the civil rights movement, "Whites were taught to fear difference."

> Today, whites embrace the differences that once disturbed them: appreciation and enjoyment have replaced uneasiness. The images whites held of black have charged in harmony with changes in aesthetic tastes. What was once disparaged and mocked is now regarded as part of legitimate culture. Any residual menace still lurking in African Americans practices and pursuits has been domesticated, leaving a black culture capable of being adapted, refined, mass-produced, and marketed. Whites not [only] appreciate black: they buy it. Having appropriated music, visual arts and the literature traditionally associated with African Americans, they have put it on the market. Black culture is now open for business. A great many blacks have become rich on the back of it. An even greater number of whites have prospered.[6]

In modern America, it is believed that rampant stereotypes of 1930s and 1940s, whether the Coon or the Mammy, have been washed away by American racial progress, struggle, and increased levels of tolerance (and intolerance for intolerance) inside and outside Hollywood. The idea that racism no longer stains popular culture and that artists can attain stardom regardless of color has achieved significant acceptance in the late 1990s and early 20th century among both popular and academic discourses. In fact, artists and others have praised popular culture in facilitating color blindness and in ridding future generations of racism. Charles Barkley, in his conversation-based book, *Who's Afraid of a Large Black Man,* celebrates not only the color blind and diverse realities of contemporary popular culture that demonstrate immense racial progress, but also its transformative possibilities. "You had a generation, the one before mine, who are now in their forties, who are in positions of power and influence in their companies in the music industries," writes Barkley. "Now you have a brother in a movie like XXX, you know what I'm saying. Just because rap has kind of churned the soil. The kid who might have been a total racist without rap is like, 'Yo, I like this, I like this. I like everything has to do with rap culture. I like Spike.

I like Jordan. I like Jay-Z. You know it's not so hard to accept.'"[7] Reflecting a color-blind discourse, Barkley links progress to the ascendance of people of color into dominant institutions and the visibility of celebrities of color. In his estimation, the popularity of hip-hop or black cinematic productions is evidence of a new racial politics. Ice Cube follows suit during his interview with Charles Barkley, sharing this celebratory vision of popular culture, one that does not account for the complexity of race and racism within contemporary America:

> I think three things transcend race: music, entertainment, and athletics. After that you've got natural disasters and tragedies and accidents, things that happen where people don't think about race, where something is bigger than what somebody is and where somebody's from, where it's just teamwork because there's an emergency and we have all get together. If everybody's house is burning down, then nobody cares what race you are. We're all going to go help, you know? Race truly goes out of consciousness too, in sports. A dude makes a spectacular play and at the instant you don't care what color he is.
>
> It's pretty much the same in the entertainment industry. In a certain instance you could care less who it is because you saw something and you loved it. Or in music. You hear a song you like and you just like it because it appeals to something in you and you don't give a damn who the artist is . . . not what race the person is, anyway. I think there are things that, on a day-to-day basis, transcend race and put us all on the same plane, you know? But to me, it's also natural for people to root for their own kind to succeed, no matter who it is.[8]

While immensely problematic on many counts, Ice Cube captures the widespread sentiment regarding race within contemporary America and hegemonic understandings of race as an individual act or taste. Of course, the persistence of racism, whether manifesting in slurs against President Barack Obama, persistent inequalities within education and the criminal justice, or the aftermath of Hurricane Katrina, illustrates the fallacies of the postracial narrative offered by Ice Cube and others.

While certainly falling short in terms of critical depth and the understanding of configurations, logic, and grammar of new racism,[9] comments such as these illustrate the complexity of popular culture in the shadows of Jim Crow and the 1960s and 1970s civil rights movement. In this sense, this book explores the nature of African American television in a postsoul moment, whereupon the production and consumptions of blackness were shaped by a shifting political and cultural landscape. According to Mark Anthony Neal, those born between the 1963 March on Washington and the

1978 Supreme Court decision overturning affirmative action at the University of California constitute "soul babies" or the "children of soul." This generation of African Americans came of age in the era of "Reaganomics and experience the change from urban industrialism to deindustrialism, from segregation to desegregation, from essential notions of blackness to meta-narratives of blackness, without any nostalgic alliance to the past."[10] Nelson George, who is credited with coining the term post-soul, describes this moment as one of tremendous transformation:

> They came of age in the aftermath of an era when many of the obvious barriers to the American Dream had fallen. Black people now voted wherever and whenever they wanted and attended integrated schools. They hurried toward a future with a different set of assumptions from any minority kids in American history. . . . As they grew up, both the black middle class and the black lower class expanded; they grew up with Wall Street greed, neo-con ideology, Atari, Gameboys, crack, AIDS, and Malcolm X as a movie hero, political icon, and a marketing vehicle.[11]

The changing landscape doesn't merely define African Americans, but society as a whole. Whereas black America can be seen as a post-soul generation in this moment, society as a whole, and particularly white America, is defined by coming of age amid new racism.

The characteristics of new racism are the shifting political, economic, and cultural faces of America embodied in the increased visibility and commodification of blackness alongside the persistent inequality, dehumanization, racial violence, and continued denial of political power to black Americans. Patricia Hill Collins describes new racism as "the juxtaposition of old and new, in some cases a continuation of long-standing practices of racial rule and, in other cases the development of something original."[12] Amy Elizabeth Ansell defines the era as one of tremendous inequality and the hegemony of cultural arguments:

> It is a form of racism that utilizes themes related to culture and nation as a replacement for the now discredited biological referents of the old racism. It is concerned less with notions of racial superiority in the narrow sense than with the alleged "threat" people of color pose—either because of their mere presence or because of their demand for "special privileges"—to economic, sociopolitical, and cultural vitality of the dominant (White) society. It is, in short, a new form of racism that operates with the category of "race." It is a new form of exclusionary politics that operates indirectly and in stealth via the rhetorical inclusion of people of color and the sanitized nature of its racist appeal.[13]

The increased visibility does not exist apart from the persistent inequality and injustice, but in fact operates on a shared plane: "The clock has been turned back on racial progress in American, though scarcely anyone seems to notice, " concludes Michelle Alexander within *New Jim Crow: Mass Incarceration in an Era of Colorblindness.* "All eyes are fixed on people like Barack Obama and Oprah Winfrey, who have defied the odds and risen to power, fame, and fortune."[14] The conditions on the ground shape each and every institution, whereupon popular culture operates as both a space for the perpetuation of the exceptions and exceptional narratives alongside those spaces of contestation. Bambi Haggins identifies this moment as one where black artists demonstrate how and why they were "laughing mad." She concludes,

> No longer was the laughter solely to keep from crying; the civil rights moment marked the beginning of black humor's potential power as an unabashed tool for social change, for the unfiltered venting of cultural and political anger, and for the annunciation of blackness. The humor, as conceived, and received within the community, spoke to a deep cultural impulse, extending beyond articulating suffering in muted tones to howling about oppression and subjugation, as well as the victories in survival amidst strike. Comics and audiences were laughing mad.[15]

African Americans on Television: Race-ing for Ratings looks at television through this post-soul era, up through the present moment, examining the contested meanings within and beyond television, reflecting on the dialectics between the representational field and the broader political, social, economic, and cultural fields. It spotlights the moments of interruption as well as those instances of the perpetuation of dominant racial discourses. *African Americans on Television: Race-ing for Ratings* thus illustrates the contradictions and limitations of a narrative of racial progress, a story that emphasizes racial acceptance and racial transcendence within television. Instead, we seek to demonstrate the ways in which race infects the textual/representational utterances, the context of audience reception, and the larger social/cultural/economic landscape. We work to underscore the cultural, political, and social meanings conveyed through the narratives offered during the last four decades, arguing that the history of African American television is a space of both racialization *and* resistance, both empowerment *and* demonization. In order to understand the multiplicity of effects surrounding the African American presence in television, as well as the problems embedded in the accompanying social discourses, it is crucial to construct a new lens through which to comprehend the larger racial, social, and political resonances of African American television. The first step toward this expanded framing is to see television as more than mere entertainment with a neutral ideological location, and instead as a powerful social regulator that maps out cultural boundaries of normativity through the narrative frames and representations that are continuously recycled and circulated for mass consumption. Even those moments that are marked as anomalous within television culture because of their seeming departure from the conventional modes of television are still confined by those modes in the ways in which they come to be initially positioned *against* convention and oftentimes ultimately assimilated into convention in order to serve market demands. The role television plays in securing this sociocultural hegemony helps to determine the limits of the ways that a large majority of the population of consumer-citizens make meaning of their world, including where they position themselves and where they position others. For better or for worse, in contemporary times, televisual epistemologies account for a considerable degree of people's social "knowledge" about the world around them due mainly to their broad accessibility, coupled with other factors including trends of separation between social groups based on race and class, as well as the raced, classed, and sexualized anxieties engendered by those trends. Television, then, becomes a site of social ordering that is arguably more powerful than other institutions of social ordering because the veil of "entertainment" effectively hides the mechanisms of social, political, and cultural hegemonies on which it operates and makes invisible the constitutive nature between mass consumer culture and systems of social marginalization. This collection seeks to lift that veil.

The traditional narrative outlined above casts the last 50 years of American popular television as one of progress, setting the standards for race relations and integration. The predominance of black artists and artists of color within consumer culture, from Bill Cosby and Oprah Winfrey to Tyler Perry and Dave Chappelle, as well as their personal and financial successes, overshadows the realities of segregated schools, police brutality, unemployment, and the white supremacist[16] criminal justice system. The deployment of evidence that purports to affirm color blindness erases those many institutions and occurrences that demonstrate the continued relevance of race. Worse yet, as argued here, dominant televisual discourses not only erase present-day inequities and persistent color lines but also facilitate, naturalize, and justify contemporary racism and white privilege. Both denying and reaffirming the relevance of race, all while maintaining a façade of color blindness, contemporary popular culture exists as a powerful vehicle of our racial status quo.

Evident in shows like *Amos 'n Andy,* and characters like Beulah and Rochester, the history of African American television is one of demeaning stereotypes. J. Fred MacDonald[17] summarizes the larger history and trajectory of African American representations during the early part of the 20th century:

> African Americans were present at the birth of television. They were regularly before TV cameras in local and network programming. Granted, they were usually seen in the context of musical entertainment. Granted, too, that blacks almost always appeared as guests rather than regulars or hosts—and when they did host their own series, blacks did not enjoy success. But these were the early days of video. Few expected overnight changes in entertainment patterns. And the fact that there were so many African-American personalities to be found in the young medium kept viable the promise of bias-free programming. There were, however, ominous signs in early TV. The most threatening was the great popularity of black entertainers when they appeared in controversial stereotyped roles.

He notes that the early history is one of caricatures and the ubiquity of the Mammy, Coon, and Uncle Tom archetypes. He notes that the Mammy was particularly omnipresent during this televisual history:

> The mammy figure—usually portrayed as a portly black maid in a white household—was a familiar stereotype. She emitted a certain human warmth that was sometimes difficult to discern beneath her aggressive self-confidence and implacable personality. In early television the black maid was a highly popular character. . . . As portrayed by Ethel Waters, followed by Hattie McDaniel for a short while, and then Louise Beavers, *Beulah* appeared for three seasons between 1950 and 1953. *Beulah* was surrounded by familiar types. Her dim-witted friend was Oriole, the black maid of the white family next door. When played by Butterfly McQueen, Oriole was a flighty woman of minimal intelligence. When Ruby Dandridge assumed the role, she added a heavy dose of her recognizable high-pitched giggles to Oriole's personality. Beulah also had a boyfriend, Bill Jackson. As played by Percy Harris, Dooley Wilson, and Ernest Whitman, he may have been the owner of a fix-it shop, but Jackson was oafish, perpetually hungry, and definitely unromantic.

Alongside the Mammy, who was the embodiment of a heavy, conscientious, and lovable stereotype of the black domestic, was the Coon, whose lack of intelligence, laziness, and overall cultural deficiencies not only provided a source of laughter and pleasure for viewers but reified racial hierarchies:

> Black men were also successful in stereotyped characterizations. Eddie Anderson had little difficulty moving his Rochester character from radio to TV on *The Jack Benny Program.* As Benny's valet, confidant, and "conscience," Rochester had been a strategic part of the broadcasting success of the program since 1937. He contributed substantially to its television popularity once Benny moved his show to video in the 1950s.
>
> Although Jack Benny and his writers had toned down considerably the minstrel-show quality originally possessed by Rochester on the radio, Anderson's character was still a stereotype. Usually the only black in the telecast, Rochester was a chauffeur and general handyman for his white boss. Anderson's naturally harsh voice gave him a vocal quality akin to the throaty "coon" dialect developed by minstrel-show endmen who cracked race jokes between themselves and the white middleman, the interlocutor. Although he was not as stark a caricature of black manhood as Sleepy Joe and Bill Jackson, Rochester did little to advance the cause of the realistic portrayal of African Americans in popular culture.

The production and consumption of television in the years before and immediately after the civil rights movement are best understood in the context of racial apartheid—Jim Crow, lynchings, and overt social, political, and economic discrimination. By the 1970s, amid protests from industry groups, actors and actresses, and television viewers, the representations available began to change. Shows like *Good Times, The Jeffersons,* and *Sanford and Son,* along with television movies like *The Autobiography of Miss Jane Pittman* and *Roots,* not only challenged the monopoly of whiteness on television, but also introduced viewers to experiences, narratives, and ideologies otherwise erased from public discourse. The 1970s and early 1980s witnessed what Christine Acham describes as a "revolution televised." This moment was defined by "numerous instances of black agency," where "African American actors and producers disrupted televisions traditional narratives about blackness and employed television as a tool of resistance against mainstream constructions of African American life."[18] These shows also demonstrated great potential for African Americans on television, convincing the industry of the interest and economic viability of black shows, especially when those shows reaffirmed dominant understanding of race. *What's Happening* and *Diff'rent Strokes,* where black bodies were the prominent focus of the programs but were cast in the frame of accepted stereotypes, are two examples of this reaffirmation of dominant assumptions about blackness.

Moving beyond typical discussions of shows, portrayals, and actors as good or bad examples of racial representations of blackness, this collection looks at the complicated and dynamic relationship between politics, racial identity, and popular culture. It considers how shows, portrayals, and actors are historically located and how the resulting representations of blackness have been responses to and reflections of the American audience's ability to confront larger issues of race, racism, and inequality in society. Responding to claims of color blindness, racial transcendence, and postracialness, we look at the consistent themes, narratives, stereotypes, frames, and emotions across time and space. Our collective voices examine specific programs and television events of each decade that, together, comprise the broad view of African Americans in television but that, individually, provide the cultural texts on which we will base our analyses and through which we will follow the development of trends, the evolution of black cultural resistance, the shift in the significance of African Americans in the television market and industry, and the changing, but enduring, face of stereotypes and racism in American television culture.

Though it is reflective of the binary thinking that our collection is interested in challenging, a good place to start our study of African American television is with a strategically oversimplified idea that all television shows exist within the continuum of two opposing poles: containment and resistance. While television shows of containment "maintain the values and representations that shape popular media discourses are determined by the dominant classes," those resistant in nature "have the capacity to subvert dominant ideologies and regimes of representations."[19] While seemingly easy and reassuring to divide the history of shows featuring African Americans into one of two inflexible, determinative categories, as either reinforcing stereotypes or challenging these same representations and as either detrimental to full inclusion within the American fabric or a necessary challenge to continued exclusion, our discussions of the shows in this collection are invested in examining the contradictions, instability, and multiple meanings through which these shows operate. This book works to demonstrate the ways that shows, over time, in different eras and contexts, both advance *and* challenge the logic and operation of American racism. At times, these shows, and the other televisual representations of blackness, naturalize/rationalize racial inequality; perpetuate stereotypes; erase the relevance of racism within America; celebrate the American Dream, racial progress, and the growth of the black middle class at the expense of the black poor; and ultimately minimize the importance of racial difference beyond cultural and commodifiable traits. Evident in our collective discussion of television is how these representations become a moment of debate and contestation. These shows are explicit manifestations of both Stuart Hall's prescient assessment of popular culture as a "struggle for ideological dominance in absence of pure victory or pure domination"[20] and S. Craig Watkins' description of popular cinema as a "perpetual theater of struggle in which the forces of containment remain in a constant state of negotiation."[21] While containing ruptures and contradictions, the history of American television is largely a story of shows, narratives, tropes, and visual languages that perpetuate the existence of white privilege and existing formations of racial order. While serving as a site of pleasure and financial gain, television also functions as a powerful vehicle in defining, constructing, and disseminating the message of dominant political and cultural ideologies.

For our purposes, the significance of television productions is not limited to their reconstitution of African American voices, communities, or experiences, but in their perpetuation, rationalization, and justification of the silencing of African American voices, the violence inflicted on African American communities, and the limited sociopolitical and socioeconomic access available to African Americans. Yet, television has also been a space of opposition, a vehicle for challenging and resisting the representations perpetuated throughout the American cultural landscape. As such, this project critically traces a cultural genealogy of African Americans in television. While it provides an inclusive historical account of how African Americans entered the genre of television and have continued to play a central role in the development of both the medium and the industry, the project also combines this fundamental history with critical analyses of the racial politics of television and the effects that television have had on popular notions of black identity in America throughout the decades since the inception of television. This collection highlights the ways in which representations of African Americans have remained consistent in spite of changes in visibility, cultural recognition, and even the types of representation. In looking at the history of African Americans on television from integration through the changes resulting from *The Cosby Show* and Fox's African American programming up to the types of televisual offerings of the last 20 years, we seek to underscore the cultural moves that have taken place amid the persistent racialization of blackness. Especially with the growth in children's television programming, reality television, and cable television, this book looks at how the changing nature of television has impacted, and continues to impact, the representations of African Americans. We bring together scholars and voices dedicated to exploring the dynamic yet interconnected history of African American representations. From *The Cosby Show* to *Scandal*, from *The Jeffersons* to *Bernie Mac*, from *Living Single* to *In Living Color*, from the Evans family to the Neelys, and from network television to cable, and now online, the space of television has been one of contested meaning over the representations of blackness. The representational struggle has not been limited to questions and challenges to the stereotypes, narratives, and images afforded to African Americans but also over what these shows teach viewers about America. In other words, the post–civil rights landscape has been one of shifting representational offerings, each of which taught viewers about blackness, whiteness, race, and America into the 21st century.

In looking at this recent history, in chronicling the key shows and themes, central debates, and representational tropes, in highlighting the ways that television has been central in both the perpetuation of, and the resistance to, American racism, this collection moves the conversation beyond a positive/negative binary. It reflects on how changing racial discourses and the increased visibility of blackness have had an equally constitutive effect on the face of both American television and American society generally going into the 21st century.

And now back to our regularly scheduled program. . . .

Notes

1. Herman Gray, *Cultural Moves: African Americans and the Politics of Representation* (Berkeley: University of California Press, 2005), p. 18.

2. Patricia Hill Collins, *Black Sexual Politics: African Americans, Gender and the New Racism* (New York: Routledge, 2005); Eduardo Bonilla-Silva, *Racism without Racists: Color-Blind Racism and the Persistence of Racial Inequality in America* (New York: Rowan and Littlefield, 2003).

3. Gray, *Cultural Moves*, p. 186.

4. Leon Wynter, *American Skin: Popular Culture, Big Business and the End of White America* (New York: Random House, 2002), front jacket.

5. Wynter, *American Skin*, p. 7.

6. Ellis Cashmore, *The Black Culture Industry* (New York: Routledge, 2000), p. 1.

7. Charles Barkley and Michael Wilbon, *Who's Afraid of a Large Black Man?* (New York: The Penguin Press, 2005), p. 131.

8. Ice Cube quoted in Barkley and Wilbon, *Who's Afraid of a Large Black Man?*, p. 132.

9. Bonilla-Silva, *Racism without Racists*.

10. Mark Anthony Neal, *Soul Babies: Black Popular Culture and the Post-Soul Aesthetic* (New York: Routledge, 2002), p. 3; Bambi Haggins, *Laughing Mad: The Black Comic Persona in Post-Soul America* (New Brunswick, NJ: Rutgers University Press, 2007), p. 5.

11. Haggins, *Laughing Mad,* pp. 4–5; Nelson George, *Hip Hop America* (New York: Viking Books, 1998), p. ix.

12. Collins, *Black Sexual Politics,* pp. 54–55.

13. Amy E. Ansell, *New Right, New Racism: Race and Reaction in the United States* (New York: New York University Press, 1997), pp. 20–21.

14. Michelle Alexander, *The New Jim Crow: Mass Incarceration in the Age of Colorblindness* (New York: New Press, 2010), p. 175.

15. Haggins, *Laughing Mad,* p. 4.

16. In eschewing muddied definitions of racism that let whites off the hook, this project understands racism in terms of white supremacy. George Fredrickson defines white supremacy as "the attitudes, ideologies, and policies associated with the rise of blatant forms of white European dominance over 'nonwhite' populations . . . making invidious distinctions of a socially crucial kind that are based primarily if not exclusively characteristic and ancestry." George Fredrickson, *White Supremacy: A Comparative Study in American and South African History* (New York: Oxford University Press, 1982).

17. J. Fred MacDonald, "Blacks in TV: Non-stereotypes versus Stereotypes," http://jfredmacdonald.com/bawtv/bawtv2.htm (accessed September 24, 2012).

18. Christine Acham, *Revolution Televised: Prime Time and the Struggle for Black Power* (Minneapolis: University of Minnesota Press, 2005), p. xii.

19. S. Craig Watkins, *Representing: Hip Hop Culture and the Production of Black Cinema* (Chicago: University of Chicago Press, 1998), p. 51.

20. Stuart Hall, "What Is This 'Black' in Black Popular Culture," in *Black Popular Culture,* ed. by Gina Dent (Seattle: Bay Press, 1992), p. 24.

21. S. Craig Watkins, *Representing,* p. 51.

Chapter 1

Consciousness on Television: Black Power and Mainstream Narratives

David J. Leonard

The post–civil rights era saw the rise of two competing and sometimes complementary visions of racial justice and racial equality. In one corner, led by the likes of Daniel Patrick Moynihan, liberal pundits and commentators lamented single-parented homes and the inability of single mothers to lift up the next generation of African American children. More specifically, these critics focused on the existence of single-mothered homes as the reason for persistent poverty, persistent inequality, and persistent gaps between blacks and whites. Yet, this was not the only perspective emanating from these dominant discourses. In another context, activists and commentators pushed aside questions about family structure and personal values to focus on the absence of community control. That is, any issue facing the black community—whether the family or education, the criminal justice system, and media—can be traced back to the absence of power and control from the black community. Progress would thus come with greater influence and control over these institutions. While these debates were not unique to television, the debates about race, politics, and the state of civil rights would be prominent on television during the 1970s.

Good Times, following in the tradition of *Sanford and Son* and *Julia,* entered into this broader discourse, not only giving life to those debates but shaping them as well. Challenging the hegemonic narrative of single-parented black

This chapter contains parts of a prior book written by the author entitled *Screens Fade to Black: Contemporary African American Cinema,* 2006. Said prior material is included herein with the permission of Praeger Publishers Inc., © 2004.

homes and even the logic of integration, *Good Times* pushed the discussions of family, representation, and community control front and center. It seems to heed the calls from members of the black community regarding the erasure of these debates and the overall experience of African Americans from the public discourse. William L. Clay, chairman of the Congressional Black Caucus, described the public discourse in the following way:

> The fact that the black community, black community workers, black organizations and the black movement are variously excluded, distorted, mishandled, and exploited by the white-controlled mass media [is obvious] to the most casual observer. . . . [The media] have not communicated to whites a feeling for the difficulties and frustrations of being a Negro in the United States . . . [or] indicated[d] the black perspective on national and local issues.[1]

Good Times enters into this space, providing viewers with a narrative that both documents and gives voice to the circumstances, trials, tribulations, and joys of a working-class African American family living in the

The Evans family and their neighbor, Wilona from CBS's sitcom, *Good Times*. Shown clockwise, from left: Ralph Carter (Michael), BernNadette Stanis (Thelma), Ja'net DuBois (Wilona), Esther Rolle (Florida), Jimmie Walker (J.J.), and John Amos (James). (CBS/Photofest)

1970s. Identifying the realities of racism, focusing on state violence, and documenting various forms of resistance, *Good Times* elucidated a shared experience often ignored by the majority of white America. While offering an intervention, the potential of the show went unfulfilled because of its reliance on bootstraps narratives, those celebrating the American Dream, and its ultimate focus on comedic laughs over pedagogical interventions. Still, *Good Times* represents an important moment in African American television history, whereupon the status quo and the accepted realities within the mainstream were both put into spotlight and challenged, leaving truth unsettled even for a moment.

Race Consciousness

While highlighting the structural inequalities plaguing black America and the daily confrontation with racism, *Good Times* is compelling because of its explicit race consciousness. This is made clear in the initial episode when Michael notes that "black is beautiful" just "not in oatmeal." In another instance, he notes, "I knew when I was born black I knew life would be difficult." Florida even connects her desire for kids to listen to her to having "respect for black power." In fact in a number of early episodes, Michael is used to highlighting tenets of black power. In many instances, he responds to the utterance of the word "boy" by noting its pejorative and racist history. In this particular episode, Florida, frustrated with J. J., calls him "boy" leading to this exchange:

Florida (*to J. J.*):	Boy.
Michael:	Boy is a white racist word.
Florida:	This ain't no time to be black.
Michael:	Racial freedom demands vigilance.
Mama:	Your mama requires silence.

While undermining the importance of black consciousness in narrating it through a child (referred to as a "militant midget"), the show's engagement with a black power ethos is particularly instructive. In "Black Jesus," Michael replaces the family's picture of Jesus with a painting from J.J. that depicts Jesus as black. When challenged by mama as to the veracity and appropriateness of this image, Michael asks, "Mama how do we know Jesus wasn't black." Citing a passage that was commonplace in the speeches of Malcolm X, Michael notes that Jesus had hair like wool. While this particular episode offers a myriad of narrative themes, the mere focus on black Jesus demonstrates the politics behind the racial consciousness within the show.

Furthermore, the family decision to hang pictures of a black and a white Jesus illustrates how DuBois's notion of twoness operates within the show. In "Of Our Spiritual Strivings," the initial chapter of *The Souls of Black Folk,* W.E.B. DuBois argues the existence of a fragmented African American consciousness, which he describes as "twoness." According to DuBois, the histories of enslavement, segregation, and state violence had resulted in a "double consciousness—two souls, two thoughts, two unreconciled strivings, two warring ideals in one dark body" (3). In other words, the desire to remain black and be accepted politically, economically, and culturally within the American landscape represents a desire "to satisfy two unreconciled ideals" that cannot be reconciled (5). James Weldon Johnson, with *Autobiography of an Ex-Colored Man,* offers a similar assessment of black identity formation, describing it as "a sort of dual personality," where African Americans are forced to reconcile a "desire to help those I considered my people or more a desire to distinguish myself . . ." (21–22; 147). Although both DuBois and Johnson oversimplify the question of identity in relying on a false binary of personal and political liberation, their ideas continue to permeate public and private discourses and academic and popular conversations.

The emphasis on black consciousness is also on display in "Michael Gets suspended." Although not central, this show begins with Florida announcing that she had dreams of marrying Errol Flynn, resulting in this exchange:

> Thelma: But Errol Flynn was white.
> Florida: Honey, in my days, those were the only stars we had to dream about. It was either Errol Flynn and Clark Cable or Step'n Fetchit and Rochester. Somehow, the sword seemed more dashing than broom.

The emphasis on invisibility, self-esteem, and identity isn't compartmentalized but connected to Michael's difficulties in school. Having announced in class that George Washington was a racist who owned slaves, Michael faces a suspension and the wrath of James. Fending off a whipping from his father, Michael justifies his pedagogical intervention by highlighting the educational deficiencies within the ghetto. He also uses this moment to highlight a number of influential African Americans—Crispus Attucks, Daniel Hale Williams, and Peter Salem, who should be taught about in school, providing all students with a better understanding of the contributions of African Americans. Unlike his mother who found inspiration in Flynn and Gable, Michael demanded greater visibility for black history and culture. While holding to the truthfulness of his educational resistance, Michael ultimately agrees to apologize to the teacher because of his desire to succeed in that space. While reminding him about his ability to learn about black history and culture in another space, James encourages him to learn what is being taught in that white-dominated space. He can exist in multiple worlds, navigating through the demands and expectations in these often contradicting and competing worlds. This is shown to be true not just for Michael but also for James who we see reading Michael's black history book.

Whether evident in references to racism, black cultural traditions, or a mere effort to invoke a positive and empowering vision of blackness (Michael's graduate cake is chocolate cake, with chocolate icing and filling with the words "Power to the people" spelled out with chocolate chips), *Good Times* links black consciousness to acceptance, inclusion and equality, building on the notion of twoness. The show's emphasis on black consciousness in the face of white supremacy and structural inequality is particularly visible in its representation of education.

Education

While embracing the language of black power and bringing into focus conversations about race so often erased from public discourse, *Good Times* was, at its core, a show about promoting the American Dream. In celebrating the black nuclear family, in highlighting education as a pathway to success, and in focusing on personal responsibility, *Good Times* identifies racial uplift as the means to overcome poverty, discrimination, and a history of racism. Although reflecting on the context of segregation, police violence, and racial animus, it concludes that through personal change and communal uplift through education and community development the stains of American racism will gradually disappear.

In "Junior the Senior," J.J. struggles in school. The episode not only highlights the importance of education in determining J.J.'s future but also how his success functions as symbolic capital. As the first potential high-school graduate, J.J.'s education represented an achievement for the entire family. Despite its importance, Florida and James remain concerned that J.J. hasn't learned anything despite his passing grades. The symbolic value of a diploma will only take him and family so far. Without preparedness and skills, J.J. faces a difficult future. Concerned, Florida and James set up a meeting with the principal demanding that he receive an education and not just be passed along. The principal explains their practice of social promotion, one that is the result of their lack of resources and pressure to continue to graduate students at sufficient rates. Graduating only prepared students would compromise their funding. Without any ability to change the system, J. J. promises to dedicate himself in the classroom because simply moving forward without learning would turn the American Dream into an American nightmare. The message about the power of education is made clear when James learns that he doesn't get the Foreman job because he has only a sixth-grade education. While a bit celebratory in terms of education as a pathway to success, *Good Times* pushes the conversation beyond individuals to look at the systemic failures of an American education system that has left children in poor communities behind. Yet, "Junior the Senior" represents the unsatisfying possibilities of *Good Times.* At one level, it offers a critical examination of the American educational system, highlighting funding/resource inequality and how social promotion contributes to the illusion of educational advancement and progress. Yet, its emphasis on bootstraps—J. J. merely trying harder/ focusing on learning—and education as a pathway to the American Dream replicates hegemonic narratives.

Writing about the film *Coach Carter,* Jared Sexton highlights the ways that popular culture deploys a narrative of individual success that emphasizes discipline, education, and proper values. "Coach Carter embeds a conservative ideology of individual achievement (which for the players is also the pathway to their rescue and/or/as escape) within his promotion of team spirit," writes Sexton. "Achievement becomes available to any and all that demonstrate the requisite traits: work ethic, respect for authority, obedience, lawful behavior, and self-discipline. Discipline, as we have seen already, is the key issue and its constant repetition across all of the films mentioned thus far is telling. The boys must be brought under control wherever we find them, but it is only in the case of *Coach Carter* that the force of law—the police, the prison— is a real and present danger, is, in fact, omnipresent and immediate" (111). While offering a more complex rendering of this narrative, *Good Times* replicates the bootstraps trope. Acknowledging the constraints and systemic obstacles, it still sells an American Dream achievable through hard work, discipline, and education.

While usually defined through the middle class, *Good Times* constructs the American Dream and a bootstrap ideal through the black working class. As with representations of black middle class that signify the possibility of the American Dream for all, and the declining significance of race, the Evans family is presented as possessing the requisite discipline and work ethic to succeed in spite of American racism. Personal investment in the American Dream and embracing a bootstraps-model work ethic are key to success; these are the qualities that make good black folks. While not dismissing racism, a common practice in those representations of the black middle class, *Good Times* embraces the idea that everyone can make it; while some, because of racism, because of class inequality, because of persistent discrimination, faced a difficult and more tortured path to the American Dream, everyone can live this life. Inequality, segregation, and violence can be overcome through education. That is a central message of *Good Times,* one that exists alongside its explicit race consciousness and pedagogical instruction about American racism.

With "IQ Test," *Good Times* again explores the American educational system, focusing on the many obstacles faced by African American youth. Excited by his impending graduation and his bright future (Michael is able to secure a scholarship not from football), the family faces a setback after Michael takes an unsuccessful IQ test. Michael's score is low, really low, leading the school to encourage him to pursue a trade rather than focus on the academic track. The context for the episode rests with the practice tracking black kids into nonacademic tracks. An important intervention, yet, the show once again backs down on its critical examination of racism, stereotyping, and tracking through its own narrative. Michael's low score is explained by his refusal to take the test because he didn't like the questions. From his perspective, the IQ test was racist because it didn't account for biases, cultural and language differences.

> They don't know it, but that IQ exam was nothing but a white racist test. . . . This one was given by the white people, made up by white people, and even graded by white people. It don't tell you how smart you are, just how white you are. That's why the average black score is fifty points lower than the average white. . . . The black community is different, it has a different language and culture altogether. . . . They ask questions on the rest like this: complete the following phrase, "cup and _____," and you have to choose from four words, *wall, saucer, table,* or *window.* . . . You know what my friend Eddy put down? *Cup* and *table,* because in his house he don't have no saucers to put under his cup.

Beyond reflecting on cultural bias and challenging long-standing stereotypes about black and white intelligence, this speech is indicative of what

Christine Acham refers to the show's "pedagogical content" given its interest in teaching and in highlighting "larger historic realities and social circumstances."[2]

To substantiate Michael's point, Thelma notes how white students score significantly lower on a Black IQ Test. Learning about these biases, Florida and James challenge the conclusion of the school's guidance counselor. Their conversation illustrates a major flaw in education in that its decision makers rely heavily on numbers, statistics generated by biased tests that disadvantage students of color all while privilege white students. Worse, these gatekeepers use these numbers and those surrounding graduate rates, college admission, and demographic distribution in jobs to justify tracking (and incarceration). Refusing to let the system crush his dream, Michael "pulls himself up by his bootstraps" in spite of the system. Representing a missed opportunity to examine the failing system of education and the need for systemic reform, *Good Times* instead returns to the values and discipline of the Evans family as the recipe for success.

Similarly, "Thelma's Scholarship" focuses on the prospect of Thelma securing a scholarship from an elite private school. While Michael laments the prospect of her attending a white school as a token and Florida bemoaning her daughter leaving the nest, the family is initially happy the school will open up its doors to Thelma. Yet, after learning that Thelma is to fill a quota (James describes it as a "coon quota") at the school, the family questions the benefits of this opportunity. Highlighting the ways in which tokenism operates in a post–civil rights context and the persistence of the white man's burden, *Good Times* challenges the political ethos that guides integration. This episode encapsulates the critical nature of *Good Times*—this represents the power of its pedagogical content (Acham, 133)—but its emphasis on autonomy, self-sufficiency, and nationalism. Thelma ultimately rejects the invitation to join Zeta Gamma sorority, which was recruiting her, and even to attend the school, because she views their tokenistic view of her as a representation of the school itself. More importantly, she realizes she doesn't need their help—their privilege, their whiteness—to succeed. Being around white people is not a privilege and opportunity in itself. Notwithstanding inequality, whiteness, and the opportunity to learn alongside white classmates was not progress not only because of the tokenism and mistreatment that defined these experiences but also because of the power within the black community.

In "the cross town bus runs all day, Doodah, Doodah," *Good Times* takes up the issue of busing but does so by emphasizing the issue of civil rights, desegregation, and educational inequality. Michael once again provides the important context, noting that his school "is one of the worst in the country." Protesting at the school board, Michael holds a sign that reads "If you can read this sign you didn't go to Harding Elementary School." In response to growing frustration about poor schools, the district initiates a voluntary busing program. Mr. Pierson, the principal at Harding Elementary School, tries to convince Florida and James to send Michael to Roger Park School, which is located in a white neighborhood. Reflecting white racist logic that "implies that black people are generally motivated to learn" all while ignoring the "disparities" that exist between schools. Mr. Pierson argues, "We've found students like Michael tend to learn when they are surrounded by other students who are highly motivated." Michael is not convinced; he argues that, "Busing is just a way of buying us off." Likewise, Thelma laments how busing will undermine the community and Michael's friendships within the neighborhood. Still, James is determined to get Michael to the white school, for there he will have the best chance of success and the best opportunity to secure the American Dream. Responding to concerns about black children leaving neighborhood schools to attend those in white neighborhood, James reminds his family of the importance of sacrifice for the sake of the American Dream and racial uplift:

> I wish y'all could hear yourselves. . . . I'd be worried about him too, but I worry less about him making his mark in the world if I know he got a chance to get a good education. . . . But two minutes ago y'all was talking just like white people do about bussing—the only reason they talk that way is because they trying to cover up the fact that they don't want to go to school with us.[3]

Unconvinced, Michael refuses to go to this school, leading James to link busing to black pride:

James: Florida, you heard the boy—he don't want to go to school. It's okay. Ain't nothing we can do if he's ashamed of being black.
Michael: What you mean—"shamed of being black"?
Florida: Oh, that was just a mistake. Your father didn't mean it.
Michael: I ain't ashamed of nothing.
Florida: Of course you're not. Maybe you're just scared to sit down in the middle of all those white kids and prove to 'em that you're just as smart as they are.
Michael: That ain't it.
James: That's all right, son. There's a lot of players in the minor leagues who would rather stay there than try and face major league pitching.

Michael:	I could get just as good grades in that school as they do, if I wanted to.
Florida:	I guess we'll never know.
Michael:	You don't think I can.
Florida:	There's only one way to prove it—still got time to catch that bus.
Michael:	You think I'm afraid of them.
James:	Must be. I don't see you moving.[4]

Beyond reducing bussing and educational (in)equality as choice and further elevating education as one of the most powerful tools available for African American uplift, the exchange here points to the ways that *Good Times* reinforces ideas of white superiority. Rather than reflecting on differential resources, its representation of bussing turns desegregation into a question of whether African Americans want to be around the best students, to accept the challenge of competing with white peers. This turn is a troubling missed opportunity to talk about resources and privileges.

Illustrating the strength of *Good Times* because of its willingness to engage in controversial political issues, to reflect on the complexity of policy debates, all while commenting on how race operates within and beyond the black community, these interventions highlight its importance within the larger history of American television. Yet, it also symbolizes a missed opportunity, a common issue that plagued *Good Times,* in that rather than pushing the conversation toward structural changes the show leaves viewers with a clear message: the burden for change, the burden of combating inequality and injustice, rests on black shoulders.

According to Christine Acham, this particular episode encapsulates the show's focus on racial uplift and the burdens placed on African Americans to pull oneself up by one's bootstraps irrespective of the quality of the shoelaces, the conditions, or even the existence of boots. "While acknowledging white society's role in disrupting school desegregation" James and the show itself "lessen the responsibility by shifting part of the blame onto the fears of black people." She continues:

When James claims that busing assault were the results of a "few sick people," he deflates the issue from an institutional level to an individual one. The issue against busing and the problems of the elementary school are primarily enunciated through Michael, the person who wields the revolutionary rhetoric but the least power in the house. This constructs militant ideology as childish. . . . The dignity, strength, and issue of double consciousness—the notion of proving yourself to the white population—are all evident. Again, however, in places the responsibility of fighting racism solely on the shoulders of black folks.[5]

As with its discussion of poverty, the story of *Good Times* is one of important interventions, significant challenges to dominant narratives and representations; it is also a story of missed opportunities and one that too often relied on dominant narratives about the American Dream and the Protestant work ethic, tropes, and ideologies that undermined its representation of American racism, educational inequality, and poverty.

Poverty

In numerous episodes, *Good Times* highlights the existence of poverty, its impact on the Evans family, and their heroic efforts to persevere in spite of injustice. Both J.J. and Michael sleep in the living room on a pullout bed. In several separate episodes, various household items break down. In "The Visitor," the family's poverty is highlighted in their living conditions; the heating unit is broken (it is 45 degrees in the house); the elevator is broken; the refrigerator is broken; half the light bulbs are out; there is no running water; and of course the washing machine is broken. *Good times* consistently pushes viewers to think about poverty in relationship to broader economic happenings within the 1970s. In "Michael Gets Suspended," J.J. references the "weak dollar" while Florida laments inflation in the form of rising food costs. In "The Gang," James comments on the horrid economy, noting, "the only thing preventing the country from going to the dogs is the cost of dog food."

One of the prominent themes of *Good Times* focused on welfare and the ways in which stereotypes about the black community impacted public discussions about public assistance. In the initial episode, viewers are introduced to the Evans family. Although a working-class family with parents and children both contributing to the economic vitality of the family, they are struggling to make ends meet. Health-care costs resulting from Florida's bout with appendicitis and tax demands push the Evans family to the brink of eviction. Although embarrassed, Florida responds by applying for public assistance. The alternatives—James hustling for dollars at a local pool hall or J.J. suggestion of stealing, prospects that Florida describes as immoral—are unacceptable. Unfortunately, Florida is denied access to welfare because James makes one hundred dollars over the limit of 4,200 for a family with three kids. Beyond illustrating the unjust nature of welfare policy and the absurdly low financial threshold for public assistant eligibility,

Good Times highlights the ways that welfare functions as a racial project. As noted by Michael Evans, "rich folks don't take welfare, they call it a subsidy," an idea that certainly plays out racially as well. In the end, James secretly converts his pool skills into some needed dollars to thwart their eviction, highlighting the power and determined ingenuity of the family, who despite the unfair rules of society continue to not only survive but also have a good time.

Good Times provides countless moments that spotlight the dialectics between employment and poverty. Notwithstanding their work ethnic, the family remains burdened by poverty. The focus on welfare illustrates the broader focus on social issues and systemic injustice. In "The Check up," James arrives home immensely stressed and frustrated about being overworked and underpaid. The economic predicament facing the family is thus linked to the issue of health disparities. Michael and Thelma both lament the fact that hypertension is the number one killer of black men, a fact that results from the stresses associated with ghetto life and the injustices of American racism. Yet, the show also takes aim at how soul food—chitterlings, pork, collard greens, and corn bread—exacerbates these systemic health disparities. Both economic inequality and cultural practices are depicted as a source of disease and unhealthiness. Foods may be source of health issues but so are racism, poverty, and injustice. The show's efforts to represent James as a strong father, to document his own dialogue with dominant stereotypes about black masculinity, points to its larger intervention against the depictions of the black family. In its narrative structure and overall tone, *Good Times* "counters the condition of father-lacking" so commonplace within dominant stereotypes.[6]

Moreover, the representations of James as a complex character, one whose identity and passions are full of contradictions and depth, encapsulate the nature of this important intervention. James is presented as having "a wide range of emotions . . . including vulnerability and sensitivity to issues surrounding the lack of fathers in his life and the larger community. Part of the appeal of James Evans Jr. to black audiences remains that he was one of the fullest and most balanced representations of black fatherhood" on and off television.[7] His importance demonstrates "the significance we have placed in American society, and the black community specifically, on the relationship between fathers and their sons and on fatherhood and masculinity."[8] Highlighting dominant inscription of black masculinity, black femininity, and black families (blackness), Mark Anthony Neal elucidates the ways that black fathers are historically represented as absent and that their absence is to blame for the problems facing the black community. *Good Times* challenges the assumptions and conclusions here, "Constructions of deviant sexuality emerge as a primary location for the production of these race and class subjectivities," writes Micki McElya in *Our Monica Ourselves: The Clinton Affair and the National Interest*. "Policy debates and public perceptions on welfare and impoverished Americans have focused relentlessly on the black urban poor—blaming nonnormative family structures, sexual promiscuity, and aid-induced laziness as the root cause of poverty and mobilizing of welfare queens, teen mothers, and sexually predatory young men to sustain the dismantling of the welfare state."[9] Throughout history, black fatherhood and motherhood are ubiquitously cited as the cause of (national) problems or as an issue that young black males have to overcome. *Good Times* provides an example of a counter narrative, and while always successful, it clearly centers a discourse on the culture of poverty and the black family within its representational field.

"The Check-up" also highlights how patriarchy, economic inequality, and those discourses that focus on single black mothers, absentee black fathers, and a culture of poverty contribute to health issues as well. James finds himself increasingly angry because he can't provide for his family, a fact that partly stems from his desire to disprove and counter societal stereotypes. Florida and Thelma suggest that they work; he expresses frustration because that doesn't address the issue of his sense of manhood and his yearning to challenge dominant stereotypes. In the absence of a sufficient paycheck and in absence of society seeing black men as breadwinners, James struggles to feel like a real man:

James: I am the man of the house and I bring home the bacon.
Florida: James you have too much dang pride.
James: What else does a man have to hold onto?

Unable to control his family's financial future, James is able to control his health. He receives a checkup at a free clinic and finds out that his high cholesterol is the result of too many salty foods. While offering a rather simplistic resolution and a half-hearted disruption of patriarchy, "The Check-up" brings together racism, poverty, and health disparities in ways uncommon to televisual culture.

In "The Enlightenment," *Good Times* documents another consequence of poverty, exploring the disparity between whites and people of color in terms of military participation. In this episode, J. J. enlists because of the financial struggles facing the Evans family. In linking these issues and in having J. J. say that he is ready for the army given the violence and squalor of the inner city, *Good Times* explains how race, class, and inequality contribute to military participation from youth of color.

Good Times also deals with housing inequality. In "The Visitor," Michael writes a letter of protest about the housing conditions that exist within the projects. His efforts lead to a representative from the housing authority (Mr. Stonehurst) to pay the Evans family a visit. Mr. Stonehurst promises that things will be fixed with 13–14 months, demonstrating the efforts of the show to highlight the larger social injustice. Similarly, the "House Hunting" episode addresses redlining and how racism prevents black families from securing the American Dream. This show also elucidates how urban renewal is further confining black families to communities with concentrated poverty. Both episodes deal with important issues, pushing viewers to understand persistent segregation and its broader consequences. Yet, both episodes also leave viewers with happy endings, which limit their critical bite. In "The Visitor," the family and Mr. Stonehurst find laughter in their poverty and misery, while "House Hunters" portrays a loan officer and the Evans family coming together to celebrate in spite of their inability to secure the home of their dreams. In an effort to show a family surviving and finding good times in spite of all the injustice and violence, *Good Times* also undermines its own criticism by often ending with happily ever after.

Crime

Another theme that is commonplace to *Good Times* is violence and criminality. The ways in which the show navigates through these issues is interesting given the predominant stereotype about black criminality and the inner city. While not ignoring violence and crime, *Good Times* decenters the issue all while challenging those cultural arguments that have historically pathologized black bodies. In "Family Guy," the issue of violence and crime is front and center all while challenging flattening narratives. Viewers see that their door has six locks on it, while Wiloma and Florida carry a police whistle to the laundry room. Yet, the show doesn't imagine the neighborhood as inherently violent or even more violent than any other community but as a place ravaged because of police failures. "This is no way to live," notes Michael. "Police won't come." Lamenting the absence of black police officers and the lack of concern about the well-being of the many hard-working families living in America's inner cities, *Good Times* positions the issue of inner-city violence and crime as an outgrowth of the culture of racism rather than a culture of poverty. After Thelma is attacked, the family calls the police. Eventually, a bumbling fool arrives at the housing, leading to the following exchange:

James: Tell me something officer, how come you didn't come around here when we first reported it.

Officer: Well, crimes are being committed so fast that we can hardly handle it. But we're making sure law enforcement is the same in chocolate city as it is out in vanilla suburbs.

J.J.:   Yeah, but in the vanilla suburbs, the cops come in with two scoops, whipped cream and a cherry. All we get here is sprinkles.

Likewise, in "J.J. Becomes a Man," viewers are pushed to think about the ubiquity of false arrests, racial profiling, and how racism within American police departments impacts the African American urban experience. Celebrating J.J.'s 18th birthday, the Evans family marks his impending adulthood as he is once again reminded of the cost of being black in America. He is arrested as he fits the profile of someone who robbed a liquor store ("he fits the description"). By documenting how part of the life cycle for African American boys is encountering a racist criminal justice system, *Good Times* highlights this important issue; yet in elucidating the realities of racial profiling and a society that sees black males as inherently criminal, the show also reinforces dominant notions of black criminal. It simultaneously invokes and reifies hegemonic stereotypes of black criminality. With "The Gang," the show represents black criminality through gang members who, despite their stereotypical and clownish demeanor, terrorize the community, scaring black youth to join their gang, and otherwise disrespect authority. The tendency to equate criminality with clownish attributes becomes commonplace in later seasons with Sweet Daddy Williams, a clownish shark/pimp character who dresses like an overdressed peacock and consistently shows himself to be ignorant. By decoupling criminal misconduct from policing, structures of inequality, and larger social forces, all while linking criminality to buffoonery, *Good Times,* especially in its later seasons, plays on dominant stereotypes, turning police misconduct and state violence into a source of laughter. In the end, the show's treatment of crime points to its unfulfilled promise and the shifting landscape in television by the late 1970s.

Good Times is not without problems. It is important to note that its innovation and willingness to provide counternarratives is found in its initial seasons. "As the seasons progressed, the frivolous episodes, out-numbered the more relevant as JJ became the focal point in the sit-com."[10] Offering generic and universal narratives, it's centering of J.J.'s buffoonish antics, and its circulation of dominant stereotypes, *Good Times* defined the changing landscape of television. Angered by the di-rection of the show and television in general, John Amos left *Good Times* in 1976 after he was killed off in a dramatic and sad episode. Ester Rolle then quit the show before the 1977–1978 season. Voicing her frustration about the show replicating long-standing stereotypes, Rolle explained the situation:

> He's [J.J.] and he doesn't work. He can't read and write. He doesn't think. The show didn't start out to be that. Michael's role of a bright, thinking child has been subtly reduced. Little by little—with the help of the artist [Jimmy Walker], I suppose, because they couldn't do that to me—they have made him more stupid and enlarged the role. [Negative images] have been quietly slipped in on us through the character of the oldest child. I resent the imag-ery that says to black kids that you make it by standing on the corner saying "Dy-no-mite!"[11]

The killing of Mr. Evans did not simply remove the empowering pres-ence of John Amos but transformed a show that worked to oppose and re-sist the pathologizing of the black poor; it sought to counter the stereotypes about black urban communities and single-mother homes. His removal from the show transformed its content, narrative and politics.

His character signified the show's class politics, its emphasis on family and struggle, collective resistance, and counter narratives; the reimagina-tion of the Evans through the trope of the single mother and the elevation of J.J. as the show's star led *Good Times* to be just another black comedy that peddled in stereotypes and narratives of shame and demonization.

While the show's transformative possibilities lessened as the show pro-gressed, it is important to understand its limited progressive orientation from the beginning. Its emphasis on education as a pathway to success, its adherence to the American Dream, its promotion of patriarchy, and its imagination of America's inner cities as a place "full of bad habits just waiting to be picked up" (Acham) illustrate how *Good Times,* in spite of its oppo-sitional voice and its points of intervention, replicated many of the tropes and narratives commonplace to American television. While addressing social and political issues, highlighting racism and celebrating race con-sciousness, its reliance on an American Dream ideal and its narrative focus on disciplinarity taught by fathers reveal the unfilled television revolution that *Good Times* promised to be to many viewers.

Paradigm Shift: New Voices or More of the Same?

By the mid- to late 1970s, the cultural popularity of black-themed and more progressive shows waned as conservatism and mainstream multiculturalism gained prominence. By the 1970s, "American movies had already undergone a change that would soon affect television's African American image," writes Donald Bogle. "The black oriented movies of the early 1970s, which had been produced for the black movie going public had been replaced as the era was drawing to a close by new crossover movies. Hollywood believed films with African Americans had to appeal to white audiences in order to succeed at the box office."[12] Television was no different in its efforts to maintain black and white audiences all while celebrating diversity and racial progress sought to deracialize the televisual landscape, scrubbing the significance of race and the persistence of racial inequality. "The same became true of the weekly primetime series in the late 1970s. Now whenever important black characters appeared, they were plucked of the African American community and dropped into a white environment be it a family or work situation: basically a nonethnic cultural setting which to the vast white audience could readily identify with."[13] Whereas *Sanford and Son* and *Good Times* focused on black characters within the black community engaging in black-oriented themes, particularly as it related to the black underclass, this new wave of shows sought to construct a different sort of blackness. J.J.'s emergence as the star of *Good Times* was indicative of one trajectory with greater emphasis on comedy and comic relief as antidote to societal ills. Laughing, even if mocking the other, was once again the source of interracial interaction. Yet, the late 1970s also saw the emergence of a new type of show that exported black bodies into white spaces. Whereas the Evans family lived in the inner city of Chicago, often confronting the intrusion of white supremacy, these new shows would focus on black presence within integrated or white spaces, leading to a whole different set of politics, one grounded in cultural difference rather than differential access to resources, one grounded in opportunity rather than inequality, and one that emphasized the declining significance of race rather than its centrality within the American social, economic, and political landscapes. Two examples of this trend were *The Jeffersons* and *Diff'rent Strokes* (as well as *Benson*) in that each repositions blackness within white and non-threatening (to whiteness; to notions of American exceptionalism) settings. In ushering in a new era, these shows replaced the paradigm established by *Good Times* during its first year of shows racially conscious and dedicated to pedagogical content, leading to a wave of shows that sought to de-emphasize race as material and political construct all while emphasizing racial progress, harmony, and the American Dream.

Notes

1. Quoted in Christine Acham, *Revolution Televised: Prime Time and the Struggle for Black Power* (Minneapolis: University of Minnesota Press, 2005), p. 127.

2. Ibid., p. 133.

3. Ibid., p. 136.

4. Ibid., pp. 137–38.

5. Ibid., pp. 138–39.

6. Mark Anthony Neal, *Soul Babies: Black Popular Culture and the Post-Soul Aesthetic* (New York: Routledge, 2002), p. 69.

7. Ibid.

8. Mark Anthony Neal, *New Black Man* (New York: Routledge, 2006), pp. 111–12.

9. Micki McElya, "Trashing the Presidency: Race, Class and the Clinton-Lewinsky Affair," in *Our Monica Ourselves: The Clinton Affair and the National Interest,* ed. by Lisa Duggan and Lauren Berlant (New York: New York University Press, 2001), p. 159.

10. Acham, *Revolution Televised,* p. 138.

11. Ibid., p. 139.

12. Donald Bogle, *Primetime Blues: African Americans on Network Television* (New York: Farrar, Straus and Giroux, 2002), p. 223.

13. Ibid.

Chapter 2

An Interview with John Amos

Tammy L. Brown

John Amos launched his career as a television actor in the 1970s, and today, he endures as an entertainment icon. From the situational comedy *Good Times* (1973) to his role as actor, director, and producer of the theatrical production *Halley's Comet* (2011),[1] Amos's work has been characterized by his versatility and longevity. He has achieved what most entertainers covet largely because of his undeniable intellect, acting ability, and comedic finesse. Leveraging his acting career as a mode of political praxis, Amos has unapologetically promoted black images that he deems empowering; however, some of his more recent film roles reveal a different approach.[2] For instance, in *The Watermelon Heist* (2003), Amos plays alongside minstrel-like characters, but his own character serves as a counterpoint. In turn, I pose the question: *What can John Amos's career teach us about black actors' complex negotiation between landing roles while remaining true to one's political and creative values?* In February 2011, I discussed this moral dilemma with Amos during a one-hour conversation at the School of Creative and Performing Arts in Cincinnati.[3]

My interview with John Amos echoes *and* expounds on Herman Gray's idea of "cultural moves," which Gray identifies as the "strategies" and "tactics" that black artists have employed to address their underrepresentation in cultural institutions and media.[4] Gray's discussion of strategies used to diversify artistic representations is quite useful, but it does not fully engage with the *long history* of black media images or how the changing political context shaped the nature and scope of black actors' battles for creative control. From the advent of television in post–World War II America through present-day artistic explorations in cyberspace (i.e., YouTube, Twitter, Tumblr, etc.), black artists' modes of resistance have varied to suit the historical moment. Amos's career illustrates the importance of this addendum to

Gray's theory. Amos embodies the multifaceted and ever-evolving tension between the entertainment industry's push to produce lucrative products that appeal to a broad audience versus black artists' desire to preserve their own political and artistic integrity. In turn, I argue that historical context—combined with black artists' individual and political values—determine the efficacy of their resistance to the entertainment industry's profit-driven mandates.

To fully understand the conflict between a black actor's commitment to artistic integrity and the economic forces that sometimes compromise that very endeavor, we must consider historical context. John Amos was both produced by and is a reflection of the culture wars of post–civil rights America. The significant racial divide between the middle and lower socioeconomic classes constituted the core of this cultural conflict. For instance, in 1974, while the unemployment rate spiked across the nation, the 15 percent unemployment rate for black Americans significantly exceeded the 7 percent unemployment rate for whites.[5] Many white Americans reaped the benefits of post–World War II prosperity, exemplified by the comforts of sprawling, suburban life. In contrast, a disproportionate number of black Americans remained within city parameters, living in cramped apartment buildings and struggling to make ends meet. The civil rights movement had pushed legislative progress toward racial equality, but the practice of racism in everyday life persisted. African Americans faced hiring and housing discrimination. Although some black families managed to purchase single-family homes along the outskirts of the city and in rural areas, many lived in housing projects in disrepair.[6] The Evans family on *Good Times,* in which John Amos played the father figure James Evans, reflected this reality of 1970s inner-city black America.[7]

Although the reality of black inner-city poverty inspired a slew of stereotypical depictions of blackness in media throughout the 1970s such as *Sanford and Son, That's My Mama,* and *What's Happening!,* John Amos aggressively challenged this practice during his two-year tenure on *Good Times.* Amos consistently voiced his disapproval of the show's inclusion of a buffoonish character in the form of J.J. In my interview with Amos, he observed, "If [the writers] put J.J in a chicken hat and have him walk into a room, [they] don't have to write anything for maybe another two pages. That's a hell of a lot of writing you save. And you extrapolate that over the amount of shows and these guys are getting like a *paid vacation.*" Amos also requested increased airtime for J.J.'s sibling characters Michael (aka "the Militant Midget") and Thelma, who he deemed more positive role models for young black children watching the show. The precocious and politically astute Militant Midget aspired to become a lawyer, and Thelma set her sights on earning a medical degree. After appearing in 61 episodes over two years, Amos eventually left *Good Times*. He attributed his exit to creative differences and his desire to pursue other projects. His career was defined by his willingness to engage in speech acts of resistance against stereotypical depictions of blackness on multiple fronts—on screen, behind the scenes, and even in absence.

John Amos's very presence on *Good Times* was indebted to comparable protest. Before the first episode was ever taped, costar Esther Rolle presented producers with the ultimatum that she would only accept the role of the mother figure Florida Evans if her character's marital status were changed from single to married. Rolle got what she wanted, and the rest is history. This example illustrates the power of individual black actors who choose to engage in intraindustry protests against images or ideas that they consider degrading. The historical and political context of the 1970s informed such debates. Amos and Rolle were obviously conversant with the prevalent "culture of poverty" theory, which blamed black Americans for their poverty all the while ignoring the strictures of institutionalized racism that produced levels of inequality. Rolle's demand that a father figure be added to the cast of *Good Times* directly challenged sociologist Daniel Moynihan's theory of alleged black family dysfunction stemming from matriarchal, single-parent homes.[8] *Good Times* was part of an era in which televisual and cinematic images loomed larger than life, and, as such, Rolle and Amos's individual activism on the set of *Good Times* carried with it broader political import.

Historical context has shaped black actors' efforts to gain political and creative control of their own depictions. Though Herman Gray's argument that contemporary black actors should pursue diverse venues of expression, beyond television, has its merits, John Amos's efforts to transform the television industry from *within* reflected the ethos of the 1970s. His courageous stance echoed the era's mantra that the "personal is political." In turn, Amos's career demonstrates the sense of agency and power that black actors wield, if they choose to do so.

* * *

February 18, 2011
School of Creative and Performing Arts
Transcribed by Stephanie Reed on March 3, 2011

Tammy Brown: Today is Friday, February 18, 2011, and I'm interviewing actor, writer, and producer John Amos at the School of Creative and Performing Arts in Cincinnati, OH. Good afternoon. Thanks for agreeing to do this interview. I'd like to start by asking you about your experience working on the television miniseries *Roots*.

John Amos: *Roots* was such an important project. It brought *our* story into the homes of America. In school, we didn't learn about black history. Working on *Roots*, I thought of my high school teachers who had ignored black history, and I felt so vindicated.

Brown: Some scholars have said that *Roots* is not historically accurate. And even Alex Haley has called *Roots* "faction"—a combination of fact and fiction. Do you think Alex Haley's creative license compromises the educational value of *Roots*?

Amos: *Roots* was watered down; it was diluted. It was made palpable for the masses. Nevertheless, it was still an effective piece of educational "edutainment" if you would. Because if you remember the subject of slavery had never been addressed with such production values and with such concern and coming from the pen of an African American author. Everything else had been, well you know, Mandingo and those types of things. They had been fantasies coming from a Eurocentric standpoint, which is that all the slaves were happy, etc. All the misconceptions that fed into the justification of slavery, they were perpetuated on a daily basis. And the thing that was disheartening is that I spoke to a group of young students just the day before yesterday, at the museum, the Underground Railroad Museum, if you would. None of them could have been older than 12 or 13, if they were that old, and I asked for a show of hands as to those young people there who had seen *Roots*. I think one hand went up, one! Hollywood's attitude is well "we've done the *Roots* thing, enough of that." In fact I even had one actress who was at an awards show, and I won't mention her name, who stood up before the microphone and said "Oh *Roots* Smoots *Roots*, enough with the *Roots* thing." This was right after *Roots* had made me. It was like hey, wait a minute; I've got the names of every concentration camp memorized and Commondance and everything else because it was drilled into me in every book, every movie: Auschwitz, Dichau, and Buchenwald. I'm not denying that that was a horrific thing; it was horrific what happened with the Khmer Rouge. It was horrific when thousands of Vietnamese were killed for no reason. Of course, those were horrific moments, but I can't say, "oh, well, ok, I'll focus so hard on your misery that I can't reflect on my own history whenever I feel like it or push for it in literature." So that was kind of disheartening.

Brown: What do you think about later depictions of slavery in film? Like *Amistad* and even *Beloved*, Oprah Winferey's attempt to bring Toni Morrison's brilliant novel *Beloved* to the screen?

Amos: I don't want to critique Oprah's work or as a producer. She's done too much, too good. She's made a whole generation aware of the power of books. She's got more people reading and introduced the public to more good books, which I think is so important, that whatever shortcomings she might have had as regard to a film producer, it's incidental. You mentioned another project?

Brown: *Amistad*, Steven Spielberg.

Amos: I thought *Amistad* was extremely well done, but it's to Debbie Allen's credit. Because Steven Spielberg had never heard of *Amistad*. Now here's an educated man and obviously one of the premiere filmmakers of all time. Because of the way he was raised in a very secular, insulated environment, how would you expect him to know about *Amistad*? So, Debbie got into a conversation with him and told him the exciting incredible historical value of *Amistad*, he goes and makes a movie. I thought it was a wonderful film. I think it's a film that should be seen by every school child in this country. You know, it should be institutionalized as much as *Schindler's List* or any other film made about any other ethnicity.

Brown: This is a good segue to think about Black History Month since it's February. When I teach at Miami University of Ohio, I always say "Black History is American History" because we would not have this country, the United States of America, as it exists today, without the labor of enslaved Africans who came here to build the wealth of this country. I'm wondering, do you see yourself as a black American icon or do you see yourself as an American icon or both?

Amos: I don't see myself as an icon. I don't know what exactly an icon is. It's someone who everyone knows and reveres. No, I see myself; my own self perception is that I'm a very lucky guy who found a profession that can be paid handsome amounts of money and receive a lot of perks for something I'd be doing anyway. I'm a storyteller; I'd be telling stories whether I was working here as an actor or whether a part of a janitorial crew. I'd have the rest of the janitors down in the men's room cracking up or over lunch, over bologna sandwiches. I'd have them cracking up because that's who I am, that's what I do; I tell stories. So, as I've matured over the years, I've learned that you must get paid for telling your stories, and if you can negotiate a way to get paid handsomely and tell only the stories you want to tell, then you're an icon.

Brown: I teach a course called "Introduction to Black World Studies," and this week we talked about the idea of racial uplift, and, specifically, we talked about the work of African American elite leaders during the 1880s into the 1920s who were working to uplift the race through a number of ways, some through socioeconomic endeavors. Let's take Marcus Garvey building the black star line.

Amos: Dubois . . .

Brown: Yes, W.E.B. Dubois and his idea of the "talented tenth" and Booker T. Washington's focus on vocational training. Another part of this discussion focused on the idea of revising the negative images of African Americans in the media, at that time, well we'll say in entertainment, minstrelsy shows, vaudeville shows, etc. So, the question is, throughout your career have you seen your work as a type of racial uplift, at all?

Amos: Well I'd like to think that those folks who saw *Good Times* that that helped destroy that misconception that all black men, particularly black fathers, have had to shed, which is: one, we don't love our children; two, we're never responsible fathers, and that most black fathers are absentee fathers. That was one of the reasons that it was the producers and quite frankly the network's obvious intention to perpetuate negative stereotypes about the black community because that's all they were comfortable with was their own misconception. They had sat down in some room somewhere and created and perpetuated and spoon-fed to each other: they're all lazy, all the women are lascivious, they don't care about their kids, they don't care about each other. And when the character J.J., as portrayed by Jimmy Walker, became so blatantly cartoonist, so blatantly buffoonish, and so blatantly, overtly, a flashback to "Stepin Fetchit" and everything else, when I had two other children in the show, one of whom aspired to become a supreme court justice. "The Militant Midget" . . .

Brown: Right, Michael . . .

Amos: Yes, Michael Ralph Carter, a wonderful actor. And Bern Nadette Stanis who played my beautiful daughter, Thelma, who aspired to become a doctor, I believe, a surgeon with a specific specialty. The writers blew right by them, not out of any ingrained sense of suppression, the necessity to suppress that imagery, but more so because it was easy for them. They were lazy. If we put J.J. in a chicken hat and have him walk into a room, we don't have to write anything for maybe another two pages. That's a hell of a lot of writing you save. And you extrapolate that over the amount of shows, and these guys are getting like a *paid vacation*. And meanwhile the show is deteriorating because my other two children who have real aspirations that can be encouragement to other young black students, whether they're in the projects or whatever. I can't be no Supreme Court justice, I can't be a doctor, I'm gonna put on a funny chicken hat and be like J. J.

Brown: Right.

Amos: Television is an extremely powerful medium, and it's been misused in many cases intentionally to perpetuate negative imagery. But it's the imagery that Oscar Micheaux first saw on film that motivated him to become a filmmaker? You asked me about the importance of movies and television. When Oscar Micheaux went to a movie back in the 20s, "Birth of a Nation," which is probably the most inflammatory movie ever made in terms of race relations in this country. He and his wife, who was a very light complected woman, were chased from the theater, and they were part of a group of black people that were literally chased from the theatre with their lives at risk because "Birth of a Nation" so embroiled the crowd and enflamed everybody, with their cartoonist stereotypes of blacks during the Reconstruction Era, that his *life* was at stake. So, he went home, and rather than pick up a gun to go back to do some drive-bys, he said "This *film thing* is incredible, the way it excites people and gets people, and just sets people off." He had been selling novels up till that time.

Brown: Right.

Amos: Well, you know this, course. I'm sure you teach this; I guess I'm preaching to the choir. But anyway, this goes back to your question about the importance of film and television. Well, he became a filmmaker. He went and bought cameras. He found out people who could operate the cameras for him and went on to become one of the most prolific filmmakers in the history of the industry. And, what I'm very proud of is that approximately seven or eight months ago the post office commemorated Oscar Micheaux with a stamp, and myself and Ruby D. were invited to New York to participate in the ceremony, the commemoration—the *acknowledgment* of his existence by the U.S. government in the form of a postage stamp. So, they gave me a laminated picture of the blowup of the stamp, and to me that's more valuable, it's more precious to me quite frankly than any trophy or nomination. I've only been nominated for a couple of deals anyway. But the bottom line is I've got a postage stamp of Oscar Micheaux, and I was part of the ceremony along with legendary icon actress Ruby D. that received that. And they said, "Well you applied your craft in the spirit of Oscar Micheaux."

Brown: That's beautiful.

Amos: So, I asked for two of them. They gave me one, and I asked for one for my son, which he has at his home. And I felt as an aspiring filmmaker, not as aspiring, he's been nominated for a Grammy already for best direction of a country music video, but as I said, as a filmmaker this is from one filmmaker, historical filmmaker to you because you are the new generation. You are the new Micheaux's. And he and his partner Sylvan Price there, I mean these are the guys who are going to be filling the movie theaters and the cinemas for years to come. When people are saying John who, you know, they'll be saying . . .

Brown: Everybody's gonna remember James Evans. Anytime a black male character dies early in a play or movie, I do the "Damn, damn, damn" line that Florida said when your character died on *Good Times*. [*laughter*] But you didn't die early; you had a nice run on *Good Times* . . .

Amos: Yes, James lasted a couple seasons, anyway.

Brown: So how do you think television and film have changed over time since the 70s? From the 70s to the present and let's say other than technology. I really appreciated your discussion regarding the content of *Good Times*. So, what do you think about the content of television and film today? Also, I want to know if you have any specific thoughts on Halle Berry winning the best actress Oscar for her role in *Monster's Ball*? She played a really destitute character, right?

Amos: I saw the movie.

Brown: And what do you think about Denzel Washington winning in the same year for *Training Day*? I personally think he should have won for *Malcolm X,* but I'm curious to hear what you think.

Amos: Number one, the awards are a political process at best. It's: Do you play the game? Do you go to the right parties; do you smile at the right people; will you play the game? If you do play the game and your movies make money, of course, then we'll give you trophy, and we'll let you into the inner circle of, you know, whatever it is. There's a certain amount of political savvy that goes with that, and I suppose if you want the trophy bad enough you'll play the game. Myself, I'm from New Jersey. I've lived in Hollywood and worked in Hollywood for a long time. . . . I have a low BS threshold. And as the young lady said who just won for *Precious.* . . .

Brown: Monique?

Amos: Yes. When Monique was initially nominated, they asked her, "Well, will you be going to the parties to campaign for the Oscars?" She said, "No, the work is on the screen, and they should go for the work." And then wiser minds prevailed and said "look, you're gonna be around for a long time; you're gonna love doing this. You're gonna love what you do, play the game." So, she reluctantly began to give interviews and go to the right parties and events or to let them know she was not against the Oscar. She just didn't want to have to do anything unnatural to win. She wasn't going to beg the people to acknowledge her work. So, I feel pretty much the same way. My work speaks for itself. And it's a political process; it has nothing to do with talent. It's a self-congratulatory club. At the end of the day, tell me who won the Oscar for best actor two years ago or best picture two years ago? Not this past year, but two years ago. Or best picture two years ago?

Brown: I'm not sure.

Amos: That goes to show you the significance of a trophy, right? And they've got so many award shows now; there's gotta be one a week. And the fact that it's no longer about talent—that does not hold true for the writing. Good scripts, like I went to see a film that didn't have one black person in it, made no reference to a black person, *The King's Speech*, which is a superb movie. A *superb* film because it dealt with King George VI who had an incredible speech impediment and how he got over it and what it took for him to get over that. That's something that everybody can relate to. I'm not saying that I'm down on movies that don't have black folks in them, but don't show me a movie that has nothing I can relate to and that is also badly written and badly acted, badly performed. I ask myself more often, "How did they get that bloody thing financed?" I want to be in the room when they sold the picture. You know: I have a dog that talks Ukrainian, and he's a spy for the CIA, and I'm like, "Ok. . . ."

Brown: For Denzel Washington, when he won the Oscar for best actor, I think it was more of a lifetime achievement award. And even the way he accepted the award, he seemed so calm, cool, and collected. . . .

Amos: Well, they weren't gonna give it to him for *Malcolm X* because that would have been to congratulate the life of Malcolm X. They would have had to acknowledge Spike Lee. They would have had to acknowledge *Malcolm X*'s influence on the world, not just the United States. They weren't ready for that yet.

Brown: For Halle Berry, in *Monster's Ball?*

Amos: The way Anthony Anderson said it, she had to let . . . what's his name?

Brown: Billy Bob Thornton?

Amos: Right, she had to let Billy Bob play quarterback before she could get an Academy Award. So, if there is any truth in that, who knows? We'll never know. It's such a political process anyway, that just kind of confirms it, doesn't it, right?

Brown: So what about the critique of a film like *Monster's Ball,* and even Monique winning for *Precious* confirms this idea that America is only willing to consume black pain? Black suffering—this voyeuristic tendency to view black suffering but an unwillingness to view black accomplishment on the screen and celebrate that. Do you think that's a valid critique?

Amos: It might have been a totally valid critique at one time, but thanks to the sensitivity of some directors, who don't have a racist agenda, that's changing—changing for the better.

Notes

1. *Halley's Comet* (2011) is a one-man theatrical play, written, produced, and performed by John Amos. In this show based on his own family history, Amos plays the role of an elderly black man who has seen *Halley's Comet* twice in his lifetime—once as a young boy perched on the shoulders of his father and again as a man in his twilight years. Amos uses the cosmic phenomenon of *Halley's Comet* as a trope to reflect on nearly a century of changes in African American history— from African American soldiers' participation in World War II through the civil rights movement through the present. I attended Amos's performance of *Halley's Comet* at the School of Creative and Performing Arts in Cincinnati, OH.

2. In *The Watermelon Heist* (2003), written by Kristine A. Tata and directed by John Amos's son K.C., John Amos plays "Old Man Amos," a mature man who is fed up with the Brown family's uncouth antics. The film opens with a reference to comedian Chris Rock's famous skit titled "Niggaz versus Black People" from Rock's second stand-up comedy album *Roll with the New* (1997). As the film's narrator, Old Man Amos suggests that the Brown family's crude behavior exemplifies Rock's argument that such behavior is not an accurate reflection of *all* black people.

3. My interview with John Amos took place on Friday, February 18, 2011. While in Cincinnati, Amos performed his one-man play *Halley's Comet,* and he led professional development workshops for high school students at the School of Creative and Performing Arts.

4. In Herman Gray's study of representations of blackness in the literary, visual, and performing arts, he explores the ways in which black artists have challenged

"histories of black exclusion, denial, and invisibility in American cultural institutions." Herman S. Gray, *Cultural Moves: African Americans and the Politics of Representation* (Berkeley and Los Angeles: University of California Press, 2005), p. 186.

5. Robert W. Fairlie and William A. Sundstrom, "The Emergence, Persistence, and Recent Widening of the Racial Unemployment Gap," *Industrial and Labor Relations Review* 52, no. 2 (1999): 252–70 cited in Algernon Austin, "For African Americans, 50 Years of High Unemployment," *Economic Policy Institute,* February 22, 2012, http://www.epi.org/publication/african-americans-50-years-high-unemployment/ (accessed September 24, 2012).

6. William Whyte brilliantly captures suburban life in post–World War II America in *The Organization Man* (1956). For a discussion of the downside of gendered roles and suburban malaise among white middle-class housewives, see Betty Friedan, *The Feminine Mystique* (1963).

7. *Good Times* is set in Chicago in a high-rise apartment building—a setting deliberately chosen to invoke the notorious Cabrini-Green housing project.

8. This concept of dysfunctional black families is based on sociologist Daniel Moynihan's notorious study titled *The Negro Family: The Case for National Action* (1965).

Chapter 3

Looking for Lionel: Making Whiteness and Blackness in *All in the Family* and *The Jeffersons*

Lisa Woolfork

All in the Family (1971–1979) and *The Jeffersons* (1975–1985) are recognized as two of the most popular television shows of the 1970s and early 1980s. *All in the Family,* in particular, is widely regarded as groundbreaking. The show ranked number one in the Nielsen ratings for five consecutive years (1971–1976). It was nominated for 41 Emmys and 21 Golden Globes and won 3 Emmys in its first season (Outstanding Lead Actress, Outstanding Comedy Series, Outstanding New Series), with many more to follow. In 1978, main characters Archie and Edith's living room chairs were installed in the Smithsonian Institution's National Museum of American History. In 1998, a 33-cent U.S. postal stamp honored *All in the Family.* Though not as acclaimed, *The Jeffersons* (a spin-off from *All in the Family*) ranked fourth in the Nielsen ratings in its first year. The following two seasons it remained in the top 30, only to rebound to the top 10 and top 20 slots in its final years. The show received 11 Emmy nominations during its 11 seasons. Isabel Sanford, who played Louise Jefferson, was nominated for Best Actress in a Comedy Series each year from 1979 to 1985. She won an Emmy in 1981: the second African American actress to do so.

Both shows brought social and cultural issues from the real world to the televised world. *All in the Family* is generally recognized as the first television show to deliberately and directly comment on the compelling social issues of its time. Similarly, *The Jeffersons,* through the character of George, revealed that black people could hold prejudices as ardently as white people

could. The protagonist's frequent use of racist language and characterizations only added to the show's verisimilitude.

Both shows departed from the popular television programming model.
The late 1960s were a socially turbulent time for the United States. In 1968,
civil rights leader Martin Luther King Jr. and Democratic presidential candidate Robert Kennedy were assassinated within months of each other. In
1969, U.S. troops began to withdraw from Vietnam but not quickly enough
to stem the tide of rebellion against the war as evidenced by the half a million protesters that marched in Washington, D.C. Students sat in, boycot-
ted, and occupied colleges and universities around the country in protest
of the war and to demand equal educational access. One consequence of
these protests was the death of students killed by national guardsmen (Kent
State, May 4, 1970) or police (Jackson State, May 14, 1970).

Despite the social upheaval of the late 1960s, the version of America
depicted by television sitcoms and dramas was calm. As Richard P. Adler
observes, there was nothing "wrong in the world that could not be set right
by a cop, a cowboy, or a doctor. At the end of 1970, for example, the ratings were dominated by melodramas such as *Ironside, Mannix, Marcus
Welby, Medical Center, Gunsmoke,* and *Bonanza.*"[1] Adler also notes that the
world of comedy programs was even further removed from the tensions
of its day, with popular shows ranging from "the slapstick and silliness
or *Here's Lucy* and *Bewitched* to the rusticated humor of *Hee Haw* and
Mayberry, RFD."[2] Such programs were deliberately escapists. As a result
of television's imperative to appease advertisers and not offend viewers,
"the characters who inhabited these programs were almost wholly devoid
of opinions, either pro or con, about any of the political or social issues
of the day."[3] This silence about current events resulted in a cognitive gap
between nightly news programs (which were riddled with disturbing yet
true events) and the easily resolved simulated problems that followed the
six o'clock news.

All in the Family, the first salvo from what would become Norman Lear's
arsenal of 1970s prime-time programming dominance, closed the gap between the reality of social tensions on the news and the portrayal of the
effects of those tensions in the life of an American family. Much has been
written about *All in the Family* and the controversies it generated. The goal
of this chapter is to illuminate certain aspects of the racial values depicted
in *All in the Family* and *The Jeffersons.* A common narrative of both programs was the racism of their flawed patriarchs. This chapter reorients the
conversation, away from discussion of interracial conflict and bigotry and
toward a perspective that allows us to peer into the racial interior of the

Bunker and Jefferson families. The aim of my approach is to reveal an alternative understanding of what race means and how it functions in both programs. To do this, I "look for Lionel." I contend that through the character of Lionel Jefferson, one can gain a fuller appreciation of the complex racial climate of *All in the Family* and *The Jeffersons.*

First appearing in the pilot episode of *All in the Family* and later evolving into a full character on *The Jeffersons,* Lionel Jefferson is both a compelling witness to and participant in the foibles of the central conflict in various episodes of both shows. Lionel featured in the pilot episodes of both shows. Altogether, he appeared in 33 episodes of *All in the Family* and in 69 episodes of *The Jeffersons.*[4] By looking for Lionel, one can discover the intricacies of racial representations, especially the intraracial variety (how racial identity is formed within a particular racial group). I will first explore the ways in which as a foundational program *All in the Family* establishes a type of racial (and racist) logic that circulates around the patriarch. Archie Bunker's racism, the venom of which is frequently tempered by his malapropisms, fosters a system within the family that permits his racist ideas to be continually diminished, critiqued, and ultimately dismissed. In addition to the show's presentation of racism as a social problem, I suggest that its depiction of whiteness as an intraracially formed idea and an identity marker is equally, if not more significantly, present. Specifically, I discuss the ways that Archie and Mike (through interactions with Lionel) cultivate two distinct forms of whiteness. In the next section, I examine the intraracial logic in *The Jeffersons* as filtered through George Jefferson, a character crafted as a black answer to Archie Bunker's white racism (Lear wanted to show a black man who could be as bigoted as Archie). Here, I consider the ways in which the family's social striving and upward mobility help them to craft a new form of black identity. In the new environment of Manhattan's Upper East Side, the Jeffersons strive to remain true to their roots.

All in the Family and *The Jeffersons* have been evaluated many times by both scholars and the mainstream press. Most commonly addressed are Archie's racism and the vigor with which he displayed it. A *Newsweek* article from 1971 sums up the shock value of Archie's racist language, claiming that Archie "speaks what was utterly unspeakable on television before him. He sees himself menaced by a rising tide of spades, spics, spooks, schwartzes, coons, colored, Chinks, Commies and their Commie crapola, jungle bunnies, jigs, pinkos, pansies, hebes, yids, Black beauties, bleeding hearts, tamale eaters, yentas, atheists, weirdos, dumb Polacks, dingbats, meatheads, fairies, fruits, fags, and four-eyes. These are the words he uses in a medium that usually minces words to the consistency of toddler food."[5]

Presented this way, Archie Bunker is a bigot whose defining characteristic is his racism and xenophobia. But there is another aspect to Archie's
hostile attitudes. In addition to being menaced by other racial groups, I
suggest that Archie's white racial identity is constantly being formed and
remolded by his racist invocation of these others. Through his acts of verbal racial profiling, of placing and putting down other races, Archie not
only exhibits racism. He is involved in the equally important task of formu-
lating and defining his own racial identity.

Lionel is the lens through which to witness the conversations that are
a part of racial identity formation in *All in the Family* and *The Jeffersons*.
The perennial arguments between Mike and Archie or Louise and George
are not just about racism as a social problem. They also become a method
by which each man (my focus on the male protagonists), as a member of a
racial group, configures his racial image of himself. The arguments about
race that are staged in *All in the Family* or *The Jeffersons* are not just displays
of bigotry, they are also ways each man simultaneously configures boundaries around (and shores up from within) whiteness in *All in the Family* or
blackness in *The Jeffersons*.

My efforts here are guided by the considerable work in African American
studies on representations of blackness as subjects (in literary or cultural
formations) or as objects (such as Toni Morrison's *Playing in the Dark*,
which addresses blacks' presence and their role in making whiteness). The
burgeoning field of Whiteness studies, a critical methodology that seeks to
make whiteness visible, informs my approach to *All in the Family*. Scholars
such as Richard Dyer, Eric Lott, and others aim to race whiteness, which
too frequently, is an unraced social position. Only rarely do white people
claim, defend, or notice their whiteness. In what follows, I aim to consider
the ways in which whiteness is subtly rendered visible.

All in the Family and Whiteness

All in the Family became the top-rated prime-time show for five consecutive
seasons, but it took a while for audiences to accept the frank language and
sensitive subjects that were staples in the Bunker household.

—Turner[6]

Prior to acquiring *All in the Family*, CBS's prime-time television lineup was
aging star vehicles featuring Lucille Ball and rural offerings like *The Bev-
erly Hillbillies*, *Green Acres*, and *Petticoat Junction*. These shows were successfully aimed at CBS's viewing audience, which was largely middle aged

and rural. However, the newly burgeoning field of market research, which among other tasks ranked viewers according to their buying potential, revealed CBS's stable yet older audience as a liability. Advertising revenues for younger audiences (like those who watched *Mod Squad* on ABC) were sold at a premium and generated vast income for the other two networks, while CBS could not compete. Eager to attract new viewers, especially the younger and urban, CBS found its answer to its flagging ratings in a show that had already been rejected by ABC. *All in the Family* would bring a different set of viewers to CBS.

Its concentration on the patriarch was nothing new in American television; many situation comedies had revolved around a dominant father. What made *All in the Family* different was that the father figure was also deeply flawed. His racist and sexist commentaries were constant features of Archie's character, as he weighed in on important public issues of the day and presented his personal and private views. CBS was willing to take the risk of this new program, but they also hedged their bets by including the following disclaimer with the first 13 episodes: "The program you are about to see is *All in the Family*. It seeks to throw a humorous spotlight on our frailties, prejudices, and concerns. By making them a source of laughter, we hope to show—in a mature fashion—just how absurd they are." The disclaimer was followed by the sound of a toilet flushing.

In her study of prime-time families, Ella Taylor notes that "The quantity of earnest explanatory publicity that accompanied the show's debut lodged it firmly in the minds of its creators, the networks, the sponsors, the FCC, and the critics, if not the viewing public at large, as a new form that dealt seriously with current social issues."[7] Taylor's overall assessment seems dismissive of *All in the Family*'s intent to engage the contemporary scene—she consistently refers to Lear's work as "'relevant' programming" thus calling into question the word "relevant." She similarly treats the word "black" when discussing *The Jeffersons*. However, her observation that *All in the Family* marks the end of idealized family portraiture in television is accurate.

All in the Family's nonidealized family is a powerful departure from America's preoccupation with its own airbrushed family imagery. This family is different not because of its bigoted father, or permissive mother, or combative son-in-law, or child-like adult daughter. *All in the Family* is a forward-thinking program, the content of which anticipates the critical work of whiteness studies as a subdiscipline of both African American studies and American studies. From the very beginning, *All in the Family*'s title is to be taken literally. When we look for Lionel at the launch of the show, we find him: right in the heart of the Bunker family. Lionel is more than an object of prejudice, more than a neighborhood kid doing odd jobs (the use of "kid" is deliberate: Lionel is in precollege at this point in 1971, attending college by the 1975 debut of *The Jeffersons*). Lionel is incorporated into this family[8] and is part of its process of making, unmaking, and remaking whiteness in the Bunker family.

In 1971, the pilot episode, "Meet the Bunkers," aired on CBS as a midseason replacement. Despite the title of the episode, the Bunker primary characters are the last to appear. Dutifully preceded by the requisite disclaimer about the mature nature of the show's humor, Edith and Archie sing the opening credits theme song that was to become an icon of the series. However, when the episode actually opens, the interaction is not between Edith and Archie but between daughter Gloria (who is busily setting the table for her parents' 22nd anniversary brunch) and her husband Mike, trying to distract her with sexual advances. Gloria rebuffs him saying that everything must be prepared by the time her parents return from church. Mike replies, "We've been living with your folks since we're married. We don't get the house alone that much!" Gloria corrects him: "Oh, we're not alone. Lionel's upstairs." After explaining that Lionel is repairing her father's television, Gloria recounts the other tasks that Lionel will perform that day: "And then later he's gonna take the present and get some fresh-cut flowers and deliver them together, just to make it more romantic."[9]

There is something remarkable in the notion that Lionel's imagined (rather than actual) presence is the significance of the show. Consider Toni Morrison's *Playing in the Dark: Whiteness and the Literary Imagination*. The study explores the ways in which "Black people ignite critical moments of discovery or change or emphasis in literature not written by them."[10] She approaches blackness as a symbolic figuration, a symbol with multiple thematic, structural, and social resonances and responsibilities. In an assessment of early American literature, Morrison demonstrates that a real or fabricated Africanist presence was crucial to these authors' sense of their American identity. A similar process is at work with Lionel Jefferson and *All in the Family*. It is through Lionel that we can explore the often-invisible process by which whiteness gains its currency as an identity.

From the very beginning of the show, even before Archie and Edith appear, actually even before *he* appears, Lionel is framed as significant to the story. He is implicated in the working out of Edith's surprise. As Gloria explains, it is his participation—taking the gift and returning it with fresh flowers—that will make the day more romantic for her mother. This arrangement is strange for the position in which it locates Lionel. He has been ensconced in the Bunker's bedroom (repairing the television); he is the reason Gloria gives for rebuffing Mike's advances (they actually *don't* have the house to themselves); he has a role to play in Edith's anniversary gift (taking it and enhancing it with flowers). All of these things take place without Lionel's physical presence; thus, the idea of Lionel (who we don't know is black yet) is framed as one who is closely linked to this family. At this point, Lionel could be anyone: a sibling, a child, a cousin. He is framed as someone who belongs. When Lionel descends the stairs and enters the living room, he immediately starts a conversation that invokes Mike's racial formulation of himself:

Lionel:	Hey, so what's new on the campus with all you angry white social democrats?
Mike:	Oh, we're shaking them up.
Lionel:	(*laughs*) Okay. (*looking around*) Hey, where's your father-in-law?
Mike:	Oh, he's at church.
Lionel:	Good.
Mike:	Why? Is he still giving you a hard time?
Lionel:	Oh, I'm used to him by now. You know his latest kick?
Mike:	What?
Lionel:	Asking me what I'm gonna be when I get to college. He likes to hear me say: "Ahm gwana be a 'lectical engineer."
Mike:	And you say that for him?
Lionel:	Give the people what they want, man. How else do I get to *become* an electrical engineer?[11]

Lionel immediately has a dual role: as trickster as well as the lens through which we see two different forms of whiteness evoked. In the first case, cued by the beginning of the conversation, Lionel's opening salvo comments on Mike's whiteness. In a jesting tone, Lionel identifies Mike as one of many angry white social democrats. The visibility of their activism and the degree to which they take themselves seriously are apparent in Mike's reaction. Mike is not offended at being called angry or white. In fact, he embraces both positions as social facts of his identity. It can be inferred here (and will be made more explicit later) that Mike is a certain type of white man. He believes that all men should be treated fairly and that there are social inequities that have privileged white over black. That he is aware of these inequities (and is majoring in sociology in order to help people) and seeks to level the playing field depict him as a type of white man different from his father-in-law, who represents another form of whiteness.

From the dialogue above, it is clear that Lionel and Archie have a long-standing relationship, though it seems based more on propinquity and time than mutual respect. When Mike asks if Archie is "still" annoying Lionel, it seems that a mild antagonism (on Archie's part, not Lionel's) is a feature of their relationship. Archie finds amusement in Lionel's college ambitions, as well as his chosen field. But what are we to make of Lionel's speaking in dialect to Archie? Why does he say "lectical" engineer rather than "electrical?" This deliberate choice to speak in a way that Archie expects to hear black speech is part of the supporting role that Lionel plays in the manufacture of whiteness in *All in the Family*. Lionel can speak Standard American English perfectly well. He toys with Archie in order to stir the pot, to keep the flame of Archie's racial anxiety lit. In addition, his performance allows Archie (who frequently malaprops his way through entire episodes) a sense of verbal superiority. Finally, he is someone Archie can laugh at which becomes a way to reinforce the declining value of his whiteness. In fact, the possibility that Lionel Jefferson can go to college to become an electrical engineer while Archie is stuck in his factory job limits the traditional value of Archie's whiteness, which was contingent on black exclusion from higher education and other public sites reserved for whites. But if Lionel tells Archie that he will study "lectical" rather than "electrical" engineering, then part of Archie's place in the world as a racial superior remains secure. This is the game that Lionel is playing when he defends his actions to Mike: Lionel is giving the people what they want, and Archie wants the deteriorating significance of his whiteness to be shored up.

In several episodes of the show's first season, Lionel appears in the Bunker home (or at an off-site location with members of the Bunker family) to reprise his role as observer/participant in the configuration of whiteness for this family. In "Gloria Discovers Women's Lib," Lionel briefly visits the Bunker family while Gloria and Mike are bitterly disputing the idea of women's equality to men.[12] Seeking aid from Lionel, Mike asks if the black community has similar issues with women's liberation. Lionel replies, "No. We're working on just liberation."[13] In "Archie Gives Blood,"[14] Lionel encounters Mike and Archie, the latter who has been pressured by Mike to donate. Archie has maintained throughout the episode that white blood and black blood are fundamentally different. Archie is surprised to see a Chinese man at the donation center but relieved when the man is revealed to be a doctor, not a donor. After Archie explains that there must be different Red Cross centers for Chinese people in Chinatown and black people in Harlem, Lionel Jefferson appears—right on cue. Mike prods Archie to restate his claim that blood banks are separated, but Archie refuses, telling Mike instead to "dummy up, dummy up, will ya?" When further pushed by Mike to share his views, Archie succumbs, saying that Lionel's presence at the blood drive is to "do odd jobs or something." Lionel, in his characteristic trickster pose (grabbing the lapels of his jacket and preening), validates Archie's point with an exaggerated, "Oh, yes! I sweeps up! I left my broom back there."[15] Mike excuses himself from the conversation. Lionel slides over to occupy Mike's vacated seat, sitting closer to Archie than before and starts in an earnest tone:

Lionel: Poor, Mike. They get all confused, don't they, those goody-goody white liberals. You tell them all men are brothers, you tell them all men come from the same God, and right away they think we got the same blood. Ain't that ridiculous?
           (*long pause, laughter, as the camera closes in on Archie*)
Archie: I know what you mean.
Lionel: Yeah, if they start pumping our blood into you white folks, who knows what would happen? You could all turn black.
Archie: Well, I tell ya, Lionel. I think that there's some doubt about that.
Lionel: You wouldn't wanna chance it, would you?
Archie: No.[16]

This brief exchange is wonderfully timed and filmed. The long pauses between the lines and the close-ups of each man enhance the conversation and emphasize its value. The comic timing and the camera work are striking: lingering on Lionel, the camera gives the audience time to see the levity of Lionel's tricksterism. When the camera concentrates its focus on Archie's face, we see him happily reckoning with an unsolicited endorsement of his position. Archie is gleeful that he has been proven right about an issue that he and Mike have disputed. Not only is Archie right and Mike wrong, Archie's validation has come from the mouth of a black man. When Lionel exits, Archie simultaneously chides Mike and praises Lionel, saying, "That kid has common sense. He knows his blood isn't the same as yours even if you don't."[17] Later, Mike confronts Lionel about his teasing (putting on) of Archie:

Mike: Lionel, you don't know the trouble you start when you put him on like that.
Lionel: Yeah, you're right, I really ought to stop, but I can't resist the temptation.[18]

Here, and on numerous episodes, Lionel relishes his role as the trickster enabler of the "loveable bigot."[19] Lionel also configures the boundaries of whiteness. For Archie's character, those boundaries were solidified as Archie engaged with Lionel in ways that cemented his ideas about whiteness. For Mike's character, the flexibility of whiteness was similarly reinforced as his and Lionel's conversations frequently differentiate between Mike's liberal and Archie's closed whiteness.

The notion that Lionel's presence indicates that a racial identity assessment process is underway is especially apparent in "Henry's Farewell," a fourth-season episode in which Henry Jefferson, George Jefferson's brother, leaves the neighborhood to open a dry-cleaning business in upstate New York. (The Jeffersons have lived next door to the Bunkers since the eighth episode of Season 1: George and Louise are Lionel's parents; Henry, his uncle, has also lived there and appeared in several episodes.) This episode marks the first appearance of George Jefferson. Lear had planned on including George's character in the early days of the series when Louise and Lionel were present. However, Sherman Hemsley's stage acting commitments (he had a lead role in the hit show *Purlie*) prevented it. George was often referred to offscreen as a black counterpart to Archie. George's absence from the show was explained by his racist refusal to visit the Bunkers. In the words of his brother, in the episode "Lionel Steps Out," George had never been in a "honky" home and "wasn't going to start at the bottom of the heap."[20]

In addition to marking the first appearance of George Jefferson (who enters Bunker's home, affectionately toasts his brother, and then leaves after insulting Archie), this episode is one of the clearest instances of the intraracial fashioning of whiteness for Mike and Archie. Though most critical work about these programs concerns interracism and the effect of having white racism so graphically depicted, it is also fruitful to evaluate the degree to which whiteness and blackness are configured in *All in the Family* and *The Jeffersons*. One should consider instances of cross-racial antagonism as more than just expressions of bigotry; they are also the methods by which Mike and Archie cultivate individual expressions of their whiteness.

For Archie, the blustery castigation of blacks and other racial minorities is a way for him to make sense of his whiteness and to preserve its value in a changing social environment. Mike, on the other hand, inverts Archie's racist invective and responds with an aggressive defense of black equity, demonstrating that he is not threatened by black social parity. This is part of Mike's strategy to create a self-generated picture of whiteness, based not on his father-in-law's closed reactionary bigotry, but instead on a more open type of whiteness that includes considerations of black life through the same lens as his own.

The central conflict in "Henry's Farewell" concerns the change of venue for Henry's good-bye party. Lionel appears early in the episode to get plates and cookies from Edith for the evening's festivities. Archie remarks that Lionel must be glad that his uncle is moving since he will now get his own bedroom. Lionel replies that he has always had his own bedroom. Archie is shocked to learn that the Jefferson home has three bedrooms while his home only has two:

Archie: You're telling me your house is bigger than mine!
Lionel: Sure, Mr. Bunker. You didn't know that? I gotta room. He got a room. (*Then, in a bass voice, to the tune of "All God's Children Got Shoes," he sings.*) All God's children got rooms . . . . (*He jives and hums the song, teasing.*)
Archie: Will you cut it out, Lionel? Geez. I ask you a simple question and you give me the Mills Brothers.[21]

Mike repeats Lionel's shucking-and-jiving routine later in the episode. Archie refuses to attend Henry's party on the grounds that he will not "set foot in no house where the head of that house don't wanna set foot in this house." When Gloria urges him to use the party as an opportunity to connect with George, Archie is adamant: "what's so perfect about getting together with a guy that treats me as if *I* was the one that was the colored guy?"[22] When Edith unwittingly offers her home for the integrated party that George refuses to host, Archie also rejects the idea. He does not want to host an integrated party.

Mike: You know, you're the last holdout. Archie, don't you see? The crisis is over!
Archie: What crisis?
Mike: Black people have arrived. They're here!
Archie: (*shouting*) I ain't letting em in![23]

There is a connection between Archie's refusal to visit the Jefferson home, or host an integrated party, and his observation that George treats him as if he were the colored guy. This is more than Archie getting a taste of his own medicine, though that is an intriguing line of inquiry. Archie has been treating colored people in hostile and dismissive ways from the throne of his armchair. Yet, it is difficult for him to believe that a black man sitting on his own armchair throne would treat a white man (or him particularly) in the same way. It is curious that Archie objects to being treated like a colored guy. This is significant because it does more than turn the tables. George's hostility toward Archie is not just Norman Lear taking a working formula (Archie's bigotry) and giving it a black mouthpiece. Beneath George's diminishing gaze, Archie feels that he has been treated as if he were colored. His whiteness (including his authority and dominance) has been diminished by the fierce consistency of George's refusal to acknowledge him, let alone engage in conversation. This helps to explain the vehemence with which he will not allow the party to take place at his home. After demanding that Edith retract the invitation to host the party at the Bunker home, Archie is stymied by his family. Gloria tells her mother that she need not obey her father's every command:

Gloria: Ma, you got some rights in this house, too. We all got rights.
Archie: I ain't denying that.
Edith: You ain't?
Archie: No. You gotta say. The little girl gotta say . . . .
Mike: (interrupts, singing) All God's chillun gotta say . . . .
Archie: (turning toward Mike) The colored guy here has gotta say . . . .[24]

This referral to Mike as the "colored guy" is different from the disempowered approach Archie took to his own temporary sense of disenfranchisement at George's rejection. In calling Mike colored, Archie reactivates the jesting and teasing tone in which Lionel informed him that the Bunker home was smaller than the Jefferson's. Mike does not respond to this colored label as an insult (which is very different from Archie's response to being treated like the colored guy). In fact, Mike's more open form of white identity allows for even more cross-racial play (thought not mockery). This permits him to use Lionel's jape to get back at Archie. His open form of whiteness has once again announced its difference from Archie's, who is shouting: "I ain't letting em in!"

Though *All in the Family* was known for its interracial conflict, the program's intraracial aspects are also worthy of attention. As I hope to have shown, *All in the Family*'s racial narrative is not just one of a loveable bigot who spouts invectively against nonwhites, gays and lesbians, women, and communists. These words are not just slurs. They are both barriers against outsiders and a fortification to protect Archie's own whiteness. Mike's whiteness needs no such reinforcement. By looking for Lionel, we can see how the main antagonists in the Bunker family make sense of their white identity. Lionel serves a similar function in the Jefferson family as his parents struggle to maintain a sense of blackness in their new social context.

The Jeffersons and Blackness

In a 1968 TV Guide interview, Diahann Carroll discussed then current image of blacks on television. Carroll, who enjoyed her own degree of television success with her show *Julia,* claimed that television had failed to adequately represent black life or its concerns: "The needs of the White writer go to the superhuman being. At the moment, we're presenting the White Negro. And he has very little Negro-ness."[25] Carroll's comment on the diminished quality of Negro-ness could be used to explain the racial neutrality of her own program. Critics have observed that *Julia,* though a historically significant contribution to prime-time television, was anemic on matters of racial value. Harry Belafonte, for instance, noted that the *Julia* show was yet another flat portrayal of black life: "for the shuffling, simple minded Amos and Andy type of Negro, television has substituted a new, one-dimensional Negro without reality."[26] One scholar has successfully summed up the prevailing view on *Julia* in her claim that, "Carroll's image in the series has come to mean Black erasure and an elision of racial tensions through an idealized assimilation of people of color within the mainstream. It is not surprising, therefore, that the show was 'originally scripted for a White actress.'"[27]

This view of *Julia* helps to contextualize the contribution of *The Jeffersons* to prime-time television. The family's role on Hauser street as the Bunkers neighbors established them in the prime-time lineup. But it is also useful to consider *The Jeffersons,* briefly, within the larger contexts of black television. My contention that Lionel's presence marks the parsing out of intraracial identity holds equally true of the Bunker and Jefferson families. For *The Jeffersons,* however, it is useful to consider the degree to which this program was permitted to concentrate on the interior world of a black family and its relation to the larger idea of blackness (both the blackness of its past and the blackness of its new present). I discuss *Julia* here to better illustrate the way in which *The Jeffersons* (though a spin-off) was *not* a derivative of either *All in the Family* or previous black television shows. Different from *Julia* (and *Good Times,* its closest chronological analog), the show offered a unique platform on which to display the inner workings of black identity. *The Jeffersons* was distinct from *Julia* in that it was deliberately and generically (as in genre) black. It was not a show that could have been as successful with a white cast. Unlike *Julia,* George, Louise, and Lionel were not meant to be incidentally black.

It is perhaps paradoxical to suggest that *The Jeffersons* should be viewed as a site for intraracial black identity formation. After all, the program was produced by Norman Lear (a white man) and featured many white writers. How much blackness could emerge in that context? As Herman Gray observes, the political and structural formations that control television production are closed systems in which a white majority rules: "For many shows based on the situations and experiences of Blacks, the conventions of television production (especially collaborative writing) serve to discipline, contain, and ultimately construct a point of view. Not surprisingly, the point of view constructs and privileges White middle-class audiences as the ideal viewers and subjects of television stories."[28] Though it is true that whites may have overly influenced the behind-the-scenes aspects of the show, I contend that blackness remained a visible, viable, and fluid construct on the show. Many Black viewers, for example, valued and appreciated the show (both as a first-run program and later in syndication)—a program that was more invested in intraracial matters than the interracial debates that dominate *All in the Family*. As Dorothy Rabinowitz observed of *The Jeffersons*'s plots, "Blacks alone pass judgment on Black problems and on Black attitudes in general. This enables a modest spirit of self-criticism to seem to prevail on these shows."[29] Though there were white writers and producers involved at that level of the show's construction, many scripts concerned matters of intraracial place, rather than interracial progress.

The intraracial value of *The Jeffersons* and its commitment to portraying blackness are apparent at many levels. In a 1976 interview with *Jet* magazine, Isabel Sanford, speaking on behalf of her character, emphasized that "despite their success, The Jeffersons have not forgotten their roots. 'At least, I haven't, and I try to remind George of that.'"[30] "We are people of means, and there are Blacks like that, but they're not portrayed enough [...] I'm glad we have an opportunity to show this."[31] Later in the same article, a viewer objected to the idea that the family's blackness was not typical, "Don't talk to me about *The Jeffersons* not being 'typical'. Every issue of *Jet* and *Ebony* has stories about Blacks who are successful in practically any deal you can mention."[32]

The visibility and viability of *The Jeffersons*'s blackness were so important for the early programming that when these aspects were downplayed in the show's latter years, people noticed. In a 1983 TV Guide article pointedly titled, "As Their Blackness Disappears, So Does Their Character," professor and scholar Mary Helen Washington lamented the shift in the show with an unusual observation: "They don't use the word 'nigger' on *The Jeffersons* any more. There are no more jokes about playing 'Pin the Tail on the Honky,' and Louise has stopped saying, 'ain't' and using double negatives. The Afros have been replaced by sleekly styled hairdos. The references to Harlem and to George's past life there have been almost totally elimi-nated."[33] In Washington's assessment, after more than 200 episodes and nearly nine years on television, the show had abandoned its Blackness in favor of assimilation and blandness. Washington faulted its producers for ruining a "once-Black show" that was more black in its early incarnation: "The reason *The Jeffersons* reruns are so popular is that there is far more of that 'soul' evident in these early episodes."[34] For Washington, the blackness of *The Jeffersons* is inherent to its success: "People I talked to in Cleveland, Detroit, Boston and New York—White and Black—agree that, for them, the show's humor and vitality are rooted in its Blackness."[35]

More recent assessments of *The Jeffersons* would concur with Washing-ton's claim that blackness was a key component of the show's success. In a 2008 book *Black Comedians on Black Comedy: How African-Americans Taught Us to Laugh*, author and comic David Littleton addresses the his-tory of black comedy through the lens of black comedic performers. In this context, *The Jeffersons* emerges as a memorable program. Comedian Mark Prince says, "I loved *The Jeffersons* because every time it came on they would show that episode of him stepping on the White man's back."[36] An-other comedian, Talent, focused on George, saying, "Here go a brotha that's f*#kin' quote, unquote making it; he doing the damn thing, but this nigga still got his niggerism at the top."[37] These comments emphasize both the interracial (stepping on the white man's back has a metaphoric quality of black dominance or even superiority, thought it also refers to the therapeu-tic massage George would perform for his white neighbor) and intraracial values of the show's privileging of a black identity. For Talent, blackness (a nigga is meant affectionately to refer to an informal/nonsanguine kin-ship connection among blacks) was an important element that the show maintained.

From the very beginning of the series, the show concerned the transi-tion of the Jefferson family from lower middle class to upper class while maintaining a black identity. The intraracial element of the family's upward mobility was privileged over interracial conflict (of which there is surpris-ingly little).[38] The predominant impulse in the early days of the show was to show the characters settling in to their new social position. Two episodes from the first season of *The Jeffersons* are particularly illustrative. This is because at this time in the series' history, the novelty of the family's new situation is still fresh. Louise, George, and Lionel are still configuring them-selves and their place as part of the black elite.[39] Louise, much more than George or Lionel, is the character whose new class status interferes with her former sense of self. In several episodes, Lionel's presence witnesses (and sometimes participates in) racial conflict and racial process. And as in *All in the Family*, the racial conflict is not an interracial clash but an intraracial one. *The Jeffersons* in its first season concerns itself with establishing an authentic newly minted form of black identity, one that is wealthy and racially whole and thoroughly black at the same time.

The initial episode of *The Jeffersons*, "A Friend in Need," focuses on Louise's adjustment to her new social environment. The plot centers on whether Louise should hire a maid, as George insists. It begins as Louise and another black woman, Diane, exit the elevator carrying grocery bags. Louise invites Diane inside for coffee. Diane initially demurs but accepts after Louise's line, "I always say: There are two things that are no fun at all unless you have company. And the other one is drinking coffee."[40] When Louise drops her bag in her hurry to answer the ringing telephone, Diane remains outside the door to pick up the strewn groceries. It is there that the comic misunderstanding is established. Neighbor Harry Bentley introduces himself to Diane and asks if she lives in the building,

Diane: No, but thanks for the compliment. I'm a maid. I work for some of the families in the building. I'm just going in for a cup of coffee with my friend. (*indicating the Jefferson's apartment*)

Harry: Oh, that's nice. Then you know the Jeffersons? (*enters the elevator*)

Diane: No. Just their maid, Louise.

Harry: Maid? Oh, I think you've. (*Elevator doors close before he can clarify.*)[41]

It is notable that Diane considers Louise a friend, even though she does not know her last name nor does she know that Louise lives, rather than works, in the building. This does not mean that the relationship is not genuine but rather that the connection the two women have formed is based on interactions that render their class difference irrelevant. For instance, Louise insists that Diane come in for coffee since Diane had "sprung for the Cokes in the laundry room yesterday." Louise does her own laundry, an illustration that the self-reliance she developed as a part of her working-class black identity is still important to her personality. It is the tension between her self-reliance (her desire to do her own domestic work) and her employment of domestic workers that drives the episode's humor. This tension is more than simply one of social class (an adjustment to a higher socioeconomic level): it reflects the ways in which multiple definitions of blackness emerge.

The main conflict manifests itself when Louise and George take opposite sides of the issue of hiring a black maid. When Lionel finally steps in to break up the argument, he ultimately agrees that his mother "could use some help around the place."[42] George's insistence in his new role as boss, employer, or even master of a household is clear in his patriarchal approach that seeks to bend everyone within the sound of his voice to his will. Hiring a maid is part of his contribution to the paternalist system. He has done right by Louise in relocating her to a posh apartment. Diane remains at the level that George and Louise have recently departed: the working class. Louise must shift her thinking and become part of the black elite: hiring a maid is part of this transition.

George attempts to train Louise to see herself differently now that they have relocated geographically and socially. Louise resists his "superior jazz," insisting that Diane is her friend, a claim with which George disagrees.

George: No, she's not. She's a domestic!
Louise: You make it sound like a disease!
George: It's a fact of life, Louise. You own an apartment in the building, and she's a maid.
Louise: Now hold it right there, Buster. Ain't you forgetting where you came from?
George: It's not a question of where I came from. It's a question of where I *am*. You are east Side and she is west Side. And I don't want no crosstown traffic in my kitchen.[43]

George has labored to build his dry-cleaning business and has made it successful. This is the reason he is comfortable and easily (and often gregariously) adopts the practices of his new upper-class environment. Thus, Louise's desire to perform her own domestic work reflects poorly on her status as a provider. Louise, on the other hand, has worked as a domestic and is aware of the strains of social stratification and the requisite performance of black obedience.

Louise: George, remember when Lionel was growing up and I did domestic work a few days a week to sorta help out?
George: Yeah, uh-huh.
Louise: Remember the folks I worked for? It was all "yes ma'am" and "no, ma'am." Now how can I ask Diane to say "yes ma'am" to me?
George: 'Cause now *you're* the ma'am. That's how life goes, Weezy. Some people gotta be the ma'ams and other people gotta be the m'am-ees.   [*Author's transcription.*]

But Louise's anxiety about hiring her friend as a maid turns out to be ill founded. When the issue reaches its climax, it turns out that Diane and Florence[44] see their work as a profession, free of the class and race issues that bother Louise. Louise has seen hiring a maid compromises her integrity and denies the person that she used to be: a black woman who worked as a domestic several days a week to support her family. For her, that position was always racially marked: she was a Black woman in a position of service and her white employers required deference. It is difficult for her to shift from that way of thinking and to force herself to assume the role of (white) employer.

Louise:	Diane, you're my friend. I can't ask you to work for me.
Diane:	Well, I'm sure glad everybody ain't as friendly as you or my children would starve to death! (*Diane turns away to exit.*)
Helen:	(*intercepts Diane*): Hi, Louise! Oh, Diane, you're here. (*putting her arm around Diane*) Here she is. I knew you would like her. Isn't she wonderful?
Louise:	Diane is *your* maid?
Helen:	Yes.
Diane:	Yes. Lucky we wasn't good friends.[45]

Florence ultimately withdraws her application to work for the Jeffersons, allowing Diane to take the job. The resolution is one that has allowed blackness to be discussed indirectly as a function of social class. It has also illustrated that a black person can have multiple versions of a black identity in their lifetime showing that blackness is a process that can shift and change. Louise has learned that she can have money, retain her values, and make friendship across the divide of social class. Diane and Florence are more than simple objects for this lesson. They are also the women that Louise once was: black women domestic workers. Louise's choice to hire Diane is a way in which she combines her former black self with her current one.

The final line of the episode is indicative of the content of many of the early season episodes. At the close, the four black women are standing together: Louise, Florence, Diane, and Helen. Florence verifies that Louise and Helen indeed live in the building, then asks: "How come we overcame and nobody told me!"[46] The laughter is rousing but also suggestive. Two of the four black women might be said to have overcome, in the sense of crossing barriers of racial limitations placed on black life. However, as this and other episodes suggest, a number of barriers *within* blackness remain to be addressed. Louise has crossed one in this very first episode, establishing intraracial concerns as more important that matter interracial.

In "Lionel Cries Uncle," the idea of intraracial solidarity is most clearly examined. The episode features a visit from Louise's uncle Ward, who has worked as a butler for an elite white New England family for many years. George, critical of this employment position, sees Ward as an Uncle Tom (a subservient black man eager to serve whites). The possible implications of Ward's name are relevant. Ward is also the name of the benevolent father figure on the long-running suburban show, *Leave It to Beaver,* and the implication of this name was not lost on viewers of *The Jeffersons.* Louise's uncle Ward is tall, elderly, kindly, dignified, and poised and has elegant manners (his kind words to the usually strident mother Jefferson reduce her to blushing titters). The viewers also recognize in Uncle Ward a wise and patient man, a stark contrast to the blustering George. The battle here as George sees it is between an Uncle Tom and its opposite, a position into which George has thrust on himself. George is self-made, pompous, and confident; all of which he believes distinguish him from the compromising Uncle Tom he believes Ward to be.

This episode stands out as an indication that iterations of blackness are a concern for the series. Unlike *Julia,* which "celebrated racial invisibility and color blindness,"[47] this episode would not work with an all-white cast. Indeed, casting aspersions of Uncle Tom are a part of a racially specific black identity formation process. The insult (and others like Oreo) is meant to police or monitor the performance of black identity on an imagined scale of authenticity. To be an Uncle Tom is to be a race traitor, to step outside the boundaries of black solidarity. More importantly, to *call* someone an Uncle Tom is to *remove oneself from similar scrutiny.* In using the aspersion Uncle Tom, George and Lionel close the circle of an authentic, uncompromised blackness around themselves.

As the title, "Lionel Cries Uncle," indicates, Lionel is a featured character, not just a witness.[48] There are two conflicts at work: the first is the tension caused by George's resistance to Uncle Ward's presence in his home. The secondary problem is ultimately subsumed by the first: Lionel becomes embroiled in trouble at school and must apologize or face expulsion. In the end, both George and Lionel come to respect Uncle Ward and to see that an authentic blackness can take many forms. Uncle Ward is not the obsequious figure George has perceived him to be. When Ralph, the white doorman carries up Uncle Ward's bags, Ward thanks him for the service, using the word "sir." This formality incenses George, who sees the courtesy as yet another example of Ward's kowtowing to white people:

George:	Look, you don't have to say "sir" to my doorman just because he's a honky.
Ward:	That had nothing to do with it. It's merely good manners.
George:	(slapping a wad of bills) Look! This is all the good manners you need. Didn't you see? I just gave him two of these and the "sirs" just came pouring out.[49]

George believes he is schooling Ward on how to maneuver with money. For George, it is not manners, but income that has propelled his family from the working-class neighborhood in Queens to a deluxe residence on the Upper East Side of Manhattan. Indeed, George sees manners as a social pleasantry that only benefits lack men like Ward who thrive in positions of servitude to whites. George sees his wealth as entitling him to live a certain way, a way that does not require the skills of politeness or manners that aided Ward in his position. As George remarked in the pilot episode (which was actually aired as part of *All in the Family*), he has "enough green to cover up the Black," meaning that his race is not a barrier to social access. For George, all you need is money.

To obtain his financial success, however, it is apparent to everyone that George indeed must compromise with his white clients. When Uncle Ward compromises, George calls it "tomming." George has described Uncle Ward as an Uncle Tom so often that even the neighbor, Harry Bentley, cordially welcomes him by saying "And you must be Mrs. Jefferson's Uncle Tom." Later when Uncle Ward asks George why he disparages him, George replies, "Just listen to yourself. Mr. Martin this. Mr. Martin that. Yes, sir. No, sir. Three bags full sir." Soon after this exchange the phone rings and George answers:

George:	Hello, Jefferson speaking. Oh, Mr. Patterson. Hello, sir. (*laughs*) No, it's no problem, we'll take care of it. We'll be glad to. Look, it's my pleasure. Whatever makes you happy is all that matters. Ok? Yes, sir! Goodbye. (*Hangs up phone.*) (*George walks to Uncle Ward, laughing, strutting.*)
George:	Ha, ha! I've been buttering that honky up for six months but it's all worth it because I finally got his business.
Ward:	How come when I do what you just did you call it "tomming?" But when you do it, it's called "business."
George:	What?! Man, don't come asking me no dumb questions like that. About "difference." You know what the difference is! The difference is uh . . .
Ward:	Yes?
George:	Look, everybody knows what the difference is. It's . . . Don't you know the difference?[50]

George cannot articulate the difference because there really is no difference between the negotiations and compromises that he makes in business and those made by Uncle Ward. What is required is that George and Lionel re-evaluate Uncle Ward, who is not an Uncle Tom in the pejorative sense they use. It turns out that Uncle Ward has his own interpretation of Uncle Tom, one that is more militant, self-determined, and community-minded than theirs. Ward tells George that Uncle Tom was based on a black man named Josiah Henson, a slave who escaped Kentucky with his family, moved to Canada, and "started the first manual training school for our people. [Henson also] helped a hundred slaves escape up North even before there was an Underground Railroad. He was a brave man, a great leader, and I'll tell you something else, George, I'd never call *you* an Uncle Tom."[51]

It is this reconceptualized version of Uncle Tom that Uncle Ward uses to keep Lionel in school and to ultimately gain Lionel's and George's respect. When Lionel is threatened with expulsion unless he apologizes for a transgression he did not commit, Lionel angrily tells Uncle Ward, George, and Louise "this is 1975 and I ain't tomming for nobody!"[52] Surprisingly, Uncle Ward agrees with him and gives him another strategy for dealing with the administration. The plan works and Lionel escapes an unjust reprimand. By embracing Uncle Ward as part of the family (and not as an object of ridicule), George and Lionel also learn that there are many ways to embrace blackness and that one version of Blackness need not contradict the other.

Conclusion

This chapter has presented the intraracial logic of two important situation comedies of the 1970s. Rather than assess the prevailing ideas about race and racial attitudes surrounding the programs, I have turned the lens inward and considered their intraracial aspects. Lionel's role in both programs has been key to witness and even enable Archie's and George's racist excesses. He is also the kid who has newly inherited an altered sense of class privilege that exceeds his former racial designation. In the spaces where you find Lionel, we see more than the interracial conflict decried by critics. We also see the unfolding of racial identities (in their own terms) for whites and blacks. In looking for Lionel, we find characters outlining the contours of their own racial identity.

Notes

1. Richard Adler, *All in the Family: A Critical Appraisal* (New York: Praeger, 1979).
2. Ibid., p. xvi.

3. Ibid.

4. As many viewers noticed, there were actually two Lionels on *The Jeffersons.* The original Lionel, played by Mike Evans (1971–1975), (1979–1981), (1985), was replaced by Damon Evans (no relation) (1975–1978).

5. "TV: Speaking about the unspeakable." The Media. *Newsweek,* November 29, 1971: p. 52.

6. Leslie Jackson Turner, "But the Republic Stood: Program Producers' Perceived Pivotal Moments in Network Television Broadcast Standards of the 1970s," *Journal of Broadcasting & Electronic Media* 44 (Winter 2000): p. 110–25.

7. Ella Taylor, *Prime-Time Families: Television Culture in Postwar America* (Berkeley: University of California Press, 1989), p. 67.

8. See figure 1. This promotional family photo was part of a larger photo spread in a 1972 issue of *Ebony* magazine with the cover story "Is Archie Bunker Really White America?" It was the first time a white person appeared on the cover of *Ebony* magazine, a fact that several angry letter to the editor writers noted the following month.

9. "Meet the Bunkers," *All in the Family,* CBS, aired January 12, 1971.

10. Toni Morrison, *Playing in the Dark: Whiteness and the Literary Imagination* (New York: Vintage, 1993), preface.

11. "Meet the Bunkers," *All in the Family,* CBS, aired January 12, 1971.

12. "Gloria Discovers Women's Lib," *All in the Family,* CBS, aired March 23, 1971.

13. Lionel's response that blacks are working on "just liberation" is funny but not fully accurate. Black women were indeed aware of the consequences of sexism and patriarchy in their lives. See work by Michele Wallace, Patricia Hill Collins, Angela Davis that addresses the role of black women in civil rights movements and other black freedom struggles.

14. Archie's preoccupation with the racial properties of blood will continue throughout the series, culminating with him receiving a blood transfusion from a black donor ("Archie's Operation," season 7, aired October 20 and 27, 1976). Later, Archie will cite his "black blood" as the reason for ultimately resisting the Ku Klux Klan, which is recruiting him for membership ("Archie and the Ku Klux Klan," season 8, aired October 16, 1977, and December 4, 1977).

15. "Archie Gives Blood," *All in the Family,* CBS, aired February 2, 1971.

16. Ibid.

17. Ibid.

18. Ibid..

19. A phrase used to describe Archie Bunker in the press and on television. This, I suggest, was one way to come to terms with the popularity of a person who in other representational contexts would be hateful and reviled.

20. "Lionel Steps Out," *All in the Family,* CBS, aired October 14, 1972.

21. "Henry's Farewell," *All in the Family,* CBS, aired October 20, 1973.

22. Carroll O'Connor, the actor who plays Archie, stumbles over this line, though the intent is as I have written it.

23. "Henry's Farewell," *All in the Family,* CBS, aired October 20,1973.

24. Ibid.

25. Richard Warren Lewis, "The Importance of Being Julia," *TV Guide,* December 14, 1968, p. 28.

26. Demetria Rougeaux Shabazz,"Negotiated Boundaries: Production Practices and the Making of Representation in *Julia,*" p. 151–64 in *The Sitcom Reader: America Viewed and Skewed,* ed. by Mary M. Dalton and Laura R. Linder (Albany: SUNY University Press, 2005), p. 159.

27. Robert Lewis Shayon, "'Julia': Breakthrough or Letdown," *Saturday Review,* April 20, 1968, p. 49.

28. Herman Gray, *Watching Race: Television and the Struggle for Blackness* (Minneapolis: University Minnesota Press, 1995), p. 71.

29. Dorothy Rabinowitz, "Watching the Sit-coms," *Commentary* 60 (October 1975):p. 201.

30. Bob Lucas, "The Jeffersons: A Black Family is Moving Up on TV," *Jet,* November 11, 1976, pp. 102–4, 114.

31. Ibid., p. 104.

32. Ibid., p. 114.

33. Mary Helen Washington, "As Their Blackness Disappears, So Does Their Character," *TV Guide* 31 (1985), pp. 4, 5, 8.

34. Ibid., pp. 4, 8.

35. Ibid., p. 8.

36. Darryl Littleton, *Black Comedians on Black Comedy: How African-Americans Taught Us to Laugh* (New York: Applause Theatre and Cinema Books, 2008), p. 120.

37. Ibid., p. 122.

38. This is not to say that George Jefferson was not bigoted against white people. Nearly every episode featuring Helen and Tom Willis, television's first interracial married couple, also included a requisite insult from George. But in terms of racism against blacks, however, there were no interracial barriers or resistance to the Jeffersons' living in the building. This contrasts with the resentment that Archie Bunker expresses when he learns that a colored family (the Jeffersons) is moving next door to him.

39. My use of the term black elite is a bit problematic. As Lawrence Graham suggests in his study, *Our Kind of People,* the black elite is an exclusive (and reclusive in some ways) social formation in black communities. George Jefferson may have merited a place in the black elite by virtue of his wealth; however, he would not be counted among their number because of his poor/working-class origins. He lacks the pedigree, college background, and participation in the organizations that comprise the core of black elite society. For my purposes, I refer to the family's new situation as one of black elite because they contend with retaining a particular form of black identity (coded here as not forgetting about one's past) while thriving financially. This also characterizes Graham's conception of black elite.

40. "A Friend in Need," *The Jeffersons,* CBS, aired January 18, 1975.

41. Ibid.

42. Ibid.

43. Ibid.

44. This is the first appearance of Florence (played by Marla Gibbs) who will become the Jefferson's maid later in the season.

45. "A Friend in Need," *The Jeffersons*, CBS, aired January 18, 1975.

46. Ibid.

47. Gray, *Watching Race*, p. 85.

48. "Lionel Cries Uncle," *The Jeffersons*, CBS, aired March 1, 1975.

49. Ibid.

50. Ibid.

51. Ibid.

52. Ibid.

Chapter 4

What's Your Name? *Roots*, Race, and Popular Memory in Post–Civil Rights America

C. Richard King

I am not sure that I actually saw *Roots* when it originally aired. I was after all eight when the epic miniseries premiered on ABC in January 1977. Nevertheless, I have a vivid memory of one particular scene, arguably among the most iconic in television history. Following a failed escape attempt, Kunta Kinte is captured and returned to the plantation, where the overseer strips him and strings him up for a whipping. The overseer does not wish to simply dole out punishment but wishes to break the young slave before his peers who have been forced to witness the impending brutality. He repeatedly asks him "What's your name?" and instructs him to respond "Toby." Initially, Kunta balks and defiantly repeats his given Mandinkan name. An act greeted again and again with the lash. In the end, severely beaten and exhausted from his escape attempt, Kunta relents and takes his new name, much to the delight of his overseer and the obvious chagrin of his fellow slaves.

The scene captures two hallmarks of *Roots:* on the one hand, it takes up slavery, a subject little discussed, perhaps even taboo, in public culture (sadly true even some 35 years after the miniseries premiered), stressing the violence and dehumanization at its core; on the other hand, it renders Africans in the diaspora as fully human, actively resisting oppression as they struggle to retain a sense of themselves and their heritage. As tempting as it is to stop here and only celebrate the significance of *Roots,* such a reading would stop short. It would discourage thinking about the miniseries in context or probing the myriad issues it has raised since its initial airing. In particular, when placed in context, we want to not only ask how it impacted television and altered images of blackness but also interrogate its import for white America and race politics more generally. Finally, as my remembrance of the series should underscore, it encourages reflection on the slipperiness of memory and how and why certain specific stories become more universal and how narratives of race, family, and nation manifest themselves in popular media in post–civil rights America.

In what follows, I offer an account of *Roots,* detailing its popularity and import, while unpacking its fundamental messages. In particular, I attend to the manner in which it altered televisual images of blackness, opened a space to engage slavery and multiculturalism, and yet remained confined by a white racial frame, an overarching set of precepts, practices, and preoccupations centered around whiteness and white Americans, which shaped its production and reception.[1]

LeVar Burton as Kunta Kinte in the ABC miniseries *Roots.* (ABC/Photofest)

An Epic Saga

Roots, based on a novel of the same title by Alex Haley, famous for his earlier *Autobiography of Malcolm X,* traces the story of the author's family from Africa to emancipation in the 19th century.[2] It chronicles the experiences of Kunta Kinte, a Mandinka, born in the village of Juffure, which today is Gambia. Africa, pictured as an idyllic, even exotic, place before Western entry, contrasts markedly with capture, middle passage, and later life in the colonies, noteworthy for pronounced hierarchy, brutality, and inhumanity. Kunta Kinte is sold into slavery and transported to North America, where he makes repeated escape attempts and experiences barbaric punishments, ranging from the whipping discussed in the opening to maiming. He later marries and has a daughter, Kizzy (Leslie Uggams), who is taken away and sold to another plantation. The narrative shifts to Kizzy, who is raped and impregnated by her new master and gives birth to a son, later known as Chicken George (Ben Vareen), so named for his prowess in the cockfighting subculture. The series closes with emancipation.

A Popular Sensation

It is easy to forget in a media landscape, marked by mass spectacles, niche audiences, and digital video recorders, the importance of network programming in the late 1970s. It is easier still to underestimate the cultural impact and popular appeal of *Roots.* By the numbers, the miniseries was a singular success. At least 80 million, and perhaps as many as 135 million, Americans watched one or more nights of the miniseries.[3] This means in excess of 60 percent of Americans at the time viewed some or the entire program. Indeed, *Roots* was an historical landmark: at the time, it was the highest rated show in the history of television; in one week, 7 of the top 10 spots for all programs were part of the miniseries; 8 of the 13 most watched shows in broadcast history were at the time episodes of *Roots;*[4] and the final episode held the record as highest rate program for six years until the finale of *M*A*S*H.*[5] It was quality television too. The miniseries "won 145 different awards, including nine Emmys."[6]

Not surprisingly, the miniseries had lingering effects across American society. Communities and corporations alike embraced the show. While 50 cities declared "*Roots* weeks" to coincide with the broadcast and May 19–21, 1977, were designated "Alex Haley days" in his home state of Tennessee, at least one department store in New York City hosted a

"*Roots* week" in May 1977, offering consumers genealogy tips and heritage lessons along with their shopping.[7] For a time, it saturated daily life, a seemingly ever-present feature of "conversations, radio call-in shows, classroom discussions, and religious sermons."[8] Individuals found inspiration in the program as well. They desired to see the places depicted in the miniseries. As a result, new tourist destinations emerged as viewers sought out locales like Gambia, where *Roots* begins its narrative.[9] At the same time, genealogy became something of a fad—and not just for African Americans: "Following the TV-special, letters to the National Archives, where Haley did genealogical research in census manuscripts, tripled, and applications to use the facilities increased by 40%."[10] And in the African American community, Kunta Kinte and Kizzy became popular baby names: "twenty babies in New York City alone were given those names in February 1977."[11] One parent noted she selected the name Kunta Kinte because she wanted her son to "be free . . . to be somebody and know he is somebody."[12]

Roots was not only popular, it was transformative. It was among the earliest miniseries and the first to be broadcast across consecutive nights.[13] Moreover, it was part of an initial wave to demonstrate the power of docudrama, "blending fact and fiction in a soap opera package."[14] And it was the first to embrace multicultural themes, laying the groundwork for the equally important miniseries like *Holocaust*. It also facilitated new directions and opportunities for African Americans on television. Other production companies, buoyed by the success of *Roots,* aggressively pursued dramatic specials featuring African American story lines, including *All God's Dangers* and *Confessions of Nat Turner.*[15] Meanwhile, ABC launched *Roots: The Next Generation,* which aired in 1979, and NBC, hoping to capitalize on the zeitgeist, broadcast *King,* a docudrama about the civil rights leader, which might be deemed a modest success at best.[16] More importantly, as other contributors to the volume demonstrate and I discuss below, *Roots* opened novel pathways for imagining African Americans and their experiences, making viable more complex narratives about African Americans as embodied and fully human characters.

"A Novel for Television"

ABC aired *Roots*, a 12-hour miniseries, over eight consecutive nights. They advertised the adaptation of Haley's best seller as "a novel for television," seeking to convey a sense of artistry and magnitude on the television event.

Although LeVar Burton may be best remembered for his role in the miniseries, *Roots* featured a cavalcade of Hollywood stars—black and white, including Richard Roundtree, Cicely Tyson, Scatman Crothers, Ben Vareen, Louis Gossett Jr., Ed Asner, Chuck Connors, Lloyd Bridges, and Lorne Greene. In addition to Burton, it also introduced the public to the talents of Maya Angelou.

For all of its success, producers had deep misgivings about the miniseries, especially the manner in which white Americans would receive it. In fact, concerns about the content prompted ABC to make the unusual move of scheduling the miniseries on consecutive nights rather than weekly as had proved successful for the format previously, such as *Rich Man, Poor Man*. This was just one of several choices that reveal the efforts of producers to create a program that resonated with the preoccupations and precepts of the white racial frame and hence ensure its appeal to largely white audience.

From the start, its producers primarily were concerned about attracting white viewers. According to Larry Sullivan, an ABC executive at the time, "Our concern was to put a lot of white people into the promos. Otherwise, we felt the program would be a turnoff." Another executive, Brandon Stoddard, echoed these sentiments, "We made certain to use actors white viewers had seen a hundred times before so they would feel comfortable."[17] Creating a comfortable feel also demanded altering Haley's novel, which producers feared had the potential to alienate whites. To avoid this, they added new characters to the miniseries whom white audiences would identify. Thus, Captain Davies (Ed Asner) was fleshed out from a rather nondescript and loathsome figure in the novel, who was rendered instead as "honorable, innocent, and naive . . . a deeply religious family man . . . who begins his voyage on the Sabbath because it 'seems like the Christian thing to do.'"[18] These changes highlight the invisible ways in which whiteness imprints cultural production. They also underscore a central tension of post–civil rights America: white only and white supremacy no longer have a place in public culture or polite discourse, but white sensibilities and sentiments still dictate the limits of acceptability and intelligibility. Importantly, while these constraints undoubtedly altered the miniseries, they did not drain the series of its capacity to offer counternarratives or refigure blackness.

Blackness

The civil rights movement, among others, modified the white racial frame, encouraging it to incorporate more positive images of African Americans. In fact, *Roots* exemplifies and advances this project. It centers on sympathetic black characters remarkable in television history: they display a range of human emotion, love and laugh, suffer and cry, struggle and strive, build families against the odds, stand up for what is right, and work hard. They are the heroes of this history, which champions the margins and encourages its audience to identify with their plight, if not them. And a century after the end of slavery and decade after the death of Jim Crow, it was easy for all Americans, certain they were on the right side of history in a nation beyond race, to want the best for these characters and to curse evil individuals and institutions, even as they enjoyed their legacies in the form of white privilege and accrued wealth. Importantly, *Roots* did not simply have black protagonists; it also opted for an alternative narrative structure. Viewers witness much of the action in *Roots* from the point of view of the African American characters, a technique that not only shifts the focus of most television narratives, decentering whiteness, but also forces the audience to "see through a black man's eyes."[19] "*Roots* may have marked the first time many whites had been able to identify with blacks as people."[20] Perspective mattered, redirecting the flow of events, the values attachable to them, and interpretations of the audience.

These shifts made the miniseries especially powerful for African Americans. In speaking of the author and the series following Haley's death, Jesse Jackson remarked, "He made history talk . . . he lit up the long night of slavery. He gave our grandparents personhood. He gave *Roots* to the rootless."[21] It not only endowed its characters but embodied agents with personhood, situating them in history. For Jackson and many others, *Roots* offered a kind of counterreading of history and society that opened up new possibilities. As Herman Gray asserts,

> For an entire generation of young blacks, *Roots,* also opened—enabled really—a discursive space in mass media and popular culture within which contemporary discourses of blackness developed and circulated . . . I would place *Roots* in dialogue with the reactivation and renewed interest in black studies and the development of African-centered rap and black urban style . . .[22]

The miniseries encouraged or at least contributed to the articulation of a counterpublic that validated submerged narratives and efforts to excavate them. What's more, these effects were not limited to the African American community: "*Roots* helped to alter slightly, even momentarily interrupt, the gaze of television's idealized white middle-class viewers and subjects . . . [and] enabled a temporary but no less powerful transitional space within which to refigure and reconstruct black television representations."[23]

Africa

Roots tells a decidedly American story, one that insists on reframing the nation, its people, and their place in the world. On one hand, it foregrounds movement and forced relocation, the dialectics between Africa and the Americas. As such, it highlights the Diasporic heritage and condition of African Americans. On the other hand, it romanticizes and rehabilitates Africa. It pictures it as a motherland, an origin point, an Eden. While arguably superficial and akin to a "Smithsonian exhibit,"[24] its representation challenged prevailing, largely imperial, images of Africa as a backward and savage place, populated by wild beasts and equally exotic and dangerous peoples. Consequently, *Roots* made it possible for Americans, especially African Americans, to reimagine Africa, encouraging trends already in motion that fostered identification and connection. Or as Manthia Diawara put it, "Africentricity could not have existed without *Roots*."[25] While media portrayals of Africa over the past three-and-half decades have often recycled familiar clichés about superstitious savages and tribal passions, the significance of the miniseries in its moment and within the African American community cannot be overstated.

Of Human Bondage

Where sympathetic black characters and telling the story from the black point of view opened a space that comforted whites and affirmed blacks, slavery, on its face, appears too negative, too extreme for prime time. After all Americans had not (and still have not) come to terms emotionally, economically, and culturally with the histories and legacies of human bondage in the United States. *Roots* not only successfully reworks blackness, it also skillfully negotiates the challenges posed by remembering slavery in a (white) nation that would rather not talk about it. As Herman Gray suggests,

> There is little doubt that the success of *Roots* helped to recover and reposition television constructions and representations of African Americans and blackness from their historic labors on behalf of white racism and myths of white superiority. But the miniseries also contributed significantly to the transformation, in popular imaginary, of the discourse of slavery and American race relations between blacks and whites. That is to say, with *Roots* the popular media discourse about slavery moved from one of almost complete invisibility (never mind structured racial subordination, human degradation, and economic exploitation) to one of ethnicity, immigration, and

human triumph. . . . this quality is precisely what made the television series a huge success.[26]

The miniseries simultaneously represented slavery and repositioned it. While it arguably romanticizes it and holds under erasure important historical elements,[27] importantly, it dramatized the violence, exploitation, and dehumanization: slaves beaten and raped, families torn apart, the dismemberment of Kunta Kinta (who lost a foot as punishment), the loss of autonomy, and perpetual servitude. But *Roots* is not a catalog of horrors or an unceasing lament; rather, as Gray asserts, it recrafts the slave narrative as a more universal tale of striving for betterment and incorporation, in which the protagonists operate without sovereignty and in the shadow of social death. In a sense, it becomes a reframed immigrant story, albeit rooted in forced migration. It is very much these positive elements of the narrative that gave the miniseries such broad appeal: it spoke a truth about past ills of slavery, showed individuals in a family unit struggling over time for a better life, and held under erasure uneasy questions raised by the lives of its heroes. In a sense, the story of the slave became an American story, joining the master narrative; it became a universal narrative available to all.

Multiculturalism

The miniseries marked a turning point not simply because it engaged slavery or refigured blackness: *Roots* established itself as one of the first docudramas to take seriously difference and as a consequence provided a foundational moment in the articulation of multiculturalism in popular media. Less than a month after the close of a year of bicentennial celebrations, its debut offered an addendum, if not an alternative, to the official national narrative. It was a supplement, attached to and in dialogue with accepted understandings of history, race, and society.

While some thought the miniseries the "most important civil rights event since the 1965 Selma, Alabama march,"[28] it did little to advance civil rights or alter race relations over the long run. Indeed, despite the hope and the hype, there was no evidence that it changed racial attitudes.[29] And, racial identity was a key variable in who consumed the miniseries and how they interpreted it: blacks were more likely to watch than whites and more likely to find it historically accurate.[30]

Nevertheless, its sympathetic attention to slavery and blackness, as well as its implicit critique, allowed it to provide a counternarrative of sorts, which not only looked to the past but also envisioned a more hybrid future. "In fact, *Roots* was partially responsible for the phenomenon of the hyphenated American, marking the moment when people of color began to change their self-understanding from black to African American."[31]

Moreover, in adding to the larger stories of American becoming, in the wake of the civil rights movement, it made an important corrective, one that encouraged all on the right side of history to read it as a triumphal expansion of the national mosaic, an enhancement of the melting pot, and a confirmation of a transcendent human spirit. Stirring in the African American experience as (white) framed in *Roots* allowed the producers to impart a "universal story,"[32] or, as the *New York Times* put it, the miniseries "speaks not only for America's black people, but for all of us everywhere."[33]

Genealogy: Personal and Popular Memory

While much of the initial trepidation and later celebration of miniseries centered around its multicultural themes anchored in the black diaspora, slavery, and silenced history, much of its attraction pivoted around family as a source of identity, heritage, and connection,[34] heightened in a social world that fostered anomie and dislocation, while placing increasing importance on identity and difference. Genealogy, as promise and practice, appealed to all. As Maya Angelou observed, "The discoveries in *Roots* have inspired Americans, both black and white, to re-examine their origins."[35] The quest was so popular that the July 4, 1977, issue of *Newsweek* featured the cover story "Everybody's search for Roots."[36] This search was a collective phenomenon but an individual pursuit and, as arguably the most significant practical outcome of the miniseries, says much about racial politics at the time. "*Roots,*" according to Helen Taylor, "is a text which may be said to chart and invite political, social, and racial identification and resistance, albeit registered at a personal, familial level."[37] Indeed, "rather than forcing white Americans to own up to the crimes of slavery, the mass media stimulated instead a fascination with the project of genealogy. Perhaps the message of *Roots* was too much about the pleasure of healing and not enough about the pain of remembering." It fostered identification and universalization over and against defamiliarization and reconciliation.[38] *Roots* added a new story, a minor addendum, to the larger national narrative, what might be seen as "a new myth . . . one which did challenge and shift . . . master narrative[s];"[39] however, the mass translation of the text into everyday life (pursuit of familial roots) blunted pursuit of more meaningful or lasting forms of collective action.

Affirming the American Dream

Even as *Roots* focused on a single African (American) family ensnared in the brutality and exploitation of slavery, the miniseries opted to tell a more familiar, affirming narrative. Even as it dwells on suffering, loss, and inequity, as a whole, the teleplay offers "a fable of American incorporation."[40] It reworked the classic American myth of individuals who through hard work, initiative, and perseverance make a better life for themselves and their families—they pull themselves up by their bootstraps. Or, as Herman Grey phrased it, the miniseries was a "realization of the American dream."[41] "*Roots* represents a variant on the Horatio Alger theme of individual striving and individual success which lies at the heart of the American Dream."[42] Framing the African diaspora in this manner demands accentuating common themes, reworking the stories of those forcibly transported and enslaved sound like those of other ethnic groups. In other words, even as *Roots* sought to faithfully offer an account of diaspora and slavery, it did so through "a generic tale of the classic immigrant success story."[43]

Importantly, for viewers, likely more so for whites than blacks, the miniseries stops at a happy place. It ends with emancipation, a kind of figurative return to Eden or a release to the promised land. Here, history and hence oppression cease as well—a variant on the all lived happily ever after closing familiar from fairy tales. This, of course, allows the universal immigrant tale to remain in place; the American Dream is untarnished. It also lets (white) viewers and (white) society off the hook. It holds under erasure the messiness of Reconstruction, the rise of Jim Crow, the enforcement of segregation, lynching, sanctioned servitude, and so on. The century between emancipation and the Civil Rights Act merit no discussion, nor do their legacies. All that matters, in the end, is individuals who rise above, who remain faithful to family against all odds, who know where they come from, and who know their true names.

Media Dialogues

Roots has not only grounded social practices, cultural identities, and collective narratives, it has also encouraged dialogues within popular culture. It has become a touchstone. To return to arguably its most iconic

character, Kunta Kinte, whose afterlife illustrates the intertextual richness of the miniseries, especially for African American expressive culture,
hip-hop artists from Lil Wayne to Missy Elliott have made reference to
Kunta Kinte in their songs, often in a manner that mirrors Kanye West's
raps, "But that is not what gives me the heart of Kunta Kinte"—an obvious reference to strength and a resilient spirit in the face of challenging
circumstances. While in *The Wire* and in *Coming to America,* the reference marks an African immigrant as alien or foreign, elsewhere in visual
culture, slavery and resistance are again more prominent. In *Boyz n the
Hood,* faced with a series of tedious jobs, asks Tré, "Who's he think you is
Kunta Kinte?" In other words, does he think you are his slave? Similarly,
in *Do the Right Thing,* Mookie declares, "slave days are over, my name
ain't Kunta Kinte." Playing off this same theme, Will Smith's character
remarks about the harshness of a punishment, "Why don't you just do
me like Kunta Kinte and cut off my foot?" And perhaps most tellingly, on
Weekend Update, Jimmy Fallon commemorated the 25th anniversary of
the miniseries with the following mash-up: "For those of you who don't
remember *Roots,* it follows a saga of Kunta Kinte from young African
tribesman, to slavery, to becoming literate, and eventually being the top of
his class at Star Fleet Academy." Here, the character and the actor become
one, as if the humanity and dignity of both characters played by LeVar
Burton were one in the same, underscoring the foundational importance
of *Roots* to more rounded and fully formed African American characters
as well as the limited number of such roles and actors to play them a
quarter of a century later. And though told in jest, the joke reminds us of
the slipperiness of memory and the fixity of racial politics in post–civil
rights America that make it possible to see all black men as interchangeable, to meld the black struggle with an imagined universal future on the
final frontier, and to celebrate the success of a story, character, and actor,
while laughing at the constrained image repertoire and equally limited
possibilities for African Americans in the 21st century.

Conclusions

One need not to have seen *Roots* when it premiered in 1977 to have been
touched by or to appreciate the manner in which it changed American
society. Unprecedented and unrivaled, the miniseries had a profound
impact on television, media images of blacks, and popular understanding of the national narrative. At the same time, in speaking to as broad an
audience as possible, *Roots* fits itself in a white racial frame. As a

consequence, the program did not foster reconciliation, reparation, or racial healing, anymore than it prompted effective engagements with persistent inequality and ongoing oppression and their amelioration. Instead, for Euro-Americans, *Roots* affirmed universal messages about family, heritage, and the American Dream, at once granting security amid the uncertainties of post–civil rights America and spawning personal curiosities about their ancestors and their personal histories. Thus, whereas African Americans found in roots an allegory of the diaspora, a larger history, and a collective struggle, Euro-Americans found inspiration to focus on the family and learn their small stories, permission in essence to turn away from the social and fixate on the self—a self extricated from the messiness of race by a universal quest for origins. For all of this, in the current moment, it is difficult to imagine a program like *Roots* being produced or if it were for it to find such a large television audience.

Notes

1. Joe Feagin, *The White Racial Frame: Centuries of Racial Framing and Counter-Framing* (New York: Routledge, 2009).

2. Alex Haley, *The Autobiography of Malcolm X* (New York: Balentine, 1965); Alex Haley, *Roots: The Saga of an American Family* (New York: Doubleday, 1976).

3. David A. Gerber, "Haley's Roots and Our Own: An Inquiry into the Nature of a Popular Phenomenon," *Journal of Ethnic Studies* 5.3 (Fall 1977): p. 87.

4. John De Vito and Frank Tropea, *Epic Television Miniseries: A Critical History* (Jefferson, NC: McFarland, 2010), p. 40.

5. Museum of Broadcast Communications. *Roots,* http://www.museum.tv/eotvsection.php?entrycode=roots.

6. Helen Taylor, "'The Griot from Tennessee': The Saga of Alex Haley's Roots," *Critical Quarterly* 37.2 (Summer 1995): p. 48.

7. Taylor, "'The Griot from Tennessee,'" p. 48; Gerber, "Haley's Roots and Our Own," p. 88.

8. Alison Landsberg, *Prosthetic Memory: The Transformation of American Remembrance in the Age of Mass Culture* (New York: Columbia University Press, 2004), p. 103.

9. Gerber, "Haley's Roots and Our Own," p. 87.

10. Ibid.

11. Landsberg, *Prosthetic Memory,* p. 103.

12. Quoted in Landsberg, *Prosthetic Memory,* p. 103.

13. Museum of Broadcast Communications. *Roots,* http://www.museum.tv/eotvsection.php?entrycode=roots.

14. Ibid.

15. Gerber, "Haley's Roots and Our Own," p. 88.

16. De Vito and Tropea, *Epic Television Miniseries.*

17. Lauren R. Tucker and Hemant Shah, "Race the Transformation of Culture: The Making of the Television Miniseries Roots Critical Studies," *Mass Communication* 9 (1992): p. 328.

18. Ibid.

19. Landsberg, *Prosthetic Memory,* p. 103.

20. Ibid.

21. Taylor, "'The Griot from Tennessee,'" p. 50.

22. Herman Gray, "The Politics of Representation in Network Television," in *Channeling Blackness: Studies on Television and Race in America,* ed. by Darnell M. Hunt (New York: Oxford University Press, 2005), p. 61.

23. Ibid.

24. Tucker and Shah, "Race the Transformation of Culture," p. 332.

25. Landsberg, *Prosthetic Memory,* p. 102.

26. Gray, "The Politics of Representation in Network Television," pp. 160–161.

27. "Responses to Roots," *Race and Class* 19.1 (1977): pp. 77–105.

28. Taylor, "'The Griot from Tennessee,'" p. 48.

29. Kenneth K. Hur and John P. Robinson, "The Social Impact of 'Roots,'" *Journalism Quarterly* 55 (1978): pp. 19–24.

30. Ibid.

31. Landsberg, *Prosthetic Memory,* p. 102.

32. Ibid., p. 105.

33. Matthew Frye Jacobson, *Roots Too: White Ethnic Revival in Post-Civil Rights America* (Cambridge: Harvard University Press, 2006), p. 42.

34. Gerber, "Haley's Roots and Our Own"; James A. Hijiya, "Roots: Family and Ethnicity in the 1970s," *American Quarterly* 30.4 (Autumn 1978): pp. 548–56.

35. Landsberg, *Prosthetic Memory,* p. 105.

36. Gerber, "Haley's Roots and Our Own," p. 88.

37. Taylor, "'The Griot from Tennessee,'" p. 60.

38. Landsberg, *Prosthetic Memory,* p. 106.

39. Taylor, "'The Griot from Tennessee,'" p. 52.

40. Jacobson, *Roots Too,* p. 43.

41. Gray, "The Politics of Representation in Network Television," p. 161.

42. Louis Kushnick, "Responses to Roots," *Race and Class* 19.1 (1977): p. 81.

43. Tucker and Shah, "Race the Transformation of Culture," p. 334.

Chapter 5

More Serious than Money: On *Our Gang, Diff'rent Strokes,* and *Webster*

Jared Sexton

My children play with skulls / and remember / for the embattled there is no place / that cannot be / home / nor is.

—Audre Lorde

This chapter will discuss the post–civil rights era television situation comedy as an oblique commentary on the racial politics of kinship in the afterlife of slavery, taking *Diff'rent Strokes* and *Webster* as case studies. It traces the black man-child characters that featured in prime-time programming throughout the 1980s to earlier figures in U.S. popular culture: the black rascals of the *Our Gang* film series of the 1920s and 1930s and, before that, Topsy of Harriet Beecher Stowe's 1852 novel *Uncle Tom's Cabin.* In the intervening years of the mid-20th century, the public witnessed sustained attempts by a new generation of black professionals and community advocates to politicize, yet again, the matter of black family preservation against ongoing attempts by state and civil society to shatter the bonds between black parents and children. It will be argued that this ongoing struggle is inscribed in the discourse of the television sitcom and returns symptomatically in its performance and reception.

Buckwheat's Return

In 1966, the late Kristin Hunter-Lattany, award-winning author of the novel *God Bless the Child,* published her second major work of fiction, *The Landlord.* The novel was adapted for the screen several years later by Bill

Gunn, and on the initiative of Norman Jewison, the film production was directed by Oscar winner Hal Foster for United Artists and released in 1970 to mixed reviews. (Its 2007 rerelease, interestingly enough, drew unanimous critical acclaim.)[2] *The Landlord* is a political satire about the belated coming-of-age of Elgar Enders (Beau Bridges), a liberal and affluent young white man—a recent critic describes him as an "indolent American princeling"[3]—who buys a rundown tenement building in a poor, predominantly black Brooklyn neighborhood in order to displace the local residents, renovate the property, and move in to his spacious new accommodations—all to assert a putative independence from the stifling blue-blooded family dynasty whose accumulated wealth made the folly possible in the first place.

Along the way, Elgar doubts the morality—though not necessarily the ethics—of his original plan as he develops obscure feelings of concern for those he would evict and, in a sense, adopts the wary tenants as his *ersatz* family, friends, and community or, at least, as his very passionate preoccupation. This change of heart is prompted in no small part by his budding intimate relationship with Lanie (Marki Bey), a young, light-skinned woman living in the building (she is described in the story as having a white father), and a brief and strained affair with Francine Johnson (Diana Sands), a somewhat older, brown-skinned woman and wife of a militant Black Power activist, Copee Johnson (Louis Gossett Jr. who garnered a nomination for the Academy Award for Best Supporting Actor). The affair results in an unplanned pregnancy, and, after giving birth to a son, Francine announces in the hospital recovery room that she will relinquish her parental rights but with a twist. She tells Elgar that she wants their newborn son put up for adoption as a *white* child. When Elgar, taken aback, asks why, Francine replies with biting candor: "Cause I want him to grow up casual, like his daddy."[4]

It turns out that Elgar, now chastened by the profound limits of his self-styled transformation, retains custody of his son and elects to raise him together with Lanie, with whom he has patched things up and will now cohabit somewhere a good distance away from the tenement where they met. With a birth mother like Francine and an adoptive mother like Lanie, it is hard to know if the unnamed son will achieve the desired results without a seam, light complexion and inherited assets notwithstanding. But the point not to be missed here has to do with the close and problematic association between racial whiteness and the versatile invocation of "the best interest of the child."[5] Or, rather, the inverse relation between ascriptions of, or proximity to, racial blackness and the presumed absence or, often enough, the enforced denial of family ties. In this sense, Foster's rendition of

Hunter-Lattany's literary intervention manages to touch a central nerve of the post–civil rights dispensation, wherein the restructuring of the welfare state and the retrenchment of conservative racial politics meet the resurgence of mass-mediated popular culture in the service of a severe agenda.

Hunter-Lattany, who would go on to pen another half-dozen novels and short story collections alongside several books for young readers, also worked successfully as a journalist for the *Pittsburgh Courier,* a lecturer on the faculty of the University of Pennsylvania Department of English, an advertising copy editor, and a television screenwriter. She knew something about the ways and means of American popular culture, in other words, and she bore witness to its troubling ideological underpinnings across a range of media for the long haul. Writing some two decades after her debut novel, well on the other side of the revolutionary Zeitgeist of the 1960s and now inhabiting an openly reactionary political context, she described sardonically as "Reaganstruction" (a title justified by the images it has produced of blacks); Hunter-Lattany observed that "today's producers and screenwriters have no governors on their racist fantasies, no authority to answer to, and no one around to set them straight."[6] What the esteemed writer–critic is referencing in the most immediate sense is the dissolution of the Black Power movement of the 1960s and 1970s and the manifold repression-absorption-co-optation of the broader, mid-century resurgence of the long-standing black freedom struggle. What she attempts to expose to a harsh light is the fundament of a cultural formation seemingly frozen in time and without spatial parameter: the black stereotype.

> Black stereotypes were put on the shelf in the 1960s and 1970s—this century's era of Rebellion and Reconstruction—because Blacks were scaring the hell out of the society and "Anything to pacify those people!" was the response. Now that the threat of Black rebellion seems to be past, now that the pacification programs have withered, and now that "affirmative action" has become a tired phrase rendered meaningless by its being stretched to accommodate a broad spectrum called "women and minorities," the Black stereotypes are being hurled at us again with a vengeance, as if TV and film producers were getting even for having to shelve their pet fantasies for so long. And they come at us unrelentingly, without the relief of any realistically human Black portrayals.[7]

"Put on the shelf," is also to say held in reserve for future use against the rebellion seeking to dislodge, dismantle, or defuse them in pursuit of a radical reconstruction of society. The return of the stereotype in popular culture appears, then, as retribution or punishment in return for wrongdoing, and it appears without relief or respite, as a state or condition of counter-insurgency. We might wonder about the demand for verisimilitude and the positive black images to which it might give rise, but the description of the predicament is astute. Indeed, one could have chosen almost at random from the portfolio of cultural imagery unleashed in the historic instance, but the present outrage was catalyzed by the return of a figure of the diminutive black man-child, tracing a line of descent from Billie Thomas's first portrayal of Buckwheat in the 1934 short film *Mama's Little Pirate* as President Franklin Roosevelt implemented the First New Deal all the way to Eddie Murphy's satiric reincarnation of the little rascal on *Saturday Night Live* in the first year of the Reagan administration's imposition of supply-side economics.

Hunter-Lattany discovers a whole set of contemporary film and television characters within this dubious genealogy, but her paradigm example is Arnold Jackson (Gary Coleman) of the hit situation comedy *Diff'rent Strokes*, running for eight seasons and 189 episodes between 1978 and 1986. The analysis, from the title onward, is suffused with a righteous indignation that lends clarity of vision and provides a safeguard against the tendency to forgo necessary judgment in the name of endless complexity. The author is interested in locating the black stereotype and identifying it properly in order to kill it forthwith. Like all of those "Black viewers who [remember] the original Buckwheat and [understand] the dangerous implications of his reincarnation on national television," she watches with "smoking psychological pistols aimed at the screen" and urges all of those of like mind to "ready our guns" for all of those stereotypes that remain alive and well in the popular imagination.[8] As a voice of the spirit of rebellion that survives in the minds of black viewers, she claims with pride a vicarious responsibility for killing Buckwheat's latter-day reincarnation.

In reality, it was Eddie Murphy himself that ordered the hit on Buckwheat, an attempt on his part to undo what had immediately become his earliest public persona. It marked an attempt on his part, that is, to interrupt the culture's predisposition to see him as the very stereotype his performance on the popular sketch comedy show was meant to satirize. What, then, are we to make of this unacknowledged alignment, this shared discontent, between Murphy and his erstwhile critics? What do they collectively understand about the necessary recourse to (figurative or symbolic) violence in order to counteract the "dangerous implications of [Buckwheat's] reincarnation on national television"? Why does it require such lethal violence to tell the difference between the black stereotype and the black actor who performs it? And why does the attempt at satire seem to fail so completely? What does this say about the force, the ungoverned fantasies, by which the conflation is achieved in the first place?

Topsy's Legacy

For all that Buckwheat may seem to suggest, pace Hunter-Lattany, about the misrepresentation of black masculinity in U.S. popular culture, it is important to note that the character was initially drawn as a girl and was played by a young actress named Carlena Beard, sister of Matthew "Stymie" Beard of the original *Our Gang* cast. In fact, even after the character was recast and played thereon by Billie Thomas, the actor most widely associated with the role, Buckwheat remained a female onscreen for another two years. To say that Thomas played the role in drag, however, would presuppose a prior gender differentiation that the unremarked nature of his performance would belie. The interchangeability of Beard and Thomas points instead toward a persistent denial, or perceived derangement, of gendered difference for the black child, and this confusion installs the black child as the backdrop before which the gendered figures of white boys and girls can be highlighted.

Like the other black rascals (e.g., Booker T. Bacon, Farina, Mango, Pineapple), Buckwheat can be played either by a young actress or by a young actor, and the character can morph from female to male (and back again?) without requiring any significant change in role. The distribution of feminine and masculine features, as it were, does not follow the conventions established by the dominant vantage. The whole system of marks is short-circuited, or hot-wired, in such a way that the black child becomes, in a sense, available for anything—seduction, betrayal, peril, disfigurement, death—a condition of social formlessness that renders the genderless child at once insubstantial (and so beyond any ethical consideration whatsoever) and pure substance (and so immune to any suffering whatsoever). The black child in this rendering is not only the constitutive outside of the social domain that indexes a relation to the coordinates of human sexuality but also the archaic point of abiogenesis preceding the advent of reproduction itself.

On this note, Buckwheat cannot but invoke Harriet Beecher Stowe's earlier literary figure Topsy, the young enslaved girl purchased by "the kind-hearted plantation owner Augustine St. Clair"[9] in her magnum opus *Uncle Tom's Cabin,* the best-selling novel of the 19th century and principal text of the international abolitionist movement. We are introduced to Topsy in Chapter XX of that famous work, wherein St. Clair presents Topsy as a challenge to the Christian faith and missionary zeal of his cousin, Miss Ophelia, whose charge it is to "bring [Topsy] up in the way she should go."[10] Unkempt and uncouth, Topsy embodies in Stowe's universe, the physical, mental, and spiritual degradation born of slavery: life among the lowly. More importantly, Topsy is parentless, a normative state of natal alienation and genealogical isolation indicating that enslaved children are, as it were, paradigmatically orphans.

In point of fact, orphan is too strong a word here because, again, it presupposes a parental bond that has been lost after the fact rather than one that is shattered in advance. As Topsy proffers her own origin story: "Never was born . . . never had no father nor mother, nor nothin.'" Topsy, before she is converted and civilized and adopted by the family that has bought her, comes from no one and nowhere; she has no sense of time, historical or biographical, and no sense of place, no hearth or home. She is perfectly deracinated or, better, she is without an original origin; her origin is nonoriginary.[11] When Ms. Ophelia queries Topsy about her knowledge of God and the source of divine creation, she replies to the point: "I spect I grow'd. Don't think nobody never made me." It will be Ms. Ophelia's principal learning objective to instill in Topsy the fundaments of her abiding faith in Christian salvation. The precondition for Topsy's conversion from ideal slave to nascent Christian lies in her willingness to develop, in the first instance, a capacity to receive love, white love—what is, on this account, tantamount to a capacity for relationality as such—against which can be registered the outrages of feelings and affection that constitute the core evil of slavery as institution.

To this end, Topsy is moved along the righteous path less by the diligent pedagogy of her pious and condescending mistress (for whom a feeling of repugnance remains in the heart) than by the pristine example of her sibling Eva, St. Clair's angelic daughter, who promises Topsy, in one of the pivotal scenes of the story, that "you can go to Heaven at last, and be an angel forever, just as much as if you were white," if only Topsy will accept Eva's enjoinder to "try to be good." Yet, beneath Topsy's seemingly characteristic incorrigibility, it is revealed, finally, that she suffers from a profound fatalism. "Couldn't never be nothin' but a nigger, if I was ever so good," she declares. "There can't nobody love niggers and niggers can't do nothin'!" Eva's outpouring, then, gives the lie to this racist axiom: "Oh Topsy, poor child, *I* love you!" It is here, where Eva, the moral centerpiece of the text, has her first and most instructive effect that the abolitionist sermon gains its coherence. Topsy's conversion is determinant for Ms. Ophelia's and St. Clair's respective changes of heart; Eva's memory becomes crucial to Uncle Tom's renewed commitment to his own Christian faith, opposing as he does unto death of the slaveholder Simon Legree and becoming thereby a martyr to the cause of Quimbo's and Sambo's (the slaves who were ordered to kill Tom) subsequent conversions and so on.

Topsy's chief role in the novel is thus to provide an object lesson in the power of white Christian love to overcome wretchedness among *both* the perpetrators *and* the victims of great moral evils, a love epitomized by the innocence of youthful white femininity. This innocence is not autochthonous, however. It is produced in the moment of juxtaposition between black and white female children in profile, Topsy ("with her usual air of careless drollery and unconcern") and Eva ("her whole face fervent with feeling"). Eva can appear "like the picture of some bright angel stooping to reclaim a sinner" only because Topsy is repeatedly described as "odd and goblin-like" in turn. Topsy plays darkness to Eva's light, crudeness to Eva's refinement, despair to Eva's hope, but most importantly incredulity to Eva's belief, reestablishing against the cynicism of the culture of slavery that the abolition of "heathenism," wherever it be found, is the proper occupation of white Christian women and men.[12]

Cultural critic Tavia Nyong'o notes in his article, "Racial Kitsch and Black Performance," that dramatic adaptations of *Uncle Tom's Cabin* became "the indispensable play of the late nineteenth-century American theater and para-theater" and remarks the particular popularity of the Topsy character therein. Most relevant for present purposes is the fact that while such stage versions "sometimes capitalized on Topsy's transformation from wild child to demure Christian" to advance the text's redemptive vision, they more commonly "misread Stowe's novel and took St. Clare at his word when he claimed [initially] to have bought Topsy as entertainment [rather than to spare her further abuse at the hands of her previous owners], and left her laughably reprobate."[13] He continues:

> As an entertainer, Topsy quickly became one of the most popular characters in the play, as necessary as Uncle Tom. Actors playing Topsy sometimes received top billing in mid-nineteenth-century productions, and Topsy's song was a hot seller in sheet music. Rival productions of *Uncle Tom's Cabin* were soon advertising two Topsies—double the fun and fidelity to Stowe's novel be damned. Topsy's conquest of the landscape of United States popular culture makes her an inaugural figure in the genealogy of performing black children.[14]

It is in this light that Buckwheat can be seen to hyperbolize (perhaps to the point of satire) for a modern film–going audience the already exaggerated attributes of the pickanniny stereotype that Stowe's sentimental novel both drew on and canonized in the antebellum period. But if Topsy "appears at a historical moment where a white supremacist and slaveholding nation was actively debating 'the character and destiny' of black folk"[15] and the character is mobilized to argue alternately, sometimes simultaneously, for ultimate assimilation or extinction; then "what is interesting about the black rascals [Buckwheat above all] is less their fit within then current racial policies of segregation" and more "the lack of fit between the racial formation of the time, ideologically considered, and the general economy of innocent pleasures to which *Our Gang* caters."[16]

That is to say, insofar as our critique focuses exclusively on Buckwheat et al. as the reproduction of stereotypes, it misses the ways in which the popular film and television series seek "a production of the appropriate ambience for the insinuation of racially unmarked innocence, an innocence predicated upon a forgetfulness of the past that is one of the greatest privileges of whiteness."[17] Buckwheat emerges not so much as a repetition of Topsy, who is firmly embedded in the partisan politics of the day, as an artifact forged in the aftermath of her transformation, or perhaps as an effect of the transformation in the postbellum white public sphere now supposed to be—or wishing it were—capable of loving black children as its own, "just as much as if [they] were white." Of course, in order to insinuate racially unmarked innocence per se, the marks of racial difference must be reiterated, and it is the function of the stereotype to manage the ambivalence generated by the operative contradiction.

We can track in this instance the procedure of a subtle political dynamic identified by historian Robin Bernstein in her recent book *Racial Innocence*. There she examines, from the antebellum period to the civil rights era in the United States, "the pivotal use of childhood innocence in racial politics."[18] Her researches in American literature, drama, and material culture across the massive upheavals of civil war, industrialization, urbanization, and the rise of mass media find that

> When a racial argument is effectively countered or even delegitimized in adult culture, the argument often flows stealthily into children's culture or performances involving children's bodies. So located, the argument appears racially innocent. This appearance of innocence provides a cover under which otherwise discredited racial ideology survives and continues, covertly, to influence culture.[19]

The emergence of the figure of the pickaninny in popular culture in the mid-19th century preserves the proslavery ideology and beyond what Bernstein calls "the libel of black insensateness"[20] in the face of abolitionism's growing moral force and political power. Insensateness is perhaps the signal attribute of the pickaninny stereotype. This is not to say that she is indestructible or even invulnerable, for she is constantly endangered, disfigured, and killed, but rather that she does not genuinely feel the pain of the injuries she receives. In a word, she does not suffer. She may experience fear or fright or threat, she may cry out, but none of this actually registers.[21] This is why and how she inhabits her condition with such strange ease. She may be wretched, as the story runs, but she knows nothing about it. It is all lost on the black juvenile, and this imputed incapacity to feel is the very source of amusement, and vindication, for white audiences.

In the *Our Gang* series, the black rascals, unlike their white counterparts, are "subjected to consistently imaginative punishments that frequently culminate in an implied off-screen death."[22] To be sure, the emerging generic conventions of the slapstick comedy film render all violence humorous, but its clear racial distribution prompts us to ask: Does the racially unmarked innocence sought onscreen serve, in the final instance, to reassert the whiteness of "the category of the child and, ultimately, the human"[23] by expelling the black juvenile from its domain over and over again? Does this depressing feature of Buckwheat's first public life in the post–Reconstruction era become an inescapable inheritance of Murphy's satirical man-child post–civil rights? And does it become a contiguous and overwhelming influence on Coleman's Arnold Jackson as well? How might the denial of black childhood—as it migrates from the stage to the silver screen to the television sitcom—supplement the unraveling mythology of the childlike black adult? How might the insensate black juvenile onstage or onscreen counteract arguments circulating in the political sphere about the realities of black suffering, first by the abolitionist movement and later by the 20th-century black freedom struggle?[24]

Like the "peculiarly genderless"[25] Topsy and the parentless nonchild juveniles (and, by implication, the childless adult slaves) for which she stands, it would seem that the black betrays no index of generational movement as well. Whether young or old, male or female, the black appears in racist culture as a figure whose traits afford no reliable measure of human differentiation. "They all look alike" is more than a notion. It describes in a phrase an entire cultural apparatus whose psychic life not only shapes the visual field but also structures the social, political, and economic spheres. "At stake in this split [between tender white children and insensate pickaninnies] was fitness for citizenship and inclusion in the category of the child and, ultimately, the human."[26] And lest we be misled by the eventual emergence in popular culture of black juvenile figures (from Buckwheat to Arnold and beyond) deemed cute by the dominant vantage, we are cautioned to recall that even "when a pickaninny was well-dressed and adorable . . . this icon of insensateness did not call for protection. Whereas the white child manifested innocence, the pickaninny deflected it: the pickaninny made not itself, but its violent context, appear innocent."[27]

Reforming the White Family

We have already had occasion to label the violent context of the 1980s "Reaganstruction." It bears repeating, however, that this context also provides the conditions of emergence and relations of production for our central point of interest, *Diff'rent Strokes* (1978–1986): the vehicle that thrust Gary Coleman into overnight celebrity and made Arnold Jackson a household name, installed the young protagonist's signature phrase ("What you talkin' bout, Willis?") as an item of common parlance, and laid the groundwork for both a successful spin-off, *The Facts of Life* (1979–1988), and its primetime heir, *Webster* (1983–1987), starring Emmanuel Lewis in the eponymous lead role. *Diff'rent Strokes* owes a good deal of its popularity to the towering influence of producers Norman Lear and Bud Yorkin, whose Tandem Productions dominated 1970s television with a series of top-rated and award-winning sitcoms: first and foremost, *All in the Family* (1971–1979), the most watched television show in the country for a record-breaking five consecutive years, but also the notable spin-offs *Maude* (1972–1978) and *The Jeffersons* (1975–1985) alongside another pair of respectable productions featuring black main characters, *Sanford and Son* (1972–1977) and *Good Times* (1974–1979). Yorkin went on to produce the modestly successful black-cast sitcom *What's Happening!!* (1976–1979) under the auspices of the short-lived TOY Productions company he cofounded with Bernie Ornstein and Saul Turteltaub.

Lear in particular exercised a progressive political influence on the culture of 1970s prime time, pursuing an array of programming that shrewdly integrated social issues into evening television for a diverse viewing audience attempting to make sense of the ongoing social, political, and economic conflicts associated with what historian (and distinguished food writer) Josh Ozersky understatedly terms "an era of change."[28] *All in the Family* staged the countervailing forces of radicalism and reaction unleashed throughout the United States, setting the rants of an unreconstructed white working-class bigot, the infamous Archie Bunker (his name signifying the very personification of silent majority *retrenchment*), against a constellation of pithy rejoinders and well-formulated critical commentary from his moderate wife, his hippy daughter and son-in-law, and his diligent, up-wardly mobile black neighbors—George and Louise Jefferson and their bright and handsome son, Lionel. *All in the Family,* garnering at its height fully one-fifth of the national population as its audience, kept in produc-tive and pleasurable tension the profound ethical questions and pressing everyday challenges posed by the new social movements for civil rights and Black Power, feminism and women's liberation, sexual revolution, and peace. In the midst of the Nixon administration's politics of backlash, the sitcom warded against the demonization and caricature afoot in the shift-ing political climate and held open a space for the normalization of, among other things, alternative family forms, gender equality, and racial integra-tion. Popular culture for Lear, then, was a site for political education and adjudication as much as it was for entertainment and escape.

The Jeffersons, as the Bunker's neighbors came to be known after relo-cating from the modest row houses of Queens to the posh high rises of Manhattan's Upper East Side, elaborated the integrationist theme adum-brated by *All in the Family,* introducing viewers to the first professional middle-class black family in American television history. And the prin-ciples, despite the patriarch's trademark antics, were unapologetic about their residence in "a deluxe apartment in the sky." *The Jeffersons* remains one of the longest-running sitcoms in general—outlasting *Friends* (1994–2004), for instance—and the single longest-running black sitcom in par-ticular, surpassing by three seasons the more celebrated *The Cosby Show* (1984–1992). Lear's work did not only attempt to symbolically desegre-gate privilege within the existing arrangements. It also sought to sustain, within generic and institutional constraints, the public discourse of social justice and economic equality articulated most forcefully by the black free-dom struggle and, in more attenuated form, the social democratic vision of the Great Society, enabling downward redistributions of wealth, power, and resources. *Sanford and Son,* set in the Watts section of South Central Los Angeles, and *Good Times,* set in the Cabrini-Green housing projects of Chicago's South Side—both locales of major civil disturbances during the long hot summers of the late 1960s—dramatized the lives of poor and working-class black families in urban ghettoes, adding a degree of texture to the grim conditions of "American Apartheid" officially acknowledged by the 1968 Kerner Report and perhaps lending a degree of urgency to the federal commission's propositions as well.

This is not to say that the sitcom, even in the hands of a Hollywood liberal like Lear, could become a cultural accompaniment to the sort of revolutionary change that defined the political horizon. Quite the contrary, the genre and the medium have tended in the historic instance to depoliticize, which is to say privatize and individualize, the social problems of the moment. Sociologist Darrell Hamamoto, writing in the twilight of the Reagan–Bush era, discusses this ideological maneuver in his aptly titled *Nervous Laughter:*

> The symbolic resolution of dilemmas inherent in interpersonal relations has long been the signal strength of the television situation comedy. [...] If macroeconomic events were beyond all comprehension and personal control, then at least a certain measure of solace, security, and autonomy might be found at the level of interpersonal relations revolving around domestic life. In the situation comedy, sociopolitical contradictions become transcoded into personal problems.[29]

There is a double movement at work here. First, sociopolitical contradictions, or macroeconomic events, are transcoded into personal problems and sequestered to the sphere of domestic life. Second, after "the dilemmas inherent in interpersonal relations" are loaded with such immense freight, they are brought to a symbolic resolution affording "a certain measure of solace, security, and autonomy." Yet, if interpersonal relations, all things remaining equal, are already complicated by *inherent* dilemmas, and so must always make do with symbolic resolutions where real contradictions remain irreducible, then the second-order ideological labor that this symbolic resolution must perform when interpersonal relations stand in for "events beyond all comprehension and personal control" becomes tenacious indeed. This, for the ideal viewer during good times, is better known in this case as the postwar liberal consensus of the brief American Century from Harry Truman to Lyndon Johnson. But just as President Dwight Eisenhower, the pivotal figure between the end of the New Deal and the rise of the New Federalism, appointed Richard Nixon as his vice president, coupling his moderately reformist domestic policies with the anticommunist politics of containment, the liberal consensus contained within itself the seeds of its undoing.

As the full effects of global economic restructuring were beginning to be widely felt across the United States (e.g., stagnating wages, rising unemployment, decreased social spending) and the radical implications of a genuine commitment to the egalitarian ideals of the social movements worked their way into the common sense, media executives, with their fingers held up to the political wind and their noses pressed to the ledger, mandated a return to the guidelines of normalcy that dominated network television programming from its inception in the 1940s through the 1960s. The permission for political experimentation inspired by the era of change was revoked. We might think of this as the cultural accompaniment of the counterrevolutionary restoration that would usher in the neoliberal orthodoxy informing the dominant discourse of the late 20th and early 21st centuries, including the ascendant doctrine of color blindness. By the time President Carter took action to address the 1978 public health scandal regarding the Love Canal toxic waste superfund in Niagara Falls, NY, "the salience of 'socially relevant' themes in the television situation comedy as seen in the 1970s gave way to the micropolitics of intimacy."[30]

Whither the Black Family

Whereas the relevancy boom of Norman Lear's 1970s attempted to catalyze in its audience an intelligent consideration of the social milieu along with a certain measure of solace, relief, and personal autonomy, the new ratings-driven programming led by NBC's newly appointed president Fred Silverman sought to crush any such consideration and sever any such linkages between education and entertainment as the decade expired. Before coming to NBC, Silverman produced the hit miniseries *Roots* for ABC, earning the latter network the honor of airing the most watched television event in history (over 70% of the viewing audience tuned in to watch the final episode) and destabilizing the long-standing position of CBS as industry leader. What is telling about the success of *Roots*, however, is less its artistic merit or political saliency in its rendering of the story of an African American family from slavery to freedom and more its capacity to circulate as commodity, demonstrating to elite decision makers that empty innovation, rather than stale repetition, was the frontier of expansion: not original, timely, or relevant but simply "new, shiny, and different." Nolan Davis, writing for the *New West,* asked at the time, "Is Kunta Kinte the New Fonzie?"[31]

Diff'rent Strokes and *Webster* entered the fray of this post–civil rights era ratings mania, in which programming selected in order to capture maximum market share was monitored on a daily basis and risks were minimized ruthlessly. What made *Diff'rent Strokes* a safe bet? To begin, it followed the integrationist theme established by *The Jeffersons* several years earlier.[32] In fact, Gary Coleman made his network television debut in a guest appearance as George Jefferson's streetwise eight-year-old nephew, linking the forthcoming sitcom directly to the ethos and environs of its predecessor. But something was lost in the gap between the launch of *The Jeffersons* in

1975—flanked as it was by *Sanford and Son* and *Good Times*—and the first season of *Diff'rent Strokes* in 1978—when these leading black working-class sitcoms, and the antagonism they inscribed, disappeared. *Diff'rent Strokes* is not just another integrationist sitcom. Rather, like its contemporaries, *Benson* (1979–1986) and *Gimme a Break!* (1981–1987), and its next of kin, *Webster,* it features lone black characters isolated in white settings with scant connection to any larger black community, history, culture, or politics. Communications scholar Catherine Squires glosses the distinction in her comprehensive study, *African Americans and the Media,* as follows:

> The networks continued to play it safe in the later '70s and early '80s, with Black TV characters. One prominent trend featured White adoptive parents and mentors who took on the task of socializing Black kids and teens. [. . .] Like the "exceptional" Black characters of the 1960s, these Black children were situated in all-White worlds. Unlike the isolated, middle-class Black predecessors like Julia, though, these characters did not live amongst Whites to prove Blacks were "just like" them, but to provide comic (and some might say racial) relief. Through their sassy, comic uses of Black slang and "street smarts," characters like Gary Coleman's Arnold livened up the "square" White environments, and safely integrated them. But like Julia, these children were divorced from contact with Black communities, suggesting that their Black origins had little to offer them.[33]

The denigrating suggestion that "Black origins [have] little to offer" children was hardly novel at this time, but it was nonetheless glowing red from the heat of public debate. The National Association of Black Social Workers (NABSW), in light of extensive analysis and direct observation by its professional membership of myriad "barriers to preserving families of African ancestry" in the pursuit of child welfare, issued a comprehensive policy statement at their Fourth Annual Conference in 1972.[34] Known primarily—and almost always reductively—in both the scholarly literature and the mass media for its trenchant (and, to date, unwavering) criticism of interracial adoption and its advocacy of race matching in child placement, the NABSW actually grounds its controversial position, including the proposal to treat interracial placement as an option of last resort, within an overarching formulation of antiblack racism as ideology, institutional practice, and structural condition.

One could, for what it's worth, interrogate the theorization of cultural identity that underwrites much of the NABSW's argument that black children receiving interracial out-of-home placements by child welfare agencies for foster care or adoption "are disengaged from their cultural background" and are therefore "denied the opportunity for optimal development and functioning."[35] One could cite, to the contrary, existing scholarship that demonstrates how, for instance, no demonstrable difference exists between black and white foster families and black children adopted interracially fare as well as black children adopted intraracially or how, to take another example, the earlier the age of adoption the higher the chances for successful adjustment, a prime rationale advanced for permitting, or even promoting, interracial adoption in lieu of extended periods in foster care awaiting eligible black adoptive families or how even the NABSW's preference for kinship care with extended family members (who are most likely to be black) over out-of-home placement in foster care or adoption (where both of the latter options are more likely to be interracial) nonetheless presents problems of oversight for those relatives not trained and monitored as registered foster families.[36] I say one could do this, for what it's worth, because the above points are merely arguments in favor of interracial placements without consideration of the bedrock motivation of NABSW's general position: protecting black families from group-based harm.[37]

For those that might think family preservation is a categorical public policy goal, the NABSW makes clear that black families, or families of African ancestry, are particularly targeted for destruction. How is this so? Clearly, it is unrelated to any racial disparities in rates of abuse or neglect. As the NABSW states: "contrary to popular opinion, parents of African ancestry are no more likely to abuse or neglect their children but they are more likely to be investigated, have children removed from their home, and receive fewer services that are often found to be substandard." Instead, it has to do with a host of institutional factors that are as readily identifiable as they are deeply entrenched. It is a well-known fact that the child welfare system in the United States has, to put it mildly, serious design flaws. Among these is the tendency to ignore abuse and neglect among the middle and upper classes and to punish abuse and neglect with undue severity among the poor.

Those with resources are not only better able to defend themselves against the intrusions of child welfare agencies, legally if need be, they are also shielded from scrutiny by a geography of privacy and a presumption of fitness even when evidence of trouble presents itself. This is especially true for instances of neglect, representing the lion's share of child welfare cases. Child welfare as a profession systematically conflates child neglect with the material effects of poverty. It fails to recognize the distinction between parental care, or lack thereof, and parental resources, or lack thereof. When cases of abuse or neglect are found to exist among families of means, those

families are much more likely to receive in-home support services leading to rehabilitation and preservation. In cases where out-of-home foster
care placement is deemed necessary, the emphasis is laid upon reunifica-
tion rather than adoption. Since black families are disproportionately poor,
it stands to reason that they are more likely to be subjected to intervention
and disruption. To this extent, the structural effects of the racial wealth gap
shape the unequal operations and outcomes of child welfare.[38]

However, the color of child welfare is overdetermined by widespread racial discrimination by policy makers, agency administrators, and casework-
ers. Legal scholar Dorothy Roberts, a leading commentator on the issue, is
unequivocal: "America's child welfare system is a racist institution."[39] That
is, even when controlling for a host of typical indicators of child endanger-
ment—from parental substance abuse to physical or sexual violence—black
families are far more likely than their white counterparts to experience
state intervention, and that intervention is far more likely to be punitive,
resulting in permanent separation of parents and children and of siblings
from one another. The disqualification of black family rights is rooted in
the what Roberts calls "the system's fundamental flaw": "The child welfare
system is designed not as a way for government to assist parents to take
care of their children but as a means to punish parents for their failures by
threatening to take their children away."[40] The child *welfare* system is more
accurately described by the official title it carries in many states throughout
the country: child *protective* services. For this reason, the system is activated
"only after children have already experienced harm and puts all the blame
on parents for their children's problems."[41] Importantly, this shift in orientation toward protection is strictly correlative with the shift in the racial
demographics in child welfare from overwhelmingly white to disproportionately black.

The group-based harm of the system's child protection orientation is
bound up with a set of popular assumptions about black family dysfunction and parental unfitness that draw on and reinforce long-standing stereotypes about deviant black mothers and absent black fathers, painting a
picture of an anomalous matriarchal structure that distorts child development and undermines community development. At bottom, these "myths
about Black mothers," dating back to proslavery ideology and, later, the
attack on Reconstruction and defense of segregation, "confirm the need
for the state to intervene in their homes to safeguard their children and to
ensure that their children do not follow their dangerous example."[42] The
careless mother, the matriarch, the welfare queen all represent the fright-
ful destiny of Topsy grown up, still suffering from outrages of feeling and

affection despite gaining family rights after emancipation. As such, the modern child welfare system inherits, in inverted form, the moral dilemma of *Uncle Tom's Cabin:* how to save black children? Like the liberal sentimental abolitionism of the 19th century, the neoliberal child welfare system of the 20th century must maintain the very segregation, and domination, of black children that its mission is meant to overcome.

Roberts helps to clarify why the problem of interracial adoption that emerged in full force in the discourse of Black Power in the 1970s is important but not essential to the historical analysis of state violence against the black family and the refraction of this violence in the products of popular culture. The crucial element here is, to borrow the phrasing of literary critic Hortense Spillers, the continuing nullification of black women's "mother right" as "a feature of human community."[43] This nullification is the hard core of the more general fact that "the laws and practices of enslavement did not recognize, as a rule, the vertical arrangements of their family,"[44] a general fact that characterizes as well the political culture and policy environment of "the afterlife of slavery"—postemancipation, post–civil rights.[45] Adopting this critical insight, family matters for the African American personality assume a different hue and cry. As such, "one aspect of the liberational urge for freed persons is not so much the right to achieve the nuclear family as it is the wish to rescue African-Americans from flight . . . essentially, to bring the *present* into view rather than the past."[46]

Perhaps, then, this is why the NABSW describes interracial out-of-home placements in the historic instance as a "particular form of genocide."[47] If to some it may seem absurd and hurtful to use the language of genocide when you look at the acts of individual loving white parents of black children, then they only need to look upstream to those processes that systematically displace black children and push them into the adoption stream in the first place. This is why, according to sociologist Barbara Rothman, "it is not absurd to think in terms of genocide when you look at social policy."[48] Accordingly, the seemingly banal micropolitics of intimacy depicted in the television sitcom, if reinscribed, or if viewed for what is already inscribed there as subtext or throwaway line or opening gambit, can follow a thread back to those occluded macroeconomic events and sociopolitical contradictions that otherwise remain beyond comprehension.

Arnold Emerges

To be sure, *Diff'rent Strokes* was a safe show, as Squires notes above. But nominal safety begs the question: safe for whom and from what? If NBC was indemnifying itself against financial risk, it did so by addressing the paramount political issue of black freedom, at least this one aspect of the liberational urge for freed persons, through a process of inoculation. Mr. Drummond (Conrad Bain), a wealthy white widower living in a Park Avenue high-rise, has agreed to look after his recently deceased black housekeeper's two sons, Arnold (Gary Coleman) and Willis Jackson (Todd Bridges). Mr. D, as he is affectionately known, describes the late Mrs. Jackson in terms redolent of the mammy stereotype: "a sweet wonderful woman. . . . like a member of the family" with a "great sense of humor." And his description of her sons as "orphans. . . . from Harlem. . . . two innocent, sweet, helpless little boys" would not be altogether unfamiliar to Stowe's Augustine St. Clair.

In season 1, episode 2, "Social Worker," the Drummond family is visited by a social worker, *Ms.* (she emphasizes, "not Mrs.") Aimsly, for a routine evaluation of postplacement adjustment. After being coached by Mr. Drummond to give positive reviews of their home life to date, the boys put on a dog and pony show to placate the stern government agent. Referring to themselves as "Happy Willis" and "Delirious Arnold," the former describes Mr. D as "a real cool dude" and the latter reveals as an obvious aside that "confidentially, the man is loaded. . . . L-O-D-I-D." Ms. Aimsly notes the material comforts of their new surrounds (we learn later in the episode that Mr. D is so rich, in fact, that he has never even heard of a garage sale). However, she is compelled nonetheless to ask: "Boys, have you ever lived in a nonblack neighborhood before?" Willis deflects this first query: "Just once when our landlord in Harlem painted our building white." Ms. Aimsly continues: "Arnold, do you miss seeing other black children your age?" And Arnold parries: "No ma'am! If I miss seeing a black kid *my* age, all I gotta do is look in the mirror."

Throughout the consultation, the boys put on airs *as* rich white children (i.e., adapted) and not the children *of* a rich white man (i.e., adopted), as evidence of Mr. D's fitness. They smile broadly, they walk arm-in-arm, they affect proper enunciation and grammar, and they use a Pollyannaish tone and idiom reminiscent of Mr. D's prep school daughter, Kimberly (Dana Plato). Ms. Aimsly, of course, sees through the amusing act, punctuated as it is by Arnold's black vernacular punch lines, but she admits to Mr. D after the fact that "the boys seem to be getting along just fine and, frankly, I'm surprised." "Why should you be?" asks Mr. D.

Ms. Aimsly: Well, it's been my observation that white children are usually happier in white families and black children with black families.

Mr. D:	Oh, really?
Ms. Aimsly:	Mm-hmm, but then it just might be that money *can* buy happiness. It must be nice to be L-O-D-I-D.

Ms. Aimsly is suggesting, of course, that Arnold and Willis have fallen in love with their own upward mobility, rather than any genuine emotional bond with their new guardian. Mr. D replies to the point: "It's true, I do have money. But I really do care a lot for those boys." And that is that.

Following this visit, however, Mr. D is so astonished by the evident facts of racial segregation in the United States that have been brought politely to bear against his studied inattention to the world beneath his 30th-floor balcony[49] that he repeats to his white housekeeper, the unflappable Mrs. Garrett, what was offered by the caseworker as a—to boot, computer-generated—truism of the profession: "black children belong with black families." Arnold inadvertently overhears this distressing fragment of the conversation and takes it, out of context, as a racist rejection of their nascent filiation. Arnold relays the message to his older brother, and Willis registers the mood of disappointment: "And all the time I thought that was one dude who was colorblind." Beyond the immediate hurt, though, Arnold is perplexed:

Arnold:	Why would he pretend to like us, Willis?
Willis:	I guess 'cause we're the latest fad in honkyland.
Arnold:	What does that mean?
Willis:	It means we better get outta here before he puts us in a jockey suit and plants us in the front lawn.

While the reference to the racist connotations of the black lawn jockey replica is meant to insinuate the young boys into the historical derogation of adult black masculinity, they are both, and Arnold in particular, too young to fit the mold. Moreover, the latest fad in honkyland has placed them, not on the exterior but on the interior of the domestic sphere of this man of means, perhaps not unlike the ceramic pickaninny figurines evoked by Topsy and Buckwheat in earlier moments. As Mr. D has already recounted for them in the opening episode the ostentatiously long list of his possessions—the elite education, the high art collection, the square footage of Manhattan real estate, the antique furniture, the hot tub, the color TV and stereo, the priceless city view—Willis is rightly concerned that he and Arnold have become part of Mr. Drummond's collection of things. Willis's clarification is lost on Arnold, of course, since Arnold is, if not unaware of, then at least underwhelmed by, the force of antiblack racism. (The general dynamic between the brothers is one in which Willis tries to impress on Arnold the cold, hard truths of the world—as he understands it in light of his 13 years—and Arnold tries to encourage Willis to lighten up.)[50] Arnold and Willis notify the social worker forthwith to indicate their dissatisfaction at Mr. Drummond's residence and announce their preference for replacement with a black adoptive family. When Ms. Aimsly puts Mr. D on notice about the impeding change, he attempts in vain to talk to the boys about their apparent change of heart. He finds them in their room watching TV, laughing, intent on ignoring him.

> Mr. D: What's so funny guys?
> Willis: The whites were attacking the Indians, and the Indians are winning.
> Arnold: Aw man, talk about a fast haircut!

This oppositional reading of a scene from the Western film genre sets the stage for what the boys believe is their defensive and reactive rejection of Mr. D in the face of his racist pronouncement, and their rejection is rendered through a curious racial transposition, like Indians repelling the aggression of white colonial expansion through armed self-defense. When Willis reiterates Arnold's reiteration of Mr. D's reiteration of Ms. Aimsly's reiteration of the professional common sense—"blacks belong with black and whites belong with white"—their newfound preference for a black family is offered without explanation and, for all intents and purposes, requires no rational justification. "It's just that things ain't working out," says Willis. Dejected and confused, but credulous, Mr. D does not press the issue, and in his very brief concession speech he simply states: "I see. Well, I only want to do what's best for you, 'cause I love you." With that, Mr. D accepts the failure of his final promise to Arnold and Willis's mother and his former housekeeper. Recall that Mrs. Garrett replaced Mrs. Jackson in her capacity, and so, as her proxy, the white woman who now occupies the position inflects the latter's wishes without account. Mrs. Garrett consoles Mr. D accordingly:

> You're very kind and loving, and you make a wonderful father. Besides, look what they got here. I'm telling you, these kids are living in the lap of luxury. [. . .] Believe me Mr. Drummond, that black couple is gonna have to be something else before those boys will give up all of this and . . . leave you.

As it turns out, that black couple, Geoffrey and Olivia Thompson, *is* something else. The head of a successful manufacturing business that provides barrels to overseas oil refineries, Mr. Drummond's luxury apartment—seven figures, two stories, four bedrooms, *and* a housekeeper—simply reminds the Thompsons of the little flat in London they use just for weekends. Now that the gross material advantages Mr. D represents with respect to their tenement in Harlem seem quaint in comparison to the Thompsons' fortune, the boys must address the racial dimensions of their prospective adoption *ceteris paribus*. And, under the circumstances, they do choose to vacate the premises. Yet, before Arnold's *faux pas* can run its course—and Arnold is designated the "big dummy" here—the rather opinionated social worker, in a moment of self-satisfaction, repeats the race-matching mantra and reveals the source of misunderstanding and catharsis begins. Importantly, it is Olivia Thompson, appearing as Arnold and Willis's prospective black adoptive mother, that rearticulates the last wishes of their recently departed black birth mother. And, according to this strange calculus of race, class, and gender, only *she,* a black woman of means, can give the (posthumous) blessing: "Black or white, its *love* that counts."

The triangulation is thus complete. Mrs. Garrett is the working-class *white* counterpart to Mrs. Jackson, the working-class *black* woman; Mrs. Thompson is the *owning-class* black counterpart to Mrs. Jackson, the *working-class* black woman. Mr. Drummond would seem to be the fourth term, the *white owning-class* male counterpart to Mrs. Jackson, the *working-class black* woman, but within the semiotic square that positions these women along axes of race and class; the missing and unspoken term is, in fact, the late Mrs. Drummond. What makes it possible for Mr. Drummond to establish the double substitution of his custodial claim is this series of relays or mediations wherein the terms of racial domination and class struggle are progressively isolated and negated. What remains, however, is the gender trouble and sexual panic of a wealthy, middle-aged, presumptively heterosexual white widower who must, on his word, take up the task of raising two young black boys—in place of the white son he always wanted and alongside his teenaged white daughter.[51] In this way, the question of interracial intimacy that had been, as noted, only recently broached in the history of American television by the late 1970s debuts in the proper sense as a matter of male bonding, intergenerational and patriarchal, in the relative absence, or management, of white women and the total absence of black women.

Here, the desire that black children might have for filiation with black caretakers or relatives, and perhaps even the larger idea and ethos of black community as such, has no positive value; it exists, on this telling, only as a reaction formation against the rejection of intimacy by white society.[52] More importantly, though, the subject of the drama has been changed from considerations of the best interests of the (black) child to the best intentions of the (white) parent. This much should give pause to the careful viewer. But, ultimately, it is the displacement of the vertical arrangements of black family in general and of black mother right in particular that makes possible the entire dialectic between white father and black sons the enduring dream of interracial fraternal bond. When Ms. Aimsly reports at the end of the episode that she will tell the computer to "go suck a lemon," she is not refuting a racist presumption, even one taken up in a misguided white liberal's attempt to provide for black child welfare. Rather, she is endorsing, and thereby giving state sanction to, the rejection of the very concern raised by the NABSW, in the name of Black Power, for the preservation of black families. It is not unreasonable to conclude, then, that *Diff'rent Strokes* is, first and foremost, *about* the death of the black mother. Whatever other ancillary themes and topics the show may take up (e.g., the growing pains of adolescence, the moral training of children, the contemporary reconfiguration of the nuclear family), the critical point is that this foundational violence is sedimented into its symbolic universe for the duration, first, by restricting the matter to the distal question of interracial adoption and, second, by preempting that question altogether with the canard of color blindness. In fact, the alternative white family formation—single parent and blended—becomes the site for the reinstitutionalization of black natal alienation, a gentrified revision of the bourgeois family that insulates interracial intimacy from the potential turbulence of its historic association with miscegenation.[53]

Arnold Redux

Noting the success of NBC's production over five seasons, ABC launched its own spin-off in 1983. *Webster* presents the story of George Papadopolous (Alex Karras, former standout defensive lineman for the Detroit Lions), a sports newscaster and former professional football player, and his wife Katherine Papadopolous (Susan Clark), a socialite, philanthropist, and consumer rights advocate. Theirs is an interethnic and cross-class marriage: George, a working-class child of Greek immigrants, and Katherine, a member of the WASP upper crust. These factors of minor internal difference will sensitize the newlywed couple to the fortune that awaits them and provide degrees of mediation for the major difference they will broach in their adoption of Webster, the son of George's former football teammate, after his parents are killed in a car accident. And the troubles involved are announced directly.

In episode 1, "Another Ballgame," Webster arrives at the Papadopolous residence special delivery by way of a courier service, rather than through the intermediaries of an adoption agency. After George receives Webster from the courier, Katherine asks apprehensively, "George, did we just buy a child?" Webster's commodity status is highlighted in this opening scene by a number of formal elements, including George's objectifying grip—arms outright with hands beneath his armpits, at the level one would position a ventriloquist's dummy—and Webster's costume-like little man suit and tie, stiff posture, and rolling eyes, silently searching the apartment. It dawns on the couple in short course what they are being asked to assume, and Katherine objects strongly to the consequent restructuring of the domestic sphere. The ensuing exchange is telling:

George:	Well, he's kinda cute.
Katherine:	That's not the point.
George:	Then I can't keep him?
Katherine:	He's not a puppy, he's a child. [...] We'll do everything we can for him. We'll find him a nice home.
George:	What is he a puppy?
Katherine:	That's not fair, George.

Webster, who has wandered into the bedroom where the adults are talking, overhears the deliberations. He feels himself an imposition in his new home and leaves the following note on his way out the door: "You have a nice house here. A boy would be happy." George tracks down Webster at the football stadium nearby and attempts to explain why he and his wife cannot or, rather, *should* not adopt him. Webster, in turn, appeals to George's latent desire for children despite his and Katherine's decision to remain childless by choice in pursuit of their respective careers. Webster pleads: "I don't eat much. I know how to make my own bed. I'm tidy." George demurs: "You can stay with us as long as it takes for us to find you a good home." Webster parries: "What am I, a puppy?" George, taking the point, asks, finally: "Don't you want a family?" Webster, undaunted, retorts: "Don't you?" So, whereas George impresses on Webster the value of living a life with people who are eager, rather than reluctant, to care for you, Webster impresses on George the improbable prospect of a life with a child who, like a puppy, actively solicits your care rather than one that, at best, makes a virtue out of necessity.

George is won over by Webster's persistence, a persistence that is curious not only for the age of seven, even in TV land, but also given the fact that Webster is, at the time we meet him, in the most immediate shock and mourning over the sudden loss of his parents, his home, and the whole of his natal surround. Together now, George and Webster attempt to prevail on Katherine, who makes defensive recourse to the pluralist idea of different strokes. She explains to Webster: "Take the zoo, for instance. Some women go to the zoo. They love to go to the zoo. They go to the zoo all the time. I am not one of those women. I don't like the zoo." Webster's task, and his stake, is to convince Katherine why a trip to the zoo, where presumably she will encounter Webster as if for the first time, can provide a source of enrichment rather than displeasure. No longer a stray animal, he is now a caged one, radical cuteness intact. The appeal to family by surrogate succeeds by and by, so much so that this very odd white couple begins to rethink their life plan, which is to say principally that the liberal feminist ideals Katherine lives by become attenuated. Over the course of the first several episodes, we witness the reconversion of the decidedly nondomestic career woman trying diligently to learn the traditional gender roles she previously rejected, making a bid, for Webster's sake, to start "homesteading in Middle America," as she puts it. Within this sweep, white masculinity can remake and reassert itself through a political rapprochement with the social effects of the movements for racial justice and gender equality, betraying a kinder, gentler white man for the new age.

The true reckoning, however, is delayed but not evaded, returning with misleading openness in episode 8, "Travis." It is not immediately clear how the title is related to the themes of the episode, except that we know Webster's father is Travis Long, George's former teammate. Travis asked George to serve as Webster's legal guardian in the event of his and his wife's untimely death, and that request comes under intense and belated scrutiny here. In the opening scene of the episode, Katherine chats after exercising with her friend Ellen, a black woman that Katherine knows well from her college days. Despite their otherwise cordial rapport, Ellen is bothered, on principle, by Katherine's interracial adoption and says so without further explanation: "I don't think a white couple should be raising a black child." When Katherine takes this news to George for discussion, her practical-minded husband counsels: "It's an opinion. . . . Does an opposing opinion automatically make you wrong? [. . .] What makes her the expert?" But Katherine has a serious contention: "Well [Ellen is] a housewife, mother of three, she's black, she has a Ph.D. in sociology specializing in the placement of minority children, and she's written this book, *Trauma and Culture Shock of the Adolescent Victims of the Liberal White Left*. [. . .] She is an expert in her field." Furthermore, Katherine concurs, "Webster has a right to know about his culture, about his background, about his heritage, about where he comes from," assuming Ellen's objection is grounded, after all, in a concern for Webster's awareness of culture, background, and heritage.

It remains perfectly ambiguous what precisely is the source of Ellen's expertise—her being black, a wife, a mother, a sociologist, a published author, or a specialist in the placement of minority children—though one would think the last would be decisive. In any event, the summary judgment of a black professional—whose rather opinionated research might be cited by Ms. Aimsly's computer—stands in for the pointed and complex debate inaugurated, or reignited, by the NABSW more than a decade earlier. And, much as in the case of *Diff'rent Strokes,* the issue is reframed beyond recognition as the very notion of black expertise on race matters, and the legitimacy of the political demands it recalls, is not so much refuted as it is circumvented. George, now impatient, says: "Do you think that kid in there has got a problem because we're white?" "I don't know," Katherine replies. "But I sure would like to find out." And so they do. Predictably, Webster does not have a problem with the fact that George and Katherine are white, but this is not revealed without routing the determination of the child's approval, already a displacement of the adjudication of his best *interest,* into an economy of sacrifice.

Katherine:	Are you ever embarrassed that George and I are your guardians?
Webster:	I'm confused. Do I do that to you?
George and Katherine, together:	No.
Webster:	Then I guess you don't do that to me.
Katherine, to George:	Maybe he doesn't understand what we're trying to say. He is only seven.

Indeed, Webster interprets his guardians' concerns wrong side up. "They're very nice, Teddy," he muses to his stuffed animal companion. "They wouldn't ever want to hurt my feelings. But I don't think they were telling the truth. I think I do embarrass them." Webster is sure that his guardians would not *want* to hurt his feelings, but they have, in raising this awkward question in so awkward a way, inadvertently done just that. In asking him about embarrassment, that is, they cause him embarrassment, a confusion or disturbance of mind. Webster seeks consolation in a young white playmate, Melanie, but her ingenue's advice only compounds the misunderstanding. Consulting the dictionary entry for "embarrassment," Webster and Melanie, through a process of elimination, land on a definition indicating "difficulty arising from the want of money to pay debts" and conclude thereby that Webster presents a financial burden to George and Katherine. Having defined, and more importantly, *quantified* the problem in this way, Webster sets out to remedy the situation by selling off his toys to neighborhood kids, raising $1.87 for the cause.

As Webster plies his wares, Katherine is shown following Ellen's advice to bone up on the scholarly research on white families raising black children, suggesting a parallel in her and Webster's respective, albeit well-meaning errors. Each of them mistakenly believes that they are a problem to the other. George remains the skeptic, dismissing outright or, rather, disavowing the very question of race-conscious parenting as nothing more than an unnecessary source of discomfiture for parents and children alike. Katherine notices the impromptu clearance sale and interrupts Webster's commerce. After learning of Webster's plan, Katherine explains: "Our problem is much more serious than money. I don't know if we're the right parents for you. I like you very much, but the truth is that you're black and we're white and I'm not sure if being together as a family is for the best." Webster reiterates his earlier stance and, again, misinterprets: "I don't mind that we're different colors. Oh, I see, *you* mind." Fed up with the sort of handwringing that characterizes the "liberal white left," George insists to Katherine: "I'm sure this arrangement is gonna work. Darling, we're not black, I can't help that, but we're the right family for Webster." "How do you know?" Katherine implores. "How can you be so sure? Make me sure."

George, meeting the demand, gathers his newly blended interracial family on the couch to settle the whole thing in a scene deeply reminiscent of Spencer Tracy's climactic soliloquy in Stanley Kramer's 1967 film, *Guess Who's Coming to Dinner?* In this instance, however, the director makes use of a flashback sequence to add an important authorial twist to the white patriarch's pronouncement. It is seven years prior, on Webster's birthday, and George has just walked off the field in the middle of a professional football game with his friend and teammate, Travis. Now at the hospital, they are buzzing with excitement about Webster's arrival when Travis asks George to be Webster's godfather. George is honored by the request but concerned about its implications.

George: Travis, you think it's okay for a white guy to bring up a black child?

Travis: I don't know about that, man. But if you're the white guy, and it's my kid in question . . . just why you being so difficult, you want the gig or not?

George: Well, I was only thinking about people. You know how people are.

Travis: People are going to think whatever they want to think. Nothing is going to change, George, not completely. If people look at what we do as some kind of social statement, then that's their problem. But I'm not giving you my kid to make a social statement. I'm giving you my kid because I love you, George Papadopolous. You got the same values, same standards, same soul. You're the closest thing to me that I can think of.

Aside from the evident way that George distances himself from responsibility for and inhabitation of the structures of antiblackness by rendering racism a problem of other people (white people? black people?), it is crucial that black people establish that considerations of race and racism do not enter their thinking when pursuing their children's best interests. Social statements on the welfare of black children are not made by black parents with meaningful personal ties to white people; they merely nominate the best person for the gig on the basis of values, standards, and soul, rather than some putatively segregationist logic of race matching. It is worth noting, on this point, that both Mrs. Jackson in *Diff'rent Strokes* and Travis Long in *Webster* are from working-class communities (Travis' recent ascent to the NFL notwithstanding), and the barriers to their stated desire for the posthumous interracial adoption of their own children are middle-class black professionals like Ellen or adherents like Ms. Aimsley or even, temporarily, Katherine herself, all educated fools. White men, whether blue bloods like Philip Drummond or *nouveau riche* white ethnics like George Papadopolous, have little trouble with the prospect of interracial adoption because they experience no compunction in their interactions with black people in general. White women with professional aspirations, under the influence of liberal feminism, are susceptible to doubt about white parental fitness, for white and black children alike. White men have heard it from the horse's mouth, as it were, and their word is their bond. Better yet, they are bonded to the ghostly word of departed black mothers and fathers to honor their singular final wishes as a testator's veto against the interference of political pressure, government mandate, or public opinion.

George: So this is why I trust this, why I'm so sure. And if you don't trust me, trust Travis Long. [...] Travis didn't say anything about easy. It wouldn't be easy if Web was white. I think we have a pretty good head start. Here's a little kid that loved us enough to sell all his toys for a buck-eighty-seven. And a woman who cared

enough to risk losing that little boy, if it would be the best thing
for Web. And a man, your pop, who was closer to me than his
own brother. I don't see easy, but I do see family, don't you?

In the symbolic universe of Reaganstruction, the vindication of white interracial adoption and the negation of the political demand for black family preservation that underwrites race-matching policy are grounded in the
earnest and profound intimacy that blacks ostensibly feel toward whites
and the moral acceptance and eventual reciprocation of that intimacy by
their white obligatees. White parents of black children cannot be interested;
in other words, they must consider the best interests of the child, however
perfunctorily, and be willing to relinquish custody in order to be rediscov-
ered in that interest and as its ultimate guarantee. If black parents choose
to give their children to white surrogates because they are kindred spirits,
then perhaps we can appreciate the acuity of the observation that "what is
called the black soul is a construction of white folk."[54]

Notes

1. Audre Lorde, "School Note," *The Collected Poems of Audre Lorde* (New York: W.W. Norton & Company, 1997), p. 217.

2. See, for instance, the online film review clearinghouse, Rotten Tomatoes, where it was rated "100% fresh." Leading critics writing for the *Chicago Sun-Times, Salon, Variety,* and the *Village Voice* all offered positive reviews.

3. J. Hoberman, "The Slums of Park Slope," *Village Voice,* September 11, 2007, http://www.villagevoice.com/2007–09–11/film/the-slums-of-park-slope/ (accessed June 1, 2012).

4. *The Landlord,* directed by Hal Foster (1970; Santa Monica, CA: MGM/UA Home Video, 1995), VHS.

5. Dorothy Roberts speaks directly to this association in *Shattered Bonds: The Color of Child Welfare* (New York: Basic Books, 2002), 67. There she writes: "White families . . . benefit from the presumption of parental fitness and valuable family ties. [. . .] [Holding] up white families as the superior standard against which all other families fail is entrenched in American culture." Throughout the text, how-ever, she speaks to the particular historical and ongoing denigration of black pa-rental fitness in general and black maternal fitness in particular.

6. Kristin Hunter Lattany, "Why Buckwheat Was Shot," *MELUS* 11 (1984): 84. Thanks to Prof. Jennifer Reich, University of Denver, for bringing this article to my attention.

7. Ibid., pp. 79–80.

8. Ibid., pp. 79, 84.

9. Tavia Nyong'o, "Racial Kitsch and Black Performance," *Yale Journal of Criti-cism* 15 (2002): p. 376.

10. All citations for this text are from Harriett Beecher Stowe, *Uncle Tom's Cabin, Or Life among the Lowly* (Salt Lake City, UT: Project Gutenberg Literary Archive Foundation, 1852, 2006, 2011), http://www.gutenberg.org/files/203/203-h/203-h.htm.

11. On the concept of the nonoriginary origin, see, for instance, Paula Marrati, *Genesis and Trace: Derrida Reading Husserl and Heideggeer* (Palo Alto, CA: Stanford University Press, 2005). This should suggest something of the generative possibilities that inhere in the political terror of this perfect deracination.

12. Stowe's novel argues that Christianity is anathema not only to slavery and its "outrages of feelings and affections" but also to racism and "the feeling of personal prejudice" it entails, even among abolitionists. Indeed, the convergence of slavery and racism is represented in the character of Simon Legree, a northern racist turned slaveholder, the quintessential godless man. In chapter XXXIX, she writes of Legree: "No one is so thoroughly superstitious as the godless man. The Christian is composed by the belief of a wise, all-ruling Father, whose presence fills the void unknown with light and order; but to the man who has dethroned God, the spirit-land is, indeed, in the words of the Hebrew poet, 'a land of darkness and the shadow of death,' without any order, where the light is as darkness. Life and death to him are haunted grounds, filled with goblin forms of vague and shadowy dread." The "goblin forms" that Legree sees in Tom and the other slaves on his plantation surely recall the "goblin-like" countenance that Miss Ophelia observes on Topsy's face up until the point of her late conversion just prior to Eva's untimely death. The question remains, obviously, about how the author, as she is wont to do, ensures her own distance toward the very racist discourse her text invariably reproduces.

13. Nyong'o, "Racial Kitsch and Black Performance," p. 376.

14. Ibid., p. 376.

15. Ibid., p. 376.

16. Ibid., p. 380.

17. Ibid., p. 381.

18. Robin Bernstein, *Racial Innocence: Performing American Childhood from Slavery to Civil Rights* (New York: NYU Press, 2011), p. 65.

19. Ibid., p. 51.

20. Ibid., p. 51.

21. Ibid., pp. 34–36. Bernstein concludes: "Pain divided tender white children from insensate pickaninnies. At stake in this split was fitness for citizenship and inclusion in the category of the child and, ultimately, the human," p. 36.

22. Nyong'o, "Racial Kitsch and Black Performance," p. 381.

23. Bernstein, *Racial Innocence*, p. 36.

24. "The unfeeling, un-childlike pickaninny is the mirror image of both the always-already pained African American adult and the 'childlike Negro'" (ibid., p. 35).

25. Nyong'o, "Racial Kitsch and Black Performance," p. 377.

26. Bernstein, *Racial Innocence*, p. 36.

27. Ibid., p. 65.

28. For a good discussion of *All in the Family* that sets it in the immediate historical context, see Josh Ozerski, *Archie Bunker's America: TV in an Era of Change, 1968–1978* (Carbondale, IL: Southern Illinois University Press, 2003).

29. Darrell Hamamoto, *Nervous Laughter: Television Situation Comedy and Liberal Democratic Ideology* (New York: Praeger Publishers, 1991), pp. 126–27. For further reading on the history of the situation comedy in American television, see Mary Dalton and Laura Linder, *The Sitcom Reader: American Viewed and Skewed* (Albany: SUNY University Press, 2005); Barbara Moore, Marvin Bensman, and Jim Van Dyke, *Prime-Time Television: A Concise History* (Westport, CT: Praeger Publishers, 2006); Joanne Morreale, *Critiquing the Sitcom: A Reader* (Syracuse, NY: Syracuse University Press, 2003); and Ella Taylor, *Prime Time Families: Television Culture in Postwar America* (Berkeley: University of California Press, 1989). For treatments of the African American presence in television in particular, see Christine Acham, *Revolution Televised: Prime Time and the Struggle for Black Power* (Minneapolis: University of Minnesota Press, 2004); Kathleen Fearn-Banks, *The A to Z of African-American Television* (Lanham, MD: Scarecrow Press, 2006); and Catherine Squires, *African Americans and the Media* (Malden, MA: Polity, 2009).

30. Hamamoto, *Nervous Laughter,* p. 126. For a discussion of this return to normalcy and its relation to internal developments in the corporate structure of the television industry, see Ozersky, *Archie Bunker's America,* chap. 6.

31. Quoted in Ozersky, *Archie Bunker's America,* p. 177.

32. Acham, *Revolution Televised,* p. 171.

33. Squires, *African Americans and the Media,* p. 224.

34. National Association of Black Social Workers (NABSW), "Preserving Families of African Descent" (2003), http://www.nabsw.org/mserver/PreservingFamilies.aspx. All subsequent quotations of the NABSW are from this source.

35. Ibid.

36. For a discussion of these and other objections to the NABSW's position, see Rachel Moran, *Interracial Intimacy: The Regulation of Race and Romance* (Chicago: University of Chicago Press, 2001), chap. 7.

37. See Roberts, *Shattered Bonds,* pt 3, for a theory of African American group-based harm in relation to the child welfare system.

38. Roberts reports that "the economic fortunes of white and Black children are just the opposite: the percentage of Black children who *ever* lived in poverty while growing up is about the same as the percentage of white children who *never* did," 46. See Roberts, *Shattered Bonds,* pt 1, for more on the intersections of race and class in child welfare.

39. Ibid., p. 99.

40. Ibid., p. 74.

41. Ibid., p. 74.

42. Ibid., p. 61.

43. Hortense Spillers, "Mama's Baby, Papa's Maybe: An American Grammar Book," *Black, White, and in Color: Essays on American Literature and Culture* (Chicago: University of Chicago Press, 2003), p. 227.

44. Hortense Spillers, "'The Permanent Obliquity of an In(pha)llibly Straight': In the Time of the Daughters and the Fathers," *Black, White and in Color: Essays on American Literature and Culture* (Chicago: University of Chicago Press, 2003), p. 249.

45. On the "afterlife of slavery" as "a racial calculus and a political arithmetic that were entrenched centuries ago," see Saidiya Hartman, *Lose Your Mother: A Journey Along the Atlantic Slave Route* (New York: Macmillan, 2007), p. 6.

46. Spillers, "Mama's Baby, Papa's Maybe," p. 249.

47. William Merritt, former president of the NABSW, quoted in Barbara Katz Rothman, "Transracial Adoption: Refocusing Upstream," *The Politics of Mulitracialism: Challenging Racial Thinking,* ed. by Heather Dalmage (Albany: SUNY University Press, 2004), p. 195.

48. Ibid., 196. Rothman explains further: "Adoption is the result of some very bad things going on upstream, policies that push women into having babies that they then cannot raise. Racism is of course the other feeder stream: more women of color find themselves placed just there, placed willingly or very much against their will. Some make adoption plans and place their babies in waiting arms; some have their children wrenched away by a deeply neglectful state, which then finds neglect. A lot of what adoption is about is poverty, a lack of access to contraception and abortions, a lack of access to the resources to raise children. In addition, a lot of what poverty is about in America is racism. Moreover, as much as the black community stands there with open arms, absorbing as many of those babies and children as it can, the same poverty that pushes all those babies and children into the adoption stream ensures that there won't be enough black homes to take them all," pp. 197–98.

49. Although this isn't entirely true, is it? Mr. D, in the same episode, quips that he's had a good day because he walked all the way home from the office through Central Park without being mugged. He also jokes, in the first episode, when bragging to Arnold and Willis about the obscene wealth they will now enjoy as his new charges, that on a clear day one can see from his balcony all the way across the Hudson River to New Jersey—likely the multiracial, multiethnic working-class neighborhoods of Jersey City—"not that anyone would want to."

50. On Arnold's role as comic relief, see Virginia Heffernan, "Revealing the Wages of Young Sitcom Fame," *New York Times,* September 4, 2006. http://tv.nytimes.com/2006/09/04/arts/television/04stro.html. There the author writes that *Diff'rent Strokes* "is the representative document of the surreal race politics of 30 years ago, which made gods of limousine liberals and allowed minstrelsy to inform black roles for children. If the 60's had radical chic, the 70's and 80's had radical cuteness. The face of this ideology in prime time was Arnold Jackson.... At the time Arnold struck audiences as an endlessly endearing trickster figure, whose Harlem-bred sensitivity to being hustled had been reduced to a sweetie-pie affectation: 'What you talkin' about, Willis?' Arnold was supposed to be shrewd and nobody's fool, but also misguided; after learning his lessons, he was easily tamed and cuddled."

51. Given the history of American film and television, one would think that *Diff'rent Strokes* would generate controversy for placing under the same roof a pubescent black boy (Willis) and a pubescent white girl (Kimberly), both aged 13. In a sense, the too obvious objection to that doubly taboo interracial, incestuous sexuality was repressed, only to return in a fascination with the perversion

attributed to the cast offscreen. All three of the former child stars—Gary Coleman, Todd Bridges, and Dana Plato—struggled with substance abuse and various legal problems that led to financial ruin. Plato additionally gained some notoriety when she posed nude for *Playboy* magazine and later starred in several soft-core pornographic films. A similar aura of perversion would attach itself to Emmanuel Lewis, star of *Webster,* with the emergence of his close and public friendship with Michael Jackson, especially as the latter faced allegations of sexual crimes against children.

52. This dynamic has been noted regarding questions of identity for black characters broadly in contemporary American television. See, for instance, Minabere Ibelema, "Identity Crisis: The African Connection in African American Sitcom Characters," *Sexual Politics & Popular Culture,* ed. by Diane Raymond (Bowling Green, OH: Bowling Green State University Popular Press, 1990). Ibelema summarizes as follows: "There is a definite pattern in all the episodes on African or racial identity. First, concern with African identity results from a personal crisis. The African American character does not project his African cultural identity in normal times. Overt awareness and projection are triggered by an event or in moments of self-doubt. Secondly, the character begins to engage in uncharacteristic behavior, rejects most social norms, and acts in exaggeratedly strange ways. In other words, overt awareness and expression of African identity is portrayed as a form of personal revolution and social rebellion. Thirdly, the character is confronted with 'evidence' that convinces him that assertion of African identity is not necessary. Fourthly and finally, the character reverts to his old ways, and the identity crisis is over," pp. 122–23.

53. A related argument is made with respect to Richard Benjamin's 1993 film *Made in America* by Robyn Weigman, "Intimate Publics: Race, Property, and Personhood," *American Literature* 74 (2002): pp. 859–85. She writes there about how "the absence of interracial sexuality . . . is critically important to the presence of white multiracial desire" in narratives of liberal whiteness for the postsegregationist era, p. 861.

54. Frantz Fanon, *Black Skin, White Masks,* trans. Richard Philcox (New York: Grove Press, 2008), p. xviii.

Chapter 6

Post-racial, Post–Civil Rights: *The Cosby Show* and the National Imagination

David J. Leonard

The 1970s, with *The Jeffersons* and several other shows during the decade, marked the emergence of the black middle-class family on television. The popularity of these shows signified not just the arrival of this community but an effort to highlight the availability of the American Dream for all and the declining significance of race. These shows would provide positive representations on television, which importantly would be done through shining a spotlight on the experiences of the black middle class. These shows would purportedly provide evidence of the black middle class, which would be cited on and off television as goodness and respectability. Without identifying blackness as a source of blame, focusing instead on cultural attributes of the underclass, and in deploying images and representations of the black middle class as evidence of good black folks, the possibility of the American Dream, and hegemony of color blindness, the existence of a binary between the black underclass and the black middle class was central to the messages, representations, and popularity of 1980s African American television. Thus, it is not about race any longer, should the offerings of contemporary African American televisual representation be believed, but about opportunity, self-determination, and personal choices. The

This chapter contains parts of a prior book written by the author entitled *Screens Fade to Black: Contemporary African American Cinema,* 2006. Said prior material is included herein with the permission of Praeger Publishers Inc., © 2004.

institutional mechanisms of race are nonexistent, and almost laughable, within the new racial order depicted within the landscape of television during the 1980s. Personal investment in the American Dream and an embrace of a bootstraps-model work ethic are key to success; these are the qualities that make good black folks.

The efforts to imagine a raceless middle-class world, especially in conjunction with a discourse that demonizes and pathologizes the black working poor, and the projects that reduce blackness to a commodifiable black cultural practice embody new racism. Imagining a black world without black people, thus, embodies new racism or the hegemonic practice of racism without racists. In other words, these shows "reproduce and disseminate the ideologies needed to justify racism."[1] With the exception of *Frank's Place* and, to a lesser degree, *A Different World,* which successfully construct the world of the black middle class as one of struggle, conflict, personal pain, and continuity, the wave of African American television shows during the 1980s and early 1990s celebrated a post-racial America defined by progress, personal responsibility, and choice. In picturing a world without race, these shows deny the racism endured by the black middle class, all rehashing bootstrap ideology and culture of poverty. *The Cosby Show* and its brethren engage the racial debates of the day with amazing clarity.

The Cosby Show

The opening credits of the initial episode of *The Cosby Show* establish the show's trajectory: in successive shots, American audiences are introduced not only to the Huxtable family, a two-parented African American family consisting of four daughters (Sandra, Denise, Vanessa, and Rudy) and a lone son (Theo) but to a regular, all-American family. With shots of the family at the park, getting out of their van with their sports equipment in hand, presumably so they can play together during one of their many family outings, the Huxtables are initially constructed as little more than an average suburban family, who just happen to be African Americans; notwithstanding the fact that as an upper-middle class (Heathcliff is a doctor and Clair is a lawyer) African American family residing in New York City, the Huxtables were certainly not average on either television or within the United States during the 1980s.

At one level, the initial credits set a certain tone for the show—one of positivity, as a clear departure from the types of representations available to African Americans during the 1980s. Whether appearing in the nightly news, as part of political campaigns, or on the front page of America's daily newspapers, "Blackness was constructed along a continuum ranging from menace on the one end to immorality on the other, with irresponsibility located somewhere in the middle."[2] In this regard, *The Cosby Show* offered a stark departure even as it affirmed dominant racial stereotypes.

Throughout the 1980s, from "scholarly and journalist treatises" to popular television and cinema, representations, and debates regarding the black "underclass anchored contemporary race talk, and spoke the language that distinguishes the aberrant underclass from the striving middle class."[3] The ubiquity of "black gang members, black male criminality, crumbling black families, black welfare cheats, black female crack users, and black teen pregnancy"[4] on and off television provided legitimacy to the Reagan Revolution, which called for a return to traditional values a return of America to its deserving (white middle-class suburban families) and not those undeserving (African Americans, poor people of color). In other words, Ronald Reagan and the New Right mobilized images of "rampaging hordes of urban black youth robbing and raping helpless and law-abiding white female victims"[5] to legitimize the systematic erosion of social welfare programs and put in their place more prisons and police all while enhancing state power. At this particular moment, with rare exception, the circulation of black images limited itself to that of menace, threat, and danger.

The Cosby Show entered into the television landscape at a moment when critics, activists, and commentators equally lamented the paucity of African Americans on television and the overall lack of diversity evident in the overrepresentations of blacks as "unimportant petty criminal roles in crime dramas."[6] Moreover, these same critics and scholars highlighted that since the 1970s, with the emergence of several black-themed shows, television had become more and more ripe with gross racial stereotypes. "As more all-black shows were developed," wrote Monica Payne, "it was felt that characters become, if anything, even more stereotyped: Viewers could conclude that 'to be Black means that one is poor, carefree and unskilled.'"[7] Visibility resulted in more and more stereotypes that included characters not only defined by a propensity to commit crimes and be from the underclass but who also consistently enacted pathological values, including "selfish materialism, social stereotyping of power relations, and amoral/irresponsible attitude toward sex and material relations."[8] Similarly, John Downing argued that the importance of *The Cosby Show* rested with it being "atypical of American television fare" since "media images of Americans of African descent have ranged from the blatantly to latently racist."[9] Timothy Havens concludes, "*The Cosby Show* changed the face of American television and set a new standard for representing African American families in non-stereotyped roles."[10]

The Huxtable Family in NBC's *The Cosby Show*. Shown clockwise from left: Keshia Knight Pulliam (Rudy), Phylicia Rashad (Clair), Sabrina Le Beauf (Sondra), Malcolm-Jamal Warner (Theo), Tempestt Bledsoe (Vanessa), Lisa Bonet (Denise), and Bill Cosby (Cliff). (NBC/Photofest)

The Cosby Show, most evident in its opening credits, offers a dramatic rupture or a transformed appearance. Blackness does not function as sign of disorder, decay, and dysfunction; blackness is not imagined as incompatible with the family but in fact complimentary; and most importantly within the banality of the Huxtables' introduction, from the generic van to the Sunday outing at the park, their blackness appears not to be a sign of otherness. The show presents the Huxtables as representatives of the national fabric. The opening segment marks a clear attempt to leave behind the negativity, the stereotypes, and the images of black criminality, which saturated the news, big-city newspaper, and shows like *Hill Street Blues*. It pointed to an intervention against the ways in which television homogenized black people as a threat, as a symbol of decay, and otherwise as a source of societal problems. To facilitate this rupture, the Huxtables needed to leave behind their blackness. The Huxtables, and by extension *The Cosby Show*, had to be different within the dominant imagination.

The Cosby Show embodies a celebration of a post–civil rights America, a validation of the American Dream, and an introduction of the black middle class to the vast majority of Americans. *The Cosby Show* "recode[d] the image of Black Americans as socially and economically successful . . . effectively mov[ing] the racial discourse of television toward the symbolic construction of racial equality and a color blind society."[11] *The Cosby Show* sought to illustrate and celebrate the existence of the black middle-class because its existence pointed to racial, economic, and national progress. Although still lagging behind the white middle-class, in terms of numbers, financial compensation, and access to power and opportunity, the post–civil rights era has seen the movement of blacks into professional, managerial, and technological fields in record numbers—in 1964, only 8.5 percent of the black employed held jobs in these sectors compared to 16.7 percent in 1983. According to these same reports from U.S. Bureau of Labor Statistics, there has been a 7 percent increase in the number of black professionals since 1973. Between 1973 and 2000, residential segregation for African Americans declined significantly, although rates were still higher than any other group, revealing the increasing likelihood of black economic success translating into residential mobility. The movement into once predominantly white communities during this period (although many communities eventually became resegregated) further enhanced economic, political, and educational opportunities for the growing black middle class. Their entry into previously blocked professions, the limited success of affirmative action and antidiscrimination laws, has facilitated not just growth in the black middle class but residential mobility, which has in turn provided access to improved schools, health care, and communal institutions.

The last three decades saw a dramatic increase in the number of African Americans attending American colleges and universities as well as moving into once predominantly white neighborhoods. U.S. census figures indicate that today 11 percent of blacks aged 25 and over have completed college, compared to 4.5 percent in 1970. Equally revealing, from 1960 when 2.8 million African Americans lived within America's suburbs to 6.2 million in 1980, there has been a dramatic change in the geographic orientation of the black community.[12] While there has been growth in the black middle-class and the movement of African Americans into leadership positions within Fortune 500 companies, the bulk of African Americans have been left behind.

In portraying African Americans as having made it and as having fulfilled the American Dream, *The Cosby Show* erases poverty, unemployment, and issues of incarceration. It obscures an 18.1 percent rate of unemployment among African Americans and the 44 percent of black youth living in poverty. It simultaneously erases the struggles and relevance of racism within the lives of the black middle class. Joe Feagin and Melvin Sikes, in *Living with Racism: The Black Middle Class Experience,* found that the black middle class faces the pervasive sting of white racism—often subtle and covert, at times blatant—on a daily basis.[13] According to their study of 209 individuals, the black middle-class experience on-the-job racism, ranging from salary inequities to discrimination in evaluations and promotions; prejudice against black renters and homebuyers by white landlords, real estate agents, homeowners, and neighbors; the channeling of black students into vocational tracks; physical assaults and institutionalized racism on college campuses; and microaggressions in the form of prejudice and discrimination in restaurants, stores, and other public places. In other words, the black middle class has not transcended race; it has not secured entry into a post-racial reality where racism and stereotypes no longer affect life's opportunities. Whether dealing with police brutality, the legacies of institutional racism, or housing segregation, racism still plays through the lives of the black middle class. For *The Cosby Show,* these conditions are neither visible nor compelling. It instead packages the black middle class as a pleasurable narrative of progress, universality, the American Dream, and universal desires for upward mobility, ironically using race as a marker of difference or hipness to sell this new and innovative show. Race does and doesn't matter at the same time.

The opening moments of *The Cosby Show* and its broader context demonstrate that at the very least a color-blind and "just world where anyone can make it and racial barriers no longer exist"[14] is presented within the world of television. According to Henry Louis Gates,

> As long as all blacks were represented in demeaning or peripheral roles, it was possible to believe that American racism was, as it were, indiscriminate. The social vision of "Cosby," however, reflecting the minuscule integration of blacks into the upper middle class (having "white money," my mother used to say, rather than "colored" money) reassuringly throws the blame for black poverty back onto the impoverished.[15]

Demonstrating "the American Dream is realistically attainable for Black Americans"[16] and the success of both Cosby himself and the fictional Huxtables provided "proof that it can be done."[17] P. W. Matabane describes *The Cosby Show* as: "epitomiz[ing] the Afro-American dream of full acceptance and assimilation into U.S. society . . . Although this achievement is certainly not inherently negative, we should consider the role television lays in the cultivation of an overall picture of growing racial equality that conceals unequal social relationship and overestimates . . . how well black are integrating into white society (if at all). The illusion of well-being among the oppressed may lead to reduced political activity and less demand for social justice equality."[18]

The juxtaposition of the narrative of *The Cosby Show* with dominant representations of blackness provides specific and concrete evidence for the declining significance of race within American popular culture. That is, if blacks could be represented in a positive way, as average Americans, that in itself was evidence for the eradication of the historic barriers on television (those that confined or shackled black image making to long-standing stereotypes). Gains since the civil rights movement could be seen with *The Cosby Show*. Presented as evidence of color blindness and America's racial transformation, the existence of positive black images was also seen as a tool of racial progress. Celebrated as a show that offered representations of the black middle class thereby challenging commonplace stereotypes of "ghetto kids or maids or butlers wise-cracking about Black life,"[19] *The Cosby Show* was praised as both evidence and a challenge to racism.

Kobena Mercer describes the demands and efforts to produce "positive black images" within popular culture to be those of a "social engineering project," where activists, commentators, and others call on or demand that black artists produce shows that challenge, if not undercut, hegemonic visions of blackness.[20] Cornel West, like Mercer, questions both the desirability and plausibility of a social engineering project, arguing, "The social engineering argument claims that since any form of representation is constructed— i.e., selective in light of broader aims—Black representation (especially given the difficulty of Blacks gaining access to positions of power to produce any Black imagery) should offer positive images, thereby countering racist stereotypes." The hidden assumption of both arguments is that we have unmediated access to what the "real Black community" is and what "positive images" are.[21] West and Mercer rightly identify these representational movements as a futile battle against racist image making, one that puts not only the responsibility and burden on African Americans to perform and embody a respectable and desired image of blackness when consumed in the public but an effort that ultimately does not produce alternative meaning. Writing about the controversy that surrounded the release of Spike Lee's *School Daze* in the 1980s, S. Craig Watkins describes it as a generational battle whereupon "an older generation of" African Americans "committed to the notion of promoting respectable—or in other words, bourgeois—images of blackness"[22] denounces, demonizes, and polices any and all representations that aren't respectable. Popular culture is obligated to elevate the community through challenging stereotypes and America's system of racism.

The celebration of *The Cosby Show* as a "positive" counternarattive to the "negativity" of television operates under a faulty assumption that positive images counter and cancel out those supposedly negative representations. The existence of positive or in this case normalized middle-class representations in many ways legitimizes those stereotypical, negative, and otherwise harmful representations. As Stuart Hall notes,

> The problem with the positive negative strategy is that adding positive images to the largely negative repertoire of the dominant regime of representation increases the diversity of the ways in which "being black is represented, but does not necessarily displace the negative. Since the binaries remain in place, meaning continues to be framed by them. The strategy challenges the binaries—but it does not undermine them. The peace-loving, child-caring Rastafarian can still appear, in the following day's newspapers, as an exotic and violence black stereotype."[23]

Secondly, the representation of the Huxtables as a happy, average family enjoying a weekend at the park, followed by images of the family's upscale (dare we say posh) brownstone (a shot of the home's exterior was the initial starting point for each and every episode), not only highlights the upper-middle class status of the Huxtables but their fulfillment of the American Dream. "Possessing the requisite moral character, individual responsibility and personal determination to succeed in spite of residual social impediments"[24] evident by their family values and their beautiful home, Cliff and Clair Huxtable symbolize the hopes, possibilities, and legitimacy of the American Dream. In fact, their story and existence elevated the greatness of the United States because it was not just whites living the American Dream but rather African Americans, who long suffered under the burdens of racism, had now achieved financial success and social/cultural acceptance. In this initial moment, we thus see that the Huxtables are "model minorities . . . celebrated and presented both to counter the dependence of the underclass and to affirm" America's purported "Commitment to racial equality."[25]

Does Race Matter for the Huxtables?

The Cosby Show success and popularity resulted from not its celebration of the American Dream and its validation of a post-racial America. It was equally successful because of its promotion of safe diversity. A review from the *Village Voice* celebrated the show's ability to deracialize the Huxtables: "No one has ever noticed that the Huxtables are black, so they rarely noticed it, too."[26] Another review concluded that, "The family's blackness . . . is simply a given—neither ignored nor flaunted but written into the show as though blackness were normal—not exotic, not stupid, not shameful, not political."[27] The social construction that defines blackness through dominant stereotypes/associated pathologies allows the absence of these stereotypical traits to render the Huxtables as white. A reviewer within *Television Quarterly* concluded that the Huxtables were not black because their behavior and values resemble those of normal people, those inhabiting middle-class white America.

> I mean, these people—these Huxtables—don't use food stamps. They not only work every day, they have super jobs. The kids don't rob or mug or steal or have babies out of wedlock. They go to the best schools. The whole family behaves, for the most part like you do. Like white folks. Cutesy-pooh.[28]

The Cosby Show wasn't simply celebrated for its comedic influences, its immense popularity, or its ability to highlight racial progress but because of its purported ability to improve race relations within American society. "Commentators in the mass media have asserted that one of the show's greatest consequences was its help in improving race relations by projecting universal values that both Whites and Blacks could identify with, using the tried-and-true situation comedy format."[29] Citing not only the narratives offered by the show and its effort to emphasize the shared themes and experiences of the Huxtables and the average white family but also the popularity of *The Cosby Show* among white viewers and commentators, critics simultaneously celebrated the show for de-emphasizing racial differences and for its efforts to facilitate improved race relations.

Ironically, many of the reviews celebrated the show for rendering race irrelevant yet simultaneously praised the show for challenging existing stereotypes. It purportedly offered positive representations of blackness, leaving one to wonder how these reviews could also celebrate the show for rendering race irrelevant.

In reflecting on the ways in which race operates within the show's narrative, it is clear that *The Cosby Show* successfully constructs race as cultural, as something as important within the Huxtables' lives but not a defining or constraining reality. Racism is irrelevant to understanding their success, experiences, or opportunities. As noted by the *New York Times:* "This particular family happens to be black but its lifestyle and problems are universal middle-class."[30] In other words, "The Huxtables' middle-class status makes their racial identity irrelevant."[31]

The Huxtables happened to be black. They might have different paintings on the wall or a different album on the turntable, but in terms of values, lifestyle, and experiences, their lives mirror those of other white middle-class communities. Race matters very little. According to Sarah Banet-Weiser, within post–civil rights (popular) culture, race "functions as an ambivalent category, where . . . it remains an important issue in terms of representation. . . ." Most importantly, "race itself no longer matters in the same way it once did but is rather an interesting means to feature the authentic, cool, or urban."[32] Similarly, Herman Gray describes the hypervisibility of blackness within 1980s television as evidence of the "pastiche of 'blackness.' "[33]

Although the Huxtables act just like whites, share the values associated with whiteness, and otherwise experience day-to-day life just like white America, the Huxtables are different in terms of cultural traditions, family history, and their relationship to a broader history of African Americans. John Downing notes that despite letting "racism off the hook,"[34] *The Cosby Show* introduced white America to "an abundance of black culture, which was expressed without fanfare, but with constant dignity."[35] *The Cosby Show* sought to emphasize humanity, shared values, and the dignity of African Americans through its subtle deployment of the cultural contributions, artifacts, styles, and aesthetics of black America. According to Alvin Poussaint, "the black culture of the characters comes through their speech, intonations, and nuances; Black music, art, and dance are frequently displayed and Black books and authors are often mentioned."[36] Decorating the family home with pictures by black artists, donning the kid's room's with posters of Fredrick Douglas, Duke Ellington, Miles Davis, Michael Jackson, Michael Jordan, and "Abolish Apartheid," and often showing the family listening to jazz, blues, and even gospel, the Huxtables are firmly situated within a black cultural tradition.

For example, in "Not Everybody Loves the Blues," Theo discovers a passion and admiration for blue's music while attending a concert at a local club. Rushing home to share his excitement with his parents, Theo quickly learns that the artist he had just seen and fallen in love with—Riley Jackson (played by B. B. King)—is a close friend of both his parents and grandparents. Despite the Huxtables' class status, and notwithstanding their professional successes, they are still connected to the blues tradition.

Likewise, the decision to make Cliff and Clair graduates of Hillman College, a fictitious historically black college, and to have Denise attend this same HBCU (historically black colleges and universities), rather than an

Ivy League School, illustrates the ways in which *The Cosby Show* invokes and deploys race though a cultural lens. In "Breaking with Tradition," Denise is confronted with the important decision about her college future. On learning that Hillman isn't on her short list of possible schools, Cliff's father reminds him that Hillman is the "oldest school in the state; it is more than a school, Hillman is your friend." Questioning the value of a Princeton (Ivy League) education, Grandpa Huxtable emphasizes that there is more to an education than prestige and reputation. Heeding the reminders provided to him by his father, Cliff likewise encourages Denise to attend Hillman because of the quality of the school and the Huxtable tradition there. While initially deciding between Brown, Princeton, Yale, Talladega, and Howard, Denise ultimately chooses Hillman because of her father and grandfather's encouragement and their lectures about family tradition. And while grandpa reiterates the importance of tradition, Denise ultimately attends Hillman not just because her parents or grandparents were alumni but because of the 8:1 ratio of males to females. *The Cosby Show* thus links the Huxtables to the history of historically black colleges and universities even without providing specifics about this history. In focusing on tradition and reducing her decision to an increased pool of potential boyfriends, the show simultaneously erases the deeper history of HBCUs as it relates to race and racism all while constructing Denise as just another teenager who makes decisions based on hormones—boys—rather than anything else. In other words, the values and importance of Hillman, whether for the grandparents, Cliff and Clair, or even Denise, do not come from institutional power; its value does not stem from being part of a longer and larger tradition of historically black colleges. Nor do its value and importance result from the histories of violence, exclusion, and segregation that have been commonplace in America's predominantly white colleges and universities. Rather, its appeal results from an abstract and individual notion of tradition. The treatment of Hillman and historically black colleges by extension reflects the broader effort of deploying safe diversity through *The Cosby Show* where difference is presented, albeit in a way where difference is never substantive or of material significance.

Other examples of cultural infusion can be seen with Sandra and Elvin naming their twins Winnie and Nelson (as in the Mandelas) and with the show incorporating numerous black artists and celebrities—Stevie Wonder, B.B. King, the Count Basie Orchestra—into the show's narrative. In "The Auction," Clair purchases a painting by Ellis Wilson, a famous African American artist, who also happens to be her great-uncle. The decision to make Wilson her great-uncle is important in that her desire to purchase the painting and put it on display in their house does not appear to be about her blackness, that of the artist, or preserving cultural identity but rather her family's history and her hopes to hang the picture just as it had been done while she was a child. For Clair, the painting, while costly at $11,500, was about "retrieving [her] heritage" and about teaching her children the importance of looking backward as well as forward. After hanging the painting on their fireplace, she announces "Welcome home Uncle Ellis." As with so many elements of the show, identity matters in a cultural sense but is confined to the private/family sphere rather than a broader historical context.

Another way that *The Cosby Show* racializes the Huxtables all while constructing a post-racial/racism, color-blind world is through providing the family with a certain amount of flava. Writing about *Hey Arnold,* Sarah Banet-Weiser aptly describes the world created on *The Cosby Show:* "Race is very seldom mentioned or directly referenced but is clearly important to the show's style and thematic element."[37] For example, in the opening scene of the pilot episode, we are introduced to the Huxtables as they eat breakfast not around the breakfast table but instead dancing around the kitchen as they prepare for breakfast. Similarly, in an extremely memorable and celebrated scene from Season 3 ("Golden Anniversary"), the Huxtables celebrate the 50th wedding anniversary of Cliff's parents by doing a lip sync performance of Ray Charles. As with the Huxtables dancing in the opening credits beginning in Season 2, the Huxtables clearly have flava. Notwithstanding their professional jobs, middle-class existence, and the overall banality of their daily lives, they are constructed as hip and cool.

Almost every season, *The Cosby Show* reworked its opening credits, putting on display a different type of Afro-Caribbean-Latin-black cultural performance. While Season 3 brought about a Latin dancing flair, Season 4 brought to life the jazz era; Season 6 put Caribbean and African dancing on display. Finally, with Season 7, the family dances in front of the Apollo Theater, a Mecca of African American performance for most of the 20th century. The blackness of the Huxtables and *The Cosby Show* isn't subtle, although it is often limited to accepted cultural performances, spice and flavor that add not only excitement but also authenticity to the show. In "Elvin Pays for Dinner," Vanessa and Rudy arrive at Sandra and Elvin's house to babysit with a perfunctory rap: "I am Vanessa. I am Rudy and we are here to babysit for you." Whether with their dancing, their performances, or their rapping, the Huxtables not only demonstrate that they have flava but do so in a way that demonstrates that this flava stems for their adoption and use of black cultural art forms. Likewise, the show's use of various hairstyles, from Denise's braids to Theo's hi-top fade with lines, reminds audiences of both the significance and insignificance of the Huxtables' blackness.

A common theme that binds together numerous episodes of *The Cosby Show* is its emphasis on values. While morality tales are common to American television in general and specific to the sitcom genre, the emphasis on values and morality takes on special meaning given the broader social debates raging about the black family, the American Dream, and the culture of poverty. According to Justin Lewis and Sut Jhally, "the Huxtables' achievement for the American Dream leads them to a world where race no longer matters. This enables white viewers to combine an impeccable liberal attitude toward race with a deep-rooted suspicion of black people."[38] Similarly, Leslie B. Innis and Joe R. Feagin conclude that its vision of blacks securing the American Dream within *The Cosby Show* leads to a different meaning within the black and white communities: "*The Cosby Show* functions for Whites in a way much different from the way it functions for Blacks. It panders to the limits of White acceptance of Black Americans in the late 20th century."[39] Innis and Feagin, as well as Lewis and Jhally, identify its celebration of the American Dream and its availability to all Americans as the basis of its popularity within white America.

While Bill "Cosby believed that he could send vital messages along with the positive images of a Black family—Children are the same all over"[40]— questions remained as to whether white audiences came to this conclusion or not. Despite claims of progress and *The Cosby Show* as both instrument and evidence of racial harmony, Lewis and Jhally found that "whites articulated the view that the Cosbys were not like most Black Americans. This contradiction is rationalized by the Whites in the study about the failure and laziness of other blacks."[41] Specifically, they argued that "The Huxtables proved that black people can succeed; yet in so doing they also prove the inferiority of black people in general (who have, in comparison with whites, failed)."[42]

Discussing the dominance of racial realists since the end of the civil rights movement, Michael Brown et al. conclude that contemporary dominant racial discourse results in very simplistic conclusions concerning racial inequality and the veritable gaps in achievement and success that emphasize cultural and communal failures. "As they see it, the problem is the lethargic, incorrigible, and often pathological behavior of people who fail to take responsibility for their own lives."[43] More importantly, "persistent and deep black poverty is attributable to the moral and cultural failure of African Americans, not to discrimination."[44] Along similar lines, Robin D. G. Kelley, in *Yo Mama's Disfunktional,* describes the discourse that has dominated the American racial landscape during the last three decades in the following way: "The clamor for 'color-blind' social policy not only delegitimizes race-based explanations for inequality but it camouflages the racist underpinnings of much contemporary political discourse. Welfare mothers, criminals, and the underclass are the most recent code words for black people," writes Kelley. "Each of these terms reflects a growing 'common sense' that black behavior—whether we call it nihilism, a culture of poverty, or plain irresponsibility—is the source of urban poverty and violence and a drain on our national resources."[45] In other words, the celebration of the Huxtables' proper family values as the most clear explanation for their economic success legitimized the discourse that pointed to the availability of the American Dream to African Americans all while demonstrating its illusiveness for those without the requisite values. "Extolling the rewards of Black, middle-class success, the series promoted individualistic explanations for the persistence of Black inequality and seduced Black and White Americans into believing that those who fail to achieve the American Dream have only themselves to blame."[46] Henry Louis Gates in the *New York Times* argued that: "While I applaud Cosby's success at depicting (at long last) the everyday concerns of black people (love, sex, ambition, generational conflicts, work and leisure) far beyond reflex responses to white racism . . . And while Cosby is remarkably successful at introducing most Americans to traditional black cultural values, customs and norms, it has not succeeded at introducing America to a truly different world."[47] It "allows whites to excuse institutional discrimination and to be become desensitized to racial inequality (Gates, 1992). They do this by asserting that if Black people fail they only have themselves to blame because any White person can point out the successful, affluence Black family on *The Cosby Show* and confirm their beliefs that affirmative action is no longer needed because Blacks now enjoy the same opportunities as Whites."[48] Jhally and Lewis argued in the *Los Angeles Times* that the "show saddles us with a new repressed form of racism" in its conclusion that every American, including people of color, can secure the American Dream as "effortlessly as the Huxtables."[49] Describing them as a "model minority" within the dominant white imagination, Herman Gray argues that the values embodied by the Huxtables were comforting and contributed to the popularity of the show.

> The African Americans were just like whites: loyal to the ethos of capitalism and bourgeois individualism and that loyalty rewarded them with the same middle-class privileges as whites. . . . Blackness was not a category requiring

structural adjustments for the disadvantages of historic and group disenfranchisement and social inequality.[50]

The Huxtables have succeeded by living the American Dream. Their path to
the land of American exceptionalism is based in their values—their emphasis, frugality, and overall interest in their children's lives.

Throughout various seasons, the show focuses a lot of attention to the
educational aspirations and struggles. Specifically, we witness Clair and
Cliff instilling in their children a commitment to their education. For example, in "Vanessa's Bad Grade," Cliff, donning his doctor's coat to remind
us of his professional class status despite his presence at the home (his office is located in the basement of the home), surveys the home, only to find
Rudy and her three dolls watching television. Without hesitation, he tells
her to take the dolls upstairs to read to them. In numerous episodes, the
Huxtables emphasize the importance of education over and over again. In
this same episode, Vanessa finds herself struggling at school, a fact we see
is a result of her lack of focus and effort toward her schoolwork. Instead of
studying, she is talking on the phone, worrying about petty teenager stuff
(in one scene she gets in a fight with Denise about clothes), and otherwise
hanging out with her boyfriend. In the end, Cliff lectures both Vanessa and
Robert about the importance of education and how they needed to focus on
their studies rather than each other. As to convey the educational message,
the episode concludes as follows: As Rudy watches Martin Luther King's
delivery of the "I Have a Dream Speech" during the March on Washington,
the entire family gathers around the television to experience the history
lesson together. While clearly an effort to integrate this historical artifact
into the show to emphasize the cultural linkages between the Huxtables
and other African Americans, it is equally important in the context of the
show's emphasis on education. Vanessa, and all black youth, not only have
opportunities otherwise not available to previous generations but have a
responsibility to fulfill the promise or better the dream provided to them
by the King generation. Such responsibility mandates dedication and maximum effort in school.

Similarly, in "The March," Theo writes a paper, which receives a poor
grade (a "C"), only to be given an opportunity to rewrite the paper for a
higher grade. Not distraught about the grade but rather that prospect of his
weekend being spent with his paper rather than his girlfriend and friends,
Theo contemplates letting the grade stand. Cliff, however, encourages him
to get his work done early so that he could spend his weekend partaking
in traditional teenage rituals: football and parties. Prior to working on the

paper, which chronicles the history of the March on Washington, Theo shares the paper with his parents and grandparents. After laying out the basic facts of the March, his paper proceeds to list all the celebrities who attended. Not surprisingly, neither his parents nor his grandparents are impressed with his effort. They criticize him for his weak effort and lack of attention of detail. His grandmother asks why he didn't talk to his family about the event, since they all attended, only to be told that he used the "Pocket Guide to U.S. History," which contained one page of information, as the basis of his paper. They suggest that facts are one thing, but what is important is to understand how people felt, what they experienced, their memories, and the overall community that developed through the March. His grandparents—true sources of historic knowledge—shared with him the mood during the March and their belief that the March on Washington was important because it gave them an opportunity to be heard. Whereas Theo previously only understood the basic facts about the March on Washington, his family educates him about the humanity of the participants, the sense of community that developed from their participation, and the overall importance of the civil rights movement and March on Washington on his family. As with other episodes, the integration of African American history comes within the private sphere, emphasis being on how it impacted the family. It is about their shared memories and how it transformed them personally rather than an opportunity to reflect on America's racial history and the continued struggle for racial justice. The emphasis on progress and personal transformation is made clear as Theo writes his revised paper which reflects on how the March on Washington, a "day of joy, hope, and pride," changed his family.

In "Theo and Cockroach," the boys prepare for their exam in Shakespeare, despite having not read the play. The fact that they are not prepared does not compel them to study, instead they chose to play in the snow and engage in some tackle hoops. Clearly, their attention is not on their exam. Eventually they turn to Macbeth, initially studying with the help of a recorded performance of the play. Failing to understand the basics of the play from the recording, they realize they are in trouble. This is followed by a failed attempt to go see the play at the New York Shakespeare Company and their turning to Denise for help. She directs them to purchase Cleland Notes, which provides a basic summary of the play, the characters, and the major themes. Confident, the boys announce that with the help of Cleland Notes, they will ace the test and get a "B." Their plan goes awry once Cliff and Clair realize that the boys read the Cleland Notes and not the play itself. Sarcastically stating that their kids would never rely on notes, they ask them what might be lost and not understood by just reading the notes. Cliff tells the boys, "Glad I didn't graduate from the Cleland School of Medicine." Worried that he may not be prepared for the exam, Theo pulls an all-nighter and reads Macbeth. When asked how the exam went, Theo tells Clair that he thinks he did OK thanks to Cleland Notes. Predicting that he got a "C," he confesses to his mom that he thinks that is pretty good "considering I didn't read." Clair then asks him if he plans to ever read Macbeth. "That test is over," notes Theo to which Clair tells him that he has to go upstairs and read the play. He is instructed to sit in his room until he finishes the play, only coming downstairs when he is ready to take an essay test administered by her.

Education is important in the Huxtable house. This may be most evident with Theo, who, in later seasons, is diagnosed with a learning disability. Despite the difficulty he experienced in school, which fuels his disinterest and resistance to learning, Clair and Cliff push him (if not force him) to continue to invest in his education. In the show's pilot episode, the show's emphasis on education is made readily apparent, especially as it relates to the responsibility of a parent to discipline and demand educational excellence. After receiving Theo's report card, where he receives 4 "Ds," Clair demands that Cliff have a talk with Theo.

Cliff: Son, your mother asked me to come up here and kill you.
Theo: Hey, I know.
Cliff: You know what?
Theo: What you are going to say. And it's under control. So, no problem!
Cliff: How do you expect to get into college with grades like this?
Theo: No problem. See, I am not going to college.
Cliff: Damn right!
Theo: I am going to get through high school and then get a job like regular people.
Cliff: Regular people?
Theo: Yeah, you know, work at a gas station, drive a bus, something like that.
Cliff: So what you are saying is your mother and I shouldn't care if you get "Ds" because you don't need good grades to be regular people.
Theo: Right.

Unable to get his point across to Theo, at this point, Cliff turns to monopoly to convey the importance of education, providing him with a lesson about expenses and income for regular people. He conveys that he may not make enough money being a regular person to live the life he imagines for himself.

Theo:	Dad, I have thought about what you said and see your point. But I have a point too. You are a doctor, and Mom is a lawyer. And you are both successful and everything. And that's great. But maybe I was born to be a regular person and have a regular life. If you weren't a doctor, I wouldn't love you any less because you are my dad. So, instead of acting disappointed because I am not like you, maybe you can just accept me for who I am and love me anyway because I am your son.
Cliff:	Theo, that is the dumbest thing I have ever heard in my life. No wonder you get Ds in everything. Now you are afraid to try. . . . Now I am telling you, you are going to try as hard as you can, and you are going to do it because I said so. I am your father. I brought you into this world; I'll take you out. . . . I just want you to do the best you can.
Theo:	I'll try. I really will!
Cliff:	I love you.
Theo:	I know.[51]

Because of their parenting, their tough love approach, and because of the values, Theo ultimately conquers his disability, completing his undergraduate and graduate degrees, only to become a teacher himself. Notwithstanding the obstacles Theo faces, his work and the values instilled in him by his parents, as well as their own expectations, facilitate his personal success.

The emphasis on values isn't exclusively evident with the show's focus on education but is also evident in representing the Huxtables as frugal. Despite their class status and the sizable income that would invariably result from their jobs as a lawyer and a doctor, the Huxtables live like regular people. In fact, they eschew excess, instilling in their children the values of thrift, modesty, and financial security. For example, in "Shirt Story," Theo hopes to impress a girl with a top-of-the-line designer shirt (Gordon Gartrel) that costs $95 only to be initially rebuffed by Clair and Cliff. "I don't even have a $95 shirt and I have a job," Cliff notes incredulously. With the $30 given to him by his father, Theo entrusts Denise to make him a replica shirt, which in the end is a huge disaster. With uneven sleeves, a crocked collar, and numerous other problems (tucked in the shirt goes down past his knees), the shirt looks like it was made for a circus clown. Distraught and embarrassed, Theo asks Cliff for help in getting a real Gordon Gartrel before his date. Although Cliff recounts a story of his wearing a hideous tie given to him by Theo to a medical convention and people ultimately not noticing the tie because they were too distracted by his knowledge and expertise, Theo is not convinced to wear the shirt on the date. He pleads for help, promising that he has learned his lesson. Believing that Theo indeed had learned a lesson, Cliff relents, telling Theo that he has not yet returned the shirt and that he can wear it (at this point, Cliff has spent $135—$95 on the designer shirt and $40 for Denise's replica). However, after accidentally walking into the living room wearing Denise's shirt, Theo tells his date: "Kristine, this is my shirt." Hearing that she loves it (It's hot), Theo decides not to change, wearing the cheap and funky replica. Most importantly, he decides to thank Denise for making him the shirt and his father for teaching. Among other things, the key lesson is that the shirt is unnecessary and wasteful. Cliff and Clair teach this lesson to Theo, reminding him that his popularity and his success in life, whether with dating or in the workforce, would be tied to his values rather than material possessions.

Similarly, in the show's initial pilot, Theo borrows $5 from his father. When he is unable to pay him back, Cliff demands that Theo clean the kitchen to pay off his debts rather than going outside to play basketball. Instilling in their children responsibility and a Protestant work ethic, Cliff and Clair teach their children to value hardwork and the value of the dollar. This is evident not just in the life lessons delivered to their children but also through their own values and role modeling. In "Say Hello to a Good Buy," the Huxtable family car breaks down. Despite their class status and their professional and financial success, the Huxtables own a clunky but practical station wagon, which after 15 years finally breaks down. The Huxtables' class status is marked by their professions, their sophisticated musical taste, the art displayed on their walls, their emphasis on education, their family structure, and their values and NOT by the material possessions they own. In this episode, Theo implores Cliff to buy a sports car. Yet, Cliff wants a sensible car such as another station wagon. More interestingly, he wants to purchase a car that is a good buy, even going to the extent of concealing the fact that he is a doctor. He hopes that he will get a better deal from the car salesman if he views him as working class.

Likewise, in "Vanessa's Rich," we see a Huxtable child with the wrong focus. Trying to make the pep squad so she can become friends with the popular girls, a feat that would ultimately change her life, Vanessa is very concerned with her image. After telling a few of the girls that Ellis Wilson's painting costs over $11,000, Vanessa gets into a fight with two of the girls after they call her a "rich girl." Recounting what happened to her parents, Vanessa expresses anger for her parents since they made her rich. "Your mother and father are rich," notes Cliff. "You have nothing." Clair, however, sees otherwise, telling Vanessa: "We are not rich. Rich is when the money is working for you not when you work for the money. And we work hard. We're proud of what we have." Emphasizing their values and work ethic, Clair concludes with the ultimate reminder of their middle-class status and their adoption of desirable American values: "You are rich not because of things you have but because you have a family that loves you."

Beyond lessons about the importance of education, managing money, and otherwise being a good person (having proper values), *The Cosby Show* focuses on, if not celebrates, Cliff and Clair as exceptional parents. Their success not only reflects their effort as parents but their good-heartedness, their emphasis on education, and their fulfillment of the American Dream.

In fact, their fulfillment of the American Dream is both the result and evidence of their commitment to being good parents. This lesson is driven home over and over again by the show. In "Theo Dirty Laundry," on learning that Theo and Justine (his girlfriend) were living together, Cliff and Clair (as well as Justine's parents) expressed their disapproval of the situation, leading Theo and Justine to decide to live separately so that they could focus on their education. Cliff and Clair are thus involved in their children's lives not only protecting them from their own bad decisions but from outside threats as well. In "That's My Joint," *The Cosby Show* illustrates that America's drug problem impacts every community regardless of class, race, or geography. While cleaning up the kitchen, Clair accidentally finds a marijuana joint within Theo's book. While never totally suspecting that it was Theo's joint (Clair: "Bet it is those kids he hangs out with"), Clair and Cliff still confront Theo only to be told that indeed the joint is not his. Although believing him (remember he is a good boy), Clair expresses concern about the values and moral character and his classmates and their potential impact on Theo. Clair even suggests taking him out of school, a proposal Cliff ultimately questions since in the South Pole penguins "would have joint in their mouth, walking around break dancing." Although his parents believe in his innocence, Theo is determined to prove to them (and America by extension) that not all African American youth are involved with drugs. In the end, Theo confronts one of his classmates, Braxton, who confesses to putting the joint in his book because he didn't bring a book to class and feared being caught by the teacher. On confirming Braxton's guilt, Theo tells him that he needs to go to his house to confess to the Huxtable parents, and, if need be, Theo was willing to fight him even though he was significantly bigger than Theo. Later that afternoon, Braxton confesses his drug problem to Cliff. On learning that indeed the joint was Braxton's and not Theo's, Cliff tells him: "I am not your father, but I do think you have a problem, son."

Encouraging him to talk to his parents, a counselor, somebody at school, or even Cliff himself, Dr. Huxtable demonstrates concern for the welfare of Theo's classmate, a stranger, a responsibility that the show conveys is necessary within the black community. Cliff is willing to be a parent to another boy, someone who is clearly lacking the requisite values to succeed. He is not alone. In the end, Theo, despite all that happens, encourages Braxton to join him the following day for a game of freeze football, as long as he comes without being high. Theo, like his father, is assisting Braxton to become a man, through discipline and proper values.

Patriarchy and the Huxtables

While seemingly avoiding race and the ubiquitous social/cultural debates of the times, *The Cosby Show* consistently addressed issues of sexism and gender roles. While often using gender and questions surrounding male-female interaction to facilitate the needed conflict and required resolution commonplace to the situation comedy genre, *The Cosby Show* successfully used the platform provided by its popularity to address issues of sexism. For example, in "Golden Anniversary," Sandra and Elvin fight about anything and everything, although Elvin's sexism and Sandra's feminist ideals are the basis of their quarreling. Elvin thinks that as a man he should pay for everything; he believes that he should pump gas for the car since this is man's work and because Sandra's hand should not smell like gas since she is responsible for making sandwiches. Demanding that he fulfill his role as a man and that Sandra act like a woman, Elvin is forced to come to grips with his patriarchal ethos. "I am confused about my duties as a man." Against the backdrop of her grandparent's 50th wedding anniversary, the show works to problematize the hegemonic notion of traditional gender roles, pointing out the absurdity of patriarchy. In this particular episode, Elvin articulates his belief that to be a gentleman means to help and assist women in tasks that they are physically incapable of performing, such as opening a jar. Yet, despite his physical strength, he is unable to open the jar, only to be forced to watch Sandra easily open the jar.

The Cosby Show comfortably engages questions of gender and gender relations within the home. While Clair is a top-notch attorney, we rarely see her at work, yet we do see her to be primarily responsible for cooking, cleaning, and parenting; compare this to Cliff, whose medical practice is based out of the home and thus is ubiquitously shown to be engaged in his work. While the show questions the sexist logic that guides the idea of gendered roles in the home, it replaces this logic through its narrative. "We seem to be hearing a statement that as women pursue their talents out-side the home, males, without loss of masculinity, can share in the family chores," writes June M. Frazer and Timothy C. Frazer. "But the action and conclusion of this program tells the audience that this is finally only a joke and that traditional family role expectations are still firmly in place."[52] For example, the opening scene of "The Auction" makes its message about sex-ist thinking clear. Sandra tells Denise that her efforts with Elvin are begin-ning to pay off since he has "finally realized that his attitudes about women could stand some improvement."[53] Denise also challenges Elvin for his sex-ist remark that cooking was women's work. She reminds Elvin, "My dad cooks. A lot of men cook." As to illustrate that Elvin's sexism is being chal-lenged by each and every woman in the family, Clair questions Elvin's logic when he judgingly asks her if she is allowed to buy an expensive painting without Cliff's permission. "It's okay if I buy this painting not because he says so, but because it is so, OKAY?"

Yet, in the end, despite the rhetorical devices, the narrative leaves a con-tradictory message: notwithstanding the fallacy of normalized gender roles, men are not incapable of cooking. Elvin sets out to prove to Clair that he can and is willing to cook—"to experience women's work." Unfortunately, the cake is not edible. Cliff can't even cut a piece as it is hard as a rock. Questioning his motives, Cliff demands that Elvin tell him the truth as to why he is in the kitchen. Able to level with Cliff man-to-man, Elvin con-fesses that he is spending time in the kitchen, an unnatural habitat for men, because it seems to be an easy way to impress Clair, to prove that he was a liberated man rather than a sexist. He tells Dr. Huxtable that he has baked Mrs. Huxtable a cake "in order to become more understanding and sensi-tive as a man."[54] Cliff teaches Elvin that the problem isn't necessarily his acceptance of patriarchy but rather his tendency to vocalize his beliefs in the company of women. He needed to learn to indulge, placate, and even pretend if necessary. He confesses to Elvin that despite Denise thinking that he cooks, and despite the fact that his family/the audience thinks he is dif-ferent, he was a real man who couldn't cook. The key was deception, "to fake cook and fool" those gullible women.[55] Cliff pretends to make spa-ghetti sauce by pouring store-bought sauce into a pot, adding some parsley and garlic, and leaves so that he can stand in front of the stove in an effort to convince his family that he is cooking some special sauce. Elvin, learning from Cliff, follows suit, cooking as only a man can: from a car. Of course, his attempt to impress Clair is ultimately unsuccessful because as a woman she knows whether food is homemade or store bought. Announcing that she knows that their secret sauce is nothing but Mrs. Farber's from a jar,

Clair tells them both "As an attorney, I would suggest you get Mrs. Farber's permission before marketing this." In the end, "the overall message . . . serves to reassure the audience that real cooking is still a female role, that a male would not serious undertake it, that the kitchen has not basically changed."[56] *The Cosby Show*'s acceptance and promotion of patriarchy bespeak its effort to highlight the normalcy of the Huxtables. Its replication of a traditional family stricture—its patriarchal orientation—points to how they are just like other average Americans. Despite hegemonic stereotypes, African Americans, as evidenced by the Huxtables, are just like white America as men and women can and do follow traditional roles.

In "Monster Man Huxtable," Clair goes on a business trip and is away from the home for a week, leaving the Huxtable family without its needed matriarch. In her absence, Cliff does not take on the role as caretaker and homemaker. Instead, Sandra returns home from graduate school so that she can set the table and give Rudy a bubble bath. Meanwhile, Elvin, who in this particular episode gets along with Sandra because she is finally acting like a woman by doing house chores and being deferential to Elvin, doesn't help Sandra with these new responsibilities but instead coaches Theo on his wrestling skills. As a man, his job is to teach Theo how to wrestle rather than give Rudy a bath or set the table.

Similarly, in "Is That My Boy," *The Cosby Show* chronicles Theo's failed attempt to follow in Cliff's footsteps onto the football field. Cliff expresses a tremendous amount of pride in the prospect of Theo playing football, which is clearly gendered as evidence by the show's title: that's my boy. His maleness/masculinity is legitimized by his participation in football, and this inspires pride from Dr. Huxtable. Moreover, the show positions sports as not only a vehicle for turning boys into men but a cultural institution that is able to properly teach boys, particularly African American youth the necessary values and discipline to secure the American Dream. Cliff argues that sport prepared him for medical school. He wasn't scared and was able to handle the stress because of football. The message is clear: African Americans, particularly the next generation, those who never experienced the levels of surveillance and control of slavery and Jim Crow "must be brought under control."[57] So, whereas Cliff and Theo learn discipline and how to be men on the sports field, women on the other hand learn their values inside the home. While Theo is on the football field learning from Cliff and presumably his coaches, Clair is busy at home counseling Rudy about the trials and tribulations of growing [she is distraught over being the youngest in the family]. What is important here is not simply the manner in which the show links sports to discipline and values or gendered this process but the ways in which it links the family to the American Dream, leaving a clear message about one of the key variables determining success or failure within the African American community: the presence of two parents.

Conclusion

At its core, *The Cosby Show* tells a story of the black middle-class, bringing into question the dilemmas of integration, assimilation, and progress. It offers insight as to the place and identity of the black middle class. It provides various levels of commentary, often in tones of demonization and ridicule, about black underclass. In bringing an African American middle-class family into the living rooms of white America, *The Cosby Show* offered comforting stories about America, the black middle-class, and the black underclass. The popularity of the show emanated as much from its orientation to middle-class stories as its tendency to erase racism, to reduce blackness to aesthetics, and to celebrate America's racial present. It was a show that recast the experiences of the black middle-class to those of happy people with happy problems because of their values, choices, and cultural attributes, in turn both denying the burdens of the black middle class and the structural realities that define their brothers and sisters' experience.

The wave of new black middle-class television shows not only sought to reinsert a middle-class black experience into the American cultural imagination, while capitalizing on consumer demand for more positive and bougie narratives, but attempted to commodify difference through safe bodies and spaces. The onslaught of television shows that constructed a color blind narrative centering on positive imagery of the black middle-class, all the while commodifying a black cultural aesthetic through insertion of jazz music, a blues tradition, or other markers of difference, sought to challenge the erasure of positive black cultural signs from the marketplace. Its celebration of black cultural aesthetics and individual mobility fulfilled dominant claims about equality in post–civil rights America. Not only had African Americans made it, but as evident with the Huxtables' economic success did not preclude cultural retention. In constructing a black middle-class world within a safe and sanitized understanding of blackness, one that marks cultural difference in commodifiable terms, *The Cosby Show* reifies dominant projects of color blindness, equality, and culture as the only difference, which in the end celebrates America at the expense of those left behind, at the expense of those who don't embody blackness in terms and ways acceptable to America.

Notes

1. Patricia Hill Collins, *Black Sexual Politics: African Americans, Gender and the New Racism* (New York: Routledge, 2004), p. 34.

2. Herman Gray, *Watching Race: Television and the Struggle for "Blackness"* (Minneapolis: University of Minnesota Press, 1995), p. 17.

3. Rhonda Williams, "Living at the Crossroads: Exploration in Race, Nationality, Sexuality, and Gender," in *The House That Race Built* (New York: Vintage Books, 1998), p. 141.

4. Gray, *Watching Race*, p. 17.

5. Ibid., p. 23.

6. Monica A. Payne, "The 'Ideal' Black Family?: A Caribbean View of the Cosby Show," *Journal of Black Studies* 25 (December 1994): p. 231.

7. Ibid.

8. Ibid.

9. Quoted in June M. Frazer and Timothy C. Frazer, "'Father Knows Best' and 'The Cosby Show': Nostalgia and the Sitcom Tradition," *The Journal of Popular Culture* 27, no. 3 (Winter 1993): p. 163.

10. Timothy Havens, "'The Biggest Show in the World': Race and the Global Popularity of The Cosby Show," *Media, Culture & Society* 22 (2000): p. 371.

11. Linda Tucker, "Was the Revolution Televised? Professional Criticism about 'The Cosby Show'; and the Essentialization of Black Cultural Expression," *Journal of Broadcasting & Electronic Media* 41, no. 1 (1997).

12. http://www.aliciapatterson.org/APF0903/Lane/Lane.html.

13. Joe Feagin and Melvin Sikes, *Living with Racism: The Black Middle Class Experience* (Boston: Beacon Press, 1995).

14. Justin Lewis and Sut Jhally, *Enlightened Racism* (Boulder: Westview Press, 1992), p. 3.

15. Henry Louis Gates, "TV's Black World Turns—But Stays Unreal," *The New York Times*, November 12, 1989. Retrieved June 9, 2012, from http://www.nytimes.com/1989/11/12/arts/tv-s-black-world-turns-but-stays-unreal.html?pagewanted = all&src = pm.

16. Tucker, "Was the Revolution Televised?," p. 13.

17. Quoted in Tucker, "Was the Revolution Televised?," p. 13.

18. Quoted in Payne, "The 'Ideal' Black Family?," p. 232.

19. Quoted in Tucker, "Was the Revolution Televised?," p. 10.

20. Kobena Mercer, *Welcome to the Jungle: New Positions in Black Cultural Studies* (New York: Routledge, 1994).

21. Cornel West, "The New Politics of Difference," in *The Cornel West Reader,* ed. by C. West (New York: Basic Civitas Books, 2000), pp. 119–39.

22. S. Craig Watkins, *Representing: Hip Hop Culture and the Production of Black Cinema* (Chicago: University of Chicago Press, 1998), p. 118.

23. Stuart Hall, *Representation: Cultural Representations and Signifying Practices* (Thousand Oaks: Sage Publications, 1997), p. 274.

24. Gray, *Watching Race,* p. 19.

25. Ibid.

26. Quoted in Tucker, "Was the Revolution Televised?," p. 12.

27. Quoted in Tucker, "Was the Revolution Televised?," p. 9.

28. Quoted in Tucker, "Was the Revolution Televised?," p. 9.

29. Leslie B. Innis and Joe R. Feagin, "The Cosby Show: The View from the Black Middle Class," *Journal of Black Studies* 25, no. 6 (July 1995): p. 692.

30. Quoted in Tucker, "Was the Revolution Televised?," pp. 10–11.

31. Tucker, "Was the Revolution Televised?," p. 11.

32. Sarah Banet-Weiser, *Kids Rule! Nickelodeon and Consumer Citizenship (Console-ing Passions)* (Durham, NC: Duke University Press, 1997), p. 144.

33. Gray, *Watching Race,* p. 39.

34. John Downing, "'The Cosby Show' and American Radical Discourse," in *Discourse and Discrimination,* ed. by Geneva Smitherman and Teun Van Dijk (Detroit: Wayne State Press, 1988), p. 68.

35. Downing, "'The Cosby Show' and American Radical Discourse," p. 61.

36. Quoted in Innis and Feagin, "The Cosby Show," p. 696.

37. Banet-Weiser, *Kids Rule!,* p. 145.

38. Lewis and Jhally, *Enlightened Racism,* p. 119.

39. Innis and Feagin, "The Cosby Show," p. 707.

40. Ibid., p. 695.

41. Ibid., p. 693.

42. Lewis and Jhally, *Enlightened Racism,* p. 95.

43. Michael K. Brown et al., *Whitewashing Race: The Myth of a Colorblind Society* (Berkeley: University of California Press, 2003), p. 6.

44. Brown et al., *"Whitewashing Race,"* p. 6.

45. Robin D. G. Kelley, *Yo' Mama's Disfunktional!: Fighting the Culture Wars in Urban America* (Boston: Beacon Press, 1997), p. 91.

46. Tucker, "Was the Revolution Televised?," pp. 2–3.

47. Quoted in Tucker, "Was the Revolution Televised?," p. 10.

48. Innis and Feagin, "The Cosby Show," p. 693.

49. Quoted in Tucker, "Was the Revolution Televised?," p. 10.

50. Gray, *Watching Race,* p. 19.

51. "The Cosby Show: Theo's Economic Lesson," season 1, episode 1 (1984).

52. Frazer and Frazer, "'Father Knows Best' and 'The Cosby Show,'" pp. 167–68.

53. Quoted in Frazer and Frazer, "'Father Knows Best' and 'The Cosby Show,'" p. 169.

54. Quoted in Frazer and Frazer, "'Father Knows Best' and 'The Cosby Show,'" pp. 169–70.

55. Frazer and Frazer, "'Father Knows Best' and 'The Cosby Show,'" p. 167.

56. Ibid.,

57. Ibid.

Chapter 7

A Different Sort of Blackness: *A Different World* in a Post-Cosby Landscape

David J. Leonard

The initial seconds of the opening montage for *A Different World* establish its ideological and representational trajectory: plastered on an abstract yet colorful wall, the words "A Different World" make clear that the world that will come to life is different from any other worlds available on television, particularly those dominated by African Americans. Followed by a series of shots of conventional symbols of college life—a water fight, a guy carrying a girl's book, students walking to class, endless bicycles, a student receiving a letter presumably from home, and lots of fun—the opening sequence established a shared point of reference for many reviewers. Yet, these commonly deployed images are set to a background that re-establishes that the show's interest rests in the experiences of African American students. While a show detailing the trials and tribulations of college life, *A Different World* deals with the dilemmas and conflicts that arise when black students arrive on a college campus, a historically black college, a place often "different from the world where they come from." Establishing the trajectory for *A Different World*, the opening montage makes clear that it will introduce viewers to the experiences of black students, although the narrative form and content structure offered will be universally understood and told in conventional ways. Beyond the structure and narrative, the history behind *A Different World* represents its conventional origin story. A spin-off of *The Cosby Show*, *A Different World*, served as a platform for Lisa Bonet, as a place for Americans to continue to watch and enjoy her character, Denise Huxtable.

More importantly, it represents an effort to advance the Cosby message: education as a vehicle to securing the American Dream; not surprisingly, given the narrative focus of *The Cosby Show,* hard work, family, and community are of principal importance to the show's narrative focus. As with *The Cosby Show,* there is a concerted effort to highlight the shared values and experiences of whites and blacks, although *A Different World* goes to great length to highlight the difference and ruptures as well. With this in mind, this chapter focuses on the ways that *A Different World* built on the foundation established by *The Cosby Show* providing viewers with a glimpse at a different world: one less concerned with whiteness and more interested in black identity formation, one less dedicated to appealing to universal stories and more focused on chronicling the trials and tribulations, joys, and successes of black college students. Refusing the demand of a sanitized and deracialized world, *A Different World* offers a counternarrative and alternative representations to much of the television landscape.

A Diverse Group

Similar to *The Cosby Show, A Different World* emphasizes the blackness of its characters by focusing on the cultural practices and historic experiences of African Americans. Of course, the decision to locate the show on a historically black college campus allowed for a consistent representation of the cultural milieu of black America, which emphasized the depth and diversity of the black community. Chronicling the experiences of African American students (as well as one white student) attending a historically black college, along with their teachers, *A Different World* documents not only the joys and struggles faced by black college students but the sense of community, identity, and cultural practices that emanate from historically black colleges. "The show imaginably used the dominant conventions of the genre to saturate its televisual world with blackness," wrote Herman Gray. In other words, the show effectively depicted blackness not through stereotypes or clichéd racial tropes but through "African American cultural and social practices, perspectives, codes, assumptions and styles."[1] For example, in "Success, Lies and Videotape" (February 8, 1990), Freddie, along with several of her peers, explores one of the buildings on a campus, a metaphoric archive of African American communal life. During their communal excavation, the students discover evidence that Hillman College was a stop on the Underground Railroad as African Americans fled slavery. Although the primary plot of this episode rests with Freddie's uncertainty concerning her career prospects, the show positions her ambivalence about her future within a broader historical context of African American history. Gray identifies this episode as yet another powerful example of the way in which this show is able "to tell a story from the perspective of black female characters."[2] Celebrating the show's final scene and its ultimate message, Gray argues:

> The episode culminates in a moving scene with Clair Huxtable and Freddie in the basement, reflecting on the horrors of slavery, the heroism of black people, especially women who were part of the Underground Railroad and the tradition of black colleges. In the end, it is Freddie who holds on for a career that she will find interesting and that will make in her words "a contribution" to black people.[3]

While utilizing a ubiquitously deployed television plot of a young person struggling to find an acceptable and well-paying job that is also fulfilling, *A Different World* invokes this story in a way that is specific and unique to the history of African Americans, illustrating how the dilemmas and questions of today's generation have a historic importance.

A Different World emphasizes the cultural diversity of the black community. *A Different World,* unlike *The Cosby Show* or few other shows exploring the black experience, represents the black community in diverse terms. While each of the characters was equally "attractive, pleasant, articulate, and smart,"[4] each in their own right represented a different segment of the black community. This allowed the show not only to present "narratives . . . through the characters, who symbolically took different sides of various issues" but to push the televisual discourse beyond racially homogenizing practices so common on television. "By deliberately casting the principal ensemble to emphasize differences in backgrounds, classes, histories, complexions, and politics, the show's producers broke with television's conventional construction of African Americans as monolithic."[5] Beyond highlighting the complexity and diversity of the black community, the representations offered by each character sought to bring into focus various identities, tensions, conflicts, and trends within the African American community.

Ostensibly the centerpiece of the show (although the show originally began as a platform for Lisa Bonet's Denise Huxtable character), Whitley Gilbert (Jasmine Guy), broke the color barrier for Southern Belles, a caricature that had been exclusively white within the popular white imagination. At one level, Whitley was America's introduction to an invisible community: "the old southern aristocracy, those light-skinned, straight-haired African Americans who took their pride in their accomplishments, their lineage, and their climb up the social ladder."[6] At another level, Whitley, whose arrogance, vanity, and selfishness were unmatched on the show, offered a certain amount of complexity and contradiction, who most importantly eschewed white definitions of beauty and social importance. "The world of Southern belles was assumed to be the terrain of white actresses only." Given the entrenched nature of racism and white supremacist ideology, "how could any woman be vain, selfish, good-looking, sexy, demanding, and so confident that she felt superior to just about everyone around her unless that women were white," asks Donald Bogle. "As the self-absorbed Whitley, who waltzed through campus life as if she were at a charity ball, Jasmine Guy overturned those assumptions about what an African American would, could or could not be."[7] While offering a sometimes clichéd and stereotypical representation of southern aristocracy, Whitley provides a new vision of blackness. Her importance, however, transcends this discursive intervention, challenging viewers to think about class, color, and countless other issues important within the African American community.

Similarly, Kim (Chanele Brown), a premed student whose dedication to school is unmatched, captured the seriousness of the show and the educational aspirations of black youth. Yet, the show doesn't simply use Kim as the "model minority" student but also developed her character as a vehicle to "acknowledge the injuries, ambivalence, and strength of African American responses to life in an oppressive racialized social order."[8] Dark-skinned Kim consistently shares "the deep injuries and pain visited on" her "because of her dark complexion."[9] The show's exploration of this history, and color coding and self-esteem, is especially powerful given its constant juxtaposition of Kim to the light-skinned Whitley, working hard not to privilege either experience over the other as more injurious but rather to highlight the pain and daily struggles experienced by each woman. With both characters, the various episodes tell stories that highlight "the complex ways in which black women's bodies are often at the intersection of race, class, and gender, both within blackness and in the relations between blacks and whites."[10]

One of the keys to success and innovation of *A Different World* stems from its ability to decenter whiteness, to narrate stories, of both triumph and conflict that is not about or even having to do with whiteness, all while acknowledging the ways in which the ongoing history of white racism impacts the lives of African Americans. For example, with Colonel Bradford Taylor (Glynn Turman) and his son, Terrence Taylor (Cory Taylor), *A Different World* highlights the heterogeneity of black masculinity. Colonel Taylor, a professor and a member of the U.S. military, embodies a traditional ideal of black manhood: strong, authoritarian, and advocating traditional values. His traditional (conservative) viewpoint puts him in direct conflict with his son Terrence who, despite his Dad's vision of what is proper/

what is manly, chooses to major in dance (in "Bedroom at the Top"). While resulting in conflict and tension, especially evident across generations, *A Different World* uses its characters to illustrate the many inscriptions of masculine identity and the potential conflict that develops from these competing identities.

Just as with Colonel Taylor and Terrence, Dwayne Wayne (Kadeem Hardison) and Ron Johnson (Daryl Bell), two students attending Hillman personify the diversity of black masculinity. Writing about black masculinity and feminism, Mark Anthony Neal highlights the importance in bringing depth and highlighting diversity to representations of black manhood.

> A New Black Man is not so much about conceiving of a more "positive" version of black masculinity . . . but rather a concept that acknowledges the many complex aspects, often contradictory, that make up progressive and meaningful black masculinity. . . . New Black Man is for those willing to embrace the fuzzy edges of a black masculinity that in reality is still under construction. . . . New Black Man can be best captured in a line from HBO film Boycott where Bayard Rustin (Erik Todd Dellums) says "I am a man of my times, but the times don't know it yet."[11]

A Different World fulfills this challenge. Dwayne, whose character evolves during the show from a nerdy B-boy (a presumed contradiction in itself), whose sole focus rests with picking up women, to a complex and dynamic man who balances his responsibilities as a man, community member, teacher, role model, friend, and leader with grace represents the fluidity and diversity of black masculinity. While his evolution certainly reflects the shifting focus of the show and its hiring of new writers after the second season, it also embodies the strength of the show in that it presents the characters as maturing and evolving throughout and between each season. Likewise, Ron, who embodies both an entrepreneurial work ethic that reflects his desire to garner respect through financial success and a sexist persona, is equally complex and contradictory. In totality, these characters are neither surface nor stereotypical. "All of the show's primary characters functioned within the ensemble to embody a variety of range of positions and experiences within blackness" writes Gray. "By imbuing the characters with such qualities and then having them play against type, the show's writers and producers seemed quite self-conscious in their intention to make their characters neither blacks in whiteface nor one-dimensional."[12] Others, like Vernon (Lou Meyers), the manager of the Pitt (the campus hangout/restaurant), and Walter Oakes (Sinbad) not only represent the range of experiences, identities, and opinions that encompass the black community but also bring into focus other sources of difference and conflict in the form of class, generation, and political viewpoints.

Similarly, Denise (Lisa Bonet) and Freddie (Cree Summers), both free-spirited optimists, and Jaleesa (Dawnn Lewis), the 26-year-old returning student, who consistently functions as the conscience and source of experience-derived wisdom for the younger students, reveal the range of identities available in this different world. More than its diversity of characters, the success and importance of A Different World stem from the depth and broader stories told through each character. "The show was most uncompromising in its construction and representation of blackness with respect to questions of difference and diversity within African American life and culture," writes Herman Gray. "On issues of gender, social class, color, location, popular culture, history, and even style, the program presented complex and diverse representation of African Americans."[13]

A Different World consistently invokes key historic events and people that define the African American experience as well as important black athletes, musicians, and leaders "that might require insider knowledge" yet were important vehicles for the shows exploration of and commentary "on contemporary issues, controversies and events within African American social and cultural discourses."[14] For example, in "Mammy Dearest" (December 5, 1991), Whitley organizes an event that exhibits the history of black women. Mammy artifacts, which depicted black women as fat, asexual maids, are included within the displays, leading to protest from Kim. During this same episode, viewers are introduced to the practice of "the dozens," an African American cultural practice where individuals banter back and forth, usually taking the form of disparaging or insulting remarks (talking trash), particularly about one's mother. The inclusion of other examples of black cultural practices, whether the inclusion of a diversity of hair styles, ranging from Afros and braids to extensions and hi-top fades, cultural performances (step show, spoken word), or clothing styles (Kente cloth, Cross Colors clothing) not only sought to illustrate the cultural styles and practices commonplace within this African American community but to convey their diversity and that of the black community.

Location, Location, Location

It is important to note how the setting for A Different World is crucial in conveying not just a diverse of representations but in conveying a level of complexity. Set at a historically black college, A Different World pushes the representational discourse beyond the private realm into the public sphere, a space historically denied to the black community within American television culture. The process of containing black-themed shows to the private sphere not only limits the types of themes and issues a show might address (e.g., those relevant to the family) but also confines the narrative and setting to an individual family unit rather than the broader community. In other words, by locating *A Different World* outside the home and within a historically black college, it was able to move in a direction otherwise not available to the bulk of black shows "that were set in domestic spaces—the house, and within the family, where they reinforced values of individualism, responsibility, and morality."[15] A college setting provides the needed tools to break down these barriers. According to Herman Gray, the show's writers and producers "saw an opportunity to use the university setting to break free of the aesthetic confinements and thematic isolation of the domestic family."[16] By using the classroom setting or including a scene showing students debating within their dorm rooms or the student union, *A Different World* alters the narrative and thematic landscape available to black television shows. Moreover, the specific history and culture of historically black colleges furthers this process in that the show's premise and location directly undermine any pretense of a fully universal experience. "Setting the show at historically black Hillman College enabled the writers to confront far more directly and consistently issues of difference without succumbing to the seductions of the zero-sum game of universal appeal at the expense of the specificity of African American diversity."[17]

A college setting thus not only opened up the thematic and aesthetic realm, all while breaking the ubiquitously accepted private/public binary, but also allowed for greater engagement with the depth and diversity of the black community. *A Different World* is able to better chronicle the diversity of experience and social location of the cast of characters because of its location and its strategic utilization of a myriad of public and private spheres. Unlike so many of the shows we have discussed, which overwhelmingly define blackness through a privatized domestic sphere, *A Different World* successfully represents the meaning, complexity, and contradictions of blackness by illustrating its shifting and dynamic presence with "the spheres of neighborhood, work, community, and volunteer associations."[18] For example, the show utilizes the classroom setting not simply as a vehicle for its seamless integration of historical information and contemporary social debates but to highlight the conflicts, contradictions, and diversity, whether materializing out of the heterogeneity of class, color, politics, or history, that embody the black community. For example, in "If I Should Die Before I Wake" (April 11, 1991), Josie (Tisha Campbell), as part of an assignment for a speech class, confesses that she is HIV positive leading her peers to question their assumptions and stereotypes about HIV and AIDS. The strength of this episode rested not only on its ability to critically engage the ways in which race, class, and sexuality impact our collective understanding about disease but to use the classroom space to organically introduce the taboo and rarely discussed issue of HIV and AIDS within the black community. The emphasis on the diversity and complexity of black community also guided the types of themes tackled by *A Different World*.

A Different World found its success with its ability to organically incorporate themes and issues that were both serious in nature and unique to a post–civil rights black experience. Avoiding the traps of black family–oriented shows, which invariably "focused on universal issues such as social relations with the family, child rearing, teenage maturation and conflicts within the domestic sphere,"[19] *A Different World* tackles a spectrum of issues and contested themes specific to the African American experience. In centering a spectrum of black voices, "it constructed a perspective from which to examine a broad range of issues of immediate relevance to African Americans."[20] Specifically, this resulted in a show that tackled a spectrum of issues ranging from sexual harassment, date rape, sexual violence, domestic violence to AIDS, South African apartheid, race relations, the 1992 Los Angeles uprising, and affirmative action. For example, in several episodes, the show explores the issue of sexual violence and harassment experienced by black college students, an issue that impacts all communities. Yet, rather than provide a universal narrative, it staged this narrative in terms specific to the black community, reflecting on both the history of sexual violence experienced by black women and the ubiquity of communal silence concerning this issue given the context of antiblack racism. It is important to understand the show's courage here given the history of American racism.

Paula Giddings concludes that oftentimes the issues of sexual harassment, child molestation, domestic violence, and rape embody "national rituals via black protagonists."[21] The historic practice of locating social problems within black male bodies has been central to white supremacist discourse, especially as it relates sexuality.

Media culture is only too happy to use black figures to represent transgressive behavior and project society's sins onto black figures. Indeed, despite the endemic problem of sexual harassment, Clarence Thomas is the representative figure for this transgression; despite the troubling problem of child molestation cutting across every race and class, Michael Jackson is the media figure who represented this inequity; despite an epidemic of violence against women, O.J. Simpson is the ultimate wife abuser, and date rape is a deplorable, frequent and well-documented phenomena, it was Mike Tyson who became "poster boy" for this offense.[22]

Refusing to avoid the issue of sexual harassment because of the potential affirmation of antiblack stereotypes and long-standing racial tropes, *A Different World* challenges the politics of respectability and demands to remain positive in the face of white racism. Adding depth and layer to these important conversations, it simultaneously exposes the impact of racism and sexism on Whitley. The show goes a long way to elucidate the ways in which race and gender intersect literally on the bodies of black women, as evident in its narrative focus on Whitley's experience in the workplace. Patricia Hill Collins (2004) argues:

> In the post civil rights era, gender has emerged as a prominent feature of what some call a "new" racism. Ironically, many African Americans deny the existence of sexism, or see it as a secondary concern that is best addressed when the more pressing problem of racism has been solved. But if racism and sexism are deeply intertwined, racism can never be solved without seeing and challenging sexism. African American men and women both are affected by racism, but in gender-specific ways.[23]

According to Jacqueline Bobo (1995), "Representations of black women in mainstream media constitute a venerable tradition of distorted and limited imagery."[24] Rather than constituting a black woman as "specific victims of the lust of [white] brutes," dominant representations have posited black women as sexually deviant, aggressive, domineering, or wretched victims— as mammies or jezebels.[25] As bell hooks reminds us: "The sexuality of black female signifiers beginning in the 18th century became an icon for deviant sexuality."[26] This history has obviously had a tremendous effect in the way U.S. society today sees black sexuality, including the way(s) it reacts to displays of black sexuality. Yet, the paradox of the sexual politics of race in America is that, "behind closed doors," writes Cornel West, "the dirty, disgusting, and funky sex associated with black people is often perceived to be more intriguing and interesting, while in public spaces talk about black sexuality is virtually taboo."[27]

These episodes don't simply depict sexual violence as an issue pitting men against women or as a manifestation of sexism but highlight the tensions that arise because of the realities of sexual violence and domestic abuse within the black community and the history of racism, stereotypes, and systematic efforts that have pathologized black men. In shining a spotlight on this issue, one that penetrates and permeates each and every community, yet doing it in a way that privileges the experiences and particularities facing the members of the black community, *A Different World* eschews the tendency of situational comedies to ignore social issues and tell universal stories. "By staging such complex questions through the experiences of African American students at Hillman, these episodes spoke to the broad concerns and relevance of these questions for all people and the particular ways they affect black middle-class men and women in the university."[28] For example, in "Bedroom at the Top" (January 30, 1992), Whitley faces unwanted sexual advances from a black male colleague. Yet, the narrative does not simply chronicle her feelings and struggles with sexism in the form of sexual harassment at the workplace but instead complicates her experience by integrating both race and class into the story. While angry and frustrated by the situation, Whitley feels a certain level of ambivalence and doubt about the situation and the lack of intervention from her white boss, wondering how race and class are playing a role here. She not only thinks about the consequences of airing dirty laundry to her white boss but questions how her social location (as an upper-class southern black woman) will impact people's perspective and reaction to the situation. In the end, *A Different World* uses this particular narrative to highlight both the issue of sexual harassment within the black community and how race, gender, class, and sexuality impact communal debates about this issue. In fact, the issues surrounding misogyny and sexism within the black community were central to several episodes of *A Different World,* eschewing the often-uttered demands for positive representations that would neither reaffirm stereotypes nor confirm racist ideologies. In "Ms. Understanding" (February 28, 1991), after the publication of a book addressing the alleged failures of black men, debates rage on campus, resulting in significant amounts of conflict and tension. Moreover, in "Somebody Say Ho!" (October 15, 1992), Terrell tapes "digit ho" on Charmaine's back after she excelled in math class, leading to tension and discussion about campus sexual harassment rules and the treatment of black women within the black community and society at large.

Likewise, in "A World Alike Campus" (February 15, 1990), an episode focusing on South African apartheid and widespread efforts on college campuses to force divestment from the Pretoria regime, the show's narrative pushes the debate beyond the conventional and obvious moralizing and political posturing. In addition to staging this particular issue at a historically black college, which given the existence of black administrators and African Americans serving on the board of trustees limits the establishment of binaries (e.g., moral and righteous black students battling against white administrators more concerned with the bottom line), the show's narrative teases out the complexity of corporate and personal responsibility through the story of Kim. A premed student, Kim, is passionate about protesting against South African apartheid and pressuring American corporations and universities into withdrawing financial support and investment until the walls of racism come down there. However, her principled opposition is put to the test when she realized her scholarship money is tied to corporate investment in South Africa. The episode concludes with numerous students, including Kim, Ron, Dwayne, Freddie, Whitley, and a South African student, speaking on the issue, elucidating the range of opinions within the black community. In personalizing this story and chronicling the issue of apartheid in South Africa, *A Different World* highlights the conflicts and contradictions of identity all while pointing to how Kim reconciles her political (and racial) identity with her career aspirations and society's class expectations for her. Rather than simply chronicle the evils of apartheid and the obvious moral outrage among Hillman students, the show's narrative points to the ways in which we are all connected to the broader global issues and the ways in which things are never as simply as they appear.

The intersection between race and class and particularly black identity and class mobility is in fact a common theme for *A Different World*. In another episode, "Here's to Old Friends" (January 11, 1990), the show addresses the widely discussed issue of selling out and how making it impacts racial identity. In this episode, Dwayne reunites with a high school buddy who is attending Pennsylvania University. Questioning the value of a Hillman (a black) education, the friend encourages Dwayne to transfer to Penn because of the academic rigor and networking possibilities available at his (white) university. After reviewing Hillman graduation rates, admission rates into graduate school, and other vital information, Dwayne realizes that his friend does not have all the facts but instead is operating from stereotypes about black college and blackness. The episode concludes with Dwayne not only deciding against transferring, but him using the opportunity to educate his friend about the value of a historically black college education not only in terms of career preparedness, quality of academic offerings, and future opportunities but in terms of "connection to community and blackness."[29] Like so many episodes, this one uses the debates about the value of a historically black college education all while engaging the discursive tension between "making it" (the American Dream) and "holding onto one's roots":

This episode represents a metaphorical intervention into the broader debates about class divisions and tensions within the African American, tensions that are increasingly out in the open as more and more black college graduates enter the middle class by way of elite educations at Ivy League universities. By constructing Dwayne and his friend as students of similar ability and promise, the writers carefully avoided a simplistic privileging of one education over the other. At the same time, the construction of these characters effectively symbolizes issues of class and difference among black students. Without indicating or blaming elite white college or judging black students who attend them, the episodes raise questions about the isolation, mobility aspirations, and relationship of all black university students to notions of community and culture. In a small way, this mirrors the central issues in the policy, social, and cultural debates about class divisions within black communities and the responsibilities of the black middle class to the black poor and the restoration of moral and civic order.[30]

Similarly, in an episode never aired ("Homey Don't ya Know me"), Lena (Jada Pinket) is forced to confront her past when her friends from Baltimore come to visit her at Hillman. Questioned as to whether she is being true to herself, her community, and her friends, Lena must confront her past, which she realizes is holding her back from her dreams. She tells one of her friends, "I am here trying to get an education so I can get something better than a city job." Ultimately she decides she must turn her back on her past, embodied by her ex-boyfriend Piccolo (Tupac Shakur), because it is not a positive influence. That is, if selling out is necessary to secure the American Dream, Lena is willing to make those sacrifices because the future looks brighter than the past.

Another example of the show's sometimes-explicit focus on black-oriented themes, even as it emphasized the diversity of the black community, rests with its engagement with the issue of colorism within the black community. Staged through specific narratives and character development, *A Different World* highlights the impact of color coding on African American youth, revealing the ways in which class status, history, the legacies of slavery, and ideals of beauty inject color consciousness within the black community. In an effort to reflect on colorism, *A Different World* "effectively challenges totalizing and narrow notions of blackness by inserting difference into contemporary and historic discourses."[31] Gray concludes "the show reaches this point by way of a brief by insightful (again, for television) tour through the history of color coding, privilege, and subordination within blackness on the basis of color skin."[32]

Unlike *The Cosby Show* that strategically told universal narratives that would appeal to white viewers and therefore downplay the cultural, social, and communal significance of their blackness, *A Different World* consistently invokes blackness as a central force to its narrative formation. For example, "Pride and Prejudice" (January 25, 1990) examines the issue of everyday racism through racial profiling. During a trip to a wealthy shopping mall, Whitley and Freddie, both light-skinned women, experience racial animus in the form of prejudice and discriminatory treatment. Distraught that despite her socioeconomic status, and her attitude/values, Whitley devises a plan to highlight the saleswoman's mistake by buying several expensive purses. It is her hope that proving her wealth and value will change the mind-set of this woman, a strategy that her friends question. Using this episode to highlight an issue experienced by many African Americans, shopping while black (the story was actually based on an incident experience by two members of the production staff), *A Different World* emphasizes the ways in which blackness mattered culturally, socially, politically, economically, and materially.

"War and Peace Hillman" (January 10, 1991) explores the meaning of the Gulf War with its story of a Hillman alumnus, Zelmer Collier (Blair Underwood), and his deployment to Iraq. While highlighting the heterogeneity of responses among the African American students and faculty on campus, this episode is not so much a commentary on the war, or an effort to patriotic platitudes, but rather as a moment to think about the disproportionate presence of African Americans within the U.S. military and the American prison system, especially in comparison to the scant presence on college campuses. Amid a time where politicians and social critics emphasized the sameness of Americans, *A Different World* identified the war as yet another example of our racial and class divisions.

Similarly, in "Cats in the Cradle" (January 16, 1992), *A Different World* explores the issue of racial violence with a narrative that has someone scrawl "Nigger" on Ron's car during a Hillman football game against a local white college. While waiting for Dwayne, who is watching the Hillman football game versus Virginia AM, Ron strikes up a conversation with three AM white students. Following a bit of trash talking, a wager between Ron and the others occurs. On their way out, the three students stop to pay Ron. After receiving his winnings, he decides to talk a little more trash.

| Ron: | Maybe you guys should get a few more brothers on the team. |
| J.C. (Jake Carpenter): | Are you saying whites can't play as well as blacks? |

Ron:	Saying, look at the score, 44–3; you do the math.
Eddie (Dean Cain):	What are you saying: blacks are superior?
Ron:	Only in football, basketball, and track. And I'll leave that physical endowment thing alone because I know how sensitive you all are.

Noting how much these people like graffiti, J.C. and Eddie respond to Ron's racial banter with violence, attempting to spray paint "Nigger" on his car, only getting to "N.I" before a fight ensues, resulting in their arrest. As to emphasize the show's message about stereotypes, racial mistrust, and misunderstanding, Ron and Eddie recount two distinct versions of the events during questioning at the campus security building, neither of which are entirely truthful. Ultimately, however, the truth does come out as Eddie confesses to vandalizing Ron's car because "of how they are."

Campus security officer (Ernie Sabella):	How are they?
Eddie:	You know.
Campus security officer:	No I don't know, tell me.
Eddie:	They have no respect. They don't care about this country at all. All they do is sit on their butt and complain.
J.C.:	And what do they have to complain about. It's because of them and their quotas that I am not in the Ivy League, where I belong.
Ron:	You all had quotas for centuries. You called them legacies, restrictive country clubs, the law.
Eddie:	My grandfather came to this county with nothing. He couldn't even speak the language, but he worked hard, and he made a place for himself and his family. Why can't you people do the same?
Dwayne:	My grandfather built this country. He fought wars for it. And most places he went he couldn't sit down to get a cup of coffee. I can't even catch a cab in New York. It doesn't matter how many degrees I get, all you people see is color. Your grandfather was an immigrant, you're an American. My grandfather was born here, duke, and your people still look at me as just another Nigger.

The tension ends as Rick (Richard Murphy), the third friend, challenges his own friends, apologizing to Ron and Dwayne. Yet, they are not moved, demanding recourse from the officer. When he doesn't act on behalf of Ron and Dwayne, questioning their culpability, Dwayne bemoans that it isn't surprising that they aren't treated fairly by the white officer.

Campus security officer: That's right. I am a white man. . . . I could be card-carrying member of the Klan. . . . Or I could have marched with Dr. King. You don't know. Maybe you should look at me as an individual and not just a color.

While certainly ironic that a security officer provides a lesson about prejudice, given the history of harassment and profiling experienced by African Americans at the hands of the police, this represents yet another moment in the episode where racism is constructed as a plague on every community, highlighting a missed opportunity to talk about systemic racism. In fact, the episode begins with Ron selling his football ticket to a ticket scalper who is Native American (Adam G.). After selling the ticket, he asks the man if he "lives on a reservation," to which he responds, "Do you live in the projects?" This of course established the show's message about stereotypes and prejudice, making clear that racism is a problem that we all must address. In this regard, the episode addresses "the exaggerated and false perceptions blacks and whites have of each other, perceptions that can lead to suspicion, hostility, and conflict."[33]

Notwithstanding this universalist message, one that is constructed as individual prejudice that can be overcome through knowledge, conversation, and social contact, this episode also offers a more complex understanding of American racism. Whereas Ron and Dwayne may be guilty of making assumptions and stereotyping, the white students promulgate dominant ideologies about race. Moreover, the show makes clear that they are the beneficiaries of a history of systemic racism, illustrating that the sins of racism are not equal. This is made further clear as the boys return to their cars, only to learn that some else had completed the graffiti, adding "G.G.E.R." to the "N.I." already on Rob's car. Racial violence remains a part of America's present, just as it defines America's racial past. Such moments were unique on American television during the eighties. These representational openings, however, were limited, in that the range of images and issues seen on television remain small. That is, in spite of the success and popularity of *The Cosby Show* and even *A Different World,* African Americans still found limited opportunities to unsettle dominant racial discourse within television culture.

Moving Forward

The success of *The Cosby Show* and *A Different world*, not simply in terms of ratings but as cultural icons identifiable and worthy of praise from blacks and whites alike, ushered in a paradigm shift within American television and culture at large. At one level, *The Cosby Show* demonstrated the potential profitability in diversifying its television lineup. According to Gray, "the recognition and engagement with blackness were not for a moment driven by sudden cultural interest in black matters or some noble aesthetic goals on the part of executives. . . ." Instead this shift was "in large part driven, as most are in network television, by economics."[34] As *The Cosby Show* amassed nationwide popularity, being the number one–rated American television show from 1985 through 1989, with 63 million people watching weekly at its pinnacle, network executives saw possibilities in the development of certain kinds of black-themed shows. In this regard, "*The Cosby Show* altered the face of the Black sitcom,"[35] as evidenced by *A Different World*. Yet, the importance and influence of *The Cosby Show* transcend its being the spoon that "stirred the melting pot"[36] on network television but is evident in the types of televisual blackness made available by the representational paradigm offered by *The Cosby Show*. In other words, *The Cosby Show* proved that certain inscriptions of blackness would be accepted, praised, and celebrated by white America; it established which types of blackness would be profitable. "Cosby's squeaky clean image as America's Black buddy or sidekick provided one social script for the types of African American men who would find acceptance in a desegregating America."[37] In this regard, what was embodied on/by *The Cosby Show* illustrated what would work within the marketplace, given the cultural, political, and racial landscape of the 1980s. "Within capitalist marketplace relations, just as representations of Uncle Ben were used to sell rice, images of Bill Cosby helped to sell products,"[38] including the ideas of the American Dream, color blindness, and post–civil rights racial equality. According to Henry Louis Gates, "the unprecedented success in depicting the lives of affluence blacks has exercised a profound influence on television . . . 'Cosby's' success has led to the flow of TV sitcoms that feature the black middle class, each of which has taken its lead from the 'Cosby Show.'"[39] More than focusing on the black middle class, *The Cosby Show* *established* a template for a commodifiable and profitable blackness which was: (1) "safe, nonthreatening;" "eminently likable;"[40] (2) "friendly and deferential . . . loyal both to dominant social values such as law and order as well as to individuals who seemingly upheld them;"[41] and (3) ultimately neither impacted nor impaired by race or racism. As a result "the new black sitcom, more often than note, ignored the pernicious manner in which race and racism penetrate the lives of the black middle-class"[42] all while demonizing the black underclass as lacking the prerequisite values and character to succeed the American Dream. *The Cosby Show* proved that as long as black people could be "happy people with happy problems,"[43] there would be a slot available on prime-time television, ushering in a wave of new shows. Yet, as we look at *A Different World*—its staging on a black college campus, its focus on identity, and diversity—we see not only increased visibility but alternative narratives. Its willingness to tackle controversial and difficult issues illustrates the televisual ruptures that *A Different World* expanded during its run. We see a different world on television. Unfortunately, the possibilities were short-lived for the sake of shows that sold a black aesthetic in the form of cultural differences of black individuals as opposed to those shows that highlighted the diverse experiences, voices, and realities that defined the black community during the 1980s and 1990s.

The hypervisibility of a commodified blackness by the mid- to late 1980s was evident with and facilitated by the popularity of *The Oprah Winfrey Show, The Arsenio Hall Show, Amen* (1986–1991), *227* (1985–1990), *Def Comedy Jam, Yo! MTV Raps,* and several African American actors who gained notoriety while appearing on integrated ensemble shows (Blair Underwood as Jonathan Rollins on *LA Law;* Philip Michael Thomas as Sonny Crockett on *Miami Vice;* Avery Brooks as Hawk on *Spencer for Hire;* and Michael Jordan as himself in countless commercials). Each, along with *The Cosby Show,* "helped to focus, organize and translate blackness into commodifiable representations and desires that could be packaged and marketed across the landscape of American popular culture."[44] The increased visibility and cultural cache afforded to blackness within network television shows set the stage for the emergence of a new type of black show during the 1990s.

Notes

1. Herman Gray, *Watching Race: Television and the Struggle for 'Blackness'* (Minneapolis: University of Minnesota Press, 1995), p. 103.

2. Gray, *Watching Race,* p. 110.

3. Ibid.

4. Ibid., p. 94.

5. Ibid., p. 98.

6. Donald Bogle, *Prime Time Blues: African Americans on Network Television* (New York: Farrar Straus Giroux, 2001), p. 319.

7. Ibid.

8. Gray, *Watching Race,* p. 98.

9. Ibid., p. 109.

10. Ibid., p. 98.

11. Mark Anthony Neal, *New Black Man* (New York: Routledge, 2006), p. 29.

12. Gray, *Watching Race*, p. 99.

13. Ibid., p. 111.

14. Ibid., p. 101.

15. Ibid., p. 60.

16. Ibid., p. 102.

17. Ibid., p. 102.

18. Ibid., p. 103.

19. Ibid.

20. Ibid., p. 103.

21. Paul Giddings, as quoted in D. L. Andrews, ed., *Michael Jordan Inc. Corporate Sport, Media Culture, and Late Modern America* (Albany: State University of New York Press), p. 154.

22. Douglas Kellner, *The Sports Spectacle, Michael Jordan and Nike: Unholy Alliance*, Retrieved May 18, 2012, from http://pages.gseis.ucla.edu/faculty/kellner/papers/MJNIKE.htm.

23. Patricia Hill Collins, *Black Sexual Politics: African Americans, Gender and the New Racism* (New York: Routledge, 2004), p. 5.

24. Jacqueline Bobo, *Black Women As Cultural Readers* (New York: Columbia University Press, 1995), p. 33.

25. Lorraine Hansberry, "This Complex of Womanhood," *Ebony*, August 1960.

26. bell hooks, *Outlaw Culture: Resisting Representation* (New York: Routledge, 1994), p. 62.

27. Cornel West, *Race Matters* (New York: Vintage Press, 1994), p. 83.

28. Gray, *Watching Race*, p. 104.

29. Ibid., p. 107.

30. Ibid., pp. 107–8.

31. Ibid., p. 109.

32. Ibid., p. 109.

33. Ibid., p. 108.

34. Ibid., p. 68.

35. Donald Bogle, *Toms, Coons, Mulattoes, Mammies, and Bucks: An Interpretive History of Blacks in American Films* (New York: Continuum Publishers, 1994), p. 300.

36. Eric Siegel as quoted in Gray, *Watching Race*, p. 68.

37. Collins, *Black Sexual Politics*, p. 167.

38. Ibid.

39. Quoted in S. Craig Watkins, *Representing: Hip Hop Culture and the Production of Black Cinema* (Chicago: University of Chicago Press, 1998), p. 148.

40. Collins, *Black Sexual Politics*, p. 167.

41. Ibid.

42. Watkins, *Representing*, p. 149.

43. Ibid.

44. Gray, *Watching Race*, p. 168.

Chapter 8

Just Another Family Comedy: *Family Matters* and *The Fresh Prince of Bel-Air*

Shiron V. Patterson

Now this is a story all about how,
My life got flipped turned upside down.

—DJ Jazzy Jeff and the Fresh Prince,
The Fresh Prince of Bel-Air.

Did I do that?
Whoa, Mama
Look what you did!

—Steve Urkel, *Family Matters*

It is evident that television has come a long way. Anyone born between televisions' inauguration and 1990 have probably seen changes that makes an individual question the past, present, and future of television, myself included. Along with the growth of television came the shows and characters presented as well. All white casts began to include characters of color. Television shows expanded their audiences and began to offer experiences that included varied settings and characters. Throughout this expansion, two of my favorite shows were created, *Family Matters* and *The Fresh Prince of Bel-Air.* As an African American female born in the 1980s, I remember the strict rules my mother had concerning television time, especially in regard to which shows I was permitted to watch. I still believe it is the reason, these two shows reflect happy memories. These shows did provide not only immense laughter but also insight into topics that remain in everyday conversations, such as: education, violence, family, and racism. Both shows placed priority on making their audiences smile; they both took time to create episodes that some may say showed audiences' life through African American eyes.

Increased access for blacks on television brought varied emotions but has allowed for welcomed visibility and profit making. For example, Will Smith came into the entertainment industry as a member of the hip-hop duo, DJ Jazzy Jeff and The Fresh Prince. The group began in 1986 and found success in their profanity-free music before Will graduated school. Fans of the duo most likely remember their most well-known and my favorite songs "Parents Just Don't Understand" and "Summertime." But after the duo's third album in 1989, Smith felt his success as a duo slipping and took the opportunity to become an actor.[1] His duo partner later joined Will as a regular character, Jazz, on *The Fresh Prince of Bel-Air*.

Since 1992, Will Smith has appeared in more than 20 movies that have cumulatively grossed more than six billion dollars. Indeed, his *Men in Back* movie trilogy has earned him on average $20,000,000 per movie plus a percentage of the total gross.[2] In addition, the talent exhibited by black actors has propelled them—Denzel Washington, Morgan Freeman, Cuba Gooding Jr., Tyler Perry, Halle Berry, Whoopi Goldberg, Angela Bassett, and Gabrielle Union—into successful careers.[3] It is important to realize that many black performers on television started their careers performing in front of smaller predominately black audiences.

The media has the power to display the images as they choose. Unfortunately, with few individuals of color in power, the available representation, images/characters/stories are often distortions.[4] Herman Gray "confirms that executives, writers, and directors tend not to place African Americans in dramatic story plots and programs."[5] Black actors are most likely to appear in situational comedies.

In 1989, ABC premiered a news special "Black in White America," produced by Ray Nunn. The special summarized the struggle that African Americans often confront when trying to become successful. Although present-day media may show more blacks that have achieved success, it is important to note that many persons of color continue to encounter many difficulties, on their journey. Correspondent George Straight concluded the special with a powerful message:

> There's a notion that white folks have done enough for black folks, but black people still remain the poorest and most segregated people in this land. So, America, don't kid yourself. When it comes to black people, there's still a lot

of unfinished business-business that won't be completed until America be-gins to live up to the promise that it made to itself more than two-hundred years ago: that every individual is free to succeed or fail based on who they are and not what they are.[6]

In a moment where children spend more time watching television than playing outside, television can play a powerful role in determining dreams and impacting sense of self.

> They watch an ideal family on TV in a perfect home with no money prob-lems they may wonder why they don't have the same. If they see things on TV that they don't have a comparison in real life, the TV image will be reality to them. When images and ideals presented at a young age take hold, and are reinforced over years of viewing, these images become reality. They may feel inadequate in comparison to the lives some seem to lead, and superior and hateful to those portrayed in a negative way, even though portrayal is not true.[7]

African American consumption of self or the Hollywood-produced African American subject is at times a very difficult process.

In this chapter, I will focus on race and humor's role in two situational comedies, *Family Matters* (1989–1998) and *The Fresh Prince of Bel-Air* (1990–1996). Specifically, I will explore the creation of each series, its repre-sentations of racism, blackness, family, and social class, all while analyzing some of the most intriguing episodes.

Family Matters (1989–1998)

The 1970s and 1980s saw an increased level of diversity on television. "Shows such as *Roots* (1977) and *The Cosby Show* (1984–1992) created an atmosphere in which African American programs could emerge."[8] Lead-ing this transformation was Bill Cosby's *The Cosby Show.* This show would emerge as model for the black family, although television would offer some level of diversity. It set the stage for greater diversity within these represen-tations; by the late 1980s, television would witness a new era of represen-tation. Whereas the parents on *The Cosby Show* were a doctor and lawyer, *Family Matters* tells the story of blue-collar workers. The show would be the most successful show since *The Cosby Show,* although *Family Matters* chronicles the trials and tribulations of a working-class African American family, refusing the tendency of other shows to avoid race. Still each, in its own ways, confirms a myriad of racial stereotypes commonplace to

American society. In this sense, stereotypes continued to limit the portrayal of black families, all while providing viewers with an up close and personal view.

A spin-off of the sitcom *Perfect Strangers, Family Matters,* would be part of the *TGIF* lineup on Friday evenings. In fact, it would be fixture for years to come. Behind *The Jeffersons,* a popular 1970s comedy, with 215 episodes, *Family Matters* is the longest running black sitcom in television history.[9] It tells the story of the fictionalized Winslow family, whose members had dissimilar personalities. *Family Matters* focuses on universal themes such as bullying and substance abuse all while providing viewers with a distinct understanding of the nature of racial conflict with society. Its ability to address difficult issues results from its deployment of humor.

The show's title reveals the centrality of family within *Family Matters.* Up through the 1970s, the family sitcom, with its focus on values and cultural transmission, reserved the familial unit for whites. It tells the story of Carl Winslow, a Chicago police officer; Harriet Winslow, an elevator operator; and their three children—Eddie, Laura, and Judy; Estelle (Carl's mother); Rachel (Harriet's sister); and Rachel's son, all reside with the Winslows. Along with the Winslow family, *Family Matters* revolves around Steve Urkel, whose nerdy and buffoonish antics provide the basis of comedic relief in the face of serious discussions. Yet, in locating the show in Chicago and telling it through a working-class black family, *Family Matters* chronicles a multigenerational black family residing together.

The show also attempts to represent family as the backbone of communities of color, countering dominant negative stereotypes about black families as both lazy and irresponsible. *Family Matters* sought to challenge dominant stereotypes. Depicting Laura and Steve as extremely intelligent individuals, the show continually works to counter stereotypes about black intelligence. For example, Steve is imaged to have genius-like abilities when it comes to science. "More than a century after the Emancipation Proclamation and decades since the U.S. Supreme Court ruled in favor of integrated public schooling, a poll of White Americans in 1990 confirmed that the majority population overwhelmingly understood Blacks in unflattering terms."[10] Over this period, 77 percent of whites held negative stereotypes about African Americans. Imaging blacks as lazy, welfare dependent, and prone for criminal activity, antiblack racism infected all aspects of society.[11] In fact "existing research reveals that African Americans are portrayed as criminals more than police officers."[12] Yet, *Family Matters* sought to challenge these assumptions, even casting Carl as police officer.

Did I Do That?

Steve Urkel received both celebration and criticism for his role in *Family Matters*. Praised for securing the American Dream, for his intellect, and for his hardwork and perseverance, Urkel was seen as evidence of exceptionalism and endless possibilities within the United States. He was praised because his role presented his scientific talents as the son of a neurosurgeon. However, Steve Urkel was too often depicted as buffoonish, lazy, and silly, continuing a long tradition within American television.[13] As Beretta Smith-Shomade argues, "Steve Urkel signified the contemporary consequence of educated Black boys—effeminacy, underdeveloped and nerdishness."[14] However, in "Dr. Urkel and Mr. Cool," viewers are introduced to Urkel's self-made "Cool Juice" and his alter ego, Stefan Urquelle, a suave and popular ladies' man. This new role downplayed his intellect and placed priority on his physical appearance. In future seasons, "Cool Juice" was transformed into "Boss Sauce." He used variations of the liquid formula to convert himself into martial artist Bruce Lee in "Substitute Son," "Random Acts of Science," and "Karate Kids." Yet, Steve Urkel "remained a studious bookworm with genius-like abilities in math and science; traits that made him a rare representation of black youth on prime-time television."[15]

Family Matters sought to capitalize on white youth fetishization of blackness, playing up an aesthetic of coolness grounded in a white construction of black identity. Jeff Ford of the British channel concluded that African American sitcoms are more popular than those focused on whites.[16] Although signifying his nerdy disposition, Steve's alter ego in many ways conveyed the importance of youth culture, fashion sensibilities, and ideas of coolness. The binary between nerdy Steve and cool Steve, and its relationship to clothing, transcended the show. For example, a middle school in Tennessee implemented a rule banning saggy pants. Those who violated the rule would find themselves "Urkeled." For students not in compliance, their pants will be cinched up with zip ties, a picture will be taken, and then placed on the school photo board. When the rule took effect, the school averaged 80 offenders per week. After five weeks, the number had lowered to 18, an 80 percent decrease.[17] *Family Matters* was not simply a show but one that was in dialogue with larger discourses about identity, respectability, stereotypes, and success.

No Humor in Racism

In "Good Cop, Bad Cop," *Family Matters* takes up the issue of racial profiling.[18] On returning home, Eddie shares that his turning violation becomes a situation in which the officer accuses Eddie of "being a black person in a white person's neighborhood." At first, Carl does not believe Eddie and thinks he is hiding evening antics because his fellow officers do not behave in such a manner. However, Carl later finds out that Eddie was correct. The officers behaved inappropriately, and Carl informed the officers that he will report them to senior administration. Even among colleagues and coworkers, racism is possible. Although comedic scenes and stories were mixed throughout the episode, the show attempted to use its characters' actions and words to influence the way the public understands issues of race and racial identities.[19]

It is important to note that the 1990s was a decade full of race-related events. These events included Rodney King's police brutality trial, which concluded with the acquittal of the police officers and the Los Angeles race riots. Shortly after, the OJ Simpson verdict furthered racial anxiety. This time it also included efforts to eliminate affirmative action. Sitcoms provided audiences an opportunity to address racial anxiety without actually confronting racism and inequality. In the episode entitled "Fight the Good Fight," Laura and Steve wanted students to gain an appreciation for black culture and other races and add a new class into the curriculum.[20] Unfortunately, all they end up receiving are threats from racist classmates including the word "nigger" written on Laura's locker. Laura breaks down in tears and wants to give up on her fight to teach others about cultural history. Dr. Alvin Pouissant of Harvard University believes that denouncing the word "nigger" can mirror bigotry and racism and promote its usage. In "a commercial culture that proclaims its dedication to free speech, it is difficult to repress language and physical expression, even if the final product is insulting."[21] However, Laura has a renewed energy to continue the fight after her grandmother tells her about black history and her struggle to obtain her first library card.

Abuse and Violence

Herman Gray states in his book *Cultural Moves: African Americans and the Politics of Representation* that beginning in the 1950s television's goal has been to gain viewership by having them identify with the image of America.[22] However, the challenge is finding familiarity in issues through viewers who are all different. Nevertheless, issues such as substance abuse transcend race, class, or gender divides. In "Tips for a Better Life," Carl tires of Eddie's incessant partying, ultimately giving his son an ultimatum to shape up or find another place to live.[23] Three weeks later, Eddie arrives home drunk, yet this time he insults both his father and best friend, Waldo. Outraged by his belligerent behavior and his drunkenness, Carl kicks Eddie out of the house. Without a place to stay, after Waldo refused to let his friend move into his house, Eddie must confront his misdeeds. Eddie realizes the negative effects of his partying and substance abuse. He reaches out for help from his friends and family.

Family Matters used its platform to foster larger conversations about race, racism, and racial tension. In perhaps the starkest episode of the series, "The Gun," shines a spotlight on "Black-on-Black violence."[24] At school, a gang of females rob Laura of her jacket at gunpoint, telling her that if she reports the crime they will kill her. Frightened, she decides to purchase a gun as self-defense. Steve begs Laura to reconsider. Laura stubbornly disagrees. After the gang brutalizes one of Laura's friends who refuses to give up her new pair of shoes, Carl not only resolves the conflict through arresting the black youth but reminding others, including the audience, that violence is never answer. This episode is indicative of a larger trend on television. Jim Pines describes this trend as television representations that imagine black as a "threat" and black as a "problem" both of which are commonplace to *Family Matters*.[25] Simon Cottle describes these types of narratives in the following way:

> It is in and through these representations, for example, that members of the media audience are variously incited to construct a sense of who "we" are in relation to who "we" are not, whether as "us" and "them," "insider" and "outsider," "coloniser" and "colonised," "citizen" and "foreigner," "normal" and "deviant," "friend" and "foe," "the West" and "the rest."[26]

Family Matters did introduce racial and contemporary issues; yet, it often relied on stereotypes, laughter, and comforting narrative. On the one hand, in challenging the image of the lazy welfare queens, and the professional class embodied by the Huxtables, *Family Matters* offered something else. On the other hand, the show rarely highlighted the trials and tribulations of a working-class family, much less their life outside of the private sphere. *Family Matters* did provide examples of African American youth with high educational levels and collegiate aspirations, which historically have been stereotyped as individuals having minimal academic presence or intelligence when compared to their white counterparts. In this regard, *Family Matters* was particularly effective as it encouraged viewers to reflect on issues of race, stereotypes, prejudices, and representation. It also set the foundation for *The Fresh Prince of Bel-Air*.

Fresh Prince of Bel-Air (1990–1996)

By the 1980s, middle-class white audiences began to trade in their network television package for cable subscriptions. As many working-class African Americans and Latino families could not afford cable, this constituency continued to rely on free channels (ABC, CBS, and NBC). Black audiences watched 44 percent more network television than nonblacks, contributing to the popularity of shows such as *The Fresh Prince of Bel-Air.*[27] *The Fresh Prince of Bel-Air* is often celebrated as the "most interesting TV series of the last decades for its innovative way of depicting its African American characters and their way to face daily problems."[28]

The 1990s saw the increased popularity of hip-hop, which spread to suburban white America. The hip-hop revolution would transform musical taste, as well as clothing, language, and icons. It sought to capitalize on the popularity of hip-hop as well as the visibility and star power by the Fresh Prince (Will Smith). Beyond the allure of hip-hop, the series capitalized on its message: racial anxiety and tension remain a reality within American society but one that can be potentially overcome.[29]

The Fresh Prince of Bel-Air offered a series of autobiographical narrative exploring integration in a post–civil rights era, albeit through slapstick comedy. "American scholars of race and television have been divided over the racial politics of the series."[30] Whereas as Robin Coleman celebrates the show for its representation of the black male and black family,[31] Herman Gray argues that its portrayal of blacks is not far-removed "from middle class White identity that promotes separate but equal racial politics."[32] Kristal Zook finds a middle ground, arguing that the show was a "trailblazer" for black-cast programs during the 1990s, providing African Americans with voice, all while exposing audiences to class and gender differences.[33]

The Bel Air Family

Born and raised as a teenager in Philadelphia, Will's mother sends him to reside in California, with his rich extended family, to avoid an unsafe and troubling environment back home. In this regard, each episode focuses on the tensions and differences between Will's life back in Pennsylvania and his new life in Bel Air. Living in a mansion with his uncle Phillip Banks, a judge, and his aunt Vivian, a college professor, is in many ways a shock to his cultural sensibilities. The professional choices of the characters are not a coincidence, reflecting their representational intervention: "we can move from news images of black criminals to fictional images of black law-yers and judges in a matter of network minutes."[34] Of course, he also finds himself learning to live with three other children, all of whom embody a distinct challenge to Will's worldview: Hillary, a twentysomething female who places emphasis on money and looks above anything else, Carlton, an extremely conservative male who embodies an individualized, educa-tion-first, bootstraps ideology, and Ashley, the youngest and most level headed of the family. Geoffrey is a black British butler who tends to the home wearing his tuxedo-like uniform, rounds out the family, further em-phasizing the class and cultural conflicts within the household.

The continued struggle to navigate his new environment, while adhering to his sense of identity and cultural purpose, is central to the show's narra-tive orientation. Gray describes this aspect of the show as "representation of differences." Will himself is a "contradictory character, one where leaks, fractures, tensions, and contradictions . . . continues to find expression."[35] As such, the success of the show reflects its ability to attract African Ameri-can viewers who identify with Will's ethnicity and cultural distinctiveness, while white audiences may find sympathy in his words and/or story. I defi-nitely remember the show being watched by my very diverse group of peers. Indeed, language was used to show the difference in social standing. Will's smaller vocabulary and limited sentence structure indicated minimal edu-cation when compared to his cousin, Carlton. This can create an impres-sion among viewers that language can define class status.[36] Nonetheless, the show's representation of the upper-class black family addressed contempo-rary racial issues prominent during the times of its television series.

Black or White?

The initial episode of *The Fresh Prince of Bel-Air* focused on Will's relation-ship with his extended family. In fact, the tension often results from his struggle to maintain his sense of self and his identity with his new life. In a conversation with Geoffrey, Will expresses his discomfort with his new zip code:

> Geoffrey: If you follow me, I will show you to your room.
>
> Will: Hey man, it's cool if you just call me Will.
>
> Geoffrey: Master William, tradition dictates that a clean unbreakable line be drawn between a family and their butler. Therefore, it is necessary for the operation of the household that you address me as Geoffrey and I, in turn, address you by your proper title, Master William.

Will:	Who are you, Robo-butler, man?
Geoffrey:	Come with me, Master William.
Will:	Yo, G. let me rap to you for a second. All this Master William stuff, I'm not down with that man.

While a goal of the show was to broaden the range of representations, "Will's way of expressing and behaving becomes disputable because the audience learns to decode Will's depiction that is closer to traditional Black stereotypes."[37] Moreover, Will expresses a widely held belief that posits wealth in opposition to blackness. To convey his sense of blackness, Will hangs a Malcolm X poster to his bedroom wall, then shows up to his uncle's formal dinner wearing colorful clothes. His attire angers his uncle. To challenge viewers' understanding of an authentic black identity, the audience learns that Uncle Phillip was politically active in the 1960s Black Power movement, having heard Malcolm X speak.

Phillip:	That's your problem, you can't take anything seriously.
Will:	Hey look man; I don't have a problem, all right. You have the problem. I remind you of who you are and what you used to be. Now I don't know, somewhere between Princeton and the office, you got soft. You forgot who you are and where you came from.
Phillip:	You think you you're so wise.
Phillip:	Look at me when I'm talking to you. Let me tell you something, son. I grew up on the streets just like you. I encountered bigotry you could not imagine. Now you have a poster of Malcolm X on your wall. I heard the brother speak. I read every word he wrote. Believe me; I know where I come from!
Will:	You actually heard Malcolm speak?
Phillip:	That's right. So before you criticize someone, you find out what he's all about.[38]

The first season focuses on a myriad of themes that center around the class-based divide between Will and his family as well as the challenges faced by African Americans residing in an upper-class white neighborhood.[39]

Black Struggles

"Mistaken Identity" explores the theme of racial profiling. Will and Carlton are stopped by two white cops while driving a family friend's Mercedes Benz.[40] Will knows exactly how the situation will conclude while Carlton is completely naïve.

Will:	Listen to me, when he comes up, keep your hands on the wheel.
Carlton:	Good evening officer, Carlton Banks.
Police:	Keep your hands on the wheel. Where are you headed?
Carlton:	We're going to Palm Springs and you? Where are you headed this fine evening?
Will:	Good Job. Now he's going to want to see your license.
Carlton:	Right.
Police:	Can I see your license?
Carlton:	What?
Will:	He's going to tell us to get out of the car.
Carlton:	You watch too much T.V.
Police:	Get out of the car.

Will predicts the treatment they experience, especially once Carlton and Will are taken to jail. The profiling and the officer's not believing his father is a judge do not impact Carlton who remains steadfast in his belief the police's actions were acting in accordance to policy. Will, on the other hand, sees the moment as just another reality of being black in a white world.[41]

In the previously mentioned ABC news special "Black in White America," a cohost Charles Thomas communicates the fear he encountered when confronted by a police officer:

It doesn't just happen to Blacks, who live in housing projects. It happens to me when I get in my car and I drive to the grocery store. I realized that if I'm stopped by a white police officer who happens to be racist, who's having a bad day, I might not see the sunset that night. But in their case, they're dying every day. When they wake up in the morning, they might not see the sunset that day, and they realize that. But it's something we live with every day, and we've lived with this for as long as we've been on this earth. You're taught this very young when you're black in America. This is part of the feeling. . . . It's real in black America.[42]

The episode entitled, "Seventy-two Hours," also illustrates the conflict between Will and Carlton based in identity, and Carlton's difficult path toward acceptance.[43]

| Will: | All right, but just out of curiosity Carlton what color are you? |
| Carlton: | Here we go again. Look just because I grew up in the best neighborhoods and pronounce the "i-n-g" at the end of words don't make me any less black. |

To emphasize the links between identity, race, class, and culture, Carlton bets Will that he can spend time in Compton with Will's best friend Jazz. Carlton soon discovers he is no match for his new environment. Carlton changes his demeanor and finds friends among Jazz's circle of acquaintances and decides to go to a party in a dangerous place. Will soon intervenes persuading Carlton that their blackness bet is ridiculous and returns home. Will realizes that in the past his friends did not define their blackness because they resided in the hood or spoke slang. Providing viewers a different perspective on representation, *The Fresh Prince* offered an intervention in the politics of identity, how authenticity plays out on black bodies, and the intersections of race, class, and culture.

Laughter Overshadowing Difference

Richard Taflinger argues that sitcoms articulate a myriad of story lines and forms of communication, providing viewers with ample issues to wrestle within 24 short minutes. Whereas dramas enter through a tone of seriousness, sitcoms use jokes and laughter to mediate the tension and difficulty. Yet, these jokes often rely on racial stereotypes that produce laughter that often revolves around "racially defined characteristics and relation of superior and inferior."[44] Worse yet, the jokes often normalized dominant ideas of acting white and acting black. This trope reflects the core of The *Fresh Prince of Bel-Air,* which found its success by portraying a lifestyle that appealed to most audiences.

It also provided a broad representation of black men but provided a very limited representation of black women. "The attention it gave to inequities in skin color and class was rarely afforded to its female characters. Instead feminine beauty was related to light skin, straight hair, relative youthfulness and middle-class status."[45] Indeed, after three seasons of the series, a light-skinned female actress replaced the original actress who played Vivian. According to bell hooks, "light skin and long, straight hair continues to be traits that define a female as beautiful and desirable in the racist White imagination and in the colonized Black mindset. . . . Stereotypically portrayed as embodying a passionate, sensual eroticism, as well as subordinate feminine nature. . . ."[46] While pushing conversions, addressing premarital sex, homosexuality, generational conflict, and countless other issues, the representations offered relied on conventional understandings of identity.

Blacks versus Social Class

Three years after the episode on Carlton and Will's Compton bet, a similar episode entitled "Blood Is Thicker than Mud" aired. It opens on the campus of a fictionalized California University, where Will and Carlton are seeking information on fraternities.[47] In the episode, both black and white fraternities are predominately represented at an informational, each with their varying missions, histories, and values. When the black fraternities perform for perspective members, they engage in a step routine for the interested parties. A step routine is a rhythmic routine that includes precise hand and feet movement, often found among historically black fraternities and sororities. When both Carlton and Will agree to rush/seek membership, in one of the fictional Black fraternities, fraternity members begin to question Carlton's blackness. The running joke is about Carlton's lifestyle and upbringing.

Throughout the episode, the fraternity pledge leader continues to challenge Carlton's authenticity; Will eventually comes to his cousin's defense. Will soon learns that the fraternity has accepted him, but Carlton has not. Embodying the power of racial stereotypes, the pledge leader denies Carlton's blackness because of his demeanor, clothes, and speech. According to the pledge leader, Carlton is not the brother they are seeking for their fraternity. Carlton is not black enough. When Carlton learns about the opinions of him, he quickly shares his thoughts with the pledge leader.

> Carlton: You think I'm a sellout? Why? Because I live in a big house or I dress a certain way. Being black isn't what I'm trying to be, it's what I am. I'm running the same race and jumping the same hurdles you are, so why are you tripping me up? You said we need to stick together, but you don't even know what that means. If you ask me . . ., you're the sellout.

His speech is followed by the audience's applause. The other fraternity members give the pledge leader a look of disappointment and then leave him standing alone. Carlton then returns home confident in his identity, approving of his blackness. When he returns home, he shares the story with his father who becomes extremely upset with the situation Carlton has endured. He questions why his hard work to provide a good life is a penalty against his blackness. The words both Carlton and Phillip share place a brief pause on the comedic lines and take a stance against stereotypes, racial ideologies, and color blindness. Viewers are then encouraged to view blackness and authenticity as separate and individual thought processes.[48]

Throughout television, race is frequently linked to the underclass, more specifically to the working poor. The aforementioned episode was an example of prejudices existence outside of the underclass. The episode brings antiblack racism to the forefront. "Anti-black racism is the racial prejudice, stereotyping, and discrimination that is directed at people of African descent, rooted in the unique history and experience of enslavement."[49]

Within representations of black upper-class (i.e., Banks family), antiblack racism is often erased as history is believed to play less of a role in their status, success/failures, and overall well-being. Antiblack racism "is manifested in the legacy of the social, economic, and political marginalization of people in society such as the lack of opportunities, lower socioeconomic status, higher unemployment, significant poverty rates and overrepresentation in the criminal justice system."[50] These areas are unfortunately believed to be irrelevant in representations of the black upper class, such as *The Fresh Prince of Bel-Air*. But during its run on television, the show attempted to address issues faced among blacks, while including the conflicts between classes, personalities, physical attributes, and ideologies while maintaining its humor.

Not Just Another Comedy

Throughout this chapter, I provided a number of examples and approaches embraced by *Family Matters* and *The Fresh Prince of Bel-Air*. Each represented African American families, stories, and identities in distinct ways and further the place and presence of blackness within dominant discourse. Both shows demonstrated how black characters, with behaviorally white characteristics, interact with the stereotypical black characters to convey the significance of race in comedic television representations. The themes throughout the shows extend to situations in which blacks of the nonfictional world are placed in a white world that exists on and off the television screen. These characters simultaneously navigated both black and white identities to appeal to a diverse audience. These black sitcoms in essence aimed to universalize the black and white experiences. All of the youth in these series continually went to school, showing strong parental roles within the families. Both shows emphasized that black youth can attend Ivy League colleges—with Steve attending MIT and Carlton's efforts to attend Princeton. It even provided me with confidence on my 10-year collegiate journey, attending both a historically black college and predominately white institutions. The adults held consistent jobs that provided the means to financially meet the needs of their families, thus suggesting the notion that higher education and hard work provide a better lifestyle.

These shows sought to point out that variations among actors/actresses of varying backgrounds are original and society should encourage diversity. Although both series attempted to display positive representation of blacks, unlike some shows of the past, neither series ignored the racial is-sues that are found in the past and present and most likely in future. The stories may have been represented through humor and appear far-removed from reality at times, but for those individuals aware of past and present inequities within society, many of the themes and situations are far from humorous and/or a laughing matter. Indeed, all who view a scene view it through their own eyes.[51]

Media are full of images and stereotypes. Bell hooks argues that the institutionalized representation of race via mass media supports oppres-sion, exploitation, and domination of blacks.[52] Images impact an individ-ual's perceptions through the process of selective interpretation. Popular culture, whose role is to bring information to the masses, impacts social reality, "that is by framing images of reality . . . in a predictable and pat-terned way."[53] In this context, television operates via agenda, which is best described as a process where the media tells audiences what to know.[54] Pop-ular culture offers skewed versions of reality, especially television shows. "Watching television is unique to the individual because of certain lifestyles and cultural norms."[55]

Family Matters and *The Fresh Prince of Bel-Air* seldom made racism the source of their humor; they did provide a means to spotlight issues of Af-rican Americans. These issues included health, racism, education, violence, substance abuse, responsibility, and respect. Despite their influence on rep-resentation among African Americans, whether family, class, and physical and personality characteristics, these shows still operated under the same political discourses that other sitcoms with white characters did, the sys-tem in which those in power inevitably control the realities available on television.

Notes

1. *Will Smith & My Work Ethnic Is Sickening*, broadcast December 2, 2007, on CBS, www.cbsnews.com.
2. www.thenumbers.com/people.
3. www.the-top-tens.com.
4. Sherryl Browne Graves, "Television and Prejudice Reduction: When Does Television as a Vicarious Experience Make a Difference?," *Journal of Social Issues* 55, no. 4 (Winter 1999).
5. Herman Gray, *Watching Race: Television and the Struggle for Blackness* (Minneapolis: University of Minnesota Press, 1995), http://216.239.59.104/search?q=cache:100wFM6UqlEJ:www.rcgd.isr.umich.edu/prba/perspectives/winter2000/cwatkins.pdf.

6. "Black in White America," aired August 29, 1989, on ABC.

7. As quoted in Yurii Horton, Raagen Price, and Eric Brown, "Portrayal of Minorities in Film, Media and Entertainment Industries," *Poverty and Prejudice: Media and Race* (June 1999), http://www.stanford.edu/class/e297c/poverty_prejudice/mediarace/portrayal.htm

8. *Television and Family—The Portrayal of Family on Television,* http://family.jrank.org/pages/1680/Television-Family-Portrayal-Family-on-Television.html

9. Ralph Richardson, *My Top 10 African American TV Shows of All Time,* http://www.thedefendersonline.com (accessed January 2010).

10. J. Fred Macdonald, *Blacks and White TV: African Americans in Television Since 1948* (Chicago: Nelson-Hall Publishers, 1992), http://jfredmacdonald.com/bawtv/bawtv21.htm.

11. Ibid.

12. http://etd.gsu.edu/theses/available/etd-07252005-120942/unrestricted/dubriel_joni_gv_summer05_ma.pdf.

13. Camille O. Cosby, *Television's Imageable Influences: The Self-perception of Young African Americans* (Maryland: University Press of America, 1994).

14. Quoted in Brittany Yelenik, *From Housekeepers to Lawyers: Breaking the Stereotype,* https://bu.digication.com/brittanyyelenik_third/Breaking_the_Stereotype (accessed April 2010).

15. Jack Curry and Walter T. Middlebrook, "Family Matters," *USA Today,* September 13, 1989, 4D, http://findarticles.com/p/articles/mi_g1epc/is_tov/ai_2419100418/.

16. Timothy Havens, "African American Television in an Age of Globalization," in *Planet Television: A Global Television Reader,* ed. by Shanti Kumar and Lisa Parks (New York: New York University Press, 2003), pp. 423–38.

17. Kontji Anthony, *Threat of Being "Urkeled" Keeps Students from Sagging,* www.wmctv.com (accessed 2010).

18. *Family Matters,* "Good Cop, Bad Cop," episode 111, first broadcast January 21, 1994, by ABC, http://www.imdb.com/title/tt0096579/epcast.

19. Herman Gray, *Watching Race,* p. 68.

20. *Family Matters,* "Fight the Good Fight," episode 42, first broadcast February 22, 1991, by ABC.

21. J. Fred Macdonald, *Blacks and White TV: African Americans in Television Since 1948* (Chicago: Nelson-Hall Publishers, 1992), http://jfredmacdonald.com/bawtv/bawtv21.htm.

22. Herman Gray, *Cultural Moves: African Americans and the Politics of Representation* (Berkley: University of California Press, 2005), p. 6.

23. *Family Matters,* "Tips for a Better Life," episode 161, first broadcast February 9, 1996, by ABC.

24. J. Fred Macdonald, *Blacks and White TV,* http://jfredmacdonald.com/ bawtv/bawtv21.htm.

25. Jim Pines, *Black and White in Colour: Black People* (British Film Institute, 1992).

26. Simon Cottle, "Introduction: Media Research and Ethnic Minorities: Mapping the Field," in *Ethnic Minorities and the Media,* ed. by Simon Cottle (Maidenhead, Berkshire: Open University Press, 2000), pp. 1–31.

27. Kristal Zook, *Color by Fox: The Fox Network and the Revolution in Black Television* (New York: Oxford University, 1999), p. 15.

28. Di Sara Corrizzato, *Undermining Traditional Black Stereotypes in "The Fresh Prince of Bel Air." Iperstoria*, http://www.iperstoria.it/?p=237 (accessed April 10, 2012).

29. Academy of Achievement, www.achievement.org/autodoc/page/jon0bio-1 (accessed June 7, 2010).

30. Timothy Havens, *Subtitling Rap: Appropriating The Fresh Prince of Bel-Air for Youthful Identity Formation in Kuwait, Gazette* 63, no. 1 (London: Sage Publications, 2000): pp. 57–72, http://myweb.uiowa.edu/thavens/FP-Kuwait.pdf.

31. Robin R. Means Coleman and Charlton D. Mellwain, "The Hidden Truth in Black Sitcoms," in *The Sitcom Reader: American Viewed and Skewed,* ed. by Mary M. Dalton and Laura R. Linder. (New York: SUNY University Press, 2005), pp. 126–27.

32. Timothy Havens, *Subtitling Rap: Appropriating The Fresh Prince of Bel-Air for Youthful Identity Formation in Kuwait,* International Communication Gazette, 02/01/2001.

33. Zook, *Color by Fox,* p. 24.

34. Justin Lewis and Sut Jhally, *Television and the Politics of Racial Representation,* http://cla.calpoly.edu/~bmori/syll/316syll/LewisJhally.html.

35. Gray, *Watching Race,* p. 91.

36. Brittany Yelenik, *From Housekeepers to Lawyers,* http://bu.digication.com/brittneyyelenik_third/Breaking_the_Stereotype (accessed 2010).

37. Di Sara Corrizzato, *Undermining Traditional Black Stereotypes in "The Fresh Prince of Bel Air." Iperstoria*, http://www.iperstoria.it/?p=237 (accessed April 10, 2012).

38. *The Fresh Prince of Bel Air,* "The Fresh Prince Project," episode no, 1, first broadcast September 10, 1990 by NBC, http://www.imdb.com/title/tt0098800/.

39. Di Sara Corrizzato, "Undermining Traditional Black Stereotypes in the Fresh Prince of Bel Air," *Iperstoria* (December 2010): p. 4.

40. *The Fresh Prince of Bel Air,* "Mistaken Identity," episode 6, first broadcast October 15, 1990, by NBC.

41. Robin Means Coleman, *African American Viewers and the Black Situation Comedy: Situating Racial Humor* (New York: Garland, 2000).

42. "Black in White America," August 29, 1989, on ABC.

43. *The Fresh Prince of Bel Air,* "Seventy Two Hours," episode 23, first broadcast March 11, 1991, by NBC.

44. Richard F. Taflinger, "A Theory of Comedy," *Sitcom: What It Is, How It Works,* http://www.wsu.edu:8080/~taflinge/theory.html. (accessed 1996).

45. Dwight E. Brooks and Lisa P. Hebert, *Gender, Race, and Media Representation,* http://www.uk.sagepub.com/upm-data/11715_Chapter16.pdf.

46. bell hooks, *Black Looks: Race and Representation* (Massachusetts: South End Press, 1992), p. 179.

47. *The Fresh Prince of Bel Air,* "Blood Is Thicker Than Mud," episode 81, first broadcast November 1, 1993, by NBC.

48. Zook, *Color by Fox,* p. 24.

49. http://www.yorku.ca/lfoster/2004–05/summer/lectures/GLOSSARY April2005.html.

50. http://www.criec.uqam.ca/pdf/Glossaire%20UNESCO%20ML.pdf.

51. Feagin, *The White Racial Frame: Centuries of Racial Framing and Counter-Framing*, www.asdic-circle.org.

52. hooks, *Black Looks*, p. 179.

53. M. McCombs, "New Frontiers in Agenda Setting: Agendas of Attributes and Frames," *Mass Communication Review* 24 (1997): pp. 32–52.

54. Bernard Cohen, *The Press and Foreign Policy* (New Jersey: Princeton University Press, 1963).

55. Narissra M. Punyant-Carter, "The Perceived Realism of African American Portrayals on Television," *Howard Journal of Communications* 19, no. 3 (2008): pp. 241–57, http://library.ttu.edu/about/facility/face/entries/social_sciences/PDF/Punyanunt-Carterhowardjournal.pdf.

Chapter 9

Single Black Female: Representing the Modern Black Woman in *Living Single*

Lisa A. Guerrero

In 1998, much was made about the debut on HBO of the female-centered sitcom *Sex and the City* (*SATC*). It was immediately embraced by critics and audiences alike and was heralded for its fresh voice and for its depiction of modern women and female friendships. That same year saw the quiet end of the successful five-year run of *Living Single,* a sitcom that too had depicted the experiences of modern women and the power of female friendships . . . and who were black. The measured difference between the marking of these two television moments, while not necessarily surprising, is still instructive in thinking about the African American presence on television, especially the specific space occupied by African American women.

Though it would be easy to dismiss any connections the two shows had to one another, it is far more interesting to consider the ways in which they did overlap, as well as the various assumptions around race, class, and womanhood that determined the different impacts each series had on American television culture. In both series, we are presented with four heroines; each set of protagonists is single, beautiful, accomplished, independent, and die-hard friends. While each set of women deals with various daily life situations that inform their positions as modern women (e.g., financial, professional, and style dilemmas), it is their pursuit of a good man and a stable romantic relationship that is presented as the main overriding goal that really grounds their position as modern women. But it is the difference in their races that determines the ways in which that ostensible common pursuit is marked as either universal, in the case of

SATC, or ethnocentric, in the case of *Living Single.* Female viewers' ability to see themselves, regardless of their race, reflected in the ordeals of Carrie, Samantha, Charlotte, and Miranda, while imagining themselves outside of those of Khadijah, Max, Regine, and Synclaire, is indicative of the complex discursive histories around the racialization of womanhood in the United States.

The social understandings around what constitutes the ideals of womanhood, the propriety of womanhood, and the position of womanhood in the United States have always been constructed along racial lines. These lines have consistently defined white womanhood as the locus of the American feminine standard, while women of color, especially black women, have consequently been marked as lesser than, even *other* than, feminine, creating the discursive space in which to elevate white womanhood through the process of devaluing womanhood of color. This mode of discursive symbiosis has provided justification for a panoply of violence, deprivations, and material inequities to be enacted on women of color in the United States. It has also served as the framework through which representations of black women and other women of color have been created and circulated within the popular imagination.

Looking specifically on representations of black women in the popular media, there has existed a clear chasm between the representational idealization of white womanhood and the representational brutalization of black womanhood that has normalized particular images of what black womanhood *is,* and what it *isn't.* Historically, the figure of the black woman in the social imagination has been mired in a host of racist and sexist rhetoric images aimed at establishing an order of womanhood that determines the supposed boundaries of what is acceptable womanhood. Focusing primarily on the arenas of sexuality, domesticity, and motherhood, in order to frame understandings around desirability, propriety, and normalcy, black women have been distorted and disfigured, in both figurative and literal terms, to maintain social myths about the superiority of white womanhood. Ironically, many of the discursive acts of distortion and disfiguration have often stood in glaring contradiction to one another. Variously, black women in the United States have been imagined and represented as *both* hypersexual *and* asexual, hardworking and industrious *and* lazy, and nurturing mother figures *and* emasculating destroyers of the normative family unit. In all cases, contradictory though they may be, the main point has been to make black womanhood as less desirable in all socially constructed standards of womanhood, sometimes to the extent that the basic inclusion within the social category "woman" has been denied to black women creating a degendered, or ungendered, discursive space that has made it easier in many ways for black women to be exploited, silenced, and violated in social, political, economic, and cultural ways without it being protested, or even recognized, by the rest of society. Drawing on this discursive infrastructure, we can begin to better understand some of the differential reactions, especially of female viewers, between the two television shows.

SATC embodied the idealized versions of modern womanhood including femininity, desirability, and, importantly, heteronormativity. Additionally, the overarching narrative frame of *SATC* was situated within a fantastically constructed urban landscape whose most fantastical feature was the almost complete absence of poor people and people of color. The predominant upper-middle class Eurocentrism of the show set it up to become a socially acceptable and culturally celebrated touchstone of turn-of-the-century womanhood. The presumption behind both the show's particular narrative focus and trajectory as well as society's enthusiastic consumption of that narrative was that womanhood, even in the 21st century, was singular and one-dimensional. Differences in race, class, and sexual desire do not disrupt the inherent nature of womanhood if we accept the narrative assumptions on which *SATC* was built and if we read its cultural worship as approval of those assumptions. And while it is possible to read its popularity as grounded somewhat in an aspirational quality of viewers' desires, the fact remains that as we look at *SATC* in relation to *Living Single,* the first show was discursively, if implicitly, positioned as defining the experience of the modern woman, while the second show was discursively positioned as singular, peripheral experiences of modern women based in race. Mapping this discursive location of *Living Single* within both a larger cultural imagination and the more specific television landscape is useful to understanding the complex challenges and effects that the show was forced to negotiate. And even while *Living Single* never achieved the cultural status of being a "universal" marker of modern womanhood like *SATC,* it did create a standard through which to imagine a new version of modern *black* womanhood that was focused on black female subjectivity and black female–centered notions of community.

Around-the-Way Girls

The premise of *Living Single* centers on the lives of four black twenty-something women who are longtime friends. The core of the group is Khadijah James played by rap star-cum-actress Queen Latifah in her first starring role as an actress. Khadijah is the editor of the fictional *Flava* magazine, a magazine devoted to urban communities, who lives in a Brooklyn brownstone with childhood friend Regine Hunter (Kim Fields), a buyer for an upscale boutique, and her cousin Synclaire James (Kim Coles), a gullible midwesterner making her way in the big city. The group is rounded out by upstart attorney Maxine "Max" Shaw (Erika Alexander), who is Khadijah's best friend and former college roommate and who, though renting an apartment across the street from the other three women, is, for all intents and purposes, a fourth roommate. Framed in broad ways as all coming from much more humble beginnings, the foursome is understood as linked by their hard work, middle-class aspirations, black racial credibility, and, of course, the lack of a good man, specifically, a good *black* man. In fact, every episode during the show's five-season run focused either centrally or peripherally on the pitfalls of romance and sex in the 1990s. The tension between professional success and romantic disaster was a recurring narrative riff for the series. In many ways, these two primary themes of the show mark a progressive departure from the ways in which black women were typically depicted on television, when they were depicted at all. All four of the main characters were professionals who were portrayed as making their respective ways without the help of men or the government like the enduring social stereotype of the "welfare queen." *Living Single* posited a version of modern black womanhood that challenged sociocultural stereotypes through the adherence to the hegemonic ideologies of meritocracy and heteronormativity with the simultaneous articulation of black cultural authenticities like hip-hop and R&B music, fashion and language trends, and institutional affiliations like HBCUs. In other words, their successful modern gendered position did not come at the expense of their race; success didn't mean "acting white." Certainly, in simplistic terms, these characters were much preferred to other less positive television representations of black womanhood. However, the relatively uncritical acceptance of both bootstraps and heteronormative logics that undergird the portraits of the main characters of the show also works in subtle ways to distinguish between socially acceptable and socially unacceptable modes of a black feminine modernity. While neither Khadijah, Max, Regine, nor Synclaire were discursively modeled after any of the standard archetypes in the pantheon of the ghettocentric cultural imagination (e.g., welfare queen, crack whore, banjee girl), these stereotypes are still significant to how the audience understands the four women. That is to say, that the normativity of the four black women of the show is implicitly grounded in opposition to those ghettocentric specters. In Foucauldian terms, the accepted normativity of Khadijah, Max, Regine, and Synclaire is both disciplined through hegemonic coding and disciplinary of those black women who are socially constructed as outside of legitimate social, racial, and gender norms. Even as their race precludes their experiences from being understood in universal terms, their maintenance of social hegemonies keeps them from being understood as locations of transgression.

Especially in terms of heteronormativity, the portrayal of black female sexuality in *Living Single* is not completely what it seems to be at first glance. On the one hand, the romantic pursuits that make up a sizable portion of the sitcom's plots do offer that rare occasion on television up until this point where black love, romance, and sex, the kind *not* contained within a family/marriage context, is normalized and not exoticized. Arguably, the depiction of nonmarital black love as normal was one of the last frontiers of representational blackness on TV. (Arguably, it still *is.*) All four women have healthy dating lives (with the possible exception of Synclaire, whose midwestern naïveté makes her bad at navigating the ins and outs of the dating world but makes her available for a romantic relationship with one of the girls' upstairs neighbors, Overton), with the search for "Mr. Right" at the center of those lives. Even Max, whose exploits are framed as more frivolous, even more masculine, than the other three, is ultimately contained (constrained?) by the stabilizing spell of heteronormative monogamy as she ends up in a relationship with another of the girls' neighbors, Kyle Barker, and pregnant with his child at the end of the series. In fact, by the end of the series, all four women have found their respective Mr. Rights, which is at once by narrative design of the genre (sitcoms require a tying up of loose ends, especially at the end of a series, in order to fulfill their responsibilities as social pacifiers) but is also an explicit acknowledgment of the necessity of an idealized monogamy, a *heterosexual* monogamy, to the maintenance of the proper social order. It also manages to forward a contemporary version of a black politics of respectability. While the four female leads are presented as modern, urban, trendy, smart women, that presentation remains loyal to normative social values of propriety. As a consequence, a critical appreciation of the characters of Khadijah, Max, Regine, and Synclaire becomes trapped within the discursive conundrum that many black representations on television are trapped within between finally being shown as normative and inevitably being strictly ordered by the normative. We can see this complicated relationship to concepts of normativity play out explicitly in two very different story lines from the show.

The first example is from "Woman to Woman" during Season 3 of the show. In the episode, Max is excited to see her old college roommate Shayla, who is in town to celebrate her wedding to Chris, whom Max unceremoniously discovers is also a woman. The tension with the normative here is played out between everyone else's seeming nonchalant embrace of gay marriage, *black female* gay marriage, and Max's thinly veiled homosexual panic. As the others throw a shower for Shayla and Chris, Max ruins the shower with her behavior and refuses to go to the wedding. (It should also be noted that Regine demonstrates her own homosexual panic during the shower by foregoing her typical, trendy, feminine style [which often accentuates her breasts] and greeting the guest of the wedding shower dressed in drab, oversize, mannish clothing. As she explains to Khadijah: "I'm thinking of our guests. You know I'm cute. And you know how enticing I usually look. Why put out the banquet if they can't eat?" Of course, in a comedic turn, she ends up still being attractive to some of the lesbian guests *because* of her manly drag.) During a confrontation with Shayla, Max attributes her behavior to being hurt by Shayla's lie. When Shayla admits that her lie was because she had been in love with Max and didn't want to ruin their friendship, Max's clear homosexual panic is given a clearer target. As it is a sitcom, the homosexual panic is largely subsumed under the jokes and plot devices of the rest of the episode. However, its presence is clear and operates to subtly secure the boundaries of normativity in which the show must stay in order to combat those social notions that link blackness to transgression. In the end, Max comes around and apologizes to Shayla saying that she wishes Shayla had given her a chance to rise to the occasion years ago in college. Though Shayla (and the audience) suspect that Max wouldn't have reacted much differently had Shayla confided in her in college, since Max's anxiety isn't about Shayla's lie, but rather her sexuality. The episode closes in a beauty shop as Shayla and Chris are getting their hair and makeup done for the wedding.[1] The scene presents a rich confluence of varied moments of normativizing: Shayla and Chris are performing normative gender roles (beauty shop) and normative family roles (marriage), even as they are seen as performing nonnormative sexual roles. Max's heterosexuality is safe and unwavering, as is her modern progressive politics of tolerance. And so, at the end of 30 minutes, the normative order has been set right.

Similarly, in the second example, it is clear that televisual representations of blackness, in particular, of black womanhood, cannot be seen as challenging the wisdom of normative social convention lest they become obvious examples of black social stereotypes. Especially for black women, it becomes an either-or proposition with little room for complex identity formations. Either you comply with social norming objectives or you become vilified as a social abnormality. Even compliance cannot fully guarantee that your race won't still be used to devalue your normative performances . . . just ask Michelle Obama. Nevertheless, following the path laid out by social norming is still the best bet at avoiding the taint of transgression, which is what Max does at the end of the series. Beginning several episodes before the series finale ("Let's Stay Together"), Max feels that something is missing from her life. Her friends, as well as the audience, assume it's a man, and one man in particular, Kyle Barker. She decides to have a baby through artificial insemination. Many jokes abound in the intervening episodes regarding Max's motherly instincts, all of the women having to raise the child, and dealing with a pregnant Max. At the same time, it is implied that Max's unorthodox, nonnormative approach to motherhood is clearly not acceptable to both her friends, who are supportive but suspectful suspicious, but also to the larger social imagination where single black mothers can only ever be a sign of transgression. Luckily, society's sense of decorum and normativity doesn't have to be offended for long as the final episode efficiently has Max discover the identity of her sperm donor to be Kyle, only then to be neatly reunited with him wherein they admit they were meant to be together.[2]

Nothing stays wrapped up like true (heterosexual) love and the nuclear family being reinforced. In the end, the series gives audiences what they want: happy endings. Again, the purpose of the sitcom genre is to stabilize narrative anxieties as a way to defer the bigger social anxieties of the audience. As a fan, I really relished the sentimental, one-dimensional happy endings that all the characters were given. However, the critic in me wonders why Max's happy ending couldn't be as a single mom? Why do the racialized gender and sexual politics in the United States require that society's normative notions of happy endings take precedence over an individual's notion of a happy ending, especially when that individual is a woman . . . and black. In offering constructions of modern black womanhood, *Living Single* not only cleared the path for future televisual representations of black women, but it also revealed, in largely subtle ways, the social restrictions that confine the bodies and identities of black women through the imagined hierarchies of propriety and respectability. One of the ways in which this tension was mediated was through the show's emphasis on black female community.

"In a '90s Kind of World, I'm Glad I've Got My Girls."

Much like *SATC* where the female leads inhabit a New York world (Manhattan) populated almost entirely by white people, the women of *Living Single* inhabit a New York world (Brooklyn) populated almost entirely by black people. Demographically, these depictions may be more accurate than not. However, the narrative purpose served by this racial homogenization is actually to place the central emphasis on the personal community of the characters and not on the broader social community in which they live; a social community poses larger, more complex sociopolitical and socioeconomic issues based on race and gender than is manageable, or desirable, in sitcoms. Given its genre convention, *Living Single*'s depiction of black female–centered community does offer an indelible articulation of both the power of women, generally, and the specific resonance of womanist communities to black women's history. Khadijah, Max, Regine, and Synclaire make up a tight-knit womanist community that is made up of, in Alice Walker's terms, "[women] who love other women sexually and/or nonsexually. Appreciate and prefer women's culture . . . and women's strength . . . committed to survival and wholeness of entire people, male and female."[3] Though not feminist in any overt political ways, *Living Single* does present a womanist community in the ways in which the women posit an alternative to the more traditional ways of thinking about black women in relationship to black men or black children, or even to white women or white children, by imagining black women in relationship to themselves and to one another. Even with the search for romantic love as the centerpiece of most of the show's plots, it is the connection that the four women share with one another that contextualizes the romantic and professional aspirations they have. Their truth-telling, yet unconditional support and love the women have for one another stands in for the larger societal support that most black women lack in both literal and ideological terms. Though the women easily give one another a hard time (it is a sitcom after all), it is never portrayed as being meant to bring any one down but rather an effort to lift them up. One of the reasons why their (micro) community functions in the way that it does, through symbiotic critique and celebration, seems to be because of the shared class trajectory of the four women. All four of them come from different variations on the "poor, humble beginnings" origin story, and all four have experienced class mobility through education, hard work, and dedication (the meritocracy trifecta). All four also seek to achieve further class mobility. The commonality of their class backgrounds allows for the show to use their friendship/community to operate as a singular sign of modern black womanhood and for class achievement, of which a monogamous, heterosexual relationship is perceived to be a characteristic to define the social apex through which black women can secure social acceptance and rid themselves of the historical palimpsest of violence and vilification: class position as social panacea. Within this model, however, the community of women provides constant reminders of the racially authentic way to pursue the class-based goals and the racially inauthentic way to pursue them, what I would call "the bougie backlash." Even from the first episode of the series, "Judging by the Cover," we see this racial authenticity radar in place when Khadijah responds to Regine's desire for "a man that knows fine wine doesn't come with a twist-off cap," when she says: "You know, I don't know how you got to be so snooty. You ain't but one generation out the projects yo' damn self!"[4] The underlying implication of the community impulse to enforce notions of racial authenticity is that upward mobility and racial realness don't have to be mutually exclusive despite social assumptions to the contrary. For the four women in *Living Single*, they have little problem imagining success in their own image in part because of the ways in which they reproduce hegemonic structures, as discussed earlier but also, in part, because they reflect off one another, their community. Generally, they aren't shown as reflecting off larger social assumptions around black women except in very broadly construed, intangible ways like when Max bolsters Khadijah's confidence by saying "You're a black woman running her own business. You defy the odds everyday."[5] Otherwise, their point of reference for their identity formation is limited to one another. This insular quality of their community could be simply construed as a convention of the genre, which is true since similar configurations can be found in almost every sitcom regardless of race or gender. I also read the insular character of their community as operating on a conscious level of protecting the representational black female body. The women love, nurture, and support one another in ways that they are not by the structures and ideologies of the greater society. Additionally, in relation to the discussion of normativity, the community of black women friends serves as a surrogate family formation that assuages societal anxieties over the transgressive potential of the black body. Generally speaking, family comedies have been the main ways in which black bodies are allowed to be translated as normative on television. The community of women on *Living Single* ends up providing a kind of makeshift family unit in which to control the possibility of urban black threat. Even though the women make up the core of this surrogate family unit, in order to maintain normative order, men must also play a role. The constructions of black masculinity in *Living Single,* as both object and subject, are instructive in understanding the show's framing of modern black womanhood.

A Good Man Is Hard to Find

Living Single balances out the emphasis on black women with the show's two male leads, Kyle Barker (T.C. Carson) and Overton Wakefield Jones (John Henton), as the women's two upstairs neighbors and eventual love interests for Max and Synclaire, respectively. Again, reflective of the overall norming impulse of the show, the two male leads provide a gendered curative that puts the women's femininity in a recognizable social structure. Kyle, a stock broker, is presented as cosmopolitan and refined, a male version of Regine, whereas Overton, the building's handyman, is presented as simple, kind, and homespun, a male version of Synclaire who will ultimately become his wife. Additionally, Kyle and Overton's relationship to one another mirrors the same kind of kinship bonds as that of the women. They are boyhood friends from Ohio who know everything about one another and support one another like brothers. In their narrative relationship to the women, Kyle and Overton are set up implicitly as standards against which the parade of men in the women's dating lives are measured. Considered largely, the depiction of modern black manhood in *Living Single* is recuperative in the same ways that the depiction of modern black womanhood is.

While there is a quality continuum on which all the women's suitors fall, Kyle and Overton included, none of the men is ever written as extreme in the qualities that eventually make most of the unfit mates for each woman. There are no abusers or addicts, no real womanizers or playas, no real chauvinists or wimps. In other words, there are very few depictions of black masculinity that reinforce social stereotypes. The rare occasions where a stereotype is played for laughs, it is momentary and not focused on any of the women's suitors. This works to stabilize black masculinity within a frame of hegemonic masculinity without playing to racialized social constructions, which allows for the integration of black manhood into dominant gender hierarchies.

One of the most interesting ways in which masculinity gets articulated in *Living Single* is through the female character of Max. As there exists a relative equilibrium of black masculine performances from the male characters of the show, Max is allowed to portray more extreme characteristics that are deemed masculine including sexual relationships with no emotional attachment, gluttony, general lack of sentiment, and aggressiveness. All of these masculinized characteristics culminate in her final denial of men altogether in her decision to have a baby on her own. Ironically, this decision to engage in this singular act of womanhood, motherhood, comes from a discovery she makes about herself at a retreat in the episode "In Your Dreams." Vishnu, the spiritual leader at the new age retreat to which Max drags Khadijah and Synclaire, after having taken Max back to every single one of her past lives (to the dismay of the other retreat participants), tells her that this is the only life in which she's been a woman. This revelation leads her to her decision about motherhood.[6] Her unconventional relationship to motherhood as an individual, trans-actional endeavor absent of sentiment, proves to be her final articulation of a masculinized performance as she is ultimately reined in by gender conventions that position her within a recognizable femininity, mainly her coupling with Kyle Barker, the serendipitous father of her child. Not only is this done in the name of the norming project discussed previously, but it is also done to guarantee that Max is not marginalized by connec-tions to historical depictions of black womanhood as emasculating and asexual. Again, black womanhood has to be recuperated. Further, that masculinity gets played out most explicitly through a female character extends the primacy of women to the narrative frame of *Living Single* wherein women are forming their identities through their pursuit of men (in part) and, in Max's case, also through the actual negotiation of mas-culine gender traits. This overarching recuperative, norming project at the heart of *Living Single* works as successfully as it does due to the genre in which it is executed.

You've Come a Long Way, Baby

Living Single was part of the new Fox network's formula to capture a younger, edgier, more urban audience in the 1990s. Along with other ul-timately successful shows like *In Living Color, The Simpsons,* and *Married with Children, Living Single* helped set a modern, diverse tone for the upstart network. The success of *Living Single* helped to catapult Queen Latifah into the arena of bankable black Hollywood stars. It also made clear that black women's lives were viable, lucrative topics that televi-sion audiences were interested in watching. But the larger question was were television networks, producers, and executives interested in showing them?

Living Single fulfilled the racial and age demographic parameters of the niche casting Fox was trying to use to establish itself against the three main networks, ABC, CBS, and NBC. At a different time and place, it would be hard to guess what the fate of *Living Single* might have been. Ignoring these larger speculations, however, there is much to be learned from *Living Single* about the place of black women on television.

Speaking generally, the largest presence of African Americans on television has always been in comedy, more specifically, situation comedy, and even more specific, family comedy. This predominant link between African Americans and the sitcom genre isn't surprising. At least, it shouldn't be. In a 30-minute format, devoted to the conventions of levity and quick resolution, sitcoms offer a simple way to culturally contain issues of race and downplay, or even ignore, the serious and complex nature of racial politics. Unlike drama, whose format and conventions open more possibilities to deal with complex issues like race (not that they necessarily take advantage of those possibilities), sitcoms offer more opportunities to deflect and defer serious conversations. So, *Living Single* becomes another in a long line of television programs that appear to be about black lives while at the same time skillfully and deliberately avoiding the larger contexts and complexities of black lives. In this case, *Living Single* presents us with the comedy of black women's lives, the significance of which is deeply paradoxical.

African American women had long been a presence in the sitcom arena but for the most part only in secondary, even peripheral, ways. However, *Living Single* was one of the very few shows that was built on the actual subjectivity of black women; in other words, it was a show that did not assume that black women only existed in relation to others' subjectivity while having none of their own. Simultaneously, though, the subjectivity that is represented in the show is an easily digestible one, it retained enough black specificity to link it to racialized notions of cool but not so much that difference became the only locus of audiences' relatability. As a consequence, *Living Single* offered a mediated black and gendered experience that for all intents and purposes operated outside of a larger social context. In many ways, *Living Single* wouldn't have been much different if all of the characters had been white (not unlike so many other black sitcoms). The coup, we are to assume, is that they *weren't* white, which is certainly significant. But is that enough? In some lights, perhaps it is. It seems as if the integration of larger social context should not become the sole responsibility of shows with black casts. If we accept that premise, however, what, then, do we expect representations of blackness on television to do? If we are satisfied with the mere presence of black bodies on our television screens without the integration of black realities to go with them, what then can "progress" mean?

Admittedly, the battle over the mere presence of black bodies on television screens isn't even one in which there has been a marked victory, especially in the specific case of black women. *Living Single* represents a significant moment in this representational trajectory of televisual blackness. Further, it remains particularly significant for the ways in which it presumed a black female sexuality that was neither transgressive nor buffoonish. The black female sexual subject had not existed on television in a fully imagined way before *Living Single* and only a few times since. The importance of this contribution of the show cannot be understated and should not be underestimated. Women's sexuality in general has not often been positioned in generous or powerful ways on television; and black women's sexuality, if allowed at all to be present on television, has predominantly been placed in positions of exploitation that tend to deny not just black female subjectivity but, frequently, black female humanity. *Living Single* posits a new model.

It did so, of course, through a comedic lens. While I would never argue that the comedy of black women's lives is not an important portrayal, I would argue that it is not the *only* important portrayal. Unfortunately, dramas focused on the modern black female subject are still few and far between. Comedy remains the most acceptable genre through which to present black womanhood, in part, we can assume, because within comedy, both literally and figuratively, audiences don't have to take black womanhood seriously. Because there isn't a balanced presence between comedic and dramatic representations of black female life in television programming, black female subjecthood is, in effect, denied an interior life, which mirrors the ways in which that interiority is denied to black women on broader social scales. Achieving this representational balance is, sadly, an ongoing and slow-going project, but *Living Single,* for its noticeable, and somewhat understandable, flaws, is more significant for its contributions to advancing this project than it is as a singular moment of television situation comedy.

Two years after the series finale of *Living Single*, UPN would introduce *Girlfriends,* a show that, in many ways, picked up where *Living Single* left off and ran with it. It, too, was a comedy but one that attempted to broach black female interiority in ways similar to the ways in which *SATC* explored the interiority of white female characters. *Girlfriends* would run for eight, not very smooth, years and would have an inauspicious end amid a television writers' strike and an impending cancellation. Apparently, black female subjectivity and black female community remain a tough sell on network television. However, in 2012, we were presented with the first television drama with a black female lead in ABC's *Scandal.* Black female subjectivity and accompanying interiority may indeed be televisually palatable to audiences as long as it's only one black female subject and as long as the black female sexuality is focused toward a white man. These are conversations for other days (and other essays in this collection). What can be stated with certainty at this point, however, is that *Scandal*'s Olivia Pope would likely never have gotten the chance to both be an extremely successful professional black woman *and* bed the "President of the United States" had it not been for *Living Single*'s Khadijah, Max, Regine, and Synclaire trying to make their way and land Mr. Right.

Notes

1. "Woman to Woman," 1996, episode 22, season 3, *Living Single* (Fox, 1993–1998), Warner Bros. Television.

2. "Let's Stay Together," 1998, episode 13, season 5, *Living Single* (Fox, 1993–1998), Warner Bros. Television.

3. Alice Walker, *In Search of Our Mothers' Gardens: Womanist Prose* (New York: Harcourt Brace Jovanovich, 1983), pp. xi–xii.

4. "Judging by the Cover," 1993, episode 1, season 1, *Living Single* (Fox, 1993–1998), Warner Bros. Television.

5. "In the Black Is Beautiful," 1993, episode 5, season 1, *Living Single* (Fox, 1993–1998), Warner Bros. Television.

6. "In Your Dreams," 1997, episode 11, season 5, *Living Single* (Fox, 1993–1998), Warner Bros. Television.

Chapter 10

The Black Family in the New Millennium: *The Bernie Mac Show, My Wife and Kids,* and *Everybody Hates Chris*

Qiana M. Cutts

The Beulah Show (1950–1952) and *Amos 'n' Andy* (1951–1953) were the first representations of African Americans on television. These shows were criticized for stereotypical portrayals of African Americans. For example, Nadine Gabbadon indicated *The Beulah Show* and *Amos 'n' Andy* were successful in blatantly misrepresenting African Americans as they reified the "coon" and "mammy" stereotypes.[1] These portrayals of African Americans were, according to Robin Means Coleman, part of the "TV Minstrelsy Era."[2] This era was the pre–civil rights era where negative perceptions of African Americans flooded televisions, and racism was entertainment for television's white viewers. As the civil rights era approached, African Americans denounced these stereotypical portrayals. However, these outcries lead not to shifting representations but to a noticeable absence of African American actors on television for about 15 years.[3] The message was clear: *If we (white viewers) can't laugh at you, we don't need to see you.* By the late 1960s, African Americans were once again visible on television, yet these images were distinctly different from those of the era of minstrelsy. Reflecting levels of realism and fantasy, television would introduce viewers to the black family.

Although Bishetta Merritt and Carolyn Stroman suggest that black families have been a staple in television programming since the 1950s, the existence of nuclear televisual black families is a 1960s intervention.[4] Sure, the history books show black actors starring in sitcoms in *The Beulah Show* and

Amos 'n' Andy, yet representations of black family are uncommon prior to Diahann Carroll's *Julia* (1968–1971). The show's portrayal of a black widowed single mother living in the suburbs faced ample critique. Erasing rac-ism and the costs and consequences of racial violence on the black family, *Julia* faced a barrage for its fantastical narrative. The 1970s also saw the debut of several other shows depicting black family life. *Sanford and Son* (1972–1977) and *Good Times* (1974–1979) focused on the experiences of black families living in America's inner cities. In contrast, *The Jeffersons* (1975–1985) focused on the experiences of a black family that had moved on up the socioeconomic ladder. These varying portrayals of black family life continued through the 1980s, 1990s, and 2000s. Shows like *The Cosby Show* (1984–1992), *227* (1985–1990), *The Fresh Prince of Bel-Air* (1991–1996), and *All of Us* (2003–2006) represented the black family across a spectrum of socioeconomic categories. In fact, these shows provide a glimpse into some form of the black family and help to define the new millennium black family that existed in stark contrast to the struggles of Florida and James Evans and Fred and Lemont Sanford.

With shifts in technology and the start of another century, 2000 marked the beginning of a new millennium. Like the millenniums before it, the third millennium, or the 21st century, included shifts in societal structures, including that of the family. For example, a survey conducted by the National Opinion Research Center entitled "The Emerging 21st Century Family" found that people were getting married at older ages than in previous years, divorce rates and out-of-wedlock childbirth had increased, and more people were living single without children.[5] The concept of the American family had shifted to reflect the current social structure where the focus on building a family had diminished. Thus, family depictions on television mirrored that shift. "The fictional family on television, in its many forms, has become one of our most enduring benchmarks for making both metric and qualitative assessments of how the American family is doing in the real world."[6] This suggests that television's portrayals of the black family would provide some insight into the realities of the black family experience. Similarly, George Gerbner and Larry Gross argue that, "television is a medium of the socialization of most people into standardized roles and behaviors. Its function is, in a word, enculturation."[7] The images of the black family have the potential to socialize black families and instruct them on how to navigate in society. These images also have the ability to define and verify others' stereotypical perceptions of black families. If we accept Gerbner's and Gross's argumentation, an analysis of fictional black families may reveal television's power to influence reality and vice versa.

There is a vast difference between the first nuclear black family on television (*Good Times*) and arguably the most popular nuclear black family (*The Cosby Show*) to ever be on television. With the exception that both shows included the two-parent–headed home with multiple children, the shows had very little in common. James and Florida Evans, a blue-collar worker and a homemaker, respectively, lived in the Chicago housing projects; Heathcliff and Claire Huxtable, a doctor and attorney, respectively, lived in an upscale New York brownstone. The families' varying socioeconomic statuses make them privy to different social realities. The Evans family struggled with employment, education, and daily living expenses but does so with a tight-knit family connection and support system. An upper-middle-class family, the Huxtables, rarely endured economic struggle. Yet, their family endured growing pains that were reflective of other upper-middle-class families, regardless of race. Nevertheless, both shows were significant cultural representations of and contributions to the definition of *the black family.*

Since 2000, variations of the black family have been represented on television in a number of sitcoms. *All of Us* centered on the lives of Robert (Duane Martin) and Neesee (LisaRaye McCoy), a divorced couple who co-parented and, at one point during the sitcom, cohabitated as friends. *Half & Half* (2002–2006) also included a divorced couple and reflected the lives of two adult women with the same father and constantly battling mothers. However, three shows—*The Bernie Mac Show* (2001–2006), *My Wife and Kids* (2001–2005), and *Everybody Hates Chris* (2006–2009)—provide portrayals of the black family that build on the representational field afforded to black family sitcoms in the preceding decades. Collectively, these shows present viewers with images of the black families that are progressive, yet still reflect some stereotypical cultural representations.

Synopsis of the Shows

The Bernie Mac Show features an upper-middle-class family led by comedian Bernie Mac, who appears as himself. As with so many other shows (*Everybody Loves Raymond,* 1996–2005; *Roseanne,* 1988–1997; *Seinfeld,* 1990–1998), it was in many ways a platform or vehicle for Mac himself; this proved to be very successful. The show experienced the most success during its first two seasons when the show drew 9.5 and 9.7 million viewers. *The Bernie Mac Show* was canceled during its fifth season after 104 episodes.

The Mac family includes Bernie's wife, Wanda (Kellita Smith), his nephew Jordan (Jeremy Suarez), and his nieces Bryanna (Dee Dee Davis) and Vanessa (Camille Winbush). The show is loosely based on Mac's stand-up routine where he often referenced his own family. As a successfully married couple with no children, Bernie and Wanda find themselves rearranging their lives in an effort to take care of their nephew and nieces, while their mom undergoes drug rehabilitation. In many regards, the show offers very clearly defined roles and identities: Bernie is the strict (and sometimes overbearing) disciplinarian; Wanda is the business-savvy executive who provides the balance between Bernie and the children; Vanessa is the difficult teenager; Jordan is the eclectic middle child whose passion for school is only matched by his athletic ineptitude; and Bryana—aka "Baby Girl"—is her Uncle Bernie's weakness.

My Wife and Kids features a middle-class family living in the suburbs. *My Wife and Kids* was popular with black viewers; however, the show initially attracted a significant nonblack audience.[8] The show ended after five successful seasons. Michael (Damon Wayans) and Janet "Jay" Kyle (Tisha Campbell-Martin) and their three children—Junior (George Gore), Claire (Jazz Raycole [Season 1] and Jennifer Freeman [Seasons 2–5]), and Kady (Parker McKenn Posey)—contend with typical family dilemmas as well as those that are a bit atypical—Junior becomes a teenage parent and husband. Michael has a successful trucking company, and Jay is an investment banker who decided to be a stay-at home in an effort to support the family. The Kyle parents work together to address issues with their children. They are presented as a loving and caring couple who use laughter to keep their relationship exciting.

Everybody Hates Chris is set in Bedford-Stuyvesant and is loosely based on the teenage years of comedian Chris Rock. Rock is also the narrator of the show. Of the three shows discussed here, *Everybody Hates Chris* is the most celebrated, having been nominated for and/or winning Golden Globe, Emmy, Teen Choice, Image, and People's Choice Awards.[9]

The Rock family is a proud working-class family headed by Julius (Terry Crews) and Rochelle Rock (Tichina Arnold). In addition to Chris, there are two other children, Drew (Tequan Richmond) and Tonya (Imani Hakim). The show documents the experiences of Chris living in the shadow of his attractive, talented younger brother, as well as his struggles with his pestering sister. He is also bullied at school where he is one of the few black students. Julius is depicted as a hardworking, thrifty, committed father and husband; Rochelle is the sassy, no-nonsense mother whose pride keeps her from working at any job where she feels disrespected or unappreciated.

While *Everybody Hates Chris* received more nominations and awards, the show on average had fewer viewers than *My Wife and Kids* and *The*

Tonya (Imani Hakim) and Chris (Tyler James Williams) from *Everybody Hates Chris*. (UPN/Photofest)

Bernie Mac Show. For example, during its most-viewed season, *Everybody Hates Chris* had 4.3 million viewers. During their most-viewed seasons, *My Wife and Kids* had 11.3 million viewers, and *The Bernie Mac Show* had 9.7 million viewers. This may be attributable to the different networks on which each show aired. *Everybody Hates Chris* aired on UPN during its first season and on The CW during the remaining seasons. *My Wife and Kids* aired on ABC, and *The Bernie Mac Show* aired on FOX. Both ABC and FOX draw larger audiences than UPN and The CW and, in particular, more diverse audiences. *My Wife and Kids* and *The Bernie Mac Show* were the first black-oriented sitcoms to enjoy such mainstream success and crossracial lines since *The Cosby Show* and *The Fresh Prince of Bel-Air* (1990–1996).[10]

Not Quite the Cosbys

The Cosby Show received as much criticism as it did acclaim.[11] While some black viewers praised the show for its portrayal of a functional black middle-class family, others denounced the show's representation of a utopian black family. A successful ob-gyn (with a home practice) and an attorney, Heathcliff and Claire Huxtable, respectively, lived in a Brooklyn Heights brownstone with their children. Their three oldest children—Sondra, Denise, and Theo—were educated at Princeton University, Hillman College (a fictional private HBCU), and New York University, respectively. *The Cosby Show* was celebrated as a televisual representation of the black family that mainstream America would like to suggest does not exist in black communities and slammed for the underlying suggestion that a benefit of black middle-class membership is the void of common racial, social, and economic issues many black families endure. Black viewers desired a sitcom that did not reinforce stereotypical notions of the dysfunctional black family but also did not paint the black middle-class family's reality with brush of perfection.[12] *The Bernie Mac Show, My Wife and Kids,* and *Everybody Hates Chris* provide some balance between the Cosbys and dysfunction; however, the extent to which these shows successfully transcend the perfection/dysfunction dichotomy is unclear. As an upper-middle-class family, Bernie and Wanda were able to provide Vanessa, Jordan, and Bryanna with the educational and social experiences similar to those the Huxtables provided to their children. Michael and Jay disciplined their children in a comedic, life lesson manner reminiscent of the Huxtables' parenting style. And Rochelle's role as the family matriarch was similar to Claire's position in the Huxtable household. Unfortunately, neither of these families was able to escape some stereotypical story lines and characterization.

Bernie Mac's philosophy of "spare the rod and spoil the child" is problematic for some viewers as his disciplinary style may be interpreted as inhumane and abusive.[13] Research suggests that African American parents, particularly of lower socioeconomic statuses, endorse physically disciplining their children more frequently than middle-income parents.[14] Research also indicated that African American mothers spank their children at much younger ages and spanked their sons more often.[15] In Season 5 of *The Bernie Mac Show,* both Bernie and Wanda are tired of the children being disobedient. For most of the series, Wanda is portrayed as the less strict parent who is willing to discipline through various methods that do not include spanking. However, Bernie believes in disciplining the children by using Big Mama's belt.

In the episode "For Whom the Belt Tolls," both Bernie and Wanda are displeased with the behavioral issues displayed by each of the children and decide to work together to solicit more positive behavior. Wanda tries several ways to guide the children to better behavior. When Jordan is caught playing golf in the backyard and ruining Wanda's club and her garden, he says to Wanda, "You're not gonna tell Uncle Bernie, are you?" Wanda replies, "Boy you ain't got to worry 'bout Uncle Bernie. You need to worry 'bout me." This response demonstrates that the children have become accustomed to Bernie being the disciplinarian as Wanda often uses the "Wait 'til your father gets home" method of discipline. Thus, they do not view Wanda as the disciplinarian. However, after several other incidents involving arguing and disobedience, Bernie decides to equip Wanda with the "weapon of ass destruction" or Big Mama's belt to help ensure that the children will fear (and respect) Wanda, which will convince them to abide by her rules. Wanda reluctantly accepts the belt and quickly learns that pulling out the belt when the children are not on task seems to be all she needs to change their behavior. The children then challenge her because they feel that she will not use the belt. Wanda uses the belt when Jordan blatantly defies her and talks back. Both Wanda and Bernie are alarmed when Wanda accidentally hits Jordan on the head. After this, Wanda keeps the belt handy, but Bernie resumes his role as the disciplinarian and uses the belt on Jordan.

In Miriam Chitiga's study of black viewers' perceptions of black sitcoms, participants commented that Bernie Mac "scolds and abuses his sister's kids" and suggested that the show sends the message that "blacks discipline their children in harsh and sometimes inhumane ways.... Bernie Mac is truly doing us great injustices."[16] These sentiments indicate that African Americans' perceptions of black parenting styles, particularly with physical and verbal discipline, do not always support the "spare the rod" mentality. Media representations of the disciplining of children within black families deserve attention because these representations are often the basis of normative perceptions of black parents as physically and verbally abusive. These perceptions then lead to the belief that black children are violent, angry, and argumentative because of black parents' disciplinary practices although recent research supports that spanking is not linked to children's externalizing behaviors.[17] Thus, theoretical links are made to support the overrepresentation of black males that are incarcerated and/or in special education classes. In addition, school systems' unbalanced discipline against black males is also theoretically supported. Therefore, viewing black parents as abusive diminishes the critical analysis of institutional racism and its impact on the disproportionate disciplinary actions against African Americans in society.

In an analysis of black cultural representation on television, Sherryl Browne Graves found that there were several stereotypical characteristics of black families on television. Siblings in black families displayed more conflicts, and the wives often challenged their husbands and were more dominant.[18] These depictions were also present in *Everybody Hates Chris*. During Season 2 of *Everybody Hates Chris*, Julius and Rochelle address Drew and Tonya's greed in the episode "Everybody Hates Superstition." The younger Rock children devise a plan to play one parent against the other in order to get what they want. Their plan works until the parents figure out what has happened. Julius and Rochelle decide that in order to be sure that the children do not get over on them again, they will make sure that they have a plan—no matter what the children ask, Julius will always say, "Go ask your mother." The suggestion that all members of the household must defer to Rochelle demonstrates Graves's claim that characterizations of black women in relationships suggest that black women emasculate their husbands and are in constant conflict with them. While Rochelle and Julius are depicted as a loving couple, the perception that Rochelle is in charge resonates throughout the seasons. This differs from Claire Huxtable's role as the matriarch of her family. Claire is soft-spoken yet firm. Motherly yet warm. Thus, while Rochelle demonstrates that she is a loving mother and wife, she is also characterized as the quick-witted, neck rolling, loud black woman who refuses to be disrespected by her husband, her children, or anyone else.

Characterizations of Black Fatherhood and Collaborative Parenting

> You and I know how true this is in the African-American community [absentee fathers]. We know that more than half of all black children live in single-parent households, a number that has doubled—doubled—since we were children. We know the statistics—that children who grow up without a father are five times more likely to live in poverty and commit crime; nine times more likely to drop out of schools and twenty times more likely to end up in prison. They are more likely to have behavioral problems, or run away from home, or become teenage parents themselves. And the foundations of our community are weaker because of it.[19]

During his 2008 Father's Day speech, President Barack Obama upset many American citizens with the aforementioned comment, particularly African Americans. Some African Americans were outraged that President Obama would make such a statement regarding black fathers, while others applauded his forthright comment regarding absentee black fathers. Noted civil rights activist Jesse Jackson denounced the president's remarks as a moral chastisement of African Americans, and, in a verbal critique captured on camera, Jackson indicated that he wanted to castrate the president—or figuratively silence him. President Obama also called for black fathers to step up and take a more active role in their children's lives. Citing his own experiences as being raised by a single mother, the president suggested that absentee black fathers could no longer afford to sit idly by while their children longed for their love, attention, and guidance.

In her focus on the American family and the shifting focus and authority, Valerie Reimer suggests that the portrayal of fathers as the head of the family and the mothers as the submissive partners in popular television sitcoms has varied since the 1960s.[20] Specifically, Reimer suggested that the roles of the mother and father have varied from the father being fearfully respectful of the mother as demonstrated in an episode of *The Cosby Show* where Rudy tries to get her dad to let her wear a dress her mother told her not to wear to the mother trading her pearls and aprons from the 1960s to jeans, sweaters, and business attire on contemporary television shows. In addition, contemporary fathers are often portrayed as the lovable good guy with good intentions but not always the best solution, while the mother is portrayed as the less submissive, take-charge mother who is able to be a successful career woman while she navigates the household.[21] The *Bernie Mac Show* and *My Wife and Kids* have elements of the characterizations described above; however, there also seems to be more of a focus on balanced parenting with the fathers being the primary disciplinarian. Bernie's profession as a comedian provided him with more time to be the stay-at-home dad, while Wanda worked a 9–5 shift as the vice president at AT&T. Michael and Jay balanced their work schedules with Jay staying home with the kids while Michael builds the business; this role is reversed when Jay decides to go back to school and leaves much of the daily interactions with the children to Michael. While job schedules sometimes dictate the visibility of one parent over the other, all three of the shows include episodes where collaborative parenting is portrayed.

Both Michael Kyle and Julius Rock were present and active in their children's lives. Similarly, Bernie Mac served as a strong father figure for his nieces and nephew. The visibility of each of the television fathers was shaped by socioeconomic status. For example, as middle- and upper- middle-class fathers, Michael Kyle and Bernie Mac were able to be more present with their children. Their class status afforded them the opportunities to spend more time with the children and to engage in various bonding activities with them (exotic family vacations, cultural events, sports and extra-curricular activities, etc.). While Julius Rock may not have been as present as the other fathers because of his numerous job responsibilities, he was present as much as his schedule permitted. For example, episodes of the *Everybody Hates Chris* often featured Julius returning from work in time to have dinner with his family and providing support to Rochelle Rock as she dealt with the daily challenges of heading the household.

Bernie Mac also faced the challenge of building a relationship that was not initially afforded by a biological connection. While Bernie shared a biological connection to his nieces and nephew, his challenge was to build a relationship as a father figure to three children that had experienced loss in so many ways. Therefore, while his class status supported his efforts to provide class-based opportunities for his nieces and nephew, his status as the uncle representing a father figure was a factor that highlighted the challenges faced by fathers in blended families.

A different characterization of black fatherhood was present in each of the sitcoms in varying ways. As previously noted, in *Everybody Hates Chris,* Julius's role was visible; however, his ability to be active often was limited because of his work schedule. Most often, Julius's main concern as a father was saving the family money. Yet, there were examples of where Julius's thrifty attitude about money was used to teach the children a life lesson. For example, in the Episode 12 of Season 1, "Everybody Hates a Part-Time Job," Chris wanted a leather jacket and worked with his dad to earn the money to purchase the jacket. The time that Julius and Chris spent working together provided Chris with another view of his father. Chris was exposed to Julius's comedic and adventurous sides and heard his father use profanity, which is something he never did at home. Arguably, the most important lesson Julius taught to Chris during this episode came at the end of the episode when Julius paid Chris for his hard work.

Chris:	After all I'd been through, I understood my father a lot more. Because when you work hard you think about every dime you spend, and I was thinking about how I was gonna spend mine. [*Julius hands Chris his payment for working.*]
Chris:	$25?
Julius:	That's right. And you earned every penny. Don't forget to ice down your arms.
Chris:	But I need $50 for the jacket.
Julius:	No you don't. You want $50. There's a difference.
Chris:	When I asked you for the jacket, you said I should get a job. And I got a job.
Julius:	The job didn't pay enough.

Chris then walks to the store to view the jacket in the display window and sees that another teenager in the neighborhood is leaving the store with the jacket. Saddened for a minute, Chris notices the store clerk putting a layaway sign in the window and decides to put the jacket on layaway. The episode ends six months later with Chris wearing the jacket but falling to the ground, presumably from the heat.

In this episode, Julius was successful in teaching Chris several lessons. Being able to see his father use profanity and humor with his coworkers helped Chris to see that different situations may call for different types of interactions. Chris also learned a lesson regarding employment hierarchy. Julius was directed by his supervisor to deliver his truck to a different location after he had worked all night. When Chris asked Julius if he was going to let the supervisor tell him what to do, Julius replied, "Either that, or I won't have nothin' to do." Julius's response was in contrast to what Rochelle might have said in the same situation, as she was known to communicate that she did not need to work because Julius had several jobs. Chris also learned about working hard and budgeting. By working with his father and putting the jacket on layaway, Chris had a stronger appreciation for his father's work ethic.

The roles of father and husband in *My Wife and Kids* are supported by the show's title. Michael Kyle is the foundation of the family and actively participates in all aspects of his children's lives. The first four episodes of Season 2 are strong examples of Michael's role as the visible/active father. The episodes—"Mom's Away" (Parts 1 and 2), "No Rules," and "Perfect Dad"—focus on Michael parenting alone while Jay is away taking care of her mother. In this series of episodes, the children challenge Michael by constantly suggesting that his parenting style is less favorable than their mother's and by suggesting that their father aims to be perfect and has too many rules. Like most episodes, Michael permits the children to learn from experience. During the "No Rules" episode, he agrees to let them go without rules. Each of the children gives in to Michael's rules after they see what life is like without rules. However, during the next episode, "Perfect Dad," they each have the opportunity to describe the father they would like to have. Michael helps them to see how each of the dads they describe has certain areas for needed improvement. This series of episodes is indicative of the parenting style adopted by Michael Kyle. He uses humor and realistic examples to help the children see why the rules are important.

Similar to Julius, Michael also uses a work-related experience to teach Junior some lessons. When Junior and his girlfriend Vanessa tell Michael and Jay that Vanessa is pregnant and they want to get married, Michael suggests that since Junior is now a man with more responsibilities, he needs to get a job. Michael hires Junior to work for him but treats him like all other employees. As a result of Junior being late for work, Michael fires him. Junior thinks Michael is being too hard on him and talks to Michael regarding the firing.

Junior:	I wanna know why you're being so hard on me.
Michael:	I'm hard on you because life is hard and I'm tryna prepare you for it. Your mother and I, we're just worried about you.
Junior:	And I appreciate that, but I get the feeling that you're mad at me all the time.
Michael:	Look, I'm not mad at you. I'm just tryna make a man outta you.
Junior:	How? By breaking my spirit, criticizing me, making me walk around with this dumb-dumb notebook? You want me to be a man but you treat me like a child.
Michael:	That's because that's what you act like, a child. You can't even get to work on time.
Junior:	I was there at nine.
Michael:	No, 9:01. You wanna impress me, be there at 8:30 or 8 o'clock.
Junior:	I'm trying Dad.
Michael:	You're not trying hard enough, Junior. You're about to be a father. If having a baby in this world doesn't motivate you, nothing will.
Junior:	You're right. And I promise, from this moment on, I'll do my best.

Michael then hugs Junior and tells him to report to work the next day. While this scene is more focused on the life-changing concept of fatherhood, it is similar to the previously discussed scene in *Everybody Hates Chris* as both fathers use their jobs and personal experiences to help teach their sons' life lessons. The fathers' use of tough love is successful in teaching their sons foundational lessons that they will be able to use later in life.

The previous excerpts challenge society's perceptions of African American fathers as absentee fathers. The examples also suggest that African American fathers are present and interact with their sons in ways that support the teaching of life lessons.[22] The interactions between Michael and Junior and Julius and Chris also support research indicating that minority fathers are portrayed as supportive, competent, and engaged with their family.[23] Michael and Julius are fictional characters; however, in a study of reality television fathers, Debra C. Smith also found that black fathers often attempt to teach their kids life lessons through their interaction and equip them with the skills to navigate society.[24]

Discussion: Representation for Us . . . and Them

Herman Gray suggests that media and popular culture are nurturing places for a marriage of theoretical abstraction and cultural representation.[25] Because the media plays such a significant role in how others view black people and how the black community views itself, critical analyses represent an important intervention against the hegemony of black caricatures and stereotypical representations. De facto segregation in the United States increases the chances that a white person's only exposure to a black person is what she/he sees on television. As comedians and actors, both Bernie Mac and Keenan Ivory Wayans had significant white fan bases. The use of comedy, laughter, and their erasure of the issues of race and class support not only contributes to the perpetuation of stereotypes but the popularity of these shows from white fans. Thomas E. Ford suggested, "Stereotypical television portrayals of African-Americans in a humorous context increase the likelihood that whites will perceive an African-American target in a stereotypical manner."[26] Black family sitcoms including families from various socioeconomic statuses and focusing on family issues are important because viewers' exposure to African Americans on television is often the driving force behind their perceptions of African Americans.[27] Narissa M. Punyanunt-Carter indicated that the media "shape[s] and influence[s] public perceptions of African Americans."[28] Therefore, the analysis of television's depictions of the black family challenges stereotypical images as definitive cultural representations.

The shows demonstrate that no matter the socioeconomic status black families are no more immune to challenges than any other family, as with Vanessa struggling to connect with her mother in spite of her drug addiction and Junior Kyle getting his girlfriend pregnant at 17 years, mirroring his parents' experience. In addition, the visibility and activeness of the black fathers in the sitcoms provide a view of black fatherhood that is often perceived to not be the norm in society. The shows also debunk the myth that black parents do not socialize their children for work, no matter the socioeconomic status. In addition, the shows provide images of African Americans in various employment fields, which are extremely important as Cynthia Hoffner, Kenneth J. Levine, and Raiza Toohey found that *wishful identification*[29] was apparent among the respondents, further solidifying that young people are influenced by the media portrayals of employment and wealth. Therefore, having the sitcoms' depiction of black families in various socioeconomic statuses provides a varied view of employment and the integrity associated with various occupations.

While the shows focus on family, parenting, and the visibility and activeness of black fathers, a critical focus on race was absent from two of the sitcoms. Producers of *My Wife and Kids* and *The Bernie Mac Show* suggested that the shows' focus on topics universal to all families, regardless of race, made them more popular to a wider audience. For example, Larry Wilmore, the executive producer and creator of *The Bernie Mac Show* indicated that he purposely created the show to appeal to a broad audience. He contended, "I just wanted to deal with universal themes and the generational push-and-pull of parent and child relationships."[30] Similarly, Dana Walden indicated that, "humor cuts across all racial boundaries."[31] Wilmore and Walden's comments regarding the use of humor and universal themes should not be taken lightly. While there are some universal themes that are prevalent in various racial contexts, the trajectory for African Americans and other groups of color as they experience these themes—family structure, discipline, relationship negotiation, economic stability, etc.—is rooted in institutional racism and discrimination. Thus, to characterize a black family as being immune to racism, particularly because of their class status, is to do a grave injustice to black and nonblack viewers.

The lack of emphasis on race was one of the challenges of two of the shows, and while *Everybody Hates Chris* dealt with race in several of the episodes, the racial undertones were rarely viewed critically and tended to become secondary factors to the overall comedic nature of the show. Racism is permanently woven into the fabric of American society,[32] and media representations of African Americans are often viewed as "Truth."[33] The perceived realism of portrayals of African Americans on television lead to continued stereotyped images and self-fulfilling prophecies.[34] Notwithstanding TVOne and the Oprah Winfrey Network (OWN), African American ownership of major television networks is limited.[35] Therefore, African Americans are not in control of the images used to characterize the black community on television. In order to challenge the dominant narrative of stereotypical black representation, writers, producers, and actors must incorporate empowering and critical instances regarding race. In addition, viewers must challenge stereotypical narratives of African Americans by demanding television shows that are complex without being stereotypical, where viewers laugh with African Americans, not at them.

Notes

1. Nadine Gabbadon, "From 'Good Times' to Bad?: Changing Portrayals of the African American Sitcom Family," Paper presented at the Annual meeting of

the International Communication Association. (Dresden, Germany: Dresden International Congress Centre, 2006), pp. 1–34.

2. Robin R. Means Coleman, *African American Viewers and the Black Situation Comedy: Situating Racial Humor* (New York: Garland Publishing, Inc, 2000).

3. Ibid.

4. Bishetta Merritt and Carolyn A. Stroman, "Black Family Imagery and Interactions on Television," *Journal of Black Studies* 23, no. 4 (1993): pp. 92–99.

5. Jennings Bryant and J. Allison Bryant, eds., *Television and the American Family, 2nd ed.* (Mahwah, NJ: Lawrence Erlbaum Associates, 2001).

6. James D. Robinson and Thomas Skill, "Five Decades of Families on Television: From the 1950s through the 1990s," in *Television and the American Family,* ed. by Jennings Bryant and J. Alison Bryant (Mahwah, NJ: Lawrence Erlbaum Associates, 2001), p. 139.

7. George Gerbner and Larry Gross, "Living with Television: The Violence Profile," *Journal of Communication* 26, no. 2 (1976): p. 175.

8. Michael Freeman, "Black-Oriented Sitcoms Gaining White Viewers: 'Bernie Mac,' 'My Wife and Kids' Cross Racial Boundaries," *Electronic Media 20,* no. 1 (2001): p. 1A.

9. *The Bernie Mack Show* and *My Wife and Kids* also were nominated for and won awards; however, *Everybody Hates Chris* received more nominations and awards from a range of organizations.

10. Ibid.

11. Leslie B. Innis and Joe R. Feagin, "The Cosby Show: The View from the Black Middle Class," *Journal of Black Studies* 25, no. 6 (1995): pp. 692–711.

12. Miriam M. Chitiga, "Black Sitcoms: A Black Perspective," *Cercles* 8 (2003): pp. 46–58.

13. Ibid.

14. Ivor B. Horn, Tina L. Cheng, and Jill Joseph, "Discipline in the African American Community: The Impact of Socioeconomic Status on Beliefs and Practices," *Pediatrics* 113, no. 5 (2004): pp. 1236–41.

15. Michael J. MacKenzie, Eric Nicklas, Jeanne Brooks-Gunn, and Jane Waldfogel, "Who Spanks Infants and Toddlers? Evidence from the Fragile Families and Child Well-Being Study," *Maltreatment of Infants and Toddlers, Children and Youth Services Review* 33 (8) (2011): pp. 1364–73.

16. Chitiga, "Black Sitcoms," p. 56.

17. Elizabeth T. Gershoff, Jennifer E. Lansford, Holly R. Sexton, Pamela Davis-Kean, and Arnold J. Sameroff, "Longitudinal Links between Spanking and Children's Externalizing Behaviors in a National Sample of White, Black, Hispanic, and Asian American Families," *Child Development* 83, no. 3 (2012): pp. 838–43.

18. Sheryl Graves, "Television, the Portrayal of African Americans, and the Development of Children's Attitudes," in *Children and Television: Images in a Changing Sociocultural World,* ed. by G. L. Berry and J. K. Asamen (Newbury Park, CA: Sage), p. 179–90.

19. Christopher Hass, "Barack Obama: Father's Day Speech," Given at the Apostolic Church of God in Chicago on June 17, 2008, https://my.barackobama.com/page/community/post/stateupdates/gG5nFK.

20. Valerie A. Reimers, "American Family TV Sitcoms. The Early Years to the Present: Fathers, Mothers, and Children—Shifting Focus and Authority," *Cercles* 8 (2003): pp. 114–21

21. Ibid.

22. Timothy A. Pehlke II, Charles B. Hennon, M. Elise Radina, and Katherine A. Kuvalanka, "Does Father Still Know Best? An Inductive Thematic Analysis of Popular TV Sitcoms," *Fathering* 7 (2009): pp. 114–39.

23. Ibid.

24. Debra C. Smith, "Critiquing Reality-Based Televisual Black Fatherhood: Critical Analysis of Run's House and Snoop Dogg's Fatherhood," *Critical Studies in Media Communication* 25 (2008): pp. 393–42.

25. Herman Gray, *Watching Race: Television and the Struggle for Blackness,* (Minneapolis: University of Minnesota Press, 1993).

26. Thomas E. Ford, "Effects of Stereotypical Television Portrayals of African-Americans on Person Perception," *Social Psychology Quarterly* 60, no. 3 (1997): pp. 266–75.

27. Narissa M. Punyanunt-Carter, "The Perceived Realism of African American Portrayals on Television," *The Howard Journal of Communication* 19 (2008).

28. Ibid., 244.

29. In Hoffner et al. article, wishful identification is defined as "psychological processes through which an individual desires or attempts to become like another person" (p. 286).

30. Ibid., p. 1A.

31. Ibid., p. 1A.

32. Derrick Bell, *Faces at the Bottom of the Well: The Permanence of Racism* (New York: Basic, 1992).

33. Clint C. Wilson, Felix Gutierrez, and Lena M. Chao, *Racism, Sexism, and the Media: The Rise of Class Communication in Multicultural America* (Thousand Oaks, CA: Safe, 2003).

34. Narissa M. Punyanunt-Carter, "The Perceived Realism."

35. Viacom purchased Black Entertainment Television (BET) for $3 billion in 2011.

Chapter 11

Blackness and Children's Programming: *Sesame Street, A.N.T. Farm,* and *The LeBrons*

David J. Leonard

The history of African American television has been one of stereotypes and contested imagery that has not been limited to adults. From *Our Gang* through *Diff'rent Strokes, Family Matters,* and countless other shows, the story of African American television has not simply been a story of representations of black manhood or womanhood (and their denial) but particular representations of black children. Throughout this volume, we explore many of these shows, elucidating how youthful bodies serve as a mechanism for both the demonization and celebration of blackness, existing as vehicles to deny and imagine an alternative future for the black community. What has been given less focus within the literature is kids'

This paper includes and builds on four essays written by D.J. Leonard—"Is the tween world ready for the Subaltern? A.N.T. Farm and the Politics of Blackness," http://newblackman.blogspot.com/2011/11/is-tween-world-ready-for-subaltern-ant.html, November 3, 2011; "Attacking Elmo and King's Beloved Community: The Conservative Right and its assault on *Sesame Street,*" http://newblackman.blogspot.com/2011/09/elmo-and-beloved-community-conservative.html, September 18, 2011; "Boxed In: The LeBrons and Stereotypes as Authenticity," http://newblackman.blogspot.com/2011/04/boxed-in-lebrons-and-stereotypes-as.html, April 28, 2011; "Scripting King James: The LeBrons and a Discourse of Blackness," http://newblackman.blogspot.com/2011/04/scripting-king-james-lebrons-and.html, April 13, 2011. Thanks to Mark Anthony Neal.

television, which, in part reflects the relatively recent focus on the kids' market from the television world. Yet, it also reflects the ways in which racial discourse has long denied the innocence, the purity of youthfulness, and the mundane realities of African American kids. Playing, friendships, youthful struggles, and the day-to-day life of African American kids are uncommon within public discourse, so it shouldn't be a surprise that such stories have remained outside of the reach of television culture. It is within this story that this chapter explores African Americans and kids' television, exploring three distinct shows, which are bound together by (1) their efforts to chronicle and explore the experiences of African American youth, (2) their systematic efforts to challenge and undermine hegemonic stereotypes, (3) with the minor exception of *Sesame Street*, their commonplace focus on the experiences of middle-class youth, and (4) to varying degrees, their avoidance of discussions of racism at the surface with greatest emphasis being on identity. Yet, the subject matter and the topics addressed by these shows in many ways reflect the orientation of kids' television culture, one that avoids controversy and topics deemed inappropriate for children. Negotiating the demands of children's television within a society that often denies the childhood for youth of color is at the core of the history of African American television.

Sesame Street

During the summer of 2011, Ben Shapiro, while making an appearance on Fox News' *Hannity*, jokingly announced his desire to cap the characters of *Sesame Street* as the lead-in for his serious critiques of the show.[1] His criticisms focus on its soft bigotry of low expectations, its promotion of gender neutral language, and its advocacy to give boys dolls and girls fire trucks. Others on *Hannity*'s great all-American panel similarly spoke about the downgrading of America's moral fabric, seemingly linking the messages of *Sesame Street* to the culture wars. *The Huffington Post* describes his criticism of *Sesame Street* in the following way:

> Chief amongst Shapiro's alleged liberal offenders is Sesame Street, the Jim Henson-created educational show carried on PBS, the public network with few conservative fans or defenders.
>
> Citing interviews with one of the show's creators, early episodes of the show featuring hippies and racial reconciliation and, more recently, incidents such as 2009's "Pox News" controversy, Shapiro writes that "Sesame Street tried to tackle divorce, tackle 'peaceful conflict resolution' in the aftermath of 9/11 and had Neil Patrick Harris on the show playing the subtly-named 'fairy shoeperson.'"

Patrick Harris, to Shapiro's chagrin, is gay. And, even scarier, Cookie Monster says cookies are only a sometimes food now; the venerable sweets machine has added fruits and vegetables to his diet, indicating a major liberal plot.[2]

On Martin Bashir's show on MSNBC, he denounced children's television for promoting "a self-esteem ethos, the idea that, to paraphrase Barney 'everyone is special'; an unearned self-esteem."[3]

The attacks on *Sesame Street* (and by extension the liberal media and big government intrusion in family matters) are nothing new. A 1992 column in *The Economist* similarly denounced *Sesame Street* as a liberal assault on American values:

> The problem comes when the sensible tolerance and respect of "Sesame Street" are mutated into something less appealing. First, it becomes a kind of hypertolerance (which argues, for example, that the canon of black female authors is as rich as that of white male authors); which is merely silly. Second, it becomes an intolerance of those who do not practice this hypertolerance (so that anyone who argues that a canon of authors who happen to be white and male is better than the one picked by sex and skin color is a racist sexist); which is pernicious. It is the intolerance that has come to be called "political correctness"—or PC.[4]

The criticisms that multiculturalism or tolerance represents a vehicle for the intolerance for dominant values (white, Christian, middle class) that have purportedly been central to America's historic greatness are common to the broader culture. Equally troubling to those critics of *Sesame Street* is not only taxpayer support for a program that is neither intended for white middle-class audiences (Shapiro notes the history behind *Sesame Street*) but in their mind a devaluing of whiteness within a multiculturalist agenda. To understand this criticism and to comprehend the Right's denunciation of *Sesame Street* mandates an examination of this larger history and the ways in which *Sesame Street* has built on the civil rights movements and those concerned with justice, equality, and fairness. In other words, the Shapiro and friends' critiques of *Sesame Street*—that it focuses on the rectifying the educational inequalities that plague America, that it seeks to celebrate difference, that it promotes self-esteem in all children irrespective of race, class, gender, and sexuality—are several reasons to celebrate the interventions provided by *Sesame Street.*

In 1979, *The New York Times* identified the primary focus of *Sesame Street* as the "4-year-old inner-city black youngster." Jennifer Mandel, in "The Production of a Beloved Community: Sesame Street's Answer to America's Inequalities," argues that while the original intended audience for the show was "disadvantaged urban youth" who suffered because of "the limited availability of preschool education," the appeal and impact of the show transcended any particular demographic. While addressing structural inequalities and countering the systemic failures in America's educational television were part of the show's mission, it more masterfully offered a utopic vision of America and the broader world. Joel Spring describes the mission of Children's Television Workshop with *Sesame Street* as one bound by a desire "to shape public morality" and offer "a standard as to what the world should be like."[5] Or as Robin D. G. Kelley might describe it, a show dedicated to the cultivation of "freedom dreams." Imagining a place of "sweet air" and "sunny days" that "sweep the clouds away," where "friendly neighborhoods" meet and "doors are open wide," *Sesame Street* is the utopia worthy of any person's imagination. Virginia Heffernan describes the show's message and transformative representational politics as follows:

> The concept of the "inner city"—or "slums," as The Times bluntly put it in its first review of "Sesame Street"—was therefore transformed into a kind of Xanadu on the show: a bright, no-clouds, clear-air place where people bopped around with monsters and didn't worry too much about money, cleanliness or projecting false cheer. The Upper West Side, hardly a burned-out ghetto, was said to be the model.
>
> People on "Sesame Street" had limited possibilities and fixed identities, and (the best part) you weren't expected to change much. The harshness of existence was a given, and no one was proposing that numbers and letters would lead you "out" of your inner city to Elysian suburbs. Instead, "Sesame Street" suggested that learning might merely make our days more bearable, more interesting, funnier. It encouraged us, above all, to be nice to our neighbors and to cultivate the safer pleasures that take the edge off—taking baths, eating cookies, reading. Don't tell the kids.[6]

The power of *Sesame Street* doesn't merely resonate with its history, its identification with Martin Luther King Jr.'s Beloved Community, its efforts to challenge differential access to educational opportunities, or even its emphasis "on the representations of diverse groups" but through its opposition to the normalization of whiteness; its power rests with its critiques of and counternarratives to hegemonic notions of identity.[7]

It is easy to come up with countless examples where *Sesame Street* sought to challenge dominant white racial frames, particularly those that reinforced the desirability and hypervisibility of white, male, heterosexual, middle-class identities. For example, in 1971, Jesse Jackson was dropped from *Sesame Street,* where he offered a call-and-response reciting of his famous "I am somebody." Surrounded by a diverse group of kids, Jackson and the kids announced:

> *I am somebody . . .*
> *I may be poor*
> *But I am somebody.*[8]

Embodying *Sesame Street*'s mission and the message of the Beloved Community, where differences should be celebrated, Jackson's appearance more importantly highlights the ways in which *Sesame Street* has historically challenged privilege and normalizing discourses. Similar themes remain central to *Sesame Street* today.

Calling on kids to dream and recognize the beauty of diversity, Will-I-Am continues the message of Jackson with "What I am." Joined by a crew of Muppets, he sings, "If what I am is what's in me, then I'll stay strong, that's who I will be."[9] Similarly Kingston, who is a favorite in our house, so often delivers not just a message about the beauty of diversity but the problematic demands of homogeneity and authenticity from popular discourses, which punish those who embrace counter or oppositional identities.[10] Kingston, who wears a sweater vest and tie, celebrates his own unique identity in "Happy to Be Me," singing, "I watch all my friends turn their hats to the back, but I kept to the front because I like it like that. Not trying to be different, just doin my own thing." With a hook of "be yourself, its easy as A-B-C . . . just happy to be me" and "I do it my way," Kingston brings to light the pressures to embrace and perform particular identities, opening up a space for a myriad of ways of being. Likewise, one of *Sesame Street*'s most celebrated segments similarly embraces the diversity that exists between and within racialized communities, questioning the discursive articulations of authenticity so commonplace within society. In 2010, "I Love My Hair" captured the imagination of many further illustrating *Sesame Street*'s power and purpose. In the song, a young black girl Muppet sings:

> Don't need a trip to the beauty shop, 'cause I love what I got on top.[11]

Kai Wright describes not only the song and video but it's significance, in the following way:

> Sesame Street got more than the kiddies' attention when it took on black women's hair. . . . An adorable black girl Muppet dances up to the camera and

starts belting an ode to herself: The girl goes on and on in unselfconscious adoration of herself. Then she sings that one of the great things about her hair is all the cool stuff she can do with it—an Afro, cornrows, braids, dread-locks. Even stick a bow in it. Good stuff Sesame Street. Good stuff.[12]

Celebrating the ways in which the song distinguishes "between *style* and *self-hate*," Wright praises it for its intervention against a larger history of white supremacy. He and others rightly note how it speaks against a larger history and discourse that has used hair (hair politics) to patholo-gize and demonize blackness. Angel Jordan, on the Root.com, further em-phasizes the important message and the larger history embedded within this song:

Sesame Street works off of a platform that permeates both childhood and adulthood—it's designed down to the smallest detail to teach children (and adults) through pictures, sounds and subliminal messaging. Thus, it's easy to see how a song like "I Love My Hair" could bring a grandmother or parent of a black child to tears. Looking past the puppet, you can clearly see and hear a positive message that says, "You are beautiful." It's a statement that seems so simple but is much more complex.

Many African-American families struggle with teaching their children to love not only themselves but also the things that make them unique: their full lips, wide noses and kinky hair. "African Americans as a people have had to battle the social idea that not only is our skin inferior, but that our hair is as well," says Karcheik Sims-Alvarado, visiting lecturer at Georgia State University's department of African-American studies. "We were treated as inferior by default simply because we were black, and because of this, we internalized these beliefs and unfortunately passed them down from genera-tion to generation."[13]

What is evident here are the ways in which *Sesame Street* challenges the normalization of whiteness, the celebration of white identity within and beyond popular culture. This brings me back to Ben Shapiro's criti-cism of *Sesame Street*. While he was positioned within the public discourse as a conservative being critical of the liberal bias of the media, the insidi-ousness of his criticism transcends that clichéd position. By denouncing *Sesame Street* for "promoting a self-esteem ethos, the idea that, to para-phrase Barney 'everyone is special'; an unearned self-esteem," Shapiro ap-pears to criticize the show for challenging and unsettling the privilege of white (heterosexual Christian) identity. Given the history of the show and the efforts to challenge, in message and in its opposition to invisibility, the systemic normalization of particular white identities, it is hard not to see his comments as part of a larger backlash against multiculturalism and any effort that unsettles the hegemony of whiteness. Even while *Sesame Street* has historically avoided the substantive realities of the impact of racism on African American youth, whether that be discrimination faced by store owners, police surveillance, or unfair treatment for teachers, the efforts to challenge the denied childhood and to undermine the erasure of youth of color represent an important intervention, one that propelled other shows into greater prominence through the 1990s and 2000s.

Disney and the Question of Color: *A.N.T. Farm*

Beginning in the 1990s, Nickelodeon sought to carve out an otherwise absent niche within commercial children's television.[14] Playing on its brand of putting children first, of challenging parent culture and embracing the diversity that defines the 21st century, Nickelodeon successfully launched several shows that embraced a multiculturalist angle. While seemingly avoiding shows that had black characters, with the development of *Dora the Explorer, Diego, Ni Hao Ka Lan,* and *Brothers Garcia,* replicating the hegemonic practice of inserting race in what is seen as a safe space (the meaning of blackness within popular culture being distinct from that of Asianness and even Latinness), Nickelodeon challenged the televisual landscape, adding immense color and diversity through its programming. While Nickelodeon has taken a multiculturalist approach (almost akin to Fox's challenge to established networks via *Roc* and *In Living Color),* Disney Channel has remained a much more white space. For all intent and purposes, Disney Channel has maintained its larger history of telling stories for and about white children, whether in its princess paradigm or tween enterprise.

Having already graduated Miley Cyrus, Selena Gomez, and Demi Lovato to various forms of stardom, it should be of little surprise that Disney has sought to infuse younger talent as a way to maintain its stranglehold on tween audiences. In recent years, this has increasingly proven difficult given the success of Nickelodeon with the emergence of Miranda Cosgrove and Victoria Justice.

Realizing the increasingly fickle marketplace, Disney has sought to change up the formula in some regard in building a show around a young African American girl, Chyna. *A.N.T. Farm* chronicles the story of three genius middle schoolers who, because of their talents and skills, attend high school as part of its advanced program. While participating in the Advanced Natural Talent Program (A.N.T.), they face numerous dilemmas resulting from their special gifts, tensions with their older schoolmates, and simply because they are kids growing up in a complex world.

Although *A.N.T. Farm* explores these issues among the three main characters, Chyna (the musical prodigy), Olive (the girl with a photographic memory), and Fletcher (the artist), the show is truly a show about Chyna. From the inclusion of her family to the endless opportunities for her to showcase her musical talents, whether it be playing the violin, jamming on the guitar, or singing a familiar pop song, the show is really one that is selling China Anne McClain, who stars as Chyna. According to one review of the show, *A.N.T. Farm* represents a continuation, albeit modified, of the proven formula of Disney's grooming stars of significant marketing potential: "Disney has turned the concept into its latest situation comedy—and a star-grooming vehicle for the very talented China Anne McClain. China, who plays Chyna, is one of the Mouse House's latest singing, dancing mini-Mileys, sure to soon grace lunchboxes and toothbrushes everywhere."[15] While certainly true, with a CD and the back-to-school Chyna accessory package is now available, the significance of this *A.N.T. Farm* transcends the commercial practices of Disney.

The introduction of an African American potential superstar in the tween marketplace, one that requires star power and crossover appeal, is important. Brooks Barnes, in *The New York Times,* describes the qualities required of a tween superstar as follows:

> Creating a breakout tween superstar takes years of careful grooming that hark back to Hollywood's studio system days. Disney, scouring audition tapes and the Web, looks for various elements: presence, a genuine interest in show business and raw talent in acting, singing or dancing. Good looks are a must, but so is a certain blandness. Tween viewers gravitate toward actresses who they think have best-friend potential; the slightest mean-girl whiff can prevent a star-in-the-making from reaching the stratosphere.[16]

Given the history of race and racism, the persistent demonization of African American women as loud, mean, and aggressive, and given the systematic erasure of young black girls from television culture, it is easy to see the ways in which the arrival of *A.N.T. Farm* can be seen as transformative and groundbreaking.

Evidenced by blog commentaries, the prospect of a Disney show starring a young African American girl led to praise and celebration. For example, Kimberly Seals Allers laments the lack of diversity available for youth of color, praising Disney for the creation of *A.N.T. Farm* because of its potential positive impact on African American girls: "As a mother, trying to raise a young black girl with positive self-esteem and self-love for her hair, her body and her mind, it's frustrating that my daughter doesn't see many images of herself on her own favorite channel. I knew things were bad when she begged me to buy her a Hannah wig (it wasn't Halloween) and complained a lot about her own thick hair," writes Allers on a parenting blog. "So I was really happy to see the new Disney show starring the very sweet and lovely, China Anne McClain. . . . And the character has a two-parent home! Whoo hoo! When she says she wants her hair to be straighter and longer and her skin lighter, it breaks my heart. I'm working super hard to do my part to counteract that. But I'm hoping a vivacious, and talented young brown girl on the TV screen every week will help a little too."[17] Allers reiterated this same theme on her own blog, Mocha Manuel, focusing on the show's potential message to young African American girls: "Anyway, I know it's up to us parents to instill in our little brown girls the self-love that the media could never do and to fill the hole of positive images with our own research and resourcefulness, but I'm hoping an A.N.T. Farm and this talented, beautiful, young black girl can help a little too. Are you hoping the same? Why are we still struggling to see positive young black girls on kids TV?"[18] Similarly, Meghan Harvey, who praised the show for a variety of girls, seemed to highlight the show's efforts to challenge stereotypes, especially as it relates to girls and African Americans:

> Smart is Cool—The girls on these shows are all smart girls who make good grades and school a priority, yet they are all cool. In fact the show Ant Farm, centers on the "ANT" program for gifted youngsters who have skipped a few grades including our lead character. And with A.N.T. Farm it's also great to see a super smart African American girl back on the Disney channel! It's about time.[19]

The concerns and hopes here are obviously real, reflecting on the damaging impact of popular culture and society at large on African American identity. It does represent an important intervention in a cultural world that normalizes whiteness as the standard of measurement all while demeaning and devaluing those who come to embody the *other* within the dominant white imagination. According to Ann DuCille, in writing about her experiences with toys and dolls, children's culture is one of hegemonic whiteness:

> Whitewashed by the images with which I was daily bombarded, for most of my childhood I little noticed that the dolls I played with, the heroes I worshipped, and the alter egos I invented did not look like me. The make-believe world to which I surrendered my disbelief was profoundly white. That is to

say, the "me" I invented, the self I day-dreamed in technicolor fantasies, was no more black like me than the dolls I played with.[20]

As such, the introduction of a show centering around a young African American girl represents a counternarrative to the cultural jamming of whiteness, albeit limited, because of broader racial realities and its emphasis on a middle-class sensibility, its elevation of a politics of respectability, and, of course, the difficult path of countering hegemonic stereotypes. Celebrations, notwithstanding, the show replicates what S. Craig Watkins describes as a commitment "to the notion of promoting respectable—or in other words, bourgeois—images of blackness."[21]

The creation of *A.N.T. Farm,* however, should not simply be thought of in terms of Disney's efforts to challenge persistent racist images within American culture or even its efforts to provide black youth with role models and positive representations. It is clearly a marketing strategy that seeks to capitalize on a market share that has ostensibly been ignored by television networks: African American families. Describing it as "shrewd marketing" "at a time when children's channels are working harder to find minority stars," Brooks Barnes highlights the economic calculations here. It is

> Signaling to parents that diversity is a priority. But Nickelodeon and Disney also want to hold a mirror to a diversifying viewer base. "We have taught children to look for themselves," Mr. Marsh said.
>
> Other actresses vying for tween superstardom are Zendaya, a biracial 14-year-old who co-stars in Disney Channel's budding dance hit, "Shake It Up." Coco Jones, 12, is an African-American singer. (Combine Jennifer Hudson with Rihanna and give the results a middle school gloss.) Ms. Jones has become a darling of Radio Disney. Nickelodeon is developing a series around Cymphonique Miller, a 14-year-old African-American singer and actress, called "How to Rock Braces and Glasses."[22]

While writing about Nickelodeon in her fantastic book *Kid's Rule: Nickelodeon and Consumer Citizenship,* Sarah Banet-Weiser's observations are applicable to Disney and, in this case, *A.N.T. Farm,* a show that imagines a world where "race is simply something that 'happens' in a kid's world."[23] Thus far, it has gone to great lengths to avoid racial conflict and tension, all while imagining blackness and whiteness as insignificant in the daily lives of American kids. In this regard, it operates through the commodification of blackness that ultimately reifies the hegemonic practice of reducing race to little more than a cultural or aesthetic marker.

Embodying Ann DuCille's idea of "mass produced difference," *A.N.T. Farm* highlights the broader approach to race within children's television culture (and popular culture as a whole). "Any time representation of race is produced it reflects a stereotype or a narrativizing of a cultural myth about race—even if ostensibly 'positive,'" writes Banet-Weiser. Or as Lisa Guerrero notes, "race merely serves as another kind of 'accessory' that signifies 'hipness,' without incurring the actual costs and consequences of real world racial signification."[24] As such, Disney "employs several different strategies of representing race: race either is represented as hip or cool, as a kind of aesthetic style or it is represented through the lens of authenticity, with 'real' tropes structuring the narrative of the program. The inclusion of explicitly racial images . . . coincides with the exclusion of a specifically racial agenda, so that inclusion functions as a kind of exclusion."[25]

A.N.T. Farm bridges these two themes together, using race as an unspoken backdrop for viewing Chyna all while constructing her as a real breath of fresh air that challenges the less desirable and less positive (yet no less supposedly real) representations of blackness within popular culture. Most importantly, it follows suit with other programs through its erasure of an explicit racial agenda. It lacks even the mere hint of the ways in which the race, class, sexuality, and gender are lived by American teenagers.

In her essay about race, gender, and the Bratz dolls, Lisa Guerrero highlights the complex relationship between children (particularly children of color) and dolls/toys/popular culture. She notes that, at one level, visibility, inclusion, and the ability to see oneself within spaces of play and consumption are important. At another level, given commercial demands and the practice of denying and erasing the real-life realities of race, gender, and class, these representations can be at best limiting, and at worst problematic, all while normalizing whiteness. Guerrero notes in "Can the Subaltern Shop: The Commodification of Difference in the Bratz Dolls":

> As much as the dolls rely on images of difference, that difference relies on naturalized notions of whiteness. The dolls may be succeeding in presenting a new, and much needed idea of difference as beautiful and coveted, but that idea still exists in opposition to the "normal," White beauty that Barbie, and the ideals reflected in her and her world, present. Ultimately, though, it is a start.
>
> However small the impact of a doll may seem, and despite some of the paradoxes of the Bratz's representation of difference, there remains an important oppositional potential about the collection. They have presented a challenge to the Anglocentric version of womanhood found in the arena of

toys that has been dominant since the 1959 introduction of Barbie. They have given face to difference and provided images through which young girls of color might find themselves reflected. And they have begun the work toward opening up a space in the popular imaginary for the normalization of multiracial identities.[26]

A.N.T. Farm, despite its shortcomings, much of which reflects the broader cultural/political landscape and the dubious motives and marketing plans of Disney, illustrates this same important instance of change. The tween world embodies the hyperemphasis on materialism and consumption, yet given the hegemony of whiteness and the lack of diversity, the arrival of China Anne McClain represents an important intervention.

Writing about television's systematic erasure of the civil rights movement and race itself within 1960s, Geneva S. Thomas illustrates the issues of erasure and racially sanitized narratives:

> New '60s-themed TV on the cuffs of controversy around number one box-office hit *The Help* should serve as a racial-GPS on what not to do. Historical inaccuracies and age-old Hollywood white-washing prove a combination clearly worthy of Oscar buzz, and lingering community outrage to tote. In this case, I'm certain black viewers would rather these shows be entirely absent of faux recollections of civil rights America. But does there exist a safe and sturdy middle ground for TV's approach to the precarious text on race? Or should we all lie in the post-primetime beds TV's '60s do-over will inevitably make—the imagined space where blackness has no real true place at all?[27]

A.N.T. Farm, while transforming the landscape of television, illustrates that the erasure of struggle, the denial of racism, and the construction of color-blind world is not limited to the 1960s, but continues into the twenty-first century. *A.N.T. Farm* is not alone as a racially sterile children's world as equally visible with online shows like *The LeBrons.*

The LeBrons: America Dream in a Postracial World

Whereas the shows above offer representations of younger kids and young black females both relatively uncommon within the larger history of televisual representations, efforts to document and explore the experiences of young black males have been more scant. With this in mind, I conclude this chapter by looking at *The LeBrons,* a show that intervenes within the larger history, while at the same time illustrating the potential in Web-based television. Challenging the widespread demonization of black youth, *The LeBrons* attempts to challenge societal stereotypes, denying the ubiquitous narratives that focus on the criminality and sexuality of black youth. Yet, one of the methods that it embraces (like *A.N.T. Farm)* is the erasure of the larger societal context that defines blackness within America; in doing so, *The LeBrons* offers a vision of blackness that is devoid of context and the material consequences of blackness, a step that appeases viewer desire for a black cool aesthetic without the baggage of American racism.

Before the initial episode of LeBron James's new Web show, *The Le-Brons,* begins, viewers get a clear glimpse of the show's purpose: advertising. However, it isn't the typical Web commercial but one that has a character from the show—Biz LeBron—using the newest HP tablet to coordinate his fashion style. The efforts to blur the line between commercials and the show itself are revealing. This is, of course, not the only instance of product placement. Within this short almost seven-minute Web show, Nike, whose commercial "The LeBrons" is the basis for the show, is visible, as are Dr. Dre's Beat headphones, which is interesting given that the show is supposed to be about LeBron's childhood.

More centrally, the show is selling LeBron, a brand that has certainly faced criticism during parts of his career. By focusing on a young man growing up in Akron, the show not only tries to reestablish his roots in Ohio but also tries to humanize LeBron by highlighting his background, where he came from, and the trials and tribulations he faced growing up before stardom. This is made clear in the show's catchy opening theme song:[28]

> You see the lights; the fame. You see the bling; but you should meet LeBron before he became king. Yeah, this is a story kinda like then; my little homie kid growing up in Akron, trying to be an athlete. We can all witness, hoping he can grow up right, handle business. Gotta show love to his friends and fam, world on his back, like an old man. 'Cause if you think he's just a ball player, you got it wrong, player. For real. Life isn't fun and games. Ladies and gentlemen, boys and girls, LeBron James. It ain't easy. . . .

Promising viewers a behind-the-scenes narrative of a less than glamorous childhood, *The LeBrons* works to reconstruct LeBron—through Kid Le-Bron—as a normal, average, kid working hard to live the American Dream. While imagining LeBron as four distinct personalities, the primary vehicle for moral lessons and engagement is Kid LeBron.

Yet, the show isn't a crass infomercial for LeBron and his corporate sponsors. It is a commercial with a narrative and a lot of moral lessons (isn't this

true of all commercial popular culture). The initial show—"The Lion"[29]—
in fact begins with James asking viewers, "Ever heard the saying two wrongs
don't make a right." Providing pedagogical context for both the episode and
the show itself, we initially meet Kid LeBron and his neighborhood friend
as they ride their bikes, only to be chased by a vicious pit bull owned by Ray
Johnson. Terrorized and fearful of this bloodthirsty dog, the kids enlist the
help from Biz LeBron. Athlete LeBron, who is seen shooting baskets, cannot
be bothered to protect the boys because he is too focused on perfecting his
game. Biz, describing the dog as a "gangsta," a "punk," and a "thug," left me
to wonder if this dog represents not a Cleveland Cavaliers ticket holder as
one blogger postulated[30] but a criminal element threatening an otherwise
tranquil community. The use of racialized and racializing terms are revealing in this instance. To describe a dog as thug and a gangsta plays on accepted racial language of black criminality. It reflects a process that not only
contributes to "black social death" but "is characterized by the seemingly
instantaneous social alienation of a delineated category of racially pathologized people."[31]

To combat the gangsta/thug threat, Biz gets a lion from the pet store to
protect Kid and the other innocents within the community. Lion confronts
the dog (we see the lion in what appears to be an interrogation room),
protecting the kids from future harm. Yet, Kid expresses discomfort on
learning from Wise LeBron that lion (a natural predator) will likely kill the
dog. He and his friend wonder if this is just as wrong as the dog inflicting
violence on the kids in the neighborhood: "two wrongs don't make a right."
Whether a message about gang violence, war, or a jab at Dan Gilbert (the
Cavs owner who infamously publicly denounced LeBron for taking his talents to South Beach), it forms the crux of the moral message in the show
about turning the other cheek and doing what is right irrespective of the
behavior of others. Sandwiched in between advertising, it encompasses the
purported agenda behind the show: "to show youths of all ages how to be
a good person."[32]

More subtly, *The LeBrons,* with its deployment of four distinct identities—Wise LeBron, Kid LeBron, Biz LeBron, and Athlete LeBron—attempts
to challenge the hegemonic process that reduces and flattens black identity.
In introducing the show, LeBron notes "It goes back to the four characters
who I feel like I am on a day-to-day basis."[33] It represents LeBron as encompassing multiple identities in an attempt to elucidate the diversity of
blackness and challenge what constitutes an authentic black identity. Greg
Tate encapsulates the context here:

Perhaps the supreme irony of black American existence is how broadly black people debate the question of cultural identity among themselves while getting branded as a cultural monolith by those who would deny us the complexity and complexion of a community, let alone a nation. If Afro-Americans have never settled for the racist reductions imposed upon them—from chattel slaves to cinematic stereotype to sociological myth—it's because the black collective conscious not only knew better but also knew more than enough ethnic diversity to subsume these fictions.[34]

At a certain level, the representations available stand in dialog with a hegemonic paradigm of racial authenticity, which, as argued by John L. Jackson in *Real Black: Adventures in Racial Sincerity,* functions as a "restrictive script" that "limit[s]" an "individual's social options."[35] At another level, the narrative choice to construct LeBron as four distinct identities constitutes a certain level of fragmentation, whereupon individual identities are compartmentalized and treated in isolation. Imagining Athlete LeBron apart from Biz and Wise LeBron reifies hegemonic stereotypes about blackness by maintaining the binary between intelligence and athleticism. More importantly, it undermines his own humanity by erasing his complexity and assigning individual identities to individual bodies.

Like Nike's commercial, the 2011 Web show is hypercommercial. Like its predecessor, it gives viewers a lot to think about in terms of black identity, commodified and otherwise. "The Nike series shows the LeBrons in characteristically 'black' behaviors from signifying stories, or 'baldheaded lies' as they're called, at the dinner table, to macking in the mirror, to dancing to Rick James's 'Superfreak,' including the requisite performance of the robot by the older LeBron brother," writes Lisa Guerrero from Leonard and King's *Criminalized and Commodified.* "It represents LeBron as not only 'hardwood maestro'; he's also funny, entertaining, and can dance well; the unstated implication being, 'just like all black people.'"[36] Yet, "He remains 'safe' because he exists in an immovable racialized space created by the public and the market culture that manages racial panics by locating blackness in confined performative geographies like athletics and entertainment, in other words, in a world of blackness that is understandable because it is the one that exists in the national imagination." While challenging hegemonic ideas, the representation of LeBron as a child, as a moral compass, and as just the average kid reifies dominant ideas about a pathological underclass as well. In imagining as like many idealized white suburban kids (he once played in the neighborhood, dreamed of a better life, and worked hard in spite of moral challenges to make it), he is imagined as not like other kids of color but instead as just another suburban white kid. Yet, he is also different from both a white normative ideal, as a fragmented, hyperblack body, and the pathological black other, represented by the pit bull.

The second installation of *The LeBrons*—"Stay on the Court"[37]—begins just as the initial episode. After the requisite HP advertisement, LeBron James highlights this week's moral lesson: "There is nothing more important than staying true to who you are." For *The LeBrons* being authentic and true means "to stay on the court."

The show begins with Athlete LeBron driving kids and his friends to the local recreation center, where they play a little hoop before heading to the pool. Athlete doesn't stay with the boys because he has to "run some drills and get mine" but before leaving imparts some knowledge to them: "remember practice makes perfect."

Heeding his advice, the boys remain on the court, until the sight of a young girl leads them off the court and over to the pool, where she happens to be along with many other scantily clad females, whose bodies become a point of emphasis for the gaze of the show.

The rest of the episode revolves around Kid trying to get the attention of Li, the young woman who drew the attention of all three boys. Kid, however, has the skills and the mentors to help him. He seeks the advice of both Wise and Biz, who are both depicted as "ladies' men." They are typical of "contemporary representations of black males" as "sex-crazed."[38] Wise fawns after the young women at the pool, chasing after them like a lecherous dirty old man as he announces "all these young girls showing skin." Countless girls, who are mesmerized by his charisma, coolness, and sexuality, on the other hand chase Biz.

Unconvinced by Wise's playbook for winning over the ladies, Kid seeks out the advice of Biz. He encourages him to impress her with his courage by jumping off a high dive. His plan almost works to perfection only to be pushed aside by a fat hairy man named Yogi giving him lip-to-mouth resuscitation, resulting in the following exchange between Athlete and Kid:

Athlete:	How was your first kiss?
Kid: Bluck:	Come on, athlete, you know that doesn't count. I made a fool of myself. I shouldn't have listened to Biz.
Athlete:	He wants the best for you. Maybe you should have listened to Wise.
Kid:	Right! If I'd listen to him, I'd be married with three kids by now.

Athlete:	Yo, stay on the court.
Kid:	You're right; forget about girls. No good at it. I'm good at [*as he rises up for a set-hot jumper*] this.
Athlete:	Stay on the court, kid.
Kid:	I got it, athlete, geez.
Athlete:	Do you?

As he walks away, Li walks toward Kid, telling him, "That was a nice shot. You're a lot better at basketball than you are at diving. How about little 1 on 1?"

Li, like Kid, is a baller, showing her skills as she blows right by him to the basket. Importantly, this final exchange reiterates the show's moral lesson about being true to oneself and not trying to front. His decision to keep it real and to stay on the court is why he ultimately gets the girl. The message is powerful because the narrative constructs an authentic black identity through athleticism and sports participation. To keep it real is to stay on the court. His manhood is tied to his game—on the court and with the ladies, which are imagined as mutually reinforcing. In other words, his success results from his staying true to his identity not as diver but as basketball player.

As with the first episode, *The LeBrons* once again explores the notion of authenticity and keeping it real, erasing the complexity and messiness of identity. "I do think there's something about 'keeping it real' that is about almost flirting with disaster in a certain kind of way. It's about a sort of boldness and a fearlessness that says, 'I'm gonna,' in a sense, 'do me,'" notes John L. Jackson. "I think 'keeping it real' is about saying, 'I'm gonna do what I need to do regardless of how the chips might fall.' I think the irony, of course, is often 'keeping it real' becomes reduced to little more than reproducing the most clichéd stereotypes of blackness, so you're demanding a sense of individualized autonomy, but you're performing it in these very stereotypical ways, in ways that are supposed to mesh with these prefabricated categories of black possibility."[39] Jackson points to the ways in which hegemonic representations of blackness, as evident here, confine identity to athletic performances. "The extent to which Americans use race as a proxy for athletic ability cannot be overstated," writes Reuben May, in *Living through the Hoop*. "Many individuals view black athletes as superior to other athletes. . . . The overrepresentation of blacks in sports . . . reinforces the notion of black males as 'natural' athletes."[40] Worse, by focusing on being true to self and staying on the court, *The LeBrons* further restricts what constitutes an authentic black identity. These narrative scripts are significant given the fact that almost 70 percent of black teenagers see sports as their path to success. *The LeBrons* embodies a racial project that, according to Thabiti Lewis, defines black masculinity "by athletic or physical prowess."[41]

While focusing on staying on the court as it relates to keeping it real, the show also teaches viewers endless stereotypes. Eric, Kid's friend, is one of the show's few white characters. Not surprisingly, he is described as a "boy genius," with his success on the court attributed to his math and science skills ("the hypotenuse is equal to the distance between the net and the ball"). Eric is able to excel because he stays true to himself—as a stereotypical white nerd, which serves him well as he is able to use principles of geometry and physics to swish a 100+ foot shot (albeit straight up in the air). Whereas Kid is successful because of his skills and talents as a baller (black identity), Eric is buckets because of his whiteness. Eric, however, is not the only stereotype.

Li, an exchange student from China, who interestingly doesn't have an accent, has brains coming out of her ears. She is a stereotypical exotic temptress in a skimpy bikini, described by one of the boys as a "Shorty" who "got it good." The show's gaze and its slow-motion effects that look her up to down emphasize her body. She is a hot anime character only; she is not a cartoon. In this regard, she is the embodiment of dominant representations of the hypersexual Asian women. While commenting about Lucy Liu and the ways in which her character (Ling) on Ally McBeal recapitulated long-standing stereotypes of Asian women, Darrell Y. Hamamoto, an associate professor in Asian American Studies from University of California, Davis, described her as "a neo-Orientalist masturbatory fantasy figure concocted by a white man whose job it is to satisfy the blocked needs of other white men. . . ."[42] Present within popular culture, pornography, the sex industry, mail-order brides, and sex tourism, hegemonic white racial framing reduces Asian women to exotic sexual bodies ready and willing to serve the sexual fantasies and needs of powerful, virile, western (white) men. Commenting on beauty norms, and the ways in which discourses of diversity and color blindness erase the consequences and significance of race within our post–civil rights movement, Carrie Smith further elucidates the impact of the hypervisible Asian temptress:

> There is also something troubling about the way that people of color are often labeled as "exotic" and categorized separately from Whites—whether it be in lists of the world's most beautiful people or in pornography. The effect of this segregation is that we now have different norms of beauty that are "racialized." People can now pick and choose which racialized norm of beauty most tantalizes them and fulfills their desires.[43]

The representational confinement for Li is representative of the very limited/limiting depictions—scripts—within *The LeBrons*. "*Scripting*, like stereotyping, often has deleterious effects. Imagine the child has internalized assumptions about his or her existence and has begun to formulate a sense of self by retaliating against misguided projections," writes Ronald Jackson in *Scripting the Masculine Body*. "The child is already contemplating achievement possibilities. Now, consider how empowered that child will be if he or she can come to understand the possibilities are limitless, the range of potential is without boundaries. Unfortunately with its scripts, and its narrative focus on authentic identities, limits those possibilities."[44]

The LeBrons, especially as a self-defined pedagogical—message—show, offers powerful lessons about identity and authenticity. In defining blackness through athleticism and athletic/sexual prowess (and Asian femininity through exotic femininity), the show reifies dominant white racial frames. It boxes in black (and Asian) identity defining success through simply staying on the court.

The LeBrons thus highlights how new media technologies provide modern black athletes (among others) tools to define their own image and message, partially apart from those restrictive scripts yet bound by the dominant discourse and accepted images.

Conclusion

In examining the history of television and representations of African Americans, the range, politics, and ideological spectrum are quite striking. Whether looking at the racist images of cartoons, the postracial fantasies of *A.N.T. Farm* and *The LeBrons*, the oppositional voices of these shows, and counternarratives of *Sesame Street*, it is quite clear that television remains a powerful source of racial pedagogy. Reflecting on identity, community, culture, and the question of race in the 21st century, television is teaching future generations as to the meaning and significance of race. The question with each show is what lessons are being learned.

Notes

1. Fox News—"Elmo & Big Bird Are Too Liberal & Make Gay Boys Want to Be Prom Queens," June 1, 2011, http://www.youtube.com/watch?v=3Ypsojc5vFg&feature=player_embedded (accessed May 18, 2012).

2. "*Sesame Street* Has Liberal Bias, New Ben Shapiro Book, Primetime Propaganda, Asserts," May 31, 2011, http://www.huffingtonpost.com/2011/05/31/sesame-street-has-liberal-bias_n_868887.html (accessed May 18, 2012).

3. "Ben Shapiro VS Martin Bashir on MSNBC," June 3, 2011, http://www.youtube.com/watch?v=5Rmc6PfwKRI&feature=related (accessed May 18, 2012).

4. "*Sesame Street*, the Acceptable Face of Political Correctness," *The Economist* 30 (January 1992): p. A30.

5. Jennifer Mandel, "The Production of a Beloved Community: *Sesame Street's* Answer to America's Inequalities," *The Journal of American Culture* 29, no. 1 (March 2006).

6. Virginia Heffernan, "Sweeping the Clouds Away," *The New York Times*, November 18, 2007, http://www.nytimes.com/2007/11/18/magazine/18wwln-medium-t.html?pagewanted=all (accessed May 18, 2012).

7. Ute Sartorius Kraidy, "Sunny Days on *Sesame Street*? Multiculturalism and Resistance Postmodernism," *Journal of Communication Inquiry* 26, no. 9 (2002).

8. "*Sesame Street*—I Am Somebody," http://www.youtube.com/watch?v=iTB1h18bHlY&feature=share (accessed May 18, 2012).

9. "*Sesame Street*: Will.i.am Sings 'What I Am,'" http://www.youtube.com/watch?v=cyVzjoj96vs (accessed May 18, 2012).

10. "*Sesame Street*: Happy to Be Me," http://www.youtube.com/watch?v=3FCUrNxnCPw (accessed May 18, 2012).

11. "*Sesame Street*: I Love My Hair," http://www.youtube.com/watch?v=enpFde5rgmw (accessed May 18, 2012).

12. Kai Wright, "*Sesame Street* Makes Me Love the Hair I Once Had," October 15, 2010, http://colorlines.com/archives/2010/10/sesame_street_makes_me_love_the_hair_i_once_had.html (accessed May 18, 2012).

13. Angel Jordan, "Loving 'I love my Hair,'" October 21, 2010, http://www.theroot.com/views/loving-i-love-my-hair (accessed May 18, 2012).

14. Sarah Banet-Weiser, *Kids Rule!: Nickelodeon and Consumer Citizenship* (Durham, NC: Duke University Press, 2007).

15. "A.N.T. Farm," http://www.pluggedin.com/tv/abc/antfarm.aspx (accessed May 18, 2012).

16. Brooks Barnes, "Tween Stars Wanted: Must Be Primed for Pressure," *New York Times*, May 10, 2011, http://www.nytimes.com/2011/05/11/arts/television/tween-stars-wanted-must-be-primed-for-pressure.html?pagewanted=all (accessed May 18, 2012).

17. Kimberly Seals Allers, "Will A.N.T. Farm Help My Young Black Girls?," May 23, 2011, http://blogs.babycenter.com/mom_stories/will-an-ant-infestation-help-young-black-girls/ (accessed May 18, 2012).

18. Kimberly Seals Allers, "Hoping an ANT Farm Will Help Young Black Girls. Finally Disney Channel!!," May 23, 2011, http://mochamanual.com/2011/05/23/hoping-an-ant-farm-will-help-young-black-girls/ (accessed May 18, 2012).

19. Meghan Harvey, "A Few Good Role Models—From Disney?," July 12, 2011, http://sheheroes.org/2011/07/a-few-good-role-models-%E2%80%93-from-disney/ (accessed May 18, 2012).

20. Ann duCille. *Skin Trade* (Cambridge, MA: Harvard University Press, 1996), pp. 11–12; Lisa Guerrero, "Can the Subaltern Shop? The Commodification of Difference in the Bratz Dolls," *Cultural Studies-Critical Methodologies* 9, (April 2009): p. 187.

21. S. Craig Watkins, *Representing: Hip Hop Culture and the Production of Black Cinema* (Chicago: University of Chicago Press, 1998), p. 118.

22. Barnes, "Tween Stars Wanted: Must Be Primed for Pressure."

23. Banet-Weiser, *Kids Rule!*, p. 170.

24. Guerrero, "Can the Subaltern Shop?," p. 190.

25. Banet-Weiser, *Kids Rule!*, p. 171.

26. Guerrero, "Can the Subaltern Shop?," p. 190.

27. Geneva Thomas, "Where Does Race Fit in TV's New '60s Stake?," August 24, 2011, http://www.huffingtonpost.com/geneva-s-thomas/naturi-naughton-mad-men_b_934380.html (accessed May 18, 2012).

28. "The LeBrons"—"Theme Song," March 14, 2011, http://www.youtube.com/watch?v=Ekm3jio—AE&feature=relmfu (accessed May 18, 2012).

29. "The LeBrons"—"Lion," April 4, 2011, http://www.youtube.com/watch?v=Q5ZNXp77RhE&feature=player_embedded (accessed May 18, 2012).

30. David Hill, "LeBron's Cartoon Debuts with Life Lessons for All," April 6, 2011, http://www.nbcmiami.com/news/sports/LeBrons-Cartoon-Debuts-119352444.html (accessed May 18, 2012).

31. Dylan Rodriguez, "The Meaning of 'Disaster' under the Dominance of White Life," in *What Lies beneath: Katrina, Race, and the State of the Nation,* ed. by The South End Press Collective (Boston: South End Press, 2007), p. 134.

32. "LeBron James Introduces New Cartoon Series 'The LeBrons,'" January 19, 2011, http://www.huffingtonpost.com/2011/01/19/lebron-the-lebrons-cartoon_n_810832.html (accessed May 18, 2012).

33. "LeBron James Introduces New Cartoon Series 'The LeBrons,'" January 19, 2011, http://www.huffingtonpost.com/2011/01/19/lebron-the-lebrons-cartoon_n_810832.html (accessed May 18, 2012).

34. Robin D. G Kelley, "Looking for the 'Real' Nigga: Social Scientists Construct the Ghetto," in *That's the Joint: The Hip-Hop Reader,* ed. by M. Forman and M.A. Neal (New York: Routledge, 2005), p. 119.

35. John L. Jackson, *Real Black: Adventures in Racial Sincerity,* (Chicago: University of Chicago Press, 2005), p. 13.

36. Lisa Guerrero, "One Nation under a Hoop: Race, Meritocracy, and Messiahs in the NBA," in *Commodified and Criminalized: New Racism and African Americans in Contemporary Sports,* ed. by D. Leonard and C.R. King (Lanham, MD: Rowman and Littlefield, 2011), p. 139.

37. "Stay on the Court," http://www.worldstarhiphop.com/videos/video.php?v=wshhC5UDG21Lf0HXOfov (accessed May 18, 2012).

38. Ronald Jackson, *Scripting the Black Masculine Body: Identity, Discourse, and Racial Politics in Popular Media* (New York: State University of New York Press, 2006), p. 81.

39. "Jonathan Jackson Interview," http://www.upenn.edu/pennnews/current/interviews/111308–1.html (accessed 2011).

40. Rueben Buford May, *Living through the Hoop: High School Basketball, Race, and the American Dream* (New York: New York University Press, 2008), p. 81.

41. Thabiti Lewis, *Ballers of the New School: Race and Sports in America* (New York: Third World Press, 2010), p. 7.

42. Darrell Y. Hamamoto, *Monitored Peril: Asian Americans and the Politics of TV Representation* (Minneapolis: University of Minnesota Press, 1994), p. 74.

43. Carrie Smith, "The New Racism and the Changing Beauty Norm," http://bad.eserver.org/issues/2006/76/raceandbeauty.html (accessed May 18, 2012).

44. Jackson, *Scripting the Black Masculine Body* (Albany: SUNY Press, 2006), p. 100.

Chapter 12

"Black" Comedy: The Serious Business of Humor in *In Living Color, Chappelle's Show,* and *The Boondocks*

Lisa A. Guerrero

As we have seen in previous chapters, the presence of African Americans in television comedy has largely followed the mainstream template of the situation comedy. Within the predictable framework of the sitcom, everyday experiences follow a trajectory of mishap and misunderstanding that can be neatly resolved in 30 minutes and provide a lighthearted moral to close out an episode. Sitcoms rely on an essence of relatability wherein audiences can connect some aspects of their own lives to those they see played out on the television screen. African American entrance into this television form did little to change the essence of this formula. By and large, in the sitcoms centered on black characters in the later part of the 20th century, their racial identity was not emphasized or meant to serve as a primary story point. While their blackness was meant to bring a different style to the format (through music, fashion, and cultural references, e.g.), it wasn't meant to bring a different *substance* to the format. That is to say, for all intents and purposes, the Huxtables were the Cleavers of the late 20th century.

In one light, this lack of attention paid to race could be seen as progress. Black characters could be finally accepted as representatives of the common man. However, in a starker light, this general lack of attention paid to race results in at least two major issues. First, the accepted "commonplaceness" of these characters was, and is, dependent on their ability to closely approximate popularly held notions of what constitutes "common" or "mainstream," in other words, whiteness. If characters' blackness doesn't disrupt the audience's notions of propriety associated with whiteness, then they are readily accepted as representative of the mainstream. In these cases, it is the implied whiteness of blackness on which popular approval is based. The second big issue that stems from this lack of attention paid to race is *the lack of attention paid to race.* Within the format of the basic sitcom, a resolution needs to be reached within 30 minutes. The humor comes from the various, and typically insignificant, obstacles that the cast encounters on the way toward an inevitably happy ending. Rarely do any significant social or political factors, particularly race, play a central, critical role in reaching a resolution in sitcoms, regardless of the racial identity of the main characters. In the world of sitcoms, race isn't explored with any critical lens toward understanding its systemic nature or its larger social impact. Consumers view sitcoms, like so many other media forms, as primarily a mode of escapism. The infiltration of real-world gravity into this particular comic medium is virtually prohibited by both the time constraint and the guiding sitcom principle of relatability.

Most white people in the United States don't think issues of race apply to them, and many people of color deal with the realities of race with constancy in their daily lives that its presence in the brief, constructed moments of levity within sitcoms isn't of particular appeal. Consequently, while sitcoms have provided ever-increasing opportunities for African Americans to establish a presence within television culture, they haven't fully offered an arena to engage race in substantive terms beyond its use to mark diversity through visual difference. The heavy lifting of dealing with social issues, especially race, has largely been left to dramas, either series or made-for-television movies, documentaries, specials, or public television programming. For the better part of the history of modern television, the substance of race apparently was no laughing matter.

In 1977, Richard Pryor tried to change all that with the debut of his show *The Richard Pryor Show* on NBC. The show was a sketch comedy program that largely dealt with socially and politically charged topics, in particular, issues dealing with race. Pryor, along with cast regulars (some of whom also served as writers for the show), including Robin Williams, Paul Mooney, Tim Reid, Sandra Bernhard, and Marsha Warfield, did not steer away from controversial topics but rather directly into them. Racism provided either the main or underlying focus of the majority of the sketches on the show. Unfortunately, viewers demonstrated little interest in confronting the humor of serious topics during their prime-time hour.

Huey, Riley, and Granddad Freeman (left to right) from *The Boondocks* TV show. (Cartoon Network/Photofest)

Subsequently, due to the combination of network interference and poor scheduling that had *The Richard Pryor Show* going head-to-head with the popular family-friendly nostalgia of the sitcoms *Happy Days* and *Laverne & Shirley,* Pryor's show lasted only four episodes. It would be another 13 years before the formula of sketch comedy and race would be tried again.

Color and Counternarratives

In 1990, the new kid on the block network, Fox, which started broadcasting only three years earlier, continued its trajectory of cutting-edge programming to appeal to a younger, hipper audience, a trajectory it had set a course for with *The Tracey Ullman Show* and *The Simpsons,* with the debut of *In Living Color.* The brainchild of brothers Damon and Keenan Ivory Wayans, *In Living Color,* capitalized on the growing popularity of the urban, hip-hop aesthetic and attitude to create a modern sketch comedy show that played willfully with sociocultural assumptions around race, class, gender, and sexuality. As the theme song suggested, "you can do what you want to do . . . in living color." While the show did not take the kind of outwardly confrontational approach toward race of its short-lived forebear, *The Richard Pryor Show*, its use of race generally, and blackness specifically, in building its comedic tableaux had the effect of steering audiences (rather gently) toward engaging assumptions around blackness that lay at the center of so many of the sociopolitical and sociocultural issues that were shaping American society at the time. Again, *In Living Color* was not imagined as topical, satiric comedy á la Richard Pryor's show, but the predominance of a black cultural sensibility within the show made it an equally important intervention into the racial homogeneity of network television.

The blueprint for the show's aesthetic is arguably its most notable innovation, as well as its riskiest in some ways. From its opening, the show foregrounded black urban culture. First, it highlighted hip-hop music, with hip-hop stars Heavy D & the Boyz performing the theme song and with a DJ (SW1) spinning records to play the show in and out of commercial breaks. Secondly, it put a spotlight on hip-hop dancing with its introduction of the Fly Girls who, choreographed by well-known hip-hop dancer/choreographer/actress Rosie Perez, provided interludes between sketches and commercials that showcased some of the most current dance styles and moves from urban culture. And thirdly, the main set where the Fly Girls and the DJ performed, and where Keenan Ivory Wayans would do the opening and closing comments of the show, made a visual impact with its backdrop that was fashioned as the rooftop of an urban brownstone replete with graffiti solidifying the verisimilitude of the urban. There was no mistaking the black cultural and racial identity the show was embracing and bringing into the living rooms of the viewing public. Accordingly, the cast was made up almost entirely by black comedians/actors, with the exception of one white actress and one white actor (notably, the show was the introduction of Jim Carrey to pop culture audiences). It was clear that for the Wayans brothers the concept of being "in living color" was one equated directly to blackness and one they took very seriously.

Along with Jim Carrey, mentioned above, the show was also responsible for launching the careers of a number of black artists including: Jamie Foxx, David Alan Grier, Tommy Davidson, and the Wayans brothers themselves, including younger brothers, Shawn and Marlon.[1] The cause of so many future success stories undoubtedly lay in the wealth of the sketches, several of which are still remembered as comedy classics. Though there is a considerable list of memorable sketches from the show, this discussion will focus on one of the most seminal, "Men on . . . ," aka "Men on Film."

Men on . . .

By almost all accounts, the general lineup of sketches on *In Living Color* would not be considered satire. Most of them are not centered on the critique of a larger social flaw, and there isn't a kind of doubling going on in them wherein a character or trait is being deconstructed or dismantled altogether in its social validity through a comedian/ actor's performance of that self-same character or trait. These are the two central characteristics that define satire, and *In Living Color* doesn't, for the most part, set out to do either of these things. That being said, it is apparent that there were obvious satiric moments within some of the sketches, intentional or not, and while not fulfilling the role of conventional satire, *In Living Color* did provide comedic counternarratives to more mainstream (read: politically correct, neoliberal) television comedy that advanced notions of diversity as long as those notions were middle class, heterosexual, and family centered, and as close to being white as possible. The counternarrative that *In Living Color* showcased elevated diverse voices and not just by the mere fact that most of the cast were African Americans. Race, class, gender, and sexuality were the primary colors in the palette that created *In Living Color,* and though arguably those "colors" were sometimes used in questionably stereotypical ways, their continued primacy week after week made *In Living Color* critical comedy or, as I will discuss later, serious black comedy, even as it wasn't completely black satire. Even so, "Men on . . . " represents a moment of the show that comes close to achieving satiric critique and definitely illustrates the power of counternarrative in the understanding of the nuance of black television.

"Men on . . . " was a recurring sketch that first appeared on the debut episode of *In Living Color* on April 15, 1990. The basic premise of the sketch is a public access show hosted by two black gay men Blaine Edwards (played by Damon Wayans) and Antoine Merriweather (played by David Alan Grier) who offer reviews of various aspects of popular culture, including movies, books, art, and sports from a male point of view. The main focus of the humor in these sketches rests in the ways Edwards and Merriweather's reviews deliberately homoeroticize all of the pop culture objects they discuss. The other central focus of the sketches' humor is the effeminate affect and flamboyant flourish of the two hosts. Wayans and Grier's portrayals of the two hosts relied almost completely on the sociocultural stereotypes of gay men. And while their portrayals of Blaine and Antoine did not appear to come from a point of derogation or derision of gay men, there were still many people who felt that Blaine and

Antoine were damaging to the LGBTQ community. Still others considered the characters small steps in the right direction, if not very complex ones. Either way, "Men on . . . " made an indelible mark on the history of both African Americans in television as well as of diverse representations in television programming.

Looking at specific examples of the "Men on . . . " sketches, there are significant ways in which they can be read as interesting critiques of hegemonic masculinity, the limits of imagined black masculinity, and heteronormativity. In the premiere sketch, "Men on Film," the tenor is established wherein Blaine and Antoine read everything through a lens of gay sexuality. On "Do the Right Thing," Blaine says: "Now I really like little Spike Lee's courage in making this film. I especially like the way he mixed the racial tension with the violence in order to give his message: "Do the right thing. Come on out the closet. Don't be afraid to be who you is. Black. White. Whatever." Antoine: "Uh huh. Ain't that the truth, Ruth!" This kind of malapropped interpretation sets up the laughs within the "Men on . . . " sketches, but they also create unexpected moments of positing alternative narratives against heternormative and hypermasculine social norms that resituate gay narratives as the dominant frame. In other words, the prevailing read of "Do the Right Thing" may not consider sexuality, but for Blaine and Antoine it is an automatic and natural consideration. Through their lens, Spike Lee's movie is clearly a coming out tale that itself has been closeted within the frame of racial tension and violence. The underlying questioning of accepted dominant narratives through Blaine and Antoine's gay-centered readings goes far in challenging the hegemony of heterosexuality within society that effectively erases GLBT voices and perspectives, rendering them socially illegitimate. The typically marginalized perspectives of the reviews offered by Blaine and Antoine in the "Men on . . . " sketches are given center stage, and new legitimacy is constructed around them.

Along with the running theme of gay "reads" (in both senses of the term) placed on pop culture objects that are assumed to be straight or, in the very least, sexually neutral, another component that makes up the framework that runs throughout all of the incarnations of the sketch is the playful, kind, homosocial bond displayed between Blaine and Antoine. This aspect is seen generally in Blaine and Antoine's banter and interaction with one another. They alternately play straight man to the other's humorous innuendos, and they give supportive affirmation to one another's world view through language, both verbal and body, and in nonsexual, physical intimacy through various lighthearted touches and pats. Also, there is usually a small disagreement between the critics included in each episode, with

Blaine frequently disagreeing with one of Antoine's assessments or making a critical comment about him. For example, in "Men on Art," as the two are discussing Andy Warhol's "Marilyn Monroe," Antoine recalls playing Marilyn in his former nightclub act "An Evening with the Stars," "with hairy legs" Blaine adds. This retort clearly upsets Antoine ("Now don't go there!"), and Blaine is quick to apologize. "I'm sorry Toine," he says sincerely. "I liked your little nightclub skits." "Did you really like it?" questions Antoine, to which Blaine definitively responds: "Cross my heart and hope to look like Whoopi Goldberg in my next life" thus ending their spat by reaffirming his affection for Antoine.

The homosociality among men gets foregrounded in these sketches but through a counternarrative of gay homosociality. Blaine and Antoine aren't depicted as lovers but rather as close friends who share a common perspective about the world, a perspective that stems from the location of their sexual identity. This is clearly no different than the socially acceptable narrative of *heterosexual* male bonding except in its sexual starting point. While society normalizes heterosexuality and heterosexual male bonding through things like professional sports' rituals, beer commercials, and the general objectification of women, it simultaneously negates the existence of other models of homosociality that are ordered around different priorities and perspectives. The "Men on . . . " sketches present that homosocial reordering. Again, the "Men on . . . " sketches, like the other sketches in *In Living Color,* aren't rightly defined as satire since social critique does not figure as one of their primary goals. However, the iteration and reiteration of counternarratives like the ones put forth in the "Men on . . . " sketches still serve to challenge the acceptance of the dominant narrative and posit viable narratives that are equally legitimate.

This move of creating spaces of legitimacy for counternarratives runs throughout many of the sketches on *In Living Color;* in the specific case of the "Men on . . . " sketches the resituating of the normalized terms of heteronormativity, hegemonic masculinity, and black masculinity is done quite sharply and to great comedic effect. Beginning with heteronormativity, the queer readings of popular culture from Blaine and Antoine disrupt the assumed stability of heterosexualized meaning within American social orders. While it might be easy to just dismiss the interpretations presented by Wayans and Grier's characters as just jokes, their queering of pop culture does actually point to the fact that *all* narratives are constructed, including dominant narratives, and are therefore unstable in their claims to be the "only," "right," or inherently "natural" narrative and that the marginalization or outright exclusion and erasure of other(ed) narratives neither keeps them from existing nor changes the conditionality of those narratives framed as "dominant." The "Men on . . ." sketches reframe our understandings of social meanings in what could be called a "homonormativity" wherein a homosexual perspective on the social order of things is normalized.

This shift in the lens that determines normativity is also central to the sketches' challenge of hegemonic masculinity, the model of masculinity that is explicitly understood to be the proper model of manhood on which the logic of social interactions rely. This masculinity is considered the standard to which all men are seen to either rise or fall. As Michael S. Kimmel has defined it:

> One definition of manhood continues to remain the standard against which other forms of manhood are measured and evaluated. Within the dominant culture, the masculinity that defines white, middle class, early middle-aged, heterosexual men is the masculinity that sets the standards for other men, against which other men are measured, and, more often than not, found wanting. . . . We equate manhood with being strong, successful, capable, reliable, in control. The very definition of manhood we have developed in our culture maintain the power that some men have over other men and that men have over women.[2]

Under this definition, masculinity is inherently understood to be, in Kimmel's words, "the flight from the feminine." When looking at "Men on . . . ," the displacement of this hegemonic masculinity occurs immediately from the opening strains of the theme song "It's Raining Men" by the Weather Girls. The characters of Blaine and Antoine are played through the feminine and articulated holistically through mannerisms, dress, language, and their desire for men. Blaine's recurrent refrain, "Don't hate me 'cuz I'm beautiful," while aimed at Antoine and their audience as a witty retort, can also be taken as an interesting comment against a system of hegemonic masculinity that would exclude diverse performances of male gender that seek to embrace perspectives and characteristics usually connected to social assumptions around female gender.

This move against hegemonic masculinity also works to reframe notions and representations of black masculinity that circulate within U.S. society. The stereotype of black masculinity in the United States has long been one of violence, brutishness, and hyper (hetero)sexuality. In the sketch, Blaine and Antoine's black masculinity suggests the limits of that stereotypical discourse. But more so than asserting a new image of black masculinity to *replace* the existing stereotype which would simply create a cycle of essentialized reductions, the counternarrative presented within the "Men on . . . " sketches merely introduce the potential for broader reimaginings around the intersections of race and gender.

As with many other instances of African American risk taking on television, the "Men on . . . " sketches fielded their share of criticism. Originally, the network even requested that the bit be cut from the show entirely out of fear of the kinds of viewer disapproval it might engender.[3] And while the sketch did remain a regular part of the show until Damon Wayans's departure at the end of Season 3, network censors asserted increasing editorial control over its content. The sketch also garnered various criticisms from both LGBTQ and black community members. The first group was largely concerned over the fact that as the only recurring gay characters on television at the time the stereotypes on which they relied would have a significant effect on larger social struggles for equality. And those in the second group criticized the depictions of black gayness as overly effeminate and flamboyant as one of the reasons why many black men found it hard to claim a gay identity for fear of being framed in these over-the-top terms.[4]

Admittedly, some of the criticisms of "Men on . . .", while not especially generous, weren't without relevance. In black comedy, it has been a central challenge to straddle the paradox of challenging stereotypes through their (hopefully) strategic deployment without reinforcing or *becoming* the stereotype. *In Living Color,* while straddling that paradox to varying degrees of success, was 100% successful in opening up the potential for black counternarratives to be both funny *and* popular (in consumer terms). And though it would be nine years after its final episode before another black comedy show took on the serious business of race, that show would be worth the wait.

Dave Chappelle's New Millennial Black Satire

Debuting in January 2003 on the Comedy Central network, *Chappelle's Show* became the very embodiment of the notion that "the star that burns brightest burns fastest." Building on some of the commercial foundations laid by *In Living Color,* while taking much of its comedic heart and direction from *The Richard Pryor Show, Chappelle's Show* lasted only three short seasons[5] but in the process became an unprecedented pop culture phenomenon and significantly changed American sociocultural considerations of racial dynamics and our national problem with race.

Unlike *In Living Color, Chappelle's Show* was wholeheartedly black satire. While arguably some of the funniest comedies to ever appear on basic cable television, the heart of that comedy stemmed from a point of social critique. Dave Chappelle deliberately and expertly deconstructed the racial aspects of various social, political, and cultural issues and did so through the creative use of racial stereotypes, histories, and ideologies. Chappelle's deft use of this satiric tactic of doubling (using an idea/characteristic/stereotype in service to dismantling the effectiveness and legitimacy of the very same idea/characteristic/stereotype) allowed him to confront serious racial issues while becoming one of, if not *the* most, wildly popular black comedian the television industry had ever seen. Many of his sketches have quickly become classics: "Clayton Bigsby, the Black White Supremacist," "The Niggar Family," "Charlie Murphy's True Hollywood Story: Rick James," "Playa Hater's Ball," "Ask a Black Dude," and, the focus here, "The Racial Draft."

The Racial Draft

This sketch is introduced at the end of the first episode of the second season. Prefaced with Chappelle's discussion of how mixed race identity always leads people to argue about what (single) race a person *really* is, he suggests we hold a draft to determine the absolute racial standing of individuals. "The Racial Draft" supposes a scenario where racial affiliation can be dislocated from its messy sociohistorical, sociopolitical, and sociocultural implications and be neatly determined by a racial team's willingness to claim you and legitimate your singular racial position. The comedic power of this particular sketch is matched, moment for moment, by its intellectual incisiveness.

The sketch is set up to mimic the pomp of the NFL draft, but instead of determining which football teams new players will join, "The Racial Draft" "will state the racial standing of these Americans once and for all." In Chappelle's vision of "The Racial Draft," the various (and limited) races into which American society has been separated are the "teams" that are vying for the right to and glory of claiming mixed-race celebrities as singularly raced members of their racial team. This basic premise frames one of the central critiques that the sketch builds, a critique of America's deep-seated social anxiety over mixed-race identity. The American desire to stabilize a person's racial identity is an intrinsic component in the maintenance of social systems of stratification and inequality. People cannot socially locate *themselves* unless they can socially locate other people. As a result, mixed-race citizens are troubling to the racial identities of *others* even as they are likely not racially troubled themselves. In Chappelle's "Racial Draft," the humor comes from the ridiculous notion of going so far as to literally draft people into your racial team. However, the implications of this joke are much more significant as they speak to American society's compulsion to put people in their proper (racial) place for the good of the national team. In other words, people are only socially legitimate when they are easily (read: essentially) identifiable. Chappelle emphasizes this important point with the portrait of the team delegates. While the larger delegations themselves seem unremarkable, though clearly determinable, in their racial appearances, the representatives for each delegation *represent* the long-held and easily racially identified stereotypes that define their respective race within the popular imagination. For example, the representative of the black delegation is a garish pimp/hustler figure named Rondell (played in pitch-perfect stereotype by Mos Def[6]); the Latino representative is an exaggeratedly accented woman who is dressed as a cross between a flamenco dancer and a hostess at a Mexican restaurant; and the Jewish representative is a Hasidic Jew. These stereotypical depictions of each race, while long holding discursive power to determine racial identities in U.S. society, are given literal power in the sketch to determine racial identities by being the ones who officially enlist people into their races. The majority of the sketch is devoted to this formal process of drafting by the representatives and informs the second main critique that undergirds the sketch, which is the precedence that *racial* determinacy takes over an individual's own determinate power to define his/her identity. The two moments in the sketch that illustrate this point most instructively are the drafting of Tiger Woods to the black race and the drafting of Colin Powell to the white race.

The first moment comes at the beginning of the sketch when the black delegation wins the first pick.

Analyst Chappelle:	Wow, that's the first lottery a black person has won in a long time.
Analyst Bill Burr:	Yes, and they'll probably still complain (*superficial laughs from all the analysts*).
Analyst Chappelle:	Man, f*** you. It comes as little surprise that the black race chooses Tiger Woods.
Analyst Robert Petkoff:	His father, black. His mother, Thai. Well, that doesn't matter anymore because now he is officially black. Dave, the Asians have got to be upset.

As Petkoff's statement makes clear, Woods has effectively had one aspect of his identity amputated and deemed socially illegitimate in the interest of racial certainty; this interest is meant to be understood as his own when the newly black Tiger states: "I'd like to say, this is a tremendous opportunity for me. To finally be part of a race, have a home. I've been so confused by cabacalasian, so many things . . . ," but his professed confusion and desire for stability stem, not from his own understanding of his mixed-race identity, rather it comes from society's inability to reconcile that mixed-race identity within the strict limitations of its racial imagination. Without a singular, knowable racial location, Tiger Woods is (1) seen as socially disruptive and racially illegitimate and (2) readily subsumed under a neat, translatable understanding of blackness by society, not by *his* choice but by the *will* of society to position him in order to map onto him the routes of race through which both he and the rest of us can navigate the expectations of our social relationships to one another. That is to say, he may think of himself as cablinasian, but society has made him black. And without that racial mandate of blackness, his identity would be unacceptable. So, in "The Racial Draft," Chappelle makes that implicit understanding explicit with Tiger's draft into the black race.

Chappelle goes further into the consequences of society's will to race when he has Tiger losing all of his endorsements as soon as he's drafted by "team Black."

Analyst Chappelle: Well, it seems as though Tiger Woods is happy to be black, and that's a good thing because I just received word that he lost all his endorsements. Ooh, that's a tough one. All of 'em . . . Amex, Tag Heuer, Wheaties, the whole shibangabang. Tough break, nigger. There's always FUBU.

The will to race is not ideologically neutral, nor is it socially inconsequential. When Tiger's identity becomes singularly raced, he immediately becomes the locus of all of the socially constructed transgressive stereotypes associated with blackness, which is to say, he's no longer useful as a commodity marker except for in those markets exclusively defined through blackness, like FUBU. So, in this case, the racial certainty brought on by the draft results in the certainty of taint and transgression. In the next example, racial certainty comes with benefit, privilege, and superiority.

When it's time for the white delegation to make its choice, Chappelle demonstrates the power that whiteness has to create the logic of a racial order in service to the maintenance of systems based on the assumptions of white superiority. In a classic moment of satiric absurdity, the white delegation chooses Colin Powell.

Analyst Bill Burr:	What?! Colin Powell is not white. He's, he's not even an eighth white. He's 100% black.
Analyst Chappelle:	Last I heard.
Analyst Bill Burr:	Wow! I gotta wonder how the blacks are gonna be taking this one? (*Picture of Colin Powell flashes across the screen with a caption beneath it reading: "Colin Powell: Whiteness under Review."*)

This moment of serious black comedy lays bare the overarching power of whiteness in a society predicated on its superiority; it is invested with the power to make all other races irrelevant at its pleasure. Since Colin Powell displays characteristics that the white race translates as its own, they feel entitled to ignore the fact of Powell's blackness and bestow a more proper racial identification of whiteness onto him. The black delegation's response to this white racial alchemy is both comically hilarious and critically incisive.

| Rondell: | (*now at the podium*) We the black delegation accept the white delegation's offer to draft Colin Powell on the condition that they also accept Condoleeza Rice as part of the deal. Final offer.
(*Enthusiastic applause erupts. Then a picture of Condoleeza Rice flashes across the screen with the caption beneath it reading: "Condoleeza Rice: Given Away by Blacks."*) |

For similar reasons to those that make the white race believe that Colin Powell is white, the black race believes that Condoleeza Rice is *not black*. Her assimilation has compromised her ability to be understood as authentically black.

After the white race accepts the deal that makes Colin Powell and Condoleeza Rice white, the black race makes a play to get Eminem. The white race vigorously objects to this proposed acquisition: white representative: "Wait a goddamned minute, Rondell! That's not part of the bargain!" The two delegations do reach a compromise, however. In exchange for Eminem remaining white, the white race returns racial claim of O. J. Simpson back to the black race. This moment of the O. J. compromise puts Chappelle's sharp comedic reflexes on display. The idea that he so deftly clarifies in this moment is that only whiteness, and whiteness alone, has the racial legitimacy and social priority to void other racial affiliations and replace them with whiteness, in other words, assimilation. However, as the exchange shows us, that process cannot be reversed. Even as Eminem takes up myriad aspects of black culture into his identity and even as he is subsequently taken up by black culture and communities as belonging, he can't be black, the fact of his whiteness precludes that kind of reverse assimilation. At the same time, O. J. Simpson's racial positioning can be shifted again and again but only at the whim of the white race. His past demonstrations of white-identified characteristics allowed for a socially valuable ideological whiteness to be bestowed on him (like Colin Powell), but his more recent transgressions can't be reconciled with those assimilative assumptions, so they must be returned to the more appropriate racial location of blackness where transgression is a socially accepted, even *expected*, characteristic. The social primacy that has been historically and ideologically built into notions of whiteness allows it the power to bestow or deny racial legitimacy to everyone else based on their proximity to positive, and socially constructed, assumptions about white racial identity. Chappelle's imagined "Racial Draft" is merely a formal and transparent approximation of processes that happen everyday as we negotiate our society's systems of racial ordering.

The example of "The Racial Draft" demonstrates both the skill and significance of *Chappelle's Show*. Unlike *In Living Color* before it, *Chappelle's Show* fully immersed itself in the mode of black satire with the goal of getting audiences to think critically about sociocultural and sociopolitical issues regarding race while also making them laugh hysterically. Because of this distinction between *Chappelle's Show* and *In Living Color,* the comedic stakes were, in many ways, much higher for Dave Chappelle. While *In Living Color's* innovation of and intervention into mainstream network television were significant in shaping the potential for black comedians and black programming into the new millennium, it did not, at least, not deliberately, challenge viewers' thinking about race in America. *Chappelle's Show* took that task head-on. Unfortunately, it was hard to keep audiences on task. After two short seasons, Dave Chappelle had become a superstar and was entering into the taping of the third season with a remarkable $50 million contract. However, with material enough for only three episodes completed, Dave Chappelle walked away from the pop culture phenomenon he had created. His reasoning, as he made clear in various interviews,[7] long after his abrupt departure, was based primarily in his recognition that people, including the show's writers and producers, network executives, as well as audiences, were missing the point of his comedy and instead were taking the stereotypes he was using satirically at face value only further fortifying the systems and ideas that Chappelle was trying to challenge. It is an inherent risk within satire that audiences will miss the aim of criticality that is embedded inside humor. And when the critical focus is race, as it is with black satire, the consequences of missing the point are the real-world legitimations of assumptions and ideologies around African Americans and other people of color that justify the continued social, political, and economic marginalization of those groups. As with Richard Pryor before him, this double-edged sword of satire proved to be too unwieldy for Dave Chappelle to work on television, but that didn't mean that other black artists wouldn't keep trying to swing it.

Radical Animation

In November of 2005, the Adult Swim channel broadcast the premiere of *The Boondocks,* a show created by Aaron McGruder and based on his comic strip of the same name. The series is an animated program that centers on two brothers, Huey and Riley Freeman, who move to the suburbs, or "the boondocks," with their granddad, Robert Freeman. The humor of the show is built on several main premises: (1) the transplant narrative of taking two black urban-centric youth and moving them to the white suburbs; (2) the generation gap between granddad and the two boys; and (3) the radical race politics of 10-year-old Huey Freeman. The general target of McGruder's satire in *The Boondocks* is very clearly race politics in America. Of particular interest to him are the ways in which the black pop culture industry and black citizens themselves participated in the various systems responsible for the continued marginalization of black people in the United States.

McGruder constructs his satiric critique by positioning 10-year-old Huey as the moral center and voice of reason among a cast of characters who are drawn as either unable or unwilling to make the distinction between the commodification of racial progress and the *actualization* of racial progress. While there is a basic, well-worn element of humor that comes from making a child the smartest person in the room, McGruder's use of it here makes a significant comment. Huey Freeman (emphasis on "free man") isn't the typical wise child character we often see in sitcoms whose youthful innocence allows them to see things in a way that adults cannot, a way that usually proves useful in teaching the adults a life lesson. Huey is intelligent, well read, and, above all, a critical thinker. He actually *is* smarter than everyone else in the room. His characterization as radical is not a kind of simplistic, t-shirt radicalism but rather a substantive, critical black radicalism informed by a deep history of radical figures from Frederick Douglass to Che Guevara, to Malcolm X. It's his critical thinking that makes him truly radical, but it is his age that makes it easy for people to discount his insight. McGruder effectively illustrates the willful societal prejudice against critical thinking in an age of blind consumerism and performative progress by making the critical perspective come from a 10-year-old boy who can be easily dismissed by those around him because of his age.

With this setup of Huey as moral and intellectual compass and everyone else as narrative foils, to lesser or greater degree, McGruder has managed unrelenting indictments against a panoply of black cultural figures and phenomena from R. Kelly, soul food, and hip-hop to BET, Tyler Perry, and the cult of Barack Obama. While these critiques are not tempered in their pointedness, they are shown, again through Huey's positioning, not as deriving from a kind of self-loathing disdain for African American people but rather from an actual deep love for them clouded by a psychic fatigue of watching them, through acts and attitudes, seemingly love themselves *so little*. This critical tension is no more apparent than in the episode entitled "Return of the King."

Return of the King

Airing during the show's first season, and premiering on what would have been Martin Luther King's 77th birthday (January 15, 2006), "Return of the King" was the most controversial episode of the season and one of the most controversial of the entire series. (The episode aired only once after heated public criticism, particularly from Rev. Al Sharpton, made the idea of it being rerun a less desirable prospect for the network.)

As a way of making the point of the episode's critique clear from the beginning, the episode opens with two epigraphs. The first is from Martin Luther King: "I want young men and young women who are not alive today . . . to know and see that these privileges and opportunities did not come without somebody suffering and sacrificing for them." The second one is attributed to anonymous and is meant to be representative of a general attitude within 21st century black popular communities: "Whatever, nigga." Setting up the ideological parameters at odds in this episode between the substance of what black civil rights struggles once were and the surface of what black consumer freedoms are today, McGruder creates a satiric fantasy where the most iconic American civil rights leader of all time returns to an America he helped to create but one that he did not imagine and for which he could not be prepared. The episode centers on the imagined scenario where Martin Luther King did not die in 1968 but rather fell into a coma, only to awaken from it some 30+ years later and be thrust into an American society where his dream hasn't been realized so much as it has been relinquished.

Initially, his return is met with the excitement one would expect for a national hero. This enthusiastic response is short lived, however, once he is seen as challenging the war response to the 9/11 attacks by maintaining his belief in the philosophy of passive resistance. For his attempts to put forth a perspective that had become beyond ill fitting in an era of neoliberalism, global capitalism, hyperconsumerism, and renewed empire, he quickly goes from beloved hero to public enemy (Martin Luther King: "What happened, Huey? What happened to our people?"). As he tries to reconcile himself to a new world where he is more useful as an old image, Huey works to convince him that African Americans need him now more than ever. Trying to rally him into action, Huey yells at him through his bedroom door, where he has refused to get out of bed, "Dr. Martin Luther King Jr.! You get outta that room and continue to fight for freedom and justice this instant!"

As the episode continues, we watch Huey, the young black radical, help King, one of history's definitive black radicals, navigate a new century where the most radical thing many African Americans engage in is consumerism, from iPods to McRib sandwiches (the latter of which is a powerful attraction to which even Martin Luther King is not immune: "Oh, snap. No they didn't. A boneless rib sandwich. What will they think of next?"). Eventually, Huey tries to persuade the dejected civil rights leader ("Huey, I just don't think I belong in this new world.") to form a black revolutionary political party that will tell people the truth "and not the pretty truth. The horrible, awful, terrible truth that hurts people's feelings. The truth that makes people angry and get up and do something." Originally, King suggests that Oprah Winfrey should lead this new party because "she's more popular." In this moment, King acknowledges the hard truth of consumer culture where much more power is wielded by media-made leadership than by cause-driven, grassroots leadership. This moment is one of many throughout the progression of the episode where McGruder's focus is made clear. He is very critical of the ways in which many people in the United States, especially black people, have willingly traded their desire to achieve sociopolitical and socioeconomic justice and equality for their ability to own the latest consumer trend.

Ultimately, the civil rights leader is convinced by Huey to again take the helm in leading black Americans toward new ways of empowerment. But though Martin Luther King is a consummate grassroots organizer, he does lack the necessary 21st century media savvy to make a campaign successful. After Huey tells him that he doesn't "have enough experience with modern media," King proceeds to prove that very point by hiring an urban promotion firm to help get the word out that ends up turning a community "action planning meeting" into an exclusive urban party where, instead of coming together to work for social change, people can go "shake their stankin' ass with Martin Luther King!" The point of the community gathering gets so lost and mired down in pop culture trend and media hype that Martin Luther King and Huey aren't even allowed in when they arrive until they pay the bouncer $50 each. When King tries to tell the bouncer who he is, in essence, the reason for the gathering in the first place, the bouncer responds "And I'm Malcolm X, nigga. You still ain't gettin' in." McGruder further develops his critique here demonstrating how a "style over substance" logic shapes the majority of people's relationships to everything in the 21st century and how in a rampant consumer society value is only determined by the ability of a person or thing, even revolution, to be commodified. People no longer know what it is they want until someone sells it to them; if they can't buy it, it can't possibly be worth it. Especially for black Americans, McGruder is critical of the ways in which they have translated the meaning of political progress into a pleasure principle of consumption. This point is driven home in the climax of the episode when Martin Luther King finally gets a chance to address his fellow African American citizens.

This closing scene was the touchstone of controversy for the whole episode. In it, McGruder depicts King using the slur "nigger" and using it *a lot.* As Huey had told him earlier in the episode, people needed to hear the "horrible, awful, terrible truth," so King goes about telling it.

> Excuse me? Brothers and sisters, please . . . (Huey in a voiceover: King looked out on his people and saw they were in great need. So he did what all great leaders do . . . he told them the truth.) WILL YOU IGNORANT NIGGERS PLEASE SHUT THE HELL UP?! (stunning the crowd into shocked silence) Is this it?! THIS is what I got all those ass-whoopings for? I had a dream once. . . . it was a dream that little black girls and black boys would one day drink from the river of prosperity freed from the thirst of oppression. But lo and behold, some four decades later, what have I found, but a bunch of trifling, shiftless, good for nothing nigger! And I know some of you don't want to hear me say that word! It's the ugliest word in the English language! But that's what I see now! NIGGERS!

McGruder's imagining of Martin Luther King using the "n-word," while unexpected and certainly jarring, does achieve a powerful moment in black satiric television. Like the generations he fought for who have succumbed to the empty equality afforded by pop culture trends, King is finally forced into the only discursive parameters that are still translatable to black people, even in the 21st century, a discourse of contempt. He attempts to make them see that after the freedoms that black people in the past had fought so hard to secure for future generations of African Americans, they, those future generations, have settled for the freedom to not care anymore. Black civil rights leaders, some of whom had participated with King in the movement, criticized the episode's depiction of King using the slur, disrespecting the memory of him and the movement he lead. Yet, McGruder was using the exaggerated, satiric depiction to make people think critically about how their disinterest in strengthening and preserving their own sociocultural and sociopolitical power in a society still based on substantive systems of racial and economic inequality is the real dishonor done to King's memory.

In many ways, "Return of the King" proves Martin Luther King's point to Huey that "I don't think I belong in this new world." McGruder posits the proposition that icons like King are only useful in the 21st century as frozen images that legitimate current apathies by establishing a belief that all of the fighting has already been done. The political goals and strategies that King (the historical figure and the character in this episode) represents are revealed to be irrelevant and ineffective in black communities in the new millennium where definitions of freedom and prosperity are impermanent, shifting at the whims of commodity, pop, and media cultures. At the end of the episode, King leaves the struggle to Huey ("Do what you can.") and moves to Canada. His speech does have the effect of inciting a movement, however. Black Americans become angered with the sociopolitical state of things, and as Huey says, "the revolution finally came." Of course, as a way to punctuate his satiric vision, McGruder has the new revolution culmination in the election of a black president—Oprah Winfrey.

Conclusion

What we see in *The Boondocks, Chappelle's Show,* and *In Living Color* alike is the impulse to foreground race and blackness, even as they do it to different degrees and to different effects. As with many of the other programs discussed in this collection, with rare exception, it is the shows created by black artists and producers that become the singular locus in the landscape of television programming where it is permissible (because it is assumed to be obvious) to address and display issues of race. Black artists and producers are seen as the sole proprietors of topics of race and racism. Naively, and more than a little dismissively, white artists and

producers don't understand race or racism as affecting them and therefore not topics that need be a part of the programs they create. Subsequently, what we also notice about *In Living Color, Chappelle's Show,* and
The Boondocks when considered together as representative of alternative
trends in black television comedy is that they took those racialized assumptions about the purview of race on television as creative challenges
to disrupt the typical models of race on television. Ironically, it was exactly this disruptive racialized character that networks found the most
appealing.

Fox, Comedy Central, and Adult Swim, the networks of *In Living Color,
Chappelle's Show,* and *The Boondocks,* respectively, all used each show as a
means to establish a certain kind of edginess around their network brand;
edginess grounded exclusively in notion of blackness. In each instance, the
individual networks positioned the character of blackness as the conduit
of hipness. While each of these networks represents (or *did* represent, in
Fox's case) a departure from the mainstream, traditional model of the alphabet networks (ABC, CBS, and NBC) that defined television for so long,
as well as the arrival of niche programming and the pursuit of younger,
fresher viewers, their "uniqueness" still relied, by and large, on terms of
whiteness. As a result, these networks identified blackness symbolically as
"the new" element that would legitimate their own positions as "the new,"
alternative response to the "old" models of television programming. But
in the final analysis of these networks' interest in these shows, it was not
what the shows *did* (bring counternarratives and critical thinking about
race to a mass audience) that made them appealing to network executives,
it was what the shows *were,* which is to say, black, that made them useful in
market terms—which are the only terms that count in television. In other
words, networks capitalized on the hipness of the blackness of these programs without relinquishing any power to it. This deliberate exploitation
by the networks of the hip character of blackness is apparent in the lack
of freedom the shows' creators were given by network executives to realize
their programs in their own terms instead of the terms that the networks
deemed more appropriate and most lucrative. In each case, after the initial
and short-lived excitement over the racialized novelty of their programs,
Wayans, Chappelle, and McGruder experienced a tightening of network
oversight on what their programs should be and should do. Eventually, the
network reins became too tight for all of them, and they abandoned the
pursuit of their shows.[8]

The common fate of these three groundbreaking shows illustrates the
ways in which the serious aspects of black comedy in these shows whether

underlying, as it was in *In Living Color,* or in your face, as it was in *Chappelle's Show* and *The Boondocks,* could not survive, at least not in the terms originally imagined by their creators, and also serve the demands of mainstream television culture. In the logic of network television, comedy is meant to be relief and to provide a comforting resolution that reassures the general American audiences that the lives that they lead and the society in which they lead them are inherently well intentioned and easily fixable. Instead, the creative pulse in the comedy in these three shows was a certain kind of discontent, both smaller—with the entertainment industry and its alternating neglect and exploitation of black talent—and larger—with American society and its sustained system of inequality against its black citizens and its other citizens of color. This kind of comedy ends up being ill fitting with the basic goal of network television which is to give the people what they want, which is actually a desire manufactured by the various elements of consumer culture, including network television. So, in actuality, the goal of network television is to give the people what network television *wants* them to want. Conversely, the serious comedy of *In Living Color, Chappelle's Show,* and *The Boondocks* tries to walk the precarious line of giving people what they want (so they'll keep watching) and giving people what they *need* (so they'll start thinking).

As stated earlier, this is the nature of serious comedy of which these three shows are prime examples. Serious comedy, not to be confused with dramatic comedy, or dramedy, is typically satiric in form, providing critique of society's shortcomings through the lens of humor. While always funny, oftentimes scathingly so (again, unlike dramedy), serious comedy isn't humor for humor's sake. And even as it sometimes employs elements of slapstick, it isn't part of a slapstick tradition, rather, its perspective draws most liberally from the structures of the American jeremiad, including lamenting the state of society and predicting the inevitable outcomes of that continued state. For African American artists, these structures are familiar tools of protest that historically have been used to great effect by political and cultural black figures to bring attention to and encourage progress toward addressing America's socioracial issues. Certainly, the character of serious black comedy is dominated by humor and not protest (it is clear that Homey the Clown isn't Frederick Douglass, Richard Wright, James Baldwin, or *The Spook Who Sat by the Door*); it is, after all, still comedy. However, the difference between serious black comedy, like the three shows highlighted here, and mainstream comedy, especially mainstream television comedy, encapsulated by the sitcom formula, is in serious black comedy's refusal to let its audience off the hook. The laughs aren't dislocated from the viewers as they can be in sitcoms. The laughs found in serious black comedy are, more often than not, uneasy, requiring viewers to question what it is they're laughing at and why they're laughing (even if that questioning is momentary). Viewers are implicated by serious black comedy, which is one of the biggest reasons why programs that try to stay true to the character of serious black comedy have a difficult time staying on the air. Generally, people don't want to devote their perpetually shrinking free time to having their comedy point out the extent of society's flaws, let alone feel guilty about one's participation in creating those flaws or think about ways to fix them. They simply want to laugh. And while the creators of these programs were definitely able to make people laugh with their comedy, it seemed not everyone got the joke.

Notes

1. The show was also responsible for launching the career of the hitherto unknown Fly Girl, Jennifer Lopez.

2. Michael S. Kimmel, "Masculinity as Homophobia: Fear, Shame, and Silence in the Construction of Gender Identity" in *The Social Construction of Difference and Inequality,* ed. by Tracy E. Ore (New York: McGraw Hill, 2011), p. 137.

3. George Alexander, *Why We Make Movies: Black Filmmakers Talk about the Magic of Cinema* (New York: Broadway, 2003), p. 143.

4. J.L. King and Karen Hunter, *On the Down Low: A Journey into the Lives of 'Straight' Black Men Who Sleep with Men* (New York: Three Rivers Press, 2005), p. 22.

5. Only the first two seasons had the official approval of Dave Chappelle. Three episodes, advertised as the *Lost Episodes* by Comedy Central, aired in July 2006 against the wishes of Dave Chappelle. These three episodes were made up of the sketches Chappelle had been working on for Season 3 of *Chappelle's Show* before his decision to leave the show. These episodes are cohosted by *Chappelle's Show* regulars, Charlie Murphy and Donnell Rawlings.

6. In 2011, musician/actor Mos Def changed his name to Yasiin Bey.

7. See, among others: Christopher John Farley, "On the Beach with Dave Chappelle," *Time Magazine,* May 15, 2005. Lisa de Moraes, "Dave Chappelle, Rematerializing Guy," *The Washington Post,* February 4, 2006. Devin Gordon, "Fears of a Clown," *Newsweek,* May 16, 2005. Josh Wolk, "Chappelle's No-Show," *Entertainment Weekly,* May 11, 2005.

8. It was announced in 2011 that *The Boondocks* would return for a fourth season on Adult Swim in 2013, after going off the air in 2010.

Chapter 13

Selling Blackness: Commercials + Hip-Hop Athletes Hocking Products

Regina N. Bradley

In 1984, soda powerhouse Pepsi used Michael Jackson to headline its burgeoning "Pepsi: The Choice of a New Generation" campaign. The video opens with a quick cutaway to Jackson's iconic wears clothes, which included his studded glove, white socks, and black shoes ensemble. This is followed by a group of children dancing to a remix of Jackson's smash hit "Billie Jean." The children, members of what Pepsi labeled "the Pepsi Generation," dance in front of a still unnoticed Jackson who is joined by the Jackson 5. They mock Michael Jackson's signature dance moves all while drinking Pepsi, visually linking their childhood playfulness and joy to the product. A young Alfonso Ribeiro, dressed like Jackson from his "Beat It" music video, performs Jackson's signature moonwalk dance. While moonwalking and drinking Pepsi, he bumps into Michael Jackson. Ribeiro, wide eyed and amazed, begins to dance with Jackson while he and the other children interact with the Jackson brothers. The commercial's chorus, "you're the Pepsi Generation," suggests a transcendence from past racial politics into a new multicultural social climate where blacks and whites are (finally) on an even playing field. This is most visible in Pepsi's use of children actors, an allusion to childhood innocence, starting anew, and the untainted possibilities of the 1980s and beyond as post–civil rights and postracial. Pepsi plays up the trope of capitalistic multiculturalism through Jackson, suggesting both black and whites can enjoy their product because Jackson—a crossover black (American) cultural icon—endorses it.

Jackson embodies the shifting representations of commercial blackness in the 1980s American imagination. He would come to signify blacks' ability to secure the American Dream and wealth, to embody and represent upper-class white privilege. Jackson seemingly breaks the glass ceiling for African American television pitchmen, resulting in the dissemination of blackness throughout the globe. Aside from Jackson's music, his endorsement of products like Pepsi suggests the accessibility and desirability of blackness to a multicultural, global audience. The use of enterprise to peddle blackness to a post–civil rights audience reflects an attempt to situate a shifting black identity removed from blatant racism into America's new multicultural narrative.

Buying blackness allowed for the consumption of black identity without acknowledging its historical and sociocultural impositions. This shift embodies what Eduardo Bonilla-Silva refers to as "color-blind racism." Bonilla-Silva writes, "because post-1960s racial practices tend to be covert, subtle, institutional, and apparently non-racial, white privilege is maintained in a 'now you see it, now you don't' fashion.'"[1] The burgeoning visuality of a black middle and upper class within popular television shows like *The Cosby Show, The Fresh Prince of Bel-Air, A Different World,* and *Family Matters* further cemented the belief that racism against blacks was deteriorating if not nonexistent. Celebrating blacks' access or crossing over to the comforts of a middle- and upper-class lifestyle of privilege once believed to be inaccessible to African Americans, television highlighted the idea that the civil rights movement had changed America. These shows reassured multiculturalism's progressive agenda. Characters like *Family Matters'* Carl Winslow, a police officer, and *The Fresh Prince of Bel-Air*'s Phillip Banks, a judge, embodied the progress of black participation in the opposite side of the law enforcement. Considering the stymied relationship between blacks and law enforcement, it was important for these shows to highlight black participation in law and order. These shows suggested nonwhite participation in the pursuit of post–civil rights American Dream.

Irrespective of the teachings of television, not all African Americans believed in the arrival of black privilege in the United States. In conversation with the Huxtables, Bankses, and Winslows were NWA, Compton Most Wanted, Ice-T, and Public Enemy. Hip-hop culture, especially rap music, provided insight into a working-class black experience minimally affected by the benefits derived from the civil rights movement. Nicknamed "the black people's CNN" by Chuck-D, rap music provided an alternative experience of post–civil rights blackness by speaking about the angst of inner-city life. America's crack epidemic, high unemployment rates, and questions about reverse discrimination due to kickback about affirmative action legislation are paired with how civil rights legislation presents a small niche for black progress. These themes were especially prevalent in the genre of gangsta rap, a nihilistic and impoverished portrayal of working-class blacks focused on the West Coast of the United States. With antiestablishment theme songs like NWA's "F*** the Police" and Ice-T's "Cop Killer," gangsta rap pushed an uncomfortable—yet wildly profitable—representation of black poverty in America. The visual component of gangsta rap, hood films, escalated rap music as the authentic voice of the black working class. The 1991 film *Boyz in the Hood* merged the gangsta rap aesthetic and film, introducing young Ice Cube of NWA fame as the conflicted yet dynamic character Doughboy. The explosion of gangsta rap, hood films, and black television speaks to America's sliding sociocultural landscape.

The entry of hip-hop into the mainstream prompted outrage and racial anxiety through the 1990s. Yet, shows like *The Fresh Prince of Bel-Air* would ease this cultural backlash. Starring rapper Will Smith, *The Fresh Prince of Bel-Air,* embodied the potential to use hip-hop as a safe vehicle for the commodification of a new black aesthetic. This is embodied in the show's opening bit, where Smith raps providing a juxtaposition of his inner-city background in Philadelphia with the elitism of the Bel Air community where his aunt and uncle reside. Smith's movement to the West Coast doubly signifies the transition of hip-hop as a black thang to a multiculturally consumed entity. The series revolves around Smith's affiliation with hip-hop through his use of slang, fashion style, and friends. Smith's rapping partner and deejay DJ Jazzy Jeff has a reoccurring role as Smith's friend Jazz. *The Fresh Prince of Bel-Air* is arguably the transitional piece of hip-hop into television culture. It makes room for other shows featuring rappers like LL Cool J (*In the House*), Queen Latifah (*Living Single*), Ice-T (*New York Undercover, Law and Order: SVU*), and Reverend Run of Run D-M-C (*Run's House*). It is important to note, however, that although Smith and *The Fresh Prince of Bel-Air* are markers of hip-hop's crossover into mainstream television they were complemented by hip-hop–focused shows like *Yo! MTV Raps* and BET's *Rap City,* which showcased rap music and videos. These shows are important in understanding the sliding focus of hip-hop culture and its audience, reflecting shifting frameworks of *what* hip-hop means to different, and often conflicting, groups of consumers. The conflicting narratives of what can be considered a contemporary black experience are embodied in commercialized black performance seen through television. The narratives presented by television shows and rap music present conflicting ideals and realities of the smaller moments that make up what Americans understand as post–civil rights. In thinking about hip-hop's role in this seeping of commercial blackness, one must consider in what other arenas of television visual culture did hip-hop and commercial blackness intersect. One of the most illustrative spaces of televisual articulations of hip-hop came in the arena of sports.

Late 20th-century black athletes were representative of these intersections, frequently teetering between the exploitation and profitability of their blackness and talent and social responsibility.

While not uncommon to see black athletes in televised college and professional sports today, the increasing visibility of black athletes dates back to the 1980s. By the 1990s, the paradigm of race-neutral athletes embodied by O. J. Simpson and Michael Jordan had been partially pushed aside for the sake of youth culture and its efforts to sell an urban hip-hop aesthetic. For many of these athletes, hip-hop and youth culture are interchangeable, often being described by commentators and spectators as reflections of hip-hop culture. These athletes' visibility doubly served as portals of accessibility to blackness by nonwhites as well as commercial viability in the American marketplace. In commercializing the black athlete, one must also layer his image with another commodified representation of blackness, rap music. Thus, the "hip-hop athlete"—an athlete who consumes, whose popularity came to pass during, or who is associated with the crossover success of rap music in America—complicates intersections with the American popular imagination and race politics. Richard Schur's definition of hip-hop is particularly useful in framing the hip-hop athlete's prominence in the American imagination: "hip-hop is relentlessly engaged with the world of sounds, images, texts, and commodities through which African Americans and others experience contemporary life."[2] Schur provides a multifaceted understanding of hip-hop as a commodified cultural medium, underscoring the ways that athletes grapple with similar themes.

Aside from televised sporting events, the increasing visibility afforded to athletes resulted from the reliance on (black) athletes to sell products within commercials. The commodification of the black body seen in current television commercials reflects the significance of a capitalistic lens used to frame this current moment of American culture. David Leonard points out how commodification of black culture is particularly embodied through the hypervisibility of professional black athletes. Leonard writes:

> The hyper commodification of the contemporary black athlete, alongside expansive processes of globalization, growth in the profitability of black bodies, and their importance within colorblind discourse, demonstrates the importance of commodification within our new racist moment . . . In the context of new racism, as manifested in heightened levels of commodification of Othered bodies, racial identity is simply a choice, but a cultural

marker that can be celebrated and sold, policed, or demonized with little questions about racial implications . . . Blackness, thus, becomes little more than a cultural style, something that can be sold on Ebay and tried on at the ball or something that needs to be policed or driven out-of-existence.[3]

In framing black athletes through a literal and figurative commercialization of their bodies, these commercials highlighted the relationship between race, commercial culture, television, and post–civil rights politics.

The Rise of the Hip-Hop Athlete

The hip-hop athlete jarringly arrived in 1991 with the emergence of the University of Michigan's all-freshman—and all black—starting lineup, known as the Fab Five. Jalen Rose, Chris Webber, Juwan Howard, Ray Jackson, and Jimmy King redressed the college basketball player, donning baggy basketball shorts, shaved heads, and black socks. The working-class background of many of these players further forced renegotiations of black athletes. In the documentary *The Fab Five* (2011), Jalen Rose adamantly spoke out against collegiate institutions like Duke University because it discriminated against inner-city prospects. Rose states: "for me, Duke was personal. I hated Duke and I hated everything I thought Duke stood for. Schools like Duke didn't recruit players like me. I felt like they only recruited black players that were Uncle Toms . . . they [black basketball players like Grant Hill] are who the world accepts. And we [inner city basketball players] are who the world hates."[4] Rose and his teammates' critique of college basketball recruiting bias paralleled similar critiques offered by many rappers about the erasure of working-class black identity from the larger American narrative. As John L. Jackson points out in *Real Black* (2005), "hip-hop is considered a rendition of performative blackness with roots in everyday urban struggles against marginalization."[5] In this sense, the Fab Five embodied the aesthetic and politics of the hip-hop athletes in that they demonstrated the need and desire to highlight the experiences of the black middle and working class.

They also aligned themselves with hip-hop through actual consumption, catching media attention for preferring to listen to gangsta rap music before games to get hype and rocking baggy jeans, fitted caps, and other styles influenced by hip-hop culture. Major corporations like Nike, who sought to capitalize on the Fab Five's hip-hop flair, embraced their commercial appeal in an effort to sell black socks and other elements of this emerging hip-hop aesthetic. This commercial exploitation by Nike of the Fab Five—who claimed to never get any compensation for the use of their image in Nike's ad campaigns—complicates not only their blackness but also its use as a marketing tool for mass consumerism.

Nike's commodification of hip-hop and black cool represented by the Fab Five were not a one-time occurrence, however. Michael Jordan changed the nature of commercial television long before the Fab Five. Jordan is the predecessor of the hip-hop athlete. His mass appeal and international stardom were solidified with his endorsement deals with McDonalds, Nike, Gatorade, and Fruit of the Loom. Indeed, Jordan's face (and blackness) was highly visible in the late 1980s and 1990s.

Jordan connects to the hip-hop athlete through time, winning his first championship with the Chicago Bulls in 1991, the same year as the introduction to the Fab Five and within the throws throes of gangsta rap music's crossover appeal. While not directly affiliated with rap music, Michael Jordan's image intersects with shifting representations of race, capitalism, and the American popular imagination. Jordan's imprint is visible in style and aesthetic, with his baggy basketball shorts and baldhead, and line of shoes known as the Air Jordan series with Nike, would also come to define a hip-hop aesthetic. Similar to Michael Jackson, Jordan's blackness is made accessible and consumable by a multicultural audience because of the products he hocks. He is aware of his brand and his audience, effectively demonstrated in his endorsement commercials. For example, Gatorade's "Be Like Mike" commercial series in 1992 offered a smiling and happy Jordan, who can be seen laughing, goofing around with children athletes, and drinking Gatorade. Lisa Guerrero writes:

> The brilliant simplicity of Gatorade's "Be Like Mike" campaign is, perhaps, the best example of the effectiveness of the racially transcendent quality of Jordan and his image. Immediately, the intimate identification of Jordan as "Mike" creates an everyman quality to the marketing. Mike's your friend; he's your buddy; he's *just like you. . . . only better* because he defies common athletic expectations, both of physicality and of character, (he even defies gravity); he's rich and successful; and he's a role model. At the same time that he is presented as the "common man," a characteristic typically limited to whiteness, in his simple perseverance for achievement and success, he is also shown to be an superlative example; it's not just that everyone, regardless of race, age, or gender, *can* dream about being that exceptional, it is that they *should* dream about being that exceptional.[6]

Jordan's image is situated between capitalism and the idealized multicultural American Dream. The "Like Mike" commercial suggests the common denominator for a consumer's likeness to Jordan, and his awesome skill set is drinking Gatorade. It is within these commercials that multiculturalism once again takes center stage, with black and white basketball players imitating Jordan's signature move—sticking his tongue out to dunk—all while incorporating footage of their shots with Jordan's game footage. Jordan presents himself as accessible by working out with the children, practicing dribbling skills and free throws with them. The lighthearted accompaniment fits the lightheartedness of the commercial, showcasing a children's choir singing "I dream I move/I dream I groove/Like Mike/I wish I can be like Mike." Jordan's identity and blackness are intertwined with his brand and its sales. Unlike the Fab Five, Jordan heavily benefited from his endorsements, raking in more than $55 million to date. Guerrero states:

> Though it was unquestionably trendy to want to "Be Like Mike" in the 1990s, that kind of hero worship of a black athlete by both fans and Wall Street was really a late 20th century phenomenon. No one had ever sold product and American Dream ideology by saying that they wanted to "Be Like Jackie," or Satchel Paige, or Wilma Rudolph, or Jack Johnson, or John Carlos and Tommie Smith. It wasn't until the original number 23 stepped on the professional hardwood and put a strangle hold on the American popular imagination that a black athlete could be conceived, in both ideological and market terms, as a living embodiment of the American Dream fantasy.[7]

Michael Jordan is arguably the first post–civil rights athlete to highlight the potential in the commercialization of black athletes, a relationship that proved to be a mutually beneficial investment between corporations and the athletes themselves.

Post-Jordan athletes depend on corporate endorsements as well. This dependency is twofold: it maintains the athletes' relevance as well as financial gain. Hip-hop culture further brands black athletes, usually through sonic accompaniment—sampling from rap music or instrumental hip-hop beats. Hip-Hop in these forms reemphasizes the athlete's blackness and, to an extent, youthfulness. In several commercials, such as Gatorade's "What's G" (2007–2010), hip-hop is represented in the voice-overs of rappers like Lil Wayne and David Banner. These rappers describe training regimes and performance of Dwyane Wade, Kevin Garnett, Serena Williams, and Michael Jordan. "What's G" parallels Gatorade "I Can Be Like Mike" commercial, yet its deployment of youth culture, athletic performance, and hard work is through a hip-hop vehicle, evident in its usage of its lexicon—"G": gangsta. Hard-hitting drum kicks, sampled snippets of cheering and clapping fans, and synthesizers emphasize the athletic performance of the black athlete and his or her blackness. This is especially relevant in positioning the black male athlete within popular cultural consumption. The hardness of the accompaniment in these types of commercials frequently reflects the hardness of the sport and thus the hardness of black manhood.

Gatorade deployed hip-hop athletes to engage their consumers with the possibility of achieving similar athletic prowess and greatness as these superstars. By pairing clips of dunks, goals, and touchdowns by professional athletes with local, everyday talent like high school athletes, Gatorade incorporated athletes as a portal, bridging their products with hip-hop thereby selling not just a drink but also ideas of race within popular imagination. Simply, Gatorade sells the idea that using their products creates a link to celebritydom.

Further, in thinking about how sports are a primary lens to frame race politics today, the hocking of mass-consumed products like Gatorade by hip-hop athletes highlights the profitability of one-dimensional, commodified blackness. The profitability of hip-hop athletes from a strictly athletic lens lies in the mutual investment of the athletes' willingness to endorse and perform as such as well as consumer's reaffirmation of this uncomplicated black identity. To an extent, hip-hop athletes' lack of complex black humanity is a reflection of the similarly flat and static representations of black humanity in commercial hip-hop. The challenge for black and white consumers, then, exists not only in the flattened representations of black athletes and rap but confronting the problematic nature of these representations. The high volume of visible black athletes reemphasizes the belief that the success of black athletes confirms a postracial moment, thereby the ideological and historic message embedded in these commercials. Class disparities and persistent racial inequalities become obscured by the consumption of products endorsed by black athletes.

Because athletes like Kobe Bryant, LeBron James, and Dwyane Wade are heavily endorsed by major corporations for their talent and blackness, they are showboated as representations of blacks' accessibility to white privilege. This demonstration of privilege envelopes what Bonilla-Silva categorizes as "whiteness stretched out and . . . seemingly inclusive."[8] This subtler representation of white privilege, then, is distributed in America's popular imagination as money. Hip-hop celebrity athletes are heralded as privileged and retain this visibility because they fulfill the expectations of white privilege extending to nonwhites. They are validated by their product endorsements. Jelani Cobb astutely points out the significance of deal and contracts for commercial rappers that can be extended to athletic spokespersons: "a rapper without a contract is a commercial without a timeslot."[9] Seeing that a chunk of celebrity athletes' visibility is literally configured within television commercials, a lack of endorsements results in a minimization of their presence, influence, and cash flow. Athletes are validated by how many products they endorse.

However, black celebrity athletes dangerously tread between expectations of pathological black manhood and self-actualization. Attached to this dangerous treading is capitalistic pursuit. Consider, for example, Kobe Bryant and Tiger Woods. Bryant, after being accused of rape, lost many of his endorsements and was quickly reduced to a black rapist with an insatiable sexual appetite. Similarly, Tiger Woods's extramarital affairs ended many of his endorsement deals, including an animated Gatorade commercial series focused around young Tiger learning to focus using Gatorade's newest line of products "Focus." The complication of such tricky negotiations results in black celebrity athletes being considered what William Rhoden calls "$40 Million Dollar Slaves." The capitalization of the black athlete's body and discourse surrounding black male athletes restrict athletes' ability to define their own identities. LeBron James is a strong example of such tensions, which are chronicled through his history of product endorsements and sponsorships.

Before James was selected as the number one draft pick in the 2003 NBA draft, he inked a $93 million endorsement deal with Nike. Similar multimillion dollar deals quickly followed, including Sprite, State Farm, and Vitamin Water. James's youthfulness, joking demeanor, and quick smile were powerful selling points as a product spokesperson. James's blackness is commercialized and, unlike Michael Jordan before him, is limited to basketball to authenticate his black identity. Lisa Guerrero points out this distinction between James and Jordan as a gauge of marketability:

> Unlike Jordan who didn't really market "blackness," except in the implicit, and highly contentious connections made between basketball and blackness, and who was marketed *beyond* blackness, always selling the "raceless" fantasy of meritocracy and excellence, LeBron is marketed differently; he is marketed *through* blackness, albeit a blackness that is largely performative. With LeBron, blackness isn't erased; in fact, part of his marketing power relies on his ability to play to America's (especially white America's) expectations of their "familiarity" with blackness.[10]

This is especially prevalent in James's State Farm ad campaigns. Each commercial series riffs off black cultural mediums of the dozens and hip-hop.

In one ad, James and friend are walking to the friend's car after a night out. They see the car is vandalized. The friend attempts to reach his insurance agent with little luck. James proceeds to chide his (noncelebrity) friend for not having State Farm. James then notices a *Kid 'n' Play* album on the ground, which the robbers overlooked. James teases his friend about still listening to *Kid 'n' Play* nearly 20 years later. The friend tries to suggest that the CD is not his, while James continues to joke (known in slang as "joning") on his taste in music. The commercial ends with James and his State Farm agent doing the "Funky Charleston," a dance made popular by *Kid 'n' Play* in the early 1990s. James's connection to hip-hop here is through *Kid 'n' Play,* a popular rap duo from the early 1990s who starred in the popular *House Party* film series. Using *Kid 'n' Play* paints rap and James as entertaining and multiculturally friendly. This friendliness presents him as accessible and thus capable of persuading his fan base and television consumers watching his commercials to buy into the accessibility of State Farm insurance.

James's media darling status, however, shifted drastically in 2010 after *The Decision,* a marketing ploy highlighting James's departure from the Cleveland Cavaliers to play for the Miami Heat. James announces his intentions to "take his talents to South Beach." In the audience are a group of children from the local YMCA. James's audience is a powerful signifier of his transcendence from local Ohio celebrity to international superstar. *The Decision* is LeBron James's last stand as an accessible, friendly, Ohio basketball player. He removes himself from the common and is thrust into a global marketplace. As David Leonard asserts, "unlike with Michael Jordan, in which the populace was told 'to be like Mike,' LeBron's greatness, his god-like status (he is King James) not only render being like him impossible . . . but concludes that surveillance as control is superfluous—we as fans should merely witness and enjoy his greatness."[11] *The Decision* pushes James past personable into a commodity. The critical uproar surrounding James's decision to make his trade negotiations an epic media event further indicate this shift in James's career from an upcoming basketball phenomenon to a franchise player. The emphasis here is *franchise. The Decision* marks James's arrival to matching Jordan's iconic status, presenting himself as a profitable brand. The difference, however, is James's showboating of this achieved iconicity—and its simultaneous embrace and criticism. David Leonard embraces the "King James" moniker, pivoting on enterprise and expected performativity of his blackness. James's royalty lies within the conflict of his visibility as a brand and his personal narrative, which his immediate post–*The Decision* endorsement commercials suggest.

In an attempt to combat or possibly utilize the sharp turnaround in James's popularity, Nike released the "Who Am I" commercial series to precede the release of James's latest cycle of shoes. In one of the first commercials, "What Should I Do," James openly addresses his critics. James replays the staging of *The Decision;* he is staged, alone and contemplative, in an interview chair surrounded by cameras. The cameras suggest James's awareness of his hypervisibility. Instead of answering questions from an awaiting press, he is focused and immersed in his own thoughts. James proceeds to look directly in the camera and asks, "what should I do?" He then proceeds to ask a series of animated rhetorical questions, including riding through what appears to be downtown Cleveland, addressing an empty hall of fame dinner and asking "should I really believe I ruined my legacy?," dressing like an old Western villain asking "should I accept my role as a villain?," and asking before abruptly fading to blackout screen "maybe I should just disappear?" ("what should I do?"). James's covers also speak to not only a vulnerability of self-definition but image constriction placed on him by his endorsements and career as a celebrity and hip-hop athlete. The ad is an acknowledgment of James's understanding and conflict with being a brand and commercialized black body. This vulnerability and lack of ownership is reflected in the multiple streams of voices and thoughts that clash throughout the ad. The overlapping streams of James's commentary reflect the overwhelmingly numerous expectations placed on him. These expectations, however conflicting, are still unified under the umbrella of James's cultural and capitalistic worth. He is still trying to sell shoes and thus hocks his products through hocking himself.

A lingering question that remains is television's role in framing the consumption of the hip-hop athlete. Outside of television commercials, hip-hop and athleticism are bound and branded by television networks like ESPN. Its popular debate show *ESPN: First Take,* for example, has revamped itself to market its debates using current rap singles and classics by artists like Swizz Beats, Ice Cube, Eric B. and Rakim, and Travis Porter. They have also had rappers like Wale, Lil Wayne, 2 Chainz, and Ice Cube sit at the debate desk as sports commentators and promoting their brand and products, further blurring commercial hip-hop and athletic discourse. Representative of rap and sports' symbiotic relationship within the popular imagination, *First Take* uses rap to validate its cool factor. ESPN uses rap music and rap artists to brand themselves as hip and culturally in tune with blackness while peddling to a multicultural audience.

The hip-hop athlete is the latest manifestation of hip-hop's commercial appeal to a multiethnic audience. They reflect sliding ideas of contemporary commercialism and blackness because of their high profitability and therefore validity in America's marketplace. Hip-hop athletes are the most visible representation of clashing ideals of blackness and commodification, frequently succumbing to corporatized narratives of black humanity seen in sports and hip-hop. These tensions of black complicity and profitable blackness frequently play out on television and therefore America's popular imagination.

Notes

1. Eduardo Bonilla-Silva, "'New Racism,' Colorblind Racism, and the Future of Whiteness in America," in *White Out: The Continuing Significance of Racism,* ed. by Eduardo Bonilla-Silva and Ashley W. Doane (New York: Routledge, 2003), p. 283.

2. Richard Schur, *Parodies of Ownership: Hip-Hop Aesthetics and Intellectual Property Law* (Ann Arbor: University of Michigan Press, 2009), p. 47.

3. David Leonard, "It's Gotta be the Body: Race, Commodity, and Surveillance of Contemporary Black Athletes," *Studies in Symbolic Interaction* 33 (2009): p. 168.

4. "The Fab Five," *30 for 30,* ESPN, aired on 13 March 2011.

5. John L. Jackson, *Real Black: Adventures in Racial Sincerity* (Chicago: University of Chicago Press, 2005), p. 177.

6. Lisa Guerrero, "One Nation under a Hoop: Race, Meritocracy, and Messiahs in the NBA," in *Commodified and Criminalized: New Racism and African Americans in Contemporary Sports,* ed. by David Leonard and C. Richard King (Lanham, MD: Rowman and Littlefield, 2011), p. 131.

7. Ibid., p. 127.

8. Bonilla-Silva, "New Racism," p. 282.

9. Jelani Cobb, *To the Break of Dawn: A Freestyle on the Hip Hop Aesthetic* (New York: New York University Press, 2007), p. 10.

10. Guerrero, "One Nation under a Hoop," p. 139.

11. Leonard, "It's Gotta Be the Body," p. 185.

Chapter 14

The Queen of Television: Oprah Winfrey in Relation to Self and as a Cultural Icon

Billye N. Rhodes and Kristal Moore Clemons

Oprah Winfrey is most often thought of as a natural, uncomplicated presence in our collective everyday lives. Rather than simply existing as a figure in popular culture, she works as a symbol. We have welcomed her into our homes as "Oprah"—*the resident expert*—and more recently, she has been branded simply as an alphabet letter: "O." For both of us, as African American females working on our doctorates at a predominantly white research-intensive university in the South (and now working in academy), we have often had limited time to watch television; yet, amid a sea of responsibilities and demands, we made watching Oprah a priority. For Kristal, Oprah represented a symbol of black womanhood, and for a period of about four years, watching Oprah was one of her daily rituals. She would justify her mild obsession with the phenomenon that is Oprah—the institution that is Oprah—as her means to decompress after dealing with the rigors, politics, and challenges of academia. Billye, on the other hand, had no interest in watching Oprah but as a result of being Kristal's roommate finally succumbed and engaged in fruitful conversations that always began with, "Did you see what happened on Oprah today?"

We've come to agree that part of what intrigues us about Oprah is her direct connection to our hometown, Chicago. We have also acknowledged that watching and critically analyzing—thereby complicating our love–hate relationship with O—are very much connected to shifting our position from regular viewer to black feminist intellectual viewer. Daily episodes that could have easily served as one person's entertainment or another's

source of information turned into sites of critique, angst, and renegotia-
tion. In show after show, we questioned the cultural meaning of Oprah;
therefore, what follows is a narrative of two black women and their relationship with a black international icon. This chapter looks at the evolution
of Oprah from a black child in the segregated South and college "queen" to
her space in mainstream media—particularly television. We explore her
impact on representations of African Americans in America through specific episodes of her 25-year network television career. Likewise, we also
reflect on Oprah's role in the changing racial discourse and the increased
visibility of blackness evident on American television. We conclude with
a dual examination of *Oprah's Next Chapter*—having created a template
for daytime television/talk shows and her position as vanguard of black
women images.

Historical Context: Oprah's Timeline

Oprah Gail Winfrey was born in Kosciusko, Mississippi—a "flyover state"
(which is a colloquial phrase for an area where black people never stay or
stop but simply fly over). She shares her birth year with one of the most
groundbreaking pieces of civil rights legislation—The U.S. Supreme
Court's *Brown v. Board of Education of Topeka* decision that ruled "separate
was not equal," ostensibly prohibiting racial segregation in public schools.
This provided a backdrop of great racial progress and mobility not only for
our society but also for the magnanimous benefits that Winfrey would reap
and sow. In 1970, she was awarded a scholarship to attend Tennessee State
University. While in college, she was crowned Miss Black Tennessee, and in
1976, she graduated with a degree in speech and performing arts. This year
also marked the next chapter in her life: she became the first black television
news anchor reporter with CBS affiliate, WTVF-TV, in Nashville. Shortly
thereafter, Oprah moved to Baltimore, Maryland, where she served as news
anchor, eventually becoming the host of *People Are Talking*, a morning talk
show. In 1983, she relocated to Chicago where she would host *A.M. Chicago*
for ABC affiliate, WLS-TV. The success of *A.M. Chicago* propelled her career in profound ways, leading to the creation of *The Oprah Winfrey Show*.

   In 1986, *The Oprah Winfrey Show* is extended to one hour and broad-
casted nationally. On the brink of becoming a household name, Oprah
began her own television production company, Harpo Productions. Her
trajectory of success was not limited to the little screen but was also seen in
Hollywood. Her prowess within the entertainment industry greatly enlarged
her territory and further defined who she was becoming as an iconic figure.

Black, Female, and Television Icon

One of the most memorable descriptions of Alice Walker's *The Color Purple* (1970) is the introduction of Sofia Butler. Through the eyes of the main character Celie, Sofia is a warrior—her "hair notty" and she "[big] . . . strong and ruddy looking, like her mama brought her up on pork."[1] This image becomes more concrete in the 1985 film adaptation when the audience first sees Oprah Winfrey charging up a road in a cloud of dust—back straight, head high, and ready for battle. She is unapologetic and unashamed. From scene to scene, we believe her power. She angrily retorts to a cowering Celie, "You ought to bash Mr. ___ head open. . . . Think about heaven later."[2] Again we see her with the mayor's wife, and on being asked to work as a maid, she emphatically states, "hell no."[3] It is here that Winfrey reaffirms the strength of a modern black woman in the late 80s. This is significant for three reasons. First, Winfrey has worked professionally in broadcast journalism since high school; however, at the hands of Quincy Jones and Steven Spielberg, this is the first time she is presented to a national, mainstream audience. Second, it is also important to note that her Oscar-nominated role was grounded in the ardent opposition of American society's white male patriarchy structure. Lastly, after Sofia, we began to see a parallel force: Oprah as a ratings-boosting talk show host, thrust from a local Chicago morning television program, on the cusp of obliterating the reign of Phil Donahue.

In September 1986, *The Oprah Winfrey Show* launches as a full-hour program. Much like the description Walker provides of Sofia, *Los Angeles Times* television critic Howard Rosenberg describes Oprah as: "a roundhouse, a full course meal, big, brassy, loud, aggressive, hyper, laughable, lovable, soulful, tender, low-down, earthy and hungry. And she may know the way to Phil Donahue's jugular."[4] This echoes the description of black women who have been caricatured as "mammy."

During this time, she is fast becoming the accepted depiction of a chattel-slave woman, which has sustained American postcolonial behaviors. Mammy is regarded by dominant society as close to traditional womanhood as a black woman can come: pious, pure, submissive, domestic, and nonthreatening. She "made her debut around 1914 when audiences were treated to a blackface version of *Lysistrata*. The comedy, titled *Coon Town Suffragettes*, dealt with a group of bossy mammy washerwomen who organize a militant movement to keep their good-for-nothing husbands at home."[5] Mammy is "distinguished . . . by her fierce independence. She is usually big, fat, and cantankerous," while alternative iterations will construct her as "sweet, jolly and good-tempered."[6] While Winfrey holds academic credentials in speech and performing arts, this platform of daytime television glorifies her as a professional counselor and expert on home and life affairs. She comfortably fits into the Mammy mold to nurture and provide factual opinions for large audiences of middle-class housewives. Unlike contemporary female journalists in her field such as Barbara Walters or Diane Sawyer, Winfrey is not necessarily heralded for her journalistic skills but the ability to articulate and *perform* as America's surrogate mother. Feminist scholar, Patricia Hill Collins, notes:

> A good deal of Winfrey's success lies in her ability to market herself within the familiar realm of the mammy, not violate the tenets of being a Black lady, yet reap the benefits of her performance for herself. [She] markets herself in the context of the synergistic relationship among entertainment, advertising, and news that frame contemporary Black popular culture. Winfrey's immense success provides a stamp of endorsement to any philosophy that she might endorse that goes far beyond any expertise she might possess on any given topic.[7]

While there is much critique, debate, and affirmation that define the public consumption of Oprah, this chapter does not focus on her personally, rather discusses the complex evolution and impact of her varied images and representations.

While Oprah certainly deals with the impact of race and gender in our society and makes personal references to her humble, Southern, Jheri curl beginnings, most of us do not think of her show as a celebration of black women or even a fair and balanced representation. Oprah has created a category of her *own* that we are to believe simply transcends everything, black and woman.

Oprah has provided a Midas touch to careers such as psychologist Dr. Phil, medical practitioner Dr. Oz, financial specialist Suze Orman, and even her best friend Gail. Oprah has set ablaze the literary world—as searches within academic journal articles for Oprah abound with notations of her Book Club as a major contributing factor to reading English. And as the tabloids once made Oprah their poster girl for weight loss and diet trends, Oprah is quoted now for quiet parables regarding "Living your best life yet." The added cherry is that all of these magic nuggets and golden children are tucked away in her magazine, *O: The Oprah Magazine,* which launched in 2000. For nearly 10 years, media has joked and/or lambasted Oprah for only featuring herself on the cover—month after month. Talk show host/comedian Ellen Degeneres even began a "Yes I Can" campaign to appear on the magazine cover; one of many tactics included her hilariously superimposed body riding in the second seat of Oprah's bicycle under the headline, "A Cover Built for Two!"[8] However, in April 2009, for the first time in the magazine's history, *O* did open the door for *another O:* first lady of the United States of America, Michelle Obama. Michelle Obama, also inextricably linked to Chicago, philanthropic activism, Ivy League intellect, and, of course, the president—surpasses all that we imagined when we fell in love with Clair Huxtable in the 1980s—representing what has been deemed the pinnacle of black womanhood.

In the August 2005 issue of *O*, Oprah wrote, "I've always had fierce respect and reverence for those whose names made history and for the millions whose names did not. People who were so resourceful, resilient, and remarkable in their will to keep moving forward. These are the roots from which I've grown."[9] These women—25 "bridges" (i.e., elders) and 45 "young'uns"—were invited to her California home in 2005 for a Legends Ball. She stated that it was "heaven in my living room. . . . the fulfillment of a dream for me: To honor where I've come from, to celebrate how I got here, and to claim where I'm going."[10] A total of 54 legends attended—all black women from every walk of life: Tina Turner, Elizabeth Catlett, Leontyne Price, Coretta Scott King, Mary J. Blige, Phylicia Rashad, Dr. Dorothy Height, and Iman were among the congregation, as well as Michelle Obama who was then simply listed as community affairs executive. Whereas her audience allowed her to come into their homes everyday, this selection of women speaks volumes regarding whom she allowed in *her* home. We have seen these women for generations as they have appeared on Broadway, in the White House, international runways, Hollywood, and on her various sets. These *legends* are reflections of how she sees herself, and ultimately what she deems acceptable representations of black women reflected to the world.

Oprah Winfrey is also cultural enterprise. Eva Illouz's (2003) *Oprah Winfrey and the Glamour of Misery: An Essay on Popular Culture* is an exercise in a cultural interpretation of Oprah. Illouz (2003) writes,

> Oprah Winfrey offers a spectacular example of the ways in which a cultural form—the Oprah Winfrey persona—has amassed an almost unprecedented role in the American culture scene. Oprah embodies not only quintessentially American values but also an American way of using and making culture.[11]

Vanity Fair once described Oprah as having arguably "more influence on the cultural than any university president, politician, or religious leader, except perhaps the Pope."[12] This Oprahization of culture was not always widely accepted by the masses. At the beginning of her career, critics slammed her talk show. Public intellectuals, political activists, feminists, and conservative moral crusaders publicly shared their disdain for her show.[13]

The Oprah Winfrey Show provided a medium for Oprah to critique the persistence of stereotypes, white racial framing, self-efficacy and gender, and antiblack racism. This set her apart from daytime peers because of her willingness and ability to access and probe sensitive areas of life in ways that appeared to move beyond sensationalism toward unpacking difficult conversations and building community. This was the core of the show: her panelists included the everyday person with dating, child-raising, or financial advice, as well as major controversial issues such as the discovery of AIDS in a small West Virginia town in 1987 or speaking with Diane Downs who killed her three children in 1988. Oprah's audience reflected the same demographic range of Harpo Studio's urban location, near West Side of Chicago on the edge of rehabilitation. She displayed the type of care that typified Mammy while promoting bootstrap skills and meritocracy suggesting that any and every person is capable of a middle-class American Dream. The latter is most evident to us when further examining the overall shift in panelists/topics for the show.

Winfrey's show ran for 25 seasons, with over 4,560 shows; surely, there is a wide breadth to consider; however, our concern began to grow in the middle years when the audience did not look so much like a rainbow and when Oprah became keenly focused on featuring celebrities such as her favorite men: John, Tom, and Denzel. We longed for the promotion of shows such as "Witnesses of Murders during the Civil Rights Era" with Mamie Till in October 1992. We wanted Oprah to continue the hard conversations day after day—to remain the critical point of access at which some of us painstakingly chipped away. As young black women concerned with our images and the open engagement of silenced conversations, this is what we looked for. And while we didn't quite see ourselves in the audience and ideas the way we continued to imagine, we did not change the channel.

Trystan Cotten and Kimberly Springer's (2010) *Stories of Oprah: the Oprahfication of American Culture* raises critical questions about society's relationship with Oprah. "Why do Americans care so much about Oprah, and how does Oprah get people to care about her?" Cotten and Springer (2010) interrogate this notion of care and write about the flexible meanings of Oprah. In Springer's (2010) chapter, "The Contours of the Oprah Culture Industry," she writes,

> In a sense, the divisions I have drawn among the cultural, economic, and political are meaningless owing to the overlap in Winfrey's cultural production. Where does Oprah the woman end and Oprah the brand begin? Attention to specificity becomes crucial in answering this question. One must be constantly and consistently vigilant to specify *which Oprah* is under examination.[14]

We, like Cotten and Springer (2010), identify Oprah as a woman whose cultural reach extends into areas of consumption, distribution, and production. She is a brand and "a culture industry in itself: television, radio, magazines, world wide web, films and publishing are all media marked by Oprahness."[15]

According to Jeanette Dates and William Barlow (1993),[16] 1950 marked a significant appearance of "African American-Focused Commercial Television." The authors list nearly 70 television programs—with the bulk of the shows based in the genres of comedy and drama—before finally naming Oprah Winfrey in 1986 as a talk show host. While others before her such as Billy Daniels (1952), Nat "King" Cole (1956), Bill Cosby (1969, 1972, 1976), Leslie Uggams (1969) (breaking the gender ceiling), Flip Wilson (1970), and Richard Pryor (1977) had led variety shows, Oprah took the baton, not professionally as an entertainer but as a popular culture news source, which broke several other ceilings. Dates and Barlow[17] note,

> ... the phenomenally successful talk show that originated in Chicago beginning in 1985, made a *Wall Street Journal* list as one of the twenty-eight rising stars in the *business* world. Called the richest woman on television in 1989, Winfrey had built and purchased a television and movie studio in Chicago from which she produced her talk show and many other television programs and films beginning in 1989. Winfrey, thus, became the third woman, and the first black woman in American history to own her own production company. Harpo coproduced "The Women of Brewster Place," which aired in early 1989. Moreover, the company owned the rights to other production possibilities, such as Toni Morrison's Pulitzer Prize-winning novel *Beloved*, Mark Mathabane's *Kaffir Boy*, a book about his life in apartheid-ridden South Africa, and Zora Neale Hurston's *Their Eyes Were Watching God*, p. 321.

However, in the 25 years since the launch of *The Oprah Winfrey Show*, we have rarely seen black women independently hosting television shows, even more rare is hosting during the daytime. Of those that have followed Oprah—Marsha Warfield (1990), Whoopi Goldberg (1992), Beatrice Berry (1993), Tyra Banks (2005), Wendy Williams (2008), and MoNique (2009), only Williams remains. Many of these shows—especially the latter—have taken more of a gossip column approach, and while they certainly cite Oprah as a major influence, they have not enjoyed the same longevity. Essentially, Oprah seems to have precipitated her own "Big Bang Theory"—as if nothing existed before her and everything that follows holds her signature. Oprah continues to use her production company and various media investments (e.g., Harpo, Oxygen, Dreamworks) to distribute *her* brand of entertainment and life-fulfilling messages. The critical significance of Oprah's impact revolves around her ability to invoke public trust from her viewers and fellow colleagues in the television industry. If we go back to the conversation of Oprah as Mammy, we see this public trust comes from the trust she has garnered from the millions of white women television viewers. We see Oprah crying with her mostly white audience members, sharing "African American communal knowledge," and teaching white women black vernacular. The not-so-subtle difference between a slave mammy and Winfrey, according to essayist Tarshia L. Stanley, is that Oprah is "paid handsomely for her milk and was clever enough to realize that she should be the distributor of her product as well."[18]

Cultural Moves and *The Oprah Winfrey Show*

On May 25, 2012, the final episode of *The Oprah Winfrey Show* aired. For many, it was akin to the farewell episodes of *The Cosby Show* and *Johnny Carson*. Viewers across the globe sat patiently to see how she would end her daytime talk show dynasty. In the shows leading up to the final episode, she reflected on some of her most memorable moments. What follows is a review of episodes that reflect what Herman Gray describes as "cultural moves" evident within *The Oprah Winfrey Show*. We look at how Oprah negotiates her sense of power and her sense of belonging and representation through her national platform.

Oprah earned her reputation as someone who would talk to *anyone* when she traveled into the South to tape a show on race with the residents of Forsyth County, Georgia, in 1987. Then known as a hotbed of racism, Forsyth County hadn't had a single black resident since before World War I. Tensions ran high, and calls for understanding were few. Oprah took the charge early in her career to provide a bridge—if not a window—to this community and its reflection within the country. She took the opportunity again just four years later with a case that brought the nation face-to-face with what we thought were private actions of those selected to serve and protect. In March 1991, Rodney King, a black man from Los Angeles, was pulled over by police after a high-speed chase. An amateur video showed seven LAPD officers hitting King more than 50 times with a baton and kicking him six times before handcuffing and arresting him. Only four of the officers were tried in April 1992: three were acquitted, and the jury failed to reach a verdict for the fourth. Los Angeles exploded for six days leading to major physical, financial, and psychological devastation of the most vulnerable areas of the city. While everyone in America had an opinion about the verdict and the LA riots, Oprah was present in Los Angeles to hear them out. And whereas journalism had been taught as an impartial science, Oprah did not turn a blind eye to the O. J. Simpson verdict, which set the country in direct opposition: black vs. white. Many believed the Simpson verdict was a reward for the injustice faced in the Rodney King trial; however, in 1997, Oprah invited Christopher Darden, the assistant prosecutor in the case, to discuss the case that further polarized America along racial lines, to garner insight about how he was called a race traitor, and to talk about how Oprah really felt when she heard "not guilty." Our aim is to illustrate that Oprah was not afraid to create time-sensitive spaces, even, and especially, in hostile environments for those hated or loved by various communities to provide their lived experiences before a national audience. It is impossible to miss that her ability to provide this space becomes a mixed bag when opening up to a generation past hers.

A Hip-Hop Town Hall

In April of 2007, after radio shock jock Don Imus was fired for his casual and absolutely racist references to the championship Rutgers women's basketball team, the country became painfully sensitized to the language we employ in the discussion of black women—not just the so-called downtrodden and welfare queens but successful college students and professionals as well. In a statement to NBC's *Today,* Imus responded to criticism by saying,

> I know that that phrase [nappy-headed hos] didn't originate in the white community. That phrase originated in the black community. And I'm not stupid. I may be a white man, but I know that these young women and young black women all through that society are demeaned and disparaged and disrespected by their own black men and that they are called that name. And

I know that, and that doesn't give me, obviously, any right to say it, but it doesn't give them any right to say it.[19]

Don Imus's controversial comments sparked conversations about the state of racial affairs in America. Oprah's two-part town hall series that aired in July 2009 included a wide breadth of music industry insiders, consumers, and critics: hip-hop father, Russell Simmons; record executive, Kevin Liles; former CEO of the NAACP and current president/CEO of the Hip Hop Summit Network, Dr. Benjamin Chavis; Grammy-winning rapper, Common; and the undergraduate Spelman College students who protested Nelly's *Tip Drill* video where the rapper is seen scanning a credit card through the backside of a female model. The purpose of this town hall was to engage and continue the critical discussion of the Imus's sentiment, while the panel specifically addressed issues of the denigration, marginalization, and sexual exploitation of women in hip-hop. Russell Simmons agreed with Oprah and said that Imus was wrong. "It is historically incorrect. Black people didn't invent 'nappy-headed hos.' Don Imus's statements were offensive to everyone." He further states, "I almost want to thank him for creating this forum. It's a long time coming." Simmons emphasized how the music did not create the conditions of the world or celebrate them but rather exposed the realities on the ground. In this regard, he used *The Oprah Winfrey Show* as a platform to challenge both the creators and consumers of hip-hop. He added,

> The Hip Hop community is a mirror, a reflection of the dirt we overlook— the violence, the misogyny, the sexism. They need to be discussed. . . . All throughout history the poets who have been a reflection of society have always been under fire. We don't like what they have to say, but some of it has to be examined. It's important that we teach artists more. It's my job to teach artists to know more and say more.

Dr. Benjamin Chavis, once CEO of the NAACP and currently the CEO of the Hip Hop Summit Network, which he cofounded with Russell Simmons, also participated in the conversation. He stated that while Imus's awful comments have presented an opportunity to discuss issues America has avoided for years, Imus should by no means be let off the hook:

> Hip Hop artists are not responsible for what Don Imus did. Don Imus was a racist. Don Imus was a sexist, and there's no way that Don Imus can blame Hip Hop for what he did. . . . That is not to excuse Hip Hop. Hip Hop is not perfect. We've got to make it better. But we make Hip Hop better by

making society better, because Hip Hop reflects the contradictions of society. There's too much poverty, there's too much injustice, and there's too much bad treatment of women in our society.

Though acknowledging his love for the music and culture, Common also admitted to Oprah that it has lost its way. "Hip Hop has been this child that we had. Our elders kind of abandoned the child at a young age and said, 'Okay, we don't really understand this. We don't relate to this,'" he said. "And now as Hip Hop has evolved and grown up, our parents are expecting Hip Hop to be perfect and to be right." Despite staying clear of such denigrating ideas in his own music, Common says he refuses to abandon the culture. "I'm going to ride with my Hip Hop people, because if I divide myself that's going to continue to keep the problem going," he says. "If criticism could come with love, we can make some progress."

On the note of progress, we cannot ignore that Oprah was willing to open the door to this new medium of voice for the current generation. However, this door was made available through the unavoidable controversy that caused a major media network to respond. Her willingness to have such a town hall had never happened before—or since—but seemed to do little to engage the complexity of hip-hop as a tool rather than as a knee-jerk reaction to squelch the drama related to its highly charged relationship with black women. The Oprah we had come to know in the earlier years may have pressed a head-on to discussion of hip-hop's relationship with white consumerism, youth entrepreneurship, and how it serves as a mirror and litmus test for social inequity. However, with hos on the main agenda, the conversation was narrowly focused on a knee-jerk reaction to squelch hip-hop's highly charged relationship with black women. To this end, one group of black women were invited to speak: students from the highly prestigious, all-female Spelman College.

During this town hall meeting, one young woman stated, "I feel that, as with the Don Imus situation, there's a lack of accountability. As rappers, I feel that accountability should be taken into consideration—as well as with Don Imus—from a racial standpoint and rappers from a sexist standpoint." The Spelman panelists collectively agreed, "it all needs to be addressed and we need to quit talking around the issues." These seven women noted that they have been called hos and that the negative stereotypes in some hip-hop songs are being applied to all black women. Unfortunately, Oprah's town hall did not uncover a solution to the problem. Many of the women from Spelman College appeared frustrated with what many of the panelists were trying to convey. Viewers were not able to hear from the perspective

of some of the worst offenders. The conversation may have taken a different turn if artists like Nelly, Lil' Kim, Ludacris, 50 Cent, or Snoop Dogg
had been present to share their perspectives on why they make the choices
they make regarding misogyny and hip-hop in addition to a more nuanced
female perspective. The group of women from Spelman's voice was absolutely valid but also closely and obviously aligned with Oprah. Of course,
we, as young black women, critically understand and have spoken/written
ad nauseam on our relationship with hip-hop as producers, bodies, and
consumers; however, without the inclusion of more voices/bodies during
this town hall, Oprah narrowly defines this contemporary form of speech
and culture through a deficit lens for a global audience. We find Oprah
missing the mark with this discussion. Oprah's cantankerous relationship
with hip-hop prevented her from equally representing both sides of the
issue. The irony is neither the entity of Oprah nor the entities of hip-hop
need one another. They both have reached their own level of influence by
appealing to those who want to hear what they have to say.

Oprah Finds Dave Chappelle Funny

In 2003, stand-up comedian Dave Chappelle was thrust into mainstream
television via his sketch program, *Chappelle's Show.* Following in the footsteps of Chris Rock (a frequent guest on *The Oprah Winfrey Show,* having
made 26 appearances), Eddie Murphy, and Richard Pryor, his show unapologetically confronted timely issues with biting humor, jabbing everyone from the Supreme Court to Hollywood. He quietly states in the sketch
"The Niggar Family," "this racism is killing me!" while doubled over in aching laughter. Chappelle experienced the same breakout success with Comedy Central that Oprah saw nearly 20 years prior when boosting ratings for
NBC; however, on the renewal of a 50 million dollar contract for two additional years, Chappelle walked away from the show, network, and America
altogether.

In 2006, Oprah snagged Chappelle for his first public interview after his
abrupt hiatus to South Africa. This was a prime opportunity for Oprah to
bridge a demographic gap as well as reveal to her audience that she too can
laugh at herself. In one of Chappelle's most popular sketches, he is ecstatic
when he receives a phone call from Oprah stating that she is pregnant with
his child. This causes Chappelle to quit his job the next day—proclaiming
he is now rich and moves to Chicago to take advantage of her wealth. The
segment concludes when Oprah gives birth to a white child that resembles
Dr. Phil—another male who has benefitted greatly from Winfrey. She replays the clip from the show for her studio audience, while Chappelle looks

down and away, visibly uncomfortable with Oprah laughing hysterically, deeming him hilarious. However, both Chappelle and Oprah are most engaged when he speaks passionately and painfully about his decision to walk away from what seemed to be so much because he believed he was not offering responsible images of black people through his television show—black men in particular.

This interview comes on the heels of Oprah receiving major backlash about snubbing hip-hop—the staple mouthpiece for young black America—by initially refusing Christopher "Ludacris" Bridges from her stage during an interview with the cast of the movie *Crash*. She publically reprimanded Ludacris for his musical lyrics—the same words that can be found in a Chris Rock or Chappelle segment—and admitted that her fear stemmed from a belief that having him as a guest signified her support of rap music.

Later in 2009, Oprah invited Shawn "Jay Z" Carter to her show. She made time to visit the infamous Marcy Projects in Brooklyn, New York, where Jay Z once sold narcotics and began his hip-hop career. Now retired from rapping and married to the über-successful powerhouse Beyoncé, Mr. Carter, dubbed "Hip-Hop Mogul," has earned face time with Oprah. We see in several clips how she is taken aback by his charm, wisdom, and humility. More than her time spent with Chappelle and Bridges, Oprah appears to be more of a student, genuinely interested in a subject for which she has never taken seriously.

Season 25

September 13, 2010, marked the beginning of the end of the Oprah era. The final season of *The Oprah Winfrey Show* surprised guests of the first episode of the season with an all-expense–paid trip to Australia. In true Oprah fashion, she started the show with an exciting monologue, "I started to think about where would I most want to go. Maybe I should take all of you with me to the other side of the world . . . We're going to Australia! We are going to Australia! You and you and you and you, are going to Australia!" This set the tone for the final season. Show after show demonstrated Oprah's ability to surprise viewers.

Halfway though the final season, *The Oprah Winfrey Show* teased viewers with the tag line "Oprah reveals shocking family secret that literally shook her to the core." Fans, who already learned that Winfrey was molested as a child and gave birth to and lost a baby at the age of 14, were in heavy suspense. This episode began with footage from a home video detailing Oprah and her longtime partner, Stedman Graham's, trip to

Milwaukee over a Thanksgiving holiday weekend. Viewers were given access to Oprah as she meets her half-sister, whom she did not know existed, for the very first time. Winfrey's mom, Vernita Lee, had put Patricia up for adoption shortly after her birth in 1963 without ever telling Oprah, then only nine years old. Patricia knew about her famous sibling since 2007. Yet, said Oprah, she "never once thought to go to the press." This episode gave the viewers new look in Oprah's childhood. Many media outlets criticized Oprah for doing this as a kind of publicity stunt. Yet, Oprah maintains she wanted to break the story herself so the media would not have the opportunity to exploit it. The idea of Oprah having to negotiate a new family member in, which she never knew about, adds a new opportunity for viewers to relate to Oprah.

Oprah's connection to the movement for civil rights has been interesting to watch throughout her long run on daytime television. She began her career fiercely addressing race. Toward the middle of her career, she scaled back on the race conversation. In recent years, however, she has once again refashioned herself yet again as a more politicized black woman. In "Oprah Honors American Heroes: The Freedom Riders Unite 50 Years Later," Oprah reflects on growing up in the segregated South. Here, she shares the stage with 178 freedom riders. In May of 1961, a racially mixed group of men and women boarded interstate buses headed to the Deep South to protest the segregation of interstate travel. Mobs viciously beat the civil rights activists. Despite the terrors they faced, the Freedom Riders succeeded when the Interstate Commerce Commission ordered that segregationist policies end in interstate bus and rail travel in September of 1961. In her opening monologue, she stated, "As an African American woman born in Mississippi in 1954 and raised in the South, I owe a deep debt of gratitude to Freedom Riders as do we all." Inspired by Oprah's experiences living in the segregated South as well as the 2011 PBS *American Experience* documentary by Stanley Nelson and the book by Raymond Arsenault, it spotlighted the terror of American racism. This space provided viewers with the opportunity to witness history, where white perpetrators of violence and black Freedom Riders could race one another, participate in dialogue, and move forward with history in hand.

Oprah's *Master Class:* The Oprah Winfrey Network

The Oprah Winfrey Network (OWN) was launched on January 1, 2011, to nearly 1.1 million viewers with a blend of daytime and prime-time shows. The cornerstone of the network—*Season 25: Oprah behind the*

Scenes—provided viewers with a behind-the-scenes look at the *Oprah Winfrey Show*. *Season 25* provided viewers with the opportunity to learn about the inner workings, hearing from Oprah, the show's executive producers, booking agents, and others who worked to make the show happen.

Despite the increased platform, Oprah's viewership declined precipitously. After just one month, viewers had dropped to a mere 287,000 viewers. In fact, interest among women over 25, the network's core demographic, fell by 20 percent each week since the debut.[20] Oprah didn't just face waning support from women but declining support from African American women. In a February 2011 *Newsweek* article entitled "Is Oprah's Network Too White?," Allison Samuels and Joshua Alston describe Oprah's race problem:

> Farah J. Griffin's 82-year-old mother, Wilhelmenia, hasn't missed an episode of The Oprah Winfrey Show since it debuted nearly 20 years ago. So when Winfrey's 24-hour Oprah Winfrey Network (OWN) debuted on Jan. 1, Griffin upgraded her mother's cable package so she could watch from her Philadelphia home. Only now, Griffin wants more for her money. "I know it's still early in the process," says Griffin, a professor of English and African-American studies at Columbia University. "That said, I really want to see more variation. I'm not saying she should just focus on black shows or black programming. But I'd like it to have shows that are interesting to women of all ages, backgrounds, and races, not just white women."[21]

Samuels and Alston go on to pose the question about whether or not Oprah's network needs more diversity. They write,

> What gives? "Oprah is the network's diversity," says Todd Boyd, a professor at USC's School of Cinematic Arts. "And that's been the way she's operated from the beginning of her career, so I'm not sure why there is even a question about more diversity. That's really not who she is or who she ever was."[22]

Christina Norman, chief executive officer for the OWN, stated,

> The folks at OWN don't see a problem, either. "Our job is to reflect the entire audience that is a part of the world vision Oprah has, and that includes blacks, whites, men, women, and everyone. One show and one network cannot do it all."[23]

Oprah took some of this criticism to heart ushering in changes at OWN. She also changed her approach and style. Ditching the sterile and constrained format of yesteryear, Oprah embraces a more informal approach, embracing the role as fan, consumer, nosey neighbor, and concerned friend. As she invites viewers into her home, scenic backyards, and island getaways, the world got to see a new side of Oprah.

This is most apparent in interviews with pop singer Rihanna (August 19, 2012) and newly ornamented Olympic gold medalist Gabrielle Douglas (August 26, 2012). Rihanna came into the media light as a teenager under the musical guidance of Jay Z. Her flourishing career nearly was interrupted in 2009 because of injuries she sustained in a domestic violence incident involving Chris Brown. Three years later, she is back atop the pop world. Proving that Oprah's "still got it," Rihanna accepted an invitation to speak with Oprah at her Barbados home. It would be her meaningful interview since Chris Brown battered her in front of the world. While she asked about the incident with Chris Brown, this interview showed a much softer Oprah. Telling Oprah that "Chris needed help," she showed greater concern for his health and wellness. She knew she would be okay resulting from her feeling that Chris needed her help. During the exchange, Oprah sat with her mouth open—much like many of her audience watching from their homes. She seemed to struggle with words and managed only to state, "I didn't expect that." Oprah did not mother Rihanna or take the road that many Oprah.com bloggers wished she would have taken with Rihanna: "I could not believe that Oprah sat there and did not try to reason with this confused girl. . . . Oprah, shame on you! You have the years and knowledge that could have at least planted a seed of knowledge in Rihanna. . . . SHAME, SHAME on you!"[24] Oprah provided no hard-hitting questions and no value judgments; there was no effort to complete Rihanna's sentences (for which Oprah is notorious for) or correct her statements. Oprah simply sat back and listened as a friend who was learning a new life lesson. When Oprah and Rihanna hugged at the conclusion of the interview, Oprah announced,

> " . . . I can always tell. You were just 100% yourself."
> With smile, Rihanna responded, "thank you."
> Oprah repeats, "100% yourself."

A refreshing approach, Oprah found freedom in a space of her own rather than one controlled by a studio audience.

The conversation with 16-year-old Gabby Douglas had an entirely different tone. Oprah opened the interview with, "As an African American woman, to another African American woman, that was the coolest damn thing." Referring to Douglas's historical gold medal during the 2012 Summer Olympics, Oprah expressed her joy and pride from Douglas's dominance in gymnastics. As with Rihanna, Gabby faced controversy amid a sea of success. Instead of celebrating her amazing grace, artistry, and talents, much of the Olympic discourse focused on hair politics. Starting the interview with a clear set of boundaries, Oprah noted: "I'm not one to play the race card. I never play the race card . . . and sometimes it's like 'wow' this is happening because of the color of my skin?" Yet, Oprah pressed Gabby to talk about how she felt being attacked by other black women because her "ponytail wasn't tight." Gabby evaded the questions; Oprah also probed about why she left her original training gymnasium at which time Douglas became visibly uncomfortable. At this point, Douglas, struck with emotion, described an instance where she was called nigger. Responding to Oprah's probes, Douglas backtracked a bit, concluding, "I don't want to focus on the negative." Almost before Gabby could complete this statement, Oprah emphatically stated, "But I do." When Gabby refused to provide additional details, Oprah announced, "I'll just ask your mother when she comes out."

In these instances, it is clear that Oprah has not invested in averting difficult conversations, a trademark of her entire career. Talking to a young woman who had just made history, Oprah pushed the conversation to a less than celebratory place. Yet, in noting that she "doesn't play the race card," and in equalizing the victimization of Douglas at the hands of both other black women and Gabby's white peers, the show leaves viewers with a very confusing and unbalanced conversation. Perhaps, if Gabby—who did insist on being called Gabrielle—were older, the interview would've played different. Perhaps, she would've taken Gabrielle's reluctance to answer as a sign of maturity rather than shyness. Perhaps, she would have engaged a historical conversation of the politics and misunderstandings of black women's hair rather than ostracizing other black women viewers by focusing on the attack and stating, "I think this is so sickening because it came from African American women." She certainly would not have resorted to asking her mother as if it were a threat.

Then, there was Iyanla Vanzant. She became a household name late in the 1990s as a self-help spiritual guide for women, particularly for black women. Her books became just as common on a shelf as bibles and recipes, and with this recognition, it was no surprise that we soon found her taking stage on *The Oprah Winfrey Show* in 1998. Her regular appearances almost ensured that soon enough she would have her own show like Phil, Oz, Suze, and Gail; however, a bitter feud ensued between the two, and communication was only to be had between lawyers. While the audiences of both women eagerly awaited a new Oprah-sanctioned program abound with spiritual enlightenment, it was painfully disappointing to see the collaboration fail and we subsequently watched Iyanla publicly self-destruct in her family and career. In response to Iyanla insisting she did not know how to handle her gifts as well as operating in the entertainment industry, particularly as a single black mother from nowhere, Oprah says to Iyanla while completely leaning into her personal space: "I know that! That's why I was trying to nurture you, I was trying to support you, I was trying to grow you." Oprah picks up her role as mentor to Iyanla and offers her a new opportunity to help viewers. They now share the stage during Oprah's *Super Soul Sunday* and *Fix My Life*.

Posing Questions for *Oprah's Next Chapter*

Oprah has demonstrated that black women do not exist as monolithic. Yet, her success has also positioned her as exceptional, as part of a very exclusive and elite cohort. Through the years, we have been able to tune in to all of the various places where she has placed microphones and cameras, still aching to hear those places that are soft and quiet. Surely, we must allow for rest and privacy—every world issue is not one that Oprah should be expected to become an expert on. However, we curiously question how her position once represented as a break from historical patriarchal norms in new ways reinscribes them for our current generation. How are the images of Mammy and Sapphire rejected or reconciled? Is a black woman who straightens her hair, curves, and her Southern accent better poised to leverage power for herself and her community? If so, who then is her community? When she grows in self and has power to sanction the success of others, who does she refuse and for what issues must she be silent to maintain power? What does Oprah owe black women and the black community as a whole, and what has her work taught us about what we can provide for ourselves?

Notes

1. Alice Walker, *The Color Purple* (Orlando, FL: Harcourt, Inc, 1970/2003), p. 30.
2. Walker, *The Color Purple*, p. 42.
3. Walker, *The Color Purple*, p. 85.
4. Howard Rosenberg, "Winfrey Zeroing in on Donahue," *Los Angeles Times*, September 1986, Web, September 26. 2012.
5. Donald Bogle, *Toms, Coons, Mulattoes, Mammies, & Bucks: An Interpretive History of Blacks in American Films* (New York: The Continuum Publishing Company, 1996), p. 9.
6. Bogle, *Toms, Coons, Mulattoes, Mammies, & Bucks*, p. 9.
7. Patricia Hill Collins, "Get Your Freak On: Sex, Babies and Images of Black Femininity," in *Black Sexual Politics: African Americans, Gender, and the New Racism*, ed. by Patricia Hill Collins (New York: Routledge, 2005), pp.142–43.

8. As a result of her relentless tenacity and enthusiasm, Degeneres did appear on the December 2009 cover of *O*.

9. Allison Samuels with Joshua Alston, "Is Oprah's Network Too White?," *Newsweek*, February 7, 2011: p. 9. *Educators Reference Complete*, Web, September 23, 2012.

10. Oprah Winfrey, "The Legends Who Lunch: How the Legends Weekend Came to Be," *O Magazine*, August 2005, p. 178.

11. Eva Illouz, *Oprah Winfrey and the Glamour of Misery: An Essay on Popular Culture* (New York: Columbia University Press, 2003), p. 1.

12. *The Church of "O,"* April 1, 2002, vol. 46, no. 4, http://www.christianityto day.com/ct/2002/april1/1.38.html.

13. Illouz, *Oprah Winfrey and the Glamour of Misery*.

14. Kimberly Springer, "Introduction: Delineating the Contours of the Oprah Culture Industry," in *Stories of Oprah: The Oprahfication of American Culture*, ed. by T. Cotten and K. Springer (Mississippi: University of Mississippi Press, 2010), p. xi.

15. Springer, "Introduction: Delineating the Contours of the Oprah Culture Industry," p. xii.

16. Jeanette Dates and William Barlow, eds. *Split Image: African Americans in the Mass Media, 2nd ed* (Washington, DC: Howard University Press, 1993).

17. Dates and Barlow, *Split Image*.

18. Tarshia L. Stanley, "The Specter of Oprah Winfrey: Critical Black Female Spectatorship," in *The Oprah Phenomenon*, ed. by Jennifer Harris and Elwood Watson (Louisville: University Press of Kentucky, 2007).

19. Imus' non-defense: the phrase "nappy-headed hos" "originated in the black community," http://mediamatters.org/research/2007/04/10/imus-non-defense-the-phrase-nappy-headed-hos-or/138562.

20. Samuels with Joshua Alston, "Is Oprah's Network Too White?"

21. Samuels with Joshua Alston, "Is Oprah's Network Too White?"

22. Samuels with Joshua Alston, "Is Oprah's Network Too White?"

23. Samuels with Joshua Alston, "Is Oprah's Network Too White?"

24. Blog comment retrieved September 23, 2012, posted September 10, 2012, by user, Willtrout retrieved from http://www.oprah.com/own-oprahs-next-chapter/Oprahs-Next-Chapter-Rihanna.

Chapter 15

Tyler Perry Takes Over TV

Bettina L. Love

I'd rather make $700 a week playing a maid than $7 being one.
—Hattie McDaniel, first black actress to win an Academy Award

Tyler Perry is one of the most powerful and influential black men in Hollywood, perhaps the most dominant black man in the history of Hollywood. He certainly is the most successful black filmmaker in the industry. Perry began his takeover of cable television in 2006, and, to date, his films have grossed over $519 million at the box office. While Perry's success is strictly an American phenomenon (his movies have earned less than $2 million abroad),[1] the American audience, specifically black Americans, have embraced Perry's work. He currently has three popular sitcoms airing on Turner Broadcasting System (TBS): *Tyler Perry's Meet the Browns*, which is in syndication after being canceled by Perry, *Tyler Perry's House of Payne*, which is also in syndication after being canceled by TBS, and *For Better or Worse*. The latter show is in its second season. *Meet the Browns* ran for five seasons. *House of Payne* aired for seven. All three of these sitcoms reach well over a million viewers a week. Perry's success in and of itself is unprecedented because he writes, produces, directs, and acts in most of his films and sitcoms. Although his success is unorthodox in that his movies and sitcoms do not appeal to middle-class America, in 2011, Forbes named Perry the highest-paid man in entertainment. He topped the list with $130 million. There were no other black actors or actresses on Forbes's list.

Furthermore, Perry's accolades in the black entertainment, film and television industry are impressive. He has won The Black Entertainment (BET) comedy awards for acting and writing and numerous National Association for the Advancement of Colored People (NAACP) Image Awards for outstanding directing, acting, and writing. However, with all of Perry's successes comes criticism. Perry's disapproval among fellow black actors, cultural critics, and black intellectuals is unmatched. In one instance, black director, actor, and writer Spike Lee spoke out against Perry's work asserting:

> Each artist should be allowed to pursue their artistic endeavors, but I still think there is a lot of stuff out today that is coonery and buffoonery. I know it's making a lot of money and breaking records, but we can do better. . . . I am a huge basketball fan, and when I watch the games on TNT, I see these two ads for these two shows (Tyler Perry's "Meet the Browns" and "House of Payne"), and I am scratching my head. We got a black president, and we going back to Mantan Moreland and Sleep 'n' Eat?[2]

Mantan Moreland and Willie Best (stage name Sleep 'n' Eat) were black minstrel era performers portraying dumb, lazy, subhuman buffoons who represented white America's racist imagination of black men.[3] Touré, a culture critic, writer, and MSNBC contributor, compared Perry's work to "cinematic malt liquor for the masses"[4] and added that Perry is "the KFC of Black cinema."[5] Most of Perry's reproaches derive from the black middle-class community and black academics. Simply put, many well-educated, middle-class to upper-middle-class blacks believe that Perry is pandering to uninformed blacks. Black intellectuals have gone on record stating that Perry's work does not speak to them or represent them.[6] His work can be considered the clash between blue-collar and middle-class blacks. Lee and Touré's sneering comments regarding Perry's films and television shows are popular among the black bourgeoisie community but do not represent the millions of black folks who watch *Meet the Browns, House of Payne,* and *For Better or Worse* weekly, and their comments are certainly not indicative of the millions of educated black folks who have made Perry a millionaire by supporting his work.

At the heart of this debate lies the question of whether it is fair to compare Perry and his work to Mantan Moreland and Sleep 'n' Eat, when millions of black folks support both Perry and his work. Furthermore, it begs the question regarding the implications of black America if Perry's success is rooted in black self-hatred and the most demeaning stereotypes of black life. Lastly, it remains to be seen whether Perry's work is nothing but the repackaging of centuries of comedic racial tropes updated for today's black audience or authentic notions of black life. This chapter aims to answer these questions by examining Perry, his life before fame, and the way in which his work relates to black America.

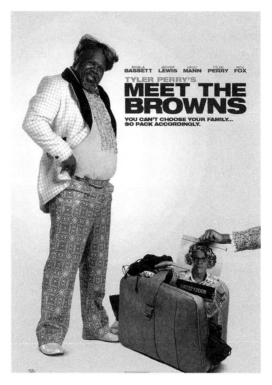

Meet the Browns, one of Tyler Perry's many television ventures. (Lionsgate Films/Photofest)

Who Is Tyler Perry and Does That Explain Anything?

Tyler Perry was born Emmitt Perry, Jr., in New Orleans, Louisiana. At the age of 16, he legally changed his first name to Tyler because he did not want the surname of his abusive father. In a 2009 interview with *Essence* magazine, Perry shared with the world details of his abusive childhood. During his dark childhood, he watched his father toss his mother around and endured physical cruelty from his father as well.[7] Perry admitted that some days the thought of killing himself or his father was the only thing that brought him relief from his abusive home. To make matters worse, a family friend molested him as a child. In order to cope with his horrific upbringing and to provide a form of therapy, Perry journaled his volatile past, which then became his first stage play, *I Know I've Been Changed.* The play, which debuted in the early 1990s, was not a commercial success at first, but it was a foreshadowing of Perry's later works and his playbook of tropes—tear-jerking scenes of redemption, distressed women, faith, forgiveness, and love—that appear in each of his films and television sitcoms.[8] *Changed,* like all of Perry's work, is rooted in Christian principles that lead Perry's characters to overcome issues of abuse and family as they find God. When the play debuted, it failed miserably; Perry was left homeless and sleeping in his car. But he persevered and revamped the play. In the late 1990s, *Changed* was in high demand on the "chitlin' circuit" (the stubborn colloquial term for the urban theater circuit that many black performers played during the age of racial segregation in the United States). Not all, but many, of these theaters were in the Southern regions of the United States. After debuting the revamped version of *Changed* in Atlanta, Georgia, Perry became an overnight success due to the relatability of his characters, the story line of redemption from childhood abuse, and his audience, black Christians who Hollywood had long ago deemed unprofitable. Before Perry, black Christians were invisible in the eyes of the television and film industry. However, Lee and others would argue that Perry's characters are mere caricatures of simpleminded coons and mammies incapable of complex thought or correct English, and therefore, Perry is selling society's most destructive stereotypes of black men and women back to black audiences.[9]

The hallmark of Perry's success is the character Mabel "Madea" Simmons. Perry contends that his characters, especially Madea, are hybrids of people in his past that embody black Southern life. The name Madea is a Southern African American portmanteau for "Mother Dear." Madea is a loud-talking, no-nonsense, pistol-toting black woman who speaks improper English and portrayed by Perry in drag. However, Perry has explained that behind that comical front, Madea jointly symbolizes the personalities of his mother and his aunt, who carried a gun to prevent Perry from being abused by his father. Perry told *Essence* magazine that "Madea represents a matriarchal figure many of us [African Americans] grew up with, one who says whatever is on her mind—and what everyone else is thinking but is too afraid to say. . . . People like her aren't around much anymore."[10] Evidenced by the success of three box-office hits, *Madea's Family Reunion, Madea Goes to Jail,* and *Madea's Big Happy Family,* perhaps the character of Madea is in fact missing in today's black experience. But do Perry's caricature creations truly serve as depictions of family members past and present or are they innocuous characters that seemingly destroy decades of racial progress and perpetuate blatant racial stereotypes about black men and women? Truthfully, the answer is both yes and no.

Black Americans are not monolithic, and there is not one particular way to be or act black—a notion that is evident in Perry's success. Perry depicts the best and worst of African American life. To many, Perry's work symbolizes a time of post–physical slavery, weighted with the enduring psychological effects of slavery and Jim Crow. Perry's characters conjure up emotions of self-hatred and the most humiliating stereotypes of black life that many African Americans have hoped to put behind them, never to be seen again. On the other side of this debate, "Black audiences and black people in general have always found the popular stereotypes of themselves to be quite funny, in a certain context."[11] For example, in the late 1920s and 1930s, black commentators, civil rights leaders, and black intellectuals denounced Lincoln Perry (no relation to Tyler Perry) who created the character Stepin Fetchit.[12] However, working-class black audiences adored Stepin Fetchit. In fact, Lincoln Perry was rumored to be the first African American actor to become a millionaire. The lure of Stepin Fetchit was painfully racist. He was known to blacks and whites as the "laziest man in the world" and a "befuddled, mumbling, shiftless fool."[13] His critics argued that whites were not laughing with Perry but at Perry and blacks in general. The racial politics of comedy suggested that whites enjoyed Stepin Fetchit because he reinforced black stereotypes.[14] Conversely, comedian Jimmy Walker, who was also criticized for portraying a coon-like character on the classic black American family sitcom *Good Times,* stated:

"The way they make it sound, it's like black people are permanently harmed by Stepin Fetchit," Walker says. "And I don't agree with that—I don't think it's a bad character. I think it's a funny character." Walker points out that the Fetchit character is actually a subversive trickster—he never got around to fetching anything.[15] In 1940, after years of trying to fight the ridicule, Lincoln Perry stepped away from acting. According to Hurst (2006), "Perry was a symbol of something black America wanted to forget, and he faded into obscurity."[16] Sixty years later, another Perry emerges to make blacks laugh and cry. Yet, unlike Lincoln Perry, who fought tirelessly to receive equal pay to white actors of his day, Tyler Perry is not taking Hollywood's leftovers.

Tyler Perry is the new and improved Lincoln Perry. In the book *Stepin Fetchit: The Life and Times of Lincoln Perry,* author Mel Watkins contends that Perry was a complex and intelligent man, who was simply misunderstood.[17] One could say the same about Tyler Perry. Tyler Perry holds a G.E.D. and has no formal education in film or television, but his success is unsurpassed. His work exploits black life, while at the same time representing elements of black life through humor, a long-time coping mechanism of black folks wrestling with being black in America. At its core, the media industry relies on stereotypes to quickly convey information and establish predictable character traits and actions.[18] Coons, Sambo, and Stepin Fetchit are all part of America's television fabric. Perry has taken these caricatures and created an empire. His exploitation of what is considered an unsavory entertainment of the past is precisely why he garners so much attention, but let's be real. Perry is not the first and he will most certainly not be the last black man to stereotypically portray blacks in the media.

The Repacking of Racial Comedy: Nothing New to See, But Something New to Laugh At

Leroy Brown, a church deacon and hospital janitor, is the protagonist of the television show *Meet the Browns*, originally a stage play written and directed by Perry that was adapted into a movie before it became a sitcom. To be blunt, the character of Leroy Brown is a modern-day coon, Sambo, and Stepin Fetchit, all wrapped up into one man. He is a dumb, inarticulate, nitwit who is almost childlike. In classic buffoon fashion, Brown opens up his home to a group of senior citizens after reading a letter from his deceased father asking him "to take care of the old." Brown understands the letter to mean to take care of old people, but Brown's father, Pop Brown, actually meant his old thunderbird in the garage. Thus, the plot centers on Brown clumsily attempting to take care of elderly housemates after a fire burns down a nearby senior home, which is called Brown Meadows. Brown's manner of dress also highlights his buffoonish persona. His outfits consist of clothing reminiscent of the 1977 film *Saturday Night Fever* with ill-fitting, bright-colored, bell-bottomed trousers paired with animal print or ruffled dress shirts. Brown is unmarried, which is the traditional relationship status for the caricature Sambo, who is typically asexual because of his childish behavior. However, Brown, who is a church-going man, many years ago, had a one-night stand with Madea, which resulted in a daughter, Cora Simmons. The show's connection to Madea is a Perry staple. A considerable portion of Perry's movies or television shows are explicitly or implicitly linked to Madea. Although Madea has never appeared on the show, she is referenced throughout. Brown has a nephew, Will, who is a doctor and the voice of reason. Will is married to Sasha, a nurse who also works at the same hospital where Brown is a janitor. There are several other characters that appear on the show, but all play a part in stirring Brown up to be over the top and simpleminded in order to provide comic relief from issues of child abandonment, molestation, and alcoholism. The serious issues that the show tackles center around two children with a very troubled past. Joaquin Ortiz and Brianna Ortiz are siblings who live with the Browns after being in foster care. Through a community service project at Brown Meadows, these two youngsters are introduced to the Brown family, who take them in. In Season 2, we learn that Brianna's mother's boyfriend molested her; the children's mother and father are in prison, and Joaquin's little league coach is a pedophile. It is important to mention that these story lines draw on Perry's childhood of molestation. Season 2 introduces Tanya Ortiz, the mother of Brianna and Joaquin. Tanya returns from jail to reclaim her children from Will and Sasha; however, at first, she only wants them so she can collect a government subsidy check or a welfare check. Also in Season 2, the father returns to tell her daughter that he loves her, but he cannot take her away from the Browns because he is still haunted by his past of drug abuse and crime. However, he does not introduce himself to Joaquin because he is the younger brother and does not remember his father. Interwoven within these emotional story lines are some of Brown's funniest lines: according to the *Meet the Browns*'s website on TBS.com, he says, "I'm a pajama thug up in this piece," "What do you mean it's too late? It ain't midnight—it's 12!" and "Colonel, don't you turn your back on the Lord! Who put shoes on your table? Who put food on your feet?" These jokes highlight just how dumb Leroy Brown is, but the mention of the "Lord" is a common theme within the show.

In contrast with Brown's buffoonish behavior, the show is saturated with biblical references that stress the importance of family and faith—two staples within the black community and Perry's audience. As mentioned earlier, Christian principles are central to Perry's work; thus, two of Season 3's central themes are forgiveness and second chances. Cora helps Tanya turn her life around as she attempts to regain custody of Joaquin and Brianna. Will and Sasha object. However, Tanya is granted custody by the courts. Yet, the same day she is given guardianship of her children, Tanya realizes the responsibility of taking care of two children, and she pretends to be on drugs again and returns the children back to Will and Sasha. Viewers also learn in Season 3 that Sasha kisses Will's mentor. When Will finds out about the kiss, he is devastated but ultimately reunites with Sasha, forgiving her for the transgression. In Season 4, Sasha has a miscarriage. Seasons 4 and 5, however, center on the love life of Cora and The Colonel. The Colonel is a former military man who lives at Brown Meadows until Season 3. By Season 5, The Colonel is married. Cora's love interest, Reggie, is the local school's football coach. He lives with his mother. Brown, Cora's father, takes great pleasure in making fun of Reggie. Brown's jokes aimed at Reggie are childish and perpetuate his buffoonish character. *Meet the Browns* aired its last episode on November 18, 2011.

Perhaps, one caveat of the show's appeal is that it is set and filmed in Atlanta, Georgia. Atlanta is a Southern city with a substantial black Southern Christian population. Furthermore, the city of Atlanta has garnered the names "Hollywood of the South" and "Black Hollywood" in large part because of Perry's accomplishments. Atlanta is where Perry launched his career and is home to his 200,000 square foot state-of-the-art studio. The city of Atlanta offers tax incentives to the television and film industry for choosing Atlanta as a set location. In 2010 and the latter part of 2011, half of all movies and television shows geared toward African American viewers were shot in Atlanta.[19] Perry is also the most frequent employer of African American actors and actresses in America.[20] *Meet the Browns* was Perry's second sitcom. After a short 10-episode pilot season of his first successful sitcom, *House of Payne,* TBS requested 100 episodes from Perry to the tune of $200 million.

The main character in *House of Payne,* also set in Atlanta, is an overweight fire chief named Curtis Payne. In addition to his inability to maintain good health because of his poor eating habits, Payne is loud, cantankerous, and obsessed with getting his nephew's family out of his house. He is also the classic coon who is socially inappropriate and perpetuates negative tropes concerning people of color with off-color jokes. Curtis Payne's wife, Ella, is a stay-at-home mother and the maternal figure of the show. She is also the religious conscience of the sitcom. Ella is an involved member of her local church and keeps the family grounded in Christian principles. She even opens her home up to feed the homeless members of her community when a local shelter is closed. Payne's nephew, C. J. Payne, who is also a fireman, comes to live with his uncle, along with his four kids, after his home burns down due to drug use by C. J.'s wife. C. J.'s wife is Janine Payne, a recovering drug addict, whom C. J. loves despite her addiction. However, in Season 1, C. J. and Janine divorce, leaving C. J. to take care of the children alone with the help of his aunt and uncle. Also in Season 1, the episode "Weeping May Endure for a Night," which stems from a biblical scripture, cast members (Brown, Cora, and Will) from *Meet the Browns* appear on the show. This episode laid the foundation for the show *Meet the Browns,* which aired two years after *House of Payne.* Much of the first season focuses on Janine's addiction and C. J. and the children adjusting to their new living situation, while Payne takes comical jabs at the members of his family who have invaded his home. Also, C. J. starts to date again but struggles with the challenges of being a single dad. Season 1 ended with Malik, C. J.'s son, stealing and wrecking Curtis's motorcycle. The climax of Season 2 is C. J. being trapped in an intense house fire, Janine being discharged from the rehabilitation center, and Malik finding Curtis's gun as he yearns to confront his school's bully. By Season 3, Perry makes his third guest appearance as Madea. Madea's presence in *House of Payne* positions the show within the Perry franchise and provides the minstrelesque entertainment for which Perry is known. Madea is the antagonist in *House of Payne*. She is one of Curtis Payne's most-known adversaries. Madea and Payne's intolerable relationship is built on Madea being loud mouthed, overbearing, and outright offensive to Payne, which is how black women have been portrayed on television for decades.

Seasons 4 and 5 focus primarily on the issues concerning the children of the show. Calvin, Curtis and Ella's son, is a work-in-progress type of character. Calvin thought of himself as a ladies' man until he met his wife Miranda, who is played by Keshia Knight Pulliam, best known for her role as Rudy Huxtable on *The Cosby Show*. In Season 6, Calvin is arrested for not paying child support for a child with a woman that is not his wife; he is later released before his child with Miranda is born. By the end of the season, Calvin, who in earlier seasons rarely attended his college classes, subsequently graduates from college. By Season 7, Calvin is a focused parent and husband. There are over a dozen recurring characters that move the show's comical aspects along, like Calvin's best friends Pookie and Peanut. Both Pookie and Peanut are foolish brutes who clash with the Payne family and Calvin's life as a husband and father. By the end of the series, Janine has truly triumphed over her addiction and has become a career-minded woman. Ella assisted Janine with rehab and overcoming her addiction. The themes of forgiveness, redemption, and unconditional love are evolved through *House of Payne* and *Meet the Browns*. Perry's third sitcom *For Better or Worse* detaches from the family-oriented slapstick styles of *House of Payne* and *Meet the Browns*. *For Better or Worse* is an adult relationship comedy drama with no laugh track but still promoting racial stereotypes and gross distortion of black life.

For Better or Worse, like most of Perry's work, is set in Atlanta. The show premiered on November 25, 2011. The first season consisted of only 10 episodes, but TBS picked up the show for a second season. The sitcom is based on Perry's film *Why Did I Get Married?* The show centers on the trials and tribulations of a boisterous married couple. Angela and Marcus Williams, who love each other deeply, are trying to rebuild their marriage after various extramarital affairs committed by both of them. Their transgressions have caused a lack of trust within their relationship. Other characters on the show are at varying stages of their relationships, and these couples offset Angela and Marcus's volatile relationship as they depict the highs and lows of dating and marriage. Angela is the star of the show for her brass personality. She is loud, overbearing, rude, and stubborn. She is the quintessential angry black woman. Historically, black women have been portrayed in popular culture as the sassy mammies from the early 1800s all the way up through the early 1990s. Sassy mammies are depictions of black women who are overbearing and constantly berating and verbally abusing their male mates. Sassy mammies are mean spirited and take pleasure in verbally emasculating black men.[21] By the early 1900s, the sassy mammy caricature evolved into the caricature of Sapphire with the creation of the character Sapphire Stevens. Sapphire Stevens was George "Kingfish" Stevens's wife on the blatantly racist radio show *Amos 'n' Andy*. Without fail, Sapphire would belittle Kingfish for his failures and reinforce negative stereotypes regarding black men as incompetent. Some of the most notable Sapphires within popular culture are Mammy (*Gone with the Wind*), Aunt Esther (*Sanford and Son*), Pam Grier (*Coffy*), and Omarosa (*The Apprentice*). Angela's primary role on *For Better or Worse* is to emasculate her husband, Marcus. In Season 1 of the show, when Angela was not yelling or punching Marcus, she was trying to hit him in the head with a frying pan or setting his clothes on fire in his car. Moreover, every character on the show is afraid of Angela, regardless of their sex. The entire first season is devoted to Angela comforting Marcus about his infidelities and the couple dealing with his ex-girlfriend and mother of Marcus's teenage daughter, Keisha. The story lines are also developed in an elementary fashion. Thus, by the end of Season 1, Marcus's business partner is dating Keisha, which makes for more outlandish scenes.

Overall, Perry's treatment of black women is debasing and rooted in the most vile black pathology and stereotypes. Madea and Angela are classic examples of the gender and racial caricature Sapphire. Through characters Janine Payne, the recovering drug addict who abandoned her kids, Sasha, the married women who kissed her husband's mentor, and Tanya Ortiz, who lost custody of her two children and served jail time, Perry portrays these black women as jezebels. Jezebels are innately promiscuous and sexually deviant. They are also poor, uneducated, and incapable of making good life decisions. The depiction of black women as jezebels was used to justify the rape of black female slaves. The slave-era jezebel was a whore who was sexually insatiable.[22] Thus, in the minds of white men, they were not raping black women because they were property, and black women desired sexual relations with white men. Perry's use of these tropes, the jezebel and Sapphire, is not as vile as that of a slave master, but he has modernized these tropes to perpetuate the most harmful stereotypes regarding black women while simultaneously teaching his audience about forgiveness and redemption.

In all of his sitcoms, the black man suffers as he waits for his wife or girl-friend to overcome her adversities. Even though Marcus cheats on his wife, he still takes her abuse. I am not arguing that Perry should display black male characters as downtrodden to even up the score between sexes or that highlighting the struggles of black women is not important. The issue is the simplicity of the characters and how they are based on enduring and hurt-ful stereotypes of black men and women.

In examining all three shows, the use of racist stereotypes is apparent and overdone. Perry's shows are plagued with simplistic story lines and low-level character development, as well as overwhelmed with comedic relief that resembles a modern-day minstrel show. Colemen refers to black actors' appearances in sitcoms rooted in racist ideologies used to justify racial injustices as "neominstrelsy."[23] Coleman and McIlwain suggest that black sitcoms regularly practice the use of stereotypical representations of blackness to promote humor.[24] According to Coleman and McIlwain, there has only been a small number of sitcoms in the last 20 years that put black-ness and the issues that impact folks of color at the forefront: *The Bernie Mac Show, The Hughleys,* and *My Wife and Kids.* These shows are notewor-thy because blackness was a significant and necessary part of the show.[25] But by far the most popular and critically acclaimed television show to bring black faces into millions of American homes was *The Cosby Show.*

The Cosby Show entered American living rooms in 1984 with the ap-proval of white Americans, who embraced the fictional Huxtable family. Bill Cosby created a black family that was "just Black enough not to of-fend and middle class enough to comfort."[26] Before *The Cosby Show,* the notion of mass applicability was seen as problematic for black sitcoms. The conventional thought at the time was that black sitcoms needed to be universal enough to reach both black and white audiences. Thus, black successful sitcoms, like *The Cosby Show,* were based on an assimilationist objective that situated black life within the context of post–civil rights. The Cosby family represented the black bourgeoisie: affluent black Ameri-cans who understood the struggles of slavery, racism, and discrimination but shifted their efforts into "celebrations of black middle class visibil-ity and achievement."[27] When *The Cosby Show* went off the air in 1992, networks struggled to create a comparable show in terms of positioning African American life within American values. Moreover, the image of black Americans was marred after eight years of being labeled America's problem child during Reaganomics—President Ronald Reagan's political attack on people of color who were poor and disadvantaged. By manipulating Americans with fear slogans like "War on Crime," "War on Drugs," "welfare queens," and "gang wars," Reagan's tactics helped cultivate a disclosure around blackness that was rooted in racist ideologies.[28] The years following Reagan's presidency, 1990–1998, began the "Neominstrelsy Era" of television.[29] During this era, television programming began to mirror America's contrived notions of blackness via the propaganda of the Reagan administration and his successor, George H.W. Bush. Neocoons filled the airwaves on networks with limited experience producing black sitcoms: *Goode Behavior, Malcolm and Eddie, Sparks, Homeboys in Outer Space* (all on UPN), and *The Wayans Brothers* (*WB*). Each of these sitcoms proliferated the caricatures of black males as coons and Sambos. In fact, *The Wayans Brothers* sitcom was so racially distasteful that a local NAACP chapter called for a boycott of the show. Thus, to contextualize Perry's work with other black comedies, actors, and sitcoms, he is traveling down a dark road that is well traveled.

In addition to Perry's use of historically black male and female caricatures, he is not the first black man to put on a dress, wear high heels, and depict a loud, violent, irrational, and outspoken black woman. Flip Wilson (Geraldine), Eddie Murphy (Mama Klump), Martin Lawrence (Big Momma and Sheneneh Jenkins), and Jamie Foxx (Wanda) have all dressed in drag to portray the most egregious stereotypes of black women. However, none have received more scrutiny than Perry. *The Boondocks* creator Aaron McGruder portrayed Perry as a cloaked homosexual hiding behind Christianity and women's clothes in his satirical animated series. In the episode "Pause," Winston Jerome is a successful black playwright and director, who is also a closeted, cross-dressing gay man and devout Christian. Furthermore, Jerome's career is based on the gun-toting matriarch Ma Dukes, who Jerome dresses in drag to play. The plot of the episode centers on Jerome casting Robert Freeman, the granddad on the cartoon, to be the lead actor in the play "Ma Dukes Finds Herself a Man" in return for sexual favors. Moreover, the larger point of the episode is that Winston Jerome, who is obviously a parody of Tyler Perry, is using Christianity to seduce men. Although the claims of Perry being a gay man are unsubstantiated, his practice of using religion as a tool to connect with his black Christian conservative audience is a large part of his success and likability. Perry uses religion to naturalize his show's stereotypic representations of black life. On that particular element, Perry's success is quite timely in that it mirrors the black megachurch movement in America. According to *Ebony* magazine, there are over 100 black megachurches in the United States, each claiming between 10,000 and 30,000 members.[30] Atlanta has two of the largest mega-church congregations: New Birth, Eddie Long's Church, and Creflo Dollar's Church, World Changers. These churches calculate combined seating to total roughly 30,000 worshippers every Sunday, which does not account for their television membership. Black megachurches and their male pastors play a unique role in Perry's success, as Perry lures his audience with stereotypical racial comedy in hopes that they will find God.

God Trumps Race: Playing the Jesus Card

In 2008, *Time* magazine referred to Perry as the "hero of the older Black Christian Community."[31] Perry told *Time* that he turned down an opportunity to produce a television comedy earlier in his career when company executives informed him that his show could not be religious. Perry said he told top executives:

> If you don't want my God here, you don't want me here either. God has been too good to me to go and try to sell out to get some money. That's O.K. I will sit in a corner and be broke with the Lord before I will sit there and have them give me millions and sell my soul. It ain't gonna happen.[32]

Perry has taken the messages from the black church's pulpit to prime-time television. Unlike many entertainers, Perry is open about his faith, and it plays a major part in his persona and appeal. For black folks, the church represents the oldest and most influential institution in the black community.[33] Research shows that church affiliation is vital among black folks, regardless of socioeconomic levels.[34] What is most remarkable about the black church as an institution is its reach beyond the church doors. Elijah Ward argues,

> But what is also striking is the influence it wields indirectly in the lives of those that are not churchgoers. Even if as adults they no longer embrace the church or religious principles, many blacks have been profoundly influenced by the church ideology and imagery with which they were raised, and this continues to influence their later beliefs and practices.[35]

Certainly, not all African Americans attend church, but the black churches' ideology of love, forgiveness, and redemption are terms most blacks identify with, and these concepts are fixtures within Perry's work. Both *Meet the Browns* and *House of Payne* have even featured award-wining gospel singers. Furthermore, Perry produced megachurch pastor

T. D. Jakes's best-selling book, *Woman Thou Art Loosed,* into a stage musical. Jakes's church in Dallas, Texas, has an estimated 30,000 members. Bishop Eddie Long, whose Atlanta-based church has over 25,000 members, also appeared in one of Perry's films, *Daddy's Little Girls.* Thus, through endorsements by megachurch pastors and his candidness regarding his faith, which is intentionally pronounced in his sitcoms, Perry carved out his audience, black churchgoers who want to see themselves and their faith represented in television. When asked in the 2008 interview with *Time* about the religious messages entrenched in his work, Perry said, "I have this unbelievable pull to have people see these movies and be healed. . . . So many people are in need of healing."[36] That unbelievable pull is embodied in Madea, Leroy Brown, and Curtis Payne, whom Perry uses as racist stereotypical baits.

To Perry, faith trumps race. Tracy Scott defended Perry's work by adding, "If you look deeper at Perry's message these characters really are bait. . . . He's using comedy to educate the masses."[37] But the questions still remain as to the nature of that education. Offensive racial comedy, no matter if it is masked within religion, is problematic in its limiting effect on the audience's potential for critical reflection.[38] Moreover, offensive racial comedy reaffirms negative stereotypes while embedding these concepts within the communal cultural consciousness of mainstream America. However, it is important to note that people read texts in various ways. Stuart Hall would argue that it is "cultural elitism" to assume that black folks cannot consume the work of Perry and cannot negotiate his messages to construct meaning in their everyday lives.[39] To be clear, I am not reducing Perry's use of racial tropes, which are destructive, but Perry's audience are not "culture dopes" unable to decode the media.[40] These viewers are decoding Perry's message just as they are decoding the work of Lee and Touré. Put another way, interpretations are fluid, and consumers have the ability to exploit and resist media messages.[41] Nonetheless, David Morley suggested that interpretive freedom oftentimes leads us to undervalue the power of the media.[42] Morley writes, "the power of viewers to reinterpret meaning is hardly equivalent to the discursive power of the centralized media institutions to construct the texts which the viewer then interprets, and to imagine otherwise is simply foolish."[43] Ji Hoon Park, Nadine Gabbadon, and Ariel Chernin concluded that offensive racial comedy naturalize one's beliefs of racial differences, which allows one to enjoy the humor.[44] The researchers added that audiences' pleasure of a certain movie or sitcom that uses racial humor requires the audiences' acceptance of racial stereotypes to find pleasure.

The popularity of *Meet the Browns, House of Payne,* and *For Better or Worse* implies that blacks are laughing with Perry and at themselves, but in order to laugh at racial stereotypes, blacks also have to accept these jokes, though not necessarily as absolute truths. Blacks have accepted racial humor because it represents the dominant ideologies of black folks that are fixed within society. The great comedian Richard Pryor was a genius at deconstructing America's racism; Pryor's fans were laughing with him because they agreed with his position on race and believed that there was not much they could do to eradicate racism. Pryor once said his fans, "I live in racist America and I'm uneducated, yet a lot of people love me and like what I do, and I can make a living from it. You can't do much better than that." He added, "White people go, Why you guys hold your things? Cause you done took everything else, motherfucker." Pryor understood that racism is a "permanent fixture" within society.[45] However, as Pryor used burlesque humor to expose America's unyielding racism and make it relatable to his audience, Perry is exploiting America's racism for his message of God, which is why Perry's shows are disappointing and embarrassing. Perry's sitcoms do not use subversive comedy to expose racism; rather, these shows perpetuate the most harmful stereotypes about black men and women in the name of God.

Perry has captured a viewing audience that is yearning for black entertainers and God; this combination makes Perry nearly unstoppable because of his faith and the limited amount of black faces on television. In the fall of 2011, there were only estimated 33 black actors and actresses on prime-time television networks.[46] That number stands in contrast to the Nielsen statistics indicating that blacks have the highest television watching rate in comparison to other ethnicities. Blacks watch an average of 7 hours 12 minutes of television each day; the national average is 5 hours 11 minutes.[47] Perry's appeal is only going to grow with the rise of black megachurches and Hollywood's absentmindedness in regard to black viewership. Perry's empire is robust and will withstand Lee and Touré's diatribes. Furthermore, in the years to come, Perry will pass the self-hating torch, freely or reluctantly, of making millions by depicting black men and women as downtrodden, uneducated, and buffoonish to other black entertainment moguls who will follow Perry's playbook. After all, the playbook that Perry uses was not created by him and will not end with him. The ideological beliefs of white supremacy are at the heart of Perry's work. And since "racism is an integral, permanent, and indestructible component of this society,"[48] there will be more Tyler Perrys to come.

Notes

1. Richard Corliss, "Madea's Big Happy Family: Tyler Perry's Drag Ball," *Time,* April 24, 2011.

2. "Tyler Perry to Spike Lee: 'Go Straight to Hell,'" *Huffington Post,* April 20, 2011.

3. Donald Bogle, *Toms, Coons, Mulattoes, Mammies, & Bucks: An Interpretive History of Blacks in American Films* (New York: Continuum, 1994).

4. Jorge Rivas, "Touré Calls Tyler Perry's Work 'Cinematic Malt Liquor for the Masses,'" *Color Lines,* September 22, 2011.

5. Valerie Boyd, "Mad about Madea: Tyler Perry Has Built an Empire. So Why Can't He Catch a Break?," *Atlanta,* September 1, 2011.

6. Ibid.

7. Pamela K. Johnson, "Diary of a Brilliant Black Man: Triumphing over Painful Memories of Childhood Abuse at the Hands of His Father, Tyler Perry Fiercely Chronicles Family Love, Forgiveness and Redemption," *Essence,* December 16, 2009.

8. Boyd, "Mad about Madea."

9. "Tyler Perry To Spike Lee: 'Go Straight to Hell,'" *Huffington Post,* April 20, 2011.

10. Johnson, "Diary of a Brilliant Black Man."

11. Gerald Early, Glenda Carpio, and Werner Sollors, "Black Humor: Reflections on an American Tradition," *Bulletin of the American Academy* Vol. 64, No. 4 (Summer 2010): pp. 29–40.

12. Ibid.

13. Roy Hurst, "Stepin Fetchit, Hollywood's First Black Film Star," *NPR,* March 6, 2006, http://www.npr.org/templates/story/story.php?storyId=5245089.

14. Early, Carpio, and Sollors, "Black Humor."

15. Hurst, "Stepin Fetchit."

16. Ibid.

17. Mel Watkins, *Stepin Fetchit: The Life and Times of Lincoln Perry* (New York: Vintage, 2005).

18. Michael Omi, "In Living Color: Race and American Culture," in *Cultural Politics in Contemporary America,* ed. by Ian Angus and Sut Jhally (London: Routledge, 1989), pp. 111–22.; Clint C. Wilson, Felix Gutierrez, and Lena M. Chao, *Racism, Sexism, and the Media: The Rise of Class Communication in Multicultural America* (Thousand Oaks, CA: Sage, 2003).

19. Debra Shigley, "Perry's Peers: For African American Filmmakers Atlanta is a Small Pond with Big Fish," *Atlanta,* September 2011.

20. Corliss, "Madea's Big Happy Family."

21. Marilyn Yarbrough and Crystal Bennett, "Cassandra and the 'Sistahs': The Peculiar Treatment of African American Women in the Myth of Women as Liars," *Journal of Gender, Race and Justice* 24 (2000): pp. 626–57.

22. Patricia Hill Collins, *Black Sexual Politics: African Americans, Gender and the New Racism* (New York: Routledge, 2005).

23. Robin R. Means Coleman, *African American Viewers and the Black Situation Comedy: Situating Racial Humor* (New York: Garland Publishers, 2000).

24. Robin R. Means Coleman and Charlton D. McIlwain, "Hidden Truths in Black Sitcoms," in *The Sitcom Reader: America Viewed and Skewed,* ed. by Mary M. Dalton and Laura R. Linder (New York: SUNY University Press, 2005): pp. 125–38.

25. Ibid.

26. Herman Gray, *Watching Race: Television and the Struggle for Blackness* (Minneapolis: University of Minnesota Press, 1995), p. 122.

27. Ibid., p. 378.

28. Bettina L. Love, *Hip Hop's Li'l Sistas Speak: Negotiating Identities and Politics in the New* (New York: Peter Lang, 2012).

29. Coleman and McIlwain, "Hidden Truths in Black Sitcoms."

30. "The New Black Spirituality," *Ebony,* December 1, 2004, pp. 136–40.

31. "God and Tyler Perry vs. Hollywood," *Time,* March 20, 2008.

32. Ibid.

33. C. Eric Lincoln and Lawrence H. Mamiya, *The Black Church in the African American Experience* (Durham, NC: Duke University Press, 1990).

34. Elijah G. Ward, "Homophobia, Hypermasculinity, and the U.S. Black Church," *Culture, Health, and Sexuality* Vol. 7, No. 5 (2005): pp. 493–504.

35. Ibid., p. 494.

36. "God and Tyler Perry," *Time.*

37. Tracy Scott, "Touré: Tyler Perry Is 'Worst Director,'" *Sister-to-Sister,* September 9, 2011.

38. Ji Hoon Park, Nadine G. Gabbadon, and Ariel R. Chernin, "Naturalizing Racial Differences through Comedy: Asian, Black and White Views on Racial Stereotypes in *Rush Hour 2," Journal of Communication* 56 (2006): pp. 157–77.

39. Stuart Hall, *Critical Dialogues in Cultural Studies* (London and New York: Routledge, 1996).

40. Stuart Hall, "Notes on Deconstructing 'The Popular,'" in *People's History and Socialist Theory,* ed. by Raphael Samuel (Boston: Routledge & Kegan, 1981), pp. 227–40.

41. Jesús Martín-Barbero, *Communication, Culture and Hegemony: From the Media to Mediations* (London: Sage, 1993).

42. David Morley, "Theoretical Orthodoxies: Textualism, Constructivism and the 'New Ethnography,'" in *Cultural Studies: From Theory to Action,* ed. by Pepi Leistyna (Malden, MA: Blackwell, 2005), pp. 171–87.

43. Ibid., p. 175.

44. Park, Gabbadon, and Chernin, "Naturalizing Racial Difference through Comedy."

45. Derrick Bell, *Faces at the Bottom of the Well: The Permanence of Racism* (New York: Basic Books, 1992), p. ix.

46. Kelli Martin, "Blacks on T.V.: Is It Getting Better or Worse," *Clutch,* May 3, 2011.

47. Cited in Martin, "Blacks on T.V."

48. Bell, *Faces at the Bottom of the Well,* p. x.

Chapter 16

B(l)ack in the Kitchen: Food Network

Lisa A. Guerrero

For the better part of modern television history, television programming devoted to cooking had been relegated to public television stations. Chefs including Julia Child, Graham Kerr (*The Galloping Gourmet*), and Martin Yan were PBS favorites who provided exotic and entertaining cooking instructions for American audiences whose palates and food attitudes had been largely shaped by the advent of television dinners and fast-food restaurants. In the minds of many American viewers, the food programming on public television, like the other programming on PBS, was seen, accurately or not, as somewhat highbrow, in other words, not appealing to the average American viewer, consumer, and home cook. Even as the roster of the PBS cooking shows grew and shifted over the years, this perception, by and large, remained the same. However, toward the later part of the 20th century, a new consumer trend began to mount, and a new popular consumer personality emerged: the foodie.

Though there is no precise origin date for this consumer personality, the rise of wealth and conspicuous consumption among Americans (at least, a portion of mainly white American public) during the 1980s mark a noticeable upswing of America's interest in distinctive food trends and products including: Dijon mustard (most notably Grey Poupon), celebrity chefs like Wolfgang Puck, and exotic foreign cuisines like sushi, Thai food, and African food. With the emergence of this new consumer type, a whole new commodity landscape was opened up. Gourmet food stores began popping up across neighborhoods all over the United States; chefs started to become the new rock stars; reservations at famous and trendy eateries began to be as coveted as Super Bowl tickets; and home cooks started to imagine that what they once did as a grinding chore could actually be transformed into a glamorous trend and a source of entertainment. With this swell in consumer interest in all things food, the public became hungry to learn how they, too, could become a part of this popular new food culture. And they didn't necessarily want to learn from the low-budget (read: low glamour) cooking programs that they saw on PBS. They wanted chefs and shows that were befitting the enormity of a pop culture trend.

"Way More than Cooking"

Giving people what, ostensibly, they wanted, in the 1990s, cable television executives came up with a plan that not only tapped into this burgeoning, eager foodie culture but would also effectively change its face and dynamic in remarkable and problematic ways. In November of 1993, Food Network (originally named TV Food Network) debuted introducing complex new chapters into both American food culture and television culture. As food culture has exploded as a pop culture trend, Food Network has paradoxically served to simultaneously democratize food culture (at least performatively, as we will see) and constantly elevate it to newer, trendier heights. Like MTV forever transformed the way many people would think about music, so too has Food Network changed the way many people think about food. Food has gone Hollywood! In other words, "*Iron Chef* killed the PBS star."[1] This transformative food project relies on changing the perspective of food from something you need for nourishment and survival to something you need for entertainment and status. This ingenious and variously dangerous shift in perspective requires a relatively rigid assumption about audience demographics, and in turn, these assumptions themselves begin to actually shape the demographic until those who were imagined both inside and outside of the particular consumer community become less imaginary and more reality.

With their slogan, "Way More than Cooking," Food Network, far from just showing the American public how to cook and what to eat and how to participate in American food culture, has also drawn a stark picture of both the transformation of food from necessity to commodity, as well as the populations whose participation in American food culture counts—and whose doesn't. In this chapter, I look at the presence (and absence) of African American food personalities on Food Network and trace the ways in which the combination of their overall scarcity and their seeming strategic deployment affects the ideological and consumptive attitudes of the American viewing public.

Before I begin my consideration of the place of blackness on Food Network, it is important to first frame the general mode of class and race that the network embraces and engenders. It is these ideological foundations of the network that dictate the ways in which blackness gets integrated into the programming and the larger effects which that integration has had on the audiences' understandings of not only American food culture but also African Americans' contributions to and participation in it.

The Hungry Masses

In 2007, it was reported that an estimated 3.5 million people were homeless, with 1.35 million of those being children.[2] Additionally, it was estimated that in 2009, 50.2 million people lived in food-insecure households, 17.2 million of those were children.[3] In other words, during 2009, for *half* of the U.S. population, food was not only *not* viewed as a commodity, it wasn't viewed as much of a reality. Despite these tragic numbers, in the postmodern era, food has become a curious case of commodity value supplanting nutritional value. Unlike most other commodities that clutter the minds of consumers, food is an object that, just out of sheer necessity and basic science, would be consumed by the public *without* it being marketed to them. However, in a consumer society, where everything can be, and is, turned into a commodity, food is no exception and gets sold to us every day in ways that remove it from the narrative of basic necessity and place it into a constructed commodity narrative of unique luxury. Considering this fundamental fact, the explosion of the commodification of food cultures at the end of the 20th century and into the new millennium suggests the overt social class project that lies at the heart of the foodie trend in popular culture.

Similar to all pop culture trends, Food Network and the foodie culture it represents presupposes the disposable income of its audience, meaning that its frame of reference naturalizes the middle-to-upper economic class positions of its viewers. The working class and working poor are erased in this demographic equation. Arguably, the erasure of a working class and working poor demographic in a majority of pop culture trends is nothing new. Pop culture is commodity driven, so the obvious targeted audiences are those with money to spend. However, the foodie culture trend, and more specifically, Food Network, is unique, as pop culture trends go, in that it seems to ignore a well-known truth in commodity culture: even as middle- and upper-class groups have bigger disposable incomes, the working and lower-middle classes and the working poor actually *spend* more of their disposable incomes. This is more logical than it sounds because at the heart of pop commodity culture what is really being sold is social identity.

A person may or may not have a particular social position in reality but through the purchasing and possession of commodities can still articulate the social identity linked to that social position. Lower social classes spend lots of money in order to detach themselves and their identities from the realities of their marginalized social positions.

But when it comes to food, the model shifts slightly. Unlike material possessions such as athletic shoes, televisions, and cars, people cannot generally (1) buy food on credit and (2) display food so as to project a particular social identity. As a consequence, food generally gets mass-marketed differently than other commodities. Instead of luxury or trendiness being foregrounded, convenience and value are the marks of most of the food marketing out there. Since mainstream advertising is largely absorbed by middle, working, and lower economic classes, it is *their* food ideologies that are most affected by this avenue of marketing. And unlike the middle class that has a certain economic stability that allows for a relative fluidity to move between the borders of the fast-food nation and the status of culinary hobbyists, the working and lower classes are, by and large, permanently fixed in that singular food culture model. Though these lower social classes may eat food, or at the very least, *need* to eat food, they don't have the resources to eat food in trendy, socially elevated ways. As a result, those groups remain inconsequential to Food Network, even as food itself remains far from inconsequential to these groups themselves. So the marketing of foodie culture occupies a different social location than that of most other mainstream food marketing. Stated another way, foodie culture isn't concerned with selling food, (even as it does) but instead is focused on selling a narrative of food as entertainment, as art, and as identity. Big Macs and frozen dinners are marketed to people who are hungry, budget minded, and short on time. Truffles and the proper method of deglazing a pan are marketed to people who have time, money, and the luxury that those two things provide in order to think creatively about their hunger.

So the demographic exclusion of the working class and working poor in Food Network's commodity project, while not wholly unexpected, still works at creating a stringently stratified perspective on the social parameters of foodie culture. That is to say that in the realm of American food culture, if you're rich, food can be looked at as play and pleasure. Nutrition and quality are foregrounded, and surplus and decadence are naturalized. Conversely, if you're poor, food is practical . . . if present at all. Efficiency and quantity are primary, and nutrition is often considered epiphenomenal. Ironically, Food Network itself recognizes this social gap in American food habits (though clearly not enough to interrogate its own participation in creating that gap) with its oft-advertised support of the Share Our Strength organization, an organization that works to end child hunger in America and make sure that every child gets the food that he or she needs to thrive. Undoubtedly, the much-needed food that the Share Our Strength organization, with the support of Food Network and its viewers, provides to families and children, while certainly desirable to *them*, will never show up as meal ideas or even ingredients on the shows of network stars like Rachael Ray, Bobby Flay, Giada DeLaurentis, and Ina Garten, (though possibly on Sandra Lee's show, which will be discussed shortly). The purpose of Food Network, in fact, is to erase those ideas and images that link food to notions of deprivation, including those who are deprived, and instead sell the image of food as a choice—an indulgent, abundant choice.

Even as Food Network has made subtle nods to the potential need for economizing when it comes to food in the face of the debilitating recession and economic downturn that faced the United States beginning in the early part of the 21st century, with shows like "Money-Saving Meals with Sandra Lee and "Ten-Dollar Dinners with Melissa D'Arabian," its representation of eating on a budget remains grounded in a specific social context that imagines budgetary constraints as a mere invitation to have fun while stretching a dollar and not as an actual obstacle to feeding one's family nutritiously or at all. Certainly, there are understandable reasons, both practical and ideological, why Food Network does not have programming focused on how to create culinary innovations with a loaf of white bread and a jar of peanut butter at the end of the month. For one, it would not appeal to audiences. Regardless of the subject, television is still regarded as a means of escape, and not only would programming like that *not* provide escape from reality, it would actually force viewers to contend explicitly with reality. Further, Food Network is aware that those people in the United States whose food reality is a loaf of bread and a jar of peanut butter at the end of the month (if that) aren't, by and large, going to be watching Food Network. Generally speaking, they don't have the leisure time, the resources, and, likely, the interest to relate to their food in such privileged ways. But even as we acknowledge these viable logics for Food Network to *not* deal with the idea of hunger in more realistic and sociopolitical terms, we can't deny that the effect of following these logics is the continued ideological containment of poorer classes outside of the larger public's consideration of who counts socially and culturally. And the use of a fundamental human need like food as the vehicle for this sociocultural exclusion and the enforcement of strict class hierarchies arguably makes Food Network one of the more problematic interventions in television and media culture in the last 30 years.

However, it is not only for the ways in which Food Network constructs particular classist frameworks for its programming that make it a problematic participant in the larger systems that marginalize particular classes and groups in the United States, it is also for the ways in which it creates a largely raceless narrative around food, food production, and food consumption in its programming and through its celebrities. In all of its programming, even within programs where race is undeniably apparent, either because of the celebrity or the cuisine, food is presented as a race-neutral cultural object. Unfortunately, in a race-based society, as the United States is, race neutral invariably gets translated as white. Food Network trades in the notion of the racelessness of food to create a commodified sense of neoliberal inclusion and equality, wherein the focus is placed on individuals and not on systems. Food is portrayed across the network as a universal language, but, as discussed above, it is definitely constructed as a specific class-based language, as well as a language constructed in specifically racialized terms. To be fair, Food Network is no different from most other cable television networks where whiteness is predominant and becomes easily normalized and rendered invisible to most viewers. However, Food Network differs in that none of its programming is scripted series (i.e., dramas and sitcoms), and therefore, though not reality television per se, all of its programming relies on notions of actuality, authenticity, and cultural neutrality.[4] In other words, Rachael Ray isn't a character (well, at least insofar as Rachael Ray isn't playing anyone but herself), she's a real person like the viewers, who just happens to know how to cook, quickly, apparently. She's presented as an average Everywoman, though what she *is* is a white upper-class woman-cum-media mogul. But even those celebrities on Food Network who aren't framed by a specifically Everywoman/man narrative are still presented as if they exemplify a kind of ordinariness that all viewers can relate to. Ironically, the relatability that Food Network carefully crafts around its personalities is almost completely belied by the everyday lifestyles many of the network celebrities are shown to have as they are strategically integrated into their respective shows, most notably with Ina Garten, Giada DeLaurentis, and Bobby Flay. While the wealth and whiteness displayed in these, and much of Food Network's other programming, is conspicuous, they are treated as commonplace, the effect of which is twofold: (1) it creates a sociocial standard when it comes to the act of food consumption and (2) it suggestively endorses the idea of food as a racial and economic privilege. Through its successful erasure of race and class, Food Network perpetuates certain understandings about the social landscape in which people think about food consumption and commodification as being generally equal among various populations, even as statistically and programmatically most people can see that food equality isn't a reality. But Food Network is able to maintain this profitable food fantasy by constructing its food narratives in a very particular sociohistorical vacuum that allows audiences to distance themselves from not only certain tediums surrounding daily food habits but also the sociohistorical and socioeconomic systems of food production and preparation in the United States. The strategic use of blackness on the network is one of the primary ways in which this distancing is enabled.

The relative absence of blackness on Food Network, while not unlike the relative absence of blackness on network television generally speaking, succeeds in denying the significant place African Americans have, both historically and contemporaneously, in the creation of American food culture and foodways. This erasure, while creating an amputated impression of American food backgrounds, does so in deliberate ways that are in keeping with long histories of using whiteness to signify notions of expertise, virtuosity, superiority, propriety, and polish. In other words, in order to cement the network's guiding narrative of elevating food to a craft, an art, an aspiration, it needs to simultaneously elevate whiteness, usually white maleness. Not surprisingly, the programming on Food Network frames American food in very Eurocentric terms, tracing food origins and traditions to primarily Western, European nations, while periodically recognizing the exotic fare of Latin America or Asia. There is little to no recognition of African cuisines within programming, despite the growing popularity of African food and restaurants among American *consumers* sparked by growing numbers of African immigrants to the United States and probably represented most notably by the often-tokenized celebrity chef, Marcus Samuelsson, who was born in Ethiopia and raised in Sweden. Neither is there much linkage drawn between the specificity of African American soul food and the development of much of what is considered American Southern food. The erasure of these African and African American cultural linkages to American food habits and histories effectively reimagines a significant portion of American food architecture as almost exclusively white, a reimagining not supported by history. Now certainly Food Network isn't The History Channel, and viewers aren't necessarily expecting to be provided with critically accurate or developed histories of food origins, routes, or social significances. Nonetheless, its lack of wider, more representative narrative frames within its programming results in two things: First, there is a barely perceptible, encompassing whitening of both the network itself as well as the perspectives it creates about food relationships within American populations. Secondly, when racial diversity and representation do occur, they have the effect of tokenism rather than inclusion. Nowhere is this latter effect more apparent than in the network's small club of black cooking personalities.

At the writing of this chapter, there are three regular programs on Food Network that are hosted by black personalities: *Down Home with the Neelys, Cooking for Real,* and *Big Daddy's House.* Married couple and BBQ restaurateurs, Pat and Gina Neely, host the first show. Sunny Anderson hosts the second show. And Aaron McCargo Jr., who is a past winner of the network's annual competition "The Next Food Network Star," hosts the last show. Besides having hosts who are African Americans among the sea of white hosts that make up the network, these shows share several other problematic characteristics that define Food Network's problem with race.

None of the hosts of these three shows is a trained chef. In and of itself, this fact isn't terribly disturbing. Not until this characteristic is placed into the context of the rest of Food Network's lineup are we able to identify the troubling narrative the network succeeds in constructing around food, cooking, and blackness. One of the first things notable about the character of the lineup is that the majority of the other personalities in the network's lineup are professionally trained chefs. While none of the shows are framed to emphasize the professionalized aspect of the food industry, the notion of expertise is deployed in various and strategic ways in order to locate the network's stars in a position of unstated authority that constructs a distinct separation between the audience and the personality. Even as the stars in these cases are presented as friendly, normal, and everyday, they are also infused with an elevated status that keeps viewers situated apart from them. And in the other cases of white personalities who have no formal training, it is their whiteness that helps to maintain a particular stratification between themselves and their viewers, even their white viewers, by spectacularizing their abilities relative to the work-a-day cook. In contrast, the shows focused on black hosts are framed in such a way as to naturalize the cooking they do. They are seen as real cooks whose ability is a natural character they possess. There are no boundaries placed between them and viewers because their cooking skills aren't institutionally legitimated by either training or race. They become relegated to the historically informed imaginary landscape of black domesticity. Of course, black people know how to cook—that's just what they do. If they can cook, certainly you can too. In this way, both the food preparation *and* the hosts themselves are presented as nonthreatening.

All of the hosts of these three programs are portrayed as a singular type: down-home, jovial, and real or authentic. There is a kind of *what you see is what you get* logic that informs the programming around the network's black hosts. This logic is reflected very clearly in the titles given to the programs. *Down Home with the Neelys, Cooking for Real,* and *Big Daddy's House*—all convey a sense of being invited in and treated as a guest. As a result, these programs place much of their emphasis on the *enjoyment* of food, particularly the viewers' enjoyment, and less on the mechanics and instruction of preparation like the other instruction programs on the network. The foregrounded quality of domesticity in the three programs with black hosts resituates blackness in a historically essentialized realm of care-taking. It's not the hosts' skills or recipes that become important within these three programs but rather the feeling of comfort with which they can provide the audience. Also important in the narrative framing of these three shows is the connections viewers are able to make to *real* cooking.

As the titles of the three programs imply, and as the title of Sunny Anderson's program makes explicit, these shows are meant to be understood as organic, not so much in the "green" food-related sense (in fact, *not at all* in the "green" food-related sense) but rather in the sense of character as being "natural" and soulful. In fact, if we look closely at the title of Anderson's show, it begs the question "what are we doing *if not* cooking for real?" But the point of the title isn't about the realness of the food or the act, but of the person performing the act and making the food. This narrative framing that is unique to this particular set of black-hosted programs, succeeds at setting them apart from the other shows devoted to cooking instruction with white hosts. Unlike the programming featuring their white counterparts, it is not the sense of skill, expertise, or innovation that gets emphasized with the Neelys, Anderson, and McCargo. Instead, what is foregrounded in their shows is the sense of the food as uncomplicated, humble home cooking and of the hosts as the food personified; they are portrayed as humble, natural cooks who are invested in the caretaking, communal aspect of food and food preparation. They are shown to be perfectly capable cooks, but it is not their cooking abilities on which the goal of the shows rely (and it *is* a singular goal for all three shows), rather it is their performative ability both to reify the naturalized authenticity ascribed to blackness, as well as to neutralize the threat of blackness by situating it in the acceptable, though ideologically charged, realm of domesticity.

Interestingly, this domesticity narrative only works, given the demographics of the viewing audience laid out in the beginning of the chapter as a white middle-class viewership, to further solidify the racial stratification of the network. This is because in many ways the stories these three programs tell are anathema to several realities for communities of color in the United States. The first is the relationship of bodies of color to domestic spaces and behaviors. While nearly everyone in the United States, regardless of race, has some connection to spaces and behaviors of domesticity, the ways in which people of color have largely been imagined within those domestic relationships are inside a frame of servitude. Historically, and to a great extent, contemporaneously, people of color are located within a domestic space that is not seen as their own, where they are translated as laborers and/or inferiors, not as equals.[5] So, in framing the only three shows on the network to feature black people prominently in a kind of welcome home narrative that capitalizes on the friendly realness of the hosts' blackness, the network endorses (whether consciously or subconsciously is impossible to determine) a particular understanding of domesticity as a racialized construct. These hosts are meant to be understood, in not-so-metaphorical terms, as *cooking for you,* an understanding that only works most effectively when the *you* that is imagined by the network executives is white. For most people of color viewing these programs, this understanding is both easily recognizable and highly discomfiting.

The second contradistinction between these three programs and certain social realities related to people of color in the United States has to do with issues of health. Again, with the narrative emphasis placed on comfort in these three shows, the food on display is, by and large, not what would immediately be identified as health conscious. Now, while it can be argued that other programs on the network also do not focus on the health-conscious aspect of food (Paula Deen's programs spring immediately to mind), there is still enough programming diversity among shows hosted by white personalities that Paula Deen doesn't become the *sole* narrative around food, which is not the case with the only three shows hosted by black personalities.

In a country where people of color live in communities disproportionately affected by food deserts (lack of sufficient access to fresh food outlets like grocery stores) and food swamps (the overabundant access to processed and fast foods, oftentimes as the *only* choice for nourishment),[6] and where African Americans disproportionately suffer from heart disease, hypertension, and diabetes, the need for not only access to better basic food opportunities but also the guidance and instruction on how to make and prepare healthier food choices seems apparent. Unfortunately, as the premier popular outlet for providing cooking instruction to a mass audience, Food Network manages to reinforce many of the most detrimental food habits plaguing communities of color, particularly African Americans, in its three shows hosted *by* African Americans. As I've said, while the Neelys, Anderson, and McCargo aren't the only hosts to focus largely on preparing dishes with high fat, high sugar content, they are the *only* African American faces associated with food on the network. To have the only four black personalities on the network present food sensibilities that are, in essence, identical to one another and that succeed in reproducing habits and choices that, on a larger scale, are effectively shortening the life chances of black men, women, and children is complicated, to say the least. While the hosts themselves are somewhat responsible for the style of cooking on display in their shows, it is ultimately the network that determines the array of shows it will have and how those shows will be focused in order to maximize ratings. In the case of the only three programs fronted by African Americans, the choices made by Food Network appear to greatly, if not entirely, disregard the mounting statistics regarding African Americans and food health in the United States to essentialize the notions of black people's relationship to food and to further normalize stereotypical representations of blackness within the popular imagination. Along with the jovial, nonthreatening, comfort food–making stereotypes foregrounded in *Down Home with the Neelys, Cooking for Real,* and *Big Daddy's House,* Food Network has also showcased blackness in one other way in the programming. And while the portrayal certainly differed from the above three shows, the narrative was no less problematic and steeped in racial stereotypes.

In October of 2008, Food Network debuted a short-run reality show entitled *The Chef Jeff Project.* The eponymous Chef Jeff was Jeff Henderson, a chef and owner of a successful catering business, Posh Urban Cuisine. Henderson is also a former drug dealer who served 10 years in prison. It was during his incarceration that he discovered his talent and passion for food, translating those attributes into a life transformation following his time in prison. The premise of the show had Henderson mentoring six at-risk youths by having them work in his catering company for one month. For all of the participants who completed the month-long internship, they were awarded scholarships to culinary institutes. Certainly, there is no way to argue that, relative to the veritable wasteland of twisted social experiments and train-wreck behavior that accounts for the majority of reality TV programming, *The Chef Jeff Project* didn't have loftier goals and better intentions. However, that does not discount the problematic issues of its narrative approach and discursive effects.

While still subtly playing on some of the sociohistorical images of blackness and domesticity that Food Network has exploited to great effect in the three regular series featuring black hosts, in *The Chef Jeff Project,* we see the narrative focus being primarily anchored by notions of criminality of blackness. The novelty of the show, and therefore its appeal, relies exclusively on the redemption narrative of moving from criminal to chef. That this particular narrative is located in blackness has been so naturalized in the social imagination as to be assumed. "Of course he was a drug dealer before he was a chef." In the popular imagination, black men obviously equate to drug dealer. This analysis is not meant to minimize Henderson's transformation but rather to question the ideological assumptions that informed Food Network's choice in commodifying that transformation.

Unlike the Neelys, Anderson, and McCargo, Henderson is a professionally trained chef. He remains as of this writing, the only African American professional chef to appear in any way, small or large, on Food Network. The fact that the only professional African American chef to make an appearance on the network also happens to be a former convicted drug dealer raises further troubling questions about the network's selective narratives of blackness that rely wholly on long-held social stereotypes. In this way, Food Network takes bell hooks's concept of "eating the other"[7] to a whole new level by collapsing the appeal of food, in a physiological sense, and the appeal of blackness, in a psychosocial sense, into a single mode of consumer desire wherein consumers are engaged in a very close approximation of actually *eating the other.* And like consumers' literal palates that crave only particular types of flavors from their foods, so too do their sociocultural palates crave only particular types of flavors from their blackness. Blackness as criminal is a veritable taste sensation. So, in many ways, Chef Jeff is only *allowed* to be legitimate as a professional chef in the eyes of the Food Network audience because he has first been legitimated within essentialized notions of blackness through his past criminality.

Additionally, the narrative arena in which the show is placed focuses less on the skills he provides as a chef and more on the skills he provides as a reformed felon. His interns, while showing varying degrees of interest in food careers, are most interested in getting or keeping their lives on track due to desperate circumstances; we are meant to understand Henderson's "I've been there" realness as that which is going to save these youths. It is a compelling and convincing narrative strategy to be sure. No one would believe that Bobby Flay could rescue these kids. Why? Because he's *just* a professional chef. As a white male, he's allowed to be *just* a professional chef. There's no authenticity that must be verified with him. He isn't forced into any essentialized social notions of whiteness. He doesn't need to be redeemed or save any at-risk youth. He can just grill a steak, and viewers will be satisfied, gastronomically and ideologically. Chef Jeff is not afforded that same luxury. He has to fulfill certain social expectations of blackness in order to succeed. He does. Therefore, he does.

His redemption narrative as translated into the redemption narrative of the overall show works in complicated ways. *The Chef Jeff Project* was one of the few, if not only, places, both then and since, where the intersection of race and class were displayed in explicit terms on Food Network. Several of the program's participants came from poor socioeconomic backgrounds, while all of them experienced poverty at one time or another caused by various circumstances. Also, the majority of the participants (four of six) were people of color. This singular representation of both class and racial diversity on the network had an equally singular narrative that framed it. Since, as a matter of course, both class and race, in explicit discursive terms, are erased within the programming of Food Network, a show like *The Chef Jeff Project,* which relied centrally on notions of class and race, required a narrative perspective that situated race and class in respectable terms. As a result, the show drew heavily on a conservative bootstraps ideology wherein redemption is brought about through hard work. The show advanced this ethic through the medium of food. Food could be the way out and forward for these people who were on the edge of society for reasons related to race, class, and, it was implied, morals; but food could only serve this purpose if it was approached in formal, disciplined (read: proper, civilized) terms. The narrative of meritocracy dominates the show elevating the idea that personal discipline and hard work are all that are needed to achieve success, while making invisible the complicated matrix of social systems of inequalities based on race, class, gender, and other differences that, more often than not, create obstacles that even the greatest amount of discipline and hard work find difficult to surmount. In this way, *The Chef Jeff Project* worked to maintain the established racial and class order of Food Network's programming sensibility even as it appeared to differ radically from the rest of the shows on the network.

It is this overarching predominance of a white upper-middle- and middle-class perspective within the range of Food Network's programming that belies the network's implied belief that food is universal. On the one hand, the network presents food as a language that everyone speaks and understands; though on the other hand, it is clear that the network is only interested in hearing a particular group of people, white middle-class *Americans,* speak it. As a result, food becomes *exclusive* instead of inclusive. It is turned into yet another thing that keeps us apart rather than bringing us together. In fact, the development of a sister channel, the Cooking Channel, makes the case even stronger that: (1) there is whiteness first *and then* there are all other races and (2) there is the United States first *and then* the rest of the globe.

As a way of concluding, I want to focus momentarily on the Cooking Channel. Though the Cooking Channel is not the focus of this chapter, it does merit a few words about its general implications regarding the continued erasure of race, especially blackness, and particularly American blackness. The framing of Food Network and the Cooking Channel break down into simplistic terms as "The U.S." and "The Global," respectively. As such, the Cooking Channel does appear to embrace diversity in a larger, more transparent way than Food Network. However, the apparent differentials of framing are really only on a cosmetic level. There are more people of color that appear regularly on the Cooking Channel, but only slightly more, and considering the overbearing whiteness of Food Network, it really wouldn't take much to have more racial diversity. But they're neutralized by emphasizing the notion of the exotic. The people of color on the Cooking Channel are, by and large, not of the United States, creating a comforting distance between U.S. audiences and any troublesome considerations about racism. In scholarly terms, it wouldn't be far off the mark to think about Food Network as "the colonial" and the Cooking Channel as "the postcolonial." In other words, Food Network denies race and its systems by trying to devalue and/or erase race altogether, while the Cooking Channel denies race and its systems by putting race on display in almost exhibitional terms so that audiences don't relate to it as a real thing. In both cases, whiteness is positioned as the fulcrum of food experiences and knowledge. And ultimately, blackness, especially American blackness, is relegated to becoming the specialty ingredient that gets used sparingly in the recipe of televisual food programming for fear that its flavor won't be palatable to American consumers.

Notes

1. This is a play on the song title "Video Killed the Radio Star," The Buggles, 1979.

2. It is difficult to measure the exact extent of homelessness and the number of people who are homeless due to various factors including the relative size of

homeless populations in comparison to entire populations, the wide geographical span of people who are homeless, and varying degrees of willingness by those who suffer homelessness to be identified. For more information, see http://homelessnessinamerica.com/.

3. Reference: http://feedingamerica.org/faces-of-hunger/hunger-101/hunger-and-poverty-statistics.aspx.

4. Other networks that rely on this type of programming include HGTV (Home and Garden Television) and DIY Network (Do-It-Yourself Network).

5. See: Patricia Turner, *Ceramic Uncles and Celluloid Mammies: Black Images and Their Influence on Culture* (Charlottesville: University of Virginia Press, 2002); Maurice M. Manring, *Slave in a Box: The Strange Career of Aunt Jemima* (Charlottesville: University of Virginia Press, 1998); Kimberly Wallace-Sanders, *Mammy: A Century of Race, Gender, and Southern Memory* (Ann Arbor: University of Michigan Press, 2009).

6. See Robert Gottlieb and Anupama Joshi, *Food Justice* (Cambridge: The MIT Press, 2010); Alison Hope Alkon and Julian Agyeman, eds., *Cultivating Food Justice: Race, Class, and Sustainability* (Cambridge: The MIT Press, 2011); Mark Winne, *Closing the Food Gap: Resetting the Table in the Land of Plenty* (Boston: Beacon Press, 2009); Julie Guthman, *Weighing In: Obesity, Food Justice, and the Limits of Capitalism* (Berkeley: University of California Press, 2011).

7. bell hooks, "Eating the Other: Desire and resistance." In *Black Looks: Race and Representation* (Cambridge: South End Press, 1992), pp. 21–39.

Chapter 17

Ratchet Responsibility: The Struggle of Representation and Black Entertainment Television

Kristen J. Warner

For more than 30 years, Black Entertainment Television (BET) epitomized the contemporary struggle within black popular culture over representation. As with communities of color as a whole, BET also negotiated the burden and politics of representation. The network's inability and outright failure to comply with the politics of respectability regarding its image and programming strategy exemplify this struggle. A term made popular by Evelyn Brooks Higginbotham, the "politics of respectability," characterizes how people of color sought acceptance from mainstream culture by demonstrating good social and moral behavior.[1] While Higginbotham focused on the politics of respectability in relationship to black church women during the early 20th century, the idea remains useful when considering minority images in the televisual landscape. Traditional notions of understanding representation, often framed within a positive/negative binary of appropriate portrayals of blackness, inform our attitudes about acceptability.

Historically, studying racial representation in television meant that scholars were analyzing and generating taxonomies of stereotypical characters of color and their trajectory from early television onward. Seminal texts such as Bogle's *Toms, Coons, Mulattoes, Mammies and Bucks: An Interpretive History of Blacks in Films,* MacDonald's *Black and White TV: African Americans in Television Since 1948,* and Gray's *Watching Race: Television and the Struggle for Blackness* are foundations to our understanding of the representations of blacks in American television. While the examination of textual representations of race has been, and remains, critical, new scholastic approaches of engaging in between the positive/negative binary—the space I call "ratchet responsibility"—may offer a more nuanced understanding of what BET means to the black community and point to why the network has had such a contentious legacy.

"Get Your Revenues Up and Keep Your Costs Down": The History of BET

Launched on January 25, 1980, by its founder Robert Johnson, the BET network became the leading provider of entertainment programming for audiences interested in black culture globally.[2] According to Viacom's website, BET reaches nearly 90 million homes in the United States, Canada, Middle East, Africa, and the Caribbean.[3] BET got its start when Johnson, at the time a cable lobbyist, enlisted the assistance of cable magnate John Malone to finance a network that targeted a demographic television that had long left untapped—African Americans.[4] According to Johnson:

> Once I understood the technology and saw that the technology could take a signal and send it all across the country simultaneously to different stations, then it became clear to me that programming could be segmented and targeted to different audiences, and so it didn't take a big leap from that to say, "Wow, wait a minute, that's what we're already doing in the black community with print." *Ebony* magazine, for instance, is a targeted magazine. To some extent, black radio is a targeted medium. I said, "Wow, you could take this concept of technology and target black programming, which has always been a dream of various individual black media types—creating a black-oriented network." The idea was talked about in various blue-sky articles that argued that cable was going to be the democratization of media, but nothing like that existed.[5]

Johnson, given the potential of black buying power evident in other mediums such as radio and print, saw tremendous opportunity with television, fueling his mission to reproduce that success in television.

Armed with a $15,000 bank loan and a $500,000 loan from Malone, Johnson set out to see if there was in fact a market within the black community to sell his product. While discussing how Malone—and other white businessmen—mentored and guided his early years of managing BET, Johnson recites one piece of advice he was given: "Get your revenues up and keep your costs down."[6] A bonafide way to maximize profits, Malone's advice meant that a successful company did not necessarily have to be a company that produced quality product. Johnson confirms this point in his discussion of programming the network.

> I followed Malone's advice, keeping my costs in line and borrowing money to continually expand the business. I kept my programming expenses low by broadcasting reruns of black sitcoms like *The Jeffersons* and music videos of black recording artists.

Johnson's strategy was to find the most cost-effective content to air that would bring in the most viewership. In an age of what John Caldwell termed "televisuality"—that is, the era of the 1980s and 1990s when visual style and auteurist pedigree worked together to target a particular kind of affluent audience member—BET thrived on recycled content and music videos as the network staple.[7] According to a *Forbes* magazine article, 70 percent of BET's lineup came from free music videos supplied by the record labels, earning the network profit margins upward of 40 percent, far higher than most cable channels.[8] As a defense, Johnson fashions himself as a businessman who happens to program a network. Johnson continues:

> As for critics who say our programming can be better, I tell them I'm not a programmer. I'm not going to go out to Hollywood with a truckload of cash and say, "All you producers, come up with the next big shows." That was never my thing, because I didn't see the connection between huge expenses in programming and advertisers stepping up their ad rates. They were only going to pay so much.[9]

Johnson's position as businessman is fully articulated here. Creating original programming and looking for trend-setting shows would never generate large enough revenues for BET. Johnson had no need for such an approach. It is an obvious point that advertising is what drives content; thus, his dismissal of the next big shows indicates his reluctance to create programming that ultimately defeated the purpose of television networks: revenue. Putting money into well-meaning, positive, and beneficial quality programming for black audiences would yield no profit. If advertisers could not envision black audiences as a viable demographic to sell products to, it ultimately defeated the purpose. Johnson describes his struggle trying to sell BET to advertisers:

> It was still a constant struggle to get the cable operators to value the black households in their neighborhood the same as they valued the white households. BET never got the same subscriber fees or advertising revenues as our

peer-group channels. Advertisers still discount the value of a black viewer, black subscriber, black reader, black consumer, but you just keep chipping away at it. I remember walking out of some advertising agency almost in tears trying to sell this product. I'm told by the advertisers, "Well, blacks don't buy that product," and then I walk into any of my friends' houses, and I see those products all over the kitchen. Or they tell me, "We don't need to reach the black consumer" or "We already reach the black consumer over regular TV. We overdeliver black households because they watch so much television."[10]

While it does not justify or excuse BET's lack of quality programming, the assumptions that advertisers made and the poor value they attributed to its viewership do suggest that its ideology is not simply shaped by one individual's perspective but rather shaped by an institutional system of disenfrachisement. This system was so influential in BET's creation that to appease cable operators into adding the network to their systems Johnson changed the original name—Black Entertainment Television to BET.[11] Put simply, BET (and its leader) may not have tried to develop better product, but the system the network functioned under did not offer any incentives to make an attempt.

If BET's content left much to be desired, its brand and link to black audiences were much sought after. And, in 2000, Johnson sold his network to Viacom for $3 billion making him the first black billionaire. Selling BET to Viacom only further strengthened the tension between Johnson and his audience. According to a *Forbes* magazine article written around the time the deal was made, "The 55-year-old executive is resented, even reviled, by some leading voices among the very audience he built his fortune catering to—black America. He has been denounced as a sell-out for striking the Viacom deal. Last March, when he fired low-rated talk show host Tavis Smiley, protesters blamed the move on the new 'white' owners at Viacom. They dismissed Johnson as 'a front man' and 'the 2001 version of the dude who drove Ms. Daisy around.'"[12] In response to his critics, Johnson countered saying, "I make too much money to be a front man."[13] Johnson taking responsibility for the large-scale changes the network made is certainly in keeping with the self-fashioned brand he made for himself. Requiring his audience and critics to consistently see him as a businessman first with loyalty to those with vested financial interests in his company and then as a man who may or may not think he owes anything to those who share his skin color is Johnson's brand. As a result of neither the critics nor Johnson budging from their ideological positions, these frequent back and forth battles endured until he retired in 2005 making his protégé Debra Lee the new CEO and president of BET.

BET's "Ratchet Responsibility": The Read a
Book Campaign and the BET Awards

For critics of BET, it was not just the programming issues that continually failed to earn their respect but ultimately the image of the network itself. With a reputation for "a lack of social conscience, a surfeit of off-color
comedy and a predilection for music videos rife with flashy cars, abundant
cleavage and gyrating derrieres," the network rarely found a positive or progressive balance.[14]

While this type of programming garnered substantial success, helping to
raise the number of new cable subscriptions each year, it did beg the question: to whom did BET belong? The decision to change the name of the
network from Black Entertainment Television to BET for the sake of cable
operators is telling. As mentioned earlier, Johnson fashioned himself as a
businessman who owed maximum profits to his investors first. The place
of black representation was something that could not be quantified and
thus bore no significance in the success formula. As Johnson puts it, "We
understood that we were not running a popularity contest for Hollywood
and we were not trying to be socially redeeming for black intellectuals. We
had the right to run our business the same way that MTV and HBO run
theirs."[15] Self-fashioning BET to resemble MTV or HBO belies the initial
motivation for creating the network in the first place. While both MTV
and HBO do have target demographics, they function as mainstream entities—something BET never could do. As the only channel devoted to black
culture, the burden placed on BET was something neither MTV nor HBO
had to confront. The *Forbes* magazine cover story on Johnson underscored
BET's ideology:

> Johnson insists BET has done plenty to improve the lot of black Americans-
> and says that isn't his job, anyway. His mission is to build a profitable busi-
> ness and run it at maximum velocity. That entails giving viewers what they
> want and doing it as cheaply as possible. If blacks can benefit along the way,
> so much the better, but that is a byproduct. "We are the only black network
> in town, so everybody has poured their burdens and obligations on BET,"
> Johnson says, "but we can't solve everybody's desires for BET. We have to be
> focused on running this as a profit maximization business."[16]

Johnson's desire to reach the lowest common denominator of audience confirms Boyce Watkins's point in the wake of BET's decision to allow the just
acquitted R&B singer R. Kelly to appear at the BET Awards. Watkins posits,
"When BET founder Bob Johnson reminded us that the 'E' in BET stands

for 'Entertainment, not education,' that is when the network officially became similar to the purely capitalist entities who exploit poor, black Americans for financial gain."[17] The tension between profit motive and creating a responsible brand image is thus always at stake with the network.

If BET considers profit motive and responsibility to black audiences a mutually exclusive set of operations, how does the network implement each of these distinct ideologies into its lineup? I want to offer two case studies that illustrate how BET attempts what I call a kind of "ratchet responsibility" that at once acknowledges sociocultural issues relevant to its demographic and also deals with those issues in the most flippant yet marketable ways. The first example of this ratchet responsibility is BET's "Read a Book" music video. According to an NPR interview, in 2007, poet Bomani "D'Mite" Armah and a few of his students from an afterschool audiovisual arts program in Washington, DC, wrote, mixed, and mastered a song titled "Read a Book."[18] Fitting squarely under the crunk genre made popular by Southern recording artists like Lil Jon, the song is essentially a list of profanity-fueled directives designed to encourage literacy, hygiene, and financial independence. Armah distributed "Read a Book" for free via Myspace attracting the attention of Reginald Hudlin, then the executive in charge of creative content at BET. Overseeing the newly created Animation Division, Hudlin transformed "Read a Book" into an animated music video. A 2007 *New York Times* article describes the song's controversial video style:

> In a gloss on the hip-hop videos frequently shown on BET, an animated rapper named D'Mite comes on with what looks like a public service message about the benefits of reading, but devolves into a foul-mouthed song accompanied by images of black men shooting guns loaded with books and gyrating black women with the word "book" written on the back of their low-slung pants.[19]

It seems absurd to make a connection between gyrating female bodies and books yet, the BET animation attempted to do just that. Unsurprisingly, "Read a Book" courted controversy with critics first asking if the video was a parody and then lambasting it for its utter disregard of positive black representation. Armah argued that the emotional responses to the video showed no shades of gray: "people either loved it or they hated it."[20] When Michel Martin pushed him to explain if the negative reactions were hate or disappointment, Armah described how critics assumed he was illiterate and uneducated. He attributed the disconnect and disappointment to a generational gap that between black audiences and their assumptions of acceptability. Ultimately, Armah argued that "Read a Book" was designed both as satire of the crunk music genre and also as a conversation starter between generations.

However, as much agency as should be attributed to Armah for creating the song, BET transformed it from a viral Internet success to a national news story. In a *New York Times* article, Denys Cowan, senior vice president of animation at BET, responded to the critics: "It's meant to be very satirical, and in a real way kind of mimics and mocks the current state of hip-hop and hip-hop videos."[21] The article paraphrased Cowan's next response, which hints at the manner ratchet responsibility emerges for BET: "He [Cowan] said the video was not part of any literacy campaign or *Schoolhouse Rock* alternative, but was intended for BET's demographic of 18- to 34-year-olds."[22] Essentially, Cowan both acknowledged that the video addressed the problematic social issues associated with hip-hop music (misogyny, violence, drug use) but stopped short of definitively suggesting that "Read a Book" was a moral tale or took responsibility for reproducing those images on his network. Cowan's play of simultaneous acknowledgment and disavowal is central to a ratchetly responsible business model because it superficially addresses issues that affect the black community but *on its own terms* with limited culpability and maximum marketability through controversy yielding maximum profits.

The second case study that illustrates BET's ratchet responsibility is the BET Awards. Established in 2001 to celebrate African Americans in entertainment, the BET Awards have a less than stellar reputation. From its shoddy production values to its notorious failure of working props, it is the disreputable character of the event that makes the BET Awards must-see television show.

The BET Awards deploys ratchet responsibility by building the show using a black family reunion aesthetic. These culturally specific events where family members who may not have seen each other all year get together, and fellowship—often over food and alcohol—with one another are ungirded by competing emotions of pride and embarrassment. They remember those who have passed on, they celebrate those prodigals who have returned, they make us all pray (whether we want to or not and regardless of whether we even all agree on who we are praying to), and they encourage the family's youth to display their skills in talent shows. Similarly, the BET Awards incorporate all of these functions in its telecast. Let me offer a few examples from the most recent 2012 ceremony.

BET's tribute to Whitney Houston—including a moving rendition of "Bridge over Troubled Water" by Houston's mother Cissy—can *only* happen on BET. If Cissy had broken down and been unable to sing, it is likely that a barrage of "it's alright; take your time" responses would have emerged from the audience. Similarly, when Whitney's mentees Monica and Brandy sung a few of her songs and the camera cut to audience reactions, the specificity of seeing both former host of BET's *Video Soul* Donnie Simpson and rapper Soulja Boy crying in response evokes empathy as well as a sense of camp aesthetic at work.

The BET Awards are significant because rarely do black folks get opportunities to celebrate particular aspects of black culture on television. Yes, the BET Awards are ultimately meaningless in terms of cultural cache—I doubt Beyonce would reject trading her award for an Oscar if given half a chance. Yet, in terms of how BET configures its image according to notions of ratchet responsibility, it does allow black audiences an opportunity to revel in culturally specific moments that could never be shown on mainstream awards broadcasts. The BET Awards is the yearly reunion where, for example, Rick James and Teena Marie can reunite, running through the audience singing "Fire and Desire"; it is the televised event where Mo'Nique can do a better version of Beyonce than Beyonce with her "Dangerously in Love" show opening. Its disreputability is the protective shield that allows it to be so fantastic and addictive.

Conclusion

In April 2012, BET hosted its annual upfronts presentation in Los Angeles. The upfronts are the presentations television networks give advertisers of their upcoming lineup of shows for the fall. BET's presentation showed off a host of original programming ranging from scripted series to talk shows to made-for-TV movies. In a press release, CEO and President Debra Lee discussed the network's new business model. "Original programming is working for us," says Lee. "Our audience wants smart, funny shows and we're venturing into dramas. We want to be the place where our audience comes to see different images of themselves and we're doing well in the ratings and our ratings keep going up."[23]

Indeed, BET made a strategic play moving into original programming after resisting under Robert Johnson's tenure. Picking up the cancelled sitcom *The Game* in 2010 after The CW network dropped it the year before proved a successful venture. According to *The Hollywood Reporter*, "In January 2010, *The Game* 2.0 premiered to a record-breaking 7.7 million viewers, the highest basic cable sitcom premiere at that time, and it averaged a 1.8 rating in its fifth season."[24] Buoyed by *The Game*'s success, BET developed more original sitcoms leading to the 2012 season with a full schedule of series, drama, and unscripted programming. What is interesting about this new paradigm is not that BET has gone back on its word regarding maximizing profits; on the contrary, original programming has ranked them in the top 20 cable networks among the 18–49 demographic.[25] Thus, while the business model has been altered, the ideology underpinning it in concert with ratchet responsibility ensures that actually very little has changed.

Notes

1. Evelyn Brooks Higginbotham, *Righteous Discontent: The Women's Movement in the Black Baptist Church 1880–1920* (Cambridge, MA: Harvard University Press, 1993).
2. "BET Networks," Viacom Networks, http://www.viacom.com/ourbrands/medianetworks/betnetworks/pages/default.aspx (accessed August 8, 2012).
3. "BET Networks," Viacom Networks.
4. Robert Johnson and Brian Dumaine, "The Market Nobody Wanted," *Fortune Small Business*, October 1, 2002, http://money.cnn.com/magazines/fsb/fsb_archive/2002/10/01/330571/index.htm.
5. Johnson and Dumaine, "The Market Nobody Wanted."
6. Johnson and Dumaine, "The Market Nobody Wanted."
7. John Caldwell, *Televisuality: Style, Crisis, and Authority in American Television* (New Brunswick, NJ: Rutgers University Press, 1995).
8. Brett Pulley, "The Cable Capitalist," *Forbes Magazine,* October 8, 2001, http://www.forbes.com/forbes/2001/1008/042_print.html.
9. Johnson and Dumaine, "The Market Nobody Wanted."
10. Johnson and Dumaine, "The Market Nobody Wanted."
11. Pulley, "The Cable Capitalist."
12. Pulley, "The Cable Capitalist."
13. Pulley, "The Cable Capitalist."
14. Pulley, "The Cable Capitalist."
15. Pulley, "The Cable Capitalist."
16. Pulley, "The Cable Capitalist."
17. Boyce Watkins, "Why There Should Be a Black Backlash against BET," *The Grio,* June 28, 2010, http://thegrio.com/2010/06/28/why-there-should-be-a-black-backlash-against-bet/.
18. Bomani Armah, Interview by Michel Martin, *Tell Me More, NPR,* September 17, 2007, http://www.npr.org/templates/story/story.php?storyId=14466377.
19. Maria Aspan, "BET Says Cartoon Was Just a Satire," *The New York Times,* August 27, 2007, http://www.nytimes.com/2007/08/27/business/media/27bet.html.
20. Armah, Interview by Michel Martin, *Tell Me More.*
21. Aspan, "BET Says Cartoon Was Just a Satire."
22. Aspan, "BET Says Cartoon Was Just a Satire."

23. Danielle Wright, *BET Networks Announces Lineup of New Shows,* BET, April 13, 2012, http://www.bet.com/news/national/2012/04/13/bet-networks-announces-line-up-of-new-shows.html.

24. Kim Masters, "Hollywood's Undercover Hitmakers: Salim and Mara Brock Akil," *The Hollywoood Reporter,* August 9, 2012, http://www.hollywoodreporter.com/news/sparkle-whitney-houston-salim-mara-brock-akil-359947/.

25. Marisa Guthrie, "Upfronts 2012: BET Orders Series with Wayans Brothers, Judge Greg Mathis," *The Hollywood Reporter,* April 12, 2012, http://www.hollywoodreporter.com/news/bet-the-game-wayans-brothers-judge-greg-mathis-311619.

Chapter 18

White Authorship and the Counterfeit Politics of Verisimilitude on *The Wire*

Michael Johnson Jr.

Many viewers are attracted to a particular television series because of its characters. Committed viewers[1] are interested in what happens to the characters—how they develop relationships and how they cope with various obstacles week after week and after season. HBO has proved itself adept in this regard, offering stories and shows that viewers are able to connect with. It is therefore not surprising that "authenticity" is heavily related to HBO's brand identity. The term itself means "worthy of acceptance, authoritative, trustworthy, not imaginary, false or imitation, conforming to an original."[2] Indeed, consumers can imbue meanings through various methods of oppositional readings of telenarratives that render those characters authentic representations of themselves, despite knowing that those characters are in fact fictional. However, as Michael Beverland makes clear, "authenticity [is] itself a self expression [that] involves consumers' desired self-identity. In this view, objects that express an inner personal truth are authentic, or 'I like that because I'm like that.'"[3] How telenarrative authenticity is achieved is directly related to how a given series is constructed and brought to fruition in production. The construction of characters, dialogue, behavior, speech, scenery, and other televisual aspects of a series all flow from origins found in a script. Thus, those who author telenarrative scripts are particularly important for a series' success and thus are important for the purposes of scholarly investigation and critical analysis.

This chapter argues that the messages communicated to *The Wire* viewers are the direct products of its heterosexual, white male writers/producers, and those messages unambiguously reproduce very specific, pathologized images of race at its intersection with queer sexuality through *The Wire*'s queer characters of color. David Simon, Ed Burns, and Jay Landsman serve as the architects of the series, along with writers George Pelecanos, Richard Price, and Dennis Lehan, while Robert Colesberry[4] was the show's executive producer. All white heterosexual men, it's *their* vision, in the form of the plot, and *their* words, in the form of the dialogue, which are spoken by *their* characters, for whom *they* selected actors during casting. The decisions of Simon et al. reflect a conscious desire to choose individuals to play specific characters based on the conformity of the actors' phenotypical appearance and congruence with *the idea of who those characters were and how they should appear, behave, and exist* within *The Wire*'s story world. Little if any scholarship has been written that critiques the racial and economic discourses, which influenced the decisions of Simon et al. Given the series popularity, and the premium that HBO places on its subscription price (and the discourses of luxury that accompany that price), the abject absence of critical analyses of queer sexuality on *The Wire* speaks volumes about how successful the pathologizing discourses of "aberrant" racialized sexualities[5] are obfuscated by the series creator(s). Those discourses take the form of messages communicated primarily through the series characters, both in terms of dialogue and also in terms outside of what they say and how they say it. Characters become especially important in the series because of how central constructions of race are to the plot, that is based in an urban setting, populated by a majority black citizenry, and whose subject matter revolves around narco-capitalist economies.

The Wire uses character-driven devices to solicit and maintain viewer interest, and it accomplishes this with finesse. And as Jason Mittell makes clear, "The boundaries between texts and the cultural practices that constitute them (primarily production and reception) are too shifting and fluid to be reified. Texts exist only through their production and their reception so we cannot make the boundary between texts and their material cultural contexts absolute."[6] Integral to this process of boundary shifting articulated by Mittell, *The Wire*'s David Simon and his writers have produced exactly the same results by creating a telenarrative whose structure is so complex as to purposefully take viewers unawares while providing them no point of reference that they can cognitively adhere. It's through this process of narrative complexity that the series has undermined previously staid conventions of the cops' drama genre, so closely associated with *CSI, Law & Order,* and even *The Shield* (however close it attempts to emulate filmic production methods found on premium cable channels). This unconventional storytelling approach has found a profitable place in the vast offerings of the multichannel cable world, and its risk taking has yielded substantial acclaim. Indeed, the profitability of the series is only matched by its scholarly popularity. There is already at least one doctoral thesis on the topic,[7] two edited volumes,[8] two special issues of academic journals,[9] and many other individual journal articles.[10] There have also been a number of academic symposia about the show: an event with the same title as this article—organized by Burroughs—held in Leeds in the United Kingdom in November 2009,[11] another at Ann Arbor, Michigan, in January 2009,[12] and most significantly one held in Harvard in April 2008.[13] The Harvard event is a useful place to start because it was here that William Julius Wilson registered the sociological significance of *The Wire*. Despite this acclaim, the series has accomplished little in terms of analysis about the political economic costs to viewers or the processes of acculturation that the series disseminates about race, homosexuality, and social hierarchies of power and privilege.

Viewers tend to feel similar to characters who are like themselves in terms of demographic characteristics such as gender, race, and age. Cynthia Hoffner and Martha Buchana argue that, "some degree of similarity

Michael Lee played by Tristan Wild in HBO's *The Wire*. (HBO/Photofest)

to media characters seems to promote a desire to be like them, possibly because certain similarities signal that it is both possible and appropriate for the viewer to become like the character in additional ways."[14] I argue that the same is true in terms of sexuality. This shared sense of similarity can be construed a number of ways for sexual minorities. But Hoffner and Buchana both note that "one of the reasons that people give for watching . . . television is that the characters' experiences suggest useful ways for the viewer to deal with their own problems."[15] Thus, homophilic queer audiences may profit from this shared sense of similarity communicated through visibly (black) queer characters like Omar Little, Shakima Greggs, and Snoop Pearson. Indeed, examining favorite characters is a common method of investigating audience reactions to media portrayals, and responses to favorite characters are informative because of their significance for viewers.[16] According to the "drench hypothesis," even one salient role model who exhibits appealing traits can have a strong impact on audience members who are drawn to that character.[17] Thus, recurring characters have enormous potential to affect the attitudes, values, and behaviors of the audience.[18]

It is through that process of selection that audiences thereby express affinity for and adopt the meanings, pleasures, and social identities promulgated for their consumption, oftentimes originating from characters (and the actors who portray them) who look, act, speak, believe, and behave nothing like them. For audiences who are both financial and cultural consumers of the messages produced for and about them but not by them, their ability to obtain recognition implicates claims by those viewers who pursue "full membership"[19] into American society through their media consumption practices. Audiences receive "help" in making their choices of telenarratives, which stems from the ability of "producers and distributors of a program exerting some, if limited, influence over who watches and some, though limited, influence over the meanings and pleasures that the audiences may produce from"[20] their telenarratives of choice.

And in the case of *The Wire,* help originates from the desk of Simon and his fellow writers. Brian Rose notes that Simon, in a type of self-congratulatory way, "fondly notes a strong following among both cops and criminals who admire the show's faithful recreation of their lives."[21] Simon unreasonably attributes the series success with "both cops and criminals." When one evaluates the substantial distance (both physically and metaphorically) between Simon and the target audiences that he says he's purportedly attempting to reach one sees an altogether different perspective. There exists no *other* evidence to suggest that the series faithfully recreates the lives of criminals and cops according to *their* perceptions, but rather those perceptions are created *for them* within the narrative. Thus, the distance between the audience's world and Simon et al.'s story world seems to coalesce into a type of verisimilitude to real life that audiences can then use as schema against which to evaluate character's authenticity. For example, Shakima Gregg's dialogue, appearance, and behaviors serve to confirm the carefully constructed and communicated messages about what a black lesbian detective should sound like, look like, and behave like in order to seem plausible. The ways in which *The Wire*'s characters are constructed reflect a purposeful and deliberate strategy by Simon et al.

For many viewers, the narrative complexity of the series is what makes *The Wire* so entertaining. It is persuasively realistic for many viewers in terms of its verisimilitude to the commonly held perceptions of what a story (about the underground drug economy) set in an urban city should look and sound like. Helena Sheehan and Sheamus Sweeney go on to articulate the centrality of David Simon and Ed Burns to *The Wire*'s success. "Their influence on the world of *The Wire* is unmistakable. Of particular note are George Pelecanos, Richard Price and Dennis Lehan. These writers share a commitment to portray 'the other America.'"[22] Here, the "other America" is one populated by bodies of color situated in the socioeconomic underclass. That Sheehan and Sweeney uncritically extol the virtues of the show's writers, because of their presumably close and authentic relationship to the streets, is problematic, especially when they invoke the author's "close proximity to the experience of 'the other America.'"[23] Sheehan and Sweeney attempt to augment the veracity of their conclusions by restating a quote by David Simon who says, "we are, none of us, from Hollywood; soundstages and back lots and studio commissaries are not in our natural habitat."[24] Notably, Sheehan and Sweeney (and almost all other scholars to date) have so far failed to address David Simon's publicly stated intent for creating *The Wire*, which was "to tell a good story that matters to *myself and the other writers*-to tell the best story we can about what it feels like to live in the American city" [emphasis added].[25] The identity of "we" in this case is a uniformly, heterosexual white male one. Simon et al.'s centrality to the creation and production of *The Wire* and its constituent parts (like dialogue, character personalities, etc.) reflect what Darnell Hunt calls "eleventh-hour window dressing . . . that facilitate[s] the business-as-usual, white world of prime-time television" that generally leaves the systems of production unexamined and thus undertheorized.[26] Indeed,

I argue that Simon et al.'s production of *The Wire* accomplishes two important functions.

First, the necessity and presence of an invariably unchanging and racially stagnant writer/production team actively impede efforts to integrate people of color into a white-controlled industry, the effect of which actually participates in discourses of postracial America and exacerbates already pervasive obstacles for people of color to survive and thrive within a white-controlled society. Second, Simon *and others'* antiracist public advocacy, taking the form of loudly, proudly, and consistently extolling the virtuous nature of the numerically dominating number of brown and black bodies on the series is just another form of acting out their own white privilege.

How can this be, one might ask, when people of color dominate the series across 60 episodes, over the course of five seasons, and in almost every acting role? The answer is that Simon and his cowriters have never failed to seize an opportunity to make their racial inclusiveness known to the public venues where discussions of race are raised.[27,] This antiracist discourse superficially appears valuable and noteworthy because of the utter absence of numerically majoritarian black/Latino casts on telenarrative series in general, and HBO *in particular.* However, these public engagements often take place in exclusively white spaces (like that of HBO boardrooms and press offices);[28] speakers[29] generally adopt the rhetoric of diversity while invoking ideals of multiculturalism as material signs of their own self-worth; and many of these conversations[30] are undertaken only to display a self-effacing radical politics, which are thinly disguised signs of social progressiveness conveniently divorced from any tangible engagement with or deeper dismantling of systems of power and racial oppression. Sheehan and Sweeney's research provides some excellent examples. According to these scholars, Simon replies to their inquiries by stating that "he is not a social crusader, claiming that he is a storyteller coming to the campfire with the truest possible stories you can tell. What people do with those stories is up to them." Simon goes on to say that, "it would be a fraud to claim that those of us spinning the stories are perfectly proletarian. We are professional writers and paid as such, and it is one thing to echo the voices of longshoremen and addicts, detectives and dealers, quite another to claim those voices as your own."[31] The subtext to this self-serving effacement is that neither Simon himself nor the rest of the series writers and producers have *ever* volunteered anything about the racial composition of the production staff and their glaring omission of people of color on a show explicitly about black and Latino lives in the inner city.

Hunt makes clear that since the 1960s whites relied on these very same mechanisms to immunize themselves from critiques of racial oppression because "the whites who controlled the entertainment industry were generally seen as left of center,"[32] and yet, this same racial demographic has still not changed. According to Hunt, white control of network television "remain[s] frozen in time" in terms of racial progress behind the camera and in the boardrooms and offices in the television industry. Hunt continues by stating that, "Network television, like the rest of Hollywood, continues to be a highly insular industry in which white decision makers reproduced themselves by hiring other whites who shared similar experiences and tastes . . . and that white males occupy nearly all of the industry 'green lighting' positions."[33] Hunt's observations are equally applicable to cable television and to both telenarratives examined in this research. Both *The Wire* and *True Blood* reflect similar racial hierarchies within their production staff and at HBO generally, despite the increasing visibility and numerical presence of people of color in front of HBO cameras. From 1969, when the first man of color took on the role of green-lighting potential programs, until 1990, there was a maximum of *five* people within that 53-year period. Similar results can be found when examining the racial composition of the directors.

Of course, Simon et al. not only produced *The Wire,* but they also were its writers. While people of color, combined, totaled only 9 percent of prime-time television writers, they often were "concentrated in situation comedies and ghettoized by network"[34] meaning that any telenarrative that fell outside of that single genre dramatically reduced the chance of people of color either having their scripts green lit (approved for a pilot) or, if they did, they were reduced to having their work appear on the least watched network. The implications for *The Wire* and its production staff are clear—the centrality of Simon and his fellow white heterosexual male writer/producer team to the series reflects the universality of the white male gaze in a presumably postracial era where people of color dominate the screen but are virtually absent from the positions of power that dictate what brown and black bodies are doing, saying, and performing. In this discursive space, *The Wire*'s racial composition between production staff and actors reveals how HBO has adjusted to an appearance of inclusivity and authenticity that "permit the privileged to have their representational cake and eat it too."[35] And as Hunt contends, "The early twenty-first century is a time when white supremacy thrives in a climate of color-blind ideology"[36] of which Simon et al. are perfect examples.

While I have concentrated on the racial composition of the production staff versus that of the actors and the implications attached to the racial hierarchy at HBO and on *The Wire* specifically, we must also examine how race is portrayed within *The Wire* narrative. While admittedly, *The Wire*'s large African American cast does include African American characters who "populate all levels of legitimate and illegitimate Baltimoreans society," some of these characters nevertheless illustrate a racial tokenism within a larger paradigm that homogenizes and normalizes blackness. The private lives of three highly visible black characters—Commissioner Burrell, Mayor Royce, and Senator Davis—are *never* seen during the five seasons of the show, and yet "Carcetti's wife, children, and home by contrast appear only during the third and fourth seasons while he mounts his improbable yet finally successful campaign against Royce."[37] Dominic West, the English actor who portrays the Caucasian detective McNulty, serves as the series' major protagonist. Anthony Andrew claims that this casting was deliberate and that "it was always accepted that you had to have a white lead, otherwise no one would watch it." Jason Vest observes that "[t]his revelation may demonstrate that Simon remains beholden to the same casting biases as network executives, who have historically assumed (often without evidence) that American television is predominantly white and middle-class audience prefers to see protagonist of his own racial and socioeconomic group."[38]

And so not only does the traditional white power system hold sway over the Baltimore Police Department of *The Wire* but also over the creators, producers, and distributors of this fictionalized narrative's critique of race relations. Indeed, Lisa Kelly has gone so far to suggest that detective McNulty, a heterosexual, Caucasian man is a "sort of stand-in for the show's creator or dramatic device offered to white viewers as a way into this 'black world'" that reflects the paradoxical reality that African American characters, even in a program largely devoted to their experiences, remain marginal because a Caucasian character must provide a window into their professional and personal lives. Vest also poignantly notes that Bubbles, the African American male, crack addict's success as an informant is not simply related to his unassuming appearance, his intimate understanding of the drug trade street codes but rather it is "rarely mentioned by McNulty or Greggs [that] Bubbles could never succeed in collecting information about the Barksdale and Stanfield organizations if he were white."[39] McNulty or Greggs characters would never have contemplated the possibility of using a white informant, given the racially dominant presence of black men in the urban location in which the narrative is set. So Vest's argument, while critically accurate, is a logical nonsequitur in terms of the narrative's story world. Yet, Bubble's race is only one example of how individual characters, in the aggregate, are directly implicated in the larger system of racial power relations between and among characters on the series, which in turn reflects on the authors of their motivations, behaviors, words, and deeds throughout the narrative's many twisting and turning plots. Thus, the issues of race and, later sexuality, become embedded in *The Wires'* characters, as much as in the narrative's plot itself.

Characters and Audience Interpretation

Racialized, working-class language, speech (particularly the Baltimore dialect), and urban street behaviors are stereotyped to resonate realistically with the way the characters were written and presumed to be portrayed. These factors are a distinct reflection of the heterosexual, socially privileged white males who constructed them. John Fiske makes clear characters are not simply reflective, nonproductive facsimiles but rather operate as "metonymic representations of social positions and the values embedded in them."[40] This assertion is particularly important when analyzing specific characters and the verisimilitude they reproduce to which audiences predictably respond. Indeed, using an almost all African American cast on *The Wire* unambiguously communicates a racial realism that is reproduced phenotypically through the actors chosen specifically for select characters. That these casting decisions were accomplished by Simon et al. and were selected according to a script written by the very same people is not a fact to be overlooked. According to Fiske, "A character is a paradigmatic set of values that are related through structures of similarity and difference. . . . character is a conjuncture of social discourses held in a metaphorical relationship to notions of individuality and embodied in the appearance and mannerisms of an individual actor or actress."[41]

Within *The Wire* story world, these paradigmatic values include racialized varieties of (1) hypermasculinity for black men, (2) female masculinity for black women, and (3) hegemonic heterosexuality for *all* white characters of either sex. Examined against these paradigmatic structures, one can see how Omar, Shakima Greggs, and Snoop Pearson personify the embodiment of difference, insofar as they both conform and deviate in predictable ways that reinforce Fiske's articulation of individuality.

Omar's unambiguous queer sexuality fails to undermine his hypermasculine performativity. He speaks with authority, carries himself, and uses mannerisms that convey a message of aggressiveness that is physically threatening and psychologically menacing (even on occasions with his own lovers). His penchant for violent robberies are often undertaken with tactical skills and techniques that often involve feats of strength that, on at least one occasion, inspire his pursuers to admire his ability to escape danger. Both Shakima Greggs and Felicia "Snoop" Pearson deviate in a number of substantial ways from hegemonic constructions of femininity compared to the rest of the cast, across all five seasons. Both black women are masculinized versions of femininity, and both are queer, although Snoop's asexuality is obscured by her appearance in exclusively violent scenes with few moments on screen in which her personality is made visible.

As Fiske makes clear, "'femininity' is from a discourse that attempts to naturalize gender construction and difference in terms of the status quo and is therefore implicitly patriarchal."[42] That both of these women occupy positions of power in a male-dominated law enforcement agency and narco-economic drug organization speaks volumes about how Fiske's articulation of femininity operates within the larger plot. As such, queer audiences can engage with these characters through identification,[43] whereby viewers willingly put themselves in the fictive space of the characters they are viewing and thus adopt similar outlook on the circumstance which those characters face within the plot. The pleasure that queer audiences experience by seeing and substituting themselves in these fictive positions is rewarding both in terms of simple entertainment and also insofar as they see themselves depicted in uncommon ways, insofar as *The Wire*'s queer characters are concerned.

By internalizing the obstacles, successes, failures, achievements, and life experiences of Omar, Shakima Greggs, and Snoop, audiences get to experience a distinctly uncommon version of black queer life that is generally invisible, inaccessible, and perpetually on the periphery of white society. That these black characters are gay and lesbian further adds a layer of complexity for queer white audiences because hegemony has minimized or marginalized queer people of color from positions of visibility and power within queer white spaces (even when located within urban locations). Indeed, queer audiences are rewarded by navigating the boundaries between these representations and their personal knowledge of the real world and by exploring the ideological relationship between these two concepts. Hoffner's research certainly seems to confirm my application of Fiske's concept of identification at least in terms of how characters and viewers related to each other. Hoffner makes clear that ". . . perceiving similarity to another person in some ways seems to promote the desire to be like that individual in other ways—especially ways that are perceived as favorable or rewarding."[44]

One needs to only look at the popularity of Omar to see how those relationships and the processes Hoffner and Fiske describe come to fruition. In the case of Omar, this reward becomes fulfilling because of how his sexuality is rendered as both conformist and provocative. Omar challenges commonly held beliefs related to same sex interracial relationships and the adoption/rejection of hegemonic black masculinity's paradoxical relationship to his periodic displays of feminized fashion. When juxtaposed against his position within the violent, hypermasculine-dominated hierarchy of an impoverished Baltimore drug world, Omar offers a glaring example of the discrete ways in which heterosexual white male authors construct both queer sexuality and black masculinity. Indeed, I would argue that having a hypermasculine black male character wear turquoise silk robes and slippers is precisely the type of performance that one might construct if one were attempting to offer viewers a comforting image of queer black masculinity. Trite attempts to complicate the threat that Omar poses to hegemonic black hypermasculinity, and hegemonic white heterosexuality does little to subvert what Raewyn Connel describes as making "straight gays" safe and thus safely consumable.[45]

Because substantial cultural differences exist between sexual minorities and the heterosexual majority within the United States, these cultural differences influence how individuals, groups, and communities relate to each other and in many ways condition queer people to participate in a patently discriminatory framework of either/or choices. For example, Diane Richardson contends that ". . . the normal gay is viewed as gender conventional, links sex with love which must occur in a marriage like relationship, defend family values, personify economic individualism, and display national pride."[46] Ultimately, the operation of these heteronormalizing processes exclude rather than expand personal autonomy, particularly for individuals (like Omar, Shakima, and Snoop) who choose to express and challenge the social construction of their identities through androgynous appearance, racial and narco-economic radicalism, and nonconformist family hierarchies. The operation of these heteronormalizing processes is tantamount to a revival of pathologized identities, set within the telenarrative urban setting of The Wire. These pathologized identities are accompanied by what John Binnie describes as "tensions over 'appropriate' forms of sexual identity—another example of the casting out of the 'queer unwanted,' seen here as potentially damaging an assimilationist agenda of respectability."[47] Those tensions appear, for example, where Shakima's partner Cheryl aspires to a homonormative, assimilationist social agenda, and yet both Cheryl and Shakima's social class precludes their economic ability to achieve those aspirations. Simon et al. offer *The Wire* as a critique of class and class-based systems of social stratification, in an explicit urban setting fraught with urban malaise, plagued by a not-so-underground drug economy.

As a product of their creation, the series and the characters who inhabit it demand that we examine how these white heterosexual men construct this world, what types of problems they see replicated in this fictive space as a type of indictment of inner-city America, and what role, if any, they see people of color playing within these locations. To ascertain and potentially comprehend these issues, I direct my analysis to how narco-capitalist regimes, socioeconomics, and discourses of urban criminality are linked to the purported social justice mission that the series writers/creators/producers have articulated.

Narco-Capitalism, Social Class, and Urban Criminality as a Racial Polemic

The Wire is as much about the narco-capitalist drug economy as it is about that economy's participants. The class-based politics embedded in the series' plots and dialogue expose an important area for discussion insofar as urban criminality is related to race. Simon et al. invoke many of the same tropes of drug dealing typically found on other telenarratives, in which the ideal of rugged individualism remains the epitome of self-made, capitalist masculinity. The African American men of the series participate just as equally in this economic endeavor as do their white counterparts in Baltimore's city hall. However, the boundaries of legality and criminality are always in play and reflect a disturbingly essentialized racial hierarchy in which white heterosexual men engage in politically unethical behavior while black men engage in exploitative drug distribution. As Amy Long makes clear *The Wire* points to Baltimore's real-world "move from an economy based on physical labor and tangible products to one based more on information, technology and services as the displacing agent that turns drug dealing into a logical occupational decision."[48] The series purports to function as a polemic that conclusively argues against capitalism's unseen influential presence that shapes all that transpires in Baltimore's economies (legal and otherwise). Marketplace structures exist in every sector on the series from narco-capitalist organizations like the Barksdale and Stanfield families to the Longshoreman Sobotka family to the political dynasties of Royce and Carcetti, all of whom have economic and political aspirations within the larger capitalist system in which their microstruggles are contrasted against macrodynamics of power, paternalism, and fiscal control of resources, people, and commodities (whether crack, prostitutes, or votes, respectively).

What makes the series especially valuable is its attention to these important issues; however, that value is undermined by some of the very methods it uses to critique those issues. Use of stereotypical tropes that equate blackness with hypermasculinity, that associate whiteness with heterosexuality, and that inseparably link femininity with female performativity do little to advance any argument for political awareness or sensitivity for social justice that some of the story arcs aim for; in fact, the racialized essentialism that the narrative reproduces in some of its characters indirectly *contributes* to the arguments against which the series purportedly argues. By racialized essentialism, I mean to say that the reduction of black male characters to stereotyped criminal figures are pitted against almost exclusively white (normalized) characters who predictably occupy positions of authority and prestige in law enforcement, the judicial system, education, and journalism over the course of five seasons goes unchallenged. While the series makes clear its indictment of the failure of Baltimore's political system to remedy its waning port and shipping economy, it almost completely fails to address the centrality of the racial composition of the legislature and citizenry. Only once does Carcetti remark anything about the seeming paradox between himself an Italian (white) man, running a majority African American city, except when his chances of achieving the governorship are threatened by African American ministers threatening to withhold their support (and thus the support of their majority African American congregations).

The series also perpetuates the image of untrustworthy, incompetent African American politicians in the form of Senator R. Clayton "Clay" Davis and his friends. Notably, the series also completely fails to address the reproduction of this racialized hierarchy in the Baltimore Police Department in which its leadership is embodied in that of white commissioner Ervin Burrell, Deputy Commissioner Stanislaus Valchek, or the Baltimore school district superintendent, also a white man, and white middle school principal Marcia Donnelly. Indeed, even the judicial system is devoid of a single black or brown face; Judge Daniel Phelan is a white male, State's Attorney Stephen E. Emper is a white male, and ASA Rhonda Pearlman and ASA Ilene Nathan are white females. And finally, the fifth and final season finds the subject of that season's story, the *Baltimore Sun* controlled by almost all white faces in the forms of Editor-in-Chief James Whitting III, Managing Editor Thomas Klebanow, State Editor Tim Phelps, Metro Editor Steven Luxenberg, and London bureau chief Robert Ruby who are all white men.

For a telenarrative whose ostensible purpose is to inspire thoughtful reflection and intellectual critique of the systems of inequality located within the other America found in inner cities across America, the lack of almost *any* dialogue about the racial hierarchies in each of the season's respective foci is irresponsible. This silence speaks volumes about a major flaw in the narrative's "social justice mission" that Rafael Alvarez identifies in David Simon's initial proposal to HBO.[49] In this sense, it is no surprise that the series equally fails to explicitly question The Greek's (Bill Raymond) role at the apex of the narco-capitalist organizations as a literal embodiment of white superiority over black men conducting transactions from street corners to hotel boardrooms. While Sheehan does note that "Narco-capitalism is seen as the only viable economic engine in neighborhoods where no other path to wealth exists. . . . Within legitimate capitalism what violence there is remains largely hidden. Only in the primitive accumulation of the drug economy is violence shown at the visible and integral part,"[50] she and her coauthor fail to note how that hidden violence has a distinctly palpable racial component.

The perfunctory violence of daily life in the narco-capitalist organizations that they identify is one that is intrinsically linked to essentialized, dominant discourses of black masculinity, whereas the violence perpetrated by many of the white characters on black characters goes un(der) criticized when its origins are obscured by the narrative's silences. Within *The Wire*'s story world, we see innumerable examples of racialized violence perpetrated by overwhelmingly black men on both black and white victims. The Barksdale organization and its enforcers are well known for their brutality. And yet similarly (perhaps even more) destructive violence perpetrated by well-meaning whites in positions of power in the educational system (Season 4), for example, Roland "Prez" Pryzbylewski against vulnerable, adolescent black boys (Dukie, Randy, Michael, and Namond), is addressed exclusively in terms of how *the victims*[51] overcome or succumb to the dysfunctional budgetary forces of the system (rather than the white educational leaders who rarely appear anytime during the season).[52] And the fact that Ed Burns, a member of Simon's production group, wrote the role of Roland "Prez" Pryzbylewski from his own experiences as a middle school teacher is part and parcel of the larger themes of the white male gaze blurring the lines between the fictive world of *The Wire* and real life. The perspective of the white male gaze finds itself reproduced in the form of straight white male detective Jimmy McNulty.

Detective Jimmy McNulty is trailing the second in command of the Barksdale drug organization, Stringer Bell, that he comes to realize the complexity of the Baltimore drug economy and its leadership when he follows Bell to the Baltimore City Community College, where Bell is taking a course on macroeconomics. And as Bell progresses in the course, his education begins to influence the practices and behaviors of the drug trade, which he oversees, later opining that "every market-based business runs in cycles. We're in the down cycle now." Indeed, Stringer Bell reads *The Wealth of Nations* and in the third season conducts meetings of his drug lieutenants according to *Robert's Rules of Order*. And in so doing, the narrative thoroughly blurs the lines between protagonist and antagonist while destabilizing the boundaries between crime and justice so much so that "the viewer cannot comfortably classify characters as good or bad depending on their occupation."[53] While that destabilization is important in terms of upending the premises by which viewers interpret class, such tactics are isolated and may very well be seen as a way of substantiating more superficial critiques later in the series.

Unfortunately, little research has surfaced that undertakes an intersectional analysis of how these characters engage with the larger discourses of power that illuminates the influences that racialized class markers have on viewers seeing these messages. Remarkably, while the series *does* address the racialized nature of class conflict between and among whites, it does so only by rendering the working-class whites as Polish and Irish ethnic others, while safely caricaturizing wealthy whites as ambiguously white in appearance. And while that too is laudable, Simon et al. accomplish little in terms of how the show's deployment of diversity and advocacy of a "social justice mission" is replicated in terms of the political economic incentives that HBO uses to encourage viewers to buy in to the series, both culturally as a type of racialized commodity and financially as a subscription-based entertainment product. Paradoxically, viewers are encouraged to buy into the series claim to originality, which lies in its open class-based politics, yet in order to do so, they must also expend capital in order to obtain access to the very claims of originality and verisimilitude on which *The Wire* is based. Simon et al.'s decision to publically pursue an agenda of racial inclusion and class-based critiques on *The Wire* is deeply undermined by the substantial omissions it possesses in terms of how race and sexuality are implicated in the political practices it purportedly examines.

Notes

1. Defined as those viewers who regularly and consistently follow a series from episode to episode and season to season without fail.

2. Michael B. Beverland, *Building Brand Authenticity* (New York: Palgrave Macmillan, 2009), p. 15.

3. Beverland, *Building Brand Authenticity,* p. 16.

4. Collectively referred to herein as "Simon et al."

5. Ferguson, Roderick A. *Aberrations in Black: Toward a Queer of Color Critique.* University of Minnesota Press, 2003.

6. Jason Mittell, "A Cultural Approach to Television Genre Theory," *Cinema Journal* 40, no. 3 (2001): p. 7.

7. T.M. Sodano, "All the Pieces Matter: A Critical Analysis of HBO's *The Wire*" (dissertation, Syracuse University, 2008).

8. Tiffany Potter, *The Wire: Urban Decay and American Television* (London: Continuum, 2009); R. Sabin and J. Gibb, *The Wire: How TV Crime Drama Got Real* (London: IB Tauris, 2011).

9. H. Cormier, "Bringing Omar Back to Life," *Journal of Speculative Philosophy* 22, no. 3 (2008): pp. 205–13; A. Brock, "Life on The Wire: Deconstructing Race on the Internet," *Information, Communication and Society* 12, no. 3 (2009): pp. 344–63.

10. P. Dreier and J. Atlas, "The Wire—Bush-Era Fable about America's Urban Poor?," *City & Community* 8, no. 3 (2009): pp. 329–41; John Kraniauskas, "Elasticity of Demand: Reflections on The Wire," *Radical Philosophy* 154 (2009): pp. 25–34; Helena Sheehan and Sheamus Sweeney, "The Wire and the World: Narrative and Metanarrative," *Jump Cut: A Review of Contemporary Media* 51 (2009).

11. Aidan Condron, "No Shame in My Game," *The Wire As Social Science Fiction?* (Leeds: University of Leeds, 2009).

12. Black Humanities Collective and the Center of Afroamerican and African Studies, "Heart of the City: Black Urban Life on *The Wire*," 2009 Symposium, University of Michigan, Ann Arbor.

13. *"The Wire" Comes to Harvard* (Cambridge, MA: Harvard University, 2009).

14. Cynthia Hoffner and Martha Buchana, "Young Adults' Wishful Identification with Television Characters: The Role of Perceived Similarity and Character Attributes," *Media Psychology* 7 (2005): 328.

15. Hoffner and Buchana, "Young Adults' Wishful Identification with Television Characters," p. 329.

16. Hoffner and Buchana, "Young Adults' Wishful Identification with Television Characters," p. 337.

17. B. S. Greenberg, "Some Uncommon Images and the Drench Hypothesis," in *Television As a Social Issue,* ed. by S. Oskamp (Newbury Park, CA: Sage, 1988), pp. 88–102.

18. M. J. Papa et al, "Entertainment-Education and Social Change: An Analysis of Parasocial Interaction, Social Learning, Collective Efficacy and Paradoxical Communication," *Journal of Communication* 50, no. 4 (2000): pp. 31–55.

19. An admittedly complex, highly contentious, and heavily debated term as Shane Phelan, Michael Warner, and many others make abundantly clear.

20. John Fiske, *Television Culture* (New York: Routledge, 1988).

21. Brian G. Rose, "The Wire," in *The Essential HBO Reader,* ed. by Gary R. Edgerton (Lexington: University Press of Kentucky, 2008), pp. 82–91.

22. Sheehan and Sweeney, "The Wire and the World."

23. Sheehan and Sweeney, "The Wire and the World."

24. Sheehan and Sweeney, "The Wire and the World."

25. J. Walker. "David Simons Says," *Reason Online,* October 2004.

26. Darnell M. Hunt, *Channeling Blackness: Studies on Television and Race in America* (New York: Oxford University Press, 2004).

27. Sheehan and Sweeny, "The Wire and the World: Narrative and Meta-narrative."

28. Particularly in public press events and in written press releases that referenced *The Wire*'s cultural success (and limited economic productivity for HBO).

29. Often Simon himself or another member of the production staff but *almost never* black or Latino actors.

30. An admittedly questionable application of the term.

31. Jason Vest, *The Wire, Deadwood, Homicide, and NYPD Blue* (Santa Barbara, CA: Praeger, 2010), p. 173.

32. Hunt, *Channeling Blackness,* p. 293.

33. Hunt, *Channeling Blackness,* p. 294.

34. Hunt, *Channeling Blackness,* p. 295.

35. Hunt, *Channeling Blackness.*

36. Hunt, *Channeling Blackness,* p. 300.

37. Vest, *The Wire, Deadwood, Homicide, and NYPD Blue,* p. 190.

38. Vest, *The Wire, Deadwood, Homicide, and NYPD Blue,* p. 192.

39. Kelly, Lisa W. "Casting The Wire: Complicating Notions of Performance, Authenticity and 'Otherness.'" Darkmatter: In the Ruins of Imperial Culture, Vol. 4. May 29, 2009.

40. Fiske, *Television Culture,* p. 158.

41. Fiske, *Television Culture,* p. 160.

42. Fiske, *Television Culture.*

43. While admittedly a theoretically problematic term, although used here, it does not engage with the full discussions over its facility as a designation of viewer internalization. According to Fiske, "a viewer implicates him or herself with a character when that character is in a similar social situation or embodies similar values to the viewer and when this implication offers the reward of pleasure. But it is always accompanied by the knowledge that implication is a willing act

of the viewer . . . and there is considerable pleasure in selectively viewing the text for points of identification and distance, in controlling ones relationship with the represented characters in the light of one's own social and psychological context," pp. 174–75.

44. Hoffner and Buchana, "Young Adults' Wishful Identification with Television Characters," p. 328.

45. Raewyn Connell, "A Very Straight Gay: Masculinity, Homosexual Experience and the Dynamics of Gender," *American Sociological Review* 57 (1992): pp. 735–51.

46. Diane Richardson, "Locating Sexualities: From Here to Normality," *Sexualities* 7, no. 4 (2004): p. 397.

47. John Binnie, "Authenticating Queer Space: Citizenship, Urbanism and Governance," *Urban Studies* 41 (2004): pp. 1807–20.

48. Amy Long, "Dealing with Drugs: Gender, Genre, and Seriality in *The Wire* and *Weeds*" (master's thesis, University of Florida, 2008), pp. 71–72.

49. Rafael Alvarez, *The Wire—Truth Be Told* (New York: Grove Press, 2009).

50. Sheehan and Sweeny, "The Wire and the World: Narrative and Metanarrative."

51. Dukie, Randy, Michael, and Namond.

52. Though much of the narrative focuses its attention on the salacious budgetary machinations of the political elites, little, if any, screen time is devoted to educational officials beyond a cursory glimpse of a (white) principal.

53. Vest, *The Wire, Deadwood, Homicide, and NYPD Blue*, p. 178.

Chapter 19

Representations of Representation: Urban Life and Media in Season Five of *The Wire*

Bhoomi K. Thakore

When thinking about the underclass,[1] particularly those represented in the HBO show *The Wire* (2002–2008) and the first-hand experiences by the low-income urban population with the social problems of crime and drugs in Baltimore, Maryland, the struggle for representation on the larger scale becomes more challenging. On many occasions, *The Wire* presented the dichotomy of Baltimore's underclass with the politically connected and economically comfortable. The extent to which the experiences of the poor in Baltimore register on the radars of the wealthy is dependent in part on the extent to which the social problems of the poor are presented in the media.[2] Further, the extent to which media production and distribution are influenced by those larger social factors that determine the racial hierarchy in the United States will determine the continued emphasis on those stories in the media that complement the white racial frame in mainstream society.[3] News reports shape views on race not only by degrading those who are being covered but also by maintaining the stereotypes among nonurban outsiders. Since these lines are drastically racial, news coverage has serious implications for the minority populations.

Media coverage is important when we consider its influences on popular opinion. Broadly speaking, media shapes our understanding of the world

This chapter is based on a work in progress by Bhoomi K. Thakore and Derrick R. Brooms, "Doing Less with Less: Race and Media in Season 5 of *The Wire*."

in which we live and the world that exists outside of us. While the professional standards of journalism had always promoted fairness and objectivity, it is apparent that this is declining in contemporary news coverage. This is especially important when considering coverage of urban issues, specifically those issues concerning poor minority groups, and how this coverage subsequently frames and perpetuates the ideologies of the dominant white upper middle class. Historically, the relationship between American racial attitudes and media coverage on issues of race has been obvious. In the 1960s, coverage of race was coupled with coverage of welfare issues. Since then, the two have continued to be one in the same, even in the news coverage of nonwhites today.[4] The effect is a reinforced ideology that paints minorities in a negative light and maintains the superiority of white ideologies.

In this chapter, I examine representations of the media in *The Wire* in the show's fifth and final season. Specifically, I examine the ways in which the Baltimore's *Sun* newspaper is used as an outlet to portray the largest issues of media ownership and production in the United States. I focus on the ways in which the show's representations of media coverage and journalistic integrity reproduce particular realities about the news media and white privilege. My ultimate aim is to shine light not only on these particular trends in the media but also the ways in which such trends can be (effectively and accurately) presented in this popular television show.

Urban Life in *The Wire's* Baltimore

Representations of urban life in *The Wire* in many ways mirror the research of William Julius Wilson.[5] In fact, series creator David Simon has noted that Wilson's 1996 book *When Work Disappears* was a strong influence on Season 2 of the show, which dealt with blue-collar workers and the international drug trade.[6] In his pivotal 1987 book, *The Truly Disadvantaged*, Wilson emphasizes the negative effect of social institutions on inner-city communities and their economies. He was among the first to point to stark income inequality between blacks and whites. In the 1970s and 1980s, a decreased number of manufacturing jobs, a workforce highly saturated by baby boomers and women, and racist hiring practices by employers disenfranchised urban black men from the workforce. This led to rampant rates of unemployment and poverty. High incarceration rates among black men led to more female-headed households. In the 1979 book *The Declining Significance of Race,* he defines this group at the bottom of the economic and educational hierarchy as the underclass. In general, Wilson called for social policy interventions in urban cities to address these holes in the social structure to serve and better equip this population.

As Anmol Chadda and William Julius Wilson have argued, *The Wire* is one of the most accurately gritty television shows to portray urban life and convey it to mainstream audiences. Chaddah and Wilson draw parallels between representations in *The Wire* and theories on the city as an ecological organism as argued by Robert Park and other Chicago School sociologists.[7] *The Wire* is meant to portray these communities as struggling against the various capitalistic social institutions that impact their daily lives.[8] Through the series, there are many direct references to the urban social problems that result of this inequality including poverty, drug addiction, underfunded schools, unemployment, gangs, and incarceration. On the other end, there were also some references to the effects on policy implementation through such addiction treatment and youth interventions, although argued by some as not accurate and not enough.[9] Further, *The Wire* incorporates discussions on the effects of social inequality on race relation and urban politics.[10]

Many universities, including Harvard, Duke, Middlebury, and University of California-Berkeley, have incorporated courses on *The Wire* into their curriculum. In these classes, the primary focus has been on the social processes that influence the lives and life chances of the characters.[11] In the course taught by Wilson at Harvard, students supplement their readings in the field of urban sociology with viewing numerous episodes of *The Wire*. This method help put a more tangible face on these urban social problems in the minds of privileged undergraduate students.[12]

As Ruth Penfold-Mounce, David Beer, and Roger Burrows suggest, *The Wire* serves as a form of "social science fiction"[13] that stimulates the sociological imagination[14] of viewers by emphasizing individual biographies and extrapolating them to social circumstances through this form of popular culture. These authors pull from the work by Andrew Abbott on lyrical sociology, defined as that which "looks at a social situation, feels its overpowering excitement and its deeply affecting human complexity, and then writes . . . trying to awaken those feelings in the minds—and even the hearts—of . . . readers."[15] In many ways, the use of these presentations of urban life for purposes of teaching and learning mirrors what I argue here as the relevance of representations of the news media in *The Wire* and the inherent problems of the news media as a social institution in America today.

White Racial Frames in the Media

Since 2004, the Pew Research Center's Project for Excellence in Journalism (PEJ) has conducted their State of the News Media reports. These reports have identified trends in journalism and other media. In their research, the PEJ have noted many bad realities for print news media in particular. Media ownership policies were severely deregulated in the 1980s, allowing many large corporations to buy up all media outlets in a metropolitan area.[16] As a result, large conglomerates like Newscorp, Disney, Comcast, CBS, and Viacom can provide access to nearly all forms of news and media in a particular market. With the increase in popularity of digital media, there has been less invested in local newspapers and the local coverage they provide on community issues. Print media is also heavily dependent on revenue, which can affect the ability of the journalists to cover important local stories. These stories are often replaced with lifestyle stories and entertainment news. In 2012, newspapers advertising revenues have maintained their state of decline. These outlets also compete with the popularity of smartphones and tablets and are forced to make the effort in keeping up with this ever-changing technology.[17] Newspapers are thus expected to keep up with other media with significantly fewer financial resources.

As a social institution, the media itself both reinforces a particular structure and serves as a socializing agent. Scholars, influenced by British Cultural Studies and the Birmingham School of Cultural Studies, have long examined the significance of representations in the media. These scholars have used the early works of Antonio Gramsci and Louis Althusser to argue that media representations are the result of power struggles between media producers and consumers.[18] These media producers maintain their power through their pandering to middle-class and working-class white Americans. As Jurgen Habermas suggests in his discussion of the bourgeoisie public sphere, marketing and advertising sectors threaten media and lead it away from its primary goal of educating the public.[19] Overall, media producers serve as the gatekeepers for representations of racial minorities in the media. While examples of these representations have recently increased, these representations continue to portray minorities in stereotypical and inaccurate ways.

On further examination of the extent to which race plays out in the media, it is evident that the inequalities have hindered minority groups from speaking out on their interests. While racist ideologies that reinforce notions of inequality by way of biological inferiority are less popular in the mainstream than they once were historically, contemporary American society continues to construct ideologies around race based on particular social constructions, stereotypes, and assumptions.[20]

The way that urban issues are framed when presented in the news perpetuates ideologies of racism and discrimination. In general, the news media uses a variety of techniques to shape the way that racial minorities are presented. First, journalists and broadcasters make conscious choices about what is covered and the prominence of certain issues over others. For example, a study by Christopher Campbell found that minorities were rarely used as citizens or as officials quoted in stories.[21] Additionally, racial minorities were more likely to appear in sports and crime stories. As Stephanie Greco Larson suggests, there is an increasing focus on "urban pathology" stories that dichotomize the city as filled with poor, violent minorities who commit various criminal acts—thus perpetuating social disorganization.[22] The popular opinion among the public of the inner city as disorganized helps perpetuate the dichotomy between us and them and further maintains inequality. More importantly, this ideology does no good for improving the central city and providing opportunities for social mobility and improved education. This tends to shift public ideology toward the notion that these are the only times when minorities are relevant or involved and presents coverage of societal race issues through a nonrepresentative white voice.[23]

Second, racial bias impacts societal understanding of issues facing communities of color. The stereotypes that exist in popular opinion are reflected in news stories and create a generalized image of a minority group. There is a tendency to focus on either bad or good minorities. Since the criteria for news media are an emphasis on the sensational, there is an increased focus on stories that emphasize conflict and violence. These stories inherently demonize and ridicule bad people of color.[24] On the other end, news stories on good people of color focus on how they achieved upward mobility and the American Dream. These help perpetuate the notion that discrimination does not exist anymore and that everyone can pull themselves up with equal access to social institutions. These narratives embody the elements of new racism which Eduardo Bonilla-Silva and others have identified.[25] They highlight how advances of American society since 1965 are used to blame those minorities who have not pulled themselves up, thus perpetuating the same type of inequality and prejudice that existed before 1965. Additionally, this sole focus by the news media ignores the inequality maintained by segregation practices of the real estate industry and underfunded schools only available to minority groups in the city.[26] The increasing influence of underground and independent media outlets has helped to some extent with their coverage of minority issues that inform and educate their target audiences.[27] Minority-owned and minority-targeted media has promoted awareness of these issues by covering them in a more accurate light. However, these media outlets maintain their influence among minorities only, as whites are still less likely to read their coverage. Even so, there is hope that this trend will help mobilize minority groups around pressing issues like immigration, employment, and wages.[28]

The ways in which the story of the local newspaper office is represented in *The Wire* mirror many of the challenges faced by real local newspaper outlets today. Local newspaper journalists are often at the mercy of their owners, many of whom are largely detached from any local issues. Often, the kinds of stories that are written and even encouraged are those that paint minorities in a negative light.[29] This is particularly relevant when taking into consideration the number of minorities in the newsroom. The American Society for News Editors conducts the Newspaper Census to identify the number of minorities in newsrooms. For the last few years, newspaper employment has remained small. As of 2012, the census identified a decline in both newspaper employment and nonwhite journalists. Additionally, on average, minorities make up approximately 20 percent of journalists, compared to an average of 30 percent minority readers in these markets.[30] These trends negatively affect coverage on stories of issues that are of particular relevance to communities of color. The abilities of an outsider to convey the particular issue and message are not always there.[31] This larger social problem became of central importance to the story line in Season 5 of *The Wire*.

Finally, media owners are also at the mercy of marketing companies. Nearly all of their revenue comes in this form, and it is also in the best interests of the advertisers to appeal to the largest demographic groups. They need stories that appeal to the white middle class so that they can assure that this group will continue to tune in. Additionally, advertisers naturally target wealthier groups because they have more money to buy the products. Since minorities are more likely to be economically disadvantaged by comparison, they are labeled as a bad minority group.[32] This is inherently ironic for journalists, who are trained to promote objectivity, fairness, and equal coverage. However, the changing norms of the newsroom tend to promote news stories that follow the criteria mentioned above. The end result is a story that presents every issue with only two sides. The "right" side is presented in the form of a government official, who is also more likely to be a white male.[33] Subsequently, the "wrong" side is the situation of those minorities, all of which is presented in a binary either–or form to the public.

There are many consequences from these types of news stories and news coverage. First, the media's influences on stereotypes and ideologies do not only influence outsiders but residents as well.[34] The media's coverage provides meanings and methods of understanding to all who consume it and will subsequently shape the way that residents in the cities will handle themselves. There is also a higher likelihood that the general public will not support welfare and affirmative action policies. Martin Gilens found that public attitudes against these programs are the direct result of this type of coverage. These stories tend to associate a black face to welfare (even though the majority of welfare recipients are white) and perpetuate the ideology that everyone in the country has equal opportunity as long as they try hard enough.[35] Further, this reinforces the stereotype that minority groups are lazy and that they choose to live this way. These stories also increase the "culture of fear"[36] by racializing crime and increasing the fear of nonwhites and also influence the government on their response to crime, such as favoring incarceration over rehabilitation.[37] The extent to which the message from these media representations is reaching white mainstream audiences is of particular concern to media owners and corporations and is further reflected in *The Wire.*

The Show

The Wire was a drama series televised on the HBO. The show aired for five seasons, from 2002 to 2008. It was made and set in Baltimore, Maryland. The plot covered life and crime in Baltimore primarily through the perspective of two groups—the police and the street gangs. In many ways, series creator, executive producer, and head writer David Simon based much of the plot on his experiences as a police reporter for the real *Baltimore Sun* and his characters in the show on individuals he knew and encountered. Simon shied away from journalists in order to tackle real social issues. Before venturing to write what we know today as *The Wire,* Simon conducted in-depth journalism (to the level of in-depth ethnography) in the 1991 book *Homicide* and the 1997 book *The Corner* with cowriter (former police officer and school teacher) Edward Burns.[38] In many ways, these ethnographies informed his writing for *The Wire* and lend to an authenticity on the part of the writers in their re-presentations of the news media.

While each season has a different focus, these two institutions are prevalent throughout the entire run of the series. Each season seemingly focuses on a mediating institution such that particular themes can be identified and are used as the narrative thread. Even within these currents, the essential theme of capitalism (capital/money) runs rampant through many of the decisions that are being made across each of these institutions. In each of its five seasons, *The Wire* incorporated a particular location or theme to the plot, including the drug trade, Baltimore ports, city government, the public schools, and local print media. As the second longest running television program to have a predominantly African American cast, it also was reflective of those individuals involved in the various levels of these social circumstances. Season 5 of *The Wire* focused on the role of local media and their coverage of local issues. In the next section, I will show some of the ways in which actual trends in news media are represented in this show.

Power Relations in the Editorial Boardroom

The fifth season of *The Wire* began with portraying how the media covers the social problems of inner-city public schools. The Baltimore public schools are a major social institution in the city, the challenges of the schools were covered in Season 4, and several of the issues continued to be pertinent in the fifth season. The editors of the *Baltimore Sun* were interested in pursuing a lengthy piece for submission to the Pulitzer Prize board concerning the schools, and this interest allows the audience to see the dynamics of the newsroom unravel. In general, Pulitzer stories cover social issues. In the meeting (5.02, "Unconfirmed Reports"), when discussing how to cover the story of the schools, a heated debate begins between the white executive editor James Whiting and black city editor Gus Haynes. Whiting emphasizes how he wants the story written in a Dickensian style or a style that emphasizes a lengthy fiction story–like report that is more about emotions, rather than a factual report that outlines real social problems. For them, it was this Dickensian style that would attract readers. This in many ways matched Wilson's descriptions, described as the "Dickensian underclass character."[39] Haynes suggests that the issue of schools is a bigger problem than the school itself and is also affected by other relevant social issues. Whiting counter-argues that the schools don't need context; thus, he dismisses the context as a "litany of excuses" that no one would read.

This scene is particularly important for a variety of reasons. By covering the story about failing schools in this way, the administrative team at the *Sun* attempts to portray the problems of inner-city schools as an individual-level issue, rather than at the structural level. This framing is significant because not only does it deflect the source(s) of the issue, but also using this story does not inform the reader about the actual problems and the various layers of the problem. The media framing[40] fails to produce the story in order to suggest a solid solution for the social problem. When Whiting asks about the budget line for this story, Haynes responds, "Johnny can't write because he doesn't have a fucking pencil." This suggests that the underlying message of the story is that "the people in the school are the problem." However, there are other systemic problems that come with the failing of the school, including drugs, crime, poverty, and subsequent lack of family structure as a direct effect of these issues. These issues were raised in Season 4 of *The Wire*, which also focused education issues within public middle schools.

The news coverage of this issue does not portray the issue in the same way that those living it see it, which is also problematic particularly for those consumers in the city. Those who are living the problem and do not feel like the media is getting it right will become alienated from the news and lose interest in how these stories are covered and reported. However, that particular market is not the target of the mainstream media. Additionally, the assumption that no one will read a story of a litany of excuses is also problematic when considering the traditional role that the newspaper had as "muckraker" to expose issues of corruption, scandal, and other social misconduct. As it is portrayed in this particular episode, it is Whiting's intention to win a Pulitzer more than it is to educate or inform the public. As a result, the shift of focus for the *Sun's* administrative team has ripple effects on the news team—and how they write and report their stories.

Additionally, the interaction between Whiting and Haynes is emblematic of the power dynamics invested within the newsroom. As Haynes is countering Whiting in the meeting, Whiting's body language of sighing and turning away while Haynes is talking represents Whiting's lack of interest in what Haynes has offered. To point, he uses his body as a kind of symbolic representation of indifference. Haynes receives pushback from the editors to cover a larger story in the same way that Simon did when covering a story about drug addicts in Baltimore who regularly farmed metal and copper from the abandoned buildings of the city.[41] While Whiting does not verbally stop Haynes from making his point, his nonverbal communication speaks clearly to who will make the final decisions. These power dynamics and the racial elements also are representative of the issue of increasing diversity in the newsroom. Although there is no direct acknowledgment through this season about Whiting's dislike of Haynes's perspective, it becomes apparent throughout the season that Haynes's race is used against him. For the most part, Haynes's racialized perspective is diminished through an ideology of color blind racism[42] as Whiting's Pulitzer pursuits allow him to circumvent race to a good extent. Haynes is disliked more so for his unique perspective on this issue of the schools—a perspective that one who has personal experience with the issue would more likely have. In the meeting, as Whiting disregards Gus's comments, he favors Templeton who is on board with Whiting's vision and appoints him lead writer on this piece.

Throughout the series, the issue of how race is covered by the news media is exemplified in a number of ways. A plot line in *The Wire* that showed three people who were shot in an inner-city drug house was pushed off the front page. This was reasoned as a result of decreasing advertising revenue, to which Mike Fletcher, a black entry-level reporter responded, "Wrong zip code. They're dead where it doesn't count. If they were white, you would have had 30 inches off the front" (5.03, "Not for Attribution"). The mindset that no one wants to hear about the murder of three people in the inner city is another direct appeal to the white middle-class readers who do not deal with such problems on a regular basis and don't want to read about them.[43]

The Fabrication of Reality

Later in the season, the focus of the Pulitzer piece is moved away from the public schools and toward the issue of homelessness that coincides with a string of homeless murders in Baltimore that the police are investigating, which in fact are being fabricated by regular character James McNulty in order to bring his superior's attention to a string of gang murders in the city. McNulty's desire to pursue major narcotics activity has been hindered due to financial cutbacks; his supervisors clearly inform him that they cannot afford to focus on these activities. For McNulty, his investigation into major narcotics activity requires that he has more funding to conduct a wiretap and police surveillance of Marlo Stanfield, the current drug lord of Baltimore. McNulty was having a difficult time in getting the newspaper reporters to pick up the story and was told that they would not be on the front-page unless they were more sensational. As regular character, detective Bunk Moreland says to McNulty, "This ain't Aruba, bitch" (5.02, "Unconfirmed Reports"). This is a direct reference to the investigation of Natalee Holloway, a white honors student who went missing during a trip to Aruba and other similar investigations of missing young white women that trump any other coverage on murders of nonwhite women. This is further exemplified when journalist Scott Templeton says to McNulty, the police officer pursuing this story, "It's not like these murders are against housewives or co-eds" (5.03, "Not for Attribution"). In an effort to circumvent the bureaucracy of the police department, McNulty decides to sensationalize his efforts through falsely promoting his reports to the *Sun* by indicating that the homeless murders were sexual in nature. This, in fact, helps to get the story of homeless murders to the first page. In effect, McNulty's fabricated story had a corollary impact on several other stories and displays the varying layers of news competition. Initially, the state legislature's decisions to pursue the persecution of Clay Davis, framed as a corrupt state senator, versus investigating 22 drug-related murders in vacated housing had ripple effects in the police department and the *Baltimore Sun* as well. The homeless murders now surface to push Davis's story to the background.

Throughout the series, Templeton was originally assigned the school's story and was then handpicked by Whiting to write a first-hand article on the homeless by spending the night with them under the highway overpass. Throughout the series and up to this point, Haynes had been suspicious of Templeton for fabricating unconfirmed sources in his stories. Templeton returns to the newsroom with his story entitled, "To Walk among Them." This story not only reads as sensational but "otherizes" the problem of homelessness as a social issue that media readers may or may not decipher correctly.[44] After reading it, Haynes challenges the story to Klebanow and asks him not to publish it. As Haynes said, "He acts like he's been living there for weeks when he was there for one night" (5.07, "Took"). When Haynes refuses to edit the piece, Klebanow announces that he will. This dramatic scene is later followed up by casual conversations between Haynes and other reporters about how the story was poorly written and should not have been published.

Later, it becomes evident that Templeton fabricated many of the details of an interview in the story that he conducted with a homeless Iraq veteran. Unlike the other instances of assumed fabrication, the homeless vet actually goes to the *Sun's* office to dispute the story. While the editors blow it off as a homeless vet who is probably too unstable to remember what he said, Haynes checks out the vet's story and now has proof of Templeton's fabrications. Later on, Templeton writes another story that includes a perfect quote from an unconfirmed source. When Haynes tells him that he will cut the quote unless he indentifies the source, Templeton complains to Klebanow who then confronts Haynes. Haynes loudly and amusingly references the newspaper's sourcing policy that requires cited sources.

Templeton's journalist tendencies reflect stories of a few journalists who were found to be fabricating details in their news reports. Examples include Stephen Glass, reporter for the *New Republic* who fabricated quotes in a story about a hacker's intrusion into a company's network, a company that did not even exist,[45] and Jayson Blair of the *New York Times,* who fabricated and plagiarized details in his coverage of numerous stories for the *New York Times* in the early 2000s.[46] Such trends are comparable to the issue of concentrated media ownership whereby their companies buy out experienced journalists in order to improve financial security. This trends leads to not only fewer voices in the newsroom but fewer voices of experienced journalists. The result is a heavier reliance on younger, inexperienced journalists who do not have the same level of experiences and, in the instances of Glass, Blair, and even Templeton, used fabricated details in the stories in order to advance their careers.

Haynes gets feedback on Templeton's stories from his friend and seasoned journalist. The journalist confirms Haynes's suspicions, but Haynes chooses to sit back on it for the time being. Templeton fabricates another story, this time claiming that he was witness to an attempted abduction of a homeless man. Seeing the holes in Templeton's story, Haynes meets with Klebanow who accuses Haynes of having a personal vendetta against Templeton. Templeton loudly exclaims in the newsroom that all of the details of his stories are in his notebook; however, entry-level journalist Alma Gutierrez later discovers that his notebook is in fact empty. This is enough for Haynes to take both the notebook and his file filled with Templeton's reports and the instances of questionable details and quotes to the editors. The editors tell him that these are not enough of a smoking gun to indicate that Templeton was lying. Perhaps as a result of Haynes' pushback, the final episode includes a scene with Haynes being demoted from city editor to the copy desk and the journalist who looked at Scott's notebook and also questioned his ethics to be transferred to the state desk.

The way in which the support of Templeton over Haynes was portrayed in the series suggests that there are dynamics involved with who is favored over others. It was understood by others in the newsroom that Templeton was seen as Whiting's pet, mostly because of how he agreed with Whiting's take on the Pulitzer story. There is also an allusion to race, which series creator David Simon likely portrayed on purpose in order to represent some of the racial dynamics that he experienced during his time at the *Baltimore Sun.* The nature of Whiting, Klebanow, and Templeton to focus more on winning a prize instead of covering important social issues is another result of concentrated media ownership. Out-of-town ownership leads to similar newsrooms as the *Sun,* where detached staff are more concerned with moving to a bigger position or bigger newspaper no matter what (Templeton), sacrificing whoever comes in their way as a result (Haynes).

Conclusion

In this chapter, I present the story lines of Season 5 of *The Wire* to identify the correlations between these representations and the reality of news media today. I argue that the bureaucratic and capitalist influences that tie hands occur at both levels of the police and of city news reporting. In this instance, it is the stories that are sensational and the ones that are assumed to win prizes that get the most attention and the most support put behind them. Those stories that affect the community and have greater implications for society are deemphasized or brushed off completely. What is highlighted throughout Season 5 is that in order to get a story in the paper it needs to happen to the right people in the right zip code. As a critically heralded television show celebrated for its unique and innovative representations of urban life, *The Wire* is an excellent case example of the effects of the media on society.

The trends that have affected media throughout the past decades are apparent in *The Wire* as much as they are in contemporary analyses of national and local news media outlets. Due to corporate downsizing and a series of administrative decisions, coverage of local issues in Baltimore were diminished and instead replaced by the sensational. The fact that these editorial choices were made for the purpose of winning a Pulitzer point to not only the type of stories that receive acclimates but those that are also perceived as socially acceptable. Further, the extent to which the (white) journalists put their professionalism on the line is coupled with the kinds of stories they choose to pursue and the ones that have the most meaning for them.

In Season 5, a collection of 22 unsolved drug-related murders is replaced and denigrated by a corrupt politician. For any community plagued with such violence, these murders are testaments to a series of social issues prevalent within the city that need to be addressed. Similarly, a fabricated and co-opted story of violence against homeless men triumphs over the political and economic corruption that rampages the city's streets, thus affecting all social classes and deteriorating the success prospects of local African American youth. However, as viewers of Season 5 learn, crime and violence come to be expected in minority neighborhoods—and these expectations are driven by highly negative stereotypes of these individuals, groups, and communities. With very few minorities in the newsroom and the hegemony of the white racial frame, people of color are subjected to dehumanizing narratives and the gaze of the white racial frame. And, with even less minorities in administrative positions, their ability to impact the hiring practices of news media corporations is neutralized even further. The ability to do more with less is hampered even more so as a result.

Herman Gray has argued that representations of African Americans on television have reached a point of proliferation and ponders if the rally for more is the result of the images themselves or the racist ways in which they are created and presented. He suggests that the maintained representation of these images in the media has had particular meaning for the development of an African American identity and one that stands up against traditional notions of racism, sexism, and general white supremacist ideologies.[47] With *The Wire*, the news media is represented in such a way as to perpetuate these traditional notions. By turning a critical eye on representations of representation, we can more closely see how this fiction reflects reality.

Notes

1. See William Julius Wilson, *The Declining Significance of Race: Blacks and Changing American Institutions* (Chicago: University of Chicago Press, 1979).

2. Robert Entman and Andrew Rojecki, *The Black Image in the White Mind* (Chicago: University of Chicago Press, 2000).

3. See Entman and Rojecki 2000; Michael Omi and Howard Winant, *Racial Formation in the United States: From the 1960s to the 1990s, 2nd ed* (New York: Routledge, 1994); Joe R. Feagin, *Systemic Racism: A Theory of Oppression* (New York: Routledge, 2006).

4. Paul Kellstadt, *The Mass Media and the Dynamics of American Racial Attitudes* (New York: Cambridge University Press, 2003).

5. Wilson 1979; William Julius Wilson, *The Truly Disadvantaged: The Inner City, the Underclass and Public Policy* (Chicago: University of Chicago Press, 1987); William Julius Wilson, *When Work Disappears: The World of the New Urban Poor* (New York: Alfred A. Knopf, Inc, 1996).

6. Drake Bennett, "This Will Be on the Midterm. You Feel Me? Why so Many Colleges Are Teaching The Wire," *Slate,* March 24, 2010, http://www.slate.com/articles/arts/culturebox/2010/03/this_will_be_on_the_midterm_you_feel_me.html (accessed September 24, 2012).

7. Anmol Chadda and William Julius Wilson, "'Way Down in the Hole': Systemic Urban Inequality and *The Wire*," *Critical Inquiry* 38 (Autumn 2011): pp. 164–88.

8. Chaddah and Wilson 2011; Anmol Chadda, William Julius Wilson, and Sudhir Venkatesh, "In Defense of *The Wire*," *Dissent* (Autumn 2008): pp. 83–86.

9. John Atlas and Peter Drieder, "Is *The Wire* Too Cynical?," *Dissent* (Summer 2008): pp. 79–82.

10. Kenneth W. Warren, "Critical Response II: Sociology and *The Wire*," *Critical Inquiry* 38 (Autumn 2011): pp. 200–207.

11. Anmol Chadda and William Julius Wilson, "Why We're Teaching 'The Wire' at Harvard," *The Washington Post,* September 12, 2010, http://www.washingtonpost.com/wp-dyn/content/article/2010/09/10/AR2010091002676.html (accessed September 22, 2012).

12. Bennett, "This Will Be on the Midterm. You Feel Me? Why so Many Colleges Are Teaching The Wire."

13. Ruth Penfold-Mounce, David Beer, and Roger Burrows, "*The Wire* As Social Science-Fiction?," *Sociology* 45 (2011): pp. 152–67.

14. See C. Wright Mills, *The Sociological Imagination,* 40th anniversary ed (New York: Oxford University Press, 2000).

15. Andrew Abbott, "Against Narrative: A Preface to Lyrical Sociology," *Sociological Theory* 25 (2007): pp. 67–99, quoted in Penfold-Mounce, Beer, and Roger Burrows, "*The Wire* As Social Science-Fiction?," p. 162.

16. Ben Bagdikian, *The New Media Monopoly* (Boston: Beacon Press, 2004); Robert McChesney, *The Problem of the Media: U.S. Communication Politics in the 21st Century* (New York: Monthly Review Press, 2004); Robert McChesney, *The Political Economy of Media* (New York: Monthly Review Press, 2008).

17. Pew Research Center's Project for Excellence in Journalism (PEJ), "State of the News Media 2012," http://stateofthemedia.org/2012/overview-4/ (accessed September 24, 2012).

18. Antonio Gramsci, in *Selections from the Prison Notebooks of Antonio Gramsci,* ed. by Q. Hoare and G. N. Smith (London: Lawrence and Wishart, 1971); Louis Althusser, "On Ideology and Ideological State Apparatuses," in *Lenin and Philosophy and Other Essays* (New York: Monthly Review Press, 1971), pp. 127–86.

19. Jurgen Habermas, *The Structural Transformation of the Public Sphere: An Inquiry into a Category of Bourgeois Society* (Cambridge: MIT Press, 1989).

20. Omi and Winant, *Racial Formation in the United States: From the 1960s to the 1990s;* Oscar Gandy, *Communication and Race: A Structural Perspective* (New York: Oxford University Press, 1998).

21. Christopher Campbell, *Race, Myth and the News* (Thousand Oaks, CA: Sage, 1995).

22. Stephanie Greco Larson, *Media and Minorities: The Politics of Race in News and Entertainment* (Lanham, MD: Rowman and Littlefield, 2006).

23. Entman and Rojecki, *The Black Image in the White Mind.*

24. Larson, *Media and Minorities;* Doris Grabber, *Mass Media and American Politics,* 6th ed. (Washington, DC: Congressional Quarterly Press, 2001).

25. For example, see Eduardo Bonilla-Silva, *Racism without Racists: Color Blind Racism and the Persistence of Racial Inequality in the United States,* 3rd ed. (Lanham, MD: Rowman and Littlefield, 2010).

26. For example, see Douglas Massey and Nancy Denton, *American Apartheid* (Cambridge: Harvard University Press, 1997); Melvin L. Oliver and Thomas Shapiro, *Black Wealth/White Wealth: New Perspectives on Racial Inequality* (New York: Routledge, 1995); Amanda Lewis, *Race in the Schoolyard: Negotiating the Color Line in Classrooms and Communities* (New Brunswick, NJ: Rutgers University Press, 2004).

27. PEJ, "State of the News Media 2012."

28. Clint Wilson and Felix Gutierrez, *Race, Multiculturalism and the Media: From Mass Communication to Class Communication* (Thousand Oaks, CA: Sage, 1995).

29. Entman and Rojecki, *The Black Image in the White Mind;* Larson, *Media and Minorities.*

30. American Society for Newspaper Editors (ASNE), "Total and Minority Newsroom Employment Declines in 2011 but Loss Continues to Stabilize," http://asne.org/Article_View/ArticleId/2499/Total-and-minority-newsroom-employ ment-declines-in-2011-but-loss-continues-to-stabilize.aspx (accessed September 22, 2012).

31. Larson, *Media and Minorities.*

32. Gregory Mantsios, "Media Magic: Making Class Invisible." In *Mapping the Social Landscape: Readings in Sociology,* ed. by Susan Ferguson (New York: McGraw Hill, 2008), pp. 450–58.

33. Entman and Rojecki, *The Black Image in the White Mind.*

34. Lyn H. Lofland, *A World of Strangers: Order and Action in Urban Public Space* (Prospect Heights, IL: Waveland Press, 1973).

35. Martin Gilens, *Why Americans Hate Welfare: Race, Media and the Politics of Antipoverty Politics* (Chicago: University of Chicago Press, 1999).

36. For example, see Barry Glassner, *The Culture of Fear: Why Americans Are Afraid of the Wrong Things* (New York: Basic Books, 1999); Eric Klinenberg, *Heat Wave: A Social Autopsy of Disaster in Chicago* (Chicago: University of Chicago Press, 2002).

37. Franklin Gilliam Jr. and Shanto Iyengar, "Prime Suspects: The Influence of Local Television News on the Viewing Public," *American Journal of Political Science* 44, no. 3 (2000): pp. 560–73.

38. Linda Williams, "Critical Response III: Ethnographic Imaginary: The Genesis and Genius of *The Wire,*" *Critical Inquiry* 38 (Autumn 2011): pp. 208–26.

39. Williams, "Critical Response III," p. 219.

40. Robert Entman, "Framing: Toward Clarification of a Fractured Paradigm," *Journal of Communication* 43, no. 4 (1993): pp. 51–58.

41. Williams, "Critical Response III," pp. 220–21.

42. For example, see Bonilla-Silva, *Racism without Racists.*

43. LeAlan Jones, Lloyd Newman, and David Isay, *Our America: Life and Death on the South Side of Chicago* (New York: Scribner, 1999).

44. Stephen F. Ostertag, "Processing Culture: Cognition, Ontology, and the News Media," *Sociological Forum* 25, no. 4 (2010): pp. 824–50.

45. Buzz Bissinger, "Shattered Glass," *Vanity Fair,* September 1998, http://www.vanityfair.com/magazine/archive/1998/09/bissinger199809 (accessed September 24, 2012).

46. Jill Rosen, "All about the Retrospect," *American Journalism Review,* http://ajr.org/article.asp?id=3020 (accessed September 24, 2012).

47. Herman Gray, *Cultural Moves: African Americans and the Politics of Representation* (Berkeley: University of California Press, 2005).

Chapter 20

La-La's Fundamental Rupture: *True Blood*'s Lafayette and the Deconstruction of Normal

Kaila Adia Story

Baby it's too late for that. Faggot's been breeding your cows, raising your chickens, even brewing your beer long before I walked my sexy ass up in this motherfucker

—Lafayette, "Sparks Fly Out," HBO, *True Blood*

The arena of performance engenders a public space in which the audience can theorize and reflect on identity. However, white racism and the white racial frame[1] in many ways have constructed the ways in which identity is translated from the performer to the audience. Historical and persistent racial segregation, the current legacy of white supremacy, and the subsequent denial by many people have all shaped the ways in which mass-mediated identities are recognized, represented, and replicated. The physical and psychological separation from one another, coupled with the repetitive performances of "blackness"[2] in both print and visual media, has led many people into a type of collective amnesia about the racist and inequitable foundations of this country, and its subsequent mediated art. In order to deconstruct the visual and performative creations that mass media have traditionally and contemporaneously generated in terms of what blackness, in conjunction with other intersectional identities (such as class, gender, and sexuality), as well as what that means for its viewers, we must always understand it as a part of our country's legacy of racism, and how racism and other socialized ills have informed these creations in the first place.

The American cultural marketplace has historically commodified identity in order to present its audiences with a salable and sanitized version of the human experience. This, usually, one-dimensional invention is made for mass consumption. The commodified construct, created to draw in mass appeal, usually misses the mark when it comes to performing actual human experience and identity. Television, created in many ways to "offer representations of experience . . . that transformed persistent ties to place, ethnicity, and class,"[3] has oftentimes served as a "major discursive site for managing difference";[4] television has served as a medium for many Americans to get a "bird's eye view" of how cultures and communities, outside their own, live. However, due to television and American society's reliance on the white racial frame and its filtering of lived experiences, people of color, LGBTQ[5] folks, women, and other citizens who exist outside of the white heterosexist hegemonic norm of identity are often one dimensional or stereotypical or mask themselves

Nelson Ellis plays Lafayette Reynolds on HBO's *True Blood*. (HBO/Photofest)

as paths to freedom for oppressed groups. Most of the popular television shows, characters, and scripts that serve to perform authentic portrayals of what it means to be black, gay, able-bodied, and so forth, fail in actuality to portray three-dimensional figures or create authentic social backdrops to represent a specific type of human experience.

However, the HBO original series hit, *True Blood,* gives us a different type of character, *Lafayette Reynolds.* Lafayette, an unapologetic, powerful, proud black gay male character, not only is an extremely authentic[6] character, in terms of representing a generalized black gay male experience, but, through the evolution of the character throughout the series, Lafayette, actually expands the viewers' socialized definitions of all three identities. In the spirit of this anthology, this essay examines how the mediated coverage of the civil rights and Black Power movements in the United States gave birth to more authentic images and symbols of blackness; however, because the undercurrent of both Black Power movement and Black Arts Movement (BAM) was based on redefining the black male as patriarch, this gave birth to the idea of a racialized hegemonic masculinity, which inevitably limited our society's notions of what it meant to be both *black* and *male.* In addition, I examine Marlon T. Riggs's cultural critical theory of *Negro Faggotry* as a practice facilitated by mainstream media to limit our definitions and deny the three-dimensionality to characters that are both *black* and *gay,* and lastly I deconstruct two episodes of the series to illuminate the ways in which Lafayette as a character is exactly what Marlon T. Riggs was yearning for 30 years ago.

Civil Rights, Black Power, Television and the Alteration of Identity

The U.S. civil rights movement (1955–1968)[7] altered the ways mainstream mass media and advertising industries represented African Americans. "The news director of a Southern television station noted that during the civil unrest of the 1960s television advanced the cause of racial equality by giving many poor blacks a chance to ameliorate their life-styles and improve their economic conditions."[8] Television gave blacks a window into the white American imagination when it came to their black bodies and persona. Not to say this was the first time that African Americans were aware of white Americans' racist and insidious attitudes when it came to them, just to say that television produced and re-produced a different kind of African American imagery. For the first time in history, the black characters on television did not match the *real* African Americans who were fighting for their rights.

With the death of Emmet Till and Rosa Parks's defiance on a city bus, the civil rights movement was born. Till's very public funeral and the ensuing news coverage of the Montgomery, Alabama, bus boycotts, placed television as a centerpiece in the daily lives of many Americans, not just as a form of entertainment but also as an escape from the civil unrest that was going on all over the nation. "Television, by the time of the Montgomery bus boycott, had become a routine diversion for millions of Americans."[9] The advent of the former radio show of the 1930s, *Amos 'n' Andy,* now had become a television program. Many Americans at the time thought that the show represented racial and visual progress.

However, "*Amos 'n' Andy* didn't seem to be about the same people shown on the evening news shows."[10] The images of African Americans juxtaposed to their racist depictions on television finally let the world know that there was another dimension to black life, the effects and consequences of racism as an ideology, practice, and quintessential American institution. This visual and lived contradiction also elucidated the transnational position of the United States as beacon of freedom, and what in actuality it was doing to its citizens that sought it. This public realization in many ways facilitated an artistic awakening with many black communities. Coupled with the revisionist energy of Black Power, the BAM was born.

With the death of Malcolm X (El Haji Malik Shabazz) in 1965 and Martin Luther King in 1968, the civil rights movement was literally decapitated. Black Power, which would soon overlap and follow their deaths, again changed the ways in which African American bodies were seen in visual culture. "Black Power was associated with a militant advocacy of armed self-defense, separation from 'racist American domination,' and pride in and assertion of the goodness and beauty of Blackness."[11] BAM initiated a movement that recreated the images of yesteryear and changed the political and cultural significance for African Americans.[12] The visual propaganda of BAM allowed African Americans to recreate a space for corporeal affirmation absent of the white racial frame, and if it did use the frame, it turned it on its racist head, recreating the same stereotypical images of black life using black militancy as its backdrop. Although BAM is known primarily as a literary movement, the visual artists during the late sixties and early seventies were heavily influenced by BAM's poetry and literature. BAM engendered black ownership of magazines, journals, publishing houses, art institutions, and theater groups and changed the ways in which black art was to be seen by black communities. Black art had to have political and cultural significance to the actual people within black communities and BAM gave artists and writers a platform to produce such works.

In addition to BAM, the Black Power movement also produced alternative images of African American imagery. Black nationalist groups, such as the *Black Panther Party for Self Defense*, challenged the white-produced distortions that African Americans would never be able to liberate themselves outside of white assistance and emphasized the ideological restraint that Euro-Americans had instilled in African Americans' minds about their culture, communities, and selves.[13] The Black Power movement put images of militant and courageous African Americans on television. Through its oftentimes racist broadcast of African Americans in the struggle for justice, mass media showed African Americans who were willing to die and use revolutionary violence to make strides in American society.[14]

The *Mammy* and *Jezebel* imagery was replaced for a time with pictures of strong and real African American women who were not only conscious of white America's framing of them but demanded that black America didn't need its handouts for its own liberation. African American men were also showcased as *strong* and *defiant* to the white racial framing of their identities. These images contradicted the *Amos 'n Andy* imagery of the thirties and built on black males' virtual absence from all media in the fifties. African American women and men gave American society a picture of black life in the United States that contradicted the imagery of black life that white media tried to preserve on television since the 1950s.

The Queer Black Body and the Politics of Respectability

Although the civil rights and Black Power movements in the United States reshaped the sociopolitical ideology of what it meant, in the American imagination, to be black, in many ways it also created a sanitized, stable, and often sanctified idea of what it meant to be black. During the Black Power movement, ideas of black male masculinity, in attempt to empower black men and black nationhood, reverted back into the reductive notions of the black male as patriarch, leaving little room for other intersectional identities to be associated with a black male identity. The sexuality of many black characters on television programming after Black Power have all virtually operated within a heteronormative framework. The adherence to traditional heteronormative gender roles and a historical gender schema, utilized in order to challenge white racist visual culture and imagery, gave birth to a virtual visual absence of the black queer body in popular media.

While black communities have revered "historical Black female figures such as Willie Mae 'Big Mama' Thornton, Ma Rainey and Bessie Smith,"[15] as musical icons who reflected bisexual expressions of sexual desire, the mass-mediated acceptance of bisexuality and/or gender nonconformity within a black body has yet to reach substantial proportions. For black male bodies in mainstream visual culture, this is also the case. At the same time that black communities have given musicians who are black and female the opportunity to gender bend and articulate their sexual desire for the same sex, they have also in some ways accepted this phenomenon in many black and male performers. Little Richard, Sylvester, Michael Jackson, Prince, Dennis Rodman, and Andre 3000 are a few black and male performers who have a "played with gender in ways that have largely been viewed as non-threatening."[16] These performers' "gender queerness has been acknowledged, mainstreamed, and largely accepted within significant portions of the Black community."[17]

However, the hegemonic and patriarchal packaging of black masculinity has had a tremendous impact on how visual culture has and has not depicted its few black gay characters. "Hegemonic masculinity embodies the most honored way of being a man, and necessitates that all men present themselves in compliance with its rules of being a man, including the subordination of women and femininity."[18] Although, both the civil rights and Black Power movements created transgressive representations of what it meant to be a black citizen in the United States, its persistence that African Americans were sexually conservative, heteronormative, and extremely religious[19] served to position the black queer body on the peripheral of mainstream visual culture. Visually redefining what it means to be black and masculine within a black sociopolitical community would in many ways benefit not only the audience of the show and/or program but in many ways might create more room for what a normative characterization of identity and experience means in mass-mediated culture. Within visual culture's box of hegemonic masculinity, the black queer body in mainstream media, then, serves to push at the edges of gender, forcing us to recognize that gender has little to do with our biological sex. The black queer body in general and the black gay man's visual performance, of his gender, blackness, and sexuality, specifically, challenge our prevailing notions of what it means to be both black and gay.

The Birth of La-La: Negro Faggotry's Evolution into the Black Gay Man

After writing the *Shakespeare Mysteries,* Charlaine Harris released her first book in the *Sookie Stackhouse* novel series, *Dead until Dark. Dead until Dark* won Harris the Anthony Award for Best Paperback Mystery in 2001. Her *Sookie Stackhouse* series follows the telepathic waitress throughout her many adventures with her undead motley crew in the northern city of Bon Temps, Louisiana. Her series not only peeked interest with readers but now has 11 books in the series and has been republished worldwide, and in September 2008, Alan Ball, the creator of the hit HBO show *Six Feet Under,* decided to turn the *Sookie Stackhouse* novels into a new HBO series.

Since *True Blood* hit the airwaves, it has created quite a stir. Its popularity stems, in part, from the fact that most of the characters comprised werewolves, vampires, shape-shifters, mediums, maenads, fairies, and the like. The stir mostly has to do with the sociopolitical undertones found within the show relating to sexuality, race, and class. Although the protagonist in the novels, as well as the show, is a white, heterosexual, young woman, the ensemble cast, which Ball made sure was racially and sexual diverse, is what has audiences tuning in every week. The character of Lafayette Reynolds, or *La-La* (which the character's mother affectionately calls him), has become a truly beloved character on the show. Although Nelsan Ellis who plays Lafayette on the show dies at the "end of the first book on which the series is inspired,"[20] the producers of the show decided to keep Lafayette on the series well into Season 6.[21] "Lafayette is a redneck-thumping, drug dealing diva with a tongue saltier than the gumbo he serves up as the grill cook at *Merlotte's*[22] honky tonk,"[23] and *True Blood* audiences are tuning in every week to see what clever, sassy, or sultry things might roll off Lafayette's tongue at any given moment. In line with mass-mediated culture's reliance of hegemonic masculinity (that not only reduces the trajectory of masculine performance but also devalues feminine performances), most black gay male characters, as well as the black male gender transgressive performer, are often stereotyped as "white negro,"[24] whose incorporations of the feminine make their performances mere minstrelsy for white consumption.

In *Black Macho Revisited: Reflections of a Snap! Queen,* Marlon T. Riggs speaks to this idea directly by naming this phenomenon Negro Faggotry.[25] "I am a Negro Faggot, if I believe what movies, TV, and Rap music say of me. Because of my sexuality, I cannot be Black. A strong, proud, 'Afrocentric' Black man is resolutely, not even bisexual."[26] To Riggs, Negro Faggotry is the minstrel performative cousin of the authentic black gay man. "My sexual difference is of no value; indeed it's a testament to weakness, passivity, the absence of real guts-balls."[27] The rampant homophobia that functioned in aggregation with reestablishing black hegemonic masculinity within the Black Power movement eroded away all other public performances of masculinity.

Riggs, who was an out and proud gay black man, proud of his black heritage and proud of his gay self, argued that the socialized and mediated public suppression of a salient and intersectional black and gay identity was more than a problem and was rooted in the African American community's need to establish an *other* within their own communities. "What lies at the heart, I believe, of Black America's cultural homophobia is the desperate need for a convenient Other *within* the community, yet not truly of the community-an Other on which blame for the chronic identity crisis afflicting the black male psyche,"[28] meaning that heteronormative black masculinity is framed and categorized off the backs of the black gay man. Therefore, the scripting of black and gay men as the "essential Other against whom Black men and boys maturing, struggling with self-doubt, anxiety, feelings of political, economic, social, and sexual inadequacy-even impotence-can always measure themselves and by comparison seem strong, adept, empowered, superior."[29]

The histrionic, playful, flamboyant, and sassy black gay man when funneled through popular media is converted into the Negro Faggot, which "parallels and reinforces America's most entrenched racist constructions around African-American identity."[30] Not only does the performance of Negro Faggotry deny black and gay characters' three-dimensionality or a variety of roles, but it also revisits old narratives of black performance, both black and white. Whites who have historically signified blackness in the minstrel tradition of performance "share with contemporary icons of Negro Faggotry a manifest dread of the deviant Other."[31] Utilizing the very characteristics and/or traits that define this deviant other, which Riggs speaks of, and imbue within this characterization the idea of an "intrinsic defect,"[32] the Negro Faggot denies the authentic portrayal of a salient black, gay, male identity. "Hence, Blacks are inferior because they are not white; Black gays are unnatural because they are not straight. Majority representations of both affirm the view that Blackness and Gayness constitute a fundamental rupture in the order of things, that our very existence is an affront to nature and humanity."[33]

While you still see the vestiges of Negro Faggotry performed in many ways by both white and black performers[34] on stages, in cinema, and on television, there has been in recent years (albeit small and not as main-stream) many more visible characterizations of the authentic black gay male character that Riggs was yearning for.[35] The ideological and visual shifting of the idea of "normal" has changed within many new sitcoms, films, and even the music industry.[36] The major movements (civil rights and Black Power) that were engendered by black Americans not only created a new idea of what blackness meant and means, but it facilitated other black activists and filmmakers, like Riggs and others, to rewrite and expand on the definition of blackness to incorporate other intersecting identities such as sexual orientation, gender, class, and so forth. All of these *cultural moves*[37] have helped to create the ideological, visual, and sociopolitical room for television (in this case, HBO) to show us an authentic portrayal of proud black gay man, who all *truebies*[38] know as Lafayette.

La-La's Counterframe: The Merging of a Black Alpha Male and Sultry Romantic

During the first season of the HBO hit *True Blood,* Lafayette, who is played by Nelsan Ellis (who has won a 2008 Satellite Award from the International Press Academy and the NewNowNext "Brink of Fame: Actor" award in 2009 for his work on the series), acted in an episode called "Sparks Fly Out," which has turned into the most quotable scene for series fans. Lafayette, who is a cook at Merlott's (the neighborhood bar and grill where all the characters' paths tend to cross), cooks an order of burgers and fries for three poor Southern heterosexual white men[39] who have, after receiving the meal, sent it back to Lafayette's kitchen, through another character Arlene. Arlene (a quintessential poor Southern white woman) tells Lafayette that the men don't want to eat the food he has cooked because they assume that the burgers are infected with HIV.

At the time that the "Sparks Fly Out" aired in 2008, its entry in the public consciousness was framed by the politically fueled public conversation about the rising rates of HIV/AIDS with black communities. This merely continued a larger history of pathologizing black sexuality, evident in media hysteria about the *down low* and black gay men. This myth, rooted in fear, ignorance, and, as Keith Boykin pointed out in his book *Beyond the Down Low,* white supremacy, all interested the producers of the series *True Blood* where they decided to play out the myth in the exchange between Lafayette and the three men.

"Is there a problem with my burger?"[40] Lafayette asks Arlene. "Just a couple of drunk rednecks that's all."[41] "Well what's they problem,"[42] Lafayette asks to Arlene. Arlene does not want to tell Lafayette about what the customers said. The audience is also unaware at this point what the problem is with the food. The viewers of the show and the character Lafayette are all informed of the commentary at the same time. After Lafayette hears why the men don't want the food, he proceeds to take off both his earrings and apron and switches politely over to the table to speak with the gentlemen. Once arriving at the table, however, Lafayette's tone, expression, and body language shift from an effeminate softness to a threatening masculine persona, and he throws the burger on their table and asks them: "Excuse me, who ordered the burger with AIDS?" Lafayette's question shocks the three men at the table, who from their reaction expected Lafayette to cower based on their passive aggressive discriminatory commentary to their waitress Arlene.

Two of the men at the table laugh at Lafayette's question, yet one gives his comrades at the table a passing dirty glance and retorts that he ordered the burger deluxe. Lafayette rolls his eyes at the man and says: "In this restaurant a hamburger deluxe comes with French fries, lettuce, tomato, mayo and AIDS."[43] When Lafayette gets to the word AIDS, he yells in order to let the other customers in the restaurant know what is happening. He wants the other customers in Merlott's to know that he is not going to tolerate discrimination of any kind, especially which is directed at him. He then turns and says to the entire restaurant, "Do anybody got a problem with that?"[44] The man at the table who has now raised his voice and says to Lafayette, "Yeah I'm an American and I got a say in who makes my food."[45]

By the second season of *True Blood,* the series had already established itself as a show that not only pokes fun at American politics but always engages its audiences with heavy social ills that we as Americans suffer from, such as domestic violence, racism, homophobia, rape, child abuse, and so forth. *True Blood* is not alone in this regard. Much of television programming is aimed at its audiences engaging with heavy-handed issues visually and empathically through the guise of entertainment and drama. However, because the show is set in a supernatural town, where humans and *sups*[46] interact, have sex, fight, and generally relate to one another, this creates the room for its audiences (and sometimes characters) to become almost more vulnerable than they would be normally when it comes to exploring their own reservations about social and political progress through the various characters' experiences with various forms of discrimination. For example, the show begins with the vampires who have now come out of the coffin and are now living *out* and *proud* among human beings and other super naturals. Viewers aware of LGBTQ struggles for marriage equality, end to don't ask don't tell, and other rights see the thematic parallels offered by *True Blood* with its narratives about vampires. In the show, vampires cannot marry humans, and there is still incredible stigma attached to a supernatural identity.

Lafayette, now enraged by the man at the table's last statement, says: "Well baby it's too late for that it's too late for that. Faggot's been breeding your cows, raising your chickens, even brewing your beer long before I walked my sexy ass up in this motherfucker."[47] Then tells the rest of the men at the table: "Everything at your goddamn table got AIDS."[48] The customer still refuses to eat the food because he swears it's infected with AIDS; Lafayette in very coy and feminine performing way bends down to ear level with the customer and says: "Well all you got to do is say hold the AIDS."[49] All of the men at the table are wide-eyed while they watch Lafayette lick the mayonnaise off the burger and then proceed to smack one of the men at the table with the licked bun on the face and say: "Here, eat it."[50] The other two men rise up from the table with the intention of beating up Lafayette for embarrassing and insulting their friend. Lafayette single-handedly beats all of the men to a bloody pulp in the restaurant, while all of the other patrons and audience watch with wonder, surprise, shock, and compassion. "Bitch you come into my house, you gonna eat my food the way I fucking make it. Do you understand me,"[51] are Lafayette's second to last words to the men. After Lafayette realizes that his business is finished with the men, he switches away from the table and smiles at the men and reminds them to make sure and not forget to "tip your waitress."[52]

Lafayette's sexuality, which defines him out of and within the show as the *deviant other,* as Riggs refers to, does not make him cower before racists or homophobes. Lafayette is the actual real character that Riggs was asking for. Lafayette is not a Negro Faggot, nor does he perform Negro Faggotry, only functioning as some type of racialized clown for comic relief. The writers of the show, its producers, and the actor who plays Lafayette on *True Blood* all had a hand in shaping the intentional three-dimensionality of the character. One of the only human characters on the show that is centered on the supernatural experience, Lafayette's humanness posits him as an other on the show. However, Lafayette accepts the growing supernatural community and his own status as a human other in *Bon Temps.*[53] If anything, Lafayette often looks and judges the other characters as crazy, nuts, or too wild for him because of their supernatural abilities and their resulting behavior.

At the beginning of Season 2, Lafayette is kidnapped by Eric, a one-thousand-year-old vampire who owns the vampire nightclub *Fangtasia.* During Season 1, Lafayette, who sold *v-blood,*[54] was caught by the vampire sheriff Eric Northman and was subsequently locked in the dungeon in the bottom of his club while he figures out the punishment that is due Lafayette. However, Lafayette, being a *clever queen*,[55] escapes and is confronted by an armed, glamoured[56] entirely too much bar maid, Ginger, who has been put in charge of watching Lafayette while Eric and his progeny,[57] Pam, are away on business. While attempting to walk out of the front door of Fangtasia, Ginger demands Lafayette to identify himself. Impersonating a heterosexual black man, Lafayette, tries to sexually seduce Ginger. He uses his deep voice as enticement as he slowly walks toward her and the gun in a very aggressive but nonthreatening way.

"Who the hell are you?"[58] Ginger asks Lafayette. Lafayette who has figured out that Ginger is human and therefore saner than the crazed sups begins to pray to God and thank Jesus because he thinks she will let him go. "Well look at you. Not only is you sexy mmmm, but you can read minds too. That get me all riled up in my nether regions."[59] Ginger, having been alerted to exactly who Lafayette is, yells: "Uh uh don't you try and flirt with me. They told me to pay special attention to the faggot drag queen in the basement."[60] Lafayette, who is now angered that he cannot use his charm or wit (attempting to perform hegemonic masculinity in order to free himself) to convince Ginger to let him go, says: "Look you skank ass bitch, you gon' let me up outta here."[61]

This scene is another where Lafayette uses both masculine and feminine communication styles and performances in order to escape from a vampire dungeon or to enact justified violence when being discriminated against. Lafayette possesses agency, demonstrating the authenticity of his character. He personifies an empowered black, gay, and male identity. Lafayette's use of black English vernacular in his speech illustrates the show's efforts to tie him, at least linguistically, to a larger black history. Lafayette's blending of the masculine and feminine not only expands the visual and ideological understanding of gender performance but also elucidates that gender is in fact an intentional performance based on notions of hegemonic masculinity and femininity and by blending the two together one expands the definitions of both. Lastly, as an out and proud gay character who not only defends himself against bigots, but also finds love with the Latino gay male character on the show, Jesus, Lafayette joins a witches' coven, and by Season 4 acts as a medium, finally becoming aware of his innate ability to exist in the physical world and communicate with the spiritual world.

Television is often thought of as providing a bird's-eye view into outside cultures and communities. Yet, it has often suffered from the ill effects of mass media and society's reliance on the white racial frame, making most of the characters on television one dimensional, stereotypical, imagined constructions based on this frame. Lafayette from the HBO series *True Blood* is not one of those types of characters. He is not a Negro Faggot, nor does he perform Negro Faggotry as Marlon T. Riggs argued about Blaine and Antoine on the television show *In Living Color*. He is three dimensional. He is an agent. He has relationships that are full of love and lust. He does not tolerate discrimination of any kind and will use his linguistic skills to make his voice heard. Lafayette is the type of character Riggs was yearning for 30 years ago, an unapologetic, powerful, proud black gay male character, which expounds on society's definitions of what it means to be black, gay, straight, male, and female.

Notes

1. Joe R. Feagin defines the white racial frame as a collective denial of race, racial relations, and sociopolitical equality in the United States by most white citizens.

2. I define blackness in the essay as the racialized, gendered, and sexual scripts rooted in the white imagination.

3. Herman S. Gray, *Cultural Moves: African Americans and the Politics of Representation* (Berkley: University of California Press, 2005).

4. Ibid., p. 89.

5. The acronym LGBTQ means Lesbian, Gay, Bisexual, Transgender, and Queer. This acronym is utilized within many alternative sexual communities as well as heterosexual communities to speak of individuals who have an alternative sexuality based on a heteronormative model.

6. I define "authentic" as a character created in television or film that closely replicates and/or mirrors the written experiences and/or themes explored in the theories, literature, and art of oppressed groups of people.

7. These dates are approximated.

8. Steven Kasher, *The Civil Rights Movement: A Photographic History 1954–68* (New York: Abbeville Press, 1996).

9. Ralph DeWitt Story, "The Equinox: When History Was Now," in *Master Players in a Fixed Game: An Extra-Literary History of Twentieth Century African-American Authors*, ed. by Ralph DeWitt Story (Boca Raton: Dissertation.com, 2001), pp. 109–62.

10. Ibid., p. 117.

11. Larry Neal, "The Black Arts Movement," *Drama Review* 12, No. 4 (1968): pp. 29–39.

12. Examples of counterframed art that appeared during the Black Arts movement were The Liberation of Aunt Jemima by Betty Saar in 1972 and No More by Onye Lockard in 1967.

13. Ralph DeWitt Story, "The Equinox," pp. 109–62.

14. Ibid.

15. M.K. Lewis Marshall and Kaila Adia Story, "Chapter 2: Gender and Black Communities," in *LGBT Psychology: Research Perspectives and People of African Descent*, ed. by M.K. Lewis Marshall and Kaila Adia Story (New York: Springer Publishing Company, 2012), pp. 21–36.

16. Ibid., p. 29.

17. Ibid.

18. Ibid., p. 26.

19. I am speaking of the Tyler Perry phenomenon that posits African American life as socioreligious and blind to the social ills of society.

20. Mike McCray, "True Blood's Lafayette Slays Gay Sterotypes," http://thegrio.com/2011/08/01/true-bloods-lafayette-slays-gay-stereotypes/ (accessed September 15, 2012).

21. Ibid.

22. Merlott's is the bar and restaurant where Lafayette works, and all of the characters on the show usually cross.

23. David Hiltbrand, "Actor Brings Extended Life to True Blood Character," http://articles.philly.com/2010-07-04/entertainment/24962696_1_true-blood-gay-club-character (accessed September 15, 2012).

24. Zine Magubane, "Black Skins, Black Masks or 'The Return of the White Negro': Race, Masculinity, and the Public Personas of Dennis Rodman and RuPaul," *Men and Masculinities* 4, no. 3 (2002): pp. 233–57.

25. Marlon T. Riggs defines the practice of "Negro Faggotry" as the stereotypical, racialized, sexual, and gendered scripts that couch black gay men as histrionic jesters and/or coons for the purposes of entertainment and to deny the humanity and authenticity of black and gay people.

26. Marlon T. Riggs, "Black Macho Revisited: Reflections of a Snap Queen," *Black American Literature Forum* 25, no. 2 (1991): pp. 389–94.

27. Ibid., p. 390.

28. Ibid., p. 390.

29. Ibid., pp. 390–91.

30. Ibid., p. 391.

31. Ibid., p. 391.

32. Ibid., p. 391.

33. Ibid., p. 391.

34. Contemporary television has created the visual room for a lot of performers who perform Negro Faggotry. Some examples of these performers are Miss Jay on *America's Next Top Model* and the gay couple in the new television show *Modern Family*, and so forth.

35. There have also been more authentic portrayals of black and gay identities such as the two Logo television series, *Noah's Arc* created by Ian Patrick Polk and *RuPaul's Drag Race* created by RuPaul Andre Charles.

36. Lady Gaga, Nikki Minaj, and the new television series, *The New Normal*, all show that there has been progress in representing more authentic portrayals of queer identity.

37. I use the term Cultural Moves from Herman Gray's book, *Cultural Moves: African Americans and the Politics of Representation.*

38. A truebie is defined as a viewer of the show *True Blood* that is obsessive about everything in the show, similar to how Star Trek viewers are referred to as trekies.

39. The viewer of the show is able to infer the class of men by the way they are dressed and by the way the other characters of the show refer to them.

40. *Sparks Fly Out*, directed by Daniel Minahan, performed by Nelsan Ellis as Lafayette Reynolds, 2008.

41. Ibid.

42. Ibid.

43. Ibid.

44. Ibid.

45. Ibid.

46. Sups is a term that is used in the show *True Blood* as a slang term for supernaturals.

47. Ibid.

48. Ibid.

49. Ibid.

50. Ibid.

51. Ibid.

52. Ibid.

53. Bon Temps is the fictitious town in which the show is set.

54. V and/or v-blood refers to vampire blood, which human characters of the show take as a recreational drug. Vampire blood has similar effects of LSD and/or acid on the human body.

55. A clever queen is a term that comes out of the subculture black house ball culture. It means a black gay man who uses his wits to convince others of what they need to do for him. See Jennie Livingston's film, *Paris Is Burning.*

56. Vampires have the ability to glamour humans. Erasing their memories and preventing them to retell any incident that preceded the glamouring.

57. A progeny is the child of a vampire parent who has turned a once human into a vampire. Progenies cannot refuse anything that their parent requests of them. They almost function as quasi-enslaved humans.

58. *Escape from Dragon House*, directed by Michael Lehmann, performed by Nelsan Ellis as Lafayette. 2008.

59. Ibid.

60. Ibid.

61. Ibid.

Chapter 21

Can the Black Woman Shout? A Meditation on "Real" and Utopian Depictions of African American Women on Scripted Television

Rebecca Wanzo

In one of our regular rambling check-ins at the office in 2005, a fellow African American woman colleague suddenly asked me, "I've been meaning to ask you, have you watched *Grey's Anatomy*? Girl, there's a REAL black woman on TV! A REAL Black woman!" "Real" is, of course, a heavily laden term, suggesting racial authenticity. Claims about authenticity and "keepin' it real" can clearly be regulatory mechanisms that construct divisions between allegedly real black people and oreos or any other derogatory expressions used to flatten out the complexity of black experience and identity. The words "authentic" and "real" are thus deeply problematic, but their deployment still can signify—in a spectrum of possible representations of black people—a deep recognition in response to a representation. And Miranda Bailey, the character my colleague referenced, was deeply recognizable to us.

Bailey, portrayed by the actress Chandra Wilson, is the African American supervisor of a group of five interns on popular prime-time melodrama *Grey's Anatomy* (2005). The very structure of her role, as well as stout body frame, has too easily led to readings of her as a "mammy," but I want to place pressure on the overdetermined nature of readings of African

American characters.[1] I've argued elsewhere that cultural critics should be leery of what I call a "just syntax."[2] While black representations are often scripted as stereotype, audiences are also primed to read black representations in relationship to these racist archetypes. But the compression of some performances into *just* a mammy and *just* a coon can capitulate to readings that refuse to recognize the two strands of resistance and ideological retrenchment that runs not only through mass culture but through broader struggles for African American agency. Given the history of black representation, black characters can be read as conforming to a stereotype every time they are servants, caregiving to nonblacks, criminals, singing, dancing, comedic, angry, poor, ill educated, perfect, self-sacrificing, magical, monstrous, victims, inspirational, violent, very masculine, very sexual, asexual, back talking, and nonspeaking. As this list makes clear, part of the success of visual racial imperialism is its omnipresence and ability to penetrate everything.

The show's African American creator, Shonda Rhimes, clearly believes she escapes these representational challenges as someone who allegedly adheres to "color-blind" casting.[3] Her postracial approach demonstrates what Frederic Jameson describes as the relationship between the ideological and utopian in mass cultural production. "Social and political anxieties," Jameson argues, are "repressed by the narrative construction of imaginary resolutions and by the projection of an optical illusion of social harmony," but "we cannot fully do justice to the ideological function of works like these unless we are willing to concede the presence [of] . . . their Utopian or transcendent potential."[4] In *Grey's Anatomy,* she reportedly refuses to cast African Americans as pimps and drug dealers (even though that is clearly not color blind casting) and constructs a multiracial hospital staff in which race and gender are no impediment to success or supervisory roles. The progressive impulses can thus contribute to erasures of political realities, and the show generically adheres to the ideological investments that propel and support its success—heteronormativity, a privileging of white protagonists, and fantasies that mask the workings of power.

Rhimes does represent an atypical model of black female subjectivity on television through the Miranda Bailey character, but like many representations before it, the legacies of progressive and regressive fantasies about race relations haunt both the construction of her character and readings of it. Many black representations are anchored by performances that may evoke lived experience, contributing to a reading of a representation as real. But the fantasies can be just as important in evoking recognition. Progressive fantasies about black female identity are deeply entwined with post–civil rights era representations of real black women on television. Bailey is one in a long line of characters who evokes the real—not only through the recognition evoked by Wilson's performance but also through idealized scripts about how black women can successfully navigate the world.

Can "Real" Black Women Be on TV?

The question of what it means to have real black people on television runs up against the broader question of how the real functions in the medium. As John Corner explains, critical discussions of realism on television address representations that are "*like* the real" and "*about* the real."[5] Producing a text that is like the real is heavily indebted to form, and both kinds of real will have content that looks realistic or gestures toward the real. Thus, a science fiction show like the reimagined *Battlestar Galactica* can nevertheless be about the real because, while set in outer space and depicting robots, it addresses questions of war, occupation, and survival in a gritty depiction of human nature. Of course, what the "real" is will constantly be debated.

Conceptualizations of the real nevertheless can bear a close resemblance to stereotype. For example, some African Americans want to privilege a black maternal, nurturing identity for African American women, one rich with folk wisdom and black mother wit. If black women lie outside of this tradition, are they not black? For some, representations of real blackness mean depicting working-class African Americans. That understanding of a real would mean that a show like *The Cosby Show*, the groundbreaking show about an upper-middle-class African American family, cannot be real—and some have made that argument.[6] By the same token, the critically acclaimed HBO show *The Wire*, which focuses on a criminal black underclass in Baltimore and the various institutions that interacted with this community, has been described as about real black people but has also been condemned as another stereotypical show about black drug dealers.[7] So, what is "real" blackness on television? How would a "real" black woman be depicted?

At the risk of reinvigorating arguments about authentic black representation, I want to make a case in this essay for the pleasures and political possibilities of a black real in cultural productions. First and foremost, we must understand that real blackness on television requires a critical mass of representations of black people so that one representation does not carry the burden of all. People of African American descent are not homogenous. Thus, no show can represent *the* real but can only represent *a* real that is

recognizable to some portion of the audience that has longed for a representation that speaks not only to lived experiences but political fantasies
and has some vague resemblance to people who look and sound like them
so that they, too, can have currency as desired objects and desiring subjects.
I thus want to make a distinction between a naming of *the* real that polices
the boundaries of authenticity and a yearning for and identification with
a real that is about the recognition of one's place within a larger group.
In other words, the kinds of representations that interest me here provide
more complex recognitory possibilities for black subjects. These kinds of
black real depictions hail individuals as part of *a* group, not as representing
the group.

Real blackness representational projects are racial projects as Michael
Omi and Howard Winant describe them: "simultaneously an interpretation, representation, or explanation of racial dynamics, and an effort to
reorganize and redistribute resources among particular racial lines."[8] Such
projects are racist when they are essentialist, suggesting that a particular
black representation encapsulates what all black people are or must be. But
I want to hold onto the idea of a "real" as a compelling affective consumptive convention for many black audience members. In other words, what
attracts people to some black representations is a sense of recognition that
something seems close to their real, and we lack vocabulary that can capture the desire other than "real." In the West, we live in a world overdetermined not by real selves but the simulacra that shapes our understanding
of the world. Since representations are, by definition, mediated, a black real
representational project is a reconfiguration of signs and codes that work
to reorganize our understanding of blackness and circulate new meanings
of blackness in the public sphere.

Thus, many shows, even those that have been accused of being unrealistic, can contain a black real. A black real (1) speaks to lived experience *or*
political fantasies and (2) depicts characters who look and sound like people in the community of some black audience members. It is also a black
real representational *project* if it attempts to redistribute racial representation in the public sphere. Looking and sounding black are expansive and
include things like a black vernacular but can also mean addressing the
variety of black experiences.

Can the Black Woman Care (for White Children)?

The most prevalent black female experience represented in film and television for many years was the black female caregiver. And all too often,

the representation did not look like the black domestic workers who were the mothers, sisters, and grandmothers in African American families. Instead, she was the mammy character, a phantasm of black devotion to white families and erasure of black ones sprung from the antebellum South and Reconstruction. A more complex understanding of a black representational real provides an explanation for why even this racist representation would have black audiences. Some members of the black audience may be drawn to the show because it circulates some aspect of a black real, not just because they are desperate for representations of black people on television. A show like *Beulah* (1950–1952), the first show with an African American woman as the title character, has little claim as a black real representational project. It is *structurally* redistributive, as it is the first show to star an African American actress (Ethel Waters, Hattie McDaniel, and, finally, Louise Beavers). However, a white male actor originated the character on radio, and the transition to black actresses did little to help the stereotypical foundations of the sassy mammy taking care of a white family. It is thus not *substantively* redistributive. But does the mammy role itself foreclose the possibility of a black real? Waters had demonstrated interiority as a mammy in the adaptation of Carson McCullers's *The Member of the Wedding* (1952). In one scene, while holding two white children, she sings, "His Eye Is on the Sparrow." One of the children begins singing the gospel song, and the scene ends with her singing with them. The camera presents a close-up of her face, and Waters performs a powerful version of a song oft-rendered in black churches. Her expression is not directed toward her charges but inward and upward, allowing for an interiority often denied to people playing roles as black caregivers. Her performance can trigger recognition of a black life outside of the white community and white desire.

I am not arguing that African American women who have been domestic servants have not cared for many of their charges. Criticisms of such representations are about the fact that these are so often the sole roles for African American women and also because these roles depict African American women as making white families the center of their identities. *Beulah* and her film and television sisters have cast a long shadow, so much so that it can be hard for African American women who express care for white characters to escape the mammy designation. Can African American women care for white children and escape the "M" word? One of the best examples of resistance to the mammy narrative on television is the civil rights era family drama, *I'll Fly Away* (1991–1993).[9] An ensemble show about a white family and their black housekeeper, the show was not structurally redistributive as network television probably would not have been sold on making the housekeeper's black family the narrative center. Regina Taylor, who played housekeeper Lily Harper, received second billing after star Sam Waterson, but Lily was clearly central to the drama. Her life away from the family was essential to the show. As Taylor said of her role, the writers "were interested in portraying a full human being" and "not just the hands that serve other people."[10] When the white child she cares for, John Morgan, accuses Lily of not loving him, she says she does but has her own family.[11] And Taylor, a dark-skinned and very attractive svelte woman, portrayed Lily as quietly strong-willed but not sassy and without the exaggerated black vernacular common to these representations. She was an entirely new model of black caregiver for television, a black real that reflected the lived experiences of many black domestics and their families.

The difference between *Beulah* and *I'll Fly Away* was a product of the wins of the civil rights movement affecting the representational possibilities on television. Herman S. Gray would describe the incorporation of black representations as a "strategic move" despite the fact that the "American national imaginary still remains deeply ambivalent about a black cultural presence."[12] This ambivalence was clear in the post–civil rights mammy show, *Gimme a Break* (1981–1987). While *I'll Fly Away* would offer a more progressive view of the past few years later, this show would depict a more retroview of the post–civil rights era present. Starring Nell Carter, a gifted musical comedy stage actress, the show focused on an African American woman who agrees to take care of her friend's husband and three daughters after her death. Nell is African American, and the Kanisky family is white. Because of the nature of the role and Nell Carter's plus-sized frame and sassy effect, the show was clearly a 1980s update of a traditional mammy narrative. Over time, Nell had more of a love life and became more involved with the black community, and because the actor who played the police chief father died, the show became organized around Nell's broader life. But as is often case in family sitcoms, when the children aged, the producers of the show decided to add a younger, cute child. Nell and Chief Kanisky took in a young white boy named Joey. After the chief's death, Joey became Nell's child exclusively.

Despite the clearly stereotypical nature of the show, it is a clear example of how a show can contain a black real, while still adhering to a racist representational logic. Produced in the 1980s, the writers of the show were clearly cognizant of the representational histories the show evoked. One explicit acknowledgment of this history was the episode "Nell's Friend." A childhood frenemy, Addy Wilson, shows up from Alabama. She provides a striking contrast to Nell. A Phi Beta Kappa with a PhD, she appears in professional garb and impresses the Kanisky girls. Nell had dropped out of high school to pursue her dreams of being a singer. Feigning modesty, Addy suggests that she is not that special, simply one of thousands of black women making it in the contemporary world. She declares, "Thank God, we finally put to rest that old stereotypical image of the black woman as an Aunt Jemima," when Nell walks in with a handkerchief around her head, a roller in the front, carrying laundry, the picture of the archetype.

Addy proceeds to put Nell down in front of the girls until Nell has had enough and directs Addy to the kitchen. Nell challenges her on her behavior, and Addy denies that she has been insulting: "After all the disappointments, I think it's wonderful you've found your niche in life as a maid in a white household." Nell stalks around the kitchen, stating that she is very fortunate because she "gives lots of love and I receive lots of love . . . this family needs me and that's all that matters." Addy looks at her with sympathy and condescension, telling her, "I do hope that you haven't forgotten that there's a whole new world out there just waiting for the modern black woman." Fed up, Nell replies, "Sugar, let's not keep that sucker waiting. World, here comes a modern black woman!" and hurls her out of the kitchen door.

This is a strikingly defensive episode, as Addy stands in for modern critiques of what Nell represents. In the scene that resolves the conflict, Nell rages at Addy for telling her she was a "failure as a modern black woman." She exclaims, "I was happy as a black woman until you walked your modern black butt in the house!" Addy eventually confesses that she is miserable and boring, a contrast to how happy Nell is, living in a house with love and fun. The decision to make the critique of representations of Aunt Jemima as an unhappy, self-important bore frames the critique as self-important. Our sympathies are with the show's protagonist. The character did indeed give and receive love on the show, but the show idealized a representation that was historically quite rare—the black female caregiver without family of her own whose kids are the ones she is paid to care for. The modern twist on the mammy is that Nell would actually adopt a white child as her own.

The black real here hinges on Carter's performance as a woman mourning lost opportunities. Nell is a high school dropout who failed to achieve her dreams. Many African Americans, despite the movement, were unable to achieve middle-class status or great economic success. The tension of a character who may look down on African Americans of a lower-class status mirrors certain tensions that sometimes arise in the black community. In not respecting Nell's position as a domestic, Addy stands for an ugly split in the African American community. Addy's politics are bad, not Nell's, and by extension, neither are the politics of the show.

A black real hinged on the audience's investment in Nell. While the premise of the show—particularly after she adopted a young white boy as her own—was peculiar, the black maternal itself was recognizable to some audience members. The black vernacular, her way of moving, and her sense of style (the Jemima appearance was anomaly, after the first season she often looked very stylish) sold a real blackness. Many television shows present a black real in stereotypical frames. But post–civil rights era television would also present a black real in more idealistic representations.

Can the Black Woman Shout?

While stereotypical roles can have a troubled relationship to black real representational projects, idealized ones can as well. Diahann Caroll's groundbreaking, non-stereotypical character in *Julia* (1968–1971) did not really address the social unrest of the period. She was a fully assimilated character, a nurse, who sometimes struggled, but the kindly, curmudgeonly boss often took care of things for her. *Julia* is an example of a show where the two strands of ideology are evident. It demonstrates the utopian hopes for racial integration, but in pursuing that hope through the generic conventions of the sitcom, it erases the complexities of black life.

Scholars have made similar claims about *The Cosby Show* (1984–1992). No black show had ever been as successful, and its success was rooted in its appeal to all audiences. But some scholars have suggested that *The Cosby Show* encourages white audiences to feel that racism has passed and that African Americans no longer face significant obstacles to their progress.[13] But if we keep in mind that no single representation can bear the burden of all representations, we can acknowledge that the show might encourage such readings but that the content itself is not responsible for such readings. In other words, a post–civil rights era climate in which white audiences are already tired of attempts at redressing racism against African Americans and resist continued arguments about racial inequalities make *The Cosby Show* inviting. Thus, the show, in itself, is not responsible for a climate that produces such readings.

But is *The Cosby Show*, and, in the context of this essay, black matriarch Clair Huxtable, an example of a black real? Can an ideal be about the real or represent the real? Clair Huxtable is perhaps the most idealized family sitcom mother ever produced. And I would suggest that she was a profoundly generative example of a black real representational project. First, Clair was recognizable historically even if she had not been seen before on television. Both she and Cliff were products of an HBCU (historically black college and university), a generation that took part in and benefitted from the civil rights movement. Their successes reflected a kind of black life that exists but was never represented. She was very much a black lady, incredibly stylish and poised. What made Clair such an impossible ideal is the absence of any discussion of how she managed to be a successful attorney, have five children, and still look so good.[14] She thus represented a real group of African Americans, but it was the invisibility of the costs and challenges of building her career and having five children while her husband had a demanding career that was the least realistic.

Clair was one of a few prominent feminist characters in 1980s sitcoms. Part of the representational work of these sitcoms was the depiction of angry, conventionally beautiful women whose rants were an anticipated object of humor and pleasure on the shows. On the one hand, when fictional journalist Murphy Brown's temper blew and she decimated an opponent for sexism or other conservative views, making the rant an object of humor made her positions palatable for a general audience. At the same time, the audience was always directed to cheer the righteous rants of both *Murphy Brown* (1988–1998) and Southern belle Julia Sugarbaker on *Designing Women* (1986–1993). Clair's anger was not a consistent feature of the humor on the show, but her anger, usually carefully regulated and controlled, was part of a black female real. The switching between a black anger vernacular of her rants and the black *lady* vernacular—still recognizable as a particular kind of blackness—highlights the kinds of public negotiations that African American women make.

An early example of such code switching takes place in the Season 2 episode "Cliff in Love." Their eldest daughter Sondra has a boyfriend, Elvin, with very traditional ideas about gender roles. She would eventually marry him. Because Elvin understands Clair as a liberated woman, he is surprised when she asks him if he wants coffee, as he was unaware she "did that kind of thing":

Elvin: You know, serve.
Clair: Serve whom?
Elvin: Serve him.
Clair: Oh. Serve him? As in serve your man? (*Her tone, which had previously been very slow and measured but quickens in pace, and her ensuing diatribe is filled with anger.*) Let me tell you something Elvin. You see, I am not serving Dr. Huxtable. OK? That's the kind

of thing that goes on in a restaurant. Now I'm going to bring him a cup of coffee just like he brought me a cup of coffee this morning. And that, young man, is what marriage is made of—it is give and take, fifty/fifty. And if you don't get it together and drop these macho attitudes, you are never gonna have anybody bringing you anything, anywhere, anyplace, anytime, EVER! (*She then asks sweetly.*) Now, what would you like in your coffee?

Clair's feminist rage is carefully dispensed. She turns it on and off seemingly easily. In contrast to Murphy Brown and, to a lesser extent, Julia Sugarbaker, Clair is not as likely to appear out of control. But the audience does get to see Clair's parental anger, her professional anger, and, very rarely, a political anger. The elegance and control of her anger is—in contrast to being a depiction of an out-of-control black womanhood—an important part of Clair's ideality.

Clair Huxtable's class position in itself was not far from some black experiences, but she was an extraordinary and transformative articulation of a black feminist political desire. As a beautiful, poised, always stylish, brilliant partner in a law firm who raised five children while maintaining a romantic, playful marriage with a man who also had a demanding career, she beat Donna Reed in every way. The traditional idealized sitcom mother had a fraction of her accomplishments. I grew up watching her, and she was the impossible ideal—not just because of what she attained but because of the representation of effortlessness. It was thus not the family structure that was necessarily the major substance of the ideal. The most fantastic element of the show was the depiction of the elegant *ease* of educated, beautiful, accomplished, and unconflicted black female adulthood. And it was as *real* a representation as anything I saw on television because the representation spoke to my desires about what should be. In his famous essay, "What Is the Black in Black Popular Culture," Stuart Hall reminds readers that popular culture is not

where we find who we really are, the truth of our experience. It is an arena that is profoundly mythic. It is a theater of popular desires, a theater of popular fantasies. It is where we are imagined, where we are represented, not only to the audiences out there who do not get the message, but to ourselves for the first time.[15]

And indeed, the most profound black real representational projects for an audience may not depict lives like their own but a structure of feeling that articulates desires, future, and possibilities that they had not previously imagined or seen. That is what it means to redistribute signs and codes of blackness in the public sphere.

Producer Shonda Rhimes, the most successful African American woman showrunner in prime-time television history, has explicitly announced her intention to redistribute the signs and codes of racial representation on television. She states that she has color blind casting, but that is not quite accurate—when she was first selling *Grey's Anatomy,* it is unlikely the central protagonist could be African American. However, it is a multiracial ensemble, and the extras are truly multicultural—perhaps reflecting a multiculturalism beyond Seattle's actual demographics. That said, the pilot appeared to offer a diversity tokenism that still wouldn't result in African American characters playing major roles in the show. *Grey's Anatomy* initially focused on five residents at the fictional Seattle Grace Hospital, and three of the four senior staff in the cast—their supervisor, the chief of staff, and the head cardiothoracic surgeon—were African Americans. The fourth senior staff member was white and the love interest for the title character. The show thus perpetuated a practice of making African American characters supervisors, leaving the starring roles to white leads. At least in this case, the show did have Asian American Sandra Oh as part of the central ensemble, a rarity on television.

In the pilot, the Bailey character appeared to be a flat characterization common to alienating supervisors—particularly black ones—on television. Bailey's nickname was the "Nazi," and Chandra Wilson spit out a monologue of cold orders and instructions, demonstrating no patience or compassion and expressing irritation with questions—a potentially deadly and stupid position to take when you are supervising new doctors. It was reminiscent of African American Peter Benton's treatment of his medical student John Carter on the hit NBC show *ER* over a decade before. But just as the show's writers and Eriq LaSalle soon shaped Benton into a complex character on the earlier hospital drama, Bailey's character would grow exponentially over the next year. The writers gave her a fuller life, and other characters would understand her as the most professional and ethical member of the staff.

What marked her as real was a combination of factors, not insignificantly that she is a black woman possessing a phenotype and frame of African American women not traditionally represented on television with nonstereotypical roles. A very short woman with a stocky frame, she is both petite and substantial. Wilson's performance would continue to emphasize the reactions that my colleague and I responded to, a familiar syntax of black woman sister talk that we exchanged in private in our offices. While Amy Long and others have suggested that she is simply mammy updated, this does not reflect the complexity the writers and actress brought to the part.[16] As she initially didn't circulate in the sexual economy of the show, her casting didn't require the model body of most of the other actors. Her stable marriage and clear thinking in relationship to unprofessional sex in the workplace also marked her as an unusual black woman in television drama—she, not the narrator, was the ethical center of the show.

As a soap opera set in a hospital, much of the show revolves around workplace sex. Bailey discovers that one of her interns is sleeping with an attending physician, who is also one of Bailey's superiors. While Bailey is preparing for a surgery, Meredith informs Bailey that she didn't know that he would be an attending when they began their relationship, and Bailey very concisely explains to Meredith why her feelings are immaterial to the structural problems produced by the affair: "You see this. What's happening right here? This is the problem with you sleeping with my boss. Not whether or not you knew him before, but how it affects *my* day. And me standing here talking to you about your sex life affects my day." She explains that when other interns learn about the affair and start complaining about the treatment she receives, the more it will disrupt her work. "So, Dr. Grey," she concludes, "I don't care what you knew, or when you knew it. Are we understood?" Bailey forecloses bonding over feelings, privileging, rightly so, the issue of structural inequality in her place of employment.

On the one hand, Bailey presented a recognizable blackness to some viewers, on the other hand, the performance of that blackness is what also marks her representation as not real on the show. Bailey's public calling out of bad behavior by people senior to her in the workplace demonstrated a shocking lack of code switching and behavior modification that marks all successful black professional performance. If part of the fantasy of Clair Huxtable was the effortlessness of contained anger, the political desire exemplified by Miranda Bailey in the early seasons of *Grey's Anatomy* is the fantasy of a life without code switching. Bailey always seems to say—often shout—what she thinks. Susan Douglas describes this as the fantasy of the sassy black woman who offers to middle-class and upper-middle-class white women viewers a fantasy where they don't need to be diplomatic, conciliatory, and nurturing, at home and at work. They "are not supposed to be too tough, have sharp tongues, point out sexism, or express anger—if we slip, you know what that makes us."[17] However, the costs of a black woman expressing anger, even though people often expect African American rage, can be quite high. Living a life without affective code switching is a fantasy of major proportions but, at the same time, reflects a real structure of feeling with which many people may identify.

Bailey's effect in the early seasons was very much about being in control and performing control, and the show eventually made that transparent. In the two-part episode "It's the End of the World/As We Know It," she goes into labor and discovers that her husband had an accident while rushing to meet her. While he is undergoing surgery, she has a breakdown and refuses to participate in delivering her baby, endangering both her health and that of her child. One of her interns, George, had made clear at the beginning of the episode that he felt that Bailey's authoritative presence comforted him, and if this was the only approach to Bailey's character, it would support the flat mammy reading of her character. But the show constantly subverts a mammy characterization; here it is subverted through transforming George into the person who presents the caregiving authority. He gently intervenes and becomes her partner in the delivery room. He tells her that there are "lots of things we have no control over . . . but this . . . this we can do." What made this episode a thoughtful moment in the development of her character is that it did not function as a contrast that humanized her character, it demonstrated how the performance of control was always part of her humanity. In a later episode, we discover that Bailey started out as a timid intern who was often ignored. Her performance of authority is part of her professional identity.

Her expression of care is also an important part of her, and those who frame her as mammy must interrogate what it means to say that black female expression of caregiving for white colleagues or subordinates always replicates that stereotype. Should we not support the expression of care and concern as ethical work behavior? She brings personal interests—as a mother and, on one memorable occasion, as a *Star Wars* fan—as she builds connections with her patients. A definitive difference between Miranda and the other characters is that for a few years she was the only one of the main characters who had to deal with the challenge of being a working parent. This is also a break with the tradition of mammy representations—the fact that she is a working mother is clearly important to her character, drawing a distinction between her relationship with the interns she supervises and her actual child. She is concerned that her mentor is mommy tracking her after she has given birth, but in that episode as she relates to a young African American patient, her maternal feelings emerge in their interactions. In the midst of soapy plots, Miranda Bailey represented working mothers, a stable marriage, the voice of professionalism, and usually common sense. But unlike some depictions of African Americans who only have folk wisdom, her common sense did not stand in place of her training and education. She was also known as a brilliant doctor. What Bailey offers is visibility and value as a black female professional in a world in which black women are often rendered invisible or less valuable. As with Clair Huxtable, Bailey offered a particular (black) feminist fantasy for everyone.

But as the show progressed, Bailey became more a part of the affective logic and the sexual economy of the show. She lost control of her emotions more often, and, unlike Clair Huxtable, her marriage could not withstand the pressure of her high-pressure career. Bailey initially had the one stable relationship on the show, but it took place primarily off-camera. For her to participate in the major plotlines of the show—which are primarily relationship oriented—the writers would have to break up her marriage and pair her with people in the hospital. Bailey's husband, Tucker, chose to stay at home and be the primary caregiver for their child, but he grew to resent his position and her hours. Eventually, they would divorce, and Bailey was paired with very handsome African American men who, arguably, are rarely the partners of women who look like her— and certainly not on television. She went on to participate in both distracting workplace interactions about relationships as well as workplace sex. By Season 9, the newest interns would call her "Booty Call Bailey" in reference to how often she disappeared into the on-call room for sex with her commuting boyfriend. The ethical authority she had when the show began had evaporated.

Bailey is thus a cautionary example of the costs and benefits of an African American character being an outsider to a generic representation— with outsider status it was possible to represent more of a black real than is usually seen on television. And when she later participates in the sexual and affective economy of the show, her character is less professional and reflects fewer of the professional negotiations that professional African American women experience. This is one of the perils of achieving full assimilation of African Americans into generically conventional representations.

And yet if we want African Americans to succeed in genre shows, we must accept that their roles can sometimes move between stereotype and the ideal, history, and utopian fantasies. These are all embedded in black real representational projects. This is clearly the case with Shonda Rhimes's third show, *Scandal*. It is perhaps the most like a classically prime-time soap of her three shows, as it features wealthy people in high positions and turns on reveals of adultery and murder. What is most new in this show is that for the first time an African American woman, actress Kerry Washington, leads a prime-time drama on a major network. The premise of the show is based on the experiences of Judy Smith, an African American crisis manager who worked as deputy press secretary under George H.W. Bush and later opened her own firm. Beyond these bare bones, the similarities end. While the show has a client-of-the-week structure, the ongoing plot in the first season involved a sex scandal in the White House. Audiences soon discover that the president Fitz and the crisis manager Olivia Pope had an affair. The writers depict the wife as a cold manipulator and Fitz and Olivia as in love and tragically separated by the higher purpose of him remaining in office because he is such a strong leader.

Fairly quickly, criticisms of the show emerged which depicted Pope as a Sally Hemings character.[18] Hemings is famous for being Thomas Jefferson's slave mistress and bearing him multiple children. The only similarity between Sally Hemings and Olivia is that they are black women who had sex with presidents who did not—or could not—marry them. In response to this reading, I will return, again, to Stuart Hall's interrogation of blackness in popular culture:

> I acknowledge that the spaces "won" for difference are few and far between, that they are very carefully policed and regulated. I believe that they are limited. I know, to my cost, that they are grossly underfunded, that there is always a price of incorporation to be paid when the cutting edge of difference and transgression is blunted into spectacularization. I know that what replaces invisibility is a kind of carefully regulated, segregated visibility. But it does not help simply to name-call it the same. That name calling merely reflects the particular model of cultural politics to which we remain attached precisely, the zero-sum game—our model replacing their model, our identities in place of their identities—what Antonio Gramsci called culture as a once and for all "war of maneuver," when, in fact, the only game in town worth playing is the game of cultural "wars of position."[19]

Just as interpreting Bailey as a mammy is extraordinarily reductive given the richness of her character, reading Pope as Hemings erases the feminist political fantasies offered by her character. She is a powerful black woman who has the wealthy and powerful begging for her services and advice. She is valued for her intellect and savvy—and, like Claire Huxtable, she always looks good doing it. We cannot escape our ghosts. And we must constantly call attention to attempts to say that the history is not with us when it is omnipresent. But accusations of sameness can be critically reductive, a willful dismissal of the utopian impulses of black real representational projects that aim to redistribute our representational signs and codes. One of the interesting gendered representational projects of Shonda Rhimes's shows is that all of her central protagonists are adulterers. This recuperation of the "dirty mistress" (as the protagonist refers to herself on *Grey's Anatomy*) is an unusual narrative focus, making sympathetic often demonized characters in both the prime-time soap and the real world. If this is a narrative thrust of her shows, is the solution to avoid casting an African American actress is to avoid evoking negative representations? I doubt that anyone interested in representational redistribution would make that suggestion.

Those of us interested in a black real would do better to first ask of a representation what kinds of signs and codes are being reworked for the public sphere? What is most interesting about black representation in the 21st century is not whether it is racist or not, or whether it evokes stereotype or not, but how the strands of a stereotype, fantasy, history, and experience all interact. Who knows when we will be free of the ghosts of mammy, coons, and sapphires. If we simply begin our analysis with the presupposition that the shadows of these representations are always there, we can focus on the idea that in fictions, as in our lives, we are constantly dealing with fictions about race and gender that cannot do justice to the complexity of human experience. When we dwell in the space between hope and failed expectations, we see with more clarity the pain and possibilities inherent in negotiation.

Notes

1. Amy Long, "Diagnosing Drama: Grey's Anatomy, Blind Casting, and the Politics of Representation," *The Journal of Popular Culture* 44, no. 5 (September 2011); Nikol Alexander-Floyd, "'But I Voted for Obama': Melodrama and Post-Civil Rights, Postfeminist Ideology in *Grey's Anatomy, Crash,* and Barack Obama's 2008 Presidential Campaign," in *Black Politics in a Time of Transition,* ed. by M. Mitchell and D. Coven (New Brunswick, NJ: Transaction Publishers, 2012), pp. 23–29.

2. Rebecca Wanzo, "Beyond a 'Just' Syntax: Black Actresses, Hollywood and Complex Personhood," *Women and Performance: A Journal of Feminist Theory* 6 (March 2006).

3. Matthew Fogel, "Grey's Anatomy Goes Colorblind," *The New York Times,* May 8, 2005, sec 2, p. 16.

4. Frederic Jameson, "Reification and Utopia in Mass Culture," *Social Text* 1 (Winter 1979): p. 141.

5. John Corner, "Presumption of Theory: 'Realism' in Television Studies," *Screen* 33 (Spring 1992): pp. 97–102.

6. For an account of readings of *The Cosby Show* as unrealistic, see Sut Jhally and Justin M. Lewis, *Enlightened Racism: The Cosby Show, Audiences, and the Myth of The American Dream* (Boulder, CO: Westview Press, 1992). Part of the critique is that the show presents an unrealistic view of social mobility in the United States about and for everyone, not just African Americans.

7. There's a great deal of critical conversation about the show, most of it positive, but for a brief outline of two sides of the debate, see opposing op-eds discussing the teaching of *The Wire* at Harvard. Ishmael Reed, "No, It Relies on

Clichés about Black and Drugs," *The Boston Globe,* http://www.boston.com/bostonglobe/editorial_opinion/oped/articles/ 2010/09/30/no_it_relies_on_clichs_about_blacks_and_drugs/?p1=Upbox_links (accessed September 28, 2012); Eugene F. Rivers and Jacqueline C. Rivers, "Yes It's the Real Thing about Urban Life," *The Boston Globe,* http://www.boston.com/ bostonglobe/editorial_opinion/oped/articles/ 2010/09/30/yes_its_the_real_thing_about_urban_life/?p1=Upbox_links (accessed September 28, 2012); and Jesse Singal, "Is 'The Wire' Racist?," *The Boston Globe,* http://www.boston.com/bostonglobe/editorial_opinion/ blogs/the_angle/2010/09/is_the_wire_rac.html (accessed September 28, 2012).

8. Michael Omi and Howard Winant, *Racial Formation in the United States: From the 1960s to the 1990s* (New York: Routledge, 1994), p. 56.

9. Time does not permit me to discuss another strong example—the post-WWII drama *Homefront* set in the fiction town of River Run Ohio. Unlike *I'll Fly Away,* the show began with equal attention to three families, the affluent Sloans who owned the town's major company, the African American Davis family who were the chauffeur and cook for the Sloans and whose son returned from the war and was the first African American to receive a good job in the factory, and the Catholic Metcalfs.

10. Michael E. Hill, "I'll Fly Away This Season's Best New Drama," *The Washington Post,* September 15, 1991, p. Y9.

11. Jerry Buck, "'Taylor-Maid' for Ending Stereotypes," *Free Lance-Star,* May 9, 1992, p. 13.

12. Herman S. Gray. *Cultural Moves: African Americans and the Politics of Representation* (Berkeley: University of California Press, 2005), p. 15.

13. See Jhally and Lewis, *Enlightened Racism.*

14. It is worth noting that in the pilot episode, the Cosby home is less elegant and looks more middle class, and Clair appears to be a stay-at-home mom.

15. Stuart Hall, "What is the Black in Black Popular Culture," in *Representing Blackness: Issues in Film and Video,* ed. by V. Smith (New York: Routledge, 1997), p. 132.

16. Long, "Diagnosing Drama," p. 1072.

17. Susan Douglas, *The Rise of Enlightened Sexism: How Pop Culture Took Us from Girl Power to Girls Gone Wild* (New York: St Martin's Griffin, 2010), pp. 127–28.

18. Stacia L. Brown, "Is Olivia Pope the New Sally Hemings?," http://www.theroot.com/buzz/olivia-pope-new-sally-hemmings (September 27, 2012); Alyssa Rosenberg, "'Scandal': Olivia Pope, Sally Hemings, and the Dangers or Race Neutrality," http://thinkprogress.org/alyssa/2012/04/20/467938/scandal-olivia-pope-sally-hemings/ (accessed September 27, 2012).

19. Hall, "What Is the Black in Black Popular Culture," p. 126.

Chapter 22

Scandal and Black Women in Television

Kwakiutl L. Dreher

Scandal, created by *Grey's Anatomy*'s Shondra Rhimes, explores the idea of black women in the enclave of (inter)national power. Critics attribute *Scandal*'s success to the corporate acuity of Judy Smith, the former first African American female assistant U.S. attorney and a deputy press secretary during the presidency of George H. W. Bush; it is Smith's genius in crisis management on which *Scandal* is based. She is the founder of Smith & Co., the firm that has worked on sensational high-profile public relations cases that include Monica Lewinsky and Michael Vick and with British Petroleum (BP) in aftermath of the Gulf oil spill. Sophia A. Nelson, author and political strategist, says of Smith, "Judy is [. . .] an outright trailblazer for black women. [. . .] Like her or not, there is none better to have in your corner when you are in political hot water, an unfavorable media spotlight, or in legal trouble."[1]

Long before Judy Smith, however, black women have enjoyed an up-close and personal relationship with heads of state and with the most powerful man in the world: the president of the United States. Many of us are familiar with all or at least some of them: Queen Nzingha (Angola, Africa), Phillis Wheatley, Elizabeth Keckley, Mary McLeod Bethune, and Patricia Roberts Harris, to name a few.[2] With the exception of Queen Nzingha, these women wielded power and influence and managed diplomacy within the most prominent home on the land, The White House. More recently, three African American women embody these merits and facilitate national comfort in appreciating an African American woman exercise that power in the intimacy of the living room: Donna Brazile, political strategist/analyst and presidential campaign manager for Albert Arnold "Al" Gore; Condoleezza Rice, the 66th secretary of state (George W.

Bush administration); and, more commanding, Michelle LaVaughn Robinson Obama, the first African American first lady of the United States. We watched their televised expertise during speeches at the Republican/Democratic National Conventions among other venues and forums. Specifically and more current, Michelle Obama demonstrated, yet again, grace, poise, and intelligence swathed in a cloak of passion at the Democratic National Convention 2012; her robust campaign for healthy eating, especially for children; and her demonstration of love and honor for her husband and the president. Her covers on magazines such as *Essence, Ebony, Vogue, Newsweek, Ladies Home Journal,* among other periodicals, all work in tandem to produce a sense of comfort and ease with black women in visual culture. These congeries of events/people play a large part in the contemporary psychocultural comfort in the relationship between Olivia Pope and the president of the United States. No wonder the green light for the series. No wonder the success of the show.

One historical marker no doubt set the stage for Rhimes's dramatization of a love affair between a black woman and the president: knowledge of the controversial liaison between Sally Hemings, an enslaved quadroon at Monticello, and Thomas Jefferson, the third president of the United States and slaveholder. Even though "rumors exploded on the national scene during the early part of Jefferson's first term as president,"[3] scientists, along with descendants of Hemings and Jefferson, scrambled to disprove/prove paternity when allegations surfaced that Jefferson fathered Hemings's children. DNA testing pushed the Hemings–Jefferson affair into the spotlight in 1998 and, as a result, opened the door to a whirlpool of discourses on the subject. Indeed, the Hemings–Jefferson liaison caused a scandal, and this liaison is in a vibrant conversation with Rhimes's project. A scene from the season finale provides a case in point. The president of the United States Fitzgerald "Fitz" Thomas Grant (Tony Goldwyn) meets with Cyrus Beene (Jeff Perry), his political advisor, and Olivia Pope to discuss strategies for managing an indiscretion committed by the president that resulted in a former intern's murder. The meeting is tense. A tape with the president asking an unidentified woman to take off her clothes has been leaked to the press. The president asks, "What will we do? What's next?" Pope offers to confess that it is she on the tape (it is). Beene scoffs at the suggestion, "maybe there's another option here; maybe something we're not seeing here." The president, then, counters with an offer that Thomas Jefferson very well could have contemplated with Sally Hemings in the privacy of his study. He says,

I could resign [. . .] we go be regular people [. . .] a man who isn't president has options. A man who isn't president can divorce his wife. A man who isn't president can have a life . . . the life he wants . . . the life he's always wanted with the woman he loves.

He walks over to his one-time lover, and they embrace against her warnings of the security cameras in the Oval Office. This woman is Olivia Pope, the skillful African American political gladiator working in the shark-infested waters of Washington politics.[4]

In that same episode, the audience witnesses, via flashback, intimate moments between Pope and Fitz, then a governor campaigning for president. Sexual tension threatens to overtake the couple in an elevator. In another instance, the desperate search for solitude outside of the flurry of the campaign forces the governor to plead with Pope to just stand with him in the hallway; finally, on a stop at a hotel on the *Grant for President* campaign trail, Pope and Grant consummate their desire. "Take off your clothes," the governor asks seductively. It is this verbal moment of intimacy that is captured on tape.[5] Fitz and Pope share another private moment on her couch in her condominium at the end of the episode. He embraces her tenderly in his arms as she curls up next to him. Both the president and Pope recognize in this moment that matters of the chief executive officer of the United States trump the personal yearning for ordinariness. "Goodbye, Livvie," he says. "Goodbye Mr. President," Pope replies.

Scandal opened to generous applause as many columnists and bloggers hailed the arrival of Pope, as she appeared as the African American female lead in a prime-time television drama. A plethora of references are made to Teresa Graves, the black actress who starred in *Get Christie Love,* a police drama centered on the fearless Christie Love and premiered on ABC in 1974. Television critic Eric Deggans, for instance, observes, "TV has come a long way since [*Get Christie Love*], when a guy flung the N-word at Christie Love, thinking she was a prostitute. But television still hasn't found much room for showcasing black women in starring roles outside comedy, until now."[6] Sarah Springer of CNN notes impressive viewer statistics, "[a]n average of 7.3 million people watched the finale, according to the Nielsen, and 1.8 million African-American viewers viewed the season finale that day. It was the No. 1 show among African-Americans for the week of May 14–May 20, 2012."[7] Kia Miakka Natisse praises the show for its presentation of a woman of color who succeeds and delivers kudos for Rhimes's turn at showcasing diversity on television. She writes, "Shonda Rhimes is a show-runner of the sort who likes to portray a colorfully diverse and integrated world, and often sidesteps issues of race within her series. [. . .] As many white-washed shows that exist on network TV, it's refreshing to watch a show where diversity is a norm and not a token effort."[8]

Kira Wills of www.starpulse.com comments on Pope's stellar performance as a crisis manager. She says,

> Shonda Rhimes' newest creation, ABC's political thriller *Scandal* [. . .] wants you to believe that Olivia Pope (Kerry Washington), a corporate fixer with some surprising and sexy ties to the President, is a superhero with a chic trench coat and stilettos instead of a mask and cape. She can intimidate gun-wielding Ukranian kidnappers with a single monologue, identify liars with her fine-tuned internal polygraph and is armed with a set of fabulously lethal cheekbones. To gain entrance to her high-end batcave, you must be a "gladiator in a suit" and you must worship her.[9]

In spite of its popularity, *Scandal* is not without its detractors. Tom Gliatto of *People* magazine scoffs at the story line's believability. He says, "Scandal is about as realistic as Mamie Eisenhower, Witch Hunter—in one episode Olivia seems to be blackmailing members of the Senate Judiciary Committee—but it has so much headlong energy, you may not care."[10] In her article, "The Trouble with 'Scandal,'" Tanya Steele puts forward that Pope's leading role becomes diluted by the end of Season 1:

> Olivia Pope established her skill set, her power, her uncompromising commitment to her work. There was no [. . .] pulling of weaves. She wasn't anyone's basketball wife. [. . .] And dressed to the nines while doing it! [. . .] Olivia Pope, who started off the series fully in charge, had become a doe-eyed mistress. How did we get here?! In the season finale, "the president" walks in and the "first lady" schools him on how they will proceed. And this came after FLOTUS schooled Olivia Pope. This was particularly demeaning. [. . .] Olivia Pope quietly stands up and has her head bowed in the corner of the frame. I'm like . . . *what in the hell is this?* This woman has gone from fierce control to utter shame. [. . .].[11]

Steele refers to a particular scene in the episode entitled "The Trial." Two years before the lover's lane expression in the Oval Office, Pope blindsides *Governor* Fitzgerald Grant with her discerning insights on his lackluster presidential campaign. When foraging for ways to attract voters, the governor howls, "People don't know where I stand. The problem is . . . "

> Your marriage! [interrupts Pope]. It looks like you don't screw your wife, which would be fine except that family values matter to Republicans. [. . .] And since [your opponent] Sally's got Jesus firmly on her side that just leaves

family, marriage, yours [. . .] looks cold . . . distant . . . dead. [. . .] People want to like who they are voting for. Voters thought Al Gore was a big stiff until he stuck his tongue down Tipper's throat. They put George W in office because he and Laura seemed like a fun couple to have a beer with.

People want to have to invite you in for dinner. And right now, you and your wife are standing in their doorway three feet apart, not looking at each other letting in the cold air. That's why you lost Iowa. It's why you'll lose New Hampshire.

Pope overhears Governor Grant's demand to Beene to fire her; she retorts, "Why did you fire me? [. . .] I am good; I am brilliant. I will eat, breathe, and live Fitzgerald Grant every minute of every day! You would be lucky to have me!" At that moment, the camera closes in on the governor and Pope, and its close-up betrays his attraction for this confident "political nun" (as dubbed by Beene). Pope, ever the astute politico, searches Governor Grant's eyes for an answer and lands on the attraction in them; she remarks, "So *this* is why you fired me." She remains on board; the governor wins New Hampshire.[12]

Pope's is a contestation demonstrating an expression of self-definition and valuation buffering her from the governor's exercise of privilege that threatens her livelihood. Patricia Hill Collins points out, "[W]hen Black women define ourselves, we clearly reject the assumption that those in positions granting them the authority to interpret our reality are entitled to do so. Regardless of the actual content of Black women's self-definitions, the act of insisting on Black female self-definition validates Black women's power as human subjects."[13] The governor projects his anxiety over his sexual attraction. Pope, nevertheless, wrestles from the governor the authority to interpret her reality and returns the gaze, insisting on her right to know why bolstered by the pronouncement of her expertise and strong work ethic. It is this self-definition that accords Pope the pass to spaces of power. That she articulates the facts behind his lifeless campaign and pauses to locate the real reason behind the governor's anxiety over her presence validates her command over unseen situations, feelings, and emotions. She will not be blindsided by the governor's entitlement, even if it is *his* space.

Meanwhile, Mellie, Grant's wife (Bellamy Young), remains invested in the political game as she realizes that going along with the program would guarantee her sociopolitical status. *Status* is her love—not her husband. She witnesses the political acumen of Pope and even invites her to an exclusive party when her husband suffers insomnia. When the president's indiscretion threatens to undermine *her* position, she yells at Pope,

I try to be pleasant. I try to be. I'm the First Lady. [. . .] You and I wanted the same thing: Fitz in the Oval. [. . .] You let that girl get into his pants! [. . .] You fell down on the job. *You broke his heart, and you left him open and vulnerable, and helpless,* and that is how that snake Billy Chambers got that shiny red Amanda apple right into Fitz' hand. I do my job. I smile, and I push him. And I make sure he has what he needs. *I do my job.* [. . .] Why couldn't *you do yours?* [. . .] I'm going to need to take my husband back because clearly I have to do *everything* myself from now on.[14]

What Tanya Steele misses in her critique of *Scandal* is the eye contact between the first lady and Pope; it gives away the first lady's awareness of the affair between Pope and her husband. Pope is called out, the secret uncovered. Mellie's slight chuckle during the pause is an unspoken trump of the secret: "What? Do you actually think I did not know that you have been sleeping with my husband?" To her astonishment, Pope fully understands that the first lady has cast a blind eye because for *her* Pope is the solid defense against undisciplined mistresses. That Pope called off the affair "broke [the President's] heart and left him open, vulnerable, and helpless" to women who may not have the emotional steadiness to carry out an extramarital affair with the president. In essence, the first lady blames Pope for the mess her husband has stepped in.

Scandal continues to agitate Steele. In her most recent critique of the second season's premier, Steele maintains her position that *Scandal* falls short of her expectations. She writes,

[. . .] in terms of Drama, it isn't delivered in a way that keeps my interest. Serial dramas have to unfold in a way that keeps you asking-[m]ainly, "how will the central character wrestle with their moral dilemma, next week?" [. . .] A power dynamic is set up when you make her lover the president of the United States. It will keep her in a weak position because he's running the world. [. . .] Her power rests in his storyline. He has to call, secure, via a "private line." She has to wait and be on the receiving end of that. It is unfortunate that her private moments are with the president.[15]

Steele, again, fails to recognize that Rhimes ensures that *Scandal* stays true to its name. The real star of the show is not the love affair between Pope and the president (as titillating as it is); rather, the stars are each scandal showcased every Thursday night. The series boasts a compelling ensemble, and Rhimes deftly illustrates the teamwork operating within a vigorous community necessary to Pope's business. For example, the deployment of Pope's management of crisis demands the concrete hands-on proficiency of Huck (Guillermo Diaz), the ordinary joe of the gladiator club. Former operative of the CIA and the consummate techie, Huck hunts down details of a scandal and moves in and out of crevices Pope and associates do not have the means or the time to enter. In one episode, his tech language is so complicated that Pope has to ask him interpret his findings for her:

> I got a signal! The kid's gen9Sd(?) is WiFi enabled. Fanboy here tracked the IP address of the dynamic host configuration protocol and was then able to ping the server's GEO(?) location vector. (Pope: English, Huck!) I found the toy which means I've found *them.*[16]

Rhimes assembles a highly functional and dedicated microcommunity for Pope wherein the expertise of fellow community members worked to maintain her status and reputation.

After all is written, however, *Scandal* is a well-crafted and brilliantly scripted series. The show's popularity no doubt stems from an African American viewer's frustration with the production of particular kinds of African American women on prime-time television. It is a show that is in direct opposition to the more popular reality shows and sitcoms that feature successful African American women: *Real Housewives of Atlanta* created by Princess Banton-Lofters, *Basketball Wives* created by Shaunie O'Neal, and *For Better or Worse* created by Tyler Perry to name a few. These shows go for the sensational as African American women exhibit behavior that would rival gladiators in a Roman coliseum. Pope "give[s] the TV audience an opportunity to meet a more balanced and layered type of black woman—minus the bad attitudes, dysfunctional relationships with rappers and ballers, and the usually required girl-on-girl boxing match."[17]

In her exploration of black women in command, Rhimes's newest creation ushers in a behind-the-scenes drama that produces the fragility of the executive suite of the highest place in the free world. Her character, Olivia Pope, pushes front and center the mental and verbal athleticism of a crisis manager who can squash a catastrophe with the speed of Serena Williams's 128-mph serve. Kira Wills notes, "'Scandal' is an over-the-top glimpse at the world of crisis management—a profession that had no booth in at high school career days because it's all cloak-and-dagger, hush-hush work."[18] As has been demonstrated, *Scandal* divests the cloak and uncovers the secrets. As Rhimes takes viewers behind the scenes of the Oval Office, we become more aware of the machinations required to maintain a sense of national peace and security within the borders of the United States. We learn that the president is a brand, and, like all brands, particular narratives have to circulate around them to sustain interest, in this drama, voter/consumer approval. The "secret" nevertheless is the team behind the brand, and in *Scandal*, Toto has pulled back the proverbial curtain to reveal the wizards behind each political concoction. Viewers become mesmerized by political chess game, the far-reaching implications of events and politico behavior, and, the execution of strategy. Throughout the season, the onus is on Pope to create and then maintain an image of (inter)national domestic bliss, while she and her "gladiators in suits" grapple with the usual suspects that run rampant in dominions of authority and influence: murder, sex, politics. What finally gets to voters and to the audience on-screen carefully has been manipulated to nurture a sense of safety and the belief that all is well in the United States of America. *New York Times* television critic Allessandra Stanley would agree, "[i]n a culture where presidents, celebrities and products alike are assessed as brands, it's perfectly natural to be more fascinated by the people shaping the image than the ones who merely claim it in public."[19]

Rhimes created the series to examine "what happens when you're very much in charge, and how everybody you know has secrets."[20] On a personal level, *Scandal* drew her interest when Rhimes experienced her own scandal. Isaiah Washington, who played Dr. Preston Burke, made a homophobic slur in a moment of frustration on the set of *Grey's Anatomy*. Even though he made a Public Service Announcement for GLAAD, stating, "[W]hen you use words that demean a person because of their sexual orientation, race or gender, you send a message of hate,"[21] Rhimes nevertheless initiated the "decision that was a long time coming" and fired Washington from the show.[22] What occurs on the backlot informs the production of the show; more to the point, it is these kinds of decisions Pope makes throughout the series.

Another point of entry to the discussion of *Scandal* is Kerry Washington's placement of her "really smart, really successful, really powerful, really put together, and really figured out" character within the "new wave of Modern Woman."[23] Just what is this new wave, and who is the modern woman riding it? As aforementioned, Pope joins an impressive lineup of African American women who have/had access to and worked within domains of power. In the public's eye, these women personify intelligence, success, power, and über-comportment in the most daunting of settings. Washington's reference to this "new wave" certainly draws attention to the third-wave feminist movement of the 1990s that boasts a focus on "female empowerment than male oppression" and "a more sexually and racially diverse movement than its predecessors."[24] Rhimes situates Pope comfortably within this movement.

A closer examination of *Scandal,* however, reminds us of the Black Women's Renaissance that found root in the early 1970s, blossomed in the 1980s, and still enjoys a healthy current in the 21st century. The fruits of the labors from this renaissance produced and celebrated African American women in the literary realm whose works made their way to the silver screen and on television. In each production, the "close-up" makes intimate the face of the African American woman. Steven Spielberg dramatizes the life of Miss Celie and Shug from Alice Walker's Pulitzer Prize–winning novel *The Color Purple* in 1985; Jonathan Demme directs Oprah Winfrey and Danny Glover in Toni Morrison's *Beloved* in 1998, the novel for which Morrison won the Pulitzer Prize for Fiction in 1988, and helped her win the Nobel Prize in Literature in 1993; Academy Award winner Halle Berry and Michael Ealy star in *The Eyes Were Watching God* based on Zora Neale Hurston's novel of the same name and produced by Oprah Winfrey and Quincy Jones in 2005; and Tyler Perry brings Ntozake Shange's choreopoem *For Colored Girls Who Have Considered Suicide When the Rainbow Is Enuf* to the silver screen in 2010. Each production generates insight into the life of the black woman as she exercises her agency via negotiations with the past (*Beloved*) and within the domestic sphere (*The Color Purple, The Eyes Were Watching God,* and *For Colored Girls*). The most formidable mark of these productions derives from the dialogue or hearing the production of words from the mouths of black women. Who can forget, for example, the words of Baby Suggs, Holy's (Beah Richards) command to the group in the clearing in *Beloved:* "My people, they do not love your hands. They only use, tie, bind, chop off and leave empty. Love your hands. Raise them up, and kiss them!"

Through Pope, Rhimes continues the legacy of the performative power of the word spoken by a black woman. For example, Amanda Tanner (Lisa Weil), the intern, accuses the president of sleeping with her; Pope dispatches her words with the coolness of a mongoose in the pilot episode; the rules of grammar cannot apply:

> My name is Olivia Pope and I want to be clear. I am not here in any official capacity, I'm only here to warn you because you should know what could happen; it could become hard for you to find employment; your face would be everywhere; people would associate you with a sex scandal; all kinds of information would easily become available to the press. For example, you have had 22 sexual partners that we know of; also there's that ugly bout of gonorrhea. And your family; your mother's mental illness, the psychotic break two

years at Bedford hospital; I'll bet that's private. She runs a daycare now right? [. . .] I'll give you some free advice: hand in your resignation and pack up your dog and your things and get in your car and go find a small city. Minneapolis, or maybe Denver. Get a little job. Meet a boring boy. Make some friends because in this town your career is over. You're done.[25]

Pope sets up her fearlessness without alienating the viewing audience; she reveals the maneuvers of crisis management. This revelation establishes the bedrock of the *Scandal*. Overall, what drives the attraction to *Scandal is* a kind of consolation or a fundamental relief that no matter the dilemma, there are ways to handle it, and that there are ways out. That "out" may require a total recreation of our lives—perhaps unexpected losses—but the *possibility* for the restoration of some semblance of stability or for a roadmap that we can take back home encourages us to go for the chance to get it right. "[P]eople screw up—we all do," says Judy Smith,[26] who harbors a heartfelt belief that "most people deserve a second chance."[27] *Scandal* tenders one blueprint on how to get it.

Notes

1. Sophia Nelson, "Judy Smith: How the Woman Who Inspired 'Scandal' Redefined Black Female Power Players in D.C," http://bit.ly/OHZj5b (accessed October 2, 2012).

2. Queen of Matamba in Angola, Africa, Nzingha's skillful negotiations between the Portuguese governor João-Correia de Sousa and her in a treaty that ensured the return of subjects taken during war and the cease of the marauding of Imgangala mercenaries in Portuguese service. She resisted colonialism by the Portuguese and fought the Portuguese slave traders. In 1641, when the Dutch seized Luanda, Nzinga wrangled an alliance with the Dutch against the Portuguese and occupied some parts of their colonies. In 1644, she defeated the Portuguese army at Ngoleme. David Sweetman, *Women Leaders in African History* (London: Heinemann, 1985), p. 39.

Across the Atlantic, moved by her poem, "To His Excellency George Washington," 1775, George Washington, commander-in-chief of the Continental Army in the United States, invites Phillis Wheatley to his home for a 30-minute chat.

Several African American women had personal relationship with the White House. Elizabeth Keckley served as the personal modiste and confidante to First Lady Mary Todd Lincoln. Before her White House years, Keckley's skill as a seamstress garnered her commissions from Varina Davis, wife of confederate president Jefferson Davis, and Mary Anna Custis Lee, wife of Robert E. Lee. In her autobiography, *Behind the Scenes Or Thirty Years a Slave and Four Years in the White House* (1868), Keckley recounts not only intimate conversations with First Lady Lincoln, she also reveals brief one-on-one moments with President Abraham Lincoln. She writes:

[. . .] on Monday evening I went to the White House to dress Mrs. Lincoln for the first grand levee. While arranging Mrs. L.'s hair, the president entered the room. [. . .] and I went up to him, proffering my hand with words of congratulation.

He grasped my outstretched hand warmly, and held it while he spoke: "Thank you. Well, Madam Elizabeth"—he always called me Madam Elizabeth—"I don't know whether I should feel thankful or not. The position brings with it many trials." (118).

According to historian Barbara McCaskill, Keckley intervened for abolitionist Sojourner Truth when President Lincoln refused to meet her. Keckley's intervention resulted in a meeting between Truth and President Lincoln on October 29, 1864, wherein they discussed the issue of slavery, http://tinyurl.com/d7h9s4b, (accessed September 9, 2012).

Mary McLeod Bethune was a personal friend of Eleanor Roosevelt, and President Franklin Delano Roosevelt appointed her to his black cabinet. Patricia Roberts Harris served three presidents. In 1963, President John F. Kennedy appointed her cochair of the National Women's Committee for Civil Rights; in 1965, she became the first African American woman to serve as U.S. ambassador to Luxembourg as Lyndon B. Johnson's appointee. In 1977, President Jimmy Carter appointed her U.S. secretary of housing and urban development. Her most famous quote is a riposte to one senator's assertion that her mid-upper-class status made her incapable of understanding the underclass. She countered, "I am one of them. You do not seem to understand who I am. I am a Black woman, the daughter of a dining-car worker. I am a Black woman who could not buy a house eight years ago in parts of the District of Columbia!"

3. Anna Gordon-Reed, *Thomas Jefferson and Sally Hemings: An American Controversy* (Charlottesville, VA: University Press of Virginia, 1997), p. 1.

4. "Grant: For the People," *Scandal,* on ABC, May 17, 2012. Internet.

5. "The Trail," *Scandal,* on ABC, May 10, 2012. Internet.

6. Eric Deggans, "With 'Scandal,' New Visibility for Black Women on TV," http://bit.ly/I4JJOu (accessed September 3, 2012).

7. Sarah Springer, "'Scandal' Updates Image of Black Women on Network Television," http://bit.ly/JRjBvn (accessed September 28, 2012).

8. Kia Miakka Natisse, "Shonda Rhimes' 'Scandal' Presents Blueprint for Survival of Blacks on Network TV," http://bit.ly/OIe5jn (accessed October 5, 2012).

9. Kira Wills, "Review of ABC's 'Scandal': Have You Been Scandalized?," http://bit.ly/PCRlfj (accessed September 28, 2012).

10. Tom Gliatto, "Scandal," *People* 77.15 (April 9, 2012): p. 40. *Academic Search Premier.* Web. http://tinyurl.com/ak9kupp (accessed September 4, 2012).

11. Tanya Steele, "The Trouble with Scandal," http://bit.ly/JRjBvn (accessed September 4, 2012).

12. "The Trail," *Scandal,* on ABC, May 10, 2012. Internet.

13. Patricia Hill Collins, *Black Feminist Thought: Knowledge, Consciousness, and the Politics of Empowerment* (New York: Routledge, 1991), p. 107.

14. "Grant: For the People," *Scandal,* on ABC, May 17, 2012. Internet.

15. Tanya Steele, "The Ongoing Trouble with 'Scandal' and Why It's Starting to Lose Me As a Viewer," http://bit.ly/OIe5jo (accessed October 5, 2012).

16. "Huck: 101," ABC.com (accessed October 6, 2012).

17. Allison Samuels, "'Scandal' and 'Styled by June': Allison Samuels's Prime-Time Saviors," http://bit.ly/Pe4Mrk (accessed August 29, 2012).

18. Kira Wills, "Review of ABC's 'Scandal': Have You Been Scandalized?," http://bit.ly/PCRlfj (accessed September 28, 2012).

19. Allessandra Stanley, "Washington Spin Doctor, Heal Thyself," http://bit.ly/SMZkHr (accessed August 30, 2012).

20. "Scandal"/"Grey's Anatomy"—Shondra Rhimes Interview, http://bit.ly/QyftlF (accessed September 10, 2012).

21. "Isaiah Washington PSA," http://bit.ly/O9l9UI (accessed September 10, 2012).

22. Michael Ausiello. "Shonda Rhimes Breaks Her Silence about Isaiah!," http://tinyurl.com/cvfh257 (accessed September 10, 2012).

23. "Scandal ABC Cliffhanger," http://tinyurl.com/7q5phzk (accessed September 10, 2012).

24. Kristin-Rowe Finkbeiner, *The F-Word: Feminism in Jeopardy* (Emeryville, CA: Seal Press, 2004), p. 90.

25. "Sweet Baby," *Scandal,* on ABC, April 5, 2012. Internet.

26. *The Daily Show with Jon Stewart,* http://bit.ly/QLIFqI (accessed October 5, 2010).

27. Jeanne Dorin McDowell, "Real 'fixer' behind 'Scandal' Steps into Spotlight," http://lat.ms/WxsQoE (accessed October 5, 2012).

Chapter 23

"Get a Crew . . . And Make It Happen": *The Misadventures of Awkward Black Girl* and New Media's Potential for Self-Definition

Phillip Lamarr Cunningham

The emergence of a Do-It-Yourself (DIY) digital film culture and the prevalence of user-generated content (UGC) sites like YouTube have dramatically altered the media landscape. As prominent media scholar Henry Jenkins notes, these occurrences have not only changed media production and consumption but also have broken down the barriers preventing entry into the media marketplace.[1] Indeed, minus the gatekeepers prevalent in traditional media forms, the Internet—especially YouTube—arguably has fostered greater diversity and inclusion within popular culture. In fact, new media technologies continue to move society closer to realizing the democratic ideal of the public sphere for which philosophers such as Jurgen Habermas have theorized.[2]

While the proverbial jury is still out on whether the Internet is a true public sphere, many see the potential for a leveling of the playing field, especially for marginalized groups. New media scholars Maria Kopacz and Bessie Lee Lawton write, "User-generated content (UGC) websites like YouTube allow anyone to post material with minimal institutional gatekeeping. They therefore hold out the promise of an outlet for alternative depictions of minorities and places where marginalizing and stereotypical racial portrayals can be challenged and redefined."[3] Considering the varying, often lackluster, degrees of returns traditional media have afforded people of color, the liberating capacity of new media certainly has appeal for a new generation of content creators. Therefore, as Jenkins suggests, the Internet has become "an important showcase for grassroots cultural production."[4]

A desire to challenge long-standing stereotypes about African Americans as participants in and partakers of popular culture while taking advantage of the potential of UGC sites are motivating factors in the creation of *The Misadventures of Awkward Black Girl,* the award-winning Web series created by actress and filmmaker Issa Rae (born Jo-Issa Rae Diop).[5] She asserts as much in an interview on the *Black Girl with Long Hair* blog, where she remarks that "Right now, pitching your idea to a network exec or an industry liaison just isn't working because they have this limited perception of black women and what they think black women want to see on screen. I think the Web is the best way to go right now, and I've seen a lot of great shows come off of the Internet."[6]

Issa Rae, star and creator of the YouTube series *The Misadventures of Awkward Black Girl.* (AP Photo/Damian Dovarganes)

Given all of the critical acclaim it has received, *The Misadventures of Awkward Black Girl* seems poised to be a game changer and for good reason. As will be evidenced here, the series exemplifies not only the capacity new media has to challenge and redefine portrayals of African American women in popular culture but also the capacity for new media to provide independent creators a measure of agency in a vast media marketplace.

Heeding the Call: The Necessity of an Awkward Black Girl

In the aforementioned interview, Issa Rae notes what prompted her to create *The Misadventures of Awkward Black Girl:* "I was frustrated with the black female characters I was seeing in the media and I realized that this 'awkward' character hadn't really been explored or portrayed in anything I'd ever seen."[7] Her frustrations with television certainly are valid, for by the time her series debuted in February 2011, none of the five broadcast networks (ABC, CBS, CW, FOX, NBC) featured a scripted series featuring an African American actress in a leading role (though there were several in which African American actresses were in important supporting roles), let alone one who could be construed as "awkward."

While basic cable channels have afforded opportunities for African American–scripted series, they also have exemplified the monolithic nature of mainstream black programming, particularly the ubiquity of filmmakers Tyler Perry and Ice Cube who created four of the seven sitcoms (*For Better or Worse, House of Payne,* and *Meet the Browns* by Perry and *Are We There Yet?* by Ice Cube, all spin-offs from their feature films) on air in 2011. Perry's hand even extended into the other sitcoms that he did not produce, as writer–producer Kellie Griffin—who helms current BET sitcom *Reed between the Lines*—was a writer and associate producer for Perry's *House of Payne* for several seasons. Moreover, the creators of the remaining sitcoms—BET's *Let's Stay Together* and TV One's *Love That Girl*—are veteran writer–producers Jacque Edmonds (*Martin, Living Single, Moesha*) and Bentley Kyle Evans (*Martin, The Jamie Foxx Show*), respectively. Thus, even in the shift from network to basic cable, creative control of African American–scripted series has remained in the hands of incredibly limited few.

Furthermore, along with these creator monopolies, traditional media forms continue to perpetuate the stereotypical representation of African American women. Dionne P. Stephens and Layli D. Phillips argue, "Although there are more representations of African American females available for consumption in the mass media than ever before, the substance of these images has changed little over the past century."[8] Nowhere is this truer than in today's sitcoms, where the roles for African American women often are variations of classic (mammy, jezebel, sapphire) and contemporary (b-girl, buppy [black urban professional], the Black American Princess [BAP], bohemian) stereotypes.[9] For example, *For Better or Worse*—one of basic cable's top-rated sitcoms and a spin-off of Tyler Perry's successful *Why Did I Get Married?* film series—features protagonist Angela Williams (Tasha Smith) who embodies many aspects of the sapphire stereotype. Marilyn Yarbrough and Crystal Bennett succinctly describe the sapphire as "the wise-cracking, balls-crushing, emasculating woman" who is "evil, bitchy, stubborn and hateful."[10] Of the most frequent stereotypes of African American women to appear in today's sitcoms, the sapphire is undoubtedly the most consistent. Marci Bounds Littlefield highlights the implications of these representations: "The crucial problem with the negative images of African American women in today's society is not merely the overabundance of these images but rather the absence of equal amounts of alternative, positive images. These images are damaging because they limit African American women's choices by excluding other options."[11] Given the frequent use of not only these stereotypes but also the writers and producers who replicate them, the likelihood of alternative images appearing on network television or basic cable seems highly unlikely.

Not only is there a reliance on stereotypes in today's African American sitcoms, but also there is very little variation in themes. In recent years, they primarily have been centered on family life. Indeed, of the African American sitcoms currently on air as of this writing, nearly all of them—save for *Let's Stay Together,* which revolves around a young engaged couple—are family oriented. Though the creators and actors of many of these series are apt to disagree, there certainly seems to be a concerted effort to revisit some of the traits—particularly a middle-class familial ethos that made *The Cosby Show* (1984–1992) the most successful African American sitcom of all time. The most overt attempt to do so is BET's *Reed between the Lines,* which stars former *The Cosby Show* star Malcolm Jamal-Warner as New York University professor Dr. Alex Reed who, alongside his wife, psychologist Dr. Carla Reed (Tracee Ellis Ross), faces the challenges of bringing a blended family together. In fact, adjusting to new family dynamics—whether it is blending families, relocating, or some other occurrence—is the central premise of all of the currently airing African American family sitcoms. As a result, in most cases, the women in these series primarily are wives attempting to balance their domestic and work lives.

Moreover, as of this writing, the number of African American sitcoms is in a state of flux. While there are still a few on air, most notably TBS sitcoms like *Are We There Yet?*, *For Better Or Worse,* and TV Land's Cedric the Entertainer and Niecy Nash vehicle *The Soul Man,* there are some indications that their statuses are tenuous at best. For example, the return of *Are We There Yet?* was uncertain for much of the year, especially after the show faced a near year-long hiatus. In 2012, TBS announced the series' return, but it has been placed in an unfavorable noonday Monday slot. Furthermore, though Perry's *For Better or Worse* has fared well in the ratings, the show perhaps signals an end to Perry's reign on TBS as his other series—*House of Payne* (2006–2012) and *Meet the Browns* (2009–2011) have ended. The nadir of these shows—coupled with TBS's recent acquisition of *Cougar Town*—has led some to fear that TBS may be following in the stead of networks such as FOX and UPN (now CW), which infamously catered to black audiences until they were able to establish ground with their desired white audiences. These concerns are valid, for *House of Payne* indeed was TBS's first foray into original scripted programming shortly after it rebranded itself as a comedy-themed network in 2004. The decline in sitcoms could be harrowing for African American actresses, for sitcoms have represented the vast majority of television shows where black women have appeared in recent years.[12]

These limited choices frustrate both African American actresses and audiences alike. *Clutch* magazine's Leslie Pitterson, for example, mirrors Issa Rae's desires for an awkward African American woman protagonist. In her rather compelling article (which Issa Rae cites as inspiration), "A Different Type of Brown Girl: Where's Our Liz Lemon?," she effectively calls for more complex African American female characters, particularly what she calls the "black nerdy girl": "[The black nerdy girl is] a rich character with loads of character development and complex storylines to boot. Give us a brown girl who gets the screen time of Ally McBeal—instead of relegating her to play the predictable, headstrong friend. With her stories of mortification, misunderstandings, and blissful triumphs, she is sure to warm the heart of any audience."[13] The desire for a character like Liz Lemon (Tina Fey), the main character of NBC's hit sitcom *30 Rock,* is not surprising. Liz Lemon—as well as the aforementioned Ally McBeal (Calista Flockhart)—is a complex, eccentric, nerdy character, a variation of what television critics have deemed the "manic pixie dream girl." While the manic pixie dream girl, who some argue is the epitome of white male fantasies, is often a problematic archetype, it is one that is featured in some of the most successful films and television series in recent years.[14] Critics have debated the inherent whiteness of the archetype, with blogger Tami Winfrey Harris suggesting, "The cult of domesticity defined idealized womanhood centuries ago—and that definition included both perpetual childhood and whiteness. The wide-eyed, girlish, take-care-of-me characters . . . are not open to many women of color, particularly black women."[15] Thus, the highly popular role that has sustained both film and television series alike is one that has proved to be quite elusive to African American actresses, especially since they very rarely and currently do not helm or star in their own series.

Issa Rae, however, may be apt to disagree. In fact, she argues that "being 'awkward' . . . is a unifying and universal thing that we all have experienced in some capacity."[16] Nonetheless, Harris is correct in her assertion that, thus far, traditional media forms generally have not permitted African American actresses to be "awkward." As such, what makes *The Misadventures of Awkward Black Girl* so unique and so promising is that it has co-opted aspects of the archetype for a new media platform—to overwhelming success.

Defying Stereotypes: Examining *The Misadventures of Awkward Black Girl*

Two occurrences usually take place when new mediums arise: users tend to drift away from older media and mass media conglomerates usually labor to ensure their control extends to the new medium. This occurred when television supplanted radio and is occurring now as the Internet gradually supplants television. Indeed, as Kopacz and Lawton suggest, the popularity of video sharing sites such as YouTube may very well replace traditional media as a primary source of news and entertainment.[17]

In particular, the Web series—short, low-budget, episodic programming specifically for the Internet—have become quite popular. As new media scholar Aymar Christian notes, the Web series is a "peculiar invention" that "exists variously as amateur and independent media and as corporate and advertising product. . . . Web series, then, exist between the conflicting and shifting currents in the new media economy. . . . They suggest the maturation of online video from one-off amateur content to more rigorous—and expensive—production."[18] More importantly (at least for our purposes), Christian contends the Web series represents a particularly useful means for marginalized creators to "correct mainstream representations."[19] With *The Misadventures of Awkward Black Girl,* Issa Rae certainly has taken advantage of the Web series' ability to do just that.

The Misadventures of Awkward Black Girl features Issa Rae as J, a sales executive for Gutbusters, a diet supplement distributor. J is a composite character who negotiates with many of the traditional female archetypes. For instance, elements of the doe-eyed manic pixie dream girl are present in J's character, particularly in moments in which she is confused or doubtful. As *New York Times* art blogger Jon Caramanica suggests, those moments are part of the series' appeal: "Much of the humor is conveyed through Ms. Rae's face: She's quick with a furrowed brow or with a wide-eyed look of incredulity."[20] At other times, J is a homegirl who channels her anger and frustration into violent freestyle raps. At one moment, J daydreams of a *Dawson's Creek* type romance to the tune of Sixpence None the Richer's syrupy "Kiss Me"; at another moment, she raps along to the Doublemint Twins' raunchy "Booty Shawts" (a parody hip-hop track performed by Issa Rae and fellow cast member Daisy Oliver) while driving to work. J's multifaceted personality makes her a more complete protagonist than many of her television sitcom counterparts, many of whom are quite one dimensional.

The series chronicles J's work and romantic lives, both of which often intersect; each is plagued by her own idiosyncrasies and social anxiety. She is joined by a cast of diverse and eccentric characters, including coworker, best friend, and Indi-American awkward girl CeCe (Sunjata Day); her equally quirky love interest "White Jay" (Lyman Johnson); her micromanaging new Latino supervisor Jesus (Michael Ruesga); and a host of other colorful characters. Indeed, few series—television or Web—can match the diversity of *The Misadventures of Awkward Black Girl*'s cast.

In many regards, the series is antithematic, owing much to its being influenced by shows such as Emmy Award–winning actor and producer Larry David's *Curb Your Enthusiasm* and *Seinfeld*, both of which are "shows about nothing."[21] Essentially, the series—like the aforementioned—is what David P. Pierson refers to as a "modern comedy of manners," wherein "the absurd does not exist in well-conceived comic gags or wisecracks [as in standard sitcoms], but rather in the small social blunders which comprise the spectrum of social manners."[22] Thus, if, as Pierson contends, the "modern comedy of manners" is primarily about characters "preoccupied with discerning, following, and sometimes evading" the social manners of their social group (i.e., white middle-class city dwellers in the case of *Seinfeld*), then *The Misadventures of Awkward Black Girl* is primarily about doing so with J's mostly African American peers. Indeed, the first season sees J vacillating between avoiding and clashing with her social circle.

In fact, J—in many of the ways Issa Rae frames herself—is an interloper in many of the social circles in which she finds herself. The viewer can easily juxtapose J with nearly every other character on the show, particularly her African American female counterparts, most of whom embody some aspect of the stereotypical representations of black women with which we are most familiar. For instance, J's primary foil for respect on the job and coworker

Fred's (Madison T. Shockley III) affections is Nina (Tracy Oliver), who is every bit the diva—the narcissistic attention seeker Stephens and Phillips suggest is one of the new dominant sexual scripts for African American women in popular culture—and J's polar opposite.[23] Light-skinned, long-haired, and domineering, Nina is made to seem abnormal because her diva attitude is displayed in such absurd fashion. For example, in Episode 10.1, "The Unexpected (Part 1)," Nina recruits her sorority sisters—the Gamma Rays, likely a nod to the women's auxiliary of the fictional Gamma Phi Gamma fraternity in Spike Lee's 1988 film *School Daze*—to help discipline her fellow Gutbusters employees after slumping sales. Parodying a scene from *New Jack City* (1991) in which volatile drug kingpin Nino Brown scolds his crew for allowing their drug haven to be infiltrated, Nina harangues and punishes her coworkers in similar fashion. Thus, in this scene and many like it, J's awkwardness is normalized, and stereotypes—particularly those of African American women—are exploited as absurd primarily because they exist alongside more well-rounded characters.

The Misadventures of Awkward Black Girl not only exploits stereotypes of African American women, but it also does so for its white characters. The series features two prominent white characters, J's initial supervisor at Gutbusters "Boss Lady" (Hanna) and the aforementioned White Jay, both of whom—like J—find themselves dealing with their own awkward nature. For both White Jay and Boss Lady, this involves negotiating between their white identities and their attraction to people of color. With Boss Lady, there is little actual negotiation taking place as she begins forsaking most vestiges of her white identity, from her appearance to her attitude. Over the course of the first season, she trades in her blond ponytail for cornrows and eventually dreadlocks. She adopts mannerisms and language that stereotypically are assigned to African American women; for example, she frequently refers to the African American women in the office as "girlfriend," uses (somewhat inappropriately) street slang, and makes references to black popular culture. Her lack of awareness and privileged position—as supervisor and, arguably, as a white woman—insulate her from any real consequences. Indeed, rather than receive chastisement or correction for her misappropriation of black identity, Boss Lady manages to effortlessly navigate her way through office politics—for which most of her ever-changing policies are to blame. Though the white woman who appropriates black mannerisms and style is not necessarily a new character in sitcoms, few have been rendered in such over-the-top fashion as Boss Lady.

White Jay, on the other hand, suffers from the same inability as J to deal with his awkwardness. His name is a clear double entendre, one that highlights both his race (J and CeCe's original intent when they began referring to him as White Jay) and his similarities with J. Unlike Boss Lady, whose obtuseness shields her, White Jay is painfully aware of his whiteness. He does not attempt to appropriate blackness like Boss Lady, but he does overcompensate in order to gain J's affections. For example, on their first date, instead of taking J to a sushi bar (as white dating expert CeCe had predicted), White Jay takes her to a soul food restaurant and a spoken word venue, neither of which appeal to J. After they both suffer through the overwrought performances and argue about each other's lack of trying, they discover that they both would have rather had sushi. As a result, even though White Jay is somewhat a hipster, he is a redeemable one as his awareness and J's own awkwardness allow him to make up for shortcomings. Again, though a character such as White Jay is certainly not new, the nuanced way in which his character is written makes him distinctive. When juxtaposed with Boss Lady, White Jay evidences a sincere (albeit flawed) approach to cross-cultural understanding and appreciation.

Not only has Issa Rae created a series that does not resemble any show currently on television, but also she has leveraged its popularity not only to keep the series going but also to take the show to new heights. After paying out of pocket for the first six episodes, she turned to crowdsourcing site Kickstarter to solicit funds to finish the first season. Ultimately, she surpassed her funding goal of $44,000, earning $56,259 from 1,960 supporters.[24] She attributes the success of both the series and successful fundraising to social media, acknowledging that "Social media is what made the show honestly. . . . Had it not been for social media, this show just wouldn't have been what it is today. I couldn't have done this 10 years ago."[25] Indeed, the series has utilized viral media in part because of Issa Rae's social media savvy, which she cultivated as a student at Stanford University.[26] Using Facebook, Twitter, and YouTube, she heavily engages her audience, even going so far as to incorporate some of their ideas. For example, as she notes in an interview with *Vibe*, fan response to the White Jay character led to his role being expanded and J's entering a relationship with him.[27] As a result, each episode of the first season currently averages more than 500,000 views, with Episode 1 at roughly 1,230,000 views as of this writing.[28]

The show later became affiliated with IAmOther.com, a multifaceted initiative helmed by famed music producer and recording artist Pharrell Williams. With IAmOther's backing, the series has been able to increase its production values.[29] This affiliation could be beneficial, as Aymar Christian suggests, "Better and more streamlined channels aimed at underserved niches, primarily people of color, women, and gay people, have created opportunities to shift the discourse of independent production from cultural and affective desire to industrial and market-oriented practice."[30]

As of this writing, the series is early into its second season, so it is difficult to discern its future. However, Jon Caramanica concedes that it is blazing the right path: "'The Misadventures of Awkward Black Girl' is a great template. Start small, build a following, raise money as proof of a concept, get bigger, garner early mainstream support, expand cautiously and, with luck, jump to a bigger screen. There's a path here waiting to be followed."[31]

Conclusion

As Marci Bounds Littlefield suggests, because popular culture holds a great deal of influence on how we view race, it is imperative that people of color not only reject misrepresentations but also produce content of their own.[32] Perhaps nowhere is the need for content creation by marginalized voices more essential than on the Internet, which is gradually becoming the broadcast medium of choice for producers and audiences alike. Indeed, as Colin Beckles argues, absence from new media threatens to create a "cybersegregation" that mirrors the one that often exists in traditional media.[33]

This need is particularly dire for African American women, who long have suffered through both misrepresentation and lack of visibility. Fortunately, sites such as YouTube—with its relatively open access and its more egalitarian audience—grants African American women a great deal of agency in shaping their own images. For Issa Rae, the process for doing so is quite simple: "I think we, as black women, need to just create the media ourselves. If you have an idea, get a crew or get your friends together and make it happen."[34]

Notes

1. Henry Jenkins, "Quentin Tarantino's Star Wars? Digital Cinema, Media Convergence, and Participatory Culture," in *Rethinking Media Change: The Aesthetics of Transition,* ed. by David Thornburn et al. (Cambridge: MIT Press, 2004), p. 287.

2. Jurgen Habermas. *The Structural Transformation of the Public Sphere: An Inquiry into a Category of Bourgeois Society* (Cambridge: MIT Press, 1995).

3. Maria Kopacz and Bessie Lee Lawton, "The Youtube Indian: Portrayals of Native Americans on a Viral Video Site," *New Media & Society* 13 (2011): p. 331.

4. Jenkins, "Quentin Tarantino's Star Wars? Digital Cinema, Media Convergence, and Participatory Culture," p. 287.

5. "'Awkward Black Girl' Web Series Grows through Social Media," *the Grio,* http://thegrio.com/2011/09/09/awkward-black-girl-web-series-grows-through-social-media/ (accessed September 9, 2011).

6. "Interview with Issa Rae; Writer, Star & Producer of Misadventures of Awkward Black Girl," *Black Girl with Long Hair,* http://blackgirllonghair.com/2011/06/interview-with-issa-rae-writer-star-producer-of-misadventures-of-awkward-black-girl/ (accessed June 13, 2011).

7. "Interview with Issa Rae; Writer, Star & Producer of Misadventures of Awkward Black Girl."

8. Dionne P. Stephens and Layli D. Phillips, "Freaks, Gold Diggers, Divas and Dykes: The Sociohistorical Development of Adolescent African American Women's Sexual Scripts," *Sexuality & Culture* 7 (2003): p. 3.

9. Angela M. Nelson, "African American Stereotypes in Primetime Television: An Overview, 1948–2007," in *African Americans and Popular Culture,* ed. by Todd Boyd (Westport, CT: Press, 2008), p. 201.

10. Marilyn Yarbrough and Crystal Bennett, "Cassandra and the 'Sistahs': The Peculiar Treatment of African American Women in the Myth of Women as Liars," *Journal of Gender, Race & Justice* 3, no. 2 (2000): pp. 625, 638.

11. Marci Bounds Littlefield, "The Media as a System of Racialization: Exploring Images of African American Women and the New Racism," *American Behavioral Scientist* 51 (2008): p. 681, doi: 10.1177/0002764207307747.

12. Nancy Signorielli, "Minorities Representation in Prime Time: 2000 to 2008," *Communication Research Reports* 26 (2009): p. 331.

13. Leslie Pitterson, "A Different Type of Brown Girl: Where's Our Liz Lemon?," *Clutch Magazine,* April 19, 2010, http://www.clutchmagonline.com/2010/04/a-different-type-of-brown-girl-where%E2%80%99s-our-liz-lemon/ (accessed July 23, 2012).

14. Esther Zuckerman, "The Week the Manic Pixie Dream Girl Broke," *The Atlantic Wire,* http://www.theatlanticwire.com/entertainment/2012/07/week-manic-pixie-dream-girl-broke/55121/ (accessed July 27, 2012).

15. Tami Winfrey Harris, "Who Is the Black Zooey Deschanel?," *Racilicious,* June 14, 2011, http://www.racialicious.com/2011/06/14/who-is-the-black-zooey-deschanel/ (accessed July 23, 2012).

16. Alyssa Rosenberg, "Issa Rae and 'Awkward Black Girl' Are the Future," *Think Progress,* July 28, 2011, http://thinkprogress.org/alyssa/2011/07/28/281328/issa-rae-and-awkward-black-girl-are-the-future/ (accessed July 27, 2012).

17. Kopacz and Lawton, "The Youtube Indian," p. 332.

18. Aymar Christian, "Fandom as Industrial Response: Producing Identity in an Independent Web Series," *Transformative Works and Cultures* 8 (2011), doi:10.3983/twc.2011.0250.

19. Christian.

20. Jon Caramanica, "Life's Hard, Web Series Gracefully Illustrates," *New York Times,* July 13, 2012, http://www.nytimes.com/2012/07/14/arts/television/issa-rae-and-awkward-black-girl-are-breaking-ground.html (accessed July 21, 2012).

21. Claudia Greene, "Rising Star: Issa Rae," *The Insider,* January 24, 2012, http://www.theinsider.com/lol/49091_Issa_Rae_interview/index.html (accessed July 30, 2012).

22. David P. Pierson, "A Show about Nothing: *Seinfeld* and the Modern Comedy of Manners," *Journal of Popular Culture* 34 (2000): p. 49.

23. Stephens and Phillips, "Freaks, Gold Diggers, Divas and Dykes," p. 15.

24. "The Misadventures of Awkward Black Girl," Kickstarter, http://www.kickstarter.com/projects/1996857943/the-misadventures-of-awkward-black-girl (accessed July 28, 2012).

25. "'Awkward Black Girl' Web Series Grows through Social Media."

26. Janel Martinez, "Issa Rae on Building an Online Audience," *Black Enterprise,* May 23, 2012, http://www.blackenterprise.com/technology/issa-rae-on-building-an-online-audience/ (accessed July 30, 2012).

27. "Issa Rae Gets Awkward for Vibe Magazine Shoot," *Vibe,* April 17, 2012, http://www.vibe.com/article/issa-rae-gets-awkward-vibe-magazine-photo-shoot (accessed July 30, 2012).

28. "The Misadventures of Awkward Black Girl, Episode 1: The Stop Sign," [n.d.], video clip, YouTube, http://www.youtube.com/watch?v=nIVa9lxkbus (accessed July 30, 2012).

29. Caramanica.

30. Christian.

31. Caramanica.

32. Bounds Littlefield, "The Media as a System of Racialization," p. 683.

33. Colin A Beckles, "Black Liberation and the Internet: A Strategic Analysis," *Journal of Black Studies* 31 (2001): p. 312.

34. "Interview with Issa Rae; Writer, Star & Producer of Misadventures of Awkward Black Girl."

Chapter 24

Performing "Blackness": Barack Obama, Sport, and the Mediated Politics of Identity

Michael D. Giardina and Kyle S. Bunds

Conscious of black stereotypes, Obama rarely falls into them. He presents himself as a very present father and husband. He projects a calm than never boils into anger. Obama's blackness is palatable, when noticeable.

—Harvey Young, 2012

Barack Obama governs a nation enlightened enough to send an African American to the White House, but not enlightened enough to accept a black man as its president.

—Ta-Nehisi Coates, 2012

In January 2009, the world looked on as Barack Obama was inaugurated as the 44th president of the United States. For much of the previous two years—as the campaign for the presidency waged across network and cable television, online spaces of digital activism, talk radio shows, town halls, and print media—viewers had been privy to one of the most explicitly racialized campaigns in modern American history. From Republican vice presidential nominee Sarah Palin implying that Obama "pals around with terrorists" to Republican campaign ads tacitly articulating Obama to incendiary remarks by Rev. Jeremiah Wright to a cavalcade of Fox News Channel pundits (e.g., Sean Hannity, Glenn Beck, Bill O'Reilly, Steve Doocy, etc.) alleging that Obama was some combination of terrorist sympathizer, socialist, Marxist, Afro-Leninist, Muslim, anti-American, and more, we witnessed a concerted effort to actively other the future president, to negatively construct his blackness as a visual if not visceral threat to the nation.[1] The cultural critic Touré put this strategy bluntly, arguing on MSNBC's *The Cycle* that four years later, at the heart of the 2012 campaign, Republicans were still openly and explicitly

> trying to use racial coding and access some really deep stereotypes about the angry black man. This is part of the playbook against Obama, the "otheriza-tion," he's not like us. I know it's a heavy thing, I don't say it lightly, but this is "niggerization." You are not one of us, you are like the scary black man who we've been trained to fear.[2]

Summarizing the political context in which these narratives emerged, veteran television news journalist Sam Donaldson argued, "Many on the political right believe this president ought not to be there—they oppose him not for his polices and political view but for who he is, an African American! These people and perhaps even certain news orga-nizations (certainly the right wing talkers like Limbaugh) encourage disrespect for this president."[3]

Although some in the chattering class predicted—or at least hoped—a postracial utopia would sweep over the United States following Obama's electoral victory, we know this to be a false state of affairs. In fact, and in many ways, we have seen just the opposite: a further entrenchment in, if not expansion of, the very racial logics his inauguration was heralded to ameliorate. Beyond structural forms of racism embedded within and ema-nating from the late 20th/early 21st century (e.g., growing levels of income inequality, rising rates of unemployment, a systemic weakening of the social safety net, etc.), consider the moments that have deeply captivated middle America during the course of his presidency with respect to racial dynamics, in both general and specific forms:

- The murder of Trayvon Martin
- The state-sanctioned execution of Troy Davis
- Harvard University professor Henry Louis Gates Jr., being arrested at his own home on suspicion of burglary, which resulted in a beer summit at the White House with Gates, the arresting officer, and the president
- Voter ID laws being brought to the fore in states such as Pennsylvania meant to keep African American and other minority voters from voting in the 2012 election
- The hypermediated spectacle over the so-called Ground Zero Mosque in New York City
- Arizona immigration bill SB1070

Additionally, and with specific respect to Obama, we have seen a demonstrable rise in racial invective used to cavil his accomplishments, minimize his stature, or call into question his very being as an American citizen. This we have become accustomed to seeing in the now-normal rehearsal of arguments that his successful entree into and renowned academic achievements at Harvard University (e.g., president of the *Harvard Law Review*) were the result of affirmative action that he has cheapened the presidency by hosting so-called "hip-hop barbeques" at the White House,[4] appearing on entertainment talk shows such as *The Tonight Show with Jay Leno, The View,* or *The Ellen DeGeneres Show,* or even wearing jeans in the Oval Office (something Ronald Reagan also did, for those keeping score) and, in a continuation of previous campaign rhetoric, that he was not born in the United States and/or is a secret Muslim who hates America. At the same time, he has been subjected to calls from the political left that he is not black enough, that he is culturally white, and that he can't adequately understand the black experience. Screened through the lens of contemporary media, it becomes an awkward bit of mental gymnastics to reconcile a commentator on Fox News referring to Obama as a "skinny, ghetto crackhead"[5] or displaying "a deep-seated hatred of white people"[6] with the rather banal images of the president that we see on our daily newscasts. Yet, the fact of his blackness, to steal a phrase from Frantz Fanon, remains ever present. Ta-Nahesi Coates frames it thusly:

> The irony of Barack Obama is this: he has become the most successful black politician in American history by avoiding the radioactive racial issues of yesteryear, by being "clean" (as Joe Biden once labeled him)—and yet his indelible blackness irradiates everything he touches. This irony is rooted in the greater ironies of the country he leads. For most of American history, our political system was premised on two conflicting facts—one, an oft-stated love of democracy; the other, an undemocratic white supremacy inscribed at every level of government. In warring against that paradox, African Americans have historically been restricted to the realm of protest and agitation. But when President Barack Obama pledged to "get to the bottom of exactly what happened," [with respect to Trayvon Martin] he was not protesting or agitating. He was not appealing to federal power—he was employing it. The power was black—and, in certain quarters, was received as such.[7]

How are we to understand the competing (if contradictory) representations of Barack Obama and the particular performances of blackness both discursively constructed in the media and deployed in a material sense by Obama himself in the historical present? What do such depictions and iterations tell us about the state of race relations in the United States? And what do they herald for the country moving forward into Obama's second term as president?

Of course, debates over Obama's blackness are not new; rather, they have been rehearsed time and again. In fact, scores of books have been written examining, deconstructing, expanding on and/or challenging him as social actor, politician, and family man[8], as well as dozens if not hundreds of scholarly journal articles taking up foreign policy, political philosophy, and race relations.[9] However, in conducting research for this chapter, we were struck most by the number of times popular culture—and especially sport—was deployed to make sense of Obama, to read him in particular ways, or render him *unreadable* in other ways. Thus, in this chapter we take up various articulations of Obama's blackness as revealed through the popular language of mediated sport—in particular, his connections to basketball and golf and the way he has been discursively if problematically constructed along similar lines as Michael Jordan (i.e., as a floating racial signifier screened through a white cultural lens[10]). We begin by discussing the performance of blackness in the historical present, especially as it relates to popular and televisual culture. From there, we engage the particular location of sport and sporting politics as it relates to dominant narratives about Obama. We conclude by pointing to a politics of possibility as embedded within his corporeal projections.

Performing Blackness

[T]o be black in a "real" way nowadays is to more closely resemble Jay-Z or Carmelo Anthony than James Baldwin or Thurgood Marshall.
                                              —Thomas Chatterton Williams, 2010

Throughout the 2008 election season and even moving into Obama's first term in office, pollster after pollster saw fit to ask whether the respondent/nation was "ready for an African American president." Where in 2000 only 38 percent of those polled voice an affirmative response, that number had gone up to 54 percent in January 2008; six months later, that number stood at 68 percent.[11] A similar poll commissioned by *CNN/Essence* magazine and conducted by Opinion Research Corp. at roughly the same time as the *CBS News* poll found that number to be even higher, at 76 percent.[12]

Yet, we've had African American presidents for decades before Obama—they just all happened to be fictional. Which is to say, within the popular imaginary of the United States, the image of an African American president had prior to 2008 become a rather ordinary occurrence in film and television. Whether it was Morgan Freeman playing the role of the thoughtful/philosophical president in the blockbuster disaster movie *Deep Impact,* Danny Glover playing a similar role in the disaster film *2012,* or Dennis Haysbert's action-hero president in the celebrated FOX drama *24,* the idea of an African American president was screened and re-screened multiple times in the last decade.[13] Beyond the genre of serious drama, we could also turn to Chris Rock's comedy *Head of State*—in which he plays a local alderman who gets recruited to run for president against a popular vice president but ends up winning the presidency by tackling serious social and economic issues (albeit in a comedic fashion)—as well as television sketch comedy shows in the form of *Saturday Night Live* or *Chappelle's Show.*

But even such comedic accounts are not new: we can go back to *The Richard Pryor Show* in 1977 and see Pryor's turn as America's first black president, in which his character takes a question from Brother Bell of *Ebony* magazine (and responds with "alaykum as-salaam" to Bell's "as-salamu alaykum, brother" greeting), discusses black ownership in and quarterbacks of NFL teams, and ponders the possibility of appointing Huey Newton (cofounder of the Black Panther Party) as director of the FBI.[14] As Coates remarked along a similar line of inquiry, "the paradoxes and problems of a theoretical black presidency were given voice" in the realm of popular culture made political by its very subject matter.[15] Yet, generally in such spaces and portrayals, as Norman K. Denzin reminds us in his important book on the cinematic construction of race and racial violence, "blackness is not given a racial identity. His blackness is not part of who he is. Race is the unnamed signifier. . . . But race is present even when it goes unnamed."[16] So while America may have been ready for an African American to be president, Obama's first term in office tell us that in some quarters America is still grappling with having a president who is *black.*[17]

But what does such a statement like this even mean? In his landmark essay on the contextual contingencies of race and its discursive performance, Stuart Hall argues that the struggle to define blackness is at its core about "the struggle over cultural hegemony, which these days is waged as much in popular culture as anywhere else."[18] To this end, understanding how the politics of racial representation is operative within and deployed in the service of the present moment—asking, along the lines of Hall, "what sort of moment it is" to pose such a question in the first place—is a key strategy for deciphering the contested terrain of Obama's blackness. As Hall put it, "we tend to privilege experience itself, *as if* black life is lived experience outside of representation" (emphasis ours).[19] Which is to say, nothing can stand outside of representation: the apparatus of representation is itself always already ideological and, through that, always already performative.

To say that race is a performance is to take up Judith Butler's theorization of politics of the performative, which understands identity to be "performatively constituted by the very expressions that are said to be its results."[20] Aligned here, the very performative act of race (i.e., racial representation) enacts the discursive conventions of race, which arise from the production of race throughout a historical moment. This (re)-iterative instantiation—the performative act in material form—exists at the intersection(s) of discourse, embodiment, and actual performance, regulating both itself and those performative moments that are to follow. As Jonathan Culler makes clear in a slightly different context: "The paradox, the dilemma of authenticity, is that to be experienced as authentic it [a particular performance] must be marked as authentic, but when it is marked as authentic it is mediated, a sign of itself, and hence not authentic in the sense of the unspoiled."[21] In other words, a discursive practice gains "authority to bring about what it names through citing the conventions of authority," such that normative (or perhaps better stated, authentic) position "takes hold to the extent that it is 'cited' as such a norm, but it also derives its power through the citations that it compels."[22]

The argument here, then, is that "race resolutely does not refer to a preconstituted body."[23] Rather, as Jonathan X. Inda has cogently articulated, "it works performatively to constitute the body itself."[24] However, this does not mean that the racial(ized) body has no material existence, only that materiality trades on the im/materiality of signification. That the racialized body—like that of Butler's gendered body—is performative "suggests that it has no ontological status apart from the various acts which constitute its reality."[25] If this is the case—race as a social fiction enacted in discursively historical moments—then the meaning of *race* and hence the constitution of racial identity ultimately performs, and simultaneously erases, a myriad cluster of resignifications, both positive and negative.[26]

Given the above, consider the ways in which Obama's blackness has come to be contested, deployed, and made meaningful over the last several years or, in other words, in which his blackness has been both essentialized and disarticulated from history. While running for the U.S. Senate in 2004, the criticism that he was not black enough dogged him in the media yet was framed as if this was a negative positionality given the racial politics of Chicago and the voter base he was thought to have needed in order to win the Democratic primary. In response to this curious projection, Obama was quoted as saying: "If I was arrested for armed robbery and my mug shot was on the television screen, people wouldn't be debating if I was African American or not. I'd be a black man going to jail."[27]

In a similar vein, during a 2008 CNN/YouTube Democratic primary debate, a question was raised addressing whether Obama was black enough (as well as if Senator Hillary Clinton was normatively feminine enough). Obama's response was forthright: "You know, when I'm catching a cab in Manhattan, in the past, I think I've given my credentials." However, he then quickly pivoted to a more mainstream, measured, and inclusive peroration:

> But let me go to the broader issue here, and that is that race permeates our society, it is still a critical problem, but I do believe in the core decency of the American people, and I think they want to get beyond some of our racial divisions. Unfortunately, we've had a White House that hasn't invested in the kinds of steps to overcome the legacy of slavery and Jim Crow in this country. And as President of the United States, my commitment on issues like education, my commitment on issues like health care, is to close the disparities and the gaps, because that's what's really going to solve the race problem in this country. If people feel like they've got a fair shake, if children feel as if the fact they have a different surname or a different skin color, is not going to impede their dreams, then I am absolutely confident that we're going to be able to move forward on the challenges that we face as a country.[28]

In both instances, Obama deployed a visual frame of reference for locating his blackness within the context of mug shots and being ignored on the street by racist cab drivers. These are not singular occurrences, either. In his press conference following the murder of Trayvon Martin (a 16-year-old boy who was shot and killed by a middle-aged man who felt threatened by him walking in his neighborhood), Obama similarly noted, "If I had a son, he'd look like Trayvon."

But beyond the visual, there exists a particular expression or performance of blackness that has come to surround the president. Coates, for one, implies that such a cultural performance is embedded within an ongoing calculus of political survival:

> Obama doesn't merely evince blackness; he uses his blackness to signal and court African Americans, semaphoring in a cultural dialect of our creation—crooning Al Green at the Apollo, name-checking Young Jeezy, regularly appearing on the cover of black magazines, weighing the merits of Jay-Z versus Kanye West, being photographed in the White House with a little black boy touching his hair.[29]

Here, Coates speaks to the heart of the matter: the political sensibility embedded within the performance of race. This calls to mind a 2007 comedy sketch on *Saturday Night Live,* in which Rev. Jesse Jackson and Rev. Al Sharpton (played by Darrell Hammond and Kenan Thompson, respectively) introduce a blackness scale by stating, "In America, unfortunately, there are degrees of blackness, scales of soul." The chart they provide "measures degrees of blackness in the eyes of others, i.e., white people." Their dialogue progresses in part:

Jackson:	Please observe, Mr. Barack Obama. There is only so much blackness the American voter can take. If you are here with the Black Eyed Peas (*points to the bottom of the chart*), then you'll be fine.
Sharpton:	But once you get into here (*points toward the top of the chart*), you're moving into Allen Iverson territory.
Jackson:	And that's unelectable. Barack, at this point and time, you're right about here: above Will Smith, but just below Bill Clinton.
Sharpton:	But this could change as the American people get to know you better. For example . . . "
Jackson:	You were raised by a single mother and your grandparents.
Sharpton:	Moving up.
Jackson:	In Hawaii.
Sharpton:	Moving down.
Jackson:	You have an African name, Barack.
Sharpton:	Moving up.
Jackson:	But it high school, you went by "Barry"
Sharpton:	Moving down.
Jackson:	You married a black woman.
Sharpton:	Moving up.
Jackson:	But in the past, you dated white women.
Sharpton:	Still moving up.

This type of discourse has become rather mainstream, while eliding an easy essentialism founded on social fictions that reiteratively instantiate a notion of authenticity with respect to blackness (e.g., that rappers Suge Knight or Chris Brown are more authentically black than actor Wayne Brady or astrophysicist Neil deGrasse Tyson). *This is a conversation that has been playing out for decades on the screen!* Consider the widely regarded scene in Spike Lee's *Do the Right Thing* between pizzeria employee Pino and Lee's Mookie, in which the outwardly racist Pino nonetheless lists his favorite athlete, actor, and musician as Magic Johnson, Eddie Murphy, and

Prince, respectively. When pressed as to how he reconciles his adoration of black celebrities with his otherwise angry disposition toward actual African Americans in his community, Pino replies:

> It's different. Magic, Eddie, Prince are not niggers. I mean, they're not black. I mean, let me explain myself. They're not really black. I mean, they're black but not really black. They're more than black. It's different.

Of the context of scenes such as this, Denzin writes, Magic, Eddie, and Prince are each read as "a black man who is not black. He is a black man who is white. Like Michael Jordan, he enacts a racially neutered identity (Andrews, 1996), a black version of a white cultural model. . . . [in which] blackness dissolves into goodness," and supplants race in favor of a color-blind utopia that doesn't exist.[30] Thomas Chatterton Williams surmises then that as a matter of context the criteria we use to designate someone as acting, or even *being* black, in the post–civil rights/hip-hop era often has little, sometimes even nothing at all, to do with a person's actual racial heritage or physical characteristics. Rather, this particular designation is often an assessment of behavioral traits, a judgment of cultural values, and a subjective projection of what is "real."[31] In *Dreams from My Father,* Obama himself writes of having to learn how to be black as a teenager in Hawaii: "Pop culture was color-coded, after all, an arcade of images from which you could cop a walk, a talk, a step, a style. I couldn't croon like Marvin Gaye, but I could learn to dance all the *Soul Train* steps. I couldn't pack a gun like Shaft or Superfly, but I could sure enough curse like Richard Pryor."[32]

At the same time, cultural anthropologist Orin Starn reminds us that Obama *complicates* this historical narrative, stating that he "calls himself a black man *of mixed heritage.*" That is, and while he consolidate his blackness by marrying a black woman, joining a black church, and working in inner-city Chicago, Starn notes that he also cultivates a wide circle of diverse acquaintances, speaks as a citizen of the world and from multiple subject positions, and moderates his outward representation and oratory to fit within a particular racial context (or audience) as politically necessary or expedient.[33] As a result of his political flexibility—or necessary dexterity— Obama has drawn the ire of some on the political black left, such as television hosts Tavis Smiley and philosopher Cornel West, who have criticized the president on similar grounds: namely, for not being perceived as doing enough for African American issues (in the case of Smiley) and for being culturally white (as in the case of West).

In other words, the limits of blackness in contemporary American dictate that Obama must be *black enough* for some but not *too black* for others, a predicament Coates would call the necessity of being "twice as good, half as black."[34] Or, put differently, the political calculus of the historical present is one that dictates that Obama situates himself with a white cultural frame, transgressing it when possible (as detailed above) and using it to his advantage when necessary. As Angela Rye, executive director of the Congressional Black Caucus, explains:

> I think that a lot of what the president has experienced is because he's black. You know, whether it's questioning his intellect or whether or not he's Ivy League. It's always either he's not educated enough or he's too educated; or he's too black or he's not black enough; he's too Christian or not Christian enough. There are all these things where he has to walk this very fine line to even be successful.[35]

As we detail in the next section, perhaps nowhere is this more apparent than in his relationship to sport or, more specifically, the way in which the racial performances Obama negotiates have been playing out in sport for decades.

Sporting Obama

I love that we have a President who can play basketball
—Paul Mooney, 2009

The watchful eye of American citizens has long been drawn to the images of the sporting president: George Washington was alleged to have been a great horseman; Theodore Roosevelt was known for mountain climbing, hunting, boxing, and his influence on the sport of football; Ronald Reagan was said to be good at almost every sport; and George W. Bush was known for his love of baseball, especially his iconic first pitch ceremony at Yankee Stadium immediately following September 11, 2001.[36] For Barack Obama, he has long been associated with the sport of basketball, going back to his memoir where he writes that his estranged father's gift of a basketball in concert with his grandfather taking him to see the University of Hawaii men's basketball team—which "had slipped into the national rankings on the strength of an all-black starting five" (p. 78)—provided him entree into a world of black masculinity that had theretofore been foreign to him. By the time he was in high school, Obama notes

I could take my game to the university courts, where a handful of black men, mostly gym rats and has-beens, would teach me an attitude that didn't just have to do with the sport. That respect came from what you did and not who your daddy was. That you could talk stuff to rattle an opponent, but that you should shut the hell up if you couldn't back it up. That you didn't let anyone sneak up behind you to see emotions—like hurt or fear—you didn't want them to see.[37]

However, and perhaps more importantly, Obama self-reflexively acknowledges the cultural pedagogy embedded within the performance of identity playing out in those spaces just two paragraphs later:

I was living out a caricature of black male adolescence, itself of caricature of swaggering American manhood. [. . .] Each of us chose a costume, armor against uncertainty. At least on the basketball court I could find a community of sorts, with an inner life all its own. It was there that I would make my closest white friends, *where blackness couldn't be a disadvantage.*[38]

It is of no surprise to us, then, that the space of popular culture in which Obama presents himself—and is himself presented—is most often related to basketball.

Consider the following: During the 2008 campaign, television news coverage of Obama playing basketball as a way to relax or as a way to engage with interviewers/supporters was commonplace. In many cases, it was used to extol the virtue of the ice in his veins or performance-under-pressure memes, as when Obama gave a speech at a U.S. military gymnasium in Kuwait and then, following his speech, picked up a basketball, played to the crowd, and drained a three-pointer on his first shot to the roaring adulation of the diverse crowd of troops. The footage became a YouTube sensation and was widely shown on network news broadcasts. Cable news outlets such as CNN began regularly covering his Election Day routine of playing basketball throughout the Democratic primary season.

Additionally, every year President Obama has filled out a bracket for the NCAA Men's and Women's basketball tournaments, giving him broad exposure on ESPN and a chance to ruminate on basketball and engage with average American viewers. He has also used March Madness as political spectacle, bringing British prime minister David Cameron to a game, taking a turn doing play-by-play on the television broadcast, and generally engaging with the fans in attendance. Along similar lines, he has filmed interviews with sports journalists such as ESPN's Bill Simmons (for the Simmons Podcast) and CBS's Clark Kellogg; in the latter instance, Kellogg (a former NCAA Division I all-American basketball player) films his interview playing a game of H-O-R-S-E (renamed as a game of P-O-T-U-S) on the White House basketball court with the president, who beats Kellogg with a series of three-pointers while cogently discussing the current state of college basketball affairs and promoting First Lady Michelle Obama's "Let's Move" campaign to fight childhood obesity.[39]

Even more explicitly, and in much the same way George W. Bush mobilized the sport of NASCAR auto racing for political benefit during his tumultuous presidency (see Newman and Giardina, 2011), we saw Obama do the same at the 2011 Quicken Loans Carrier Classic. The inaugural event, which was held on November 11, 2011, in celebration of Veterans Day, featured a college basketball game between the University of North Carolina and Michigan State University playing on the deck of the USS Carl Vinson (a U.S. aircraft carrier berthed in San Diego). Wearing specially made camouflage uniforms and playing before a crowd of 3,000 uniformed U.S. Navy sailors and select dignitaries—including the president and his family—the two teams celebrated the troops, the event's corporate sponsors, and the spectacle of commercial fantasy that had the parallel effect of reinforcing Obama's image as commander-in-chief. The event was part and parcel of the growing normalization of military themes and spectacles dominating U.S. sporting and popular culture (e.g., the U.S. Army Experience interactive marketing pavilion at NASCAR events, the NFL 9/11 anniversary weekend celebration, increased militarization of local police forces, the commercialization of militaristic nationalism, and so forth) that has occurred in the post-9/11/01 moment.

Not only does the sporting body of Obama reflect on a certain facet of the American narrative in the present tense, but it also puts forth a very prescribed—if not ascribed—image of acceptable black (sporting) masculinity. We have seen this before, specifically, in the case of Michael Jordan, arguably the most celebrated (African American) athlete in recent history. Along with celebrities like Oprah Winfrey and Bill Cosby, Jordan helped to "focus, organize, and translate Blackness into commodifiable representations and desires that could be packaged and marketed across the landscape of American popular culture."[40] Specific to sport (and especially basketball) in the 1980s and 1990s, Denzin argues that this meant "translating Blackness into a nonthreatening Reaganesque masculinity for male youth."[41] Ruben A. Buford May provides context to this argument by noting in regard to the NBA in the 1980s, "Most of the public viewed the league, made up of 70% African American players, 'as a space of racial threat and criminal menace' owing to the widely publicized incidences of violence and drug use by the league's players."[42] This deleterious image was perpetuated largely by the media-driven narrative that black basketball players were simply an extension of the out-of-control inner-city ghetto of the kind represented in a slew of films such as *Heaven Is a Playground, Menace II Society, Boyz N the Hood, Grand Canyon,* and so on. As May went on to explain:

> In a 1980s Reagan era, undergirded by a philosophy of individual responsi-
> bility and the criminalization of Black males, these social pathologies were
> viewed largely as a result of individual choice rather than stemming from
> historical discrimination and social inequality, the context in which these
> social pathologies arise.[43]

Related to sport, C. L. Cole argues that the context of the 1980s produced the notion of the sport/gang dyad, in which "Sport and gangs [became] represented not only as channels for what [was] understood to be the corporeal predispositions of African-American youth but as the available substitutes for the 'failed black family.'"[44] In the parlance of modern identities, she continues, gang members, whose deviance was coded through discourses of laziness, violence, sexual promiscuity, and poverty, work to "produce what/who are normal and acceptable: the urban African-American athlete."[45]

Jordan, in order to be profitable for both himself and his corporate sponsors, had to be different than what the average (white, middle-class) consumer viewed a basketball player to be at that point in history. Jordan was flashy on the court to be sure and dominated his sport like few others had theretofore, but off the court he starred in family-oriented advertisements for brands such as McDonalds, Coca-Cola, and Hanes and in movies such as *Space Jam* (with Bugs Bunny no less). The "marketing of black masculinity," as Mary G. McDonald put it, shaped up thusly:

> With an assist from Nike, fresh meanings were associated with Black mascu-
> linity in an effort to court White middle-class audiences. New narratives sug-
> gested that NBA athletes possessed exceptional skill, hard work, dedication,
> and determination. The presentation of NBA players as idealized athletic
> heroes committed to competition and meritocracy also suggests the New
> Right's understanding of a racially harmonious country.[46]

Obama positions himself over and against this paradigm the closer he gets to the seat of power. Where before in his memoir he once spoke of clashes with his high school basketball coach ("there are white folks, and then there are ignorant motherfuckers like you," he wrote of one heated exchange with his coach) and the racial dynamics on the team, by 2008 he was appearing with Bob Costas on HBO's *Real Sports* with a much different tone: he speaks in almost reverential tones about teamwork, playing fair, listening to his coaches, etc. Even more telling is his admission that he gave up playing a creative style in order to play a more team-oriented game. This segued into a discussion about family dynamics and the worth of a man: he explained to Costas how he came to be accepted by his then future wife's brother (Craig Robinson, now a Division I basketball coach at Oregon State University) as a man suitable for his sister by playing basketball—Robinson witnessed a generous passer and all-around player, the consummate team player (as opposed to a selfish or flashy ball hog, for example).

Ironically, however, the deeper into his presidency Obama got, and despite the oft-deployed basketball narratives, his tendency toward the sport of golf soon became an important theme in media coverage of him and his politics. In some ways cliché, his introduction to the American golf fan base was through sharing the cover of an issue of *Golf Digest* with Tiger Woods, who had been hailed by Oprah Winfrey as "America's son" at the height of political debates concerning multiculturalism in the late 1990s.[47] In the accompanying cover story by Don Van Natta (a best-selling author and investigative journalist affiliated with ESPN), we learn how Obama first picked up the game and what it meant for him to do so while residing in a zip code associated with the South Side of Chicago. He writes:

> In 1998, Obama finally decided to invest in a new set of clubs. At a golf discount store in the Chicago suburbs, he found a set on sale for $350. He wrote a check, but the cashier informed him that the store's check-processing company had rejected it. There was more than enough money in Obama's account, but the company had flagged Obama's South Side zip code, 60619, before the matter was resolved, recalls Shomon. "It didn't matter that his credit was perfect."[48]

Unsurprisingly, Van Natta leaves the anecdote to sit on own without critically considering what the discrimination against Obama really means. Instead, his article talks about how Obama became an avid golfer and plays as much as he can because he fell in love with the game. However, a telling statement to both the zip code story and the narrative surrounding why Obama plays golf comes a bit later on, "For Obama, golf was appealing because he believed the game would help him connect with his colleagues in the state Senate as well as his constituents in far-flung places like downstate Illinois."[49] This very telling connection between the sport of golf as a way to make connections in the predominately white senate and among constituents helps us understand how golf was deployed as a political tool.

Yet, in an odd twist of fate, it is precisely Obama's playing of golf—and not basketball—that comes to be used against him in the world of right-wing political machinations. For much of his presidency, Fox News channel has kept a running tab on the number of rounds of golf he has played and has deployed it within interview segments to assail the president as an elitist and out of touch with regular Americans. Republican presidential candidate Mitt Romney has also deployed such language, stating during a televised Republican primary debate in Florida on January 24, 2012, that "he plays 90 rounds of golf, when you have 25 million people out of work"; former UN ambassador (and, in a just world, war criminal) John Bolton has similarly used the golf cudgel to mock him for not scheduling an official trip to Israel.

But the heart of the matter is not really the sports he decides to play despite the fact that they stand as physical embodiments of a very long history of ideology in the United States. Rather, what really gets to the heart of the matter when we discuss Barack Obama and his legitimacy as an American, as a black man in America, or as a corporeal embodiment of "transnational American blackness"[50] is the complicated political entanglements he must negotiate, or perform, his way through. Returning to Hall's asking the question of "what sort of moment it is" to pose the question of Obama's blackness, the answer lies in a deeply divided country in which race can still be mobilized as a means to some other end. As Andrew Sullivan explained,

> The demographics tell a basic story: a Black man is President and a large majority of white Southerners cannot accept that, even in 2009. They grasp conspiracy theories to wish Obama—and the America he represents—away. Since white Southerners comprise an increasing proportion of the 22% of Americans who still describe themselves as Republican, the GOP can neither dismiss their crankery nor move past it. The fringe defines what's left of the Republican center. . . . The chilling implication is that a large number of Americans believe the President has no right to be in office and has fraudulently maneuvered himself there.[51]

Given the *realpolitik* of the times, is it any wonder that Obama so carefully manages his blackness? Is it any wonder that he treads so cautiously on issues related to race? While we might concur with some of his critics on the left that a more forceful progressive agenda is warranted, we are not blind to historical circumstance and political constraints. *And neither, we believe, is he.*

By Way of a Conclusion

As we write this chapter, the 2012 presidential election is a mere two months away. As it stands, Barack Obama leads the Republican nominee, Mitt Romney, by several percentage points in national polls, and has a strong yet not insurmountable lead in important swing states such as Ohio and Florida. Given the last four years of repeated if not constant assault on his race and citizenship—not to mention the outright lies about his public policy initiatives—across the spectrum of television and other forms of media, this ranks as nothing short of amazing. Hundreds of millions of dollars have been spent in the last year alone on targeted television advertisements that are by any fair judgment misleading, false, racist, xenophobic, and so forth—and yet his popularity persists.

Thus, we believe Cornel West is wrong in suggesting that Barack Obama is culturally white, for West most assuredly knows the performative utterance embedded within his charge. Rather, what West's criticism illuminates is the very fact(s)[52] of Obama's blackness and the limits of blackness in the present moment. Obama is neither culturally white nor culturally black, for both are performative fictions. Rather, he has positioned himself within and against such fictions for the very fact of his political survival. And in doing so, he has revealed the instabilities of race—of blackness—and "calls attention to those constitutive instabilities that contest the naturalizing effects of discourse."[53] In the last analysis, we might suggest that Barack Obama overcame the political realities of being American's first black president by using the fiction of race against itself, by turning it in on itself. At the end of the day, his very existence as a global citizen of empire elected to the most powerful position on earth may not ultimately result in the type of systemic change his constituent publics have hoped for, but let us not deny the change that his election heralded nor the means by which it happened.

Notes

1. Michael D. Giardina, "Barack Obama, Islamophobia, and the 2008 U.S. Presidential Election Media Spectacle," in *Teaching against Islamophobia*, ed. by J. L. Kincheloe, S. R. Steinberg, and C. D. Stonebanks (New York: Peter Lang, 2010), pp. 135–60.

2. Andrew Kirell, "MSNBC's Toure: Romney Engaging in the 'Niggerization' of Obama," August 16, 2012, http://www.mediaite.com/tv/msnbcs-toure-to-panel-romney-engaging-in-the-niggerization-of-obama/ (accessed September 5, 2012).

3. Michael Calderone, "Sam Donaldson Rejects Comparison to Reporter Who Interrupted Obama," June 16, 2012, http://www.huffingtonpost.com/2012/06/16/sam-donaldson-tucker-carlson-daily-caller-obama-interrupted_n_1602526.html (accessed September 4, 2012).

4. This was how Fox News channel referred to Obama's 50th birthday party.

5. J. Jillian Rayfield, "Obama Called 'Skinny, Ghetto Crackhead' on Fox News," December 23, 2011, http://tpmmuckraker.talkingpointsmemo.com/2011/12/obama_called_skinny_ghetto_crackhead_on_fox_news.php (accessed September 6, 2012).

6. Ryan Nakashima, "Glenn Beck Signs $100 Million, 5-Year Radio Deal," June 11, 2012, http://www.usatoday.com/money/media/story/2012-06-11/Glenn-Beck-100-million-5-year-contract/55522332/1 (accessed September 4, 2012).

7. Ta-Nehisi Coates, "Fear of a Black President," September 2012, http://www.theatlantic.com/magazine/archive/2012/09/fear-of-a-black-president/309064/ (accessed September 12, 2012).

8. Jodi Kantor, *The Obamas* (New York: Back Bay Books, 2012); David Maraniss, *Barack Obama: The Story* (New York: Simon & Schuster, 2012); David Remnick, *The Bridge: The Life and Rise of Barack Obama* (New York: Vintage, 2012); David Sanger, *Confront and Conceal: Obama's Secret Wars and Surprising Use of American Power* (New York: Crown, 2012); Terry Smith, *Barack Obama, Postracialism, and the New Politics of Triangulation* (New York: Palgrave Macmillan, 2012); Jeffrey Toobin, *The Oath: The Obama White House and the Supreme Court* (New York: Doubleday, 2012); Bob Woodward, *The Price of Politics* (New York: Simon & Schuster, 2012).

9. Thomas Edge, "Southern Strategy 2.0: Conservatives, White Voters, and the Election of Barack Obama," *Journal of Black Studies* 30, no. 3 (2010): pp. 426–44; Pearl K. Ford, Tekla A. Johnson, and Angie Maxwell, "'Yes We Can' or 'Yes We Did'? Perspective and Retrospective Change in the Obama Presidency," *Journal of Black Studies* 30, no. 3 (2010): pp. 462–83; Marco A. Gandasegui, "President Obama, the Crisis, and Latin America," *Latin American Perspectives* 38, no. 4 (2011): pp. 109–21; Craig Hayden, "Beyond the 'Obama effect': Refining the Instruments of Engagement through U.S. Public Discourse," *American Behavioral Scientist* 55, no. 6 (2012): pp. 784–802; Christopher J. Metzler, "Barack Obama's Faustian Bargain and the Fight for America's Racial Soul," *Journal of Black Studies* 40, no. 3 (2010): pp. 395–401; Nancy Murray, "Obama and the Global War on Terror," *Race & Class* 53, no. 2 (2011): pp. 84–93; Bart Schultz, "Obama's Political Philosophy: Pragmatism, Politics, and the University of Chicago," *Philosophy of the Social Sciences* 39, no. 2 (2009): pp. 127–73; Robert C. Rowland, "The Fierce Urgency of Now: Barack Obama and the 2008 Presidential Election," *American Behavioral Scientist* 54, no. 3 (2010): pp. 203–21.

10. David L. Andrews, "The Fact(s) of Michael Jordan's Blackness: Excavating a Floating Racial Signifier," *Sociology of Sport Journal* 13, no. 2 (1996): pp. 125–58.

11. CBS News, "CBS Poll: Ready for a Black President?," June 18, 2008, http://www.cbsnews.com/2100-500160_162-4151937.html (accessed September 12, 2012).

12. Paul Steinhauser, "Poll: 76 Percent Say U.S. Ready for Black President," April 4, 2008, http://edition.cnn.com/2008/POLITICS/04/03/poll.black.president/index.html (accessed September 12, 2012).

13. Beyond that, we could also include James Earl Jones playing a black president in the 1972 film *The Man.*

14. Additionally, in Eddie Murphy's celebrated 1983 stand-up film *Delirious,* the comedian riffed on the idea of Jesse Jackson becoming the first black president in the 1984 election.

15. Coates, "Fear of a Black President."

16. Norman K. Denzin, *Reading Race: Hollywood and the Cinema of Racial Violence* (London: Sage, 2002), p. 99.

17. Coates, "Fear of a Black President." In the article, Coates also quotes one of Obama's own pollster, Cornell Belcher, who reinforces this (strategic) line of thinking: "The thing is, a *black man* can't be president in America, given the racial aversion and history that's still out there. However, an extraordinary, gifted, and talented young man who happens to be black can be president."

18. Stuart Hall, "What Is This 'Black' in Black Popular Culture?," in *Stuart Hall: Critical Dialogues in Cultural Studies,* ed. by D. Morely and K. Chen (London: Routledge, 1996), p. 471. As Hall goes on to define it, cultural hegemony is "always about shifting the relations of power in the relations of culture; it is always about changing the dispositions and the configurations of culture power, not getting out of it."

19. Hall, "What Is This 'Black' in Black Popular Culture," p. 468.

20. Judith Butler, *Bodies That Matter: Feminism and the Subversion of Identity* (New York: Routledge, 1990), p. 25; this paragraph and the one that follows draw directly from Michael Giardina, "'Bending in like Beckham' in the Global Popular: Stylish Hybridity, Performativity, and the Politics of Representation," *Journal of Sport & Social Issues* 27, no. 1 (2003): pp. 68–69.

21. Jonathan Culler, "Semiotics of tourism," *American Journal of Semiotics* 1, no. 1 (1981): p. 137.

22. Judith Butler, *Bodies That Matter: On the Discursive Limits of "Sex"* (New York: Routledge, 1993), p. 13.

23. Jonathan X. Inda, "Performativity, Materiality, and the Racialized Body," *Latino Studies Journal* 11, no. 3 (2000): p. 75.

24. Ibid.

25. Butler, *Gender Trouble,* p. 173.

26. Inda, "Performativity, Materiality, and the Racialized Body."

27. M. Davey, "A Surprise Senate Contender Reaches His Biggest Stage Yet," *The New York Times,* September 19, 2004, p. A1.

28. "YouTube Debate: Is Obama Black Enough? Hillary Woman Enough," July 23, 2007, http://www.youtube.com/watch?v=utf4-LPhUz0 (accessed September 22, 2012).

29. Coates, "Fear of a Black President."

30. Denzin, *Reading race,* p. 100.

31. Thomas Chatterton Williams, "What Obama and Drake Have to Do with Being Black," http://www.theroot.com/views/what-obama-and-drake-have-do-being-black (accessed September 22, 2012).

32. Barack Obama, *Dreams from My Father: A Story of Race and Inheritance* (New York: Three Rivers Press, 2004), p. 75.

33. Orin Starn, "Orin Starn Discusses Tiger Woods' Scandal in the Media," December 1, 2010, http://www.youtube.com/watch?v=-I95ck2_CNQ (accessed September 22, 2012).

34. Coates, "Fear of a Black President."

35. J. Gehrke, "CBC Staff: Opposition to Obama Is Racist," June 11, 2012, http://washingtonexaminer.com/cbc-staff-opposition-to-obama-is-racist/article/1342346 (accessed September 22, 2012).

36. John Sayle Watterson, *The Games Presidents Play: Sports and the Presidency* (Baltimore: The Johns Hopkins University Press, 2006).

37. Obama, *Dreams from My Father,* p. 79.

38. Obama, *Dreams from My Father,* pp. 79–80, emphasis ours.

39. K. Hechtkopf, "Obama, Clark Kellogg Play Basketball at White House," April 3, 2010, http://www.cbsnews.com/8301-503544_162-20001717-503544.html (accessed September 23, 2012).

40. Herman Gray, *Watching Race: Television and the Struggle for Blackness* (Minneapolis: University of Minnesota Press, 1995), p. 68.

41. Norman K. Denzin, "More Rare Air: Michael Jordan on Michael Jordan," *Sociology of Sport Journal* 13, no. 4 (1996): p. 320.

42. Rueben A. Buford May, "The Good and Bad of It All: Professional Black Male Basketball Role Models for You Black Male Basketball Players," *Sociology of Sport Journal* 26, no. 4 (2009): p. 444.

43. Ibid.

44. C.L. Cole, "American Jordan: P.L.A.Y., Consensus, and Punishment," *Sociology of Sport Journal* 13, no. 4 (1996): p. 69.

45. Cole, "American Jordan," p. 70.

46. Mary G. McDonald, "Michael Jordan's Family Values: Marketing, Meaning, and Post-Reagan America," *Sociology of Sport Journal* 13, no. 4 (1996): p. 348. Spatial considerations limit our discussion. For more, see David Leonard's discussion of the "absurdity of colorblind rhetoric" as it relates to sport in "The Next M.J. or the Next O.J.? Kobe Bryant, Race, and the Absurdity of Colorblind Rhetoric," *Journal of Sport & Social Issues* 28, no. 3 (2004): pp. 284–313.

47. C.L. Cole and David L. Andrews, "America's New Son: Tiger Woods and America's Multiculturalism," in *Sports Stars: The Cultural Politics of Sporting Celebrity,* ed. by D.L. Andrews and S.J. Jackson (London: Routledge, 2001).

48. Don Van Natta, "The New First Golfer," January 16, 2009, http://upstart.bizjournals.com/culture-lifestyle/culture-inc/2009/01/16/Barack-Obamas-Golf-Game.html (accessed September 1, 2012).

49. Ibid.

50. Radhika Parameswaren, "Facing Barack Obama: Race, Globalization, and Transnational America," *Journal of Communication Inquiry* 33, no. 3 (2009): pp. 195–205.

51. Andrew Sullivan, "Obama Still Isn't President in the South: Denying the Leader's American Birth Is Just Another Form of Racism," *The Times* (London), August 9, 2009, p. 4.

52. I take this usage from David L. Andrews, "The Fact(s) of Michael Jordan's Blackness."

53. Luis F. Miron and Jonathan X. Inda, "Race as a Kind of Speech Act," *Cultural Studies: A Research Annual* 5, no. 1 (2000), p. 95.

"New Normal" in American Television? Race, Gender, Blackness, and the New Racism

Paula Groves Price

The chapters in this volume have provided in-depth analyses of the complex interplay of raced, classed, and gendered representations of African Americans on television in shifting social contexts. In many respects, the textual discussions and critiques embodied in this collection speak truth to the old adage that "the more things change, the more they stay the same," especially when it comes to issues of blackness. In this epilogue, I revisit some of the prominent themes discussed in *African Americans on Television: Race-ing for Ratings* by briefly examining the most recent representations of black manhood and womanhood found in television as markers of what we can expect in the future. Framed within the context of what Patricia Hill Collins calls the "new racism,"[1] this chapter critically explores the sociopolitical implications of black representations to ideology and social policy and the future of black representations on television.

The New Racism in Television

The "old racism" commonly found in American television shows since the 1950s has been well documented.[2] Featuring old stereotypes of African Americans as mammies, Sambos, hoodlums, and Jezebels, television has been notorious for perpetrating harmful images of African Americans into the homes of the American mainstream. These images of African American men as buffoons and thugs and of African American women as asexual, ugly caregivers, or hypersexualized hussies have been instrumental in (re)inscribing ideologies of inequality and white supremacy. While many of the same images can be readily seen on television today, as has been discussed in this volume, they often appear under the guise of reality television, black popular culture, or postracial ensemble shows.

> In the post-civil-rights era, Black popular culture and mass media have both grown in importance in creating ideologies of inequality. Black popular culture consists of the ideas and cultural representations created by Black people in everyday life that are widely known and accepted. In contrast, mass media describes the appropriation and repackaging of these ideas for larger audience consumption. Black popular culture as examined here is indicative of larger political and economic forces on the macro level that in turn influence the micro level of everyday behavior among African Americans. Conversely everyday behavior becomes the stuff that is mined by Black popular culture and a mass media with an insatiable appetite for new material.[3]

In other words, black popular culture, created largely by and for black communities often features African American responses to oppression. Contextualized within culture, black consumption of black popular culture is largely dependent on insider, taken for granted assumptions about experience, positionality, and the counternarrative. Mass media, in their repackaging for larger outsider audiences, often decontextualize the sociopolitical conditions that instigate responses, commodify black popular culture, and present behaviors as everyday reality. The selling of reality shows such as *Love and Hip Hop, The Bad Girls Club, Basketball Wives, The Real Housewives of Atlanta,* and the like rely on the high drama of fighting, arguing, and the seemingly everyday violent behaviors of African American people. When consumed by the mainstream operating from/through a white racial frame, these decontextualized responses to oppression are understood as merely black behavior. Mass media, therefore, work to reinscribe racist ideologies of blackness by framing it as black culture to the world. Gloria Ladson Billings reminds us, however, that "true culture supports its people; it doesn't destroy them."[4]

So what is "new" about the "new racism"? The new racism is located in a time and space controlled by global capitalism, transnational corporations, and an unprecedented redistribution of wealth to the hands of a small minority while the numbers of people (mostly of color) in poverty expands to new heights. Under the new racism, media conglomerates—the transnational mass media corporations which control music, television, publishing, internet, movies, and radio—drive much of the world economy and politics. Sometimes called American media colonialists,[5] the top five media conglomerates control the global production and distribution of media while simultaneously controlling local and regional markets. The images and racial ideologies seen across the world are largely dependent on the decisions made by Comcast, Disney, News Corp, Time Warner, and CBS/Viacom.

The fall 2012 television season is host to several new and old shows with African American men and women. As has historically been the case, network television (ABC, CBS, NBC, FOX) shows with African American representation are usually couched within the context of whiteness, offering black characters supporting roles in the form of sidekick, friend, assistant, or coworker. In our current media environment, however, network media (and images) no longer dominate the social landscape. Cable television stations, satellite channels, video streaming, and Internet shows now vie for the attention of audiences across the globe. The cable cousins of the networks (CW, VH1, BET, TV Land, etc.) are often home to the shows that feature blackness or majority black casts in the form of situation comedies, dramas, and reality shows. While there seems to be infinitely more choices

Cast of NBC'S *The New Normal.* Shown back row from left: Ellen Barkin (Jane), Bebe Wood (Shania), and NeNe Leakes (Rocky). Front row from left: Justin Bartha (David), Georgia King (Goldie), and Andrew Rannells (Bryan). (NBC/Photofest)

in terms of stations, channels, and types of programs, the fact remains, however, that the production, distribution, and delivery of nearly all media emerge from five media corporations.

With a few exceptions, every television show discussed in this volume has been produced, distributed, and broadcast by one of the major mass media conglomerates. Comcast, the largest of the media giants, controls NBC, USA network, E! Entertainment, and Oprah Winfrey's OWN, to name a few. The Walt Disney Company controls ABC, the Disney Channel, ESPN, Lifetime, and numerous local and cable channels, film companies, interactive websites, publishing houses, theme parks, and consumer merchandising companies. Time Warner controls popular cable channels CNN, WB, CW, TBS, TNT, and HBO in addition to numerous additional cable channels, film companies, magazines, and interactive media.[6] Viacom is home to CBS and popular cable stations BET, MTV, VH1, Nickelodeon, TV Land, and Comedy Central among others. News Corporation is home to the myriad of Fox local, cable, and international stations as well as the parent company of DirecTV.[7] These massive media corporations undoubtedly hold incredible power in determining what images, ideologies, and agendas are released to the public.

In the era of new racism, liberal ideologies of color blindness and meritocracy become the overarching tropes that dominate, masking the policies and practices (such as deregulation) that allow corporations and the extremely wealthy to reap record profits while the poor struggle to survive with less. Under the new racism, racism doesn't feel like racism because it has been normalized under seemingly color blind moral codes of decency, behavior, and meritocratic values. The images translated on screen become dominant narratives of whiteness, middle-class status, and heteronormativity juxtaposed by reality programming to support racist ideologies of blackness and deviancy. It turns discussions of opportunity and equality into debates about morals and values. From mainstream standpoints, the reality genre offers a window into the everyday reality of subcultures and communities that are rarely visited or seen in network television. The images projected carry great ideological power, as these shows appear to be unscripted, and with real people and not actors, they become the basis from which many long-held beliefs are confirmed or formed.

Undoubtedly, the images found in the (black) reality genre today are dominated by classed images of black women as Sapphires or bitches and of black men as players and criminals.[8] Portrayed as loud, aggressive, rude, confrontational, and lacking moral character, the controlling image of the bitch becomes a central feature of understanding the breakdown and drama endemic to black relationships and families. Coupled with the dominant image of the black man as the player and criminal, unable to resist temptations of additional women, fast money, and playing, the raced and classed portrayals of black men and women become the opposite of white gender ideology. According to Patricia Hill Collins, these images carry great consequences as they become linked to justifications for treatment of African Americans and social policy.

> Under the colorblind ideology of the new racism, Blackness must be *seen* as evidence for the alleged colorblindness that seemingly characterizes contemporary economic opportunity. A meritocracy requires evidence that racial discrimination has been eliminated. The total absence of Black people would signal the failure of colorblindness. At the same time that Blackness must be visible, it must also be contained and/or denuded of all meaning that threatens elites. Rejecting traditional racist discourse that sees racial difference as rooted in *biology,* these representations of criminals and bad mothers, of sidekicks and modern mammies work better in a context of desegregation in which cultural difference has grown in importance in maintaining racial boundaries. Poor and working class African American men are not *inherently* inclined to crime, such images suggest. Rather the *culture* in which they grow up, the authentic black culture so commodified in the media, creates images of criminality that explains the failures of integration by placing the blame on the unassimilability of African Americans themselves. The joblessness, poor schools, racially segregated neighborhoods, and unequal public services that characterize American society vanish, and social class hierarchies in the United States, as well as patterns of social mobility within them, become explained solely by issues of individual values, motivation, and morals.[9]

Media and television shows not only become the medium by which hegemonic ideologies of color blindness and meritocracy become reified, but they also become the vehicle by which power structures can justify unequal treatment and stratification. White mainstream is able to shift attention away from structural inequality and racism and place blame solely on the shoulders of African Americans (for their deviant behaviors); African Americans at times internalize these ideologies and spend their time blaming each other rather than the systems and structures that support racism.

So, in this current climate of new racism marked by globalization, corporate control of popular culture, politics, and social policy, what is the future of African American television and, more importantly, African American communities?

A *New Normal* in the Future of Black Television?

As an African American critical race hip-hop feminist, I find myself conflicted in my own projections of the future. I'm pessimistic and frustrated by the slowness of social change, angry about the incredible redistribution of wealth and power to the hands of few transnational corporations while the public remains oblivious, and yet I'm also hopeful that in the future images of African Americans in the media will include more nuanced and critical representations of African American life. In many ways, my hope is an "audacious hope,"[10] my recognition that although it involves raging against an unyielding machine, we must continue to demand better, as the stakes are too high to acquiesce. My audacious hope, however, is not a blind faith in progress, as I believe that despite the context of the new racism there is always space for resistance. Current programming provides us a space to critique what is, but it also allows us the opportunity to anticipate what could be. If we demand it, if we fight for it, they will come.

While much of the current reality television lineup is mired with problematic images of African Americans, I am optimistic that this genre may become more critical of larger relations of power in society through more strategic counternarratives. Hip-hop has always been about different voices, resistance, and critique. In an era where the reality show is now viewed as the new record deal, the hip-hop feminist in me believes that the reality show circuit will endure some of the same trials and tribulations of hip-hop music. Ultimately, as we hold our peers and ourselves accountable for our own complicity and complacency in propagating imagery to the world, we will also play a more active role in the contextualization of those images.[11] As social media such as Twitter and Facebook continue to be the new platforms for cultural critique and social mobilizing that are accessible to the masses, I hold hope that the images and narratives will shift because African American consumers will resist.

The fall 2012 lineup of new shows on NBC also offer an interesting glimpse into the future directions networks might be willing to go *if* American audiences indicate a willingness and ability to confront larger issues of inequality, gender, and race. *Guys with Kids* attempts to shift some of the ideologies of black masculinity and the absent father by featuring an African American middle-class working two-parent family, where the father is a stay-at-home dad to four children, and the African American mother is a professional career woman. The few episodes that have aired, however, are mired in color blind ideologies and whiteness. If it survives, it seems unlikely to push the envelope with respect to race, as it seems exclusively focused on gender and family relations.

Premiering on September 10, 2012, *The New Normal* is a comedy centered on a white middle-/upper-class gay couple and their surrogate. Critiquing mainstream notions of family normalcy that are focused on heteronormativity, whiteness, and middle-class status, *The New Normal* attempts to problematize taken for granted ideologies that control the mainstream. And while it is guilty of reproducing some of the same images and stereotypes commonly found on network television—the gay effeminate fashionista partnered with a masculine could pass for straight partner, the sassy strong black female assistant (ironically played by reality TV star NeNe Leakes), the ditsy romantic blonde, and the bigoted baby boomer grandmother—the overt scripting of race-conscious dialogue is one of the more interesting components of the show. The show is very cognizant of its location in an Obama presidency and finds multiple opportunities to display hot political issues related to marriage equality, women's rights to control their own body, and racism.

Episode 4, which aired on September 25, 2012, titled "Obama Mama," explicitly critiques color blind ideologies and racism as the characters debate core components of the ideologies that drive Republican and Democratic party politics. Filled with references to Mitt Romney and Barack Obama's campaigns, the characters question their own lack of living the principles of equality and diversity that they support in the abstract. Critiquing the dominant ideology that middle-class whites often profess to prove that they are not racist by touting the number of black friends that they have, *The New Normal* finds ways of critiquing whiteness in the presence and absence of blackness. Shows like *The New Normal*, while projecting limited images of blackness, demonstrate the potential disruption to dominant ideologies because of their explicit commitment to voicing inequality, hypocrisy, and white racism.

The future of African Americans in television will most likely follow many of the same formulas that have dominated the airwaves for many years—dramas that feature black criminals and sidekick police detectives, situation comedies with elements of "coonery buffoonery,"[12] and color blind ensemble shows with token black friends. So long as audiences support these types of programs, mass media corporations will continue to offer the programming that provides them the greatest profits and ratings.

While it is unlikely that the FCC will do much to reverse the deregulatory policies that created the incredibly powerful media corporations, growth in the areas of the Internet and independently produced shows that are outside of the purview of mass media conglomerates also provide pockets of hope for change. Media conglomerates have made headway in extending their corporate hands across the Internet, but their power and influence are not nearly as pronounced as they are in controlling television, film, print, and radio. Web shows such as *The Misadventures of Awkward Black Girl*, as discussed in this volume, will likely increase as independent artists work to produce and disseminate their crafts outside of corporate models. Ultimately, the future of African American television is in the hands of audiences. Following critical race notions of interest convergence, mass media will shift and change the images reproduced if it sees it is in its best interest. In a global economy, interests rest with economic profits and ratings. While the current *New Normal* seems to rest on critiquing gender ideologies by providing more representations of masculinity, femininity, and gay and lesbian characters, there is hope that the nuanced discussions of inequality that emerge as a result will also include more critical dialogue of racism and class inequality. A new normal in African American images will come to pass when consumers take more responsibility for their own complicity in supporting mass media by demanding change. Given the connections between media images, ideology, and social policy, the world, and African Americans in particular, cannot afford to keep the old normal alive.

Notes

1. Patricia Hill Collins, *Black Sexual Politics: African Americans, Gender, and the New Racism* (New York: Routledge, 2005).

2. *Ethnic Notions*, directed by Marlon Riggs, California Newsreel, 1987; *Color Adjustment*, directed by Marlon Riggs. California Newsreel, 1991.

3. Collins, *Black Sexual Politics*, p. 17.

4. Gloria Ladson Billings, *Multiplication Is for White People: Raising Expectations for Other People's Children* (New York: The New Press, 2012), p. 7.

5. William Hoynes and David Croteau, *The Business of Media: Corporate Media and the Public Interest, Second Edition* (Thousand Oaks, CA: Pine Forge Press, 2006).

6. William Hoynes, David Croteau, and Stefania Milan, *Media/Society: Industries, Images, and Audiences*, 4th edition (Thousand Oaks, CA: Sage Publishing, 2012).

7. Who Owns What? *Columbia Journalism Review*, http://www.cjr.org/resources/?c=newscorp (September 30, 2012).

8. Jennifer L. Pozner, *Reality Bites Back: The Troubling Truth about Guilty Pleasure TV* (Berkeley: Seal Press, 2010).

9. Collins, *Black Sexual Politics*, p. 178.

10. Mark Hicks and Gretchen Generett, "Barriers to Transformative Collaboration for Justice within Cross-Cultural Communities," in *Handbook of Research in the Social Foundations of Education*, ed. by S. Tozer et al. (New York: Routledge, 2011), p. 686.

11. Gwendolyn D. Pough. "An Introduction of Sorts for Hip Hop Feminism," in *Home Girls Make Some Noise: Hip Hop Feminism Anthology,* ed. by Pough et al. (Mira Loma, CA: Parker Publishing, 2007).

12. "Spike Lee on Tyler Perry's Movies Shows! Its Coonery Buffoonery," December 29, 2009, http://www.youtube.com/watch?v=Ciwhh3fB6vE (accessed October 1, 2012).

About the Editors and Contributors

Editors

DAVID J. LEONARD is an associate professor and chair in the Department of Critical Culture, Gender, and Race Studies at Washington State University. He is the author of the just released *After Artest: Race and the Assault on Blackness* (SUNY Press, 2012). He is also author of *Screens Fade to Black: Contemporary African American Cinema* (Praeger, 2006); he is co-editor of *Visual Economies of/in Motion: Sport and Film* (Peter Lang, 2006), and *Commodified and Criminalized: New Racism and African Americans in Contemporary Sports* (Rowman and Littlefield, 2011). His work has appeared in *Journal of Sport and Social Issues, Cultural Studies: Critical Methodologies, Game and Culture,* as well as several anthologies. Leonard is a regular contributor to *NewBlackMan,* Feminist Wire, *Huffington Post, and Urban Cusp. He is frequent contributor to Ebony, Slam, and Racialicious as well as a past contributor to Loop21, The Nation, Layupline, The Grio, and The Starting Five.* He blogs *@No Tsuris.* Follow him on *Twitter @drdavidjleonard.*

LISA A. GUERRERO is an associate professor in the Department of Critical Culture, Gender, and Race Studies at Washington State University. Dr. Guerrero is the editor of *Teaching Race in the 21st Century: College Teachers Talk about Their Fears, Risks, and Rewards* (Palgrave Macmillan, 2008) and has published essays on various topics including: African American "Chick Lit," LeBron James, and Michelle Obama. Her book *Satiric Subjectivities: Double Conscious Satire in Contemporary Black Popular Culture* is forthcoming from Temple University Press.

Contributors

REGINA N. BRADLEY is a PhD candidate in African American literature. She analyzes post-1980 African American literature, black satire, race and sound, and hip-hop. Regina earned her BA in English from the Albany State University (GA) and an MA in African American and African Diaspora Studies from Indiana University, Bloomington. Her current project, "Race to Post: Negotiating White Hegemonic Capitalism and Black Empowerment in 21st Century Black Popular Culture," identifies negotiations of white hegemonic capitalism and black empowerment in 21st century African American popular culture.

TAMMY L. BROWN is assistant professor of Black World Studies and History at Miami University of Ohio. Currently a postdoctoral fellow in the Department of American Studies at the University of North Carolina-Chapel Hill, she is a historian, poet and visual artist, whose historical research informs her creative work. Her book, *City of Islands: West Indian Immigrants in New York,* is forthcoming from UNC Press.

KYLE S. BUNDS is a doctoral fellow at the Center for Physical Cultural Studies at Florida State University. His research interests are focused on the political economy of water and water rights in Africa.

KRISTAL MOORE CLEMONS received her PhD in Education-Culture, Curriculum and Change from the University of North Carolina at Chapel Hill and a graduate certificate in Women's Studies from Duke University. Her work uses women's studies, cultural studies, and history to develop interpretive and critical perspectives on education and popular culture, both inside and outside of schools. She is an assistant professor of History at Tallahassee Community College.

PHILLIP LAMARR CUNNINGHAM is currently visiting assistant professor of Media Studies at Quinnipiac University. His scholarly work has appeared in the *Journal of Graphic Novels and Comics, Journal of Popular Music Studies,* and *Journal of Sport and Social Issues,* and in several anthologies.

QIANA M. CUTTS is a professor of Practice at Argosy University Atlanta. Her work examines diversity/multiculturalism in education, identity exploration of black lesbian-identified women, and media representations of women of color.

KWAKIUTL L. DREHER is associate professor of English and Ethnic Studies at the University of Nebraska-Lincoln. She is program liaison for the African American and African Studies Program within the Institute for Ethnic Studies. Her book, *Dancing on the White Page: Black Women Entertainers Writing Autobiography,* was published by SUNY press in 2008. She currently is at work on her second book project that involves the study of black men in entertainment. Her research interests include African American literature since 1970, including auto/biography, film, visual, and popular culture, and mass-marketed popular literature (romance).

MICHAEL D. GIARDINA is an assistant professor in the College of Education and the associate director of the Center for Physical Cultural Studies at Florida State University. He is the author or editor of a dozen books, including most recently *Sport, Spectacle, and NASCAR Nation: Consumption and the Cultural Politics of Neoliberalism* (with Joshua Newman; PalgraveMacmillan, 2011). He is the associate editor of the *Sociology of Sport Journal* and special issue editor of *Cultural Studies<=>Critical Methodologies.*

MICHAEL JOHNSON JR. is a PhD candidate and Ronald E. McNair Fellow at Washington State University where he currently teaches both introductory and upper division, interdisciplinary undergraduate courses in the Department of Critical Culture, Race and Gender Studies. His first book, *Tickle My Fancy, Fat Man: Emerging Images of Race and Queer Desire on HBO,* is currently under contract with Lexington Press, in its Critical Studies in Television Series.

C. RICHARD KING is a professor of Critical Culture, Gender, and Race Studies at Washington State University in Pullman. He is author/editor of several books, including *Team Spirits: The Native American Mascot Controversy* and *Postcolonial America.*

BETTINA L. LOVE is an assistant professor in the Department of Elementary and Social Studies at the University of Georgia. Her research focuses on the ways in which urban youth negotiate hip-hop music and culture to form social, cultural, and political identities. A continuing thread of her scholarship involves exploring new ways of thinking about urban education and culturally relevant pedagogical approaches for urban learners. More specifically, she is interested in transforming urban classrooms through the use of nontraditional educational curricula (e.g., hip-hop pedagogy, media literacy, hip-hop feminism, and popular culture). Building on that theme,

Dr. Love also has a passion for studying the school experiences of queer youth, along with race and equity in education. Her first book, *Hip Hop's Li'l Sistas Speak*, explores how young women navigate the space of hip-hop music and culture to form ideas concerning race, body, class, inequality, and privilege.

SHIRON V. PATTERSON was raised in Phoenix, Arizona, and is an independent scholar who aims to encourage youth of color to trust their talents, while fostering confidence to support the realization of their potential. She received an EdD from Washington State University in Curriculum & Instruction with a concentration in Cultural Studies and Social thought in Education, an MA from Michigan State University in K-12 Education Administration, and a BS from Langston University in Elementary Education.

PAULA GROVES PRICE is an associate professor in the Cultural Studies and Social Thought in Education Program at Washington State University where she teaches courses in critical race theory, critical ethnography, educational philosophy, and qualitative research. Her areas of expertise are in African American and indigenous education, hip-hop pedagogy, black feminist epistemology, critical race theory, and the social foundations of education. Dr. Price is also the editor of the *Western Journal of Black Studies*. She received her PhD from the University of North Carolina Chapel Hill in the Social Foundations of Education and her BA in Social Welfare and Interdisciplinary Field Studies at the University of California Berkeley.

BILLYE N. RHODES received her PhD in Education-Culture, Curriculum and Change from the University of North Carolina at Chapel Hill. She is lover of art, teaching, and proponent of community activism. Her research interests include educational sociology, critical race theory, black feminism, critical ethnography, and critical multicultural education. She is a professor and academic specialist in the Doctor of Education program at the College of Professional Studies at Northeastern University.

JARED SEXTON is associate professor and director of the Program in African American Studies at the University of California, Irvine, where he is also affiliated with the Department of Film and Media Studies, the Critical Theory Institute, and the Center in Law, Society and Culture. He has published articles in journals such as *American Quarterly, Radical History Review,* and *Social Text* and chapters in various anthologies on contemporary politics and popular culture. He is author of *Amalgamation Schemes:*

Antiblackness and the Critique of Multiracialism (University of Minnesota Press, 2008) and coeditor of *Critical Sociology* 36 (2010): 1, a special issue on "Race and the Variations of Discipline."

KAILA ADIA STORY is an assistant professor and the Audre Lorde Endowed Chair in Race, Class, Gender, and Sexuality Studies in the Departments of Women's and Gender Studies and Pan African Studies at the University of Louisville.

BHOOMI K. THAKORE is a PhD candidate in the Department of Sociology at Loyola University Chicago and a Clinical Research Associate at Northwestern University. In her dissertation, she uses audience study methodology and focuses on contemporary representations of South Asians in American popular media. Her additional research interests include intergroup relations, racial attitudes, and racial microaggressions.

REBECCA WANZO is associate professor of Women, Gender, and Sexuality Studies at Washington University in St. Louis. She is the author of *The Suffering Will Not Be Televised: African American Women and Sentimental Political Storytelling.* Her research interests include African American literature and culture, feminist theory, cultural studies, and critical race theory.

KRISTEN J. WARNER is an assistant professor in the Department of Telecommunication and Film at the University of Alabama where she teaches courses on race and gender in television and film as well as courses on film and television history and style. Her research primarily focuses on production cultures of casting as it relates to race and representation within the Hollywood film and television industry.

LISA WOOLFORK is an associate professor of English at the University of Virginia. Her research and teaching interests include African American literature, African American studies, American literature, and digital media representations.

Index

mL   3-1